Dedication:

To Max Jacob Fauth and Laine Ellen Fauth

To Suzanne Babbie

Research Methods for **Criminal Justice** and **Criminology**

EIGHTH EDITION

Michael G. Maxfield
John Jay College of Criminal Justice,
City University of New York

Earl R. Babbie
Chapman University

Australia • Brazil • Mexico • Singapore • United Kingdom • United States

CENGAGE Learning®

Research Methods for Criminal Justice and Criminology, Eighth Edition
Michael G. Maxfield, Earl R. Babbie

Senior Product Director: Marta Lee Perriard

Senior Product Manager:
Carolyn Henderson Meier

Project Manager: Seth Schwartz

Content Developer: Julie Anderson,
Lumina Datamatics

Marketing Manager: Mark Linton

Senior Content Project Manager:
Christy Frame

Senior Art Director: Helen Bruno

Senior Manufacturing Planner: Judy Inouye

Production and Composition:
Christian Arsenault, SPi Global

Text Researcher: Rashmi Manoharan,
Lumina Datamatics

Copy Editor: Elise Schneider

Text Designer: Pam Verros

Cover Designer: Helen Bruno

Cover Image: Large crowd of people:
Mitchell Funk/Getty Images; Charts: Roy
Scott/Getty Images; Network abstract:
Maria Kazanova/iStockPhoto.com.

Library of Congress Control Number: 2016962411

Student Edition:
ISBN-13: 978-1-337-09182-4
Loose-leaf: 978-1-337-09239-5

Cengage
20 Channel Center Street
Boston, MA 02210
USA

Cengage is a leading provider of customized learning solutions with employees residing in nearly 40 different countries and sales in more than 125 countries around the world. Find your local representative at **www.cengage.com**.

Cengage products are represented in Canada by
Nelson Education, Ltd.

To learn more about Cengage Solutions,
visit **www.cengage.com**.

Purchase any of our products at your local college store or at our preferred online store **www.cengagebrain.com**.

Printed at CLDPC, USA, 08-19

Contents

Preface

One of my[1] most oddly rewarding teaching experiences took place not in the classroom but on the streets of downtown Indianapolis. On my way to a meeting with staff from the Indiana Department of Correction, I recognized a student from the previous semester's research methods class. Ryan was seated on a shaded bench, clipboard in hand, watching pedestrians make their way down the sidewalk. After we had exchanged greetings, I learned that Ryan had landed a summer internship with the city's planning department and was currently at work conducting a study of pedestrian traffic.

"Ha!" I exclaimed, recalling student complaints about how research methods are not relevant (what I have since referred to as "Ryan's lament"). "And you whined about how you were never going to use the stuff we talked about in class." Ryan responded that the systematic study of pedestrians was interesting, and he admitted that some course topics did, in fact, relate to his work as an intern. He also said something about not really knowing what actual research involved until he began his current project. Ryan remained attentive to people passing by while we chatted for a few minutes. I was pleased to see that he was a careful observer, applying some of the skills he had learned in my course only a few weeks after the semester's end.

Later, thinking more about the encounter, I recognized the need to change my approach to teaching the course. Ryan clearly enjoyed his experience in doing research, but had not recognized how much fun research could be until leaving the classroom. As a result, I restructured the course to involve students more actively in the research process. I resolved to be more diligent in linking fundamental concepts of research methods to a broad spectrum of examples, and to show students how they, like Ryan, could apply systematic inquiry and observation techniques

to a wide variety of situations in criminal justice and other policy areas.

Goals and Objectives

Criminal justice has always been a fascinating topic for students, partly because it is the stuff of news stories, fiction, and much popular entertainment. Criminal justice research goes beyond the headlines to address important questions of *who*, *what*, *why*, and *how*. *Who* is involved as offender, victim, and justice professional? *What* is the nature and frequency of different kinds of crime and disorder problems? *What* new problems are emerging? *Why* are incidents happening in particular places? *Why* are offenders involved in particular patterns of behavior? *How* are different kinds of offenses committed? *How* should justice agencies prevent and respond to problems of crime and safety?

Our primary goal in writing a new edition of the text is unchanged: to help students learn how to conduct research to answer these and related questions. Toward that end, certain principles have guided our revision of each edition:

- provide a careful description of the varied options for doing research in criminal justice.
- clarify and demystify what is traditionally a challenging subject for students at all levels.
- illustrate research methods with examples that are informative and interesting.
- incorporate new approaches that reflect methodological developments in the field.
- emphasize the application of criminal justice research to real-world problems and justice policy examples.
- bridge the gap between authors, instructors, and students by drawing on examples of our own research, especially those conducted with student colleagues.

When I began collaborating with Earl Babbie to produce this textbook, I joined a colleague whose

---

[1] In this Preface, the first-person singular refers to Michael Maxfield, while the first person plural refers to Michael Maxfield and Earl Babbie.

writing embodied my efforts to engage students in the learning process. Earl's classic text, *The Practice of Social Research*, has always been an enviable model of clarity, generating student interest while presenting a rigorous treatment of social science research methods. In the spirit of Earl's text, we have sought to convey the excitement of doing research that Ryan discovered as he observed pedestrians in downtown Indianapolis.

Organization of the Text

The eighth edition of *Research Methods for Criminal Justice and Criminology* has 14 chapters:

- Chapter 1, "Crime, Criminal Justice, and Scientific Inquiry," introduces research methods. Material in this chapter describes how social scientific inquiry differs from other ways of learning things. This chapter also advises students on how to select research topics, conduct a literature review, and write a research proposal.
- Chapter 2, "Foundations of Criminal Justice Research," summarizes principles of social science research and examines different general approaches to research. This chapter also describes the important role of theory in all research. We dispel myths about theory by describing it as a logical guide to scientific inquiry. Examples illustrate how theory drives applied and basic research.
- Chapter 3, "Ethics and Criminal Justice Research," examines how justice research has the potential to harm subjects and the obligations of researchers to minimize the risk of such harm. Examples illustrate the range of ethical issues and steps researchers take to address them.
- Chapter 4, "General Issues in Research Design," describes basic features of all research studies that must be considered when planning a research project.
- Chapter 5, "Concepts, Operationalization, and Measurement," considers the central topic of measurement in criminal justice research. All research requires some sort of measurement, and this chapter examines key elements of this important topic.

- Chapter 6, "Measuring Crime," focuses on a central dependent and independent variable in criminal justice research. This provides an in-depth example of measurement more generally, while describing different ways crime is measured and why the various measures are necessary.
- Chapter 7, "Experimental and Quasi-Experimental Designs," examines how we plan research that has explanatory and applied purposes. Research design involves a collection of building blocks that can be combined in different ways. We emphasize the flexibility of research designs, drawing on interesting and creative examples.
- Chapter 8, "Sampling," describes approaches to selecting subjects for research. We cover the two general categories of probability and nonprobability sampling, describing different subtypes in each category. The basics of probability theory are introduced as key principles underlying sampling and statistical significance.
- Chapter 9, "Survey Research," explores traditional survey research, other types of interviewing, and how changes in technology continue to affect how surveys are conducted.
- Chapter 10, "Qualitative Interviewing," describes different applications of qualitative and specialized interviewing. Earl and I are pleased that Amber Horning joined us in this chapter, drawing on her own work and research by others to examine this family of data gathering techniques.
- Chapter 11, "Field Observation," includes discussion of traditional approaches as well as structured environmental surveys. Examples illustrate the use of the different approaches.
- Chapter 12, "Agency Records, Content Analysis, and Secondary Data," covers data extracted from administrative records as well as data series regularly collected by researchers and government agencies. Examples illustrate the wide range of research opportunities supported by data from different secondary sources.
- Chapter 13, "Evaluation Research and Problem Analysis," focuses on applied research that aims to improve criminal justice policy. The chapter describes how problem analysis is

increasingly used in justice agencies to address crime and related problems.

- Chapter 14, "Interpreting Data," introduces data analysis techniques widely used in criminal justice research. Descriptive and explanatory approaches are explained and illustrated with examples.

What's New in This Edition

In preparing this eighth edition, we stayed with what has proven to be a popular formula, but also responded to suggestions from several people – reviewers, colleagues, and instructors – who used earlier editions.

Terrorism

Terrorist attacks in the United States and other countries have been prominent in news stories. At the same time, distinguishing terrorism from terrorist acts, and terrorist acts from crime and other kinds of violence remains challenging. In this edition we incorporate systematic research on terrorism to illustrate the key features a research-based approach offers for understanding this important problem. In particular, the Global Terrorism Database (GTD) at the University of Maryland is a good example of carefully defining terrorist acts and systematically collecting large-scale global data. New examples from the GTD are included in Chapter 6, "Measuring Crime," and Chapter 12, "Agency Records, Content Analysis, and Secondary Data," since the GTD is an excellent example of content analysis.

In Chapter 12, Marrisa Mandala raises an important question about political assassinations as terrorist acts. Arguing that murders of public officials are a specific type of terrorist acts, Mandala describes her efforts to examine country-level differences in the correlators of assassinations and other attacks. This offers important lessons in the challenges of assembling international data for research purposes.

Web-based Samples and Surveys

Chapters 8, "Sampling," and 9, "Survey Research," are updated to reflect fundamental changes in how large-scale surveys can be conducted. Traditional methods texts lament the potential for bias in using online samples, without recognizing that sampling and interviewing methods reflect available technology. Past explosive growth in peoples' on-line presence has leveled off at a near saturation point, so concerns about limited access are much less important. We describe examples of web-based samples in Chapter 8. Chapter 9 includes a new box that shows how online samples and surveys can be used to conduct experiments of how people interpret behavior of children by systematically varying descriptions of behavior and photos of children.

Technology and Data Collection

Web-based samples and surveys are examples of how more general advances in technology can be used by researchers. Other examples include the growing presence of video cameras in U.S. cities, and increasing coverage of Google maps and similar products worldwide. We describe some examples of these, including the use of geo-coded cameras to track evidence of wildlife poaching in Africa. Similar techniques have been used to trace the likely routes of graffiti artists in other countries.

Applied Research

Research methods for criminal justice and criminology are commonly used by justice professionals and criminal justice activists, but they don't call it "research." We describe evidence generation as a process where justice professionals systematically collect data to better understand a problem of interest. They don't complete research projects, but they use research methods in a systematic way. This is an important message for students in criminal justice who move on to careers in justice agencies or related organizations. Evidence-based practice is important, but so is practice-based evidence. Chapter 13 presents one great example: participatory crime analysis in South African townships. Similar techniques could be used in many communities to better understand crime and disorder problems.

Expanded Examples of Student Research

Reviewers and colleagues have commented favorably on the use of examples from student research in earlier editions, a feature that serves multiple purposes. First, it amplifies what some instructors call the "over-the-shoulder" tone of the text, in which readers feel they are experiencing more than simply words on a printed page. Second, student research examples embody the kind of collaborative supervision that exists between graduate students and faculty. Third, although I have great familiarity with the details of my students' work, such details are rarely described in published articles. Being able to report them adds behind-the-scenes information not readily available elsewhere. Finally, Earl and I believe the examples presented here are topical and inherently interesting to readers. Among the examples in this edition are projects that address terrorism, violence reduction in New York City, human trafficking, and sex offenders.

Chapter by Chapter Changes

We have made a variety of changes in each chapter of the text:

- **Chapter 1** was extensively reworked in the 8th edition. We have received positive feedback on these revisions, but have updated some references and examples. This chapter has become somewhat of a tutorial on how to plan a research project, review the literature, and write a research proposal.
- **Chapter 2** is similarly revised so the balance of material from Chapters 1 and 2 is smoother. Some examples and references have been updated.
- **Chapter 3** updates material on the institutional review boards that oversee the protection of human subjects in the course of social science research. The American Society of Criminology has finally adopted a code of ethics and we describe it here. We also revised some discussion of ethical questions that stem from working with active offenders.
- **Chapter 4** offers a more streamlined treatment of three important principles for designing social science research: causation, units of analysis, and the time dimension.
- **Chapter 5** revises figures that illustrate principles of measurement. We also clarified material describing validity, a perennial

source of confusion. Some examples have been revised.

- **Chapter 6** updates the various ways to conceptualize and measure different types of crime. We added a subsection on the Global Terrorism Database that does two things. First, it illustrates the difficulties of developing cross-national measures. Second, it introduces the concept of open-source data, describing extensive procedures used to clean and verify open-source measures. We also added an opening vignette that details some of the coding procedures for open-source reports.
- **Chapter 7** presents new examples for double-blind experiments and cohort designs. References and other examples are selectively updated.
- **Chapter 8** updates the continuing changes in technology that require new approaches to sampling. We added a new box on Amazon's Mechanical Turk (MTurk), describing its use as a source of purposive samples. Some research finds that MTurk samples are more representative than samples of university students and other groups commonly used in criminal justice research.
- **Chapter 9** has extensive revisions. First, it reflects continuing change in survey research methods. We reduced and updated our discussion of mail and phone surveys. Descriptions of two national crime surveys are streamlined. Other examples and references were revised. A new box describes an example of combining an MTurk sample with complex surveys through an on-line survey platform. Combining this with the box from Chapter 8 produces a brief primer on how to develop online samples and questionnaires.
- **Chapter 10**, by Dr. Amber Horning, has been slightly revised following comments from reviewers.
- **Chapter 11** includes several new examples of field observation, including technologies such as GPS-enabled cameras for recording observations. We've added another example of using Google Street View for observational data. New York City's annual shadow count of the homeless illustrates the plant-capture

technique for enhancing reliability of field observations.

- **Chapter 12** adds the GTD as an example of content analysis. The chapter includes new discussion of a "criminology of place" in describing hot spots. In a new box, Marrisa Mandala describes her work using secondary data in analyzing terror-related assassinations.
- **Chapter 13** introduces the concept of evidence generation. A new box by Sheyla Delgado and Jeffrey Butts describes a large-scale evaluation of Cur Violence in New York City using field interviewing and creative sampling techniques. We've updated our discussion of politics in applied research. In a new box, Tinus Kruger summarizes participatory crime analysis as an applied research method.
- **Chapter 14** updates crime data in selected examples.

Learning Tools

To make this book more accessible to students with a range of interests and abilities, we have included learning tools in each chapter:

- **Learning Objectives** Chapters open with learning objectives that are keyed to the summaries presented later in each chapter. This feature will help students pull material together as they read through and review each chapter.
- **Marginal Key Terms** This edition includes marginal key terms accompanied by brief definitions. These marginal key terms are a subset of those pulled together at the end of each chapter, which in turn are defined fully in the glossary.
- **Chapter Summary** Adapted from different sections in earlier editions, chapter summaries are keyed to the learning objectives that open each chapter.

Ancillary Materials

A number of supplements are provided by Cengage Learning to help instructors use *Research Methods for Criminal Justice and Criminology* in their courses and to help students prepare for exams. Supplements are available to qualified adopters. Please consult your local sales representative for details.

Online Instructor's Manual

The manual includes learning objectives, key terms, a detailed chapter outline, a chapter summary, review questions and exercises, assignments, discussion questions, "What If" scenarios, and media tools. The learning objectives are correlated with the discussion topics, student activities, and media tools.

Downloadable Word Test Bank

The enhanced test bank includes a variety of questions per chapter—a combination of multiple-choice, true/false, completion, essay, and critical thinking formats, with a full answer key. The test bank is coded to the learning objectives that appear in the main text, and identifies where in the text (by section) the answer appears. Finally, each question in the test bank has been carefully reviewed by experienced criminal justice instructors for quality, accuracy, and content coverage so instructors can be sure they are working with an assessment and grading resource of the highest caliber.

Cengage Learning Testing

Powered by Cognero, the accompanying assessment tool is a flexible, online system that allows you to:

- import, edit, and manipulate test bank content from the text's test bank or elsewhere, including your own favorite test questions;
- create ideal assessments with your choice of 15 question types (including true/false, multiple-choice, opinion scale/Likert, and essay);
- create multiple test versions in an instant using drop-down menus and familiar, intuitive tools that take you through content creation and management with ease;
- deliver tests from your LMS, your classroom, or wherever you want—plus, import and export content into and from other systems as needed.

Online PowerPoint Lectures

Helping you make your lectures more engaging while effectively reaching your visually oriented students, these handy Microsoft PowerPoint®

slides outline the chapters of the main text in a classroom-ready presentation. The PowerPoint slides reflect the content and organization of the new edition of the text and feature some additional examples and real-world cases for application and discussion.

Acknowledgments

Many colleagues have offered suggestions, comments, and advice on this and earlier editions, including: Patricia Brantingham (Simon Fraser University), Judith Collins (Michigan State University), Jeffrey Butts (John Jay College of Criminal Justice), Robyn Dawes (Carnegie Mellon University), Joel Miller (Rutgers University), Mangai Natarajan (John Jay College of Criminal Justice), Jon Shane, (John Jay College of Criminal Justice), Cathy Spatz Widom (John Jay College of Criminal Justice), and Sung-suk Violet Yu (John Jay College of Criminal Justice).

A number of former students at the Rutgers University School of Criminal Justice have offered advice, feedback, and contributions for this and earlier editions. They have now moved on to their own academic careers as faculty or other researchers. I thank Dr. Gisela Bichler (California State University, San Bernardino), Dr. Stephen Block (Central Connecticut State University), Dr. Sharon Chamard (University of Alaska), Dr. Niyazi Ekici (Turkish National Police), Dr. Shuryo Fujita (California State University, San Bernardino), Dr. Galma Jahic (Istanbul Bilgi University, Turkey), Dr. Jarret Lovell (California State University, Fullerton), Dr. Nerea Marteache (California State University, San Bernardino), Dr. Marie Mele (Monmouth University), Dr. Nancy Merritt (National Institute of Justice), Dr. Melanie Angela Neuilly (Washington State University), Dr. Dina Perrone (California State University, Long Beach), Dr. Gohar Petrossian (John Jay College of Criminal Justice), Dr. James Roberts (University of Scranton), Dr. William Sousa (University of Nevada, Las Vegas), and Dr. Christopher Sullivan (University of Cincinnati). Dr. Carsten Andresen (Travis County Department of Community Corrections and Supervision) merits special thanks for generously sharing information about his own research.

With my move to John Jay College in 2010, I have enjoyed contributions and suggestions from new students, many of whom are now researchers in academic and other settings: Dr. Amber Horning (William Paterson University), Dr. Michelle Cubellis (Central Connecticut State University), Dr. Brittany Hayes (Sam Houston State University), Dr. Alana Henninger (RTI International), Dr. Leonid Lantsman (U.S. Department of State), Dr. Daiwon Lee (New York City Police Department), Dr. Bryce Peterson (Urban Institute), Sheyla Delgado (Research and Evaluation Center, John Jay College), Dr. Julie Viollaz (Interpol, United Nations), Marissa Mandala (New York City Police Department), and Mawia Khogali. Special thanks to Dr. Jeffrey Butts, Director of the Research and Evaluation Center at John Jay College, for being a gracious colleague and host.

Finally, Earl and I are very grateful for the patient, professional assistance from content developer Julie Anderson (Lumina Datamatics), and the professionals at Cengage: Carolyn Henderson Meier, Christy Frame, Seth Schwartz, and the entire book team.

An Introduction to Criminal Justice Inquiry

What comes to mind when you encounter the word *science*? What do you think of when we describe criminal justice as a social science? For some people, science is mathematics; for others, it is white coats and laboratories. Some confuse it with technology, or equate it with difficult courses in high school or college.

For the purposes of this book, we view science as a method of inquiry—a way of learning and knowing things about the world around us. Like other ways of learning and knowing about the world, science has some special characteristics. We'll examine these traits in this opening set of chapters. We'll also see how the scientific method of inquiry can be applied to the study of crime and criminal justice.

Part One lays the groundwork for the rest of the book by examining the fundamental characteristics and issues that make science different from other ways of knowing things. Chapter 1 begins with a look at native human inquiry—the sort of thing all of us have been doing all our lives. We'll also consider different research purposes and the basics of how to design a research project.

Chapter 2 deals specifically with the social scientific approach to criminal justice inquiry and the links between theory and research. The lessons of Chapter 1 are applied in the study of crime and criminal justice. Although special considerations arise in studying people and organizations, the basic logic of all science is the same.

Ethics is one of those special considerations we face in studying people. In Chapter 3, we'll see that most ethical questions are rooted in two fundamental principles: (1) research subjects should not be harmed and (2) their participation must be voluntary.

The overall purpose of Part One is to construct a backdrop for the more specific aspects of designing and doing research. By the time you complete the chapters in Part One, you'll be ready to look at some of the more concrete aspects of criminal justice research.

CHAPTER 1

Crime, Criminal Justice, and Scientific Inquiry

People learn about their world in a variety of ways, and we often make mistakes along the way. Science is different from other ways of learning and knowing. We'll consider errors people commonly make and how science tries to avoid them, discuss different purposes of research, and describe how to design a research project.

Learning Objectives

1. Understand why knowledge of research methods is valuable to criminal justice professionals.
2. Describe the different ways we know things.
3. Distinguish inquiry as a natural human activity—from inquiry through systematic empirical research.
4. Recognize that much of our knowledge is based on agreement rather than on direct experience.
5. Explain how tradition and authority are important sources of knowledge.
6. Understand the role of experience and systematic observation in criminal justice research.
7. Recognize that social science guards against, but does not prevent, political beliefs from affecting research findings.
8. Distinguish the different purposes of research.
9. Understand how to design a research project.
10. Be able to conduct a review of research literature.
11. Describe how to write a research proposal.

Sexual Assault in Jails and Prisons

Responding to reports of sexual assault in prisons and jails, the Prison Rape Elimination Act became law in 2003. The act enhanced penalties for sexual violence in most detention facilities and required the Department of Justice to collect systematic data on the problem. The newspaper article "County Misreports Data About Sexual Violence in Juvenile Jails" is an example of how sexual assault continues to be a problem in San Diego, California (Maass, 2012). Researchers have conducted studies to better understand the problem and assess ways to reduce sexual violence.

Allen Beck and associates (2010) describe data collected from a sample of prisons and jails by the Bureau of Justice Statistics. They report that 4 percent of prison inmates and 3 percent of jail inmates were victims of sexual assault in the previous 12 months or since being admitted to the facility. Projecting those percentages to all prisons and jails nationwide produces an estimate of 88,500 adult victims. In addition, the researchers report that approximately 3 percent of prison inmates and 2 percent of those in jail had sexual contact with facility staff, often willingly.

Nancy La Vigne and other researchers from the Urban Institute (2011) describe their research on how to prevent sexual assault in jails. Working with three facilities, they described efforts to improve supervision of inmates and corrections officers, install surveillance cameras, and train corrections officers in crisis intervention. Based on their evaluation, La Vigne and associates recommended that jail administrators use a systematic process to assess problems in specific facilities, design changes that address those problems, and collect data to assess the effects of the new actions.

This example illustrates how researchers take steps to better understand the scope of a problem and then try different approaches to reduce it. The Urban Institute analysts went one step further in their efforts to train corrections officials to do their own applied research. Jail managers were consumers of research produced by La Vigne and associates and also gained some of the skills needed to become producers of applied studies in their own facilities.

Introduction

Criminal justice professionals are both consumers and producers of research.

Spending a semester studying criminal justice research methodology may not be high on your list of "Fun Things to Do." Perhaps you are or plan to be a criminal justice professional and are thinking, "Why do I have to study research methods? When I graduate, I'll be working in probation, or law enforcement, or corrections, or court services—not conducting research! I would benefit more from learning about probation counseling, or police management, or corrections policy, or court administration." Fair enough. But as a criminal justice professional, you will need at least to be a consumer of research. One objective of this book is to help you achieve this. And as we will soon see, justice professionals often produce research as well.

For example, in the section "Two Realities," we will see how findings from one of the first experimental studies of policing appeared to contradict a traditional tenet of law enforcement—that a visible patrol force prevents crime. Acting as a consumer of research findings, a police officer, supervisor, or executive should be able to understand how the research was conducted and how the study's findings might apply in his or her department. Because police practices vary from city to city, a police executive would benefit from knowledge of research methods and of how to interpret findings.

Most criminal justice professionals, especially those in supervisory roles, routinely review various performance reports and statistical tabulations. In the past 30 years or so, thousands of criminal justice research and evaluation studies have been conducted. The National Criminal Justice Reference Service (https://ncjrs.gov) was established in 1972 to archive and distribute research reports to criminal justice professionals and researchers around the world. Many such reports are prepared specifically to keep the criminal justice community informed about new research developments. More recently, the Center for Problem-Oriented Policing (POP Center, http://www.popcenter.org) and CrimeSolutions.gov were created to share applied research on various law enforcement and general justice problems. By understanding research methods, decision makers are better equipped to critically evaluate research reports and to recognize when methods are properly and improperly applied. See the box titled "Home Detention" for an example of how knowledge of research methods can help policy makers avoid mistakes.

Another objective of this book is to help you produce research. In other courses or in your job, you may become a producer of research. For example, probation officers sometimes test new approaches to supervising or counseling clients, and police officers try new methods of addressing particular problems or working with the community. Many cities and states have a compelling need to assess how to better serve adults and juveniles returning from periods of incarceration after reforming sentencing laws. Determining whether such changes are effective is an example of applied research. A problem-solving approach, rooted in systematic research, is being used in more and more police departments and in many other criminal justice agencies. Many items on the POP Center website are the product of applied research conducted by police departments. Therefore, criminal justice professionals need to know not only how to interpret research accurately, but also how to produce accurate research.

HOME DETENTION

Home detention with electronic monitoring (ELMO) was widely adopted as an alternative punishment in the United States in the 1980s. The technology for this new sanction was made possible by advances in telecommunications and computer systems. Prompted by growing prison and jail populations, not to mention sales pitches by equipment manufacturers, criminal justice officials embraced ELMO. Questions about the effectiveness of these programs quickly emerged, however, and led to research to determine whether the technology worked. Comprehensive evaluations were conducted in Marion County (Indianapolis), Indiana. Selected findings from these studies illustrate the importance of understanding research methods in general and the meaning of various ways to measure program success in particular. ELMO programs directed at three groups of people were studied: (1) convicted adult offenders, (2) adults charged with a crime and awaiting trial, and (3) juveniles convicted of burglary or theft. People in each of the three groups were assigned to home detention for a specified time. They could complete the program in one of three ways: (1) successful release after serving their term; (2) removal due to rule violations, such as being arrested again or violating program rules; or (3) running away, or "absconding." The agencies that administered each program were required to submit regular reports to county officials on how many individuals in each category completed their home detention terms. The table below summarizes the program completion types during the evaluation study:

	Convicted Adults	Pretrial Adults	Juveniles
Success	81%	73%	99%
Rule violation	14	13	1
Abscond	5	14	0

These figures, reported by agencies to county officials, indicate that the juvenile program was a big success; virtually all juveniles were successfully released.

Now consider some additional information on each program collected by the evaluation team. Data were gathered on new arrests of program participants and on the number of successful computerized telephone calls to participants' homes:

	Convicted Adults	Pretrial Adults	Juveniles
New arrest	5%	1%	11%
Successful calls	53	52	17

As the above table shows, many more juveniles were arrested, and juveniles successfully answered a much lower percentage of telephone calls to their homes. What happened?

The simple answer is that the staff responsible for administering the juvenile program were not keeping track of offenders. The ELMO equipment was not maintained properly, and police were not visiting the homes of juveniles as planned. Because staff were not keeping track of program participants, they were not aware that many juveniles were violating the conditions of home detention. And because they did not detect violations, they naturally reported that the vast majority of young burglars and thieves completed their home detention successfully.

A county official who relied on only agency reports of program success would have made a big mistake in judging the juvenile program to be 99 percent successful. In contrast, an informed consumer of such reports would have been skeptical of a 99 percent success rate and searched for more information.

Source: Adapted from Maxfield and Baumer (1991) and Baumer, Maxfield, and Mendelsohn (1993).

What Is This Book About?

This book focuses on how we know what we know.

This book focuses on how we learn and know things, not on what we know. Although you will come away from the book knowing some things you don't know right now, our primary purpose is to help you look at how you know things.

Two Realities

Ultimately, we live in a world of two realities. Part of what we know could be called our "experiential reality"—the things we know from direct experience. For example, if you dive into a glacial stream flowing from the Canadian Rockies, you don't need anyone to tell you that the water is cold; you notice that by yourself. And the first time you step on a thorn, you know it hurts even before anyone tells you. The other part of what we know could be called our "agreement reality"—the things we consider real because we've been told they're real and everyone else seems to agree they're real. A big part of growing up in any society, in fact, is learning to accept what everybody around us "knows" to be true. If we don't know those same things, we can't really be a part of the group. If you were to seriously question a geography professor as to whether the sun really sets in the west, you'd quickly find yourself set apart from other people. The first reality is a product of our own experience; the second is a product of what people have told us.

To illustrate the difference between agreement and experiential realities, consider preventive police patrol. The term *preventive* implies that when police patrol their assigned beats they prevent crime. Police do not prevent all crime, of course, but it is a commonsense belief that a visible, mobile police force will prevent some crimes. In fact, the value of patrol in preventing crime was a fundamental tenet of police operations for many years. O. W. Wilson, a legendary police chief in Chicago and the author of an influential book on police administration, wrote that patrol was indispensable in preventing crime by eliminating incentives and opportunities for misconduct (Wilson and McLaren, 1963:320). A 1967 report on policing by President Lyndon Johnson's President's Commission on Law Enforcement and Administration of Justice (1967:1) stated that "the heart of the police effort against crime is patrol. . . . The object of patrol is to disperse policemen in a way that will eliminate or reduce the opportunity for misconduct and to increase the probability that a criminal will be apprehended while he is committing a crime or immediately thereafter."

Seven years later, the Police Foundation, a private research organization, published results from an experimental study that presented a dramatic challenge to conventional wisdom. Known as the "Kansas City Preventive Patrol Experiment," this classic study compared police beats with three levels of preventive patrol: (1) control beats, with one car per beat; (2) proactive beats, with two or three cars per beat; and (3) reactive beats, with no routine preventive patrol. After almost one year, researchers examined data from the three types of beats and found no differences in crime rates, citizen satisfaction with police, fear of crime, or other measures of police performance (Kelling et al., 1974).

Researchers and law enforcement professionals alike were surprised by these findings. For the record, the Kansas City researchers never claimed to have proved that preventive patrol had no impact on crime. Instead, they argued that police should work more closely with community members and that routine patrol might be more effective if combined with other strategies that used police resources in a more thoughtful way. Subsequent research has supported that last statement. An experimental study of foot patrol in Philadelphia found that assigning foot patrol officers based on analytically identified "hot spots" of crime produced a 23 percent reduction in violent crime after 12 weeks (Ratcliffe et al., 2011).

Additional studies conducted in the 1970s cast doubt on other fundamental assumptions about police practices. A quick response to crime reports made no difference in arrests, according to a research study in Kansas City (Van Kirk, 1977). And criminal investigation by police detectives rarely resulted in an arrest (Greenwood, 1975).

We do not attack routine law enforcement practices in mentioning these examples. Rather, we want to show that systematic research on policing has illustrated how traditional beliefs—agreement reality—can be misleading. Simply increasing the number of police officers on patrol does not reduce crime, because police patrol often lacks direction. Faster response time to calls for police assistance does not increase arrests, because there is often a long delay between the time when a crime occurs and when it is reported to police. Clever detective work seldom solves crimes; investigators get most of their information from reports prepared by patrol officers, who, in turn, get their information from victims and witnesses. These early studies informed more recent research that examines how sorting cases into "solvability" categories can improve investigations and lead to more arrests. (Robb et al., 2011).

Traditional beliefs about patrol effectiveness, response time, and detective work are examples of agreement reality. In contrast, the research projects that produced alternative views about each law enforcement practice represent experiential reality. These studies are examples of **empirical**[1] research, the production of knowledge based on experience or observation.

In each case, researchers conducted studies of police practices and based their conclusions on observations and experience. Empirical research is a way of learning about crime and criminal justice; explaining how to conduct empirical research is the purpose of this book.

The Role of Science

Science offers an approach to both agreement reality and experiential reality. Scientists have certain criteria that must be met before they will agree on something they haven't experienced personally. In general, an assertion must have both *logical* and *empirical* support: It must make sense, and it must agree with actual observations. For example, why do earthbound scientists accept the assertion that it's cold on the dark side of the moon? First, it makes sense because the surface heat of the moon comes from the sun's rays. Second, scientific measurements made on the moon's dark side confirm the assertion. Scientists can accept the reality

of things they don't personally experience—they accept an agreement reality—but they have special standards for doing so.

More relevant to this book, however, is that science offers a special approach to discovering reality through personal experience. Epistemology is the science of knowing; methodology (a subfield of epistemology) might be called "the science of finding out." This book focuses on criminal justice **methodology**—how social science methods can be used to better understand crime and criminal justice problems. To understand scientific inquiry, let's first look at the kinds of inquiry we all do each day.

Personal Human Inquiry

Everyday human inquiry draws on personal experience and secondhand authority.

Most of us feel more comfortable if we understand what's going on around us and are able to predict our future circumstances. We seem quite willing, moreover, to undertake this task using causal and probabilistic reasoning. First, we generally recognize that future circumstances are somehow caused or conditioned by present ones. For example, we learn that getting an education will affect how much money we earn later in life and that speeding may result in an unhappy encounter with an alert traffic officer. As students, we learn that studying hard will result in better examination grades.

Second, we recognize that such patterns of cause and effect are probabilistic in nature. The effects occur more often when the causes occur than when the causes are absent—but not always. Thus, as students, we learn that studying hard produces good grades in most instances, but not every time. We recognize the danger of exceeding the speed limit without believing that every time we do so will produce a traffic ticket.

Empirical From experience. Social science is said to be empirical when knowledge is based on what we experience.

Methodology The study of methods used to understand something; the science of finding out.

---

[1]Words set in boldface are defined in the glossary at the end of the book.

ARREST AND DOMESTIC VIOLENCE

In 1983, preliminary results were released from a study on the deterrent effects of arrest in cases of domestic violence. The study reported that male abusers who were arrested were less likely to commit future assaults than offenders who were not arrested. Conducted by researchers from the Police Foundation, the study used rigorous experimental methods adapted from the natural sciences. Criminal justice scholars generally agreed that the research was well designed and executed. Public officials were quick to embrace the study's findings that arresting domestic violence offenders deterred them from future violence.

Here, at last, was empirical evidence to support an effective policy in combating domestic assaults. Results of the Minneapolis Domestic Violence Experiment were widely disseminated, in part due to aggressive efforts by the researchers to publicize their findings (Sherman and Cohn, 1989). The attorney general of the United States recommended that police departments make arrests in all cases of misdemeanor domestic violence. Within five years, more than 80 percent of law enforcement agencies in U.S. cities adopted arrest as the preferred way of responding to domestic assaults (Sherman, 1992:2).

Several things contributed to the rapid adoption of arrest policies to deter domestic violence. First, the experimental study was conducted carefully by highly respected researchers. Second, results were widely publicized in newspapers, in professional journals, and on television programs. Third, officials could understand the study, and most believed that its findings made sense. Finally, mandating arrest in less serious cases of domestic violence was a straightforward and politically attractive approach to a growing problem.

Sherman and Berk (1984), however, urged caution in uncritically embracing the results of their study. Others advised that similar research be conducted in other cities to check on the Minneapolis findings (Lempert, 1984). Recognizing this, the U.S. National Institute of Justice sponsored more experiments—known as replications—in six other cities. Not everyone was happy about the new studies. For example, a feminist group in Milwaukee opposed the replication in that city because it believed that the effectiveness of arrest had already been proved (Sherman and Cohn, 1989:138).

Results from the replication studies brought into question the effectiveness of arrest policies. In three cities, no deterrent effect was found in police records of domestic violence. In other cities, there was no evidence of deterrence for longer periods (6–12 months), and in three cities, researchers found that violence actually escalated when offenders were arrested (Sherman, 1992:30). For example, Sherman and associates (1992:167) report that in Milwaukee "the initial deterrent effects observed for up to thirty days quickly disappear. By one year later [arrests] produce an escalation effect." Arrest works in some cases but not in others. As in many other cases, in responding to domestic assaults, it's important to carefully consider the characteristics of offenders and the nature of the relationship between offender and victim.

After police departments throughout the country embraced arrest policies following the Minneapolis study, researchers were faced with the difficult task of explaining why initial results must be qualified. Arrest seemed to make sense; officials and the general public believed what they read in the papers and saw on television. Changing their minds by reporting complex findings was more difficult, but continues to be important. Long-term follow-up studies have found that arrested offenders were more likely to be victims of homicide (Sherman. Lawrence W. and Harris, 2013). Even more sobering, domestic violence victims of arrested offenders were more likely than victims of non-arrested offenders to have died within 23 years after the experiment (Sherman. Lawrence W. and Harris, 2015).

The concepts of causality and probability play a prominent role in this book. Science makes causality and probability explicit and provides techniques for dealing with them more rigorously than does casual human inquiry. Science sharpens the skills we already have by making us more conscious, rigorous, and explicit in our inquiries.

However, our attempts to learn about the world are only partly linked to personal inquiry and direct experience. Another, much larger, part comes from the agreed-on knowledge that others give us. This agreement reality both assists and hinders our attempts to find out things for ourselves. Two important sources of secondhand knowledge—tradition and authority—deserve brief consideration here.

Tradition

Each of us inherits a culture made up, in part, of firmly accepted knowledge about the workings of the world. We may learn from others that planting corn in the spring will result in the greatest assistance from the gods, that the circumference of a circle is approximately twenty-two sevenths of its diameter, or that driving on the left side of the road (in the United States) is dangerous. We may test a few of these "truths" on our own, but we simply accept the great majority of them. These are the things that "everybody knows."

Tradition, in this sense, has some clear advantages for human inquiry. By accepting what everybody knows, we are spared the overwhelming task of starting from scratch in our search for regularities and understanding. Knowledge is cumulative, and an inherited body of information and understanding is the jumping-off point for the development of more knowledge.

At the same time, tradition may hinder human inquiry. If we seek a fresh understanding of something everybody already understands and has always understood, we may be marked as fools for our efforts. More to the point, however, it rarely occurs to most of us to seek a different understanding of something we all "know" to be true.

Authority

Despite the power of tradition, new knowledge appears every day. In addition to our own personal inquiries, throughout life we learn about the new discoveries and understandings of others. Our acceptance of this new knowledge often depends on the status of the discoverer. For example, you are more likely to believe a judge who declares that your next traffic violation will result in a suspension of your driver's license than to believe your parents when they say the same thing.

Like tradition, authority can both help and hinder human inquiry. We do well to trust the judgment of individuals who have special training, expertise, and credentials in a matter, especially in the face of contradictory arguments on a given question. At the same time, inquiry can be greatly hindered by the legitimate authorities who err within their own special province. Biologists, after all, do make mistakes in the field of biology, and biological knowledge changes over time. Most of us assume that over-the-counter medications are safe when taken as directed, trusting the authority of drug manufacturers and government agencies. However, in the late nineteenth century, our trust might have led us to buy a bottle of Bayer Heroin, then available as an over-the-counter pain relief medication (Inciardi, 1986). The box titled "Arrest and Domestic Violence" illustrates the difficult problems that can result when criminal justice policy makers accept too quickly the results from criminal justice research. More generally, as Albert Einstein wrote, "Unthinking respect for authority is the enemy of truth" (quoted in Highfield and Carter, 1994: 79).

Inquiry is also hindered when we depend on the authority of experts speaking outside their realm of expertise. For example, consider the political or religious leader, lacking any biochemical expertise, who declares marijuana to be a dangerous drug. The advertising industry plays heavily on this misuse of authority by having popular athletes endorse various consumer products.

Both tradition and authority, then, are double-edged swords in the search for knowledge about the world. Simply put, they provide us with a starting point for our own inquiry, but they may lead us to start at the wrong point or push us in the wrong direction.

Errors in Personal Human Inquiry

Everyday personal human inquiry reveals a number of potential biases.

Aside from the potential dangers of relying on tradition and authority, we often stumble when we set out to learn for ourselves. Let's consider some of the common errors we make in our own casual inquiries and then look at the ways science provides safeguards against those errors.

Inaccurate Observation

The keystone of inquiry is observation. We can never understand the way things are without first having something to understand. We have to know *what* before we can explain *why*. On the whole, however, people are rather sloppy observers of the flow of events in life. We fail to observe things right in front of us and mistakenly observe things that aren't so. Do you recall, for example, what your instructor was wearing on the first day of this class? If you had to guess now, what are the chances you would be right?

In contrast to casual human inquiry, scientific observation is a carefully directed activity. Simply making observations in a more deliberate way helps to reduce error. If you had gone to the first class meeting with a conscious plan to observe and record what your instructor was wearing, you'd have been more accurate.

In many cases, using both simple and complex measurement devices helps to guard against inaccurate observations. Suppose, for example, that you had taken a photograph of your instructor on the first day. The photo would have added a degree of precision well beyond that provided by unassisted human senses.

Overgeneralization

When we look for patterns among the specific things we observe around us, we often assume that a few similar events are evidence of a general pattern. The tendency to overgeneralize is probably greatest when there is pressure to reach a general understanding, yet overgeneralization also occurs in the absence of pressure. Whenever overgeneralization does occur, it can misdirect or impede inquiry.

Imagine you are a rookie police officer newly assigned to foot patrol in an urban neighborhood. Your sergeant wants to meet with you at the end of your shift to discuss what you think are the major problems on the beat. Eager to earn favor with your supervisor, you talk to the manager of a popular store in a small shopping area. If the manager mentions vandalism as the biggest concern, you might report that vandalism is the main problem on your beat, even though residents and other store managers believe that drug dealing is the main problem and that it contributes to local burglary, car break-ins, and robbery, as well as vandalism. Overgeneralization would lead to misunderstanding and simplification of the problems on your beat.

Criminal justice researchers guard against overgeneralization by committing themselves in advance to a sufficiently large sample of observations and by focusing on how representative those observations are. The **replication** of inquiry provides another safeguard. Replication means repeating a study and checking to see whether similar results are obtained each time. The study may also be repeated under slightly different conditions or in different locations. The box titled "Arrest and Domestic Violence" describes an example of replication and why it can be especially important in applied research. Replication results either support earlier findings or cause us to question the accuracy of an earlier study.

Selective Observation

One danger of overgeneralization is that it may lead to selective observation. Once we have concluded that a particular pattern exists and have

> **Replication** Repeating a research study to test the findings of an earlier study, often under slightly different conditions or for a different group of subjects.

developed a general understanding of why, we will be tempted to pay attention to future events and situations that correspond with the pattern and to ignore those that don't. Racial, ethnic, and other prejudices are reinforced by selective observation.

Researchers often specify in advance the number and kind of observations to be made before marking a conclusion to a particular project. For example, if we wanted to learn whether women were more likely than men to support long prison sentences for sex offenders, we would have to make a specified number of observations on that question. We might select 200 people to be interviewed. Even if the first 10 women supported long sentences and the first 10 men opposed them, we would continue to interview everyone selected for the study and record each observation. We would base our conclusion on an analysis of all the observations, not just those of the first 20 respondents.

Illogical Reasoning

People have various ways of handling observations that contradict their judgments about the way things are. Surely one of the most remarkable creations of the human mind is "the exception that proves the rule," an idea that makes no sense at all. An exception can draw attention to a rule or to a supposed rule, but in no system of logic can it prove the rule it contradicts. Yet we often use this pithy saying to brush away contradictions with a simple stroke of illogic.

What statisticians call the "gambler's fallacy" is another illustration of illogic in day-to-day reasoning. According to this fallacy, a consistent run of either good or bad luck is presumed to foreshadow its opposite. Thus, an evening of bad luck at poker may kindle the belief that a winning hand is just around the corner—a mistaken belief that has kept many a poker player in a game for too long. Conversely, an extended period of good weather may lead us to worry that it is certain to rain on our weekend picnic.

Although we all sometimes use embarrassingly illogical reasoning, scientists avoid this pitfall by using systems of logic consciously and explicitly. Chapters 2 and 4 examine the role of logic in science.

Ideology and Politics

Crime is, of course, an important social problem, and a great deal of controversy surrounds policies for dealing with crime. Many people feel strongly one way or another about the death penalty, gun control, and long prison terms as approaches to reducing crime. There is ongoing concern about racial bias in police practices and sentencing policies. Being tougher on sex offenders seems to be a favorite topic of state legislatures. Ideological or political views on such issues can undermine objectivity in the research process. Criminal justice professionals in particular may have difficulty separating ideology and politics from a more detached, scientific study of crime.

Criminologist Samuel Walker (1994:16) compares ideological bias in criminal justice research to theology: "The basic problem . . . is that faith triumphs over facts. For both liberals and conservatives, certain ideas are unchallenged articles of faith, almost like religious beliefs that remain unshaken by empirical facts."

Most of us have our own beliefs about public policy, including policies for dealing with crime. The danger lies in allowing such beliefs to distort how research problems are defined and how research results are interpreted. The scientific approach to the study of crime and criminal justice policy guards against, but does not prevent, the research process becoming colored by ideology, theology, and blind acceptance of authority. In empirical research, so-called articles of faith are compared with experience.

To Err Is Human

We have seen some of the ways that we can go astray in our attempts to know and understand the world and some of the ways that science protects its inquiries from these pitfalls. Social science differs from our casual, day-to-day inquiry in two important respects.

First, social scientific inquiry is a conscious activity. Although we engage in continuous observation in daily life, much of it is unconscious or semiconscious. In social scientific inquiry, conversely, we make a conscious decision to observe, and we stay alert while we do it.

Second, social scientific inquiry is a more careful process than our casual efforts; we are more wary of making mistakes and take special precautions to avoid doing so.

Do social science research methods offer total protection against the errors that people commit in personal inquiry? Of course not. Not only do individuals make every kind of error we've looked at, but social scientists as a group also succumb to the pitfalls and stay trapped for long periods of time.

Purposes of Research

We conduct criminal justice research to serve different purposes.

Criminal justice research, of course, serves many purposes. Explaining associations between two or more variables is one of those purposes; others include exploration, description, and application. Although a given study can have several purposes, it is useful to examine them individually because each has different implications for other aspects of research design.

Exploration

Much research in criminal justice is conducted to explore a specific problem, known as **exploratory research**. A researcher or official may be interested in some crime or criminal justice policy issue about which little is known. Or perhaps an innovative approach to policing, court management, or corrections has been tried in some jurisdiction, and the researcher wishes to determine how common such practices are in other cities or states. An exploratory project might collect data on some measure to establish a baseline with which future changes will be compared.

For example, heightened concern about bullying might prompt efforts to estimate the level of bullying in high schools. How many reports are made to high school teachers? Do parents complain that their children have been subjected to intimidation at school? Does bullying take different forms when the targets are male or female? Are gay, lesbian, and bisexual students particular

targets? Are students suspected of bullying involved in delinquency? Does bullying have an effect on school attendance? These are examples of research questions intended to explore different aspects of the problem of bullying. Exploratory questions may also be formulated in connection with how parents and schools respond to the problem. How many schools have created special anti-bullying education programs? Are services available to victims? The government publication, *Indicators of School Crime and Safety*, offers an overview of information on bullying and other dimensions of school safety, with the following purpose:

> The report is not intended to be an exhaustive compilation of school crime and safety information, nor does it attempt to explore reasons for crime and violence in schools. Rather, it is designed to provide a brief summary of information from an array of data sources and to make data on national school crime and safety accessible to policymakers, educators, parents, and the general public. (Robers, Kemp, Rathburn et al., 2014:2).

Exploratory studies are also appropriate when a policy change is being considered. Stricter enforcement of laws and longer prison sentences were common policy responses to drug abuse for many years, and jails and prisons were soon filled with newly arrested and sentenced drug offenders. This prompted a search for alternatives to incarceration, such as diversion coupled with treatment. One of the first questions public officials typically ask when they consider a new policy is "How have other cities (or states) handled this problem?"

Exploratory research in criminal justice can be simple or complex, using a variety of methods. For example, a mayor seeking to learn about drug arrests in his or her city might simply phone the police chief and request a report. In contrast, estimating how many high school seniors have used marijuana requires more sophisticated survey methods. Since 1975, different federal agencies have conducted annual nationwide surveys of students regarding drug use.

Description

A key purpose of many criminal justice studies is to describe the scope of the crime problem or policy responses to the problem. In **descriptive research**, a researcher or public official observes and then describes what was observed. Criminal justice observation and description, methods grounded in the social sciences, tend to be more accurate than the casual observations people may make about the crime rate or how violent teenagers are today. Descriptive studies are often concerned with counting or documenting observations; exploratory studies focus more on developing a preliminary understanding about a new or unusual problem.

Descriptive studies are frequently conducted in criminal justice. The FBI has compiled the Uniform Crime Report (UCR) since the 1930s. UCR data are routinely reported in newspapers and widely interpreted as accurately describing crime in the United States. For example, 2008 UCR figures (Federal Bureau of Investigation, 2009) showed that Nevada had the highest rate of auto theft (611.6 per 100,000 residents) in the nation, and Maine had the lowest (89.3 per 100,000 residents).

Because criminal justice policy in the United States is largely under the control of state and local governments, many descriptive studies collect and summarize information from local governments. The UCR is one example of this. For an even longer period, since 1850, the federal government has conducted an annual census of prisoners in state and local correctional facilities. Like the decennial U.S. census, it gathers basic characteristics of a population—in this case, the population of people in detention (jail or prison) and on probation or parole.

Descriptive studies in criminal justice have other uses. A researcher may attend meetings of neighborhood anticrime groups and observe their efforts to organize block watch committees. These observations form the basis for a case study that describes the activities of neighborhood anticrime groups. Such a descriptive study might present information that officials and residents of other cities can use to promote such organizations themselves. Or consider research by Heith Copes, Andy Hochstetler, and Michael Cherbonneau (2012), in which they describe how carjackers use different techniques to overcome victim resistance.

Explanation

A third general purpose of criminal justice research is to explain things. Reporting that urban residents have generally favorable attitudes toward police is a descriptive activity, but reporting why some people believe that police are doing a good job while other people do not is an example of **explanatory research**. Similarly, reporting why Nevada has the highest auto theft rate in the nation is explanation; simply reporting auto theft rates for different states is description. A researcher has an explanatory purpose if he or she wishes to know why the number of 14-year-olds involved in gangs has increased, as opposed to simply describing changes in gang membership.

Application

Researchers also conduct criminal justice studies of an applied nature. **Applied research** stems from a need for specific facts and findings with policy implications. Another purpose of criminal justice research, therefore, is its application to public policy. We can distinguish two types of applied research: evaluation and problem analysis.

First, applied research is often used to evaluate the effects of specific criminal justice programs. Determining whether a program designed to reduce burglary actually had that intended effect is an example of evaluation. In its most basic form, evaluation involves comparing the goals of a program with the results. For example, if one goal of increased police foot patrol is to encourage citizens to report crimes to police, then an evaluation of foot patrol might compare levels of reporting before and after increasing the number of those police officers. Jerry Ratcliffe and associates (2011) did something similar in their evaluation of foot patrol in Philadelphia.

In most cases, evaluation research uses social science methods to test the results of some program or policy change. In this regard evaluation has much in common with explanatory research. Because crime problems persist and seem to change frequently, officials are constantly seeking new approaches, and it is becoming more common for public officials or researchers to evaluate new programs.

The second type of applied research is the analysis of general justice policies and more specific problems. What would happen to court backlogs if we designated a judge and prosecutor who would handle only drug-dealing cases? How many new police officers would have to be hired if a department shifted to two-officer cars on night shifts? These are examples of *what if* questions addressed by problem analysis. Answering such questions is sort of a counterpart to program evaluation. Problem analysis is different from other forms of criminal justice research, primarily in its focus on future events. Rather than observing and analyzing current or past behavior, policy analysis tries to anticipate the future consequences of alternative actions.

Similarly, justice organizations are increasingly using techniques of problem analysis to study patterns of cases and devise appropriate responses. Perhaps the best-known example is problem-oriented policing, in which crime analysts work with police and other organizations to examine recurring problems. Ron Clarke and John Eck (2005) have prepared a comprehensive guide for this type of applied research.

Our brief discussion of distinct research purposes is not intended to imply that research purposes are mutually exclusive. Many criminal justice studies have elements of more than one purpose. Suppose you want to examine the problem of bicycle theft at your university. First, you need some information that describes the problem of bicycle theft on campus. Let's assume your evaluation finds that thefts from some campus locations have declined but that there has been an increase in bikes stolen from racks outside dormitories. You might explain these findings by noting that bicycles parked outside dorms tend to be unused for longer periods and that there is more coming and going among bikes parked near classrooms. One option to further reduce thefts would be to install more secure bicycle racks. A policy analysis might compare the costs of installing the racks with the predicted savings resulting from a reduction in bike theft.

Incidentally, the POP Center has published an extremely useful guide on the problem of bicycle theft (Johnson, Sidebottom, and Thorpe, 2008).

In addition to its substantive value, this guide is an example of applied research that can be conducted and used by justice professionals. Visit the POP Center website (http://www.popcenter.org) for more information and examples. You may wish to conduct a study of bicycle theft of your own.

How to Design a Research Project

Designing research requires planning several stages, but the stages do not always occur in the same sequence.

We've now seen how casual human inquiry can set us up for making mistakes, and we have summarized basic research purposes. But what if you were to undertake a research project yourself? Where would you start? Then where would you go? How would you begin planning your research? College courses on research methods in criminal justice often require students to design a research project. The rest of this chapter covers the basics of planning research and writing a proposal for doing research.

Every project has a starting point, but it is important to think through later stages even at the beginning. Figure 1.1 presents a schematic view of the social scientific research process. Think of this as a sort of map that provides an overview of the whole process before we launch into the details of particular components of research.

The Research Process

At the top of the diagram in Figure 1.1 are interests, ideas, theories, and new programs—the possible beginning points for a line of research. The letters (*A*, *B*, *X*, *Y*, and so forth) represent concepts such as deterrence or burglary. Thus you might have a general interest in finding out why the threat of punishment deters some, but not all, people from committing crimes, or you might want to investigate how burglars select their targets. Question marks in the diagram indicate that you aren't sure things are the way you suspect they are. We have represented a theory as a complex set of relationships among several concepts (*A*, *B*, *E*, and *F*).

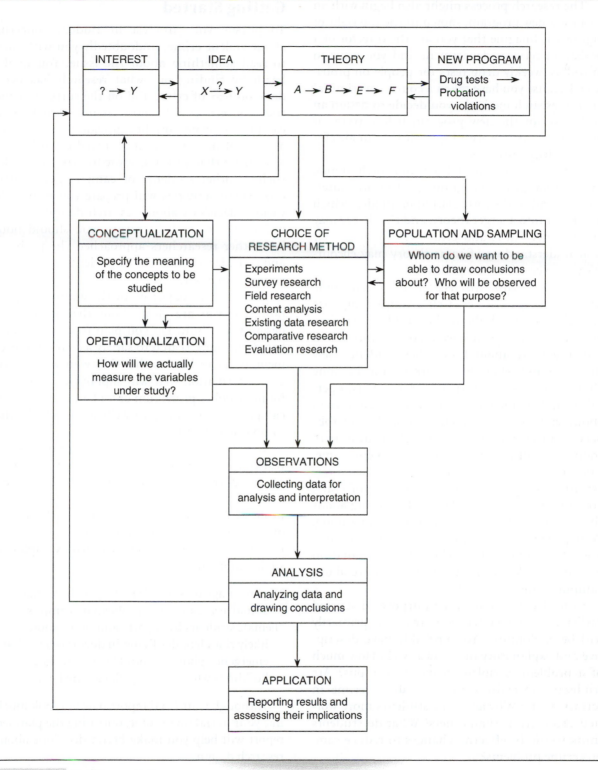

FIGURE 1.1 The Research Process

The research process might also begin with an idea for a new program, shown in the top right of Figure 1.1. Imagine that you are the director of a probation services department and you want to introduce weekly drug tests for people on probation. Because you have taken a course on criminal justice research methods, you decide to design an evaluation of the new program before trying it out. The research process begins with your idea for the new drug-testing program.

Notice the movement back and forth among these several possible beginnings. An initial interest may lead to the formulation of an idea, which may be fit into a larger theory, and the theory may produce new ideas and create new interests. Or your understanding of some theory may encourage you to consider new policies.

To make this discussion more concrete, let's take a specific research example. Suppose you are concerned about the problem of crime on your campus; you have a special interest in learning more about how other students view the issue and what they think should be done about it. Going a step further, let's say you perceive that students are especially concerned about violent crimes such as assault and robbery and that many students feel the university should be doing more to prevent violent crime. The source of this idea might be your own interest after being a student for a couple of years. You might develop the idea while reading about theories of crime in a course you are taking. Perhaps you recently read stories about a crime wave on campus. Or maybe some combination of things makes you want to learn more about campus crime.

Considering the research purposes discussed earlier in this chapter, your research primarily will be exploratory. You probably have descriptive and explanatory interests as well: How much of a problem is violent crime on campus? Are students especially concerned about crime in certain areas? Why are some students more worried about crime than others? What do students think would be effective changes to reduce campus crime problems?

Getting Started

To pursue your interest in student concerns about violent crime, undoubtedly you will want to read something about the issue. You might begin by finding out what research has been done on fear of crime and on the sorts of crime that concern people most. Items posted on a campus website might provide information about violent crimes that occurred recently. It is also likely that you will want to talk to people, such as other students or campus police officers. These activities will prepare you to handle various decisions about research design. As you review the research literature, you should note how other researchers approached the problem and consider whether the same designs will meet your research objective.

What is your objective, by the way? It's important that you are clear about that before you design your study. Do you plan to write a paper based on your research to satisfy a course requirement, or as an honors thesis? Is your purpose to gain information that will support an argument for more police protection or for better lighting on campus? Do you want to write an article for the campus newspaper or blog?

Usually, your objective for undertaking research can be expressed in a report. We recommend that you make an outline of such a report as the first step in the design of any project. You should be clear about the kinds of statements you will want to make when the research is complete. Here are two examples of such statements:

"X percentage of State U students believe that sexual assault is a big problem on campus."

"Female students living off campus are more likely than females living in dorms to feel that emergency phones should be installed near buildings where evening classes are held."

Although your final report may not look much like your initial image of it, outlining the planned report will help you make better decisions about research design.

Conceptualization

We often talk casually about criminal justice concepts such as deterrence, recidivism, crime prevention, community policing, and child abuse—but it's necessary to specify what we mean by these concepts to do research on them. Chapter 5 will examine this process of **conceptualization** in depth. For now, let's see what it might involve in our hypothetical example.

If you are going to study student concerns about violent crime, you must first specify what you mean by *concern about violent crime*. This ambiguous phrase can mean different things to different people. Campus police officers are concerned about violent crime because that is part of their job. Students may have two other kinds of concerns. On the one hand, students might be concerned about crime in much the same way they are concerned about other social problems, such as immigration, health care, and the global economy. They recognize these issues as problems society must deal with, but they don't feel that the issues affect them directly; we could specify this concept as *general concern about violent crime*. On the other hand, students may feel that the threat of violent crime does affect them directly, and they express some fear about becoming a victim; let's call this *fear for personal safety*.

Of course, you need to specify all the concepts you wish to study. If you want to study the possible effect of concern about crime on student behavior, you'll have to decide whether you want to limit your focus to specific precautionary behavior—such as keeping doors locked or to general behavior, such as going to classes, parties, and football games.

Choice of Research Method

A variety of methods are available to the criminal justice researcher. Each method has strengths and weaknesses, and certain concepts are studied more appropriately by some methods than by others.

A survey is the most appropriate method for studying both general concern and fear for personal safety. These are things that people think about, and that usually can't be observed directly. You might interview students or ask them to fill out an online questionnaire. As we'll see in Chapter 9, surveys are especially well suited to the study of individuals' attitudes and opinions. Thus, if you wish to examine whether students who are afraid of crime are more likely to believe that campus lighting should be improved than students who are not afraid, a survey is a good method. Alternatively, you might conduct in-depth interviews with a smaller number of students or with a focus group—topics addressed in Chapter 10.

Other methods described in Part Three may be appropriate. Through content analysis (discussed in Chapter 12), you might examine entries on a campus blog and analyze the writers' recommendations to improve campus safety. Field research (see Chapter 11)—in which you observe whether students tend to avoid dark areas of the campus—will help you understand student behavior in avoiding certain areas of the campus at night. Or you might study official complaints made to police and college administrators about crime problems on campus. As you read Part Three, you'll see how other research methods might be used to study this topic. Often the best study design is one that uses more than one research method, taking advantage of their different strengths.

Operationalization

Having specified the concepts to be studied and chosen the research method, you now must develop specific measurement procedures. **Operationalization**, discussed in Chapter 5, refers to the concrete steps, or operations, used to measure specific concepts.

If you decide to use a survey to study concern about violent crime, your operationalization will take the form of questionnaire items. You might operationalize fear for personal safety with the question "How safe do you feel alone on the campus after dark?" This could be followed by boxes indicating the possible answers "Safe" and "Unsafe." Student attitudes about how to improve campus safety could be operationalized with the item "Listed below are different actions that might be taken to reduce violent crime on campus. Beside each description, indicate whether you favor or oppose the actions described." This could be followed by several different actions, with "Favor" and "Oppose" boxes beside each.

Population and Sampling

In addition to refining concepts and measurements, decisions must be made about whom or what to study. The population for a study is that group about whom we want to be able to draw conclusions. Groups are usually made up of people, but we may wish to study a group of drug rehabilitation clinics. We are almost never able to study all the members of the population that interests us, so we often sample subjects for study. Chapter 8 describes methods for selecting samples that adequately reflect the population that interests us. Notice in Figure 1.1 that decisions about population and sampling are related to decisions about the research method to be used.

In the study of concern about violent crime, the relevant population is the student population of your college. As you'll discover in Chapter 8, however, selecting a sample requires you to get more specific than that. Will you include part-time as well as full-time students? Students who live on campus, off campus, or both? If your purpose is to study concern about sexual harassment, you might consider limiting your population to female students. If hate crimes are of special interest, you will want to be sure that your study population includes minorities and others who are thought to be particularly targeted by hate crimes.

Observations

Having decided what to study, among whom, and by what method, you are ready to make observations—to collect empirical data. The chapters in Part Three, which describe various research methods, discuss the different observation methods appropriate to each.

For a survey of concern about violent crime, you might prepare an electronic questionnaire and have it completed by a sample selected from the student body. Or you could have a team of interviewers conduct the survey over the telephone. The relative advantages and disadvantages of these and other possibilities are discussed in Chapter 9.

Analysis

We manipulate the collected data for the purpose of drawing conclusions that reflect on the interests, ideas, and theories that initiated the inquiry. Chapter 14 describes a few of the many options available to you in analyzing data. Notice in Figure 1.1 that the results of your analyses feed back into your initial interests, ideas, and theories. In practice, this feedback may initiate another cycle of inquiry. In the study of student concern about violent crime, the analysis phase will have both descriptive and explanatory purposes. You might begin by calculating the percentage of students who feel afraid to use specific parking facilities after dark and the percentage who favor or oppose each of the different things that might be done to improve campus safety. Together, these percentages will provide a good picture of student opinion on the issue.

Moving beyond simple description, you might examine the opinions of different subsets of the student body: men versus women; freshmen, sophomores, juniors, seniors, and graduate students; and students who live in dorms versus off-campus apartments. You might then conduct some explanatory analysis to make the point that students who are enrolled in evening classes are most in favor of improved campus lighting.

Application

The final stage of the research process involves using the research you've conducted and the conclusions you've reached. To start, you will probably want to communicate your findings so that others will know what you've learned. You will usually prepare some kind of written report. Perhaps you will make oral presentations in class or at a professional meeting. Or, you might create a Web page that presents your results. Other students will be interested in hearing what you have learned regarding their concerns about violent crime on campus.

Your study might also be used to actually do something about campus safety. If you find that a large proportion of students you interviewed believe that a parking lot near the library is poorly lighted, university administrators could add more lights, or campus police might patrol the area more frequently. Crime prevention programs might be launched in dormitories if residents are more afraid of violent crime than students who live in other types of housing. Students in a Rutgers University class on crime prevention focused on car thefts and break-ins surrounding the campus in Newark, New Jersey. Their semester project presented specific recommendations on how university and city officials could reduce the problem.

Thinking About Research Problems

One of the most important, yet surprisingly difficult, parts of the research process is specifying and framing your interest in a particular problem or question.

What are you interested in understanding? Surely you have several questions about crime and possible policy responses. Why do some juvenile gangs sell drugs, while others steal cars? Why do particular neighborhoods near campus seem to have higher rates of burglary? How often are guns found in stop-and-frisk operations? Do sentencing policies discriminate against minorities? Do cities with gun control laws have lower murder rates? Is burglary more common in single-family homes or in apartment buildings? Are sentences for rape more severe in some states than in others? Are mandatory jail sentences more effective than license suspension in reducing repeat drunk-driving offenses? Think for a while about the kinds of questions that interest and concern you.

To give you ideas about the many possible subjects for research, here are topics of papers written by students in a class Maxfield taught at John Jay College in fall 2010:

- Risk assessment in juvenile parole hearings
- The effect of religion and culture on attitudes about suicide
- Determining the extent to which arrest frequency is associated with substance addiction and mental illness

- Links between domestic violence and indirect spouse abuse after separation
- An exploratory study of pimps in Atlantic City, New Jersey
- An experimental study of attitudes toward sex offenders in Spain
- Whether sexual abuse by Catholic priests is a product of sexual preference or situational factors
- Community disorganization and crime on Native American lands

In most cases, researchers find themselves reworking or clarifying research problems as they learn more about a topic. That was the case for students in Maxfield's class. Amber Horning, the student studying pimps, was surprised to learn that only a minority of prostitutes in Atlantic City had anything like the classic worker/manager relationship with a pimp. That led to reframing the research to begin by classifying the different ways prostitutes worked with pimps and others playing pimp-like roles. (By the way, Amber Horning is the author of Chapter 10 on qualitative interviewing in this text.)

In most cases, you're advised to begin with your own interests and experiences, and then learn more about what research has been done. For example, a student with considerable experience in correctional settings examined the third topic listed earlier. She began with her observation that people arrested frequently for minor offenses often seem driven more by substance abuse and mental health problems than any overt criminal intent. The student then conducted research to learn more about existing research on jail populations, and she revised her topic as she read more of the research literature.

Students sometimes have difficulty narrowing interests to researchable questions. We are all concerned about crime and justice problems to some degree, but our casual interests can be misleading. Reading research about crime and justice problems is a good way to get ideas about research topics and to see how social science addresses problems that are treated more casually in popular literature. The box "Getting Ideas About Research Topics" offers more advice in this regard.

GETTING IDEAS ABOUT RESEARCH TOPICS

Many people will have some idea what sort of research questions they're interested in, no matter how general the idea may be. Even so, it can be difficult for beginning researchers to get started. Here are some tips for finding and fleshing out preliminary ideas about research topics.

DO AN INTERNET SEARCH, BUT USE SPECIALIZED TOOLS

For example, type the following phrase into a Google search panel: "sex offender residency restrictions." In April 2013, this entry produced an estimated 203,000 results that included mass media stories, links to legislation, and many other types of sites. Now, type the same phrase into a Google Scholar search panel (go to http://scholar.google.com). In April 2013, this search yielded about 238 results of scholarly books and articles on the topic. Reading examples of these results, or mass media stories for that matter, will give you ideas about how to begin research on sex offender residency restrictions.

REPLICATE AN EXISTING STUDY

Jacqueline Berenson and Paul Appelbaum (2010) examined where sex offenders lived in two New York counties. They were interested in laws that required sex offenders to live a minimum distance from places like schools and other public facilities, as well as the effects that such laws have on housing choices for sex offenders. Two findings were noteworthy. First, 73 to 97 percent of existing housing units in the two counties were off-limits to sex offenders because they were too close to specified facilities. Second, and as a consequence of the first finding, most sex offenders living in the two counties were in violation of the restrictions. What about in your city or county?

Because data on where sex offenders live are widely available, you could conduct a similar kind of study in a different place.

FOLLOW UP ON RECOMMENDATIONS FOR FURTHER RESEARCH

Many research articles and books conclude by describing how subsequent research can add to knowledge. So if you find an article interesting, you might get an idea from the authors' suggestions for further research. For example, Norman White and Rolf Loeber (2008) examined links between bullying in school, placement in special education programs, and later involvement in serious delinquency. They found that later delinquency often followed bullying, regardless of placement in special education programs. Their research was based on interviews over a period of years with students in Pittsburgh, Pennsylvania, schools. Near the end of their article, they recommend that future research use systematic observations of behavior in different types of school activity (White and Loeber, 2008:393). If you are interested in the problem of bullying or violence in middle schools, reading articles that report research on the topic could give you ideas about designing your own study.

ASK YOUR PROFESSOR

If one of the requirements for your research methods course is to write a research proposal or actually do some research, you should find out what topics are of special interest to your instructor. This does not mean you should engage in idle flattery. Instead, think of your instructor as both an expert and a professional scholar, someone who is probably doing research for a book, scholarly article, or dissertation. Your professor is an expert in what research might need to be done in a particular area. So don't hesitate to ask for ideas. Be sure to use focused questions, such as "What sorts of topics are you interested in?" That's better than asking something like "Can you give me some ideas? I don't know where to begin."

Reviewing the Literature

Researchers begin a research project with a review of the literature.

Research should be seen as an extension of what has been learned previously about a particular topic. A review of the literature will tell you what's already known and not known. In most cases, you should organize your search of the literature around the key concepts you wish to study. Alternatively, you may want to study a certain population: corrections officers, sex offenders, drug counselors, computer hackers, and so forth. In any case, you'll identify a set of terms that represent your core interests.

With the expansion of information and search tools on the Internet, conducting a literature review has become simultaneously easier and more challenging. It's easier in the sense that much information can be accessed through the Internet without having to visit brick-and-mortar libraries. Most colleges and universities now have online access to academic journals. Reports by government agencies and private organizations are readily available to anyone with online access.

Reviewing what others have found about a problem has become more difficult largely for the same reason—it's easy to access a seemingly endless supply of documents. This has produced a related problem of how to sort through all the information, separating research findings from the demented ramblings of ideologues and everything in between. After providing guidelines on how to find relevant literature, we'll suggest some cautionary strategies.

General Strategies

Doing a literature review is basically a process of accumulating, sorting through, and synthesizing information. We do this every day in different, usually informal ways. Doing a literature review for research is more systematic and deliberate, much like the research process itself. It's best to keep notes of articles, books, websites, or other resources as you review them. Also keep in mind that research literature accumulates; research studies usually build on previous studies, as we noted in the box "Getting Ideas About Research Topics."

Getting Started Start with a book or article that deals with your topic and expand from there. We'll call this your source document. Expanding can mean going backward (consulting readings cited in your source document), or forward, in which you find later research that is based on your source document. For example, if you're interested in terrorism, you might read the book *Outsmarting the Terrorists* by Ronald Clarke and Graeme Newman (2006). In conducting your literature review, you would read selected references shown in the book's bibliography.

But you would also be interested in later research that expands on what Clarke and Newman wrote in 2006. One of the best ways to do this is to use the website Google Scholar (http://scholar.google.com). Type "clarke newman outsmarting" in the search box, and one of the first references that pops up should be their book. In March 2016, this search showed that 221 subsequent publications have cited the book. Clicking on "cited by 221" produces a list of these publications, together with links to further information about the books or journals that cite Clarke and Newman. For example, in 2015 Joshua Freilich and associates examined how various criminological theories of crime were useful in understanding terrorist attacks. Their research built on the early book by Clarke and Newman. This is an example of how you can find out about more current research that's been published since your source document.

Being Selective Sources like Google Scholar offer a built-in quality control by limiting your search to academic journals and related publications. However, you may want to find other types of materials, such as government reports or studies published by other types of organizations. Ronald Clarke and Phyllis Schultze (2005:24) offer a useful warning and guidelines:

> Unlike scholarly books and journal articles, websites are seldom reviewed or refereed. You need to be critical of the information you use when it comes to the Web, because anyone can make a website that looks expert. In general, rely more heavily on those sites sponsored by colleges and universities, government agencies, and professional organizations.

Some college or university libraries provide more detailed suggestions on how to evaluate information you discover in your research. For example, the Meriam Library at California State University Chico (2010) describes evaluation criteria referred to as the "CRAAP Test":

Currency: Information timeliness.
Relevance: Does the information apply to your specific topic?
Authority: The source of the information.
Accuracy: Is the information based on fact or opinion?
Purpose: Why does the information exist? Why is it presented?

Using a Library   Although it is no longer necessary to visit a physical library to access many published research materials, libraries and librarians remain critical resources for research. Librarians can help you develop strategies for searching the literature and evaluating the different sources you find. Ronald Clarke and Phyllis Schultze (2005) offer excellent advice on how to use different types of libraries. For research on crime and justice, the Don M. Gottfredson Library of Criminal Justice at Rutgers University, under the direction of Phyllis Schultze, is the best single library resource available anywhere, with unmatched physical and online resources. Visit the library through the World Criminal Justice Library Electronic Network (http://andromeda.rutgers.edu/~wcjlen/WCJ/).

How to Read Scholarly Research

You don't read a social research report the way you'd read a novel. You can, of course, but it's not the most effective approach. Journal articles and books are laid out somewhat differently, so here are some initial guidelines for reading each.

Reading a Journal Article   In most journals, each article begins with an abstract. Read it first. It should tell you the purpose of the research, the methods used, and the major findings. The abstract serves two major functions. First, it gives you a good idea as to whether you'll want to read the rest of the article. If you're reviewing the literature for a paper you're writing, the abstract tells you whether that particular article is relevant.

Second, the abstract establishes a framework within which to read the rest of the article. It may raise questions in your mind regarding method or conclusions, thereby creating an agenda to pursue in your reading. Several journals in criminal justice now present abstracts in a standard format that makes it easier to learn about each published article. Abstracts are presented under four headings: *Objectives, Methods, Results, and Conclusions.*

After you've read the abstract, you might go directly to the summary and/or conclusions at the end of the article. That will give you a more detailed picture of what the article is all about. Jot down any new questions or observations that occur to you.

Next, skim the article, noting the section headings and any tables or graphs. You don't need to study any of these items in your skimming, although it's fine to review anything that catches your attention. By the end of this step, you should start feeling familiar with the article. You should be pretty clear on the researcher's conclusions and have a general idea of the methods used in reaching them.

If you decide to read the entire article carefully, you'll have a good idea of where it's heading and how each section fits into the logic of the whole. Keep taking notes. Mark any passages you think you might like to quote later on. After reading the article thoroughly, it's a good idea to skim it quickly one more time. This way, you get back in touch with the forest after having focused on the trees.

If you want to fully grasp what you've just read, find someone else to explain it to. If you're doing the reading in connection with a course, you should have no trouble finding someone willing to listen. However, if you can explain it coherently to someone who has no prior contact with the subject matter, you'll know you have an absolute lock on the material.

Reading a Book-Length Report   The approach for articles can be adapted to reading a book-length report, sometimes also called a research monograph. These longer research reports cover the same basic terrain and use roughly the same structure. Instead of an abstract, the preface and opening chapter of the book lay out the purpose, method, and main findings of the study. The preface is usually written more informally, and so may be easier to understand than an abstract.

As with an article, it's useful to skim through the book, getting a sense of its organization, its use of tables and graphs, and its main findings. You should come away from this step feeling somewhat familiar with the book. Take notes as you go along, writing down things you observe and questions that are raised.

As you settle in to read the book more carefully, you should repeat this same process with each chapter. Read the opening paragraphs to get a sense of what's to come, and then skip to the concluding paragraphs for the summary. Skim the chapter to increase your familiarity with it, and then read more deliberately, taking notes as you go.

It's sometimes okay to skip portions of a scholarly book, but this depends on your purpose in reading it in the first place. Perhaps only a few portions of the book are relevant to your research. However, if you're interested in the researcher's findings, you must pay some attention to the methods used (e.g., who was studied? How? When?) in order to judge the quality of the author's conclusions.

The Research Proposal

Research proposals describe planned activities, and include a budget and time line.

If you undertake a research project—an assignment for this course, perhaps, or a study funded by your university or a research foundation—you probably will have to provide a research proposal describing what you intend to accomplish and how. We now offer advice on how you might prepare such a proposal. As we do this, think of the research proposal as another way to get an overview of the research process.

Elements of a Research Proposal

Some funding agencies have specific requirements for a proposal's elements, structure, or both. For example, in its research solicitation announcement for graduate research fellowships, the National Institute of Justice (NIJ) describes what should be included in research proposals regardless of topic (http://www.nij.gov/nij/funding/fellowships/graduate-research-fellowship/faqs.htm). Your instructor may have certain requirements for preparing a research proposal in this course. Here are some basic elements that should be included in almost any research proposal.

Problem or Objective What exactly do you want to study? Why is it worth studying? Does the proposed study contribute to our general understanding of crime or policy responses to crime? Does it have practical significance? If your proposal describes an evaluation study, then the problem, objective, or research questions may already be specified for you. For example, in its request for research on research and evaluation in connection with changes in policing, the NIJ asked that proposals address specific topics described in a report on policing in the twenty-first century. One set of questions centered on training and education in police use of force (National Institute of Justice, 2016:10).

Literature Review As we described in the previous section, research begins by reviewing what others have said about your topic.

Research Questions What specific questions will your research try to answer? Given what others have found, as stated in your literature review, what new information do you expect to find? It's useful to view research questions as a more specific version of the problem or objective described earlier. Then, of course, your specific questions should be framed in the context of other research findings.

Subjects for Study Whom or what will you study in order to collect data? Identify the subjects in general terms, and then specifically identify who (or what) is available for study and how you will reach them. Is it appropriate to select a sample? If so, how will you do that? If there is any possibility that your research will have an impact on those you study? If so, how will you ensure that they are not harmed by the research? Finally, if you will be interacting directly with human subjects, you will probably have to include a consent form, as we describe in Chapter 3.

PUTTING IT ALL TOGETHER

"Driving While Black"

INTRODUCTION

Racial profiling of drivers on the nation's streets and highways became a prominent issue in the late 1990s. Concern was fueled by compelling stories of minority motorists stopped by police for minor traffic violations, then subjected to aggressive questioning, searches, and even arrest. One of the most highly publicized examples involved:

> . . . Robert Wilkins, a Harvard Law School graduate and a public defender in Washington, D.C., who went to a family funeral in Ohio in May 1992. On the return trip, he and his aunt, uncle, and 29-year-old cousin rented a Cadillac for the trip home. His cousin was stopped for speeding in western Maryland while driving 60 miles per hour in a 55-mile-per-hour zone of the interstate. The group was forced to stand on the side of the interstate in the rain for an extended period while officers and drug-sniffing dogs searched their car. Nothing was found. Wilkins, represented by the ACLU, filed suit and received a settlement from the state of Maryland. (Ramirez, McDevitt, and Farrell, 2000:6)

What came to be known as "driving while black" generated a number of lawsuits and eventually legislation at the state and federal level.

The underlying question was whether police traffic stops targeted African American and other minority drivers in a discriminatory way. Because the U.S. Constitution prohibits law enforcement officers from discriminatory behavior based on race, allegations of racial profiling generated a number of legal challenges and court cases.

By their nature, lawsuits revolve around individual cases, such as that of Robert Wilkins, and whether evidence of discrimination was present in Wilkins's encounter with the Maryland State Police. In this sense, court cases tend to seek idiographic explanations of what happened in an individual case. Eventually, however, social scientists became involved in trying to assess the scope of racial profiling and what sorts of things might be associated with the practice. And social scientists focused more on nomothetic explanations of what kinds of things accounted for more general patterns of police actions in traffic stops.

Racial profiling also offers examples of different types of errors in traditional human inquiry. You might recognize the role overgeneralization plays in most forms of prejudice. Selective observation is another example. If police believe minorities are more often involved in drug or weapons smuggling, they will selectively stop cars driven by minorities. Assuming the extreme case where police stop only minorities, they will only be able to detect possible weapons or

Measurement What are the key variables in your study? How will you define and measure them? Do your definitions and measurement methods duplicate (that's okay, incidentally) or differ from those of previous research on this topic?

Data Collection Methods How will you collect the data for your study? Will you observe behavior directly or conduct a survey? Will you undertake field research, or will you focus on the reanalysis of data already collected by others? Criminal justice research often includes more than one such method.

Analysis Briefly describe the kind of analysis you plan to conduct. Spell out the purpose and logic of your analysis. Are you interested in precise description? Do you intend to explain why things are the way they are? Will you analyze the impact of a new program? What possible explanatory variables will your analysis consider, and how will you know whether you've explained the program impact adequately?

References Be sure to include a list of all materials you consulted and cited in your proposal.

drug offenses among minority motorists. In that case, race profiling might become a self-fulfilling prophecy.

This box is the first of a running example that appears throughout the book. We examine racial profiling for several reasons. First, it was a highly publicized issue that promoted policy action and research throughout the United States. Second, for most people, a traffic stop is their most common experience of coming under suspicion of police. A much larger proportion of people have a contact with police through a traffic stop than a criminal arrest. Further, in the words of David Harris (1999), "almost any black person any place in the country" could describe a personal experience of what was believed to be a discriminatory traffic stop. Third, police and other public officials challenged accusations of discrimination, claiming any disproportionate traffic stops of black motorists reflected different rates of traffic violations. This raised questions about how to determine whether individual traffic stops or patterns of traffic stops were based on the race of drivers or on something else. In this way, measuring patterns of traffic stops and the reasons underlying those patterns became an important research topic.

Finally, researchers at New Jersey's Rutgers University conducted their own research on race profiling in New Jersey, a state that came to symbolize race profiling for many people. Maxfield collaborated with colleagues George Kelling and Carsten Andresen to conduct research on the New Jersey State Police (Maxfield and Andresen, 2002; Maxfield and Kelling, 2005). And Carsten Andresen completed his own dissertation research on this topic (Andresen, 2005). Thus, the running example reflects some direct experiences in the messy realities of criminal justice research, realities that are not usually depicted in published studies.

HOW DO WE KNOW?

Let's consider what we have covered so far and examine how these general issues in research are reflected in the questions about racial profiling on the nation's highways.

- What percentage of cars stopped have minority drivers (descriptive)? What affects police decisions to stop particular vehicles (explanatory)? What changes should be made in police practices regarding traffic stops (applied)?
- How do we come to believe that discriminatory practices underlie patterns of police traffic stops? What evidence supports that belief? And what evidence supports claims that police actions are not affected by race or ethnicity?
- In addition to those mentioned above, what errors of traditional human inquiry might be involved? What about ideology and politics?
- Are particular theories available to guide our inquiry?
- Quite a lot of research has been conducted on municipal policing and police actions with respect to crime, but state police and traffic enforcement have hardly been studied at all. Can findings from other police actions help understand traffic enforcement?

How might the problem of racial profiling illustrate other topics described in this chapter?

Formats for citations vary. Your instructor may specify certain formats or refer you to specific style manuals for guidelines on how to cite books, articles, and web-based resources.

Schedule   It is often appropriate to provide a schedule for the various stages of research. Even if you don't do this for the proposal, do it for yourself. If you don't have a time line for accomplishing the stages of research and keeping track of how you're doing, you may end up in trouble.

Budget   If you are asking someone to give you money to pay the costs of your research, you will need to provide a budget that specifies where the money will go. Large, expensive projects include budgetary categories such as personnel, equipment, supplies, and expenses (such as travel and copying). Even for a more modest project you will pay for yourself, it's a good idea to spend some time anticipating any expenses involved: office supplies, photocopying, transportation, and so on.

As you can see, if you are interested in conducting a criminal justice research project, it is a good idea to prepare a research proposal for your own purposes—even if you aren't required to do so by your instructor or a funding agency. If you are going to invest your time and energy in such a project, you should do as much planning as you can to ensure a return on that investment.

Knowing Through Experience: Summing Up and Looking Ahead

Empirical research involves measurement and interpretation.

This chapter introduced the foundation of criminal justice research: empirical research, or learning through experience. Doing scientific research in criminal justice is different from the ordinary ways we learn about things, because ordinary modes of inquiry have some built-in limits. The coming chapters describe how science tries to avoid such limits and biases.

We also considered the different purposes we may have in mind for conducting criminal justice research, ranging from exploration to examining links between policy action and justice problems.

Our advice on how to design a research project will be useful in two respects. First, consider it an annotated outline of what a typical research report would include. In that capacity, this can be useful if you are going to prepare a research report or proposal for this course. Second, Figure 1.1 and our discussion of how to design a research project offer an introduction and overview to later chapters.

The box "Putting It All Together: Driving While Black" presents the first installment of an example of criminal justice research we will consider throughout the book. This running example will illustrate some features of topics discussed in each chapter, drawing largely on research completed by Michael Maxfield and former colleagues at Rutgers University. In this chapter's example, we introduce the topic and compare how researchers approach it to how it has been presented in courts and the media generally.

Finally, much of criminal justice research centers on two basic activities: measurement and interpretation. Researchers measure aspects of reality and then interpret the meaning of what they have measured. All of us are observing all the time, but measurement refers to something more deliberate and rigorous than ordinary human inquiry. Parts Two and Three of this book describe ways of structuring observations to produce more deliberate, rigorous measures.

The other key to criminal justice research is interpretation. Much of interpretation is based on data analysis, which is introduced in Part Four. More generally, however, interpretation very much depends on how observations are structured, a point we will encounter repeatedly.

As we put the pieces together—measurement and interpretation—we are in a position to describe, explain, or predict something. And that is what social science is all about.

SUMMARY

- Knowledge of research methods is valuable to criminal justice professionals as consumers and producers of research.

- The study of research methods is the study of how we know what we know.

- Inquiry is a natural human activity for gaining an understanding of the world around us.

- Much of our knowledge is based on agreement rather than on direct experience.

- Tradition and authority are important sources of knowledge.

- Empirical research is based on experience and produces knowledge through systematic observation.

- Scientists avoid illogical reasoning by being as careful and deliberate in their thinking as they are in their observations.

- The scientific study of crime guards against, but does not prevent, ideological and political beliefs from influencing research findings.

- Different research purposes are exploratory, descriptive, explanatory, and applied.

- The research process is flexible, involving different steps that are best considered together. The process usually begins with some general interest or idea.

- A careful review of previous literature is an essential part of the research process.

- A research proposal provides an overview of why a study will be undertaken and how it will be conducted. It is a useful device for planning and is required in some circumstances.

KEY TERMS

Key terms are introduced in each chapter and are defined in the book's glossary.

Applied research *(p. 13)*
Conceptualization *(p. 17)*
Descriptive research *(p. 13)*
Empirical *(p. 7)*
Explanatory research *(p. 13)*
Exploratory research *(p. 12)*
Methodology *(p. 7)*
Operationalization *(p. 17)*
Replication *(p. 10)*

REVIEW QUESTIONS AND EXERCISES

1. Review the common errors of personal inquiry discussed in this chapter. Searching the Internet or a newspaper, find an article about crime that illustrates one or more of those errors. Discuss how a social scientist would avoid making that error.

2. Briefly discuss examples of descriptive research and explanatory research about crime rates in a large city near your college or university.

3. Often, things we think are true and supported by considerable experience and evidence turn out not to be true, or at least not true with the certainty we expected. Criminal justice seems especially vulnerable to this phenomenon, perhaps because crime and criminal justice policy are so often the subjects of mass and popular media attention. If news stories, movies, and television shows all point to growing gang or drug-related violence, it is easy to assume that these are real problems identified by systematic study. Choose a criminal justice topic or claim that's currently prominent in news stories or entertainment. Using Google Scholar or some other bibliographic tool, search the Internet for two research studies that examine the topic in systematic ways we described in this chapter. Briefly summarize the studies' findings.

CHAPTER 2

Foundations of Criminal Justice Research

We'll see what distinguishes scientific theory from everyday reasoning and how the social scientific approach to criminal justice research is linked to theory. We'll also lay a foundation for understanding the research techniques discussed throughout the rest of the book.

Learning Objectives

1. Summarize the three fundamental features of social science: theory, data collection, and data analysis.
2. Describe why social scientists are interested in explaining aggregates, not individuals.
3. Understand that social scientists are primarily interested in discovering relationships that connect variables.
4. Understand the difference between idiosyncratic and nomothetic explanations.
5. Distinguish between inductive and deductive forms of reasoning.
6. Distinguish between quantitative and qualitative approaches to research.
7. Recognize that intersubjective agreement, not objectivity, is a fundamental norm of science.
8. Describe the traditional image of social science theory.
9. Understand how scientific inquiry alternates between induction and deduction.
10. Describe how observations contribute to theory development in grounded theory.
11. Discuss how criminological theories draw on other social sciences, and sometimes on the natural sciences.
12. Describe how theory and public policy can be closely linked.

Theory and Serial Sex Offenders

Criminologists Eric Beauregard, D. Kim Rossmo, and Jean Proulx (2007) studied 69 incarcerated serial sex offenders in Canada. The research had two objectives. First, the researchers developed a descriptive model of how sex offenders "hunted" for victims. Drawing on lengthy interviews with subjects, they systematically classified the different search methods and places where offenders looked for victims. Rational choice and routine activity theories of crime helped Beauregard and colleagues classify sex offender actions into summary categories for their descriptive model:

Victim Search Methods

- Offender's routine activities
- Victim's routine activities
- Choice of a hunting field
- Victim selection preferences

Offender Attack Methods

- Attack location choice
- Method to bring victim to crime location
- Crime location choice

The second objective was to see if this descriptive model was potentially useful in *profiling* serial sex offenders. If the researchers could identify patterns of behavior based on what they learned from convicted sex offenders, then it might be possible to profile the actions of active offenders at large. Profiling is a form of prediction based on observed regularities. Results showed clear patterns and sequences of offense stages. Sex offenders' behavior was limited to certain situations where they encountered victims. For example, 57 percent of offenders chose public areas such as parks or shopping malls as their "hunting field"—where they searched for possible victims. In this regard, these serial sex offenders were quite different than sex offenders generally, who tend to limit their search to family members and acquaintances (Leclerc, Wortley, and Smallbone, 2011).

This example illustrates three ways in which theory is involved in criminal justice research. First, Beauregard and associates drew on existing theories to frame their analysis of serial sex offender behavior. We will see further examples of this *deductive* use of theory. Second, findings from the preliminary model "also make a contribution to the theoretical assumptions regarding offender profiling" (Beauregard, Rossmo, and Proulx, 2007:461). This is *inductive* theory building, pulling together research findings to make more general statements and predictions. Third, criminal justice theory and policy have much in common.

Each depends on general explanations and patterns of behavior.

Also notice how this example examines aggregates of sex offenders, not individuals. Finally, the researchers are interested in relationships between types of places and sex offender behavior.

Introduction

Criminal justice in particular, and human behavior in general, can be studied scientifically.

The evolution of social science has brought a greater emphasis on systematic explanation and a reduced emphasis on description. For example, political scientists now focus on explaining political behavior rather than describing political institutions. The growth of such subfields as econometrics has had this effect in economics, as has historiography in history. Criminal justice and criminology have followed this same trend. Research on the causes of crime and the effects of criminal justice policy has supplanted an earlier emphasis on describing strategies for police investigation or corrections management.

This book is grounded in the position that human behavior can be subjected to scientific study as legitimately as can the physicist's atoms or the biologist's cells. The study of crime and criminal justice concentrates on particular types of human behavior, and so is no less amenable to scientific methods. Our attention now turns to the overall logic of social scientific inquiry in criminology and criminal justice. That logic is fundamentally rooted in the use of theory to guide inquiry.

At the same time, criminal justice research often examines questions that cannot easily be reduced to scientific measures. Sometimes researchers are more interested in gaining a detailed understanding about a particular individual or small number of people. (e.g., Amber Horning's research on pimps sought to learn more about the range of their roles in linking sex workers and consumers; see Chapter 10). Addressing such questions requires approaches to gathering information that differ from those used by natural scientists.

Foundations of Social Science

Social scientific inquiry generates knowledge through logic and observation.

Science is sometimes characterized as "logico-empirical." This ungainly term carries an important message: The two pillars of science are (1) logic or rationality and (2) observation. A scientific understanding of the world must make sense and must agree with what we observe. Both of these elements are essential to social science and relate to three key aspects of the overall scientific enterprise: *theory, data collection,* and *data analysis.*

As a broad generalization, scientific theory deals with the logical aspect of science, data collection deals with the observational aspect, and data analysis looks for patterns in what is observed. This book focuses mainly on issues related to data collection—demonstrating how to conduct empirical research—but social science involves all three elements. Later in this chapter, we consider the theoretical context of designing and executing research. Chapter 14 presents a conceptual introduction to the statistical analysis of data.

Let's turn now to some of the fundamental issues that distinguish social science from other ways of looking at social phenomena.

Theory, Not Philosophy or Belief

Social scientific theory has to do with what is, not what should be. This means that scientific theory—and, more broadly, science itself—cannot settle debates on value or worth. Social science cannot determine, for example, whether prosecutors who are elected (as in most states) are "better" than prosecutors who are appointed by a state official (as in New Jersey) except in terms of some agreed-on criteria. We could determine scientifically whether elected or appointed prosecutors are more respected by the citizens they serve. But we could do that only if we agreed on some measures of citizen respect, and our conclusion would depend totally on those measures.

By the same token, if we agree that, say, conviction rate or average sentence length is a good measure of a prosecutor's quality, then we will be in a position to determine scientifically whether a prosecutor in one city is better or worse than a prosecutor in another city. Again, however, our conclusion will be inextricably tied to the agreed-on criteria. As a practical matter, however, people are seldom able to agree on criteria for determining issues of value, so science is seldom of any use in settling such debates.

As an example, consider the dilemma of how to identify a good parole officer. On the one hand, a parole officer whose clients are rarely cited for violations and returned to prison might be considered a good officer. However, parole officers might attain low violation rates by ignoring misbehavior among clients they are supposed to supervise—in effect, by not supervising them at all. Therefore, we might view a parole officer who frequently cites parolees for violations as being especially attentive to his or her job. We might also consider other factors. Someone who routinely cites parolees for trivial rule infractions would not necessarily be considered a good officer, especially if such actions swell already crowded prison populations. In a study of parole and community supervision of offenders, the National Research Council (2007) considered this question in examining the purposes of parole.

Thus, social science can assist us in knowing only what is and why. It can be used to address the question of what ought to be only when people agree on the criteria for deciding what makes one thing better than another. But this agreement seldom occurs. With that understanding, let's turn now to some of the fundamentals that social scientists use to develop theories about what is and why.

Regularities

Ultimately, social science aims to find patterns of regularity in social life. This assumes, of course, that life is regular and not chaotic or random. That assumption applies to all science, but it is sometimes a barrier for people when they first approach social science.

Certainly, at first glance, the subject matter of the physical sciences appears to be more regular than that of the social sciences. A heavy object, after all, falls to Earth every time we drop it. In contrast, a judge may sentence one person to prison and give another probation, even though both are convicted of the same offense. Driving 10 miles per hour over the speed limit will produce a speeding ticket in Ohio, but not in New Jersey.

A vast number of norms and rules in society create regularity. For example, only persons who have reached a certain age may obtain a driver's license. Only lawyers are considered for positions on the U.S. Supreme Court. Informal and formal prescriptions, then, regulate or regularize social behavior.

In addition to regularities produced by norms and rules, social science deals with other types of regularities based on observation. For example, teenagers commit more crimes than middle-aged people. When males commit murder, they usually kill another male, but female murderers more often kill a male. On average, white urban residents view police more favorably than nonwhites do. Judges receive higher salaries than police officers. And probation officers have more empathy for the people they supervise than prison guards do.

What About Exceptions?

The objection that there are always exceptions to any social regularity does not mean that the regularity itself is unimportant. A police officer in a large city might earn more than a judge in a small town, but overall, judges earn more than police officers. The pattern still exists. Social regularities represent *probabilistic* patterns, and a general pattern does not have to be reflected in 100 percent of the observable cases to be a pattern.

This rule applies in the physical as well as the social sciences. In genetics, for example, the mating of a blue-eyed person with a brown-eyed person will *probably* result in a brown-eyed offspring. The birth of a blue-eyed child does not challenge the observed regularity, however. Rather, the geneticist states only that a brown-eyed offspring is *more likely* and, furthermore, that a brown-eyed offspring will be born in only a certain percentage of cases. The social scientist makes a similar, probabilistic prediction: Women overall are less likely to murder anybody, but when they do, their victims are most often males.

Aggregates, Not Individuals

Social scientists primarily study social, rather than individual, patterns. All regular patterns reflect the aggregate or combined actions and situations of many individuals. Although social scientists study motivations that affect individuals, **aggregates** are more often the subject of social science research.

A focus on aggregate patterns rather than on individuals distinguishes the activities of criminal justice researchers from the daily routines of most criminal justice practitioners. Consider, for example, the task of processing and classifying individuals newly admitted to a correctional facility. Prison staff administer psychological tests and review the prior record of each new inmate to determine security risks, program needs, and job options. A researcher studying whether white inmates tend to be assigned to more desirable jobs than nonwhite inmates would be more interested in patterns of job assignment. The focus would be on *aggregates* of white and nonwhite persons, rather than the assignment for any particular individual.

Social scientific theories typically deal with aggregate, not individual, behavior. Their purpose is to explain why aggregate patterns of behavior are so regular even when the individuals who perform them change over time. In another important sense, social science doesn't even seek to explain people. Rather, it seeks to understand the systems within which people operate—the systems that explain why people do what they do. The elements in such systems are not people, but variables.

A Variable Language

Our natural attempts at understanding usually take place at the concrete, idiosyncratic level. That's just the way we think. Suppose someone says to you, "Women are too soft-hearted and weak to be police officers." You are likely to "hear" that comment in terms of what you know about the speaker. If it's your old Uncle Albert, who, you recall, is also strongly opposed to daylight savings time, cell phones, and indoor plumbing, you are likely to think his latest pronouncement simply fits into his dated views about things in general. If, however, the statement comes from a candidate for sheriff who is trailing a female challenger, and who has begun making other statements about women being unfit for public office, you may "hear" his latest comment in the context of this political challenge.

In both of these examples, we try to understand the thoughts of a particular, concrete individual. In social science, however, we go beyond that level of understanding to seek insights into classes or types of individuals. In the two preceding examples, we might use terms like *old-fashioned* or *bigoted* to describe the person who made the comment. In other words, we try to identify the actual individual with some set of similar individuals, and that identification operates on the basis of abstract concepts.

One implication of this approach is that it enables us to make sense out of more than one person. In understanding what makes the bigoted candidate think the way he does, we can also learn about other people who are "like him." This is possible because we have not been studying *bigots* as much as we have been studying *bigotry*.

Here's another example. Consider the problem of whether police should make arrests in cases of domestic violence. The object of a police officer's attention in handling a domestic assault is the individual case. Of course, each case includes at least two people, and police are concerned with preventing further harm to the parties involved. The officer must decide whether to arrest someone or to take some other action. The criminal justice researcher's subject matter is different: Does arrest as a general policy prevent future assaults? The researcher may study an individual case (victim and offender), but that case is of interest only because arrest policy might be invoked, which is what the researcher is really studying.

This is not to say that criminal justice researchers don't care about real people. They certainly do. Their ultimate purpose in studying domestic violence cases is to identify ways to protect potential victims from future assaults. But in this example, victims and offenders are most relevant for what they reveal about the effectiveness of the arrest policy. As researchers, our interest centers on variables and aggregates, not on individuals.

Variables and Attributes

Social scientists study variables and the attributes that compose them. Social scientific theories are written in a variable language, and people get involved mostly as the carriers of those variables. Here's how social scientists define attributes and variables:

Attributes are characteristics or qualities that describe some object such as a person. Examples are "bigoted," "old-fashioned," "married," "unemployed," and "intoxicated." Any quality we might use to describe ourselves or someone else is an attribute.

Variables are logical groupings of attributes. Thus, for example, "male" and "female" are attributes, and "gender" is the variable composed of the logical grouping of those two attributes. The variable "occupation" is composed of attributes like "dentist," "professor," and "security guard." "Prior record" is a variable composed of a set of attributes such as "prior convictions," "prior arrests without convictions," and "no prior arrests." It's helpful to think of attributes as the categories that make up a variable. Figure 2.1 provides a schematic view of what social scientists mean by variables and attributes.

Variables Logical groupings of attributes. The variable "gender" includes the attributes of "female" and "male."

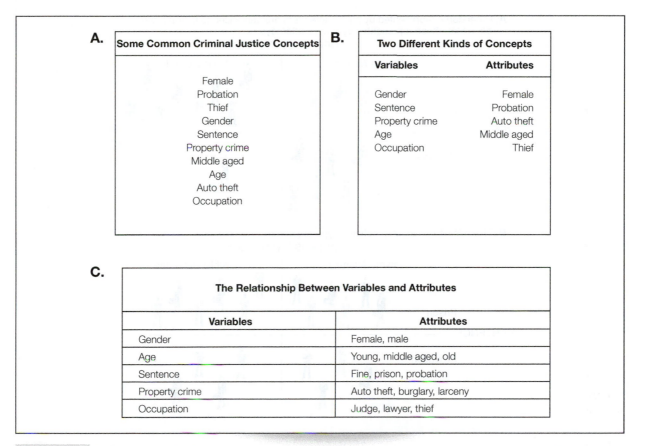

A.

Some Common Criminal Justice Concepts
Female
Probation
Thief
Gender
Sentence
Property crime
Middle aged
Age
Auto theft
Occupation

B.

Two Different Kinds of Concepts	
Variables	**Attributes**
Gender	Female
Sentence	Probation
Property crime	Auto theft
Age	Middle aged
Occupation	Thief

C.

The Relationship Between Variables and Attributes	
Variables	**Attributes**
Gender	Female, male
Age	Young, middle aged, old
Sentence	Fine, prison, probation
Property crime	Auto theft, burglary, larceny
Occupation	Judge, lawyer, thief

FIGURE 2.1 Variables and Attributes

The relationship between attributes and variables lies at the heart of both description and explanation in science. For example, we might describe a prosecutor's office in terms of the variable "gender" by reporting the observed frequencies of the attributes "male" and "female": "The office staff is 60 percent men and 40 percent women." An incarceration rate can be thought of as a description of the variable "incarceration status" of a state's population in terms of the attributes "incarcerated" and "not incarcerated." Even the report of family income for a city is a summary of attributes composing the income variable: $47,124, $64,980, $86,000, and so forth.

The relationship between attributes and variables becomes more complicated as we try to explain things. Here's a simple example involving two variables: type of defense attorney and sentence. For the sake of simplicity, let's assume that the variable "defense attorney" has only two attributes: "private attorney" and "public defender." Similarly, let's give the variable "sentence" two attributes: "probation" and "prison." Now let's suppose that 90 percent of people represented by public defenders are sentenced to prison and the other 10 percent are sentenced to probation. And let's suppose that 30 percent of people with private attorneys go to prison and the other 70 percent receive probation. This is shown visually in Figure 2.2A.

Figure 2.2A illustrates a relationship between the variables "defense attorney" and "sentence." This relationship can be seen by the pairings of attributes on the two variables. There are two predominant pairings: (1) persons represented by private attorneys who are sentenced to probation and (2) persons represented by public defenders who are sentenced to prison. But there are two other useful ways of viewing that relationship.

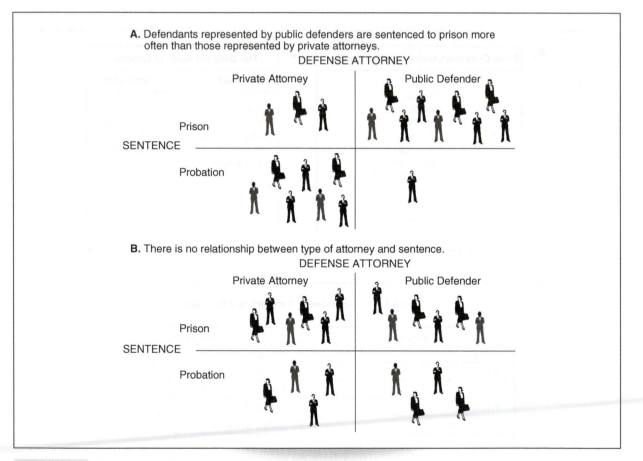

A. Defendants represented by public defenders are sentenced to prison more often than those represented by private attorneys.

DEFENSE ATTORNEY

Private Attorney   Public Defender

Prison

SENTENCE

Probation

B. There is no relationship between type of attorney and sentence.

DEFENSE ATTORNEY

Private Attorney   Public Defender

Prison

SENTENCE

Probation

FIGURE 2.2 Illustration of Relationships Between Two Variables

First, imagine that we play a game in which we bet on your ability to guess whether a person is sentenced to prison or probation. We'll pick the people one at a time (not telling you which ones we've picked), and you have to guess which sentence each person receives. We'll do it for all 20 people in Figure 2.2A. Your best strategy in this case is to always guess prison because 12 out of the 20 people are categorized that way. Thus, you'll get 12 right and eight wrong, for a net success score of four.

Now suppose that we pick a person from Figure 2.2A and we have to tell you whether the person has a private attorney or a public defender. Your best strategy now is to guess prison for each person with a public defender and probation for each person represented by a private attorney. If you follow that strategy, you will get 16 right and four wrong. Your improvement in guessing the sentence based on knowing the type of defense attorney illustrates what it means to say that the variables are related. You would have made a probabilistic statement based on some empirical observations about the relationship between type of lawyer and type of sentence.

Second, let's consider how the 20 people would be distributed if type of defense attorney and sentence were unrelated. This is illustrated in Figure 2.2B. Notice that half the people have private attorneys and half have public defenders. Also notice that 12 of the 20 (60 percent) are sentenced to prison—six who have private attorneys and six who have public defenders. The equal distribution of those sentenced to probation and those sentenced to prison, regardless of type of defense attorney, allows us to conclude that the two variables are unrelated. Here, knowing what type of attorney a person had would not be of any value to you in guessing whether that person was sentenced to prison or probation.

Variables and Relationships

We will look more closely at the nature of the relationships between variables later in this book. For now, let's consider some basic observations about variables and relationships that illustrate the logic of social scientific theories and their use in criminal justice research.

Theories describe relationships that might logically be expected among variables. This expectation often involves the notion of causation: A person's attributes on one variable are expected to *cause* or encourage a particular attribute on another variable. In the example just given, having a private attorney or a public defender seemed to cause a person to be sentenced to probation or prison, respectively. Apparently, there is something about having a public defender that leads people to be sentenced to prison more often than if they are represented by a private attorney.

Type of defense attorney and sentence are examples of independent and dependent variables, respectively. These two concepts are implicit in causation, which is the focus of explanatory research. In this example, we assume that criminal sentences are determined or caused by something; the type of sentence depends on something and thus is called the **dependent variable**. The dependent variable depends on an **independent variable**; in this case, sentence depends on type of defense attorney.

Notice, at the same time, that type of defense attorney might be found to depend on something else—our subjects' employment status, for example. People who have full-time jobs are more likely to be represented by private attorneys than those who are unemployed. In this latter relationship, the type of attorney is the dependent variable, and the subject's employment status is the independent variable. In cause-and-effect terms, the independent variable is the cause, and the dependent variable is the effect.

How does this relate to theory? Our discussion of Figure 2.2 involved the interpretation of data. We looked at the distribution of the 20 people in terms of the two variables. In constructing a theory, we form an expectation about the relationship between the two variables based on what we know about each. For example, we know that private attorneys tend to be more experienced than public defenders. Many people fresh out of law school gain a few years of experience as public defenders before they enter private practice. Logically, then, we would expect the more experienced private attorneys to be better able to get more lenient sentences for their clients. We might explore this question directly by examining the relationship between attorney experience and sentence, perhaps comparing inexperienced public defenders with public defenders who had been working for a few years. Pursuing this line of reasoning, we could also compare experienced private attorneys with private attorneys fresh out of law school.

Notice that the theory has to do with the variables "defense attorney," "sentence," and "years of experience," not with individual people per se. People are the carriers of those variables. We study the relationship between the variables by observing people. Ultimately, however, the theory is constructed in terms of variables. It describes the associations that might logically be expected to exist between particular attributes of different variables.

The vignette that opens this chapter, "Theory and Serial Sex Offenders," illustrates how researchers used theory to guide their inquiry to research behaviors by sex offenders.

Differing Avenues for Inquiry

Social scientific research is conducted in a variety of ways.

Three broad and interrelated distinctions underlie many of the variations of social scientific research: (1) idiographic and nomothetic explanations, (2) inductive and deductive reasoning, and (3) quantitative and qualitative data. Although they might appear to be competing choices, a good researcher masters each of these orientations.

Idiographic and Nomothetic Explanations

All of us go through life explaining things; we do it daily. In our everyday explanations, we engage in two distinct forms of causal reasoning, although we do not ordinarily distinguish them. Sometimes we attempt to explain a single situation exhaustively. You might have done poorly on an exam because (1) you had forgotten there was an exam that day, (2) it was in your worst subject, (3) a traffic jam caused you to be late to class, or (4) your roommate kept you up the night before with loud music. Given all these circumstances, it is no wonder that you did poorly on the exam.

This type of causal reasoning is **idiographic** explanation. *Idio* in this context means "unique, separate, peculiar, or distinct," as in the word *idiosyncrasy*. When we complete an idiographic explanation, we feel that we fully understand the many causes of what happened in a particular instance. At the same time, the scope of our explanation is limited to the case at hand. Although parts of the idiographic explanation might apply to other situations, our intention is to explain one case fully.

Now consider a different kind of explanation. For example, every time you study with a group, you do better on an exam than if you study alone. Your favorite team does better at home than on the road. Traffic around your campus is heavier on weekdays than on the weekend. This type of explanation—called **nomothetic**—seeks to explain a class of situations or events rather than a single one. Moreover, it seeks to explain efficiently, using only one or just a few explanatory factors. Finally, it settles for a partial rather than a full explanation of a type of situation.

In each of the preceding nomothetic examples, you might qualify your causal statements with phrases such as "on the whole" or "usually." You usually do better on exams when you've studied in a group, but there have been exceptions. Your team has won some games on the road and lost some at home. And during last Saturday's home football game, traffic was terrible, much worse than any day the previous week. Such exceptions are an acceptable price to pay for a broader range of overall explanation.

Both idiographic and nomothetic approaches to understanding can be useful in daily life. They are also powerful tools for criminal justice research. The researcher who seeks an exhaustive understanding of the inner workings of a particular juvenile gang or the rulings of a specific judge is engaging in idiographic research. The aim is to understand that particular group or individual as fully as possible.

Rick Brown and Ron Clarke (2004) sought to understand thefts of a particular model of Nissan trucks in the south of England. Most stolen trucks were never recovered. Their research led Brown and Clarke to a shipping yard where trucks were taken apart and shipped to ports in France and Nigeria as scrap metal. They later learned that trucks were reassembled and sold to individuals and small companies. In the course of their research, they linked most thieves in England and most resellers abroad to legitimate shipping and scrap metal businesses. Even though Brown and Clarke sought answers to the idiosyncratic problem of stolen trucks in one region of England, they came to some tentative conclusions about loosely organized international theft rings.

In contrast to the idiographic study of Nissan truck theft, Aki Roberts and Steven Block (2012) examined differences in temporary and permanent motor vehicle theft in 310 U.S. cities. In a temporary theft the stolen vehicle is eventually recovered, while vehicles are not recovered in permanent thefts. The authors found that different types of factors were related to temporary and permanent theft. Temporary theft was more common in cities with more young male residents, and a larger number of households that did not own vehicles. Roberts and Block attributed this to a larger pool of people interested in joyriding, and greater demand for temporary (albeit illegal) transportation. Permanent theft was higher in cities where more adult property offenders lived, and cities closer to the U.S. border with Mexico. Revealing these different patterns for permanent and temporary vehicle theft illustrates the nomothetic approach to understanding.

Social scientists have access to two distinct logics of explanation. We can alternate between searching for broad, albeit less detailed, universals (nomothetic) and probing more deeply into more specific cases (idiographic).

Inductive and Deductive Reasoning

The distinction between inductive and deductive reasoning exists in daily life, as well as in criminal justice research. You might take two different routes to reach the conclusion that you do better on exams if you study with others. Suppose you find yourself puzzling, halfway through your college career, over why you do so well on exams sometimes and poorly at other times. You list all the exams you've taken, noting how well you did on each. Then you try to recall any circumstances shared by all the good exams and by all the poor ones. Do you do better on multiple-choice exams or essay exams? Morning exams or afternoon exams? Exams in the natural sciences, the humanities, or the social sciences? After you studied alone or in a group? It suddenly occurs to you that you almost always do better on exams when you studied with others than when you studied alone.

This is known as the inductive mode of inquiry. **Inductive reasoning** (induction) moves from the specific to the general, from a set of particular observations to the discovery of a pattern that represents some degree of order among the varied events under examination.

There is a second, and very different, way you might reach the same conclusion about studying for exams. As you approach your first set of exams in college, you might wonder about the best ways to study. You might consider how much you should review the readings and how much you should focus on your class notes. Should you study at a measured pace over time, or pull an all-nighter just before the exam? Among these musings, you might ask whether you should get together with other students in the class or study on your own. You decide to evaluate the pros and cons of both options. On the one hand, studying with others might not be as efficient because a lot of time might be spent on material you already know. Or the group might get distracted from studying. On the other hand, you can understand something even better when you've explained it to someone else. And other students might understand material that you've been having trouble with and reveal perspectives that might have escaped you.

So you add up the pros and the cons and conclude, logically, that you'd benefit from studying with others. This seems reasonable to you in theory. To see whether it is true in practice, you test your idea by studying alone for half your exams and studying with others for half.

This second approach is known as the deductive mode of inquiry. **Deductive reasoning** (deduction) moves from the general to the specific. It moves from a pattern that might be logically or theoretically expected to observations that test whether the expected pattern actually occurs in the real world. Notice that deduction begins with *why* and moves to *whether*, whereas induction moves in the opposite direction.

Both inductive and deductive reasoning are valid avenues for criminal justice and other social scientific research. Moreover, they work together to provide ever more powerful and complete understandings.

Quantitative and Qualitative Data

Simply put, the distinction between quantitative and qualitative data is the distinction between numerical and nonnumerical data. When we say that someone is witty, we are making a qualitative assertion. When we say that that person has appeared three times in a local comedy club, we are attempting to quantify our assessment.

Most observations are qualitative at the outset, whether it is our experience of someone's sense of humor, the location of a pointer on a measuring scale, or a check mark entered in a questionnaire. None of these things is inherently numerical. But it can be useful to convert observations to a numerical form. Quantification often makes our observations more explicit, makes it easier to aggregate and summarize data, and opens up the possibility of statistical analyses, ranging from simple descriptions to more complex testing of relationships between variables.

Quantification requires focusing our attention and specifying meaning. Suppose someone asks whether your friends tend to be older or younger than you. A quantitative answer seems easy. You think about the ages of each of your friends, calculate an average, and see whether it is higher or lower than your own age. Case closed.

Or is it? Although we focused our attention on "older or younger" in terms of the number of years people have been alive, we might mean something different with that idea—for example, "maturity" or "worldliness." Your friends may tend to be a little younger than you in age but to act more mature. Or we might have been thinking of how young or old your friends look or of the variation in their life experiences, their worldliness. All these other meanings are lost in the numerical calculation of average age.

In addition to greater detail, nonnumerical observations seem to convey a greater richness of meaning than do quantified data. Think of the cliché "He is older than his years." The meaning of that expression is lost in attempts to specify how much older. In this sense, the richness of meaning is partly a function of ambiguity. If the expression meant something to you when you read it, that meaning came from your own experiences, from people you have known who might fit the description of being "older than their years." Two things are certain: (1) your understanding of the expression is different from ours, and (2) you don't know exactly what either of us means by the expression.

A psychology graduate student at John Jay College in New York City, Miriam was born in Frankfurt, Germany. Her mother was a child soldier in the civil conflict that eventually formed Eritrea from a region of Ethiopia in the Horn of Africa. An uncle in Saudi Arabia helped Miriam's mother obtain asylum in Germany, where she met the man who was to become Miriam's father. Her parents divorced when Miriam was about seven years old; her father moved to Las Vegas, while she stayed with her mother. Miriam was increasingly unsettled by the acute brand of prejudice faced by many immigrants in Germany, especially those from Muslim countries. After eventually overcoming strong objections from her mother, Miriam moved to the United States to join her father; she was 14 years old. Miriam obtained her undergraduate degree from the University of Nevada and set out for New York in September 2009 to begin her graduate work.

We would probably agree that Miriam sounds like someone who is both worldly and "older than her years." However, the brief description of Miriam's experiences, although it fleshes out the meaning of the phrase, still does not equip us to say how much older or even to compare Miriam with someone else without the risk of disagreeing as to which one is more "worldly."

This concept can be quantified to a certain extent, however. For example, we could make a list of life experiences that contribute to what we mean by worldliness:

Getting married
Getting divorced
Having a parent die
Being fired from a job
Moving to another country

We could quantify people's worldliness by counting how many of these experiences they have had; the more such experiences, the more worldly we say they are. If we think that some experiences are more powerful than others, we can give those experiences more points than others. Once we decide on the specific experiences to be considered and the number of points each warrants, scoring people and comparing their worldliness is fairly straightforward.

To quantify a concept like worldliness, we must be explicit about what we mean. By focusing specifically on what we will include in our measurement of the concept, as we did here, we also exclude the other possible meanings. Inevitably, then, quantitative measures will be more superficial than qualitative descriptions. This is the trade-off.

What a dilemma! Which approach should we choose? Which is better? Which is more appropriate to criminal justice research?

The good news is that we don't have to choose. In fact, by choosing to undertake a qualitative or quantitative study, researchers run the risk of artificially limiting the scope of their inquiry. Both qualitative and quantitative methods are useful and legitimate. And some research situations and topics require elements of both approaches.

Theory 101

Theory and observation go together in science—but sometimes theory precedes observation, and other times observation comes before theory.

We now consider the relationship between **theory** and research in more depth. First, we'll get started with some of the basics of theory. Next, we'll consider an example of the scientific method as it is traditionally taught. Then, we will take a closer look at two models for describing how theory and research work together in the practice of social science. Finally, we consider at some length the important links between theory, research, and policy.

We already have used some of the common terms associated with social science theory. Most people have a general idea of what they mean in everyday language. In this chapter, however, we will examine their meanings more precisely to prepare for our later examination of the links between theory and criminal justice research.

Theory

A **theory** is a systematic explanation for the observed facts and laws that relate to a particular aspect of life—juvenile delinquency, for example, or perhaps social stratification or political revolution. Joseph Maxwell (2013:48) defines theory as "a set of concepts and the proposed relationships among these, a structure that is intended to represent or model something about the world."

Objectivity and Subjectivity

We recognize that some things fall into the realm of attitudes, opinions, and subjective points of view. For example, the question of whether Bach or Beethoven was the better composer is a subjective matter, dependent on the experiences and tastes of the person who is making such a judgment. But the existence of this publication on your computer or in your hands is an objective matter, independent of your experience of it. Objective is typically defined as "independent of mind," but our awareness of what might objectively exist comes to us through our minds. As a working principle, social scientists prefer the phrase **intersubjective agreement** instead of **objectivity**. If several of us agree that something exists, then we treat that thing as though it had objective existence. This view of intersubjective agreement as a working version of objectivity is consistent with our earlier consideration, in Chapter 1, of agreement reality.

Hypotheses

A **hypothesis** is a specified expectation about empirical reality, derived from propositions. If we continue the present example, a theory might

Theory   A systematic explanation for observed facts and laws that describe and predict.

Intersubjective agreement   Norm of science whereby different researchers studying the same problem arrive at the same conclusion.

contain the hypothesis "Second-generation immigrant youths have higher delinquency rates than first-generation immigrant youths do." Such a hypothesis could then be tested through research, as we will see below, in an example drawing on social disorganization theory and delinquency.

Another way to think of a hypothesis is as a tentative answer to a research question. For example, we may want to do research to answer the question "What is the relationship between immigration status and arrest for assault?" Then we present a tentative answer to that question as a hypothesis: "Second-generation immigrant youths will be more likely to be arrested for assault than will first-generation immigrant youths."

Paradigms

No one ever starts out with a completely clean slate to create a theory. When we mentioned juvenile delinquency as an example of a topic for theory construction, you probably already had some implicit ideas about it. If we had asked you to list some concepts relevant to a theory of juvenile delinquency, you would have been able to make suggestions. We might say that you already have a general point of view—a frame of reference or paradigm. A **paradigm** is a fundamental model or scheme that organizes our view of something.

This may strike you as uncomfortably similar to the definition of theory, and this is a natural point of confusion. The primary distinction is based on organization and structure. A paradigm is a structured but broader way of viewing things that affects how we approach research problems. It may be helpful to think of a paradigm as a pair of tinted glasses; everything we look at reflects the tint, no matter how we structure our observations. A theory serves to structure more carefully what we see through the paradigm's lenses, but what we see is still tinted. Whereas a paradigm offers a way of looking, a theory aims at explaining what we see.

Although a paradigm doesn't necessarily answer important questions, it tells us where, and

often how, to look for the answers. And as we'll see repeatedly, where you look largely determines what you find. Thomas Kuhn (1996:37) describes the importance of paradigms this way:

> One of the things a scientific community acquires with a paradigm is a criterion for choosing problems that, while the paradigm is taken for granted, can be assumed to have solutions. To a great extent these are the only problems that the community will admit as scientific or encourage its members to undertake. Other problems, including many that had previously been standard, are rejected as metaphysical, as the concern of another discipline, or sometimes as just too problematic to be worth the time. A paradigm can, for that matter, even insulate the community from those socially important problems that are not reducible to the puzzle form, because they cannot be stated in terms of the conceptual and instrumental tools the paradigm supplies.

Kuhn's chief interest was in how science advances. Although some progress involves the slow, steady, and incremental improvement of established paradigms (Kuhn calls this "normal science"), he suggests that important scientific progress takes the form of paradigm shifts, as established, agreed-on paradigms are discarded in favor of new ones. Thus, for example, Newtonian physics was replaced by Einstein's relativity in what Kuhn calls a "scientific revolution."

The Traditional Model of Science

The traditional model begins with theory and then uses deductive reasoning.

Theory plays a critical role in the traditional model of science. The scientist begins with an interest in some aspect of the real world. Suppose we are interested in discovering some of the broad social factors that contribute to the concentration of crime in urban areas. What kinds of social

Paradigm A fundamental model or frame of reference that we use to organize our observations and reasoning.

problems and characteristics of urban areas are associated with higher levels of crime?

As we think about this question, we might come up with things like population density, crowded housing conditions, poverty, unemployment, limited economic opportunities, weakened family ties, and the absence of appropriate role models. These are some of the ideas that influenced the development of social disorganization theories of crime. In the early twentieth century, sociologists began to examine the social disruption produced by rapid population growth in the city of Chicago. What came to be known as the "Chicago School" of criminology began with more general studies of the roots of a broad spectrum of social problems.

Conceptualization

Sociologists Ernest Burgess and Robert Park started by describing Chicago's growth as a pattern of concentric zones (Burgess, 1925; Park and Burgess, 1921). At the core was the city's central business district, or downtown area. As Chicago expanded, the city developed in a pattern of circles radiating from the core. Each area, from the downtown core to outlying suburbs, displayed particular patterns of land use. Commerce and industry were concentrated in downtown areas, while wealthy families occupied residential areas in outer circles. Lower-income migrants to Chicago settled in transition zones between the core and more distant areas.

Transition zones were so labeled because of the continuous flow of people in and out of the areas. Higher-income residents tended to move outward to avoid the influx of industrial activity expanding from the city's core area. Outward-moving families were replaced by lower-income immigrants from Europe (and later white and black migrants from depressed southern states) who came to the United States to pursue economic opportunity or escape political oppression. Persons moving into transition zones found housing that was deteriorating and crowded, but close to the factory jobs that had attracted them to Chicago. As their economic situation improved, they moved outward and were replaced by new "in-migrants," thus continuing the cycle of transition.

Burgess argued that these patterns of population movements and neighborhood conditions weakened families, social institutions, and other collective ties, thus producing a general phenomenon he called "social disorganization." Several problems were believed to result from social disorganization, including higher rates of disease, mental illness, and crime. These ideas form the basis of the social disorganization theory of crime.

However, the social conditions in transition zones that Burgess described suggest other possible explanations for the higher rates of crime in these areas. For example, if early-twentieth-century immigrants from Europe were concentrated in transition zones, such groups might have brought cultural differences to urban areas that contributed to crime and other social ills. In other words, crime in transition zones might not have been a consequence of social disorganization, but the result of a concentration of individuals from particular cultural backgrounds in those areas.

How should we settle the question of whether social disorganization or cultural differences accounted for the concentration of crime in transition zones? The next step in the traditional model of science helps us move toward an answer.

Operationalization

Operationalization means specifying steps, procedures, or operations for actually identifying and measuring the variables we want to observe. In the present example, operationalization involves deciding how to measure things like crime, social disorganization, and cultural background.

While Park and Burgess were developing their general theories of urban growth and its social consequences, sociologists Clifford Shaw and Henry McKay began a series of studies that tested the social disorganization explanation for crime in transition zones. Their landmark study, originally published in 1942, described how important concepts were operationalized (Shaw and McKay, 1969).

First, they chose three indicators of delinquency to measure crime, each obtained from official city records: (1) alleged delinquents brought before juvenile court, (2) juveniles committed to institutions, and (3) alleged delinquents detained by police but not brought before a juvenile court.

Second, social disorganization was measured even less directly, as is often the case in social research. Indicators were constructed from census data and information provided by local agencies. These indicators included families on relief (an earlier version of welfare and unemployment payments), average monthly rent, home ownership, occupational status, and ethnicity. One measure of ethnicity was whether a head of household was born in another country, referred to as "foreign-born"; another was the percentage of black families.

These indicators made it possible to compare delinquency with social disorganization and ethnic background. But how could Shaw and McKay determine which of these two factors was more important in explaining delinquency? Recall the concept of transition zones: People were continuously moving into and out of the neighborhoods between core commercial zones and more wealthy residential areas. The notion of transition implies population movement, and the mobility of urban residents in Chicago offered an answer.

Shaw and McKay compared changes in delinquency rates over time, focusing on three periods: 1900–1906, 1917–1923, and 1927–1933. They also examined delinquency among different ethnic groups within each zone. On the one hand, they suggested, if cultural differences accounted for crime, then delinquency rates in outer zones should increase as people from different cultural backgrounds moved out of transition zones and into more stable residential areas. On the other hand, if social disorganization produced delinquency, then the pattern of lower rates in outer zones and higher rates in transition zones should remain stable despite the outward movement of ethnic groups.

Park and Burgess identified five concentric zones in Chicago: Zones I and II were the inner core and transition areas; farther out, zone III included the homes of working-class families; zone IV was a middle-income residential area; and zone V was a suburban or outer area. Within each zone were several distinct neighborhoods. Shaw and McKay divided the city into 140 areas of approximately one square mile each, so that several areas were included in each of the five zones. These 140 areas represented units of analysis.

Observation

The final step in the traditional model of science involves actual observation—looking at the world and making measurements of what is seen. Having developed theoretical expectations and created a strategy for observation, we next look at the way things are. Our observations may be structured around the testing of specific hypotheses, or the inquiry may be less structured. For Shaw and McKay, it meant poring through published statistics in search of data relevant to their operationalization and then grouping data on delinquency and other indicators according to 140 geographical areas.

Comparing delinquency between ethnic groups, they found that rates were higher for all groups in core areas and transition zones. Although there was wide variation within groups—foreign-born, black, and native white—similar rates for each group were found in similar types of zones. Comparing rates over time, Shaw and McKay (1969:162, 315) found that when foreign-born families moved to outer zones, delinquency rates remained lower in those areas than in inner zones. Summarizing these findings, they concluded:

> In the face of these facts it is difficult to sustain the contention that, by themselves, the factors of race, nativity, and nationality are vitally related to the problem of juvenile delinquency. It seems necessary to conclude, rather, that the significantly higher rates of delinquents found among the children of Negroes, the foreign born, and more recent immigrants are closely related to existing differences in their respective patterns of geographical distribution within the city. . . .

Moreover, the fact that in Chicago the rates of delinquents for many years have remained relatively constant in the areas adjacent to centers of commerce and heavy industry—despite successive changes in the nativity and nationality composition of the population—supports emphatically the conclusion that the delinquency-producing factors are inherent in the community.

Although subsequent research has challenged some of the conclusions Shaw and McKay reached, social disorganization theory continues to influence theory and research in criminal justice and other fields. For example, though most research on social disorganization has been conducted in the United States, Valdimarsdottir and Bernburg (2015) found that its basic mechanisms operate in Iceland. Their findings are all the more remarkable since they show that: "... social disorganization research can be generalized to a small homogeneous country with a developed welfare system" (p. 236). As a general rule, social science theories become stronger with evidence that they apply in a variety of social settings.

Contemporary environmental theories of crime, which emphasize such concepts as urban form and its influence on human behavior, are rooted in the earlier work of Park and Burgess and Shaw and McKay (e.g., see Brantingham and Jeffery, 1991). Dutch researchers have found that the presence of neighborhood businesses in large cities helps reduce social disorganization (Steenbeek et al., 2012).

Notice how Shaw and McKay's research was based on a more general theory of the links between the conditions of urban neighborhoods and a broad class of social ills. They had certain expectations about the patterns they would find in the numbers if a particular theoretical explanation was accurate. Operationalizing delinquency as an example of a social problem, they found higher rates of delinquency in transition zones, regardless of ethnic or cultural composition. In themselves, of course, these particular data did not prove the case; they did not provide definitive evidence that social disorganization produced delinquency. These data, however, were part of a body of evidence that Shaw and McKay amassed.

We have considered this example at some length for three reasons. First, it illustrates the traditional deductive model of scientific research—moving from theory, to operationalization, to observation. Second, it is more realistic than the hypothetical physics experiments you might recall from a science class. Finally, contemporary research in criminal justice continues to build on this theoretical view of the relationship between crime and the urban environment.

Figure 2.3 provides a schematic diagram of the traditional model of scientific inquiry. In it, we see

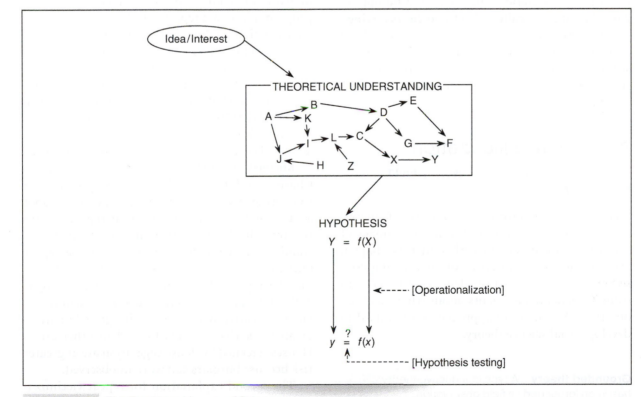

FIGURE 2.3 The Traditional Image of Science

the researcher beginning with an interest in something or an idea about it. Next comes the development of a theoretical understanding of how a number of concepts, represented by the letters A, B, C, and so on, may be related to each other. The theoretical considerations result in a hypothesis, or an expectation about the way things should be in the world if the theoretical expectations are correct. The notation $Y = f(X)$ is a conventional way of saying that Y (e.g., delinquency) is a function of or is in some way caused by X (e.g., substandard housing). At that level, however, X and Y have general rather than specific meanings.

In the operationalization process, general concepts are translated into specific indicators. Thus, the lowercase x is a concrete indicator of capital X. As an example, census data on the number of housing units that lack indoor plumbing (x) are a concrete indicator of substandard housing (X). This operationalization process results in the formation of a testable hypothesis: For example, did the rate of delinquency among Italian immigrants actually decline as they moved from substandard housing in transition zones to better housing in outer residential areas? Observations aimed at finding out are part of what is typically called **hypothesis testing**.

This traditional model of science provides a clear and understandable guide to how we can study something carefully and logically. However, theory and research in criminal justice are related in other ways.

An Inductive Illustration

Research also reasons inductively to build theory from observations.

Shaw and McKay's work illustrates the deductive reasoning that underlies the traditional image of science. As we described earlier in this chapter, criminal justice researchers often use inductive reasoning to accumulate evidence that leads them to make general statements about what has been observed. An inductive approach is often used to develop social science theory.

Grounded theory   A type of inductive theory based on (grounded in) field observation.

Social scientists may begin constructing a theory by observing aspects of social life, seeking to discover patterns that may point to more or less universal principles. Barney Glaser and Anselm Strauss (1967) coined the term **grounded theory** to describe this inductive method of theory construction. Field research—the direct observation of events in progress—is frequently used to develop theories. Or research drawing on data from surveys might reveal patterns of results that suggest particular theoretical explanations. Here's an example.

Crime Concentration

Criminal justice researchers increasingly have recognized that much crime is concentrated among offenders, places, victims, and even things that are stolen. A landmark study of youths in Philadelphia underscored the concentration of delinquency among a relatively small number of youths (Wolfgang, Figlio, and Sellin, 1972). Researchers have also formulated the concept of hot spots, relatively small places where a number of crimes are concentrated (Weisburd, 2015). Research done mostly in England discovered that some individual people or places are repeatedly victimized by crime. For example, Ken Pease reports that about 2 percent of victims of property crime in England account for over 40 percent of property crime victimizations (Pease, 1998:3). Tracking insurance claims for vehicle theft, the Highway Loss Data Institute (2016) reports the BMW M6 convertible was at most risk of car theft; theft rates were 9.4 times higher than average. The Smart for Two was at least risk of theft.

Michael Townsley, Ross Homel, and Janet Chaseling (2003) carried this one step further in wondering whether some burglaries in hot spot areas might be conceived as "near repeat victimizations." In doing so, they drew on their understanding of two different mechanisms for repeat burglary victimization. First, people and places may be repeatedly victimized because of inherently unequal risks, referred to as *risk heterogeneity*. Houses located in areas where burglars live are at greater risk than targets located in other areas. Houses screened by dense vegetation are at greater risk because burglars can work unobserved.

The second explanation for repeat victimization assumes that offenders learn something about individual dwellings from breaking into them. After burglars break into a particular house or apartment, they know how to break into it later. When offenders learn how to get into a dwelling, it reduces the element of uncertainty associated with a lesser-known target. Burglars also know what's available to be taken at a later time. This mechanism of repeat burglary is known as *event dependency*, where the event of a later burglary is partly dependent on what was learned during the first.

The idea of a near-repeat burglary recognizes how each of these two mechanisms might contribute to a burglary hot spot. Risk heterogeneity means that homes in areas where burglars operate are at greater risk. So if a burglary occurs a couple of doors down from an earlier burglary, that's a near-repeat that occurs because burglars are working in a particular neighborhood. With respect to event dependency, Townsley and associates proposed that burglars learn something about an area in the course of breaking into one home. That means dwellings near those already targeted are at greater risk, because offenders have learned something about features of the area that offer clues for selecting additional targets. Burglars may learn something about the street layout, how to blend into an area, and the routine coming and going of area residents.

The researchers examined police burglary reports from five urban and suburban areas in Queensland, Australia. As it happens, police records in Australia and the United Kingdom are more uniform and much more detailed than police records for most areas in the United States. Repeat burglaries were defined as those addresses that had two or more burglaries over 34 months. *Near-repeats*, identified through a fairly complex statistical estimation process, were burglaries that occurred within about 200 yards of a previous burglary over the 34-month study period.

Next, Townsley and associates enlisted the help of a real estate agent to learn something about the residences in their study area. This was an important part of a research strategy to learn how physical features of areas were related to burglary rates. They distinguished newer suburban developments with similar housing from more established areas that tended to have older,

more varied housing. The agent also helped researchers estimate the market value and age of houses in different neighborhoods, and whether or not areas were large-scale developments. The researchers used qualitative interviews to gather this information.

Analyzing the official police data, Townsley and associates found that repeat victimization was more common in areas with older homes, where the types and features of houses varied quite a lot. This was consistent with previous research suggesting that event dependency was the mechanism. Once burglars had targeted an older home, subsequent burglaries were more likely to strike the same dwelling, presumably because offenders knew how to break in and what they would find.

Findings were different in newer, larger developments. Here researchers found higher levels of near-repeat burglaries. Burglars were more likely to strike houses close to a home previously victimized than they were to return to the original target.

Considering this pattern of results, Townsley and associates proposed a mechanism of *contagion* for understanding repeat and near-repeat burglary:

> One way to think of the relationship between housing diversity and target vulnerability is through the infection analogy. . . . Housing diversity is an indicator of how contagious burglary victimization is, in that similar areas allow transmission of burglaries, whereas diverse areas restrict transmission. (2003:630)

Just as infectious diseases spread when people are packed together, as on an airplane or bus, burglary moves through a neighborhood made up of many newer homes of similar design. Once burglars have learned how to break into one house, they can more easily strike another nearby house of similar design. But in older neighborhoods where houses are more varied, burglars tend to return to the same target.

The researchers used inductive reasoning to develop their contagion theory of burglary. Examining patterns of offenses across different types of neighborhoods led them to compare the spread of crime to the spread of disease.

Finally, the researchers linked their findings to theoretical foundations of environmental criminology, emphasizing the central role of place. Just as Burgess—along with Shaw and McKay—found delinquency rates linked to urban zones, Townsley, Homel, and Chaseling now proposed that features of housing settlement patterns affect how burglaries spread through a community.

Inductive Theory in Practice

Consider a different way of looking at inductive theory building, suggested by Barbara Hart, legal director of the Pennsylvania Coalition Against Domestic Violence.[1] Speaking on the topic of how to increase the utilization of criminal justice research by justice professionals, Hart argued that the development of grounded theory was common among many practitioners. By this she meant that probation officers, judges, case managers, victim services counselors, and others tend to formulate general explanations to fit the patterns they observe in individual cases. As Hart put it, "Practitioners engage in theory building as they interpret experience." Others refer to a "theory of action" that embraces experience-based theories that guide public officials (Santos and Santos, 2015).

A theory of action may then guide the future actions of justice professionals, until they discover cases or patterns of cases that don't fit their theory. See the box titled "Grounded Theory and Community Prosecution" for an example.

In summary, the scientific norm of logical reasoning provides a bridge between theory and research—a two-way bridge. Scientific inquiry in practice typically involves an alternation between deduction and induction. During the deductive phase, we reason toward observations; during the inductive phase, we reason from observations. Both logic and observation are essential. In practice, both deduction and induction are routes to the construction of social theories.

---

[1]From remarks at the Family Violence Cluster Conference, National Institute of Justice, Washington, DC, July 12, 1995.

Theory, Research, and Public Policy

Theory in criminal justice guides both research and public policy.

Because crime is an important social problem, and not simply a social artifact of interest to researchers, much research in criminal justice is closely linked to public policy. It is interesting and important to determine why some people commit crimes while others do not, but such research takes on added meaning when we consider how new knowledge can be used to formulate policy. Research on criminal justice policy is an example of applied research; research results are applied to specific questions about how government officials and the general public should respond to crime.

Criminal justice theory is just as important in structuring applied research questions as it is in directing basic research. Theory, research, and criminal justice policy are linked in two ways. First, theory is used to guide basic research. The results from this research may point to specific policies. For example, early research by Burgess, Shaw, and McKay evolved into theories of crime and place. Weisburd and associates (2012) summarize these in their book, *The Criminology of Place*. As research knowledge about crime concentration has grown, police departments are increasingly focusing on places, not people. This has led to hot spots policing, a tactic that has been found to reduce crime (Braga et al., 2014).

To understand the second way criminal justice theory and policy are related, consider the similarities between a *hypothesis* and a specific program. Earlier in this chapter, we described hypotheses as specified expectations about empirical reality. This is also true of public policy programs; they are specified expectations about what empirical reality will result from a particular policy action. Theories of social disorganization include "if-then" statements such as "If an urban neighborhood exhibits signs of social disorder, then crime and delinquency in that neighborhood will be higher compared with neighborhoods having fewer signs of social disorder." This implies a public policy if-then statement: "If we implement a new program to reduce social disorder in an

GROUNDED THEORY AND COMMUNITY PROSECUTION

BY BARBARA BOLAND

Like community policing, community prosecution differs from traditional ways of handling crime in two respects. First, community policing and prosecution involve working with community organizations and ordinary residents. Second, police and prosecutors try to identify patterns of crime and related problems rather than just respond to individual incidents as they occur. "Look for patterns, and look for help" is one way to summarize this approach: focus on problems rather than incidents; cooperate with community residents and others rather than responding to a crime report or prosecuting a case in isolation of other organizations.

A community prosecutor who worked in a Portland, Oregon, neighborhood initially assumed that the concerns of area residents centered on serious crime problems produced by repeat offenders. However, conventional notions about crime and appropriate responses were quickly changed once the prosecutor began talking with neighborhood residents. They wanted something done about prostitution, public drinking, drug use, vandalism, littering, assaults, garbage, and thefts from cars—problems that did not match the traditional notions of serious crime.

One particular area in the neighborhood, Sullivan's Gulch, illustrates what troubled residents. A natural depression where two railroad lines intersect, Sullivan's Gulch had long attracted transients who set up illegal camps in the area, sometimes remaining for extended stays. By the late 1980s, the number of illegal campers had exploded. Gulch dwellers wandered into nearby commercial and residential areas to buy and consume liquor, to litter, loiter, urinate, and fight. None of these problems were serious crimes, and such nuisance reports were seldom recorded in crime counts. But they nonetheless troubled neighborhood residents and undermined efforts to revitalize commerce in the area. After talking with area residents and business owners and thinking about the problem, the community prosecutor reasoned that traditional approaches like stepped-up patrol, police visibility, and arrests might work for a time. The increased police presence could not be maintained over a long period, however, and problems would no doubt reappear after police moved on to other areas.

Instead, the prosecutor arranged an initial police sweep to disperse campers from the Gulch. This was accompanied by a city-sponsored clean-up that removed tents, derelict structures, and countless truckloads of debris. The next step was a cooperative effort among police and area residents. Signs reading "No Camping" on one side and listing nearby homeless shelters on the reverse were posted in the area. Citizens were enlisted to patrol the Gulch on a regular basis and to notify police about the appearance of any campsites. Encouraged by the support they had received from police and the prosecutor's office, area residents were diligent in watching for campers and dissuading new arrivals from setting up camp.

Resident concerns about Sullivan's Gulch offer a classic example of the links between disorder and crime, as described in the article "Broken Windows" by James Wilson and George Kelling (1982) and a later book by Wesley Skogan (1990). The "broken windows" theory of crime holds that: "serious crime flourishes in areas where disorderly behavior goes unchecked" (Wilson and Kelling, 1982:34).

Listening to the concerns of residents and business owners near Sullivan's Gulch and observing the area firsthand, the neighborhood prosecutor "built" a theory. His theory was based on street-level experience, experience that differed from the prevailing suite-level perspective of traditional prosecution. The theory was inductive, grounded in observations that were then used to formulate more general statements about the links between disorder and serious crime in an area of Portland. And these links suggested a theory of action that guided justice policy.

Source: Adapted from Boland (1996:36–37).

The possibility of racial bias in policing has been a topic for criminal justice research for many years. Most researchers link discriminatory treatment to discretion—the ability of police and other criminal justice actors to make decisions that are not routinely subject to review. Lloyd Ohlin (1993) describes how police discretion was "discovered" by large-scale observational studies of criminal justice agencies conducted in the 1950s by the American Bar Foundation. One classic study by Albert Reiss (1971) drew on these observation studies, and reported what appeared to be discriminatory treatment by police in large cities. Later research by Douglas Smith and Christy Visher (1981) found police were more likely to make arrests of black suspects, but, recalling Shaw and McKay, that much of this appeared linked to neighborhoods in which incidents occurred. Robert Sampson (1986) reported similar findings in a study of juvenile justice—social and economic characteristics appeared to confound relationships between race and police action to detain juveniles.

Research on the links between race and the actions of criminal justice officials has expanded in many directions. But in most cases, theoretical explanations of minority overrepresentation among people arrested or incarcerated took one of two forms: (1) overrepresentation of minorities among the population of offenders or (2) overt discrimination by justice officials.

Despite this theoretical heritage, concern about racially biased traffic enforcement emerged from widely publicized "horror stories," not from systematic research. One of the best-known legal researchers on the topic, David Harris (1999), describes several examples. In this way, mass media reports and individual lawsuits about discriminatory traffic enforcement led to research and a kind of inductive theorizing as social scientists sought to piece observations together in an effort to find general explanations. In this way, reports of bias promoted exploratory research that has gradually led to theory development to help understand possible mechanisms.

Engel, Calnon, and Bernard (2002) were among the first to identify lack of theory as an obstacle to understanding. They claim that basing research on horror stories is equivalent to assuming the horror stories are themselves typical of police actions in traffic enforcement. As a remedy, they present a variety of social science theories that might account for

urban neighborhood, then crime and delinquency will decline." Complementary if-then statements such as these underlie the rationale for community policing and the actions taken by Boland's community prosecutor (see the box on grounded theory earlier in this chapter). With community-based crime control strategies, police and prosecutors take action against neighborhood problems of social disorder that may contribute to crime and delinquency.

So theory, research, and policy are related in two similar ways: (1) theory structures research, which, in turn, is consulted to develop policy; and (2) policies take the form of if-then statements, which implies that they are subject to empirical tests. This chapter's installment of our running example, "Putting It All Together: Theories of Discretion and Discrimination," illustrates how theory has helped researchers formulate and test explanations for patterns of traffic stops. Conversely, some researchers have argued that the lack of theory to guide research has been a problem in studies of racial profiling.

disproportionate stops of minority motorists, then suggest how research might be structured to test those theories. Here are two brief examples:

1. *Behavior is the product of underlying attitudes.* Rooted in psychological theory, this perspective assumes that police stop minority drivers because of underlying prejudices. Testing this would require measuring these underlying attitudes by administering a standard questionnaire.

2. *Organizational behavior and myths.* Organization theory would claim that the actions of individual police in traffic stops are the result of organization policies. As an explanation of racial profiling, this perspective would mean that police managers encourage individual police to stop minority drivers. Further, Crank and Langworthy (1992) describe how organizations have traditions, myths, and beliefs that can affect actions by individuals. If organization beliefs assume that minorities are more often involved in drug or weapons violations, those beliefs can influence actions by police in traffic enforcement.

TRAFFIC ENFORCEMENT IS DIFFERENT

In his work on the New Jersey State Police, Carsten Andresen (2005) drew on two bodies of theory to guide his two basic research questions: (1) what influences police decisions to stop a particular vehicle, and (2) what influences the actions police take after making a stop.

Andresen adapted a theory of police discretion to address the first question: In the absence of clear directives, police can choose which cars to stop based on whatever criteria they wish to use. He tested this explanation by interviewing troopers and observing their actions while accompanying troopers on a large number of routine patrols.

A synthesis of theories rooted in the psychology of interactions guided Andresen's research on the second question. He reasoned that a traffic stop is a transaction between police and drivers. Like other transactions, the parties involved in a traffic stop negotiate, though not as obviously as we might negotiate when buying some item at a garage sale. Troopers sought some concession of fault or contrition from the driver. In exchange, they gave cooperative drivers a break by not issuing a ticket or by writing a ticket for a lesser traffic violation. Negotiations broke down if drivers were aggressive, denied traffic violation, or complained that everyone else was speeding too; these drivers usually received a traffic citation.

Andresen used theory in two ways. Observing patterns of "bargaining" between police and drivers, he began to form some more general explanation through inductive reasoning. Then he consulted research literature in other areas, drawing on the organizational psychology theory of reciprocity to "deduce" an explanation for the patterns he observed but had been able to only partly explain.

Criminological Evolution: Ecological Theory and Crime Prevention Policy

We conclude this chapter by offering an example of how theory, research, and policy are intertwined. Further, we believe after reading the final section of this chapter, you will be able to trace principles of contemporary criminological theory to foundations from the Chicago School, discussed earlier.

In his introduction to a collection of case studies on situational crime prevention, Ronald Clarke (1997b) describes how this approach to criminal justice policy evolved from more general ecological theories of crime. The word ecological is significant; just as humans and other organisms are affected by environmental forces in nature (e.g., weather, global climate change, and water quality), human behavior is partially a function of the physical and social environment in which that behavior takes place. Environmental criminologists link criminal behavior to physical and social space.

As described by Paul and Patricia Brantingham (Brantingham and Brantingham, 1991), applying principles of social ecology to criminology has two components. First, the physical features of a city—urban form—are partly the results of conflict over space, a scarce resource. Cities are densely populated because land costs are high and many people want to locate near workplaces, stores, and entertainment venues. Second, human behavior is affected by physical form. People behave differently in the downtown areas of large cities, for example, than they do in suburban shopping malls (Wikström, 1995).

Different urban forms present greater or lesser opportunities for crime by bringing potential offenders and victims close to each other. For example, the Brantinghams (1991:49) describe how dispersed shopping areas and strip malls are especially vulnerable to high rates of property crime. This is because such shopping areas are designed to provide convenient access to large numbers of people in automobiles. And just like shoppers, property offenders value ease of access and anonymity—and are therefore attracted to dispersed shopping centers and strip developments in large metropolitan areas.

Notice how these fundamental principles of ecological theory are consistent with social disorganization theory: Crime is more common in urban transition zones where the physical environment (crowded housing) is unpleasant and the social environment (poverty, unemployment, and disease) is undesirable.

Ecological theories rooted in research by Shaw and McKay eventually affected the thinking of architects and city planners, whose work focuses on the design of buildings, streets, parks, and other physical features of the urban landscape. One of the most influential works that blended concepts of urban design and criminal justice was Oscar Newman's book *Defensible Space* (1972). Newman argued that urban housing should be constructed to enhance residents' ability to monitor and control their environment. Too often, the design of large public housing projects in U.S. cities made it difficult for residents to distinguish threatening strangers from neighbors going about their business.

Around the same time Newman's book appeared, similar ideas about the link between urban design, human behavior, and crime were influencing the development of crime prevention policy in England. Drawing on the economics paradigm of rational choice, researchers in the British Home Office Research Unit extended Newman's ideas about how the physical environment affects potential victims (be they people or places), proposing that decisions made by criminals are also influenced by urban design (Clarke and Mayhew, 1980; Cornish and Clarke, 1986). Offenders may not formally weigh the costs and benefits of committing a crime, but Cornish and Clarke assert that offenders do evaluate potential targets and make choices based at least in part on opportunities.

Such reasoning led Clarke and others to propose crime prevention policies that try to reduce the opportunities for crime. This approach is called "situational crime prevention," defined by Clarke (1997b:4) as "opportunity reducing measures that are (1) directed at highly specific forms of crime (2) that involve the management, design, or manipulation of the immediate environment in as systematic and permanent a way as possible (3) so as to increase the effort and risks of crime and reduce the rewards as perceived by a wide range of offenders." Clarke describes several examples of situational crime prevention techniques. The effort required to steal cars can be increased by the use of steering wheel locks; the rewards of theft from automobiles can be reduced if car owners install removable stereo systems; the risks (to thieves) of auto theft can be increased by more thoughtful design of parking lots.

This example illustrates the deductive approach to moving from theory to policy development. Situational crime prevention policies were deduced, over a period of years, from ecological theories that described the relationships between crime and the physical and social environment of urban areas.

Now consider how Clarke's description of the steps involved in designing specific situational crime prevention programs illustrates the inductive approach to policy development (Clarke, 1997b:5):

1. Collect data about the nature and dimensions of the specific crime problem;
2. [A]nalysis of the situational conditions that . . . facilitate the commission of the crimes in question;

3. [S]ystematic study of possible means of blocking opportunities for these particular crimes, including analysis of costs;

4. [I]mplementation of the most promising, feasible economic measures; and

5. [M]onitoring of results and dissemination of experience.

Steps 1 and 2 involve collecting data and searching for patterns; steps 3 and 4 are equivalent to formulating a tentative conclusion and operating hypothesis based on the observed patterns. Step 5 is the applied research counterpart to hypothesis testing: monitor and evaluate results, and then report whether the program achieved its intended objectives.

Throughout this chapter, we have seen various aspects of the links between theory and research in criminal justice inquiry. In the deductive model, research is used to test theories. In the inductive model, theories are developed from the analysis of research data. Although we focused on two logical models for linking theory and research, criminal justice researchers have developed a great many variations on these themes. Sometimes theoretical issues are introduced merely as a background for empirical analyses. Other studies cite selected empirical data to bolster theoretical arguments.

The ground we covered in this chapter reinforces our claim that there is no simple recipe for conducting criminal justice research. It is far more open-ended than the traditional view of science would suggest. Ultimately, science rests on two pillars: logic and observation. As we'll see throughout this book, they can be fit together in many patterns.

SUMMARY

- Social science involves three fundamental aspects: theory, data collection, and data analysis.
- Social scientists are interested in explaining aggregates, not individuals.
- Although social scientists observe people, they are primarily interested in discovering relationships that connect variables.
- Explanations may be idiographic or nomothetic.
- Science is a process involving an alternation of deduction and induction.
- Data may be quantitative or qualitative.

- Although people speak of science as being "objective," it's more a matter of intersubjective agreement—different scientists agree on their observations and conclusions.
- The traditional image of science includes theory, operationalization, and observation.
- Social scientific theory and research are linked through two logical methods: (1) deduction involves the derivation of expectations or hypotheses from theories, and (2) induction involves the development of generalizations from specific observations.
- In grounded theory, observations contribute to theory development.
- Theory in criminology and criminal justice is frequently adapted from other disciplines in the social and, less often, natural sciences.
- Criminal justice theory, research, and policy are linked in two ways: (1) theory influences basic research, which may suggest new policy developments; and (2) policies are formulated like hypotheses and may therefore be subject to empirical tests.

KEY TERMS

Aggregates *(p. 32)*
Attributes *(p. 33)*
Deductive reasoning *(p. 37)*
Dependent variable *(p. 35)*
Grounded theory *(p. 44)*
Hypothesis *(p. 39)*
Hypothesis testing *(p. 44)*
Idiographic *(p. 36)*
Independent variable *(p. 35)*
Inductive reasoning *(p. 37)*
Intersubjective agreement *(p. 39)*
Nomothetic *(p. 36)*
Objectivity *(p. 39)*
Paradigm *(p. 40)*
Theory *(p. 39)*
Variables *(p. 33)*

REVIEW QUESTIONS AND EXERCISES

1. In his book *Crime and Everyday Life*, Marcus Felson (2002) expands on "routine activity theory" as an explanation for why crime occurs. According to this theory, crimes happen when three elements come together: (a) a motivated offender, (b) an attractive victim, and (c) absence of capable guardians. Select one property crime and one violent crime. Apply routine activity theory to explain examples of each. Are you using theory in an inductive or deductive way?

2. Review the relationships between theory and research discussed in this chapter. Select a research article

from an academic journal, and classify the relationship between theory and research you find there.

3. David Lester (2012) describes how researchers examined change in suicide rates in England following the reformulation of household gas used for cooking and heating. Beginning in the 1960s, household gas was "detoxified"—its carbon monoxide content was sharply reduced to make it less toxic when inhaled. Based on your understanding of theory as discussed in this chapter: (a) Do you think suicide rates would have changed? If so, how? (b) Explain what mechanisms you think might be at work.

CHAPTER 3

Ethics and Criminal Justice Research

We'll examine some of the ethical and scientific considerations that must be taken into account for the design and execution of research. We'll also consider different types of ethical issues and ways of handling them.

Learning Objectives

1. Recognize how criminal justice research is shaped by ethical considerations.
2. Understand that what is ethically "right" and "wrong" in research is ultimately a matter of what people agree is right and wrong.
3. Understand why researchers may not recognize whether their own work adequately addresses ethical issues.
4. Summarize how ethical questions usually involve weighing the possible benefits of research against the potential harm to research subjects.
5. Understand the norm of voluntary participation and how it can conflict with generalizability.
6. Describe examples of the special ethical questions sometimes raised by criminal justice research.
7. Discuss how informed consent addresses many ethical questions.
8. Distinguish anonymity and confidentiality as ways to protect the privacy of research subjects.
9. Summarize the ethical principles presented in the *Belmont Report*.
10. Describe why prisoners and juveniles require special ethical considerations.
11. Understand the role of institutional review boards (IRBs) in protecting human subjects.

Ethics and Research with Pimps

Human trafficking of women for sex work is a criminal justice topic that has attracted considerable attention in news reports and popular culture. It is also widely reported that young American-born children, often runaways, are coerced into sex work by predatory pimps. Here's an example from a Cleveland newspaper:

> Eric Turnstone warned the buyer that the next time he made a sale to her, he'd charge a lot more. But that day in 2010 he settled for $300, saying it would at least give him some pocket change. What Turnstone sold, inside a Starbuck's in Cleveland's Warehouse District, was a 16-year old girl. Yes, that's correct. He *sold* a girl—to a madam in the commercial sex industry. . . . [I]ncreasingly, pimps are coercing vulnerable teens into the sex trade. They flatter the girls by telling them they're pretty, develop their trust and entice them to leave their families. (Bernstein, 2012; emphasis in original)

Mass media accounts typically describe exploitation and sexual slavery. The problem is real, of course, but criminal justice research has revealed that the situation is more complex. In their study of sex trafficking in Asia, researchers Ko-lin Chin and James Finckenauer (2012) interviewed female sex workers in 10 cities in Asian countries and the United States. Through their research, they found that women generally knew they would be sex workers in other countries, and as many as 40 percent of women interviewed in China had worked in prostitution before leaving the country.

The image of pimps as exploiters who use violence and threats to coerce sex workers is similarly over-simplified. A paper I wrote with Anthony Marcus and colleagues (2012) describes some of the findings of two years of ethnographic research in New York City and Atlantic City, New Jersey. Among other things, we learned that adolescents become involved in sex work for many reasons, and relationships between females and pimps acting as "market facilitators" can be complex. Also, I recently completed a year-long project that involved interviewing former and current sex-market facilitators or pimps in Harlem. This work will be discussed more in later chapters. Here I note some of the ethical questions that come up in conducting research on the commercial sex market.

When recruiting and interviewing people from hard-to-reach populations, the first issue was assuring them that the interview was confidential. Those currently pimping were particularly cautious, and in a few cases, they were even worried that I was an undercover police officer. Besides the actual assurance of confidentiality, subjects may also be assured of confidentiality based on how they are recruited, whether they are asked to give oral versus written consent, and where the interviews take place.

For the pimp project in Harlem, we drew on a few contacts in the community to identify people to interview. One contact grew up in the area, and another was a regular fixture in the community. They endorsed us as legitimate researchers to their friends, acquaintances, and sometimes even strangers. Our contacts hung around during the interviews, which assured potential subjects that the situation was safe. Contacts were essential for establishing the kind of trust necessary for this type of research.

The ethical principle of voluntary participation can be tricky in research on criminal behaviors or lifestyles. We had to work carefully with our institutional review board. For example, it is customary to have subjects sign a document indicating that they agree to participate in the research. Because the people we interviewed were hesitant to sign anything, we used a type of verbal consent.

Location played a role in establishing trust. I conducted a number of interviews outside around housing projects in Harlem and inside two nonprofit organizations. I used empty office space in one of the nonprofits; with the exception of a few chairs, there was no furniture in these offices. Further, tangled wires stuck out of the ceiling, and a phone occasionally rang. One subject asked us outright if this was a sting operation; questions like this never arose when the interviews were conducted outdoors (which is where most of the interviews took place).

We asked our subjects to use fake names when discussing their sex workers, their friends, and themselves. We told them that if a question made them uncomfortable they could skip it. For the pimp project, none of the subjects asked to skip a question, but they sometimes edited their own stories, especially when prior arrests or convictions or gang affiliations came up in conversation, saying things such as, "I am in a gang, but I don't wanna say which one."

Interviews with sex workers and pimps may reveal sensitive information about trauma, violence, other crime, and prior arrests or convictions. It can also be difficult to verify whether someone is an adult or juvenile. Interviewees may lie about their age, and you cannot ask hard-to-reach populations for identification; you have to trust them. This can be tricky, because research on juveniles requires special protections.

Interviewees can also be enticed by monetary incentives, especially if they are in need of money. We paid subjects $20 to $30 per interview. Despite popular images of pimps living the high life, this was rare among those we encountered; many of them were struggling financially.

Finally, many ethical issues in criminal justice research are concerned with protecting vulnerable populations. Our subjects were vulnerable in complex, multiple ways. Working in the commercial sex market, they engaged in illegal behavior that was often intertwined with other illegal markets. We suspect that some were juveniles, but we could not verify ages. Many subjects lived and worked in communities troubled by violence and drug markets.

As you read about research ethics in this chapter, think about how this research with pimps and sex workers raises questions about ethics. Also consider how research should be structured to comply with basic principles of ethics. What sorts of protection should be provided to subjects? Who should determine whether those protections are adequate? How should they do that?

BY AMBER HORNING

Introduction

Despite our best intentions, we don't always recognize ethical issues in research.

Most of this book focuses on scientific procedures and constraints. We'll see that the logic of science suggests certain research procedures, but we'll also see that some scientifically "perfect" study designs are not feasible because they would be too expensive or take too long to execute. Throughout the book, we'll deal with workable compromises.

Before we get to scientific and practical constraints on research, however, it's important to explore another essential consideration in doing criminal justice research in the real world—ethics. Just as certain designs or measurement procedures are impractical, others are constrained by ethical problems. We introduce the issue of ethics by quoting from Earl Babbie's book, *The Practice of Social Research* (2004:62):

> Several years ago, I was invited to sit in on a planning session to design a study of legal education in California. The joint project was to be conducted by a university research center and the state bar association. The purpose of the project was to improve legal education by learning which aspects of the law school experience were related to success on the bar exam. Essentially, the plan was to prepare a questionnaire that would get detailed information about the law school experiences of individuals. People would be required to answer the questionnaire when they took the bar exam. By analyzing how people with different kinds of law school experiences did on the bar exam, it would be possible to find out what sorts of things worked and what didn't. The findings of the research could be made available to law schools, and ultimately legal education could be improved.
>
> The exciting thing about collaborating with the bar association was that all the normally aggravating logistical hassles would be handled. There would be no problem getting permission to administer questionnaires in conjunction with the exam, for example, and the problem of nonresponse could be eliminated altogether.
>
> I left the meeting excited about the prospects for the study. When I told a colleague about it, I glowed about the absolute handling of the nonresponse problem. Her immediate comment turned everything around completely. "That's unethical. There's no law requiring the questionnaire, and participation in research has to be voluntary." The study wasn't done.

It now seems obvious that requiring participation would have been inappropriate. You may have recognized that before you read the comment by Babbie's colleague.

All of us consider ourselves ethical—not perfect perhaps, but more ethical than most of humanity. The problem in criminal justice research—and probably in life—is that ethical considerations are not always apparent to us. As a result, we often plunge into things without seeing ethical issues that may be obvious to others and even to ourselves when they are pointed out. Our excitement at the prospect of a new research project may blind us to obstacles presented by ethical considerations.

Any of us can see immediately that a study asking juvenile gang members to demonstrate how they steal cars is unethical. You'd speak out immediately if we suggested interviewing people about drug use and then publishing what they said in the local newspaper. However, as ethical as we think we are, we are likely to miss the ethical issues in other situations—not because we're bad, but because we're human.

Most of this chapter deals with the ethics of criminal justice research. In part, it presents some of the broadly agreed-on norms describing what's ethical in research and what's not. More important than simply knowing the guidelines, however, is becoming sensitized to the ethical component in research so that you'll look for it whenever you plan a study. It's worth noting in this context that many professions operate under ethical constraints and that these constraints differ from one profession to another. Thus, priests, physicians, lawyers, reporters, and television producers operate under different ethical constraints. In this chapter, we'll look only at the ethical principles that govern social research.

Political considerations in research are also subtle, ambiguous, and arguable. Notice that the law school example involves politics as well as ethics. Although researchers have an ethical norm that participation in research should be voluntary, this norm clearly grows out of U.S. political norms protecting civil liberties. In some nations, the proposed study would have been considered quite ethical.

In the last part of this chapter, we'll look at two research projects that raised serious ethical questions. Because there is often no "correct" take on a given situation, we won't give you a definitive answer about what is and is not acceptable. Each example is important, and should stimulate discussion of how it illustrates the principles of research ethics.

Ethical Issues in Criminal Justice Research

A few basic principles encompass the variety of ethical issues in criminal justice research.

In most dictionaries and in common usage, ethics is typically associated with morality, and both deal with matters of right and wrong. But what is right and what is wrong? What is the source of the distinction? For various individuals, the sources vary from religion, to political ideology, to pragmatic observations of what seems to work and what doesn't.

Webster's New World Dictionary (2001) is typical among dictionaries in defining **ethical** as "conforming to the standards of conduct of a given profession or group." Although the relativity embedded in this definition may frustrate those in search of moral absolutes, what we regard as moral and ethical in day-to-day life is no more than a matter of agreement among members of a group. And, not surprisingly, different groups agree on different ethical codes of conduct. If someone is going to live in a particular society, then it is extremely useful to know what that society considers ethical and unethical. The same holds true for the criminal justice research "community."

Anyone preparing to do criminal justice research should be aware of the general agreements shared by researchers about what's proper and improper in the conduct of scientific inquiry. Ethical issues in criminal justice can be especially challenging, because our research questions frequently examine illegal behavior that people are anxious to conceal. This is true of offenders and, sometimes, people who work in criminal justice agencies.

The sections that follow explore some of the more important ethical issues and agreements in criminal justice research. Our discussion is restricted to ethical issues in criminal justice research, not ethics in criminal justice policy and practice. Thus, we will not consider such issues as the morality of the death penalty, acceptable police practices, the ethics of punishment, or codes of conduct for attorneys and judges. If you are interested in substantive ethical issues in criminal justice policy, consult Jocelyn Pollock (2012)

or the journal *Criminal Justice Ethics* published at John Jay College of Criminal Justice.

No Harm to Participants

Weighing the potential benefits from doing research against the possibility of harm to the people being studied—or harm to other people—is a fundamental ethical dilemma in all research. For example, biomedical research can involve potential physical harm to people or animals. Social research may cause psychological harm or embarrassment in people who are asked to reveal personal information. Criminal justice research has the potential to produce both physical and psychological harm, as well as embarrassment. Although the likelihood of physical harm may seem remote, it is worthwhile to consider possible ways it might occur.

Harm to subjects, researchers, or third parties is possible in field studies that collect information from or about persons engaged in criminal activity; this is especially true for field research. For example, studies of drug crimes may involve locating and interviewing active users and dealers. Scott Jacques and Richard Wright (2008) studied active drug sellers in Atlanta and St. Louis, recruiting subjects by spreading the word through various means. Collecting information from active criminals presents at least the possibility of violence against research subjects by other drug dealers.

Potential danger to field researchers should also be considered. For instance, Peter Reuter, Robert MacCoun, and Patrick Murphy (1990) selected their drug dealer subjects by consulting probation department records. The researchers recognized that sampling persons from different Washington, DC, neighborhoods would have produced a more generalizable group of subjects, but they rejected that approach because mass media reports of widespread drug-related violence generated concern about the safety of research staff

> **Ethical**   Conforming to the norms or standards of a group.

(1990:119). Whether such fears were warranted is unclear, but this example does illustrate how safety issues can affect criminal justice research. More generally, Barbara Paterson and associates (1999) describe guidelines for assessing possible threats to researcher safety in qualitative field research, while Bruce Jacobs (2006) summarizes how different approaches to fieldwork can reduce potential dangers.

A more sobering example of potential safety concerns is a notorious series of experimental studies of bystander intervention by Bibb Latané and John Darley (1970). These researchers staged crimes that, in some instances, could have produced harm to either subjects or research staff. They were interested in circumstances when witnesses to a "crime" would or would not intervene. In one experiment that staged a liquor store holdup, a bystander called police, who responded with drawn guns.

Other researchers acknowledge the potential for harm in the context of respect for ethical principles. The box titled "Ethics and Extreme Field Research" gives examples of subtle and not-so-subtle ethical dilemmas encountered by a Rutgers University graduate in her dissertation research on drug use in rave clubs. For more information on this research, see Dina Perrone's book *The High Life* (2009).

Applying a broader perspective, John Monahan and associates (1993) distinguish three different groups at potential risk of physical harm in their research on violence. First are research subjects themselves. Women at risk of domestic violence, for example, may be exposed to greater danger if assailants learn they have disclosed past victimizations to researchers. Second, researchers might trigger attacks on themselves when they interview subjects who have a history of violent offending. Third, and most problematic, is the possibility that collecting information from unstable individuals might increase the risk of harm to third parties. The last category presents a new dilemma if researchers learn that subjects intend to attack some third party. Should researchers honor a promise of confidentiality to subjects or intervene to prevent the harm?

The potential for psychological harm to subjects exists when interviews are used to collect information. For example, crime surveys that ask respondents about their experiences as victims of crime might remind them of a traumatic, or at least unpleasant, experience. Surveys may also ask respondents about illegal behaviors such as drug use or crimes they have committed. Talking about such actions with interviewers can be embarrassing.

Researchers have taken special steps to reduce the potential for emotional trauma in interviews of domestic violence victims (Bumiller, 2010). One of the most interesting examples involves the use of self-completed computer questionnaires in the British Crime Survey (Mirrlees-Black, 1999). Rather than verbally responding to questions from interviewers, respondents read and answer questions on a laptop computer. This procedure affords a greater degree of privacy for research subjects.

Although the fact often goes unrecognized, subjects can also be harmed by the analysis and reporting of data. Every now and then, research subjects read the books published about the studies they participated in. Reasonably sophisticated subjects can locate themselves in the various indexes and tables of published studies. Having done so, they may find themselves characterized—though not identified by name—as criminals, deviants, probation violators, and so forth.

Largely for this reason, information on the city of residence of victims identified in the National Crime Victimization Survey is not available to researchers or the public. The relative rarity of some types of crime means that if crime victimization is reported by city of residence, individual victims might recognize the portrayal of their experience or might be identified by third parties.

Recent developments in the use of crime mapping software have raised concerns about the privacy of crime victims. Many police departments now use some type of computer-driven crime map, and some have made maps of small areas available to the public on the Web. Kounadi, Bowers, and Leitner (2014) discuss how the increased availability of online crime maps produces concerns for privacy by enabling people to identify where crime victims live. Some cities, such as New York, present maps that show general frequencies and patterns of incidents (http://maps.nyc.gov/crime. Accessed March 2016). But Chicago makes it possible to see details for individual incidents at the city block level (http://gis.chicagopolice.org/clearmap/startpage.htm# Accessed March 2016).

By now, it should be apparent that virtually all research runs some risk of harming other people somehow. A researcher can never completely guard against all possible injuries, yet some study designs make harm more likely than others do. If a particular research procedure seems likely to produce unpleasant effects for subjects—asking survey respondents to report deviant behavior, for example—the researcher should have firm scientific grounds for doing so. If researchers pursue a design that is essential and also likely to be unpleasant for subjects, they will find themselves in an ethical netherworld, forced to do some personal agonizing.

As a general principle, possible harm to subjects may be justified if the potential benefits of the study outweigh the harm. Of course, this raises a further question of how to determine whether possible benefits offset possible harms. There is no simple answer, but as we will see, the research community has adopted certain safeguards that help subjects to make such determinations themselves.

Not harming people is an easy norm to accept in theory, but it is often difficult to ensure in practice. Sensitivity to the issue and experience in research methodology, however, should improve researchers' efforts in delicate areas of inquiry. Review Dina Perrone's observations in the box "Ethics and Extreme Field Research" for examples.

Voluntary Participation

Criminal justice research often intrudes into people's lives. The interviewer's telephone call or the arrival of an email link to a questionnaire signals the beginning of an activity that respondents have not requested and that may require a significant portion of their time and energy. Being selected to participate in any sort of research study disrupts subjects' regular activities.

A major tenet of medical research ethics is that experimental participation must be voluntary.

The same norm applies to research in criminal justice. No one should be forced to participate. But this norm is far easier to accept in theory than to apply in practice.

For example, prisoners are sometimes used as subjects in experimental studies. In the most rigorously ethical cases, prisoners are told the nature—and the possible dangers—of the experiment; they are told that participation is completely voluntary; and they are further instructed that they can expect no special rewards (such as early parole) for participation. Even under these conditions, volunteers often are motivated by the belief that they will personally benefit from their cooperation. In other cases, prisoners—or other subjects—may be offered small cash payments in exchange for participation. To people with very low incomes, small payments may be an incentive to participate in a study they would not otherwise endure. Amber Horning notes this point in her discussion of research on pimps.

When an instructor in an introductory criminal justice class asks students to fill out a questionnaire that she or he plans to analyze and publish, students should always be told that their participation in the survey is completely voluntary. Nonetheless, students might fear that nonparticipation will somehow affect their grade. The instructor should, therefore, be especially sensitive to the implied sanctions and make provisions to obviate them. For example, students could be asked to drop the questionnaires in a box near the door prior to the next class.

Notice how this norm of voluntary participation potentially works against certain scientific concerns or goals. The goal of generalizability may be threatened if experimental subjects or survey respondents are only the people who willingly participate. The same is true when subjects' participation can be bought with small payments. Research results may not be generalizable to all kinds of people. Most clearly, in the case of a descriptive study, a researcher cannot generalize the study findings to an entire population unless a substantial majority of a scientifically selected sample actually participates—both the willing respondents and the somewhat unwilling.

Qualitative interviewing and field research (the subjects of Chapters 10 and 11) have their

ETHICS AND EXTREME FIELD RESEARCH

BY DINA PERRONE
California State University, Long Beach

As a female ethnographer studying active drug use in a New York dance club, I have encountered awkward and difficult situations. The main purpose of my research was to study the use of ecstasy and other drugs in rave club settings. I became a participant observer in an all-night dance club (The Plant) where the use of club drugs was common. I covertly observed activities in the club, partly masking my role as a researcher by assuming the role of club-goer.

Though I was required to comply with university institutional review board guidelines, published codes and regulations offered limited guidance for many of the situations I experienced. As a result, I had to use my best judgment, learning from past experiences to make immediate decisions regarding ethical issues. I was forced to make decisions about how to handle drug episodes, so as not to place my research or my informants in any danger. Because my research was conducted in a dance club that is also a place for men to pick up women, I faced problems in getting information from subjects while watching out for my physical safety.

DRUG EPISODES AND SUBJECT SAFETY

I witnessed many drug episodes—adverse reactions to various club drugs—in my visits to The Plant. I watched groups trying to get their friends out of "K-holes" resulting from Ketamine or "Special K." I even aided a subject throwing up. Being a covert observer made it difficult to handle these episodes. There were times in the club when I felt as though I was the only person not under the influence of a mind-altering substance. This led me to believe that I had better judgment than the other patrons. Getting involved in these episodes, however, risked jeopardizing my research.

During my first observation, I tried to intervene in what appeared to be a serious drug episode but was warned off by an informant. I was new to the club and unsure what would happen if I got involved. If I sought help from club staff or outsiders in dealing with acute drug reactions, patrons as well as the bouncers would begin to question why I kept coming there. I needed to gain the trust of the patrons in order to enlist participants in my research. Furthermore, the bouncers could throw me out of the club, fearing I was a troublemaker who would summon authorities.

As a researcher, I have an ethical responsibility to my participants, and as a human being, I have an ethical responsibility to my conscience. I decided to be extra cautious during my research and to pay close attention to how drug episodes are handled. I would first consult my informants and follow their suggestions. But if I ever felt a person suffering a drug episode was at risk while other patrons were neither able nor inclined to help, I would intervene to the best of my ability.

SEXUAL ADVANCES IN THE DANCE CLUB

The Plant is also partly a "meat market." Unlike most bars and dance clubs, the patrons' attire and the dance club entertainment are highly erotic. Most of the males inside the club are shirtless, and the majority of females wear extremely revealing clothes. In staged performances, males and females perform dances with sexual overtones, and clothing is partly shed. This atmosphere

own ethical dilemmas in this regard. Often, a researcher who conducts observations in the field cannot even reveal that a study is being done, for fear that this revelation might significantly affect what is being studied. Imagine, for example, that you are interested in whether the way wireless headphones are displayed in a discount store affects rates of shoplifting. Therefore, you plan a field study in which you will make observations of store displays and shoplifting. You cannot very well ask all shoppers whether they agree to participate in your study.

promotes sexual encounters; men frequently approach single women in search of a mate. Men had a tendency to approach me—I appeared to be unattached, and because of my research role, I made it a point to talk to as many people as possible. It's not difficult to imagine how this behavior could be misinterpreted.

There were times when men became sexually aggressive and persistent. In most instances, I tended to walk away, and the men usually got the hint. However, some men are more persistent than others, especially when they are on Ecstasy. In situations in which men make sexual advances, Terry Williams and colleagues (1992) suggest developing a trusting relationship with key individuals who can play a protective role. Throughout my research, I established a good rapport with my informants who assumed that protective role. Unfortunately, acting in this role has had the potential to place my informants in physically dangerous circumstances.

During one observation, "Tom" grabbed me after I declined his invitation to dance. Tom persisted, grabbed me again, then began to argue with "Jerry," one of my regular informants who came to my aid. This escalated to a fist fight broken up only after two bouncers ejected Tom from the club.

I had placed my informant and myself in a dangerous situation. Although I tried to convince myself that I really had no control over Jerry's actions, I felt responsible for the fight. A basic principle of field research is to not invite harm to participants. In most criminal justice research, harm is associated mainly with the possibility of arrest or psychological harm from discussing private issues. Afterward, I tried to think about how the incident escalated and how I could prevent similar problems in the future.

ETHICAL DECISION RULES EVOLVING FROM EXPERIENCE

Academic associations have formulated codes of ethics and professional conduct, but limited guidance is available for handling issues that arise in some types of ethnographic research. Instead, like criminal justice practitioners, those researchers have to make immediate decisions based on experience and training, without knowing how a situation will unfold. Throughout my research, I found myself in situations that I would normally avoid and would probably never confront. Should I help her get through a drug episode? If I don't, will she be okay? If I walk away from this aggressive guy, will he follow me? Does he understand that I wanted to talk to him just for research?

The approach I developed to tackle these issues was mostly gained by consulting with colleagues and reading other studies. An overarching theme regarding all codes of ethics is that ethnographers must put the safety and interests of their participants first, and they must recognize that their informants are more knowledgeable about many situations than they are. Throughout the research, I used my judgment to make the best decisions possible when handling these situations. To decide when to intervene during drug episodes, I followed the lead of my informants. Telling men that my informant was my boyfriend and walking away were successful tactics in turning away sexual advances.

The norm of voluntary participation is an important one, but it is sometimes impossible to follow. For cases in which researchers ultimately feel justified in violating it, it is all the more important to observe the other ethical norms of scientific research.

Anonymity and Confidentiality

The clearest concern in the protection of the subjects' interests and well-being is the protection of their identity. If revealing their behavior or responses would injure them in any way, adherence to this norm becomes crucial. Two techniques—anonymity and confidentiality—assist researchers in this regard, although the two are often confused.

Anonymity A research subject is considered anonymous when the researcher cannot associate a given piece of information with the person. Anonymity addresses many potential ethical difficulties. Studies that use field observation techniques are often able to ensure that research subjects cannot be identified. Researchers may also gain access to nonpublic records from courts, corrections departments, or other criminal justice agencies in which the names of persons have been removed.

One example of anonymity is a Web-based survey in which no login or other identifying information is required. Respondents anonymously complete online questionnaires that are then tabulated. Likewise, a telephone survey can be anonymous if residential phone numbers are selected at random and respondents are not asked for identifying information. Interviews with subjects in the field are anonymous if the researchers neither ask for nor record the names of subjects.

Ensuring anonymity makes it difficult to keep track of which sampled respondents have been interviewed, because researchers do not record respondents' names. Nevertheless, in some situations, the price of anonymity is worth paying. In a survey of drug use, for example, we may decide that guaranteeing anonymity will enhance the likelihood and accuracy of responses. A useful compromise is to record street names for subjects, as Amber Horning describes in the opening vignette, "Ethics and Research with Pimps."

Respondents in many surveys cannot be considered anonymous because an interviewer collects the information from individuals whose names and addresses are known. Other means of data collection may similarly make it impossible to guarantee anonymity for subjects. If we wished to examine juvenile arrest records for a sample of ninth-grade students, for example, we would need to know their names even though we might not be interviewing them or having them fill out a questionnaire.

Confidentiality means that a researcher is able to link information with a given person's identity, but essentially promises not to do so publicly. In a survey of self-reported drug use, for example, the researcher is in a position to make public the use of illegal drugs by a given respondent, but the respondent is assured that this will not be done. Similarly, if field interviews are conducted with juvenile gang members, researchers can certify that information will not be disclosed to police or other officials. Studies using court or police records that include individuals' names may protect confidentiality by not including any identifying information.

Some techniques ensure better performance on this guarantee. To begin, field or survey interviewers who have access to respondent identifications should be trained in their ethical responsibilities. As soon as possible, all names and addresses should be removed from data collection forms and replaced by identification numbers. A master identification file should be created linking numbers to names to permit the later correction of missing or contradictory information. This file should be secured and made available only for legitimate purposes.

Whenever a survey is confidential rather than anonymous, it is the researcher's responsibility to make that fact clear to respondents. He or she must never use the term anonymous to mean *confidential*. Note, however, that research subjects and others may not understand the difference. For example, a former assistant attorney general in New Jersey once demanded that Maxfield disclose the identities of police officers who participated in an anonymous study. It required repeated explanations of the difference between "anonymous" and "confidential" before the lawyer finally understood that it was not possible to disclose identities, because it was not possible to identify participants. In any event, subjects should be assured that the information they provide will be used for research purposes only and not be disclosed to third parties.

Deceiving Subjects

We've seen that the handling of subjects' identities is an important ethical consideration. Handling our own identity as a researcher can be tricky, too. Sometimes it's useful and even necessary to identify ourselves as researchers to those we want to study. It would take a master con artist to get people to participate in a laboratory experiment or complete a lengthy questionnaire without letting on that research was being conducted. We should also keep in mind that deceiving people is unethical; in criminal justice research, deception needs to be justified by compelling scientific or administrative concerns.

Sometimes, researchers admit that they are doing research but fudge about why they are doing it or for whom. For example, Cathy Spatz Widom, Sally J. Czaja, and Mary Ann Dutton (2008) interviewed victims of child abuse many years after their cases had been heard in criminal or juvenile courts. Widom and associates were interested in whether child abuse victims were more likely than a comparison group of nonvictims to be victims of crime later in life. Interviewers could not explain the purpose of the study without potentially biasing responses. Still, it was necessary to provide a plausible explanation for asking detailed questions about personal and family experiences. Widom's solution was to inform subjects that they had been selected to participate in a study of human development. She also prepared a brochure describing her research on human development that was distributed to respondents.

Deception is sometimes used in experimental studies, but subjects eventually learn they were deceived. For example, Raymond Paternoster and associates studied whether students who witnessed staged cheating on a course assignment were more likely to cheat themselves compared to students who were not exposed to staged cheating. After the experiment was completed, participants were "debriefed" and informed about the deception:

> If you were a participant in the memory/recall study that took place in the computer labs of LeFrak Hall, the experiment involved an element of deception. You were recruited under the idea that the study was about your ability to remember and recall words. The actual purpose of the study was to examine the effect of peers on cheating behavior. There was a confederate of the researcher in the sessions, who was a professional actor hired by the researcher. (Paternoster, McGloin, Nguyen et al., 2013:496)

Although we might initially think that concealing our research purpose by deception would be particularly useful in studying active offenders, James Inciardi (1993), in describing methods for studying "crack houses," makes a convincing case that this is inadvisable. First, concealing our research role when investigating drug dealers and users implies that we are associating with them for the purpose of obtaining illegal drugs. Faced with this situation, a researcher would have the choice of engaging in illegal behavior or offering a convincing explanation for declining to do so. Second, masquerading as a crack house patron exposes the researcher to the considerable violence that is common in such places. Because the choice of committing illegal acts or becoming a victim of violence is really no choice at all, Inciardi (1993:152) offers the following advice to researchers who study active offenders in field settings: "Don't go undercover."

Analysis and Reporting

As criminal justice researchers, then, we have ethical obligations to our subjects of study. At the same time, we have ethical obligations to our colleagues in the scientific community; a few comments on those obligations are in order. In any rigorous study, the researcher should be more familiar than anyone else with the technical shortcomings and failures of the study. Researchers have an obligation to make those shortcomings known to readers. Even though it's natural to feel foolish admitting mistakes, researchers are ethically obligated to do so.

Any negative findings should be reported. There is an unfortunate myth in social scientific reporting that only positive discoveries are worth reporting. As editor of the *Journal of Research in Crime and Delinquency*, Michael Maxfield confesses to sometimes believing that as well. This is not restricted to social science. For example, Helle Krogh Johansen and Peter Gotzsche (1999) describe how published research on new drugs tends to focus on successful experiments. Unsuccessful research on new formulations is less often published, which leads pharmaceutical researchers to repeat studies of drugs already shown to be ineffective. Largely because of this bias, researchers at the Harvard University School of Dental Medicine have established the *Journal of Negative Observations in Biomedicine*, dedicated to publishing negative findings from biomedical research (http://www.jnrbm.com. Accessed March 2016). In social science, as in medical research, it is often as important to know that two things are not related as it is to know that they are.

Similarly, researchers should avoid the temptation to save face by describing findings as the product of a carefully planned analytic strategy when that is not the case. Many findings are unexpected, even though they may seem obvious in retrospect. Suppose you uncover an interesting relationship by accident—so what? Embroidering such situations with descriptions of fictitious hypotheses is dishonest, and tends to mislead inexperienced researchers into thinking that all scientific inquiry is rigorously preplanned and organized. Fortunately, evaluation researchers recognize the value of reporting unexpected findings and have developed evaluation approaches that increase the likelihood of discovering unanticipated benefits (Tilley, 2000).

In general, science progresses through honesty and openness and is retarded by ego defenses and deception. We can serve our fellow researchers—and the scientific community as a whole—by telling the truth about all the pitfalls and problems experienced in a particular line of inquiry. With luck, this will save others from the same problems.

Legal Liability

Two types of ethical problems expose researchers to potential legal liability. First, assume you are making field observations of criminal activity, such as street prostitution, that is not reported to police. Under criminal law in many states, you might be arrested for obstructing justice or being an accessory to a crime. Potentially more troublesome is the situation in which participant observation of crime or deviance draws researchers into criminal or deviant roles themselves—smuggling cigarettes into a lockup to obtain the cooperation of detainees, for example.

The second and more common potential source of legal problems involves knowledge that research subjects have committed illegal acts. Self-report surveys or field interviews may ask subjects about crimes they have committed. If respondents report committing offenses they have never been arrested for or charged with, the researcher's knowledge of them might be construed as obstruction of justice. Or, research data may be subject to subpoena by a criminal court. Because disclosure of research data that could be traced to individual subjects violates the ethical principle of confidentiality, a new dilemma emerges.

Fortunately, federal law protects researchers from legal action in most circumstances, provided that appropriate safeguards are used to protect research data. The National Institute of Justice includes the following information on its human subjects protection Web page (http://www.nij.gov/nij/funding/humansubjects/confidentiality.htm. Accessed April 2016):

> NIJ policy provides for the protection of the privacy and well being of individuals who are participants in NIJ research studies through the statutory protection provided to private information under the authority of 42 U.S.C. § 3789g the other DOJ regulations on the Confidentiality of Identifiable Research and Statistical Information found in 28 CFR Part 22. These regulations are

1. Protect the privacy of individuals by limiting the use of private, identifiable information for research or statistical purposes.

2. Protect private information provided by individuals from use in any judicial, legal, or administrative process without the individual's prior consent.

3. Improve the scientific quality of NIJ research programs by minimizing the subject's concerns over the use of the data.

4. Clarify for researchers the limitations on the use of privately identifiable information for only research or statistical purposes.

These provisions not only protect researchers from legal action but also can be valuable in assuring subjects that they cannot be prosecuted for crimes they describe to an interviewer or field worker.

Somewhere between legal liability and physical danger lies the potential risk to field researchers from law enforcement. Despite being upfront with crack users about his role as a researcher, Inciardi (1993) points out that police could not be expected to distinguish him from his subjects. Visibly associating with offenders in natural settings brings some risk of being arrested or inadvertently being an accessory to crime. Thus, Inciardi on one occasion fled the scene of a robbery and on another was caught up in a crack house raid. Another example is the account Bruce Jacobs (1996) gives of his contacts with police while he was studying street drug dealers. Exercises presented at the end of the chapter ask you to think more carefully about the ethical issues involved in Jacobs's contact with police.

Special Problems

Certain types of criminal justice studies present special ethical problems in addition to those we have mentioned. Applied research, for example, may evaluate some existing or new program. Evaluations frequently have the potential to disrupt the routine operations of agencies being studied. Obviously, it is best to minimize such interferences whenever possible.

Staff Misbehavior While conducting applied research, researchers may become aware of irregular or illegal practices by staff in public agencies. They are then faced with the ethical question of whether to report such information (see final discussion example). For example, investigators conducting an evaluation of an innovative probation program learned that police visits to the residences of probationers were not taking place as planned.[1] Instead, police assigned to the program had been submitting falsified log sheets and had not actually checked on probationers.

What is the ethical dilemma in this case? On the one hand, researchers were evaluating the probation program and so were obliged to report

reasons it did or did not operate as planned. Failure to deliver program treatments (home visits) is an example of a program not operating as planned. Investigators had guaranteed confidentiality to program clients—the offenders assigned to probation—but no such agreement had been struck with program staff. On the other hand, researchers had assured agency personnel that their purpose was to evaluate the probation program, not individuals' job performance. If researchers disclosed their knowledge that police were falsifying reports, they would violate this implied trust.

What would you have done in this situation? We will tell you what the researchers decided at the end of this chapter. However, you should recognize how applied research in criminal justice agencies can involve a variety of ethical issues.

Research Causes Crime Because criminal acts and their circumstances are complex and imperfectly understood, some research projects have the potential to produce crime or influence its location or target. Certainly, this is a potentially serious ethical issue for researchers.

Most people agree that it is unethical to encourage someone to commit an offense solely for the purpose of a research project. What's more problematic is recognizing situations in which research might indirectly promote offending. Scott Decker and Barrik Van Winkle (1996) discuss such a possibility in their research on gang members. Some gang members offered to illustrate their willingness to use violence by inviting researchers to witness a drive-by shooting. Researchers declined all such invitations (1996:46). Another ethical issue was the question of how subjects used the $20 cash payments they received in exchange for being interviewed (1996:51):

> We set the fee low enough that we were confident that it would not have a criminogenic effect. While twenty dollars is not a small amount of money, it is not sufficient to purchase a gun or bankroll a large drug buy. We are sure that some of our subjects used the money for illegal purposes. But, after all, these were individuals who were regularly engaged in delinquent and criminal acts.

You may not agree with the authors' reasoning in the last sentence. But their consideration of how

---

[1]Information about this example is from personal communication between the researchers and Maxfield.

cash payments would be used by active offenders represents an unusually careful recognition of the ethical dilemmas that emerge in studying active offenders.

Anthony Braga (2016) describes a more serious example, in which street worker interventions to curb gang violence in Phoenix were associated with an increase in actual shootings. Similarly, a research on a gang violence program in Boston found 14 percent higher shootings in gangs that received program treatment compared to those that did not.

A different type of ethical problem is the possibility of crime displacement in studies of crime prevention programs. For example, consider an experimental program to reduce street prostitution in one area of a city. Researchers studying such a program might designate experimental target areas for enhanced enforcement, as well as nearby comparison areas that will not receive an intervention. If prostitution is displaced from target areas to adjacent neighborhoods, the evaluation study contributes to an increase in prostitution in the comparison areas.

In a review of more than 200 evaluations of crime prevention projects, Rob Guerette and Kate Bowers (2009) report that the scope of displacement is limited. An earlier study by René Hesseling (1994) shows that the type of crime prevention action makes a difference, with displacement more common for target-hardening programs. For example, installing security screens on ground-floor windows in some buildings seemed to displace burglary to less protected structures. Similarly, adding steering column locks to new cars tended to increase thefts of older cars (Felson and Clarke, 1998).

In any event, when it does occur, displacement tends to follow major policy changes that are not connected with criminal justice research. Researchers cannot be expected to control actions by criminal justice officials that may benefit some people at the expense of others. However, it is reasonable to expect researchers involved in planning an evaluation study to anticipate the possibility of such things as displacement and bring them to the attention of program staff.

Withholding Desirable Treatments Certain kinds of research designs in criminal justice can lead to different kinds of ethical questions. Suppose, for example, researchers believe that diverting domestic violence offenders from prosecution to counseling reduces the possibility of repeat violence. Is it ethical to conduct an experiment in which some offenders are prosecuted but others are not?

You may recognize the similarity between this question and those faced by medical researchers who test the effectiveness of experimental drugs. Physicians typically respond to such questions by pointing out that the effectiveness of a drug cannot be demonstrated without such experiments. Failure to conduct research—even at the potential expense of subjects not receiving the trial drugs— would therefore make it impossible to develop new drugs, or to distinguish beneficial treatments from those that are ineffective and even harmful.

One solution to this dilemma is to interrupt an experiment if preliminary results indicate that a new policy or drug does in fact produce improvements in a treatment group. For example, Michael Dennis (1990) describes how such plans were incorporated into a long-term evaluation of enhanced drug treatment counseling. If preliminary results had indicated that the new counseling program reduced drug use, researchers and program staff were prepared to provide enhanced counseling to subjects in the control group. Dennis recognized this potential ethical issue and planned his elaborate research design to accommodate such midstream changes. Similarly, Martin Killias, Marcelo F. Aebi, and Denis Ribeaud (2000) planned to interrupt their experimental study of heroin prescription in Switzerland if compelling evidence pointed to benefits from that approach to treating drug dependency.

Research in criminal justice, especially applied research, can pose a variety of ethical dilemmas, only some of which we have mentioned here. Our running example box, "Putting It All Together," illustrates various ethical questions that emerge in conducting research on racial profiling and traffic enforcement.

Promoting Compliance with Ethical Principles

Codes of ethics and institutional review boards are two main ways of promoting compliance with ethical principles.

No matter how sensitive they might be to the rights of individuals and the possible ways in which subjects might be harmed, researchers are not always the best judges of whether safeguards used are adequate. In 1974, the National Research Act was signed into law after a few highly publicized examples of unethical practices in medical and social science research.[2] A few years later, what has become known as the **Belmont Report** prescribed a brief but comprehensive set of ethical principles for protecting human subjects (National Commission for the Protection of Human Subjects of Biomedical and Behavioral Research, 1979). In only six pages, three principles were presented:

1. *Respect for persons*: Individuals must be allowed to make their own decisions about participation in research, and those with limited capacity to make such decisions should have special protection.

2. *Beneficence*: Research should do no harm to participants and seek to produce benefits.

3. *Justice*: The benefits and burdens of participating in research should be distributed fairly.

Copious federal regulations have stemmed from these three principles. But in most cases, the research community has adopted two general mechanisms for promoting ethical research practices: codes of professional ethics and institutional review boards.

Codes of Professional Ethics

If the professionals who design and conduct research projects can fail to recognize ethical problems, how can such problems be avoided? One approach is for researchers to consult one of the codes of ethics produced by professional associations. Formal codes of conduct describe what is considered acceptable and

---

[2]We'll consider one of these examples near the end of this chapter.

unacceptable professional behavior. The American Psychological Association (2010) code of ethics is quite detailed, reflecting the different professional roles of psychologists in research, clinical treatment, and educational contexts.

Many of the ethical questions that criminal justice researchers are likely to encounter are addressed in the ethics code of the American Sociological Association (1999). The National Academy of Sciences publishes a very useful booklet on a variety of ethical issues, including the problem of fraud and other forms of scientific misconduct (Committee on Science, Engineering, and Public Policy, 2009).

The two national associations representing criminology and criminal justice researchers in the United States have developed codes of ethics. The Academy of Criminal Justice Sciences (ACJS) based its code of ethics on that developed by the American Sociological Association. ACJS members are bound by a very general code that reflects the diversity of its membership: "Most of the ethical standards are written broadly, to provide applications in varied roles and varied contexts. The Ethical Standards are not exhaustive— conduct that is not included in the Ethical Standards is not necessarily ethical or unethical" (Academy of Criminal Justice Sciences, 2000:1).

After years of inaction, followed by failed attempts to draft a code, members of the American Society of Criminology (ASC) approved a code of ethics in 2016, one that like the ACJS code drew extensively on the code for sociology. The preamble to the new code begins with language remarkably similar to some of our commentary in Chapter 1: "Criminology is a scientific discipline and criminologists subscribe to the general tenets of science and scholarship" (American Society of Criminology, 2016:1). The code then presents basic principles, and a section on respecting the rights of research populations:

ASC members

a. comply with appropriate federal and institutional requirements pertaining to the proper review and approval for research that involves human subjects, materials, and procedures;

b. do not mislead respondents to purposes for which research is being conducted;

Conducting research on racial profiling potentially involves researchers in a variety of ethical questions. First, researchers in New Jersey (Andresen, 2005; Maxfield and Kelling, 2005), North Carolina (Smith, Tomaskovic-Devey, Zingraff et al., 2003), and Pennsylvania (Engel, Calnon, Liu et al., 2004; Engel, Calnon, Tillyer et al., 2005) interacted with human subjects, primarily police, supervisors, command officers, and administrative staff. Second, all projects required access to confidential files maintained by state police agencies. Third, when Rutgers researchers accompanied New Jersey state troopers on patrol, they came into contact with private citizens, often people stopped for some traffic offense. Fourth, accompanying troopers on routine patrol exposed researchers to high-speed driving on congested highways and other potential dangers. Finally, it became clear that voluntary participation by state troopers was not always entirely voluntary.

POLICE AS HUMAN SUBJECTS

Studying state troopers as they patrolled New Jersey highways raised ethical issues that are somewhat different from those involving private individuals and their everyday lives. On the one hand, researchers simply observed what public servants are paid to do. Troopers patrol in public view and interact with drivers as part of their daily routine. In a sense, researchers became not much different from curious bystanders who are naturally drawn to real-life examples of the stuff of television dramas.

But field research observing police is different in certain respects. Researchers accompanied troopers for an extended time, listening in on their conversations with each other and on messages broadcast over the radio. Troopers drive on public roads, but much of what happens inside patrol units is private, just as the general public enjoys some measure of privacy inside personal vehicles. Riding with state police revealed candid actions and comments. Maxfield and Andresen learned firsthand what sorts of driving infractions were routinely overlooked and which ones were certain to warrant a traffic stop. Researchers witnessed actions that were inconsistent with New Jersey State Police regulations, and heard a fair share of racist and sexist comments.

Researchers in Pennsylvania had access to all records of police stops. Among other things they were interested in whether some troopers stopped higher proportions of minority drivers. However, researchers wanted to protect the identity of individual troopers; they wished to study only aggregate patterns, not individual police. Accordingly, after they received traffic stop records, the identifying badge number of the trooper who made the stop was deleted from each data record.

CONFIDENTIAL INFORMATION

At the time of the research in New Jersey, state police were under scrutiny by the U.S. Department of Justice. Federal officials and their representatives had access to information about police stops; some of this was shared with Rutgers researchers who were bound to

c. ensure participants' rights of personal anonymity unless they are otherwise waived; and

d. ensure confidentiality of any data not obtained from records open to public scrutiny (American Society of Criminology, 2016:3).

The code goes into a bit more detail affirming that ASC members will take other steps to protect human subjects.

It took many years of debate before the code was adopted. Even then, some ASC members

protect the confidentiality of this information. In addition, all patrol cars in New Jersey were equipped with video cameras and microphones to record interactions between troopers and motorists. Andresen and Maxfield reviewed samples of these taped encounters that were otherwise available only to state police supervisors and commanders.

CONTACTS WITH THE GENERAL PUBLIC

Accompanying state police on patrol means that researchers witness interactions between the police and the public. In most cases Rutgers staff remained in the patrol vehicle but observed and listened in via the video and audio monitor inside each patrol vehicle. Although researchers could record license plate numbers to potentially identify individuals, this served no purpose in their research. Andresen recorded information on approximate age, gender, and ethnicity of each driver stopped; this was sufficient for his research purposes.

As you might expect, people stopped for traffic violations are sometimes upset and not on their best behavior. Occasionally, troopers flirted with female drivers. On one occasion, Andresen reports a female driver lifted her shirt and flashed a trooper during a traffic stop. The trooper laughed and allowed the driver to leave.

POTENTIAL HARM TO RESEARCHERS

Municipal police departments throughout the country allow researchers and other observers to accompany officers on patrol. However, before research by Andresen and Maxfield, few private individuals had been permitted to accompany New Jersey State Police on the road. The official reason most often cited was potential threats to the safety of researchers. State police officials were most concerned about two situations: traffic stops that might escalate into violent encounters and the possibility of high-speed chases. We were usually asked to wear body armor. We were told to remain in the patrol vehicle during traffic stops unless instructed otherwise by troopers. On one occasion, Maxfield was riding with a trooper who was dispatched to an expressway toll booth to possibly intercept an armed suspect fleeing other police units. The trooper first drove to a building housing the toll booth's supervisor and asked Maxfield to wait there until further notice.

A few incidents involved speeds in excess of 100 mph, usually as troopers hurried to accident scenes. In such cases researchers were more frightened than at actual risk. Engel et al. (2004) describe how their selection of sites for stationary observation in Pennsylvania was guided in part by safety concerns. Maxfield learned that safety was also a criterion used by state police in selecting "fishing holes"—areas where radar and laser units parked to monitor speeding.

INFORMED CONSENT?

Police departments are often described as paramilitary organizations, with strict provisions for command and control. In situations like this, informed consent is a slippery concept. If a supervisor orders a trooper to host an observer, that doesn't seem much like voluntary consent. Andresen reports accompanying a few troopers who were clearly involuntary hosts. An individual trooper may be reluctant to decline participation if they expect that such a decision would raise the proverbial eyebrows of supervisors.

So informed consent is, somewhat paradoxically, important in studying police in much the same way as it is in studying prisoners—police and prisoners may be subject to subtle forms of coercion to participate.

raised strong objections to some sections. The wide variety of approaches to doing research in this area probably has something to do with it. Criminologists also encounter a range of ethical issues and have diverging views on how those issues should be addressed. Finally, we have seen examples of the special problems that criminologists face in balancing ethics and research.

Despite their pronouncement, professional codes of ethics for social scientists cannot be expected to prevent unethical practices in criminal justice research any more than the American Bar Association's Code of Professional Responsibility eliminates breaches of ethics by lawyers. For this reason, and in reaction to some controversial medical and social science research, the U.S. Department of Health and Human Services (HHS) has established regulations protecting human research subjects. These regulations do not apply to all social science or criminal justice research. However, it is worthwhile to understand some of their general provisions. Much material in the following section is based on the Code of Federal Regulations, Title 45, Part 46, revised June 23, 2005. And those regulations are themselves rooted in the *Belmont Report* (National Commission for the Protection of Human Subjects of Biomedical and Behavioral Research, 1979).

Institutional Review Boards

Government agencies and nongovernment organizations (including universities) that conduct research involving human subjects must establish review committees, known as an institutional review board (IRB). These IRBs have two general purposes. First, board members make judgments about the overall risks to human subjects and whether these risks are acceptable, given the expected benefits from actually doing the research. Second, they determine whether the procedures to be used include adequate safeguards regarding safety, confidentiality, and general welfare of human subjects.

Under HHS regulations, virtually all research that uses human subjects in any way—including simply asking people questions—is subject to IRB review. The few exceptions sometimes include research conducted for educational purposes and studies that collect anonymous information only. However, even those studies may be subject to review if they use certain special populations (discussed later), or procedures that might conceivably harm participants. In other words, it's safe to assume that most research is subject to IRB review if original data will be collected from individuals whose identities will be known. You will understand why if you consider the various ways subjects might be harmed and the difficulty of conducting anonymous studies.

Federal regulations and IRB guidelines address other potential ethical issues in social research. Foremost among these is the typical IRB requirement for dealing with the ethical principle of voluntary participation.

Informed Consent   The norm of voluntary participation is usually satisfied through **informed consent**—informing subjects about research procedures and then obtaining their consent to participate. Although this may seem like a simple requirement, obtaining informed consent can present several practical difficulties. It requires that subjects understand the purpose of the research, possible risks and side effects, possible benefits to subjects, and the procedures that will be used.

If you accept that deception may sometimes be necessary, you will realize how the requirement to inform subjects about research procedures can present something of a dilemma. Researchers usually address this problem by telling subjects at least part of the truth, or offering a slightly revised version of why the research is being conducted. In Widom's study of child abuse, subjects were partially informed about the purpose of the research—human development (in which victimization by child abuse is a component), which the subjects were not told.

Another potential problem with obtaining informed consent is ensuring that subjects have the capacity to understand the descriptions of risks, benefits, procedures, and so forth. Researchers may have to provide oral descriptions to participants who are unable to read. For subjects who do not speak English, researchers should be prepared to describe procedures in participants' native language. And if researchers use specialized terms or language common in criminal justice research, participants may not understand the meaning and thus will be unable to grant informed consent. For example, consider this statement: "The purpose of this study is to determine whether less restrictive

Informed consent   Agreement to participate in research after being informed about goals, procedures, and potential risks.

sanctions such as restitution produce heightened sensitivity to social responsibility among persistent juvenile offenders and a decline in long-term recidivism." Can you think of a better way to describe this study to delinquent 14 year olds? Figure 3.1 presents a good example of an informed consent statement that was used in a study of juvenile burglars. Notice how the statement describes research procedures clearly and unambiguously tells subjects that participation is voluntary.

Other guidelines for obtaining informed consent include assuring participants of confidentiality. However, it is more important to understand how informed consent addresses key ethical issues in conducting criminal justice research. First, it ensures that participation is voluntary. Second, by informing subjects of procedures, risks, and benefits, researchers are empowering them to resolve the fundamental ethical dilemma of whether the possible benefits of the research offset the possible risks of participation.

Special Populations Federal regulations on human subjects include special provisions for certain types of subjects, called **special populations**, and two of these are particularly important in criminal justice research: juveniles and prisoners. Juveniles, of course, are treated differently from

Special populations Groups such as juveniles and prisoners who require special protections if they are research subjects.

You and your parents or guardian are invited to participate in a research study of the monitoring program that you were assigned to by the Juvenile Court. The purpose of this research is to study the program and your reactions to it. In order to do this a member of the research team will need to interview you and your parents/guardians when you complete the monitoring program. These interviews will take about 15 minutes and will focus on your experiences with the court and monitoring program, the things you do, things that have happened to you, and what you think. In addition, we will record from the court records information about the case for which you were placed in the monitoring program, prior cases, and other information that is put in the records after you are released from the monitoring program.

Anything you or your parents or guardian tell us will be strictly confidential. This means that only the researchers will have your answers. They will not under any conditions (except at your request) be given to the court, the police, probation officers, your parents, or your child!

Your participation in this research is voluntary. If you don't want to take part, you don't have to! If you decide to participate, you can change your mind at any time. Whether you participate or not will have no effect on the program, probation, or your relationship with the court.

The research is being directed by Dr. Terry Baumer and Dr. Robert Mendelsohn from the Indiana University School of Public and Environmental Affairs here in Indianapolis. If you ever have any questions about the research or comments about the monitoring program that you think we should know about, please call one of us at 274-0531.

Consent Statement

We agree to participate in this study of the Marion County Juvenile Monitoring Program. We have read the above statement and understand what will be required and that all information will be confidential. We also understand that we can withdraw from the study at any time without penalty.

Juvenile _____ Date: _____

Parent/Guardian _____

Parent/Guardian _____

Researcher _____

FIGURE 3.1 Informed Consent Statement for Evaluation of Marion County (Indiana) Juvenile Monitoring Program

Scott Decker and Barrik Van Winkle faced a range of ethical issues in their study of gang members. Many of these should be obvious given what has been said so far in this chapter. Violence was common among subjects and presented a real risk to researchers. Decker and Van Winkle (1996:252) reported that 11 of the 99 members of the original sample had been killed since the project began in 1990. There was also the obvious need to assure confidentiality to subjects.

Their project was supported by a federal agency and administered through a university, so Decker and Van Winkle had to comply with federal human subjects guidelines as administered by the university institutional review board (IRB). And because many of the subjects were juveniles, they had to address federal regulations concerning that special population.

Foremost among these was the normal requirement that informed consent for juveniles include parental notification and approval.

You may immediately recognize the conflicting ethical principles at work here, together with the potential for conflict. The promise of confidentiality to gang members is one such principle that was essential for the researchers to obtain candid reports of violence and other law-breaking behavior. But the need for confidentiality conflicted with initial IRB requirements to obtain parental consent for their children to participate in the research:

> This would have violated our commitment to maintain the confidentiality of each subject, not to mention the ethical and practical difficulties of finding and informing each parent. We

adults in most aspects of the law. Their status as a special population of human subjects reflects the legal status of juveniles, as well as their capacity to grant informed consent. In most studies that involve juveniles, consent must be obtained both from parents or guardians and from the juvenile subjects themselves.

In some studies, however, such as those that focus on abused children, it is obviously not desirable to obtain parental consent. Decker and Van Winkle faced this problem in their study of St. Louis gang members. See the box "Ethics and Juvenile Gang Members" for a discussion of how they reconciled the conflict between two ethical principles and satisfied the concerns of their university's IRB.

Prisoners are treated as a special population for somewhat different reasons. Because of their ready accessibility for experiments and interviews, prisoners have frequently been used in biomedical experiments that produced serious harm (Mitford, 1973). Recognizing this, HHS regulations specify that prisoner subjects may

not be exposed to risks that would be considered excessive for nonprison subjects. Furthermore, undue influence or coercion cannot be used in recruiting prisoner subjects. Informed consent statements presented to prospective subjects must indicate that a decision not to participate in a study will have no influence on work assignments, privileges, or parole decisions. If an IRB reviews a project in which prisoners will be subjects, at least one member of that IRB must be either a prisoner or someone specifically designated to represent the interests of prisoners to help ensure that these ethical issues are recognized. Figure 3.2 presents selected requirements from the City University of New York for using prisoners as research subjects.

Regarding the item 5.4 in Figure 3.2, randomization is generally recognized as an ethical procedure for selecting subjects or deciding which subjects will receive an experimental treatment. HHS regulations emphasize this in describing special provisions for using prison subjects: "Unless

told the Human Subjects Committee that we would not, in effect, tell parents that their child was being interviewed because they were an active gang member, knowledge that the parents may not have had. (Decker and Van Winkle, 1996:52)

You might think deception would be a possibility—informing parents that their child was selected for a youth development study, for example. This would not, however, solve the logistical difficulty of locating parents or guardians, some of whom had lost contact with their children. Furthermore, it was likely that even if parents or guardians could be located, suspicions about the research project and the reasons their children were selected would prevent many parents from granting consent. Loss of juvenile subjects in this way would compromise the norm of generality as we have described it in this chapter and elsewhere.

Finally, waiving the requirement for parental consent would have undermined the legal principle that the interests of juveniles must be protected by a supervising adult. Remember that researchers are not always the best judges of whether sufficient precautions have been taken to protect subjects. Here is how Decker and Van Winkle (1996:52) resolved the issue with their IRB:

> We reached a compromise in which we found an advocate for each juvenile member of our sample; this person—a university employee—was responsible for making sure that the subject understood (1) their rights to refuse or quit the interview at any time without penalty and (2) the confidential nature of the project. All subjects signed the consent form.

Source: Adapted from Decker and Van Winkle (1996).

---

5. Criteria for IRB Approval

In order to approve research involving prisoners as subjects, the CUNY IRB must find and document that . . . research involving prisoners as subjects meets the following criteria:

5.2   Any possible advantages accruing to the prisoner through his or her participation in the research, when compared to the general living conditions, medical care, quality of food, amenities and opportunity for earnings in the prison, are not of such a magnitude that his or her ability to weigh the risks of the research against the value of such advantages in the limited choice environment of the prison is impaired.

5.3   The risks involved in the research are commensurate with risks that would be accepted by non-prisoner volunteers.

5.4   Procedures for the selection of subjects within the prison are fair to all prisoners and immune from arbitrary intervention by prison authorities or prisoners. Unless the Principal Investigator (PI) provides to the Board justification in writing for following some other procedures, control subjects must be selected randomly from the group of available prisoners who meet the characteristics needed for that particular research project.

5.5   The information is presented in language which is understandable to the subject population.

5.6   Adequate assurance exists that parole boards will not take into account a prisoner's participation in the research in making decisions regarding parole, and each prisoner is clearly informed in advance that participation in the research will have no effect on his or her parole.

5.7   Where the Board finds there may be a need for follow-up examination or care of participants after the end of their participation, adequate provision has been made for such examination or care, taking into account the varying lengths of individual prisoners' sentences, and for informing participants of this fact.

Source. Adapted from: City University of New York, H. R. P. P. (2013, 31 July). *CUNY HRPP Policy: Prisoners as Research Subjects*. (http://www.cuny.edu/research/compliance/human-subjects-research-1/hrpp-policies-procedures/Prisoners.pdf). Accessed 4 May 2016.

FIGURE 3.2   Excerpts from City University of New York Policy on Prisoners as Research Subjects

the principal investigator provides to the [IRB] justification in writing for following some other procedures, control subjects must be selected randomly from the group of available prisoners who meet the characteristics needed for that particular research project" (45 CFR 46.304[4]).

Institutional Review Board Requirements and Researcher Rights

Federal regulations contain many more provisions for IRBs and other protections for human subjects. Some researchers believe that such regulations actually create problems by setting constraints on their freedom and professional judgments. Recall that potential conflict between the rights of researchers to discover new knowledge and the rights of subjects to be free from unnecessary harm is a fundamental ethical dilemma. At the very least it is inconvenient to have outsiders review a research proposal. Or a researcher may feel insulted by the implication that the potential harm or inconvenience to human subjects may outweigh the potential benefits of research.

Sometimes, people who review research for IRB approval are not familiar with different types of criminal justice research. For example, one of Maxfield's colleagues at John Jay College planned to survey jail inmates at two time points, with the second described as a follow-up interview. She described her frustration with IRB comments in part:

> The review letter from the IRB board gave me an impression that at least some of the IRB members were not familiar with research studies conducted by John Jay College faculty members. For example, the board members did not appear to know what a longitudinal study was. Board members wanted to know what kinds of medical procedures would be discussed in the follow-up survey. Later I learned that the IRB members customarily reviewed biomedical studies, and assumed that a follow-up survey signaled a medical study. (personal communication)

In fact, much of the original impetus for establishing IRBs had to do with medical experimentation on humans. Many social research study designs are regarded as exempt from IRB review under federal guidelines (45 CFR 46.101[b]). Here are those most relevant for criminal justice research:

1. Research conducted in established or commonly accepted educational settings, involving normal educational practices.

2. Research involving the use of educational tests (cognitive, diagnostic, aptitude, and achievement), survey procedures, interview procedures, or observation of public behavior, unless (i) information obtained is recorded in such a manner that human subjects can be identified, directly or through identifiers linked to the subjects; and (ii) any disclosure of the human subjects' responses outside the research could reasonably place the subjects at risk of criminal or civil liability or be damaging to the subjects' financial standing, employability, or reputation.

3. Research involving the use of educational tests (cognitive, diagnostic, aptitude, and achievement), survey procedures, interview procedures, or observation of public behavior if (i) the human subjects are elected or appointed public officials or candidates for public office; or (ii) any personally identifiable information will be maintained as confidential throughout the research and thereafter.

4. Research involving the collection or study of existing data, documents, records, pathological specimens, or diagnostic specimens, if these sources are publicly available or if the information is recorded by the investigator in such a manner that subjects cannot be identified, directly or through identifiers linked to the subjects.

5. Research and demonstration projects that are conducted by or subject to the approval of department or agency heads, and that are designed to study, evaluate, or otherwise examine (i) public benefit or service programs; (ii) procedures for obtaining benefits or services under those programs; (iii) possible changes in or alternatives to those programs or procedures; or (iv) possible changes in methods or levels of payment for benefits or services under those programs.

These exempt categories include quite a number of common models for doing criminal justice research. However, *exempt* means that research proposals do not have to be subject to *full* IRB review. In most cases, researchers who believe that their projects qualify for exemption under these categories must still have IRBs review the research to verify that exemption.

If this strikes you as confusing, you may be reassured to learn that researchers, IRBs, and federal regulators are often confused as well. As noted earlier in this chapter, the National Institute of Justice has developed a useful set of resources to guide researchers. Given the unclear language of HHS regulations, many university IRBs have become extremely cautious in reviewing research proposals. See Richard Shweder's (2006) discussion for examples of problems resulting from this. Professional associations and research-oriented federal agencies have tried to offer guidance on what is and is not subject to various levels of IRB approval. Joan Sieber (2001) prepared an analysis of human subjects issues associated with large surveys for the Bureau of Justice Statistics. Always alert for possible restrictions on academic freedom, the American Association of University Professors (2006) published a useful summary of how IRBs have come to regulate social science research.

There is some merit in such concerns; however, we should not lose sight of the reasons IRB requirements and other regulations were created. Researchers are not always the best judges of the potential for their work to harm individuals. In designing and conducting criminal justice research, they may become excited about learning how to better prevent crime or more effectively treat cocaine addiction. That excitement and commitment to scientific advancement may lead researchers to overlook possible harms to individual rights or well-being. You may recognize this as another way of asking whether the ends justify the means. Because researchers are not always disinterested parties in answering such questions, IRBs are established to provide outside judgments. Also, recognize that IRBs can be sources of expert advice on how to resolve ethical dilemmas. Decker and Van Winkle (1996) shared their university's concern about balancing confidentiality against the need to obtain informed consent from juvenile subjects; together, they were able to fashion a workable compromise.

Virtually all colleges and universities have IRBs. Consult the City University of New York website on research compliance (http://www.cuny.edu/research/compliance.html; accessed 4 May 2016) for an example, or visit the IRB website at your institution.

Another reason for creating regulations to protect human subjects—and IRBs to monitor compliance with those regulations—is the perceived failure of other means, together with ethical controversies raised by some actual studies (Mertens and Ginsberg, 2008). In the next section, we will briefly describe two research projects that provoked widespread ethical controversy and discussion. These are not the only two controversial projects that have been done; they simply illustrate ethical issues in the real world.

Two Ethical Controversies

Two examples of controversial studies illustrate key issues in ethics.

The first project studied sexual behavior in public restrooms, and the second examined how "prisoners" and "guards" reacted in a simulated prison setting.

Trouble in the Tearoom

As a graduate student, Laud Humphreys became interested in studying homosexual behavior. He developed a special interest in the casual and fleeting homosexual acts engaged in by some non-homosexuals. In particular, his research interest focused on male homosexual acts between strangers who met in the public restrooms in parks, called "tearooms" among homosexuals. The result was the publication of the classic, *The Tearoom Trade* (Humphreys, 1975).

What particularly interested Humphreys about the tearoom activity was that the participants seemed to lead otherwise conventional lives as "family men." Thus, it was important to them that they remain anonymous in their tearoom visits. How would you study something like that?

Humphreys' approach took advantage of the social structure of the situation. Typically, the tearoom encounter involved three people: The two men actually engaged in the homosexual act and a lookout, called the "watchqueen." Thus, Humphreys began to show up at public restrooms, offering to serve as watchqueen whenever it seemed appropriate. Because the watchqueen's payoff was the chance to watch the action, Humphreys was able to observe behavior in natural settings, just as he would if he were studying drug dealers or jaywalking.

To round out his understanding of the tearoom trade, Humphreys needed to know something more about the people who participated. Given that the men probably would not have been thrilled about being interviewed by their watchqueen, Humphreys came up with a different solution. Whenever possible, he noted the license plate numbers of participants' cars and tracked down their names and addresses through the police. Humphreys then visited the men at their homes, disguising himself enough to avoid recognition and claiming that he was conducting a survey. In that fashion, he collected the personal information he was unable to get in the restrooms.

Humphreys' research provoked considerable controversy, both within and outside the social scientific community. Some critics charged Humphreys with a gross invasion of privacy in the name of science; what men did in public restrooms was their own business and not Humphreys'. Others were concerned about the deceit involved; Humphreys had lied to the participants by leading them to believe he was only a voyeur. People who believed that the tearoom participants were fair game for observation because they were in a public facility nonetheless protested the follow-up survey. They argued that it was unethical for Humphreys to trace the participants to their homes and to interview them under false pretenses. Still others justified Humphreys' research. The topic, they said, was worth studying and couldn't be studied any other way. They regarded the deceit as essentially harmless, noting that Humphreys was careful not to harm his subjects by disclosing their tearoom activities.

Of course, social norms about sexual orientation have changed in the decades since Humphrey's book was published. But the tearoom trade controversy has never been resolved. It remains a topic of debate regarding research ethics because it stirs emotions and reveals ethical issues people disagree about. What do you think? Was Humphreys ethical in doing what he did and how he did it? Are there parts of the research you feel were acceptable and other parts that were not? Whatever your opinion, you are sure to find others who disagree with you.

The Stanford Prison Experiment

The second research controversy differs from the first in many ways. Whereas Humphreys' study involved participant observation, this study setting was in the laboratory. And whereas the first study examined a form of human nonconformity, this one focused on how people behave in formal institutions.

Few people would disagree that prisons are dehumanizing. Inmates forfeit freedom, of course, but their incarceration also results in a loss of privacy and individual identity. Violence is among the realities of prison life that people point to as evidence of the failure of prisons to rehabilitate inmates.

Although prison problems have many sources, psychologists Craig Haney, Curtis Banks, and Philip Zimbardo (1973) were interested in two general explanations. The first was the dispositional hypothesis: Prisons are brutal and dehumanizing because of the types of people who run them and who are incarcerated in them. Inmates have demonstrated their disrespect for legal order and their willingness to use deceit and violence; persons who work as prison guards may be disproportionately authoritarian and sadistic. The second was the situational hypothesis: The prison environment itself creates brutal, dehumanizing conditions independent of the kinds of people who live and work in the institutions.

Haney and associates set out to test the situational hypothesis by creating a functional prison simulation in which healthy, psychologically normal male college students were assigned to roles as prisoners and guards. The "prison" was constructed in the basement of a psychology department building: three 6 × 9 foot "cells" furnished with only a cot, a prison "yard" in a corridor, and a 2 × 7 foot "solitary confinement cell." Twenty-one subjects were selected from 75 volunteers after screening to eliminate those with physical or psychological problems. Offered $15 per day for their participation, the 21 subjects were randomly assigned to be either guards or prisoners.

All subjects signed contracts that included instructions about prisoner and guard roles for the planned two-week experiment. "Prisoners" were told that they would be confined and under surveillance throughout the experiment, and their civil rights would be suspended; however, they were guaranteed that they would not be physically abused.

"Guards" were given minimal instruction, most notably that physical aggression or physical punishment of "prisoners" was prohibited. Together with a "warden," they were generally free to develop prison rules and procedures. The researchers planned to study how both guards and prisoners reacted to their roles, but guards were led to believe that the purpose of the experiment was to study prisoners.

If you had been a prisoner in this experiment, you would have experienced something like the following after signing your contract: First, you would have been arrested without notice at your home by a real police officer, perhaps with neighbors looking on. After being searched and taken to the police station in handcuffs, you would have been booked, fingerprinted, and placed in a police detention facility. Next, you would have been blindfolded and driven to "prison," where you would have been stripped, sprayed with a delousing solution, and left to stand naked for a period of time in the "prison yard." Eventually, you would have been issued a prison uniform (a loose overshirt stamped with your ID number), fitted with an ankle chain, led to your cell, and ordered to remain silent. Your prison term would then have been totally controlled by the guards.

Wearing mirrored sunglasses, khaki uniforms, and badges and carrying nightsticks, guards supervised prisoner work assignments and held lineups three times per day. Although lineups initially lasted only a few minutes, guards later extended them to several hours. Prisoners were fed bland meals and accompanied by guards on three authorized toilet visits per day.

The behavior of all subjects in the prison yard and other open areas was videotaped; audiotapes were made continuously while prisoners were in their cells. Researchers administered brief questionnaires throughout the experiment to assess emotional changes in prisoners and guards. About four weeks after the experiment concluded, researchers conducted interviews with all subjects to assess their reactions.

Haney and associates (1973:88) had planned to run the prison experiment for two weeks, but they halted the study after six days because subjects displayed "unexpectedly intense reactions." Five prisoners had to be released even before that time because they showed signs of acute depression or anxiety.

Subjects in each group accepted their roles all too readily. Prisoners and guards could interact with each other in friendly ways because guards had the power to make prison rules. But interactions turned out to be overwhelmingly hostile and negative. Guards became aggressive, and prisoners became passive. When the experiment ended prematurely, prisoners were happy about their early "parole," but guards were disappointed that the study would not continue.

Haney and colleagues justify the prison simulation study in part by claiming that the dispositional/situational hypotheses could not be evaluated using other research designs. Clearly, the researchers were sensitive to ethical issues. They obtained subjects' consent to the experiment through signed contracts. Prisoners who showed signs of acute distress were released early. The entire study was terminated after less than half of the planned two weeks had elapsed when its unexpectedly harsh impact on subjects became evident. Finally, researchers conducted group therapy debriefing sessions with prisoners and guards and maintained follow-up contacts for a year to ensure that subjects' negative experiences were temporary.

Two related features of this experiment raise ethical questions, however. First, subjects were not fully informed of the procedures. Although we have seen that deception, including something less than full disclosure, can often be justified, in this case deception was partially due to the researchers' uncertainty about how the prison simulation would unfold. This relates to the second and more important ethical problem: Guards were granted the power to make up and modify rules as the study progressed, and their behavior became increasingly authoritarian. Comments by guards illustrate their reactions as the experiment unfolded (Haney, Banks, and Zimbardo, 1973:88):

> "They [the prisoners] didn't see it as an experiment. It was real and they were fighting to keep their identity. But we were always there to show them just who was boss."
>
> "During the inspection, I went to cell two to mess up a bed which the prisoner had made and he grabbed me, screaming that he had just made it. . . . He grabbed my throat, and although he was laughing, I was pretty scared. I lashed out with my stick and hit him in the chin (although not very hard), and when I freed myself I became angry."
>
> "Acting authoritatively can be fun. Power can be a great pleasure."

How do you feel about this experiment? On the one hand, it provided valuable insights into how otherwise normal people react in a simulated prison environment. Subjects appeared to suffer no long-term harm, in part because of precautions taken by researchers. Paul Reynolds (1979:139) found a certain irony in the short-term discomforts endured by the college student subjects: "There is evidence that the major burdens were borne by individuals from advantaged social categories and that the major benefactors would be individuals from less advantaged social categories [actual prisoners], an uneven distribution of costs and benefits that many nevertheless consider equitable."

On the other hand, researchers did not anticipate how much and how quickly subjects would accept their roles. The experiment had to be halted prematurely. In discussing their findings, Haney and associates (1973:90) note: "Our results are . . . congruent with those of Milgram[3] who most convincingly demonstrated the proposition that evil acts are not necessarily the deeds of evil men, but

---

[3]Here the authors refer to controversial research on obedience to authority by Lester Milgram (1965).

may be attributable to the operation of powerful social forces." This quote illustrates the fundamental dilemma—balancing the right to conduct research against the rights of subjects. Is it ethical for researchers to create powerful social forces that lead to evil acts? You can get a good impression of what guards and prisoners experienced by viewing videos of "arrest" and "prison" scenes. Search on the Internet for "video Stanford prison experiment."

Discussion Examples

Research ethics, then, is an important and ambiguous topic. The difficulty of resolving ethical issues cannot be an excuse for ignoring them, however. You need to keep ethics in mind as you read other chapters in this book and whenever you plan a research project.

To further sensitize you to the ethical component of criminal justice and other social research, we've prepared brief descriptions of 10 real and hypothetical research situations. Can you see the ethical issue in each? How do you feel about it? Are the procedures described ultimately acceptable or unacceptable? It would be very useful to discuss these examples with other students in your class.

1. A researcher studies speeding on urban expressways by using a small radar gun to detect speeders, while an assistant records the license plate numbers of cars traveling more than 10 miles per hour over the posted limit. The speeders' addresses are traced, and they receive a mailed questionnaire with a cover letter beginning: "You were observed traveling more than 10 miles per hour over the speed limit on [date and location]."

2. Researchers make field observations of social activities as part of a study of police strategies to reduce certain crimes in specified neighborhoods. While making observations during a weekday afternoon, a researcher witnesses a residential burglary. The incident is recorded in field notes but not reported to police.

3. In a federally funded study of a probation program, a researcher discovers that one participant was involved in a murder while on probation. Public disclosure of this incident might threaten the program, which the

researcher believes, from all evidence, is beneficial. Judging the murder to be an anomaly, the researcher does not disclose it to federal sponsors or describe it in published reports.

4. As part of a course on domestic violence, a professor requires students to telephone a domestic violence hotline, pretend to be a victim, and request help. Students then write up a description of the assistance offered by hotline staff and turn it in to the professor.

5. Studying aggression in bars and nightclubs, a researcher records observations of a savage fight in which three people are seriously injured. Ignoring pleas for help from one of the victims, the researcher retreats to a restroom to write up notes from these observations.

6. This quote is from a report on crack dealers by Bruce Jacobs (1996:364–365, n.5):

I informed police of my research, realizing that I could not withhold information from authorities if they should subpoena it. This never happened, perhaps because I told police that the research was about street life and urbanism rather than about gangs and crack distribution per se. Although technically this was a violation of the law, many other sociologists studying deviant populations have done the same thing to acquire valid observational data. . . . In addition, my university's Human Subject Review committee approved this research because I obtained written informed consent from all respondents and included safeguards to protect their anonymity and confidentiality.

7. In a study of state police, researchers learn that officers have been instructed by superiors to "not sign anything." Fearing that asking officers to sign informed consent statements will sharply reduce participation, researchers seek some other way to satisfy their university IRB. What should they do?

8. While visiting a police department as part of an evaluation of community policing sponsored by the National Institute of Justice, two researchers accompany a police captain to a local restaurant for lunch. The captain insists on paying. The tab is less than half the listed price of menu items ordered by the captain and the two researchers.

9. A researcher studying juvenile gangs is asked by a federal funding agency not to publish findings indicating that gang members are less often involved in illegal drug sales than are nongang members.

10. In the example mentioned in the section "Staff Misbehavior," the researchers disclosed to public officials that police were not making visits to probationers as called for in the program intervention. Published reports describe the problem as "irregularities in program delivery."

SUMMARY

- In addition to technical and scientific considerations, criminal justice research projects are shaped by ethical considerations.

- What's ethically "right" and "wrong" in research is ultimately a matter of what people agree is right and wrong.

- Researchers are not always the best judges of whether their own work adequately addresses ethical issues.

- Most ethical questions involve weighing the possible benefits of research against the potential for harm to research subjects.

- Scientists agree that participation in research should, in general, be voluntary. This norm, however, can conflict with the scientific need for generalizability.

- Criminal justice research may generate special ethical questions, including the potential for legal liability and physical harm.

- Most scientists agree that research should not harm subjects unless they willingly and knowingly accept the risks of harm through the principle of informed consent.

- Anonymity and confidentiality are two ways to protect the privacy of research subjects.

- Compliance with ethical principles is promoted by professional associations and by regulations issued by the Department of Health and Human Services (HHS).

- HHS regulations include special provisions for two types of subjects of particular interest to many criminal justice researchers: prisoners and juveniles.

- Institutional review boards (IRBs) play an important role in ensuring that the rights and interests of human subjects are protected. But some social science researchers believe that IRBs are becoming too restrictive.

KEY TERMS

Anonymity *(p. 62)*
Belmont Report *(p. 67)*
Confidentiality *(p. 62)*
Ethical *(p. 57)*
Informed consent *(p. 70)*
Special populations *(p. 71)*

REVIEW QUESTIONS AND EXERCISES

1. Obtain a copy of the American Society of Criminology (2016) code of ethics at this website: http://www.asc41.com/code_of_ethics_copies/ASC_Code_of_Ethics.pdf. Read the document carefully. How would the code apply to Laud Humphreys' tearoom research? What about the prison simulation? Especially note the "General Principles" section beginning on page 1.

2. As mentioned in the opening box for this chapter, Ko-lin Chin and James Finckenauer (2012) conducted research on sex trafficking of Chinese women. As you might imagine, this study required the researchers to consider a number of ethical questions on protecting human subjects, including researcher safety. As the authors describe, their work was guided by principles developed by the World Health Organization (2003). Download a copy of the WHO report and discuss how it illustrates our discussion of ethics in criminal justice research. http://www.who.int/gender-equity-rights/knowledge/9789242595499/en/

3. Review the box "Ethics and Juvenile Gang Members," noting that Decker and Van Winkle developed an informed consent form for their subjects. Try your hand at preparing such a form, keeping in mind the various ethical principles discussed in this chapter.

Structuring Criminal Justice Inquiry

PART 2

Posing questions properly can be more difficult than answering them. Indeed, a properly phrased question often seems to answer itself. We sometimes discover the answer to a question in the very process of clarifying the question for someone else.

Basically, scientific research is a process of achieving generalized understanding through observation. Part Three of this book will describe some of the specific methods of observation for criminal justice research. But first, Part Two deals with the posing of proper questions—the structuring of inquiry.

Chapter 4 addresses some of the fundamental issues that must be considered in planning a research project. It examines questions of causation, the units of analysis in a research project, the important role of time, and the kinds of things we must consider in proposing to do research projects.

Chapter 5 deals with the specification of what it is we want to study—a process known as conceptualization—and the measurement of the concepts we specify. We'll look at some of the terms that we use casually in everyday life, and we'll see the importance of being clear about what we really mean by such terms when we do research. Once we are clear on what we mean when we use certain terms, we are in a position to create measurements of what those terms refer to. The process of devising steps, or operations, for measuring what we want to study is known as operationalization.

Chapter 6 focuses on a specific but important measurement problem: measuring crime. We'll see many different approaches to measuring crime through conceptualization and operationalization, and discuss the strengths and weaknesses of each. In doing so, we'll refer to standards of measurement quality described in Chapter 5.

Chapter 7 concentrates on the general design of a criminal justice research project. A criminal justice research design specifies a strategy for finding something out—for structuring a research project. Chapter 7 describes commonly used strategies for experimental and quasi-experimental research. Each is adapted in some way from the classical scientific experiment.

CHAPTER 4

General Issues in Research Design

Here, we'll examine some fundamental principles about conducting empirical research: causation, and variations on whom or what is to be studied, when, and how. We'll also take a broad overview of the research process.

Learning Objectives

1. Recognize how explanatory scientific research centers on the notion of cause and effect, and why this is a probabilistic model of causation.

2. Describe the three basic requirements for establishing a causal relationship in science, together with what is a necessary cause and a sufficient cause.

3. Understand the role of validity and threats to validity of causal inference.

4. Summarize the four classes of validity threats, and how they correspond to questions about cause and effect.

5. Discuss how a scientific realist approach bridges idiographic and nomothetic approaches to causation.

6. Describe different units of analysis in criminal justice research.

7. Explain how the ecological fallacy relates to units of analysis.

8. Understand the time dimension, together with the differences between cross-sectional and longitudinal research.

9. Describe how retrospective studies may approximate longitudinal studies.

Parts-Marking and Auto Theft

Ronald Clarke and Mike Maxfield conducted a study to examine the effect of parts-marking on auto theft. Their work was commissioned by the National Highway Traffic Safety Administration (NHTSA). Beginning in 1987, NHTSA required that certain body and other parts be marked with vehicle identification number (VIN) on cars subject to high rates of theft. Though the question "Does parts-marking produce a decline in auto theft?" seemed straightforward at first, Clarke and Maxfield began by breaking that general question into a series of research questions:

- Has the decline in auto theft since 1987 been greater than the decline in other crimes?
- What have been the trends in thefts *from* cars? Have they been different than theft *of* cars?
- Which cars are required to have parts marked?
- Has there been a greater decline in thefts of cars that are required to have marked parts compared to those where parts-marking is not required?
- Which cars have other forms of security, such as transponder keys and electronic immobilizers?
- How does the trend in cars equipped with other forms of security compare to trends in cars with parts-marking?

These are a few of the several questions that were formulated to guide a research project that became considerably more complex than Clarke and Maxfield initially thought. Their work illustrates many of the topics covered in this chapter. Asking whether car theft declined over time more than other crimes involved the *time dimension* and a basic question about *causation*. If car theft had not declined more than other crimes, it was unlikely that federal requirements for parts-marking could have caused a decline.

Different units of analysis were involved. Clarke and Maxfield were basically interested in *aggregate* trends of car theft over a long period of time. But they had to determine which individual cars fit into different categories, which required examining *model years*, such as 2009 Ford Mustangs equipped with 5-liter engines.

These and other general issues in research design were initially addressed at early stages of the project. But as Clarke and Maxfield learned more, they had to adjust their approach and develop new measures. That's an example of our opening statement to this part of the book: Posing questions properly is often more difficult than answering them.

It is common for researchers to make adjustments as they move from planning to executing a particular research project. Review this box as you read the chapter. Consider another example of a seemingly simple question that can become more complex:

Has the growth of online shopping contributed to an increase in identity theft? Or think of another example of a seemingly simple research question that becomes more complex as you begin to think through it.

Introduction

Causation, units, and time are key elements in planning a research study.

Science is an enterprise dedicated to "finding out." Topics examined in this chapter address important considerations in planning all types of scientific inquiry—how to design a strategy for finding out something. Often, criminal justice researchers want to find out something that involves questions of cause and effect. They may want to learn more about things that make crime more likely to occur, or about policies that they hope will reduce crime in some way.

Let's say you are interested in studying corruption in government. That's certainly a worthy and appropriate topic for criminal justice research. But what specifically are you interested in? What do you mean by "corruption"? What kinds of behavior do you have in mind? And what do you mean by "government"? Whom do you want to study: All public employees? Judges? Sworn police officers? Elected officials? What is your purpose? Do you want to find out how much corruption there is? Do you want to learn why corruption exists? Do you want to compare corruption in different agencies? In different cities or states? These are the kinds of questions that need to be answered in research design. Read the vignette titled "Parts-Marking and Auto Theft" for an example of how a single question can lead to many more.

In practice, all aspects of research design are interrelated. They are separated here and in subsequent chapters so that we can explore particular topics in detail. We start with a discussion of causation in social science, the foundation of explanatory research. We then examine units of analysis—the *what* or *whom* to study. Deciding on units of analysis is an important part of all research, partly because people sometimes inappropriately use data

measuring one type of unit to say something about a different type of unit.

Next, we consider alternative ways of handling time in criminal justice research. It is sometimes appropriate to examine a static cross section of social life, but other studies follow social processes over time. In this regard, researchers must consider the time order of events and processes in making statements about cause.

Causation in the Social Sciences

Causation is the focus of explanatory research.

Cause and effect are implicit in much of what we have examined so far. One of the chief goals of social science researchers is to explain why things are the way they are. Typically, we do that by specifying the causes: Some things are caused by other things.

The general notion of causation is both simple and complex. On the one hand, we could have ignored the issue altogether. We could simply plug in the terms *cause* and *effect* and have little difficulty understanding them. On the other hand, an adequate discourse on causation would require a whole book or even a series of books. We decided to adopt a middle ground, providing more than a commonsense perspective on causation but not attempting to be definitive.

Much of our discussion in this section describes issues of causation and validity for social science in general. Recall from Chapters 1 and 2 that criminal justice research and theory are most strongly rooted in the social sciences. Furthermore, social science research methods are adapted from those used in the physical sciences. Many important and difficult questions about causality and validity occupy researchers in criminal justice. But our basic approach requires stepping back a bit to consider the larger picture—how we can or cannot assert that some cause actually produces some effect.

At the outset, it's important to keep in mind that cause in social science is inherently **probabilistic**, a point we introduced in Chapter 2. We say, for example, that certain factors make delinquency more or less *likely* within groups of people. Thus, victims of childhood abuse or neglect are *more likely* to report alcohol abuse as adults (Schuck and Widom, 2001). Burglary is *less likely* in neighborhoods where opportunities for informal guardianship are greater (Reynald, 2011).

Criteria for Causality

We begin our consideration of cause by examining what criteria must be satisfied before we can infer that one thing causes another. Recall the discussion of idiographic and nomothetic modes of explanation in Chapter 2. We now consider criteria for inferring idiographic causation, then criteria for inferring cause in the nomothetic mode of explanation.

Joseph Maxwell (2013:122–123) writes that criteria for assessing an idiographic explanation are (1) how credible and believable it is and (2) whether alternative explanations ("rival hypotheses") were seriously considered and found wanting. The first criterion relates to logic as one of the foundations of science. We demand that our explanations make sense, even if the logic is sometimes complex. The second criterion reminds us of Sherlock Holmes's dictum that when all other possibilities have been eliminated, the remaining explanation, however improbable, must be the truth.

Regarding nomothetic explanation, we examine three specific criteria for causality, as described by William Shadish, Thomas Cook, and Donald Campbell (2002):

1. Two variables must vary together; they must be empirically correlated.
2. The cause must occur before the effect.
3. The empirical correlation between cause and effect is not due to some other factor.

The first requirement in a causal relationship between two variables is that the two variables be empirically correlated with each other—they must occur together. It makes no sense to say that exploding gunpowder causes a bullet to leave the muzzle of a gun if, in observed reality, a bullet does not come out after the gunpowder explodes.

As straightforward as it may seem, criminal justice research has difficulties with this requirement. In the probabilistic world of nomothetic models of explanation, at least, we encounter few perfect measures of correlation. Most judges sentence repeat drug dealers to prison, but some don't. Many gang members use illegal drugs, but many do not. We are forced to ask, therefore, how strong the empirical relationship must be for that relationship to be considered causal.

The second requirement for inferring a causal relationship between two variables is that the cause precede the effect in time. It makes no sense to imagine something being caused by something else that happened later on. A bullet leaving the muzzle of a gun does not cause the gunpowder to explode; it works the other way around.

As simple and obvious as this criterion may seem, criminal justice research suffers many problems in this regard. Often, the time order connecting two variables is simply unclear. Which comes first: drug use or crime? And even when the time order seems clear, exceptions may be found. For example, we normally assume that obtaining a master's degree in management is a cause of more rapid advancement in a state department of corrections. Yet corrections executives might pursue graduate education after they have been promoted and recognize that advanced training in management skills will help them do their job better.

The third requirement for a causal relationship is that the observed empirical correlation between two variables cannot be attributed to the influence of some third variable that causes both of them. For example, we may observe that drug markets are often found near bus stops, but this does not mean that bus stops encourage drug markets. A third variable is at work here: Groups of people naturally congregate in reasonably close proximity at bus stops, and street drug markets are often found where people naturally congregate. In fact, Sung-suk Violet Yu (2011) describes a number of variables that are involved in a complex relationship between bus stops and crime.

To sum up, most criminal justice researchers consider two variables to be causally related—one causes the other—if (1) there is an empirical correlation between them, (2) the cause precedes the effect in time, and (3) the relationship is not found to result from the effects of some third variable on each of the two initially observed. Any relationship that satisfies all these criteria is causal.

Necessary and Sufficient Causes

Recognizing that virtually all causal relationships in criminal justice are probabilistic is central to understanding other points about cause. Within the probabilistic model, it is useful to distinguish two types of causes: necessary and sufficient. A

necessary cause is a condition that must be present for the effect to follow. For example, it is necessary for someone to be charged with a criminal offense before a person can be convicted. But being charged is not sufficient. Some people who are charged are ruled innocent. You must plead guilty or be found guilty by the court. Figure 4.1A illustrates a necessary cause: It is necessary to be charged before one can be convicted.

A *sufficient* cause, in contrast, is a condition that more or less guarantees the effect in question. Thus, for example, pleading guilty to some criminal charge is a sufficient cause for being convicted. It is also possible to be convicted through a trial, but pleading guilty is sufficient. Figure 4.1B illustrates this state of affairs.

FIGURE 4.1A Necessary Cause

FIGURE 4.1B Sufficient Cause

The discovery of a cause that is both necessary and sufficient to produce some result is the most satisfying outcome in research. If we are studying juvenile delinquency, we want to discover a single condition that (1) has to be present for delinquency to develop and (2) always results in delinquency. Then we will surely feel that we know precisely what causes juvenile delinquency. Unfortunately, we seldom discover causes that are both necessary and sufficient. Most causal relationships that criminal justice researchers work with are probabilistic and partial—we are able to partly explain cause and effect in some percentage of cases we observe.

Validity and Causal Inference

Scientists assess the truth of statements about cause by considering threats to validity.

Paying careful attention to cause-and-effect relationships is crucial in criminal justice research. Cause and effect are also key elements of applied studies, in which a researcher may be interested, for example, in whether a new mandatory sentencing law actually causes an increase in the prison population.

When we are concerned with whether we are correct in inferring that a cause produced an effect, we are concerned with the **validity** of causal inference. In the words of Shadish, Cook, and Campbell (2002:34), validity is "the approximate truth of an inference. . . . When we say something is valid, we make a judgment about the extent to which relevant evidence supports that inference as being true or correct." They emphasize that *approximate* is an important word, because one can never be absolutely certain about cause.

It is rarely possible to conclusively establish the validity of causal inference. We cannot make any sort of absolute judgment about whether our statements about cause are true. Instead, social scientists try to address different **validity threats** in causal inference—reasons we might be incorrect in stating that some cause produced some effect. As Maxwell (2013:123) puts it, "A key concept for validity is thus the *validity threat*: a way you might be wrong" (emphasis in original). Here we will

summarize the threats to four general categories of validity: statistical conclusion validity, internal validity, construct validity, and external validity. Chapter 7 discusses each type in more detail, linking the issue of validity to different ways of designing research.

Statistical Conclusion Validity

Statistical conclusion validity refers to our ability to determine whether a change in the suspected cause is statistically associated with a change in the suspected effect. This corresponds with the first criterion for inferring cause: Are two variables related to each other? If we suspect that using illegal drugs causes people to commit crimes, one of the first things we will be interested in is the common variation between drug use and crime. If drug users and nonusers commit crime at equal rates, and if about the same proportions of criminals and noncriminals use drugs, there will be no statistical relationship between measures of drug use and criminal offending. That seems to end our investigation of the causal relationship between drugs and crime. Review the vignette at the opening of this chapter for another example, the first research question considered by Clarke and Maxfield.

Basing conclusions on a small number of cases is a common threat to statistical conclusion validity. For example, suppose a researcher studies ten drug users and ten nonusers, comparing the numbers of times these subjects are arrested for other crimes over a six-month period. The researcher might find that over a six-month time period the 10 users were arrested an average of three times, while nonusers averaged two arrests. There is a difference in arrest rates, but is it a significant difference? Statistically, the answer is no because so few drug users were included in the study. Researchers cannot have much confidence in statements about

Validity   Whether statements about cause or measures are correct.

Validity threats   Possible sources of false conclusions about cause or measurement.

cause if their findings are based on small differences for a small number of cases.

Threats to statistical conclusion validity might also have the opposite effect, suggesting that covariation is present when in fact there is no cause-and-effect relationship. The reasons for this are again somewhat technical and require a basic understanding of statistical inference. However, some of the superstitious behavior exhibited by gamblers provides a rough-and-ready example.

Let's say you like to play the state lottery; nothing serious, you simply buy a couple of tickets each week. Many people play a system whereby they pick numbers that correspond to their date of birth or their license plate number. Expecting these lucky numbers to influence your chances of winning the lottery is an example of failing to recognize that winning numbers are picked by a random process. If you always pick your favorite uncle's birthday—say, July 7, 1977 (7777)—and buy two tickets per week for five years, your lucky number might come up simply by chance in the random system used to pick winning numbers. But there is no statistical conclusion validity to the inference that your method will cause you to win the lottery. Your winning will be due to the random effects of how numbers are selected.

Internal Validity

Even if we have found that two variables appear to be related to each other, **internal validity** threats can challenge causal statements about the observed covariation. An observed association between two variables has internal validity if the relationship is, in fact, causal and not due to the effects of one or more other variables. Whereas statistical conclusion threats are most often due to random error, internal validity problems result from nonrandom or systematic error. Simply put, threats to the internal validity of a proposed causal relationship between two variables usually arise from the effects of one or more *other* variables. Notice how this validity threat relates to the third requirement for establishing a causal relationship: eliminating other possible explanations for the observed relationship.

If, for example, we observe that convicted drug users sentenced to probation are rearrested less often than drug users sentenced to prison, we might be tempted to infer that prison sentences cause recidivism. Although imprisonment might have some impact on whether someone commits more crimes in the future, in this case it is important to look for other causes. One likely candidate would be prior criminal record. Convicted drug users without prior criminal records are more likely to be sentenced to probation, whereas persons with previous convictions more often receive prison terms. Research on criminal careers has found that the probability of reoffending increases with the number of prior arrests and convictions (Blumstein et al., 2010). In this case, a third variable—prior convictions—may explain some or all of the observed tendency of prison sentences to be associated with recidivism. Prior convictions are associated with both sentence—prison or probation—and subsequent convictions.

External Validity

Are findings about the impact of mandatory arrest for family violence in Minneapolis similar to findings in Milwaukee? Can community crime prevention organizations successfully combat drug use throughout a city, or do they work best in areas with only minor drug problems? Electronic monitoring may be suitable as an alternative sentence for convicted offenders, but can it work as an alternative to jail for defendants awaiting trial? Such questions are examples of issues in **external validity**: Do research findings about cause and effect apply equally to different cities, neighborhoods, and populations?

In a general sense, external validity is concerned with whether research findings from one study can be reproduced in another study, often under different conditions. Because crime problems and criminal justice responses can vary so much from city to city or from state to state, researchers and public officials often are especially interested in external validity. For example, a Kansas City evaluation found sharp reductions in gun-related crimes in hot spots that had been targeted for focused police patrols (Sherman, Shaw, and Rogan, 1995). Because these results were promising, similar projects were launched in two other cities—Indianapolis (McGarrell et al., 2001) and Pittsburgh (Cohen and Ludwig, 2003). In both cases, researchers found that police actions targeting hot spots for gun violence reduced gun-related crimes and increased seizures of illegal firearms. Having similar findings in Indianapolis and Pittsburgh enhanced the external validity of original results from Kansas City.

Construct Validity

This type of validity is concerned with how well an observed relationship between variables measured by a researcher represents the underlying causal process of interest. In this sense, **construct validity** refers to generalizing from what we observe and measure to the real-world things in which we are interested. The concept of construct validity is thus closely related to issues in measurement, as we will see in Chapters 5 and 6.

To illustrate construct validity, let's consider the supervision of police officers—specifically, whether close supervision causes police officers to write more traffic tickets. We might define "close supervision" in this way: A police sergeant drives his own marked police car in such a way as to always keep a patrol car in view.

This certainly qualifies as close supervision, but you may recognize a couple of problems. First, two marked patrol cars present a highly visible presence to motorists, who might drive more prudently and thus reduce the opportunities for patrol officers to write traffic tickets. Second, and more central to the issue of construct validity, this represents a narrow definition of the construct "close supervision." Patrol officers may be closely supervised in other ways that cause them to write more traffic tickets. For example, sergeants might closely supervise their officers by reviewing their ticket production at the end of each shift. Supervising subordinates by keeping them in view is only one way

of exercising control over their behavior. It may be appropriate for factory workers, but it is not practical for police, representing a very limited version of the construct "supervision."

The classic Kansas City Preventive Patrol Experiment, discussed in Chapter 1, provides another example of construct validity problems. Recall that the experiment sought to determine whether routine preventive patrol reduced crime and fear of crime, and increased arrests. This causal proposition was tested by comparing measures of crime, fear, and arrests in proactive beats (with twice the normal level of preventive patrol), reactive beats (with no preventive patrol), and control beats (with normal levels of preventive patrol). Researchers found no significant differences in levels of crime, fear, or arrests.

Richard Larson (1975) discussed several difficulties with the experiment's design. One important problem relates to the visibility of police presence, a central concept in preventive patrol. It is safe to assume that the ability of routine patrol to prevent crime and enhance feelings of safety depends partly on the visibility of police. It makes sense to assume further that withdrawing preventive patrol, as was done in the reactive beats, reduces the visibility of police. But by how much? Larson explored this question in detail and suggested that two other features of police operations during the Kansas City experiment partially compensated for the absence of preventive patrol and produced a visible police presence.

First, the different types of experimental beats were adjacent to one another; one reactive beat shared borders with three control and three proactive beats. This enhanced the visibility of police in reactive beats in two ways: (1) police in adjoining proactive and control beats sometimes drove around the perimeter of reactive beats, and (2) police often drove through reactive beats on their way to some other part of the city.

Second, many Kansas City police officers were skeptical about the experiment and feared that withdrawing preventive patrol in reactive beats would create problems. As a result, police who responded to calls for service in the reactive areas more frequently used lights and sirens when driving to the location of complaints. A related action was that police units not assigned to the calls for service nevertheless drove into the reactive beats to provide backup service.

Each of these actions produced a visible police presence in the reactive beats. People who lived in these areas were unaware of the experiment and, as you might expect, did not know whether a police car was present because it was on routine patrol, was on its way to some other part of the city, or was responding to a call for assistance. And, of course, the use of lights and sirens makes police cars much more visible.

Larson's point was that the *construct* of police visibility is only partly represented by routine preventive patrol. A visible police presence was produced in Kansas City through other means. Therefore, the researchers' conclusion that routine preventive patrol does not cause a reduction in crime or an increase in arrests suffers from threats to construct validity. Construct validity is a frequent problem in applied studies, in which researchers may oversimplify complex policies and policy goals. That is basically a measurement problem, as we will see in Chapter 5.

Validity and Causal Inference Summarized

The four types of validity threats can be grouped into two categories: bias and generalizability. Internal and statistical conclusion validity threats are related to systematic and nonsystematic bias, respectively. Problems with statistical procedures produce nonsystematic bias, while an alternative explanation for an observed relationship is an example of systematic bias. In either case, bias calls into question the inference that some cause produced some effect.

Failing to consider the more general cause-and-effect constructs that operate in an observed cause-and-effect relationship results in research findings that cannot be generalized to real-world behaviors and conditions. And a cause-and-effect relationship observed in one setting or at one time may not operate in the same way in a different setting or at a different time.

Shadish, Cook, and Campbell (2002:39) summarized these four validity threats by linking them to the types of questions that researchers ask in trying to establish cause and effect. Test your understanding by writing the name of each validity threat after the appropriate question from Shadish, Cook, and Campbell.

1. How large and reliable is the covariation between the presumed cause and effect?
2. Is the covariation causal, or would the same covariation have been obtained without the treatment?
3. How generalizable is the locally embedded causal relationship over varied persons, treatments, observations, and settings?
4. What general constructs are involved in the persons, settings, treatments, and observations used in the experiment?

Does Drug Use Cause Crime?

To illustrate issues of validity and causal inference, we will consider the relationship between drug use and crime. Drug addiction is thought to drive people—who are desperate for a fix and unable to secure legitimate income—to commit crimes in order to support their habits.

Understanding causal statements about drug use and crime requires carefully specifying two key concepts (drug use and crime) and considering the different ways these concepts might be related. Jan Chaiken and Marcia Chaiken (1990) provide unusually careful and well-reasoned insights that will guide our consideration of links between drugs and crime. Let's begin with issues in basic research on the drugs–crime connection, and then discuss the implications of this research for criminal justice policy.

First is the question of temporal order: Which comes first, drug use or crime? Research summarized by Chaiken and Chaiken provides no conclusive answer. In an earlier study of prison inmates, Chaiken and Chaiken (1982) found that 12 percent of their adult subjects committed crimes after using drugs for at least two years, while 15 percent committed predatory crimes two or more years before using drugs.

Regarding an empirical relationship, many studies have found that some drug users commit crimes and that some criminals use drugs. Trevor Bennett and associates (2008) conducted summary analysis of 30 research studies on drug use and crime. They found that drug users were over three times more likely to be involved in crime than nonusers. So a statistical association between drug use and crime clearly exists.

What about the possible influence of other factors—things that might be related to both drug use and crime? Chaiken and Chaiken (1990:234) conclude that "drug use and crime participation are weakly related as contemporaneous products of factors generally antithetical to traditional United States lifestyles." Stated somewhat differently, drug use and crime (as well as delinquency) are each deviant activities produced by other underlying causes. A statistical association between drug use and crime clearly exists. But the presence of other factors indicates that the relationship is not directly causal, thus bringing into question the internal validity of causal statements about drug use and crime.

To assess the construct validity of research on drugs and crime, let's think for a moment about different patterns of each behavior, rather than assume that drug use and crime are uniform behaviors. Many adolescents in the United States experiment with drugs, and just as many—especially males—commit delinquent acts or petty crimes. A large number of adults may be occasional users of illegal drugs as well. Many different patterns of drug use, delinquency, and adult criminality have been found through research in other countries. Stephen Pudney (2002) and Trevor Bennett and Katy Holloway (2005) report on varying patterns of use in England and Wales. Because there is no simple way to describe either construct, searching for a single cause-and-effect relationship misrepresents a complex causal process.

Both construct and external validity are concerned with generalizations. Problems with the external validity of research on drugs and crime are similar to those revolving around construct validity. The relationship between occasional marijuana use and delinquency among teenagers is different from that between occasional cocaine use and adult crime; in turn, each

relationship varies from that between heroin addiction and persistent criminal behavior among adults.

The issue of external validity comes into sharper focus when we shift from basic research that seeks to uncover fundamental causal relationships to criminal justice policy. Chaiken and Chaiken argue that any uniform policy to reduce the use of all drugs among all population groups will have little effect on serious crime. Bennett and associates reach similar conclusions, arguing that government antidrug policy should distinguish more carefully between types of drug use (2008:117–118).

Basic and applied research on the relationships among drug use and crime readily illustrates threats to the validity of causal inference. It is often difficult to find a relationship, because there is so much variation in drug use and crime participation (statistical conclusion validity threat). A large number of studies have demonstrated that when statistical relationships are found, both drug use and crime can be attributed to other, often multiple, causes (internal validity threat). Different patterns among different population groups mean that there are no readily identifiable cause-and-effect constructs (construct validity). Because of these differences, policies developed to counter drug use among the population as a whole cannot be expected to significantly impact serious crime (external validity).

None of the above is to say that there is no cause-and-effect relationship between drug use and crime. However, research has clearly shown that there is no simple causal connection.

Introducing Scientific Realism

In our final consideration of cause and effect in this chapter, we revisit the distinction between idiographic and nomothetic ways of explanation. Doing research to learn what causes what usually involves nomothetic explanations. We wish to find causal explanations that apply generally to situations beyond those we actually study in our research. At the same time, researchers and public officials are often interested in understanding specific causal mechanisms in more narrowly defined situations—what we have described as the idiographic mode of explanation.

Scientific realism bridges idiographic and nomothetic approaches to explanation by seeking to understand how causal *mechanisms* operate in specific *contexts*. Traditional approaches to finding cause and effect usually try to isolate causal mechanisms from other possible influences—something you should now recognize as attempts to control threats to internal validity. The scientific realist approach views these other possible influences as contexts in which causal mechanisms operate. Rather than try to exclude or otherwise control possible outside influences, scientific realism studies how such influences are involved in cause-and-effect relationships.

For example, earlier in this chapter, we noted that electronic monitoring as a condition of probation might apply to some populations but not others. We framed this as a question of external validity in the traditional way of considering nomothetic causation. A scientific realist approach would consider the causal mechanism underlying electronic monitoring to be effective in some contexts, but not in others. As another example, we reviewed at some length the cause-and-effect conundrum surrounding drug use and crime. That review was framed by traditional nomothetic research to establish cause and effect. A scientific realism approach to the question would recognize that drug use and crime co-occur in some contexts, but not in others.

We say that scientific realism bridges idiographic and nomothetic modes of explanation because it exhibits elements of both. Because it focuses our attention on very specific questions, scientific realism seems idiographic. Nicholas Zanin, Jon Shane, and Ronald Clarke (2004) asked, "Will redesigning the Interstate 78 exit in Newark, New Jersey cause a reduction in suburban residents seeking to buy heroin in a nearby neighborhood?" But their analysis and interpretation addressed a more general question of causation: "Can the design of streets and intersections be modified to make it more difficult for street drug markets to operate?" Changing an expressway exit ramp to reduce drug sales in Newark is a specific example of cause and effect that is rooted in the more general causal relationship between traffic patterns and drug markets.

These illustrations of the scientific realist approach to cause and effect are examples of research for the purpose of application, a topic treated at length by British researchers Ray Pawson and Nick Tilley (1997). Application is a type of explanatory research, as we indicated in Chapter 1. In later chapters, we call on scientific realism as a strategy for designing explanatory research (Chapter 7) and conducting evaluations (Chapter 13).

Sorting out causes and effects is one of the most difficult challenges of explanatory research. Our attention now turns to two other important considerations that emerge in research for explanation and other purposes: units of analysis and the time dimension.

Units of Analysis

To avoid mistaken inferences, researchers must carefully specify the people or phenomena that will be studied.

In criminal justice research, there is a great deal of variation in what or who is studied—technically called **units of analysis**. Individual people often are units of analysis. Researchers may make observations describing certain characteristics of offenders or crime victims, such as age, gender, or race. The descriptions of many individuals then are combined to provide a picture of the population that comprises those individuals.

For example, we may note the age and gender of persons convicted of drunk driving in Fort Lauderdale over a certain period. Aggregating these observations, we might characterize drunk-driving offenders as 72 percent men and 28 percent women, with an average age of 26.4 years. This is a descriptive analysis of convicted drunk drivers in Fort Lauderdale. Although the description applies to the group of drunk drivers as a whole, it

Units of analysis The things—what or whom—being studied in a research project.

is based on the characteristics of individual people convicted of drunk driving.

The same situation could exist in an evaluation study. Suppose we wish to determine whether an alcohol education program reduces repeat arrests of first-time drunk-driving offenders. First, we administer the education program to half the persons convicted of drunk driving in Fort Lauderdale over a period of two months; the other half does not receive the program. Next, we observe drunk-driving arrest records for 12 months, keeping track of people who were previously convicted and of whether they received the alcohol education program. Combining our observations, we find that 5 percent of those who received the program were arrested again, and that 20 percent of those who did not receive alcohol education were rearrested within a year. The purpose of the study is to evaluate a program, but individual drunk drivers are still the units of analysis.

Units of analysis in a study are typically also the units of observation. Thus, to study what steps people take to protect their homes from burglary, we might observe, perhaps through interviews, individual household residents. Sometimes, however, we "observe" units of analysis indirectly. For example, we might ask individuals about crime prevention measures for the purpose of describing households. We might want to find out whether homes with double-cylinder deadbolt locks are burglarized less often than homes with less substantial protection. In this case, our units of analysis are households, but the units of observation are individual household members who are asked to describe burglaries and home protection to interviewers.

Some studies try to describe or explain more than one unit of analysis. In these cases, the researcher must anticipate their desired conclusions with regard to which units of analysis. For example, we may want to discover what kinds of college students (individuals) are most successful in their careers; we may also want to learn what kinds of colleges (organizations) produce graduates who are the most successful.

Here's an example that illustrates the complexity of units of analysis. Murders usually involve one individual who kills another individual.

However, when Charis Kubrin and Ronald Weitzer (2003:157) asked, "Why do these neighborhoods generate high homicide rates?" the unit of analysis in that phrase is neighborhood. You can probably imagine some kinds of neighborhoods (e.g., poor and urban) that would have high homicide rates and some (e.g., wealthy and suburban) that would have low rates. In this particular conversation, the unit of analysis (neighborhood) would be categorized in terms of variables such as economic level, locale, and homicide rate.

In their analysis, however, Kubrin and Weitzer were also interested in different types of homicide: in particular, those that occurred in retaliation for some earlier event, such as an assault or insult. Can you identify the unit of analysis common to all of the following excerpts (Kubrin and Weitzer, 2003:163)?

1. "The sample of killings. . . ."
2. "The coding instrument includes over 80 items related to the homicide."
3. "Of the 2,161 homicides that occurred from 1985 [to] 1995. . . ."
4. "Of those with an identified motive, 19.5 percent (n = 337) are retaliatory."

In each of these excerpts, the unit of analysis is *homicide* (also called killing). Sometimes, as in the first excerpt, you can identify the unit of analysis in the description of the sampling methods. A discussion of classification methods might also identify the unit of analysis, as in the second excerpt (80 ways to code the homicides). Often, numerical summaries point the way: 2,161 homicides; 19.5 percent (of the homicides).

To explore this topic in more depth, let's consider several common units of analysis in criminal justice research.

Individuals

Any variety of individuals may be the units of analysis in criminal justice research. This point is more important than it may initially seem. The norm of generalized understanding in social science should suggest that scientific findings are most valuable when they apply to all kinds of people. In practice, however, researchers seldom study all kinds of people. At the very least, studies typically are limited to people who live in a single country, although some comparative studies stretch across national borders.

As the units of analysis, individuals may be considered in the context of their membership in different groups. Examples of circumscribed groups whose members may be units of analysis at the individual level are *police, victims, defendants in criminal court, correctional inmates, gang members,* and *active burglars.* Note that each term implies some population of individual persons. Descriptive studies with individuals as their units of analysis typically aim to describe the population that comprises those individuals.

Groups

A variety of groups may also be the units of analysis for criminal justice research. It's important to understand that this is not the same as studying the individuals within a group. If we study the members of a juvenile gang to learn about teenagers who join gangs, the individual (teen gang member) is the unit of analysis. But if we study all the juvenile gangs in a city to learn the differences between big gangs and small ones, between gangs selling drugs and gangs stealing cars, and so forth, the unit of analysis is the social group (gang).

Police beats or patrol districts might be the units of analysis in a study. A police beat can be described in terms of the total number of people who live within its boundaries, total street mileage, annual crime reports, and whether the beat includes a special facility such as a park or high school. We can then determine, for example, whether beats that include a park report more assaults than beats without such facilities—or whether auto thefts are more common in beats with more street mileage. Here, the individual police beat is the unit of analysis.

Other examples of units at the group level are *households, city blocks, census tracts, cities, counties,* and *other geographic regions.* Each of these terms also implies some population of groups. *Street gang* implies some population that includes all street gangs. The population of street gangs could be described, say, in terms of its geographic distribution throughout a city. An explanatory study of street gangs might discover, for example, whether large gangs are more likely to engage in inter-gang warfare than small gangs.

Organizations

Formal political or social organizations may also be the units of analysis in criminal justice research. An example is correctional facilities, which implies a population of all correctional facilities. Individual facilities might be characterized in terms of their number of employees, status as state or federal prisons, security classification, percentage of inmates who are from racial or ethnic minority groups, types of offenses for which inmates are sentenced to each facility, average length of sentence served, and so forth. We might determine whether federal prisons house a larger or smaller percentage of offenders sentenced for white-collar crimes than do state prisons. Other examples of formal organizations as units of analysis are *police departments, courtrooms, probation offices, drug treatment facilities,* and *victim services agencies.*

When social groups or formal organizations are the units of analysis, their characteristics often derive from the characteristics of their individual members. Thus, a correctional facility might be described in terms of its inmates: gender distribution, average sentence length, ethnicity, and so on. In a descriptive study, we might be interested in the percentage of institutions housing only females. Or, in an explanatory study, we might determine whether institutions housing both males and females report, on the average, fewer or more assaults by inmates on staff compared with male-only institutions. In each example, the correctional facility is the unit of analysis. By contrast, if we ask whether male or female inmates are more often involved in assaults on staff, then the individual inmate is the unit of analysis.

Some studies involve descriptions or explanations of more than one unit of analysis. Consider, for example, an evaluation of community policing programs in selected neighborhoods of a large city. In such an evaluation, we might be interested in how *citizens* feel about the program (individuals), whether arrests increased in *neighborhoods* with the new program compared with those without it (groups), and whether the *police department's* budget increased more than the budget in a similar city (organizations).

Social Artifacts

Yet another potential unit of analysis may be referred to as "social artifacts," or the products of social beings and their behavior. Stories about crime in newspapers and magazines or on television reflect one class of social artifacts. A newspaper story might be characterized by its length, placement on front or later pages, size of headlines, and presence of photographs. A researcher could analyze whether television news features or newspaper reports provide the most details about a new police program to increase drug arrests.

Social interactions are also examples of social artifacts suitable for criminal justice research. Police crime reports are an example. We might analyze assault reports to determine how many involved three or more people, whether assaults involved strangers or people with some prior acquaintance, or whether they occurred more often in public or in private locations.

At first, crime reports may not seem to be social artifacts, but consider for a moment what they represent. When a crime is reported to the police, officers usually record what happened from descriptions by victims or witnesses. For instance, an assault victim may describe how he suffered an unprovoked attack while innocently enjoying a cold beer after work. However, witnesses to the incident might claim that the "victim" started the fight by insulting the "offender." The responding police officer must interpret who is telling the truth in sorting out the circumstances of a violent social interaction. The officer's report becomes a social artifact that represents one among the population of all assaults.

Records of different types of social interactions are common units of analysis in criminal justice research. Criminal history records, meetings of community anticrime groups, presentence investigations, and interactions between police and citizens are examples. Notice that each example requires information about individuals, but that social interactions between people are the units of analysis.

In an annual report on juveniles arrested, Charles Puzzanchera describes examples of how arrests represent social artifacts. His comments also illustrate some of the confusion that stems from the different units counted in social artifacts:

> The number of arrests is not the same as the number of people arrested because an unknown number of individuals are arrested more than once during the year. Nor do arrest statistics represent the number of crimes that arrested individuals commit because a series of crimes that one person commits may culminate in a single arrest. . . . (Puzzanchera, 2014:2)

The Ecological Fallacy

At this point, it is appropriate to introduce two important concepts related to units of analysis and causation: the ecological fallacy and reductionism. The first concept—the **ecological fallacy**—refers to the danger of making assertions about individuals based on the examination of groups or other aggregations. Such assertions are often made in connection with causation, where researchers observe associations between aggregate units and make statements about causality between individual units.

Suppose we are interested in learning about robbery in different police precincts of a large city. Let's assume that we have information on how many robberies were committed in each police precinct of Chicago for the year 2015. Assume also that we have census data describing some of the characteristics of those precincts. Our analysis of such data might show that a large number of 2015 robberies occurred in the downtown precinct, and that the average family income of persons living in downtown Chicago was substantially higher than in other precincts in the city. We might be tempted to conclude that high-income, downtown residents are more likely to be robbed than are people who live in other parts of the city—that is, robbers select richer victims.

In reaching such a conclusion, we run the risk of committing the ecological fallacy by using observations aggregated into police precincts to make some statement about the socioeconomic status of individual robbery victims. We refer to this as a fallacy because lower-income people who did not live in the downtown area might also have been robbed there in 2015. Victims might be commuters to jobs in the loop, people visiting downtown theaters or restaurants, passengers on subway or elevated train platforms, or homeless persons who are not counted by the census. Our problem is that we examined police precincts as our units of analysis, but we wish to draw conclusions about individual people.

The same problem will arise if we discover that incarceration rates are higher in states that have a large proportion of elderly residents. We will not know whether older people are actually imprisoned more often. Or, if we find higher suicide rates in cities with large nonwhite populations, we cannot be sure whether more nonwhites than whites committed suicide.

Don't let these warnings against the ecological fallacy lead you to commit what is called an "individualistic fallacy." Some students approaching criminal justice research for the first time have trouble reconciling general patterns of attitudes and actions with known individual exceptions. If, for example, you read a news story about a Utah resident visiting New York who is murdered on a subway platform, the fact remains that most visitors to New York and most subway riders are not at risk of murder. Similarly, mass media stories and popular films about drug problems in U.S. cities frequently focus on drug use and dealing among African Americans. But that does not mean that most African Americans are drug users, or that drugs are not a problem among whites.

The individualistic fallacy can be especially troublesome for beginning students of criminal justice. News media and television police dramas often present unusual or highly dramatized versions of crime problems and criminal justice policy. These messages may distort the way many people initially approach research problems in criminal justice.

Reductionism

A second concept relating to units of analysis is reductionism. Basically, reductionism is an overly strict limitation on the concepts and variables to be considered as causes of the broad range of human behavior represented by crime and criminal justice

policy. Economists may tend to consider only economic variables (marginal value, expected utility); sociologists may consider only sociological variables (values, norms, roles); psychologists may consider only psychological variables (personality types, compulsive personality disorder). For example, why did homicide by juveniles decline from 1994 through 2010, after an increase from 1984 through about 1994? Was it the result of changes in family structure? Fluctuation in economic opportunities for teenagers? Diminished fascination with images of violence, power, and flashy lifestyles among drug dealers in popular media? Social scientists from different disciplines tend to look at some explanations for crime problems and ignore the others. Explaining crime solely in terms of economic factors is economic reductionism; explaining crime solely in terms of psychological factors is psychological reductionism.

Reductionism of any type tends to suggest that particular units of analysis or variables are more relevant than others. If we consider the changing family structure as the cause of increased juvenile crime, our unit of analysis will be families. An economist, though, might use the 50 states as the units of analysis and compare juvenile crime rates and economic conditions. A psychologist might choose individual juveniles as the units of analysis to determine how watching violent films affects personality development.

Like the ecological fallacy, reductionism involves the use of inappropriate units of analysis. The appropriate unit of analysis for a given research question is not always clear and is often debated by social scientists, especially across disciplinary boundaries.

The box titled "Units of Analysis in the National Youth Gang Survey" offers several additional examples of using inappropriate units of analysis. It also illustrates that lack of clarity about units of analysis in criminal justice results in part from difficulties in directly measuring the concepts we want to study.

Units of Analysis in Review

The purpose of this section has been to specify what is sometimes a confusing topic, in part because criminal justice researchers use a variety of different units of analysis. Although individual people are often the units of analysis, that is not always the case. Many research questions can more appropriately be answered through the examination of other units of analysis.

Understanding the logic of units of analysis is more important than memorizing some list of the units. It is irrelevant what we call a given unit of analysis—a group, a formal organization, or a social artifact. It is essential, however, that we be able to identify what our unit of analysis is. We must decide whether we are studying assaults or assault victims, police departments or police officers, courtrooms or judges, and prisons or prison inmates. Without keeping this point in mind, we run the risk of making assertions about one unit of analysis based on the examination of another.

To test your grasp of the concept of units of analysis, here are some examples of real research topics. See if you can determine the unit of analysis in each. (The answers are given at the end of this chapter.)

1. "Taking into account preexisting traffic fatality trends and several other relevant factors, the implementation of the emergency cellular telephone program resulted in a substantial and permanent reduction in the monthly percentage of alcohol-related fatal crashes" (D'Alessio, Stolzenberg, and Terry, 1999:463–464).

2. "Our analysis provides, at best, extremely weak support for the hypothesis that curfews reduce juvenile crime rates. Of the offense and victimization measures, only burglary, larceny, and simple assault arrests significantly decreased after cities adopted curfew statutes. These decreases occurred only for revised laws, and only the reductions in larceny appeared in both the county and city–county samples" (McDowall, Loftin, and Wiersema, 2000:88).

3. "The survey robbery rate was highest in Canada and the Netherlands, and lowest in Scotland. . . . In 1999 the survey robbery rate was lowest in the United States" (Farrington, Langan, and Tonry, 2004:xii).

4. "On average, probationers were 31 years old, African American, male, and convicted of drug or property offenses. Most lived with family, and although they were not married, many were in exclusive relationships (44 percent) and had children (47 percent)" (MacKenzie et al., 1999:433).

5. "Seventy-five percent ($n = 158$) of the cases were disposed at district courts, and 3 percent ($n = 6$) remained pending. One percent of the control and 4 percent of the experimental cases were referred to drug treatment court" (Taxman and Elis, 1999:42).

6. "Drawing on detailed spatial data on the location and characteristics of a sample of 132 [cannabis] cultivation sites, we examine the patterns in site location against three measures of distance and examine their implications for the number of plants grown" (Bouchard, Beauregard, and Kalacska, 2013:37).

7. "Although Albania and Kosovo experienced the steepest decline in homicide rates in the last decade, they still, along with Montenegro, showed higher levels in comparison to European countries . . . in 2009" (del Frate and Mugellini, 2012:146).

8. "Of all the files opened for Arabs, 32 percent were crimes against the person, whereas of all the files opened for Jews, 30 percent were in that category. Proportionally, more files of property and drug offenses were opened for Jews than for Arabs. In addition, Arabs are over-represented in public order offenses" (Mesch and Fishman, 1999:184).

9. "Stories about women perpetrating crimes against children were more likely to appear on the first page of the newspaper, 7.5% versus 1%" (Grabe et al., 2006:149).

10. "Approximately half of the burglars (54 percent) admitted to 50 or more lifetime burglaries. . . . Included in this group are 44 offenders who had committed at least 100 such crimes. At the other extreme are 11 individuals who had participated in nine or fewer residential break-ins" (Wright and Decker, 1994:13).

UNITS OF ANALYSIS IN THE NATIONAL YOUTH GANG SURVEY

In 1997, the third annual National Youth Gang Survey was completed for the federal Office of Juvenile Justice and Delinquency Prevention (OJJDP). This survey reflects keen interest in developing better information about the scope of youth gangs and their activities in different types of communities around the country. As important and useful as this effort is, the National Youth Gang Survey—especially reports of its results—illustrates how some ambiguities can emerge with respect to units of analysis.

A variety of attempts, often creative, are used to gather information from or about active offenders. Partly this is because it is difficult to systematically identify offenders for research. Studying youth gangs presents more than the usual share of problems with units of analysis. Are we interested in gangs (groups), gang members (individuals), or offenses (social artifact) committed by gangs?

Following methods developed in earlier years, the 1997 National Youth Gang Survey was based on a sample of law enforcement agencies. The sample was designed to represent different types of communities: rural areas, suburban counties, small cities, and large cities. Questionnaires were mailed to the police chief for municipalities and to the sheriff for counties (National Youth Gang Center, 1999:3). Questions asked respondents to report on gangs and gang activity in their jurisdiction—municipality for police departments, and unincorporated service area for sheriffs' departments. Here are examples of the *types* of questions included in the survey:

1. How many youth gangs were active in your jurisdiction?
2. How many active youth gang members were in your jurisdiction?
3. In your jurisdiction, what percent of street sales of drugs were made by youth gang members? [followed by list: powder cocaine, crack cocaine, marijuana, heroin, methamphetamine, other]
4. Does your agency have the following? [list of special youth gang units]

The Time Dimension

Because time order is a requirement for causal inferences, the time dimension of research requires careful planning.

We saw earlier in this chapter how the time sequence of events and situations is a critical element in determining causation. Time is also involved in the generalizability of research findings. Do the descriptions and explanations that result from a particular study accurately represent the situation of 10 years ago or 10 years from now? Or do they represent only the current state of affairs? In general, observations may be made more or less at one time point, or they may be deliberately stretched over a longer period. Observations made at more than one time point can look forward or backward.

Cross-Sectional Studies

Many criminal justice research projects are designed to study some phenomenon by taking a cross section of it at one time and analyzing that cross section carefully. Exploratory and descriptive studies are often **cross-sectional studies**.

Cross-sectional studies Data collected at a single time point.

Notice the different units of analysis embedded in these questions. Seven are stated or implied.

1. Gangs: item 1
2. Gang members: items 2, 3
3. Jurisdiction (city or part of county area): items 1, 2, 3
4. Street sales of drugs: item 3
5. Drug types: item 3
6. Agency: item 4
7. Special unit: item 4

Now, consider some quotes from a summary report on the 1997 survey (National Youth Gang Center, 1999). Which ones do or do not *reasonably* reflect the actual units of analysis from the survey?

- "Fifty-one percent of survey respondents indicated that they had active youth gangs in their jurisdictions in 1997." (page 7)
- "Thirty-eight percent of jurisdictions in the Northeast, and 26 percent of jurisdictions in the Middle Atlantic regions reported active youth gangs in 1997." (extracted from Table 3, page 10)
- "Results of the 1997 survey revealed that there were an estimated 30,533 youth gangs and 815,986 gang members active in the United States in 1997." (page 13)

- "The percentage of street sales of crack cocaine, heroin, and methamphetamine conducted by youth gang members varied substantially by region.... Crack cocaine sales involving youth gang members were most prevalent in the Midwest (38 percent), heroin sales were most prevalent in the Northeast (15 percent), and methamphetamine sales were most prevalent in the West (21 percent)." (page 27)
- "The majority (66 percent) of respondents indicated that they had some type of specialized unit to address the gang problem." (page 33)

The youth gang survey report includes a number of statements and tables that inaccurately describe units of analysis. You probably detected examples of this in some of the statements shown here. Other statements accurately reflect units of analysis measured in the survey.

If you read the 1997 survey report and keep in mind our discussion of units of analysis, you will find more misleading statements and tables. This will enhance your understanding of units of analysis.

Source: Information drawn from the National Youth Gang Center (1999).

A single U.S. census, for instance, is a study aimed at describing the U.S. population at a given time. A single wave of the National Crime Victimization Survey (NCVS) is a descriptive cross-sectional study that estimates how many people have been victims of crime in a given time.

A cross-sectional exploratory study might be conducted by a police department in the form of a survey that examines what residents believe to be the sources of crime problems in their neighborhood. In all likelihood, the study will ask about crime problems in a single time frame, with the findings used to help the department explore various methods of introducing community policing.

Cross-sectional studies for explanatory or evaluation purposes have an inherent problem. We have seen that inferring cause requires that a cause precede an effect in time, but cross-sectional studies produce observations made at only one time. For example, a survey might ask respondents whether their home has been burglarized and whether they have any special locks on their doors, hoping to determine if special locks prevent burglary. Because the questions about burglary victimization and door locks are asked at only one time, it is not possible to determine whether burglary victims installed locks after a burglary—or whether special locks were already in place but did not prevent the crime. Some of the ways we can deal with the difficult problem of determining time order will be discussed in the section on approximating longitudinal studies.

Longitudinal Studies

Research projects known as **longitudinal studies** are designed to permit observations over an extended period. An example is a researcher who interviews a group of subjects every six months for five years. Analysis of newspaper stories about crime or numbers of prison inmates over time are other examples. In the latter instances, it is irrelevant whether the researcher's observations are made over the course of the actual events under study or at one time—for example, examining a year's worth of newspapers in the library or 10 years of annual reports on correctional populations.

Three special types of longitudinal studies should be noted here: trend, cohort, and panel studies. **Trend studies** look at changes within some general population over time. An example is a comparison of the FBI's Uniform Crime Report (UCR) figures over time, showing an increase in reported crime from 1960 through 1993 and then a decline through 2010. Or a researcher might want to know whether changes in sentences for certain offenses were followed by increases in the number of people imprisoned in state institutions. In this case, a trend study might examine annual figures for prison population over time, comparing totals for the years before and after new sentencing laws took effect.

Cohort studies examine more specific populations (cohorts) as they change over time. Typically, a cohort is an age group, such as those people born during the 1990s, but it can also be based on some other time grouping. Cohorts are often defined as a group of people who enter or leave an institution at the same time, such as persons entering a drug treatment center during July, offenders released from custody in 2013, or high school seniors in March 2016.

In a classic cohort study, Marvin Wolfgang and associates (Wolfgang, Figlio, and Sellin, 1972) studied all males born in 1945 who lived in the city of Philadelphia from their 10th birthday through age 18 or older. The researchers examined records from police agencies and public schools to determine how many boys in the cohort had been charged with delinquency or arrested, how old they were when first arrested, and what differences there were between delinquents and nondelinquents in school performance.

Panel studies are similar to trend and cohort studies, except that observations are made on the same set of people on two or more occasions. The NCVS is a good example of a descriptive panel study. A member of each household selected for inclusion in the survey is interviewed seven times at six-month intervals. The NCVS serves many purposes, but it was developed initially to estimate how many people were victims of various types of crimes each year. It is designed as a panel study so that persons can be asked about crimes that occurred in the previous six months; two waves of panel data are combined to estimate the nationwide frequency of victimization over a one-year period. Panel studies are often used in evaluation research, in which the same persons are interviewed both before and after a new program is introduced.

Longitudinal studies can be expensive and difficult to conduct. Panel studies face a special problem: panel attrition. Some of the respondents studied in the first wave of a study may not participate in later waves. The danger is that those who drop out of the study may differ in some way compared to those who remain in the study, and may thereby distort the results of the study. Suppose we are interested in evaluating the success of a new drug treatment program by conducting weekly drug tests on a panel of participants for a period of 10 months. Regardless of how successful the program appears to be after 10 months, if a substantial number of people drop out of our study, we can expect that treatment was less effective in keeping them off drugs.

Approximating Longitudinal Studies

It may be possible to draw conclusions about processes that take place over time even when only cross-sectional data are available. It is worth noting some of the ways to do that.

Sometimes, cross-sectional data imply processes that occur over time on the basis of simple

Longitudinal studies Data collected at multiple time points.

logic. Consider, for example, a study of gun ownership and violence by Swiss researcher Martin Killias (1993). Killias compared rates of gun ownership, as reported in an international crime survey, to rates of homicide and suicide committed with guns. He was interested in the possible effects of gun availability on violence: Do nations with higher rates of gun ownership also have higher rates of gun violence?

Killias reasoned that inferring causation from a cross-sectional comparison of gun ownership and homicides committed with guns would be ambiguous. Gun homicide rates could be high in countries with high gun ownership rates because the availability of guns was higher. Or, people in countries with high gun ownership rates could have bought guns to protect themselves, in response to homicide rates. Cross-sectional analysis would not make it possible to sort out the time order of gun ownership and gun homicides.

But does that reasoning hold for gun suicides? Killias argued that the time order in a relationship between gun ownership and gun suicides is less ambiguous. It makes much more sense that suicides involving guns are at least partly a result of gun availability. But it is not reasonable to assume that people might buy guns in response to high gun suicide rates.

Logical inferences like those made by Killias may also be made whenever the time order of variables is clear. For example, if we discover in a cross-sectional study of high school students that men are more likely than women to smoke marijuana, we can conclude that gender might affect the propensity to use marijuana, not the other way around. Thus, even though our observations are made at only one time, we are justified in drawing conclusions about processes that take place across time.

Retrospective and Prospective Studies

Retrospective research asks people to recall their pasts, and is another common way of approximating observations over time. In a study of recidivism, for example, we might select a group of prison inmates and analyze their history of delinquency or crime. Or, suppose we are interested in whether college students convicted of drunk driving are more likely to have parents with drinking problems than are college students with no drunk-driving record. Such a study is retrospective, because it focuses on the histories of college students who have or have not been convicted of drunk driving.

The danger in this technique is evident. Sometimes people have faulty memories. Retrospective recall is one way of approximating observations across time, but it must be used with caution. Retrospective studies that analyze records of past arrests or convictions suffer from different problems; records may be unavailable, incomplete, or inaccurate.

A more fundamental problem in retrospective research hinges on how subjects are selected and how subject selection affects the kinds of questions such studies can address.

Imagine that you are a juvenile court judge, and you're troubled by what appears to be a large number of child abuse cases in your court. Talking with a juvenile caseworker, you wonder whether the parents of these children were abused or neglected during their own childhood. Together, you formulate a hypothesis about the intergenerational transmission of violence: victims of childhood abuse later abuse their own children. How might you go about investigating that hypothesis?

Given your position as a judge who regularly sees abuse victims, you will probably consider a retrospective approach that examines the backgrounds of families appearing in your court. Let's say you and the caseworker plan to investigate the family backgrounds of 20 abuse victims who appear in your court during the next three months. The caseworker consults with a clinical psychologist from the local university, and obtains copies of a questionnaire that has been used by researchers to study the families of child abuse victims. After interviewing the families of 20 victims, the caseworker reports to you that 18 of the 20 child victims have a mother or father who was abused as a child. It seems safe to conclude that your hypothesis about the intergenerational transmission of violence is strongly supported, because 90 percent (18 out of 20) of abuse/neglect victims brought before your court come from families with a history of child abuse.

Think for a moment about how you approached the question of whether child abuse breeds child abuse. You began with abuse victims and retrospectively established that many of their parents had been abused. However, this is different from the question of how many victims of childhood abuse later abuse their own children. That question requires a **prospective** approach, in which you begin with childhood victims and then determine how many of them later abuse their own children.

To clarify this point, let's shift from the hypothetical study to actual research that illustrates the difference between prospective and retrospective approaches to the same question. Rosemary Hunter and Nancy Kilstrom (1979) conducted a study of 255 infants and their parents. The researchers began by selecting families of premature infants in a newborn intensive care unit. Interviews with the parents of 255 infants revealed that either the mother or the father in 49 of the families had been the victim of abuse or neglect; 206 families revealed no history of abuse. In a prospective follow-up study, Hunter and Kilstrom found that within one year, 10 of the 255 infants had been abused. Nine of those 10 infant victims were from the 49 families with a history of abuse, while one abused infant was from the 206 families with no background of abuse.

Figure 4.2A illustrates these prospective results graphically. Infants in 18 percent (nine out of 49) of families with a history of abuse showed signs of abuse within one year of birth, while less than 1 percent of infants born to parents with no history of abuse were themselves abused within one year. Although that is a sizable difference, notice that the 18 percent figure for continuity of abuse is very similar to the 19 percent rate of abuse discovered in the histories of all 255 families.

Now consider what Hunter and Kilstrom would have found if they had begun with the 10 abused infants at time two and then checked their family backgrounds. Figure 4.2B illustrates this retrospective approach. A large majority of the 10 infant victims (90 percent) had parents with a history of abuse.

You probably realize by now that the prospective and retrospective approaches address fundamentally different questions, even though the questions may appear similar on the surface:

Prospective: What percentage of abuse victims later abuse their children? (18 percent; Figure 4.2A)

Retrospective: What percentage of abuse victims have parents who were abused? (90 percent; Figure 4.2B)

In a study of how child abuse and neglect affect drug use, Cathy Spatz Widom and associates (Widom, Weiler, and Cotler, 1999) present a similar contrast of prospective and retrospective analysis. Looking backward, 75 percent of subjects with a drug abuse diagnosis in semiclinical interviews were victims of childhood abuse or neglect. Looking forward, 35 percent of childhood victims and 34 percent of nonvictims had a drug abuse diagnosis.

More generally, Robert Sampson and John Laub (1993:14) comment on how retrospective and prospective views yield different interpretations about patterns of criminal offending over time:

> Looking *back* over the careers of adult criminals exaggerates the prevalence of stability. Looking *forward* from youth reveals the success and failures, including adolescent delinquents who go on to be normal functioning adults. This is the paradox noted [by Lee Robins] earlier: adult criminality seems to be always preceded by childhood misconduct, but most conduct-disordered children do not become antisocial or criminal adults. (Robins, 1978) (emphasis in original)

Our intention here is not to suggest that retrospective studies have no value. Rather, we want to point out how the time dimension is linked to the framing of research questions. A retrospective approach is limited in its ability to reveal how causal processes unfold over time. Therefore, a retrospective approach is not well suited to answer questions such as how many childhood victims of abuse or neglect later abuse their own children. A retrospective study can be used, however, to compare whether childhood victims are more likely than nonvictims to have a history of abuse in their family background.

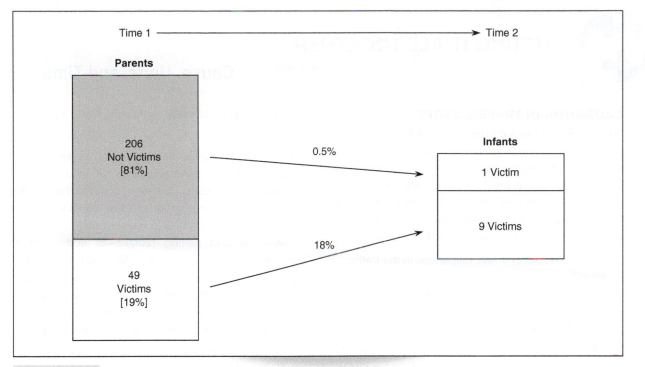

FIGURE 4.2A Prospective Approach to a Subject

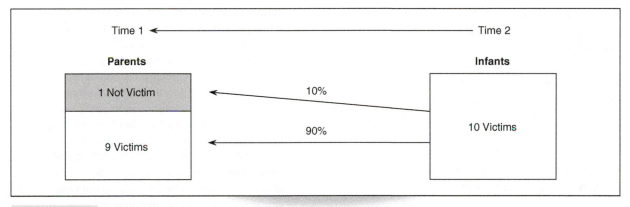

FIGURE 4.2B Retrospective Approach to a Subject

Source: Adapted from Hunter and Kilstrom (1979), as suggested by Widom (1989).

The Time Dimension Summarized

Joel Devine and James Wright (1993:19) offer a clever metaphor that distinguishes longitudinal studies from cross-sectional ones. Think of a cross-sectional study as a single photograph, a trend study as a slide show, and a panel study as a video. A cross-sectional study, like a photo, produces an image at one point in time. This can provide useful information about crime—burglary, for example—at a single time, perhaps in a single place. A trend study is akin to a slide show—a series of photos in sequence over time. By viewing a slide show, we can tell how some indicator—change in burglary rates—varies over time. But a trend study is usually based on aggregate information. It can tell

PUTTING IT ALL TOGETHER

CAUSATION IN TRAFFIC STOPS

What causes observed proportions of traffic stops by race of driver? That is the central question confronted by researchers and public officials who tried to sort out the problem of racial profiling. Studies in three states framed these questions somewhat differently, but each was concerned with one descriptive question, then a family of causal questions:

1. Are there racial or ethnic disparities in the traffic stops?
2. If yes, what causes these disparities?
   - Overt discrimination by police?
   - Something else?

The first question refers to covariation as a criterion for cause. It is necessary to show disparities, or disproportionality by race before determining that discrimination exists. In other words, if minority motorists are not being stopped or ticketed in greater proportion to their numbers in the population, then discrimination does not exist.

Regarding the second question, most news reports and horror stories assumed some form of discrimination was responsible for any observed disparities. In fact, some researchers seemed to believe that discrimination was the only possible reason for disparities in traffic stops (e.g., Lamberth, 2003). Others recognized that different explanations could be at work. For example, Smith et al. wrote:

> . . . discussions of racial disparity in policing require a good faith effort to account for non-discriminatory sources of racial disparity in stops associated with driving behavior before reaching a conclusion that a particular police

force is guilty of racial profiling in traffic stops. (2003:39)

You should recognize this statement as an implicit challenge to the internal validity of inferring that discrimination causes disparity. In fact, Smith and associates found a number of other variables to be associated with disparities in traffic stops.

Maxfield and Kelling (2005:5–6) addressed a more narrow research question: Why was the proportion of minority drivers stopped substantially higher for one segment of the New Jersey Turnpike than for other segments? Their research considered five possible causal factors in addition to actual discrimination:

- *Deployment:* Do more troopers happen to be deployed in areas with high proportions of minority drivers?
- *Behavior:* In comparison to whites, do minority motorists disproportionately engage in illegal driving practices that bring them to the attention of the New Jersey State Police?
- *Instrumentation:* Are New Jersey State Police troopers now more accurately and/or more consistently reporting the race and ethnicity of traffic violators in comparison to past practices?
- *Evasion:* Are white traffic offenders on the turnpike more able to avoid detection by the New Jersey State Police than minority traffic offenders?
- *Interaction:* Is the continuity over time of racially disproportionate stops in the stop data caused by some mix of the above hypotheses?

Similar alternative explanations were considered by most other researchers in most other areas of the country. In later chapters, we describe steps taken to address these questions.

UNITS

Studying traffic enforcement and the possibility of race-based discrimination involves several different units of analysis. The studies done in Pennsylvania and North Carolina collected data on several units, moving from the least to the greatest level of aggregation:

- Traffic stops: driver characteristics and reasons for stop
- Trooper: aggregate characteristics of all drivers and stops; plus data on individual trooper
- Small-area segment: aggregate characteristics of all troopers, drivers, and stops; plus data on road segment and individual area
- Station or county: aggregates from lower-level units; plus summary data on county residents

Then, of course, studies done in different states reflected the laws and other features of each state. For example, in Pennsylvania troopers are prohibited from stopping cars traveling less than 7 mph above the posted speed limit. New Jersey has no stated policy, but informal norms tolerate speeding up to about 15 mph over the posted limit on many expressways.

TIME DIMENSION

The time dimension revealed certain trends in traffic enforcement. In North Carolina, researchers found a sharp decline in traffic enforcement during 1999, when the state legislature was considering laws to monitor the possibility of racial profiling (Smith et al., 2003:28–29). This documents what Engel and associates term "disengagement," where police cut back on enforcement activities to avoid getting into trouble.

The time dimension was one factor triggering research in New Jersey. The figure below shows, over a two-year period, what proportion of drivers stopped for moving violations was black. Two generally stable trend lines are presented. The lower one shows data for the entire New Jersey Turnpike, while the upper line represents the southern segment, about 50 miles long. You can see that the proportion of stopped drivers who were black is about twice as high for the southern segment as for the entire Turnpike. The size and stability of this difference was one of the main reasons for launching the New Jersey study. The time dimension here played a role in documenting the persistence of race disparities over time.

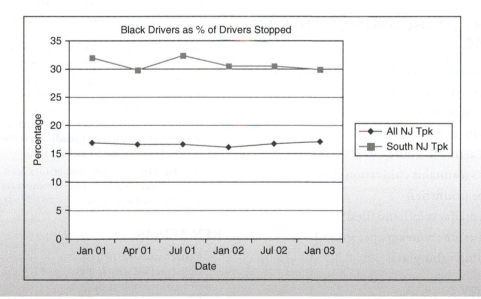

us something about aggregations of burglary over time; but it cannot, for instance, indicate whether the same people are committing burglaries at an increasing or decreasing rate, or whether there are more or fewer burglars with a relatively constant rate of crime commission. A panel study, like a video, can capture moving images of the same individuals and give us information about individual rates of offending over time.

These, then, are some of the ways time figures in criminal justice research and some of the ways researchers have learned to cope with it. In designing any study, you need to look at both the explicit and implicit assumptions they are making about time. Are you interested in describing some process that occurs over time, such as whether mandatory jail sentences reduce drunk driving? Or are you simply going to describe how many people were arrested for drunk driving in the past year? If you want to describe a process that occurs over time, will you be able to make observations at different points in the process, or will you have to approximate such observations, drawing logical inferences from what you can observe now?

Our "Putting It All Together" example for this chapter illustrates many of the general issues in research design we have discussed so far.

ANSWERS TO THE UNITS-OF-ANALYSIS EXERCISE

1. Social artifacts (alcohol-related fatal crashes)
2. Groups (cities and counties)
3. Groups (countries)
4. Individuals (probationers)
5. Social artifacts (court cases)
6. Groups (cannabis cultivation sites)
7. Groups (countries)
8. Social artifacts (offense files)
9. Social artifacts (newspaper stories)
10. Individuals (burglars)

SUMMARY

- Explanatory scientific research centers on the notion of cause and effect.
- Most explanatory social research uses a probabilistic model of causation. X may be said to cause Y if it is seen to have some influence on Y.

- X is a necessary cause of Y if Y cannot happen without X having happened. X is a sufficient cause of Y if Y always happens when X happens.
- Three basic requirements determine a causal relationship in scientific research: (1) the independent and dependent variables must be empirically related to each other, (2) the independent variable must occur before the dependent variables, and (3) the observed relationship cannot be explained away as the effect of another variable.
- When scientists consider whether causal statements are true or false, they are concerned with the validity of causal inference.
- Four classes of threats to validity correspond to the types of questions researchers ask in trying to establish cause and effect. Threats to statistical conclusion validity and internal validity arise from bias. External and construct validity threats may limit our ability to generalize from an observed relationship.
- A scientific realist approach to examining mechanisms in context bridges idiographic and nomothetic approaches to causation.
- Units of analysis are the people or things whose characteristics researchers observe, describe, and explain. The unit of analysis in criminal justice research is often the individual person, but it may also be a group, an organization, or a social artifact.
- Researchers sometimes confuse units of analysis, resulting in the ecological fallacy.
- Cross-sectional studies are those based on observations made at one time. Although such studies are limited by this characteristic, inferences often can be made about processes that occur over time.
- Longitudinal studies are those in which observations are made at many times. Such observations may be made of samples drawn from general populations (trend studies), samples drawn from more specific subpopulations (cohort studies), or the same sample of people each time (panel studies).
- Retrospective studies sometimes can approximate longitudinal studies, but retrospective approaches must be used with care.

KEY TERMS

Cohort study (p. 100)
Construct validity (p. 89)
Cross-sectional study (p. 98)
Ecological fallacy (p. 95)
External validity (p. 88)
Internal validity (p. 88)
Longitudinal study (p. 100)
Panel study (p. 100)
Probabilistic (p. 85)

REVIEW QUESTIONS AND EXERCISES

1. Discuss one of the following statements in terms of what you have learned about the criteria of causation and threats to the validity of causal inference. What cause-and-effect relationships are implied? What are some alternative explanations?

   a. Guns don't kill people; people kill people.
   b. Capital punishment prevents murder.
   c. Marijuana is a gateway drug that leads to the use of other drugs.

2. Several times, we have discussed the relationship between drug use and crime. Describe the conditions that would lead us to conclude that drug use is:

   a. A necessary cause
   b. A sufficient cause
   c. A necessary and sufficient cause

3. In describing different approaches to the time dimension, criminologist Lawrence Sherman (1995) claims that cross-sectional studies can show differences and that longitudinal studies can show change. How does this statement relate to the three criteria for inferring causation?

4. William Julius Wilson (1996:167) cites the following example of why it's important to think carefully about units and time. Imagine a 13-bed hospital, in which 12 beds are occupied by the same person for one year. The other hospital bed is occupied by 52 people, each staying one week. At any given time, 92 percent of beds are occupied by long-term patients (12 out of 13); but over the entire year, 81 percent of patients are short-term patients (52 out of 64). Discuss the implications of a similar example, in which "jail cell" is substituted for "hospital bed."

CHAPTER 5

Concepts, Operationalization, and Measurement

It's essential to specify exactly what we mean (and don't mean) by the terms we use. This is the first step in the measurement process, and we'll cover it in depth.

Learning Objectives

1. Understand the role of concepts as summary devices for bringing together observations and experiences that have something in common.

2. Explain how concepts are mental images that do not exist in the real word.

3. Describe how operationalization specifies concrete empirical procedures for measuring variables.

4. Recognize that operationalization begins with study design but continues through the duration of research.

5. Explain why measurement categories must be mutually exclusive and exhaustive.

6. Distinguish different levels of measurement and the properties of different levels.

7. Understand precision, reliability, and validity as dimensions of measurement quality.

8. Summarize how creating specific, reliable measures may not reflect the complexity of the concepts we seek to study.

9. Understand how multiple measures of a concept can improve reliability and validity.

10. Describe composite measures and explain their advantages.

Measuring Neighborhood Characteristics

Criminologists have always been interested in how features of neighborhoods might be linked to crime problems. We saw some of this in Chapter 2, where we discussed early research on crime in Chicago neighborhoods. Researchers traditionally have used measures of social and economic characteristics, such as those collected every 10 years in the U.S. Census. Census tracts and blocks are small areas into which measures of demographic, social, and economic characteristics are aggregated. Much criminological research has used census data to examine what kinds of neighborhood characteristics are related to crime.

Another way to measure neighborhood characteristics is to observe them. Whereas census data are collected through questionnaires completed by neighborhood residents, more recent research has sent researchers into the field to observe characteristics such as housing conditions, the presence of graffiti and litter, and the types of buildings in an area. However, such measures are difficult and costly to obtain. Field observers (more on this in Chapter 10) must be trained and sent to walk or drive streets. Robert Sampson and Stephen Raudenbush (1999) describe an example where observers drove around Chicago neighborhoods, making video recordings of people and conditions on sampled streets.

An alternative is to view the existing images of city streets available on the Web through Google Street View (GSV). If you have not used GSV on the Google Maps site, you may have seen such images through some other application on a smart phone or other mobile device. Try it now, by going to http://www.google.com/maps.

The most complete coverage is available for major cities in the United States, but GSV increasingly covers many smaller cities and places in other countries. Type an address in the search window. Or see a couple of buildings at John Jay College of Criminal Justice by typing in the following address: 899 Tenth Ave, New York, NY. You'll see a map or satellite image, depending on how your browser is set up. You should also see a photo in a separate panel that shows the intersection of Tenth Avenue and 59th Street in New York City. You can pan the image with your mouse to look around the area. You can also virtually travel up or down New York City streets, seeing continual images along the way.

What results for New York and most other major cities is a photo archive of everything that can be seen from a car (Google's camera-equipped vehicles) traveling down the street. This has tremendous potential for researchers by offering a low-cost method for making observations of large areas.

But what about the quality of measures developed through such images? More fundamentally, what concepts can be measured by GSV images? As you read this chapter—the first of two on measurement—think about GSV as a source of measures for different concepts. For example, images might produce measures for housing conditions, but they are not very useful for measuring socioeconomic characteristics such as household income or family size. Much of this chapter describes how to create measures that are valid and reliable. How might you determine the reliability and validity of such measures? It would be helpful to try out GSV while reading this chapter. Or see the recent study by Quinn et al. (2016) that used GSV to measure neighborhood physical disorder in New York City. One of the compelling features of GSV is that you can make observations of streets in Moscow, Russia, while sitting at a computer in Moscow, Idaho.

Introduction

Because measurement is difficult and imprecise, researchers try to describe the measurement process explicitly.

This chapter describes the progression from a vague idea about what we want to study to being able to recognize it and measure it in the real world. We begin with the general issue of conceptualization, which sets up a foundation for our examination of actual measurement—a process known as *operationalization*. We then turn to different approaches to assessing measurement quality. The chapter concludes with an overview of strategies for combining individual measures into more complex indicators. Our examination of measurement continues in Chapter 6, where we'll focus on different strategies for measuring crime.

As you read this chapter, keep in mind a central theme: communication. Ultimately, criminal justice and social scientific research seek to communicate findings to an audience—professors, classmates, journal readers, or coworkers in a probation services agency, for example. As we described in Chapter 1, moving from vague ideas and interests to a completed research report involves communication at every step, from general ideas to more precise definitions of critical terms. With more precise definitions, we can begin to develop measures to apply in the real world.

Conceptions and Concepts

Clarifying abstract mental images is an essential first step in measurement.

If you hear the word *recidivism*, what image comes to mind? You might think of someone who has served time for burglary and who breaks into a house soon after being released from prison. Or, in contrast to that rather specific image, you might have a more general image of habitual criminals. Someone who works in a criminal justice agency might have a different mental image. Police officers might think of a specific individual they have arrested repeatedly for a variety of offenses, and a judge might think of a defendant who has three prior convictions for theft.

Ultimately, *recidivism* is simply a term we use in communication—a word representing a collection of related phenomena that we have either observed or heard about somewhere. It's as though we have file drawers in our minds containing thousands of sheets of paper, and each sheet has a label in the upper right-hand corner. One sheet of paper in your file drawer has the term *recidivism* on it, and the person who sits next to you in class has one, too.

The technical name for those mental images, those sheets of paper in our file drawers, is *conception*. Each sheet of paper is a **conception**— a subjective thought about things that we encounter in daily life. But those mental images cannot be communicated directly. There is no way we can directly reveal what's written on our mental images. Therefore, we use the terms written in the upper right-hand corners as a way of communicating about our conceptions and the things we observe that are related to those conceptions.

For example, the word *crime* represents our conception about certain kinds of behavior. But individuals have different conceptions; they may think of different kinds of behavior when they hear the word *crime*. For example, police officers in most states would include possession of marijuana among their conceptions of crime, whereas residents of states where recreational marijuana use is permitted would not. Recent burglary victims might recall their own experiences in their conceptions of crime, whereas more fortunate neighbors might think about the murder story in yesterday's newspaper.

Because conceptions are subjective and cannot be communicated directly, we use the words and symbols of language as a way to communicate our conceptions and the things we observe that are related to those conceptions.

Concepts are the words or symbols in language that we use to represent these mental images. We use concepts to communicate with one another, to share our mental images. Although a common language enables us to communicate, it is important to recognize that the words and phrases we use represent abstractions. Concepts are abstract because they are independent of the labels we assign to them. Crime as a concept is abstract, meaning that in the English language, this label represents mental images of illegal acts. Of course, actual crimes are real events, and our mental images of crime may be based on real events or what we see in movies. However, when we talk about "crime" without being more specific, we are talking about an abstraction. Thus, for example, the concept of crime proposed by Michael Gottfredson and Travis Hirschi (1990:15)—using force or fraud in pursuit of self-interest—is abstract. "Crime" is the symbol or label they have assigned to this concept.

Let's discuss a specific example. What is your conception of "serious crime"? What mental images come to mind? Most people agree that rape, bank robbery, and murder are serious crimes. What about a fistfight that results in a concussion and facial injuries? Many of us would classify it as a serious crime, but not if the incident took place in a boxing ring. Is burglary a serious crime? It doesn't rank up there with drive-by shooting, but we would probably agree that it is more serious than shoplifting. What about drug use or drug dealing?

Our mental images of serious crime may vary depending on our backgrounds and experiences. If your home has ever been burglarized, you might be more inclined than someone who has not suffered that experience to rate it as a serious crime. If you have been both burglarized and robbed at gunpoint, you would probably think the burglary was less serious than the robbery.

Disagreement over the seriousness of drug use continues. Younger people, whether or not they have used drugs, may be less inclined to view drug use as a serious crime, whereas police and other public officials might rank drug use as very serious. Alaska, California, and Washington are among the states that have legalized the use of marijuana. However, the U.S. Department of Justice views marijuana use as a crime, creating problems for marijuana dispensaries in accepting credit cards and creating bank accounts (Popper, 2016).

"Serious crime" is an abstraction, a label we use to represent a concept. However, we must be careful to distinguish the label we use for a concept from the reality that the concept represents. There are real robberies, and robbery is a serious crime, but the concept of crime seriousness is not real. The use of marijuana for recreational or medical purposes is real, but the concept of its seriousness is abstract.

To link conceptions, concepts, and measurement, consider Abraham Kaplan's (1964) discussion of three classes of things that scientists measure: direct observables, indirect observables, and constructs. The first class, direct observables, includes those things that we can observe simply and directly, such as the color of an apple or the words in a crime report. Indirect observables require "relatively more subtle, complex, or indirect observations" (1964:55). We note that a police officer has written "robbery" in the place for "offense type" on a crime report and has thus indirectly observed what crime has occurred. Newspaper stories, court transcripts, and criminal history records provide indirect observations of past actions. Finally, constructs are theoretical creations based on things that cannot be observed directly or indirectly. IQ is a good example: It is

> **Concept** Words or symbols in language that we use to represent mental images.

constructed mathematically from the answers to questions on an IQ test. It measures the theoretical concept of intelligence, which cannot be observed directly.

Kaplan (1964:49) defined concept as a "family of conceptions." A concept is, as Kaplan noted, a construct. The concept of serious crime, then, is a construct created from your conception of it, our conception of it, and the conceptions of all those who have ever used the term. The concept of serious crime cannot be observed directly or indirectly. We can, however, meaningfully discuss the concept, observe examples of serious crime, and measure it indirectly.

Conceptualization

Day-to-day communication is made possible through general but often vague and unspoken agreements about the use of terms. Usually, other people do not understand exactly what we wish to communicate, but they get the general drift of our meaning. For example, although we may not fully agree about the meaning of the term serious crime, it's safe to assume that the crime of bank robbery is more serious than the crime of bicycle theft. A wide range of misunderstandings is the price we pay for our imprecision, but somehow we muddle through. Science, however, aims at more than muddling, and it cannot operate in a context of such imprecision.

Conceptualization is the process by which we specify precisely what we mean when we use particular terms. Suppose we want to find out whether violent crime is more serious than nonviolent crime. Most of us would probably assume that is true, but it might be interesting to find out whether it's really so. Notice that we can't meaningfully study the issue, let alone agree on the answer, without some precise working agreements about the meanings of the terms we are using.

Conceptualization The mental process of making fuzzy and imprecise notions, such as concepts, more specific and precise.

They are working agreements, in the sense that they allow us to work on the question.

We begin by clearly differentiating violent and nonviolent crimes. In violent crimes, an offender uses force or threats of force against a victim. Nonviolent crimes either do not involve any direct contact between a victim and an offender, or involve contact but no force. For example, pickpocketing involves direct contact but no force. In contrast, robbery involves at least the threat to use force on victims. Burglary, auto theft, shoplifting, and the theft of unattended personal property such as bicycles are examples of nonviolent crimes. Assault, rape, robbery, and murder are violent crimes.

Indicators and Dimensions

The end product of the conceptualization process is the specification of a set of indicators of what we have in mind, indicating the presence or absence of the concept we are studying. To illustrate this process, let's discuss the broader concept of crime seriousness. This concept is more general than serious crime because it implies that some crimes are more serious than others.

One good indicator of crime seriousness is harm to the crime victim. Physical injury is an example of harm, and physical injury is certainly more likely to result from violent crime than from nonviolent crime. What about other kinds of harm? Burglary victims suffer economic harm from property loss and perhaps damage to their homes. Is the loss of $800 in a burglary an indicator of more serious crime than a $10 loss in a robbery in which the victim was not injured? Victims of both violent and nonviolent crimes may suffer psychological harm. Charles Silberman (1978:18–19) described how people feel a sense of personal violation after discovering that their home has been burglarized. Jerry Ratcliffe (2014) discusses a variety of ways to think about harm, proposing groups and subgroups of harm types based on analysis of data from Philadelphia. In addition, he describes examples of harms that might be produced by police actions, such as investigative stops and frisks.

The technical term for such groupings is **dimension**—some specifiable aspect of a concept. Thus, we might speak of the "victim harm dimension" of crime seriousness. This dimension could include indicators of physical injury, economic loss, or psychological consequences. And we can easily think of other indicators and dimensions related to the general concept of crime seriousness. If we consider the theft of $20 from a poor person to be more serious than the theft of $2,000 from a wealthy oil company CEO, victim wealth might be another dimension. Also, consider a victim identity dimension. Killing a burglar in self-defense would not be as serious as threatening to kill the president of the United States.

Thus, it is possible to subdivide the concept of crime seriousness into several dimensions. Specifying dimensions and identifying the various indicators for each of those dimensions are both parts of conceptualization.

Specifying the different dimensions of a concept often paves the way for a more sophisticated understanding of what we are studying. For example, we might observe that fistfights among high school students result in thousands of injuries per year, but that the annual costs of auto theft cause direct economic harm to hundreds of insurance companies and millions of auto insurance policyholders. Recognizing the many dimensions of crime seriousness, we cannot say that violent crime is more serious than nonviolent crime in all cases.

As it happens, defining and measuring crime seriousness is an important issue in criminal justice policy and research. Domestic assaults and acquaintance rape are examples of violent crimes that are often treated differently than physical or sexual violence among strangers, suggesting a victim–offender relationship dimension. For instance, the battered-woman defense has been used in trials of women who kill a spouse or lover following an extended period of violence (Williams, 1991). Such mitigating circumstances mean that some types of murder are treated differently than others, based in part on motivation and the relationship between victim and offender. The

tendency of courts to punish rapists less harshly if they had some prior relationship with their victims has led to growing protests (Lopez, 1992). Research on sexual assaults targeting women in college has found that victims less often recognize that acquaintance rape is a crime (Fisher, Cullen, and Turner, 2000). Studies have shown that death penalties were more often imposed on blacks convicted of killing whites, which indicates that victim race is related to sentencing and might, therefore, be considered an indicator of crime seriousness (Baldus, Pulaski, and Woodworth, 1983; Baldus et al., 2011). Later in this chapter, we will discuss specific attempts to develop measures of crime seriousness.

Confusion over Definitions and Reality

To review briefly, our concepts are derived from the conceptions (mental images) that summarize collections of seemingly related observations and experiences. Although the observations and experiences are real, our concepts are mental creations. The terms associated with concepts are merely devices created for communication. The term *crime seriousness* is an example. Ultimately, that phrase is only a collection of letters and has no intrinsic meaning. We could have as easily and meaningfully created the term *crime pettiness* to serve the same purpose.

Often, however, we fall into the trap of believing that terms have real meanings. That danger seems to grow stronger when we begin to take terms seriously and attempt to use them precisely. And in the presence of experts—who appear to know more about what the terms really mean—the danger is all the greater. It's easy to yield to the authority of experts in such a situation.

Once we have assumed (mistakenly) that terms have real meanings, we begin the task of discovering what those real meanings are and what constitutes a genuine measurement of them. We make up conceptual summaries of real observations because the summaries are convenient—so convenient, however, that we begin to think they are real. The process of regarding as real things that are not is called **reification**. The reification of concepts in day-to-day life is very common.

Creating Conceptual Order

The design and execution of criminal justice research requires that we clear away the confusion over concepts and reality. To this end, logicians and scientists have found it useful to distinguish three kinds of definitions: real, conceptual, and operational. The first of these reflects the reification of terms, and, as Carl G. Hempel (1952:6) has cautioned:

> A "real" definition, according to traditional logic, is not a stipulation determining the meaning of some expression but a statement of the "essential nature" or the "essential attributes" of some entity. The notion of essential nature, however, is so vague as to render this characterization useless for the purposes of rigorous inquiry.

A "real" or "essential nature" definition is inherently subjective. The specification of concepts in scientific inquiry depends instead on conceptual and operational definitions. A **conceptual definition** is a working definition specifically assigned to a term. In the midst of disagreement and confusion over what a term really means, the scientist specifies a working definition for the purposes of the inquiry. Wishing to examine socioeconomic status (SES), for example, we may simply specify that we are going to treat it as a combination of income and educational attainment. With that definitional decision, we rule out many other possible aspects of SES: occupational status, money in the bank, property, lineage, lifestyle, and so forth.

Conceptual definition The working definition of a concept or term.

Operational definition A statement specifying what operations should be performed to measure a concept.

The specification of conceptual definitions does two important things. First, it serves as a specific working definition we present so that readers will understand exactly what we mean by a concept. Second, it focuses our observational strategy. Notice that a conceptual definition does not directly produce observations; rather, it channels our efforts to develop actual measures.

As a next step, we must specify exactly what we will observe, how we will do it, and what interpretations we will place on various possible observations. These further specifications make up the **operational definition** of the concept—a definition that spells out precisely how the concept will be measured. Strictly speaking, an operational definition is a description of the "operations" undertaken in measuring a concept.

Pursuing the definition of SES, we might decide to ask the people we are studying three questions:

1. What was your total household income during the past 12 months?

2. How many persons are in your household?

3. What is the highest level of school you have completed?

Next, we need to specify a system for categorizing the answers people give us. For income, we might use the categories "under $50,000" and "$50,000–$75,000." Educational attainment might be similarly grouped into categories, and we might simply count the number of people in each household. Finally, we need to specify a way to combine each person's responses to these three questions to create a measure of SES.

The end result is a working and workable definition of SES. Others might disagree with our conceptualization and operationalization, but the definition has one essential scientific virtue: it is absolutely specific and unambiguous. Even if someone disagrees with our definition, that person will have a good idea of how to interpret our research results because what we mean by the term SES—reflected in our analyses and conclusions—is clear.

Here is a diagram showing the progression of measurement steps from our vague sense of what a term means to specific measurements in a scientific study:

Conceptualization

↓

Conceptual definition

↓

Operational definition

↓

Measurements in the real world

To test your understanding of these measurement steps, return to the beginning of the chapter, where we asked you what image comes to mind in connection with the word *recidivism*. Recall your own mental image, and compare it with Tony Fabelo's (1995) discussion in the box titled "What Is Recidivism?"

Operationalization Choices

Describing how to obtain actual empirical measures begins with operationalization.

The research process usually is not a set of steps that proceed in order from first to last. This is especially true of operationalization, the process of developing operational definitions. Although we begin by conceptualizing what we wish to study, once we start to consider operationalization, we may revise our conceptual definition. Developing an operational definition also moves us closer to measurement, which requires that we think about selecting a data collection method as well. In other words, operationalization does not usually proceed according to a systematic checklist.

To illustrate this fluid process, let's return to the issue of crime seriousness. Suppose we want to conduct a descriptive study that shows which crimes are more serious than others.

One obvious dimension of crime seriousness is the penalties assigned to different crimes by law. Let's begin with this conceptualization. Our conceptual definition of crime seriousness is, therefore, the level of punishment that a state criminal code authorizes for different crimes. Notice that this definition has the distinct advantage of being unambiguous. We're making progress, which leads us to an operational definition something like this:

> Consult the Texas Criminal Code. (1) Those crimes that may be punished by death will be judged most serious. (2) Next will be crimes that may be punished by a prison sentence of more than one year. (3) The least serious crimes are those with jail sentences of less than a year and/or fines.

The operations undertaken to measure crime seriousness are specific. Our data collection strategy is also clear: Search the Web or go to the library, make a list of crimes described in the Texas Code, and classify each crime into one of the three groups.

Note that we have produced rather narrow conceptual and operational definitions of crime seriousness. We might presume that penalties in the Texas Code consider additional dimensions like victim harm, offender motivation, and other circumstances of individual crimes. However, the three groups of crimes include very different types of incidents, and so do not tell us much about crime seriousness.

An alternative conceptualization of crime seriousness might center on what people think of as serious crime. In this view, crime seriousness is based on people's beliefs, which may reflect their perceptions of harm to victims, offender motivation, or other dimensions. Conceptualizing crime seriousness in this way suggests a different approach to operationalization: You will present descriptions of various crimes to other students in your class and ask them to indicate how serious they believe the crimes are. If crime seriousness is operationalized in this way, a questionnaire is the most appropriate data collection method.

We must make many other decisions before actually taking measurements of crime seriousness. How should crimes be described, and how should students indicate whether a crime is serious or not? Will crime descriptions simply be ranked from most to least serious, or will we try to make more precise measurements about how, for example, rape compares with smoking marijuana?

BY TONY FABELO

The Senate Criminal Justice Committee will be studying the record of the corrections system and the use of recidivism rates as a measure of performance for the system. The first task for the committee should be to clearly define recidivism, understand how it is measured, and determine the implications of adopting recidivism rates as measures of performance.

DEFINING RECIDIVISM

Recidivism is the reoccurrence of criminal behavior. The rate of recidivism refers to the proportion of a specific group of offenders (for example, those released on parole) who engage in criminal behavior within a given period of time. Indicators of criminal behavior are re-arrests, reconvictions, or reincarcerations.

Each of these indicators depends on contact with criminal justice officials, and will therefore underestimate the reoccurrence of criminal behavior. However, criminal behavior that is unreported and not otherwise known to officials in justice agencies is difficult to measure in a consistent and economically feasible fashion.

In 1991, the Criminal Justice Policy Council recommended to the legislature and state criminal justice agencies that recidivism be measured in the following way:

Recidivism rates should be calculated by counting the number of prison releases or number of offenders placed under community supervision who are reincarcerated for a technical violation or new offense within a uniform period of at-risk street time.

The at-risk street time can be one, two, or three years, but it must be uniform for the group being tracked so that results are not distorted by uneven at-risk periods.

Reincarceration should be measured using data from the "rap sheets" collected by the Texas Department of Public Safety in their Computerized Criminal History system. A centralized source of information reduces reporting errors.

Measurement as "Scoring"

Operationalization involves describing how actual measurements will be made. The next step, of course, is making the measurements. Royce Singleton, Bruce Straits, and Margaret Miller Straits (2010:100) define measurement as "the process of assigning numbers or labels to units of analysis in order to represent conceptual properties. This process should be quite familiar to the reader even if the definition is not."

Think of some examples of the process. Your instructor assigns number or letter grades to exams and papers to represent your mastery of course material. You count the number of pages in this week's history assignment to represent how much time you will have to spend studying. The American Bar Association rates nominees to the U.S. Supreme Court as qualified, highly qualified, or not qualified. You might rank last night's date on the proverbial scale of 1 to 10, reflecting whatever conceptual properties are important to you.

Another way to think of measurement is in terms of scoring. Your instructor scores exams by counting the right answers and assigning some point value to each answer. Referees keep score at basketball games by counting the number of one-point free throws and two- and three-point field goals for each team. Judges or juries score persons charged with crime by pronouncing "guilty" or "not guilty." City murder rates are scored by counting the number of murder victims and dividing by the number of city residents.

Measurement is distinct from operationalization in that measurement involves actually making observations and assigning scores (numbers or other labels) to those observations. Making

SYSTEMWIDE RECIDIVISM RATES

Recidivism rates can be reported for all offenders in the system—for all offenders released from prison or for all offenders placed on probation. This I call *systemwide recidivism rates*. Approximately 48 percent of offenders released from prison on parole or mandatory supervision, or released from county jails on parole, in 1991 were reincarcerated by 1994 for a new offense or a parole violation.

For offenders released from prison in 1991 the reincarceration recidivism rate three years after release from prison by offense of conviction is listed below:

Burglary	56%	Assault	44%
Robbery	54%	Homicide	40%
Theft	52%	Sexual assault	39%
Drugs	43%	Sex offense	34%

For the same group, the reincarceration recidivism rate three years after release by age group is listed below:

17–25	56%
26–30	52%
31–35	48%
36–40	46%
41 or older	35%

THE MEANING OF SYSTEMWIDE RECIDIVISM RATES

The systemwide recidivism rate of prison releases should not be used to measure the performance of institutional programs. There are many socio-economic factors that can affect systemwide recidivism rates.

For example, the systemwide recidivism rate of offenders released from prison in 1995 declined because of changes in the characteristics of the population released from prison. Offenders are receiving and serving longer sentences, which will raise the average age at release. Therefore, "performance" in terms of systemwide recidivism will improve but not necessarily due to improvements in the delivery of services within the prison system.

On the other hand, the systemwide recidivism rate of felons released from state jail facilities should be expected to be relatively high, since state jail felons are property and drug offenders who tend to have high recidivism rates.

observations, of course, is related to the data collection method—which, in turn, is implied by operationalization. However, the measurement process begins much earlier, usually with conceptualization.

Many people consider measurement to be the most important and difficult phase of criminal justice research. In part, it is difficult because so many basic concepts in criminal justice are not easy to define as specifically as we would like. Without being able to settle on a conceptual definition, we find operationalizing and measuring things challenging. This is illustrated by the box titled "Jail Stay."

Different operationalization choices also can produce different results. Here are three brief examples, developed with the excellent assistance of students in a research methods class at John Jay College of Criminal Justice in New York City (CRJ 715-03, October 9, 2003).

First, in comparing a general-purpose survey of crime victimization with specialized studies of family conflict, Murray Straus (1999) reported that domestic assault rates are over 16 times higher in surveys of family conflict. He attributes this to an explicit focus on crime in crime surveys, whereas studies of family conflict do not cue respondents with the keyword *crime*. As a result, physical violence among family members appears to be much more prevalent in Straus's research than in general crime surveys. The opposite is true of injuries—Straus reports that less than 4 percent of family violence incidents produced an injury, compared with 75 percent in the National Crime Victimization Survey (NCVS). These divergent findings make sense. Straus finds higher rates of less-severe violence, whereas crime surveys reveal lower rates of more severe violence.

Recall from Chapter 1 that two of the general purposes of research are description and explanation. The distinction between them has important implications for the process of definition and measurement. If you have formed the opinion that description is a simpler task than explanation, you may be surprised to learn that definitions can be more problematic for descriptive research than for explanatory research. To illustrate this, we present an example based on an attempt by one of the authors to describe what he thought was a simple concept.

In the course of an evaluation project, Maxfield wished to learn the average number of days people stayed in the Marion County (Indiana) jail. This concept was labeled "jail stay." People can be in the county jail for three reasons: (1) They are serving a sentence of 1 year or less, (2) they are awaiting trial, or (3) they are being held temporarily while awaiting transfer to another county or state or to prison. The third category includes people who have been sentenced to prison and are waiting for space to open up, or those who have been arrested and are wanted for some reason in another jurisdiction.

Maxfield vaguely knew these things but did not recognize how they complicated the task of defining and ultimately measuring jail stay. So the original question—"What is the average jail stay?"—was revised to "What is the average jail stay for persons serving sentences and for persons awaiting trial?"

Just as people can be in jail for different reasons, an individual can be in jail for more than one reason. For example, let's consider a hypothetical jail resident we'll call Allan. He was convicted of burglary in July 2002 and sentenced to a year in jail. All but 30 days of his sentence were suspended, meaning that he was freed but could be required to serve the remaining 11 months

Second, according to the FBI Uniform Crime Report (UCR), about 7 million larcenies were reported in 2001 (Federal Bureau of Investigation, 2002), whereas the NCVS estimated over 14 million larcenies nationwide for the same year (Rennison, 2002). FBI data count only crimes reported to police, whereas the NCVS includes incidents not reported. Less than half of larcenies are reported, accounting for most of the difference. But for motor vehicle theft, the patterns are reversed: over 1,226,000 vehicle thefts were recorded in the 2001 UCR, compared with fewer than 1,009,000 in the NCVS. A different operationalization rule is at work here. The NCVS measures crimes against households and cannot count thefts of vehicles owned by businesses or other organizations; these crimes do appear in UCR counts.

Third, in the box titled "What Is Recidivism?" Tony Fabelo argues that there should be a uniform at-risk period for comparing recidivism for different groups of offenders. It's possible to examine one-, two-, or three-year rates, but comparisons should use standard at-risk periods. Varying the at-risk period produces, as we might expect, differences in recidivism rates. Evaluating a Texas drug-abuse treatment program, Michael Eisenberg (1999:8) reports rates for different at-risk periods:

	1-Year	2-Year	3-Year
All participants	14%	37%	42%

Note that the difference between one- and two-year rates is much larger than that between two and three-year rates. Operationalizing "recidivism" as a one-year failure rate would be much less accurate than operationalizing the concept as a two-year rate, because recidivism rates seem to stabilize at the two-year point.

if he got into trouble again. It did not take long. Two months after being released, Allan was arrested for robbery and returned to jail.

Now it gets complicated. A judge imposes the remaining 11 months of Allan's suspended sentence. Allan is denied bail and must wait for his trial in jail. It is soon learned that Allan is wanted by police in Illinois for passing bad checks. Many people would be delighted to send Allan to Illinois; they tell officials in that state they can have him, pending resolution of the situation in Marion County. Allan is now in jail for three reasons: (1) serving his sentence for the original burglary, (2) awaiting trial on a robbery charge, and (3) waiting for transfer to Illinois.

Is this one jail stay or three? In a sense, it is one jail stay because one person, Allan, is occupying a jail cell. But let's say Allan's trial on the robbery charge is delayed until after he completes his sentence for the burglary. He stays in jail and begins a new jail stay. When he comes up for trial, the prosecutor asks to waive the robbery charges against Allan in hopes of exporting him to the neighboring state, and a new jail stay begins as Allan awaits his free trip to Illinois.

You may recognize this as a problem with units of analysis. Is the unit the person who stays in jail? Or are the separate reasons Allan is in jail—which are social artifacts—the units of analysis? After some thought, Maxfield decided that the social artifact was the more appropriate unit because he was interested in whether jail cells are more often occupied by people serving sentences or people awaiting trial. But that produced a new question of how to deal with people like Allan. Do we double-count the overlap in Allan's jail stays, so that he accounts for two jail stays while serving his suspended sentence for burglary and waiting for the robbery trial? This seemed to make sense, but then Allan's two jail stays would count the same as two other people with one jail stay each. In other words, Allan would appear to occupy two jail beds at the same time. This was neither true nor helpful in describing how long people stay in jail for different reasons.

Exhaustive and Exclusive Measurement

Briefly revisiting terms introduced in Chapter 2, an attribute is a characteristic or quality of something. "Female" is an example, as are "old" and "student." Variables, by contrast, are logical sets of attributes. Thus, "gender" is a variable traditionally composed of the attributes "female" and "male." The conceptualization and operationalization processes can be seen as the specification of variables and the attributes composing them. Thus, "employment status" is a variable that has the attributes "employed" and "unemployed"; or, the list of attributes could be expanded to include other possibilities such as "employed part-time," "employed full-time," and "retired."

Every variable should have two important qualities. First, the attributes composing it should be *exhaustive*. For the variable to have any utility in research, researchers must be able to classify every observation in terms of one of the attributes composing the variable. We will run into trouble if we conceptualize the variable "sentence" in terms of the attributes "prison" and "fine." After all, some convicted persons are assigned to probation, some have a portion of their prison sentence suspended, and others may receive a mix of prison terms, probation, suspended sentences, or perhaps community service. Notice that we can make the list of attributes exhaustive by adding "other" and "combination." Whatever approach we take, we must be able to classify every observation.

At the same time, attributes composing a variable must be *mutually exclusive*. Researchers must be able to classify every observation in terms of one and only one attribute. Thus, for example, we need to define "prison" and "fine" in such a way that nobody can be classified as both at the same time. That means we must be able to handle the person whose sentence includes both a prison term and a fine. In this case, attributes could be defined more precisely by specifying "prison only," "fine only," and "both prison and fine."

Levels of Measurement

Attributes composing any variable must be mutually exclusive and exhaustive. Attributes may be related in other ways as well. Of particular interest is that variables may represent different levels of measurement: nominal, ordinal, interval, and ratio. Levels of measurement tell us what sorts of information we can gain from the "scores" assigned to the values of a variable.

Nominal Measures Variables whose attributes have only the characteristics of exhaustiveness and mutual exclusiveness are **nominal measures**. Examples are gender, race, city of residence, college major, Social Security number, and marital status. Although the attributes composing each of these variables—"male," "female," and "transgendered" for the variable "gender"—are distinct from one another and exhaust the usual possibilities among people, they have none of the additional structures mentioned later. Nominal measures merely offer names or labels for characteristics.

Imagine characterizing a group of people in terms of a nominal variable and grouping them physically by the appropriate attributes. Suppose we are at a convention attended by hundreds of state court judges. At a social function, we ask them to stand together in groups according to the states in which they live: all those from Vermont in one group, those from California in another, and so forth. (The variable is "state of residence"; the attributes are "live in Vermont," "live in California," and so on.) All the people standing in a given group have at least one thing in common; the people in any one group differ from the people in all other groups in that same regard. Where the individual groups are formed, how close they are to one another, and how they are arranged in the room is irrelevant. All that matters is that all the members of a given group share the same state

of residence and that each group has a different shared state of residence.

Ordinal Measures Variables whose attributes may be logically rank-ordered are **ordinal measures**. The different attributes represent relatively more or less of the variable. Examples of variables that can be ordered in some way are opinion of police, occupational status, crime seriousness, and fear of crime.

Let's pursue the earlier example of grouping state court judges at a social gathering and imagine that we ask all those who have sat on appellate courts to stand in one group, all those serving felony trial courts to stand in another group, and all those who sit on misdemeanor trial courts to stand in a third group. This manner of grouping people satisfies the requirements for exhaustiveness and mutual exclusiveness. In addition, however, we might logically arrange the three groups in terms of the level of court where they serve (the shared attribute). We might arrange the three groups in a row, ranging from highest court to lowest court. This arrangement provides a physical representation of an ordinal measure. If we know which groups two individuals are in, we can determine what level of court they sit on.

Note that in this example, the distance between the groups is irrelevant. They might stand 5 feet apart or 500 feet apart; the appellate and felony trial court groups could be 5 feet apart, and the misdemeanor trial court group might be 500 feet farther down the line. These physical distances have no meaning. The felony group, however, should be between the misdemeanor group and the appellate group, or else the rank order is incorrect.

Interval Measures When the actual distance that separates the attributes composing variables does have meaning, the variables are **interval measures**. The logical distance between attributes can then be expressed in meaningful standard intervals.

For example, in the Fahrenheit temperature scale, the difference, or distance, between 80 degrees and 90 degrees is the same as that between 40 degrees and 50 degrees. However, 80 degrees Fahrenheit is not twice as hot as 40 degrees, because the zero point in the Fahrenheit scale is arbitrary; zero degrees does not really mean lack of heat. Similarly, minus 30 degrees on this scale doesn't represent 30 degrees less than no heat. This is true for the Celsius scale as well. In contrast, the Kelvin scale is based on an absolute zero, which *does* mean a complete lack of heat.

Criminal justice researchers often combine individual nominal and ordinal measures to produce a composite interval measure. We'll see examples at the end of this chapter.

Ratio Measures Most of the social scientific variables that meet the minimum requirements for interval measures also meet the requirements for **ratio measures**. In ratio measures, the attributes that compose a variable, besides having all the structural characteristics mentioned previously, are based on a true zero point. Examples from criminal justice research are age, dollar value of property loss from burglary, number of prior arrests, blood alcohol content, and length of incarceration.

Returning to the example of various ways to classify judges, we might ask them to group themselves according to years of experience in their present position. All those new to their job would stand together, as would those with one year of experience, those with two years on the job, and so forth. The facts that members of each group share the same years of experience and that each group has a different shared length of time satisfy the minimum requirements for a nominal measure. Arranging the groups in a line from those with the least to those with the most experience meets the additional requirements for an ordinal measure, and permits us to determine whether one person is more experienced, is less experienced, or has the same level of experience as another. If we arrange the groups so that there is the same distance between each pair of adjacent groups, we satisfy the additional requirements of an interval measure and can say how much more experience one judge has than another. Finally, because one of the attributes included—experience—has a true zero point (judges just appointed or elected to their job), the phalanx of judges also meets the requirements for a ratio measure, permitting us to say that one person is twice as experienced as another.

Comparing two people in terms of a ratio variable, then, allows us to conclude (1) whether they are different (or the same), (2) whether one is more than the other, (3) how much they differ, and (4) what the ratio of one to another is. Figure 5-1 summarizes this discussion by presenting a graphic illustration of the four levels of measurement.

Implications of Levels of Measurement

To review this discussion and to understand why level of measurement may make a difference, consider Table 5.1. It presents information on crime seriousness adapted from a survey of crime severity conducted for the Bureau of Justice Statistics (Wolfgang et al., 1985). The survey presented brief descriptions of more than 200 different crimes to a sample of 60,000 people. Respondents were asked to assign a score to each crime based on how serious they thought the crime was compared with bicycle theft (scored at 10).

The first column in Table 5.1 lists some of the crimes described. The second column shows a nominal measure that identifies the victim in the crime: home, person, business, or society. Type of victim is an attribute of each crime. The third column lists seriousness scores computed from survey results, ranging from 0.6 for trespassing to 35.7 for murder. These seriousness scores are interval measures because the distance between, for example, auto theft (at 8.0) and accepting a bribe (at 9.0) is the same as that between accepting a bribe (at 9.0) and obstructing justice (at 10.0). Seriousness scores are not ratio measures; there is no absolute zero point, and three instances of obstructing justice (at 10.0) do not equal one rape with injury (at 30.0).

The fourth column shows the ranking for each of the 17 crimes in the table; the most serious crime, murder, is ranked 1, followed by rape with injury, and so on. The rankings express only the order of seriousness, however, because the difference between murder (ranked 1) and rape (ranked 2) is smaller than the distance between rape and robbery with injury (ranked 3).

Finally, the crime descriptions presented to respondents indicated the value of property loss for each offense. This is a ratio measure with a true zero point, so that 10 burglaries with a loss

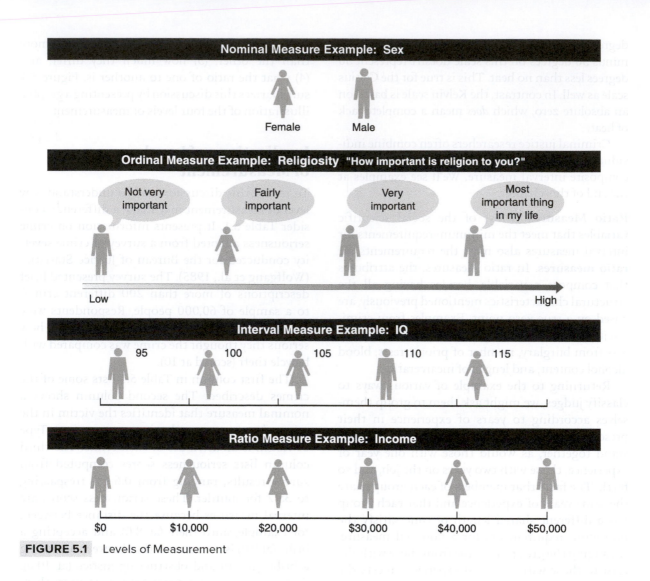

Nominal Measure Example: Sex

Female   Male

Ordinal Measure Example: Religiosity "How important is religion to you?"

Not very important   Fairly important   Very important   Most important thing in my life

Low ————————————————————————————————→ High

Interval Measure Example: IQ

95   100   105   110   115

Ratio Measure Example: Income

$0 $10,000 $20,000 $30,000 $40,000 $50,000

FIGURE 5.1   Levels of Measurement

of $1,000 each have the same property value as one arson offense with a loss of $10,000.

Different statistical techniques require variables that meet certain minimum levels of measurement. For example, we could compute the average property loss from the crimes listed in Table 5.1 by adding up the individual numbers in the fifth column and dividing by the number of crimes listed (17). However, we would not be able to compute the average victim type because that is a nominal variable. In that case, we could report the modal—the most common—victim type, which in Table 5.1 is society.

Researchers may treat some variables as representing different levels of measurement. Ratio measures are the highest level, followed by interval, ordinal, and nominal. A variable that represents a given level of measurement—say, ratio—may also be treated as representing a lower level of measurement—say, ordinal. For example, age is a ratio measure. If we wish to examine only the relationship between age and some ordinal-level variable, such as delinquency involvement (high, medium, or low), we might choose to treat age as an ordinal-level variable as well. We might characterize the subjects of our study as being

TABLE 5.1 Crime Seriousness and Levels of Measurement

Crime	Victim	Seriousness Score	Rank	Value of Property Loss
Accepting a bribe	Society	9.0	9	0
Arson	Business	12.7	6	$10,000
Auto theft	Home	8.0	10	$12,000
Burglary	Business	15.5	5	$100,000
Burglary	Home	9.6	8	$1,000
Buying stolen property	Society	5.0	12	0
Heroin sales	Society	20.6	4	0
Heroin use	Society	6.5	11	0
Murder	Person	35.7	1	0
Obstructing justice	Society	10.0	7	0
Public intoxication	Society	0.8	15	0
Rape and injury	Person	30.0	2	0
Robbery and injury	Person	21.0	3	$1,000
Robbery attempt	Person	3.3	13	0
Robbery, no injury	Person	8.0	10	$1,000
Shoplifting	Business	2.2	14	$10
Trespassing	Home	0.6	16	0

Source: Adapted from Wolfgang, Figlio, Tracy, and Singer (1985).

young, middle aged, and old, specifying the age range for each of those groupings. Finally, age might be used as a nominal-level variable for certain research purposes. Thus, people might be grouped together as teenagers if their ages are between 12 and 20.

The analytic uses planned for a given variable, then, should determine the level of measurement to be sought, with the realization that some variables are inherently limited to a certain level. If a variable is to be used in a variety of ways that require different levels of measurement, the study should be designed to achieve the highest level possible. Although ratio measures (such as number of arrests) can later be reduced to ordinal or nominal measures, it is not possible to convert a nominal or ordinal measure to a ratio one. More generally, you cannot convert a lower-level measure to a higher-level one. That is a one-way street worth remembering.

Criteria for Measurement Quality

The key standards for measurement quality are reliability and validity.

Measurements can be made with varying degrees of precision, which refers to the fineness of the distinctions made between the attributes that compose a variable. Saying that a woman is "43 years old" is more precise than that she is "in her forties." Describing a felony sentence as "18 months" is more precise than "over one year."

As a general rule, precise measurements are superior to imprecise ones, as common sense would suggest. But precision is not always necessary or desirable. If it is sufficient for your research purpose to know that a felony sentence is over one year, then any additional effort invested in learning the precise sentence would be wasted. The operationalization of concepts, then, must be guided partly by an understanding of the degree of precision required. If your needs are not clear, be more precise rather than less.

Don't confuse precision with accuracy. Describing someone as "born in Stowe, Vermont" is more precise than "born in New England," but suppose the person in question was actually born in Boston? The less precise description, in this instance, is more accurate; it's a better reflection of the real world. This is a point worth keeping in mind. Many criminal justice measures are imprecise, so reporting approximate values is often preferable.

Precision and accuracy are obviously important qualities in research measurement, and they probably need no further explanation. When criminal justice researchers construct and evaluate measurements, they pay special attention to two technical considerations: reliability and validity.

Reliability

In the abstract, **reliability** is a matter of whether a particular measurement technique, applied repeatedly to the same thing, will yield the same result each time. In other words, measurement reliability is roughly the same as measurement consistency or stability. Imagine, for example, a police officer standing on the street, guessing the speed of cars that pass by, and issuing speeding tickets based on that judgment. If you received a ticket from this officer and went to court to contest it, you would almost certainly win your case. The judge would no doubt reject this way of measuring speed, regardless of the police officer's experience. The reliability or consistency of this method for measuring vehicle speed is questionable at best. If the same police officer used a laser speed detector, however, it is doubtful that you would be able to beat the ticket. The laser device is judged a much more reliable way of measuring speed.

Reliability Consistency; obtaining the same results when measuring something more than once.

Reliability, though, does not ensure accuracy any more than precision does. The speedometer in your car may be a reliable instrument for measuring speed, but sometimes speedometers can be off by a few miles per hour, especially at higher speeds. If your speedometer shows 65 miles per hour when you are actually traveling at 70, it gives you a consistent but inaccurate reading that might attract the attention of police officers with more accurate laser guns.

Measurement reliability is often a problem with indicators used in criminal justice research. Numerous studies have shown that measures of crime based on police records often suffer from reliability problems. A classic example is the study by Richard McCleary, Barbara Nienstedt, and James Erven (1982:362), which analyzed changes in police records of burglary following a change in how burglary reports were investigated in a large city. Under the new system, detectives formally investigated burglaries that previously had been examined only by patrol officers. Burglaries declined sharply as soon as the new investigation procedures were implemented. The reason for the decline was that some patrol officers counted some crimes as burglaries that did not meet the official definition of burglary. When a smaller number of detectives began to investigate burglaries, they were more consistent in applying the official definition.

Other examples of reliability problems can be found in criminal justice research and policy settings. How accurate are judges' evaluations in determining which defendants are at risk of fleeing before trial? A study by Sheila Royo Maxwell (1999) found that the factors used by judges in deciding whether to release defendants on their own recognizance were neither reliable nor effective predictors of the likelihood that defendants would fail to appear in court. Inconsistency in the administration of blood alcohol tests in certain states has forced researchers to search for new measures of drunk driving (Heeren et al., 1985; Voas, Romano, and Peck, 2009). Forensic DNA evidence increasingly is being used in violent crime cases. National Research Council studies (1996, 2009) found a variety of errors in laboratory procedures, including sample mishandling, evidence contamination, and analyst bias. These are measurement reliability problems that can lead to unwarranted exclusion of evidence or to the conviction of innocent people (Roth, 2010).

Reliability problems crop up in many forms. Reliability is a concern every time a single observer is the source of data, because we have no way to guard against that observer's subjectivity. We cannot tell for sure how much of what's reported represents true variation and how much is due to the observer's unique perceptions.

Reliability can also be an issue when more than one observer makes measurements. Survey researchers have long known that as a result of their own attitudes and demeanor, different interviewers get different answers from respondents. Suppose we want to classify different types of right-wing extremist organizations in terms of some standard coding scheme, such as a set of categories created by the National Institute of Justice. However, a supporter of Mayors Against Illegal Guns and a member of the National Rifle Association would be unlikely to code all groups into the same categories.

These examples illustrate problems of reliability. Similar problems arise when we ask people for information about themselves. Sometimes we ask questions that people don't know the answers ("How many times have you seen a police officer in the last month?"). Sometimes we ask people about things that are totally irrelevant to them ("Are you satisfied with the FBI's guidelines on the positioning of AMBER Alert signs?"). And sometimes we ask questions that are so complicated that a person who has a clear opinion on the matter might interpret the question differently when asked a second time.

How do we create reliable measures? Because the problem of reliability is a basic one in criminal justice measurement, researchers have developed a number of techniques for dealing with it.

The Test–Retest Method   Sometimes it is appropriate to make the same measurement more than once. If there is no reason to expect the information to change, we should expect the same response both times. If answers vary, however, then the measurement method is, to the extent of that variation, unreliable. Here's an illustration.

In their classic research on delinquency in England, Donald West and David Farrington (1977) interviewed a sample of 411 males from a working-class area of London at age 16 and again at age 18. The subjects were asked to describe various aspects of their lives, including educational and work history, leisure pursuits, drinking and smoking habits, delinquent activities, and experience with police and courts.

Because many of these topics involve illegal or at least antisocial activity, West and Farrington were concerned about the accuracy of information obtained in their interviews. They assessed reliability in several ways. One was to compare responses from the interview at age 18 with those from the interview at age 16. For example, in each interview, the youths were asked at what age they left school. In most cases, there were few discrepancies in stated age from one interview to the next, which led the authors to conclude: "There was therefore no systematic tendency for youths either to increase or lessen their claimed period of school attendance as they grew older, as might have occurred if they had wanted either to exaggerate or to underplay their educational attainments" (1977:76–77). If West and Farrington had found less consistency in answers to this and other items, they would have had good reason to doubt the truthfulness of responses to more sensitive questions. The test–retest method suggested to the authors that memory lapses were the most common source of minor differences.

Although this method can be a useful reliability check, it is limited in some respects. Faulty memory may produce inconsistent responses if there is a lengthy gap between the initial interview and the retest. In their study of childhood victimization, Christine Walsh and associates (2008) addressed this problem by asking their respondents about experiences of violence and then retesting by repeating the questions to their sample only four weeks later. A different problem can arise when trying to use the test–retest method to check the reliability of attitude or opinion measures. If the test–retest interval is short, then answers given in the second interview may be affected by earlier responses if subjects try to be consistent.

Inter-Rater Reliability It is also possible for measurement unreliability to be generated by research workers—for example, interviewers and coders. To guard against interviewer unreliability, it is common practice in surveys to have a supervisor call a subsample of the respondents on the telephone and verify selected information. West and Farrington (1977:173) checked inter-rater reliability in their study of London youths and found few significant differences in results obtained from different interviewers.

Comparing measurements from different raters works in other situations as well. For example, Michael Geerken (1994) presents an important discussion of reliability problems that researchers are likely to encounter in measuring prior arrests through police "rap sheets." Duplicate entries, the use of aliases, and the need to transform official crime categories into a smaller number of categories for analysis are among the problems that Geerken cites. One way to increase consistency in translating official records into research measures—a process often referred to as coding—is to have more than one person code a sample of records and then compare the consistency of coding decisions made by each person. This approach was used by Michael Maxfield and Cathy Spatz Widom (1996) in their analysis of adult arrests of child abuse victims.

In general, whenever researchers are concerned that measures obtained through coding may not be classified reliably, they should have each independently coded by different people. In the hypothetical study of newspaper editorials about a proposed work release center, coding decisions that generate disagreement should be evaluated more carefully and resolved. If we find a great deal of disagreement, our operational definitions of how to code newspaper editorials should be carefully reviewed and made more specific.

Split-Half Method As a general rule, it is always a good idea to make more than one measurement of any subtle or complex social concept, such as prejudice or fear of crime. This procedure lays the groundwork for another check on reliability.

Suppose you've created a questionnaire that contains 10 items you believe measure prejudicial beliefs about African Americans and delinquency. Using the split-half technique, you randomly assign those 10 items to two sets of 5 items. Each set should provide a good measure of prejudice, and the sets should agree in the way they classify the respondents. If the two sets of items measure people differently, then that, again, points to a problem in the reliability of how you are measuring the variable.

In their longitudinal study of links between childhood experiences and adolescent delinquency, Woodward and Fergusson (2000) used interview data that included something like an abbreviated IQ test. IQ tests are usually quite lengthy, reflecting the need to include a large number of test items to measure multiple dimensions of intelligence. One consequence is that it's not possible to use standard IQ tests in a survey that includes a number of other questions. So researchers commonly use subsets of questions from standard intelligence tests. For example, if a standard intelligence test includes 20 items, two subsets of 10 items each can be randomly presented to half of the subjects in a survey—split-half. Then scores on each subset of items are computed and compared across the split-halves. In their study, Woodward and Fergusson report a split-half reliability value of 0.93, roughly indicating that 93 percent of scores between the two halves were consistent.

The reliability of measurements is a fundamental issue in criminal justice research, and we'll return to it in the chapters to come. For now, however, we hasten to point out that even total reliability doesn't ensure that our measures actually measure what we think they measure. That brings us to the issue of validity.

Validity

Recall that in Chapter 4 we considered the concept of validity with respect to inferring cause. Validity is also an important criterion for measurement quality. In conventional usage, the term validity means that an empirical measure adequately reflects the meaning of the concept under consideration. Put another way, measurement validity involves whether you are really measuring what you say you are measuring. As we have discussed, an operational definition specifies the operations you will perform to measure a concept. Does your operational definition accurately reflect the concept you are interested in? If the answer is yes, you have a valid measure. A laser speed detector is a valid measure of vehicle speed, but a wind velocity indicator is not, because the volume of air displaced by a slow-moving truck will register higher than that displaced by a fast-moving sports car.

Although methods for assessing reliability are relatively straightforward, it is more difficult to demonstrate that individual measures are valid. Because concepts are abstract and not real, we cannot directly demonstrate that measures—which are real—are actually measuring an abstract concept. Nevertheless, researchers have some ways of dealing with the issue of validity.

Face Validity   First, there's something called **face validity**. Particular empirical measures may or may not jibe with our common agreements and our individual mental images about a particular concept. We might debate the adequacy of measuring satisfaction with police services by counting the number of citizen complaints registered by the mayor's office, but we'd surely agree that the number of citizen complaints has something to do with levels of satisfaction. If someone suggested that we measure satisfaction with police by finding out whether people like to watch videos of police chases on the Internet, we would probably agree that the measure has no face validity; it simply does not make sense.

A good example of face validity is a study of food-buying habits by Ditte Johansen and associates (2006). They were interested in learning whether people who drank wine ate healthier foods than people who drank beer. The researchers measured what people drank and what they ate by examining the electronic records of food and beverage purchases that are produced when cashiers read "discount" cards. Johansen and colleagues reasoned that people ate and drank what they bought, thus appealing to the face validity of their measures.

There are many concrete agreements among researchers about how to measure certain basic concepts. The Census Bureau, for example, has created operational definitions of such concepts as family, household, and employment status that seem to have a workable validity in most studies using those concepts.

Criterion-Related Validity   Criterion-related validity involves comparing a measure with some external criterion. A measure can be validated by showing that it predicts scores on another measure that is generally accepted as valid; this is sometimes referred to as convergent validity. The validity of College Board exams, for example, is shown in their ability to predict the success of students in college.

Robert Voas, Eduardo Romano, and Raymond Peck (2009) offer a good example of criterion-related validity in their efforts to validate a measure of alcohol-related auto accidents. Of course, conducting a blood alcohol laboratory test on everyone involved in auto accidents would be a valid measure. But this is not routinely done, so Voas and colleagues tested an alternate measure adapted from one used to estimate alcohol-related *fatal* accidents: single-vehicle accidents occurring between midnight and 3:00 A.M. The validity of this measure was shown by comparing it with the blood alcohol test results obtained from samples of drivers involved in nonfatal accidents at two test sites: Long Beach, California, and Fort Lauderdale, Florida. Because the two measures agreed closely, Voas and associates claimed that the proxy or surrogate measure would be valid in other sites.

Another approach to criterion-related validity is to show that our measure of a concept is different from measures of similar, but distinct concepts. This is called *discriminant* validity, meaning that measures can discriminate different concepts. For example, Jacinta Gau (2011) investigated differences in more specific perceptions of police and more general beliefs in procedural justice. She found that measures of obligation to obey legal authorities, part of procedural justice, were distinct from measures of trust in police. This meant that people could endorse procedural justice while distrusting police.

Sometimes, it is difficult to find behavioral criteria that can be used to validate measures as directly as in the examples described here. In those instances, however, we can often approximate such criteria by considering how the variable in question theoretically ought to relate to other variables.

Construct Validity   **Construct validity** is based on the logical relationships among variables. Let's suppose, for example, that we are interested in studying fear of crime—its sources and consequences. As part of our research, we develop a measure of fear of crime, and we want to assess its validity.

In addition to our measure, we will also develop certain theoretical expectations about the way the variable "fear of crime" relates to other variables. For instance, it's reasonable to conclude that people who are afraid of crime are less likely to leave their homes at night for entertainment than people who are not afraid of crime. If our measure of fear of crime relates to how often people go out at night in the expected fashion, then that constitutes evidence of our measure's construct validity. However, if people who are afraid of crime are just as likely to go out at night as people who are not afraid, then that challenges the validity of our measure. This and related points about measures of fear are nicely illustrated by Jason Ditton and Stephen Farrall (2007) in their analysis of data from England.

Tests of construct validity, then, can offer a weight of evidence that our measure either does or doesn't evaluate the quality we want it to measure, without providing definitive proof. We have suggested here that tests of construct validity are less compelling than tests of criterion validity. However, there is room for disagreement about which kind of test should be done in a given situation. It is less important to distinguish these two types than to understand the logic of validation that they have in common; if we are successful in measuring some

variable, then those measurements should relate to other measures in some logical fashion.

Content Validity   Finally, **content validity** is the degree to which a measure covers the range of meanings included within the concept. For instance, this question has frequently been used in surveys to measure fear of crime:

How safe do you feel (or would you feel) walking alone in this area after dark? Would you say very safe, fairly safe, fairly unsafe, or very unsafe?

Although this question may provide a valid measure of fear in connection with street crime, it is not a good measure of fear of burglary, auto theft, or airplane hijacking. The concept of fear of crime is broader than the concept represented in the question.

Multiple Measures   Another approach to validation of an individual measure is to compare it with alternative measures of the same concept. The use of multiple measures is similar to establishing criterion validity. However, the use of multiple measures does not necessarily assume that the criterion measure is always more accurate. For example, many crimes that are committed never result in an arrest, so arrests are not good measures of how many crimes are committed by individuals. Self-report surveys have often been used to measure delinquency and criminality. But how valid are survey questions that ask people how many crimes they have committed?

The approach used by Donald West and David Farrington (1977) and by others is to ask, for example, how many times someone has committed robbery and how many times someone has been arrested for that crime. Those who admit having been arrested for robbery are asked when and where the arrest occurred. Self-reports can then be validated by checking police arrest records. This works two ways: (1) it is possible to validate individual reports of being arrested for robbery, and (2) researchers can check police records for all persons interviewed to see if there are any records of robbery arrests that subjects do not disclose to interviewers.

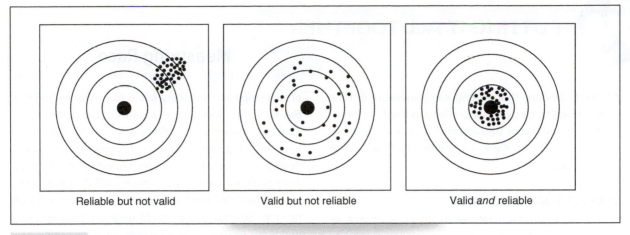

| Reliable but not valid | Valid but not reliable | Valid *and* reliable |

FIGURE 5.2 Analogy to Validity and Reliability

Figure 5.2 illustrates the difference between validity and reliability. Think of measurement as analogous to hitting the bull's-eye on a target. A reliable measure produces a "tight pattern," regardless of where it hits, because reliability is a function of consistency. Validity, in contrast, relates to the arrangement of shots around the bull's-eye. The failure of reliability in the figure can be seen as a random error; the failure of validity is a systematic error. Notice that neither an unreliable nor an invalid measure is likely to be very useful.

This chapter's installment of our running example, "Putting It All Together: Measuring Race," discusses reliability and validity of different approaches to measuring the race of drivers.

Composite Measures

Combining individual measures often produces more valid and reliable indicators.

Sometimes it is possible to construct a single measure that captures the variable of interest. For example, asking auto owners whether their cars have been stolen in the previous six months is a straightforward way to measure auto-theft victimization. But other variables may be measured more accurately by more than a single indicator. A "property crime" index might combine burglary, larceny, and motor vehicle theft, whereas a "violent crime" index would be a composite of murder, rape, robbery, and assault.

Composite measures are frequently used in criminal justice research for three reasons. First, the researcher is often unable to develop single indicators of complex concepts, despite carefully designing studies to provide valid and reliable measurements of variables. This is especially true regarding attitudes and opinions that are measured through surveys. For example, we saw that measuring fear of crime through a question that asks feelings of safety on neighborhood streets measures some dimensions of fear, but certainly not all of them. This leads us to question the validity of using that single question to measure fear of crime.

Second, we may wish to use a rather refined ordinal measure of a variable, arranging cases in several ordinal categories from very low to very high on a variable such as degree of parental supervision. A single data item might not have enough categories to provide the desired range of variation, but an index or scale formed from several items would.

Finally, indexes and scales are efficient devices for data analysis. If a single data item gives only a rough indication of a given variable, considering several data items may give us a more comprehensive and more accurate indication. For example, the results of a single drug

It's pretty obvious that getting some measure of race is necessary to study racial profiling in traffic enforcement. But you might be surprised to learn that measuring race is not easy. The difficulty begins with conceptualization.

CONCEPTUALIZING RACE

At the most general level, we might think of race as a genetic or biological trait, however even that is an oversimplification. Margaret Winker (2004) reports that studies to classify the world's population by genotype find as much genetic variation within race groups as across them. For medical purposes, Winker recommends that individuals self-designate race so the resulting categories ". . . most closely match what they believe reflects their personal and cultural background" (p. 1613).

Self-designation of race and ethnicity—how people view their own race or ethnic background is the approach followed by the Census Bureau and other federal agencies. But even this has run into problems in the past. Rachel Swarns (2004) describes how people whose heritage is Hispanic or Latino frequently select "some other race" when presented with the five standard census categories: Alaskan native, American Indian, Asian, black, white.

A final way to conceptualize race is to think of how people appear, perhaps appealing to the phrase, "people of color." Thinking about how people appear,

or racial appearance, may seem to border on bigotry. But isn't this how police would conceptualize race? That is, if police are profiling drivers based on race, how would police ultimately measure race? Police don't have access to genotyping or other genetic data. They can't very well ask people to self-designate their race before deciding whether or not to make a traffic stop. So if we are trying to measure race in a way that helps us detect the possibility of racial profiling by police, we would do well to mimic how police are likely to "measure" race.

OPERATIONALIZING RACE AND ETHNICITY

Two general approaches have been used to operationalize the concepts of race and ethnicity: self-report and observed race. You can see these correspond to the second and third conceptualizations.

Most researchers have relied on some kind of observation. But most researchers have encountered problems in identifying Hispanic drivers, falling back on a white/nonwhite dichotomy, perhaps supplemented with Asian. Different studies illustrate different approaches to measuring race by observation. Pennsylvania researchers placed two observers in cars parked on the edges of roadways (Engel et al., 2004). In North Carolina, teams of researchers rode in vans, acting as mobile observers, and recorded the race of drivers on selected road segments. Researchers in New Jersey (Lange et al.,

test would give us some indication of drug use by a probationer. Examining results from several drug tests would give us a better indication, but the manipulation of several data items simultaneously can be very complicated. In contrast, composite measures are efficient data reduction devices. Several indicators may be summarized in a single numerical score, even while perhaps

very nearly maintaining the specific details of all the individual indicators.

Typologies

Researchers combine variables in different ways to produce different composite measures. The simplest of these is a **typology**, sometimes called

2005) used digital cameras to photograph drivers. Images were viewed on computers by teams of raters who classified them as white, black, Asian, American Indian, or other; Hispanic/not-Hispanic was coded separately.

Self-reported race was also measured in New Jersey. The New Jersey Turnpike is a toll road. When data were collected in 2000 and 2001, drivers were required to stop at a booth when they exited the turnpike to pay a toll. Standing behind toll booth attendants, researchers asked samples of drivers exiting the turnpike to report their racial/ethnic group from six choices: Asian, black, white, American Indian, Hispanic/Latino, or other.

Finally, the race of stopped drivers was recorded by New Jersey troopers and appeared on all traffic stop data records. This was collected by observation. These three sources of data provided three different measures of race. Here is a summary tabulation extracted from Lange et al. (2005:209); data are shown for the southern segment of the turnpike, the same area described in Chapter 4.

	Tollbooth survey	Police stop data	Photo coding, speeders only
White	66%	52%	58%
Black	15	29	26
Hispanic	11	10	7
Other	9	10	9

The last column presents race breakdown of drivers for cars that were further classified as speeding, in this case exceeding the posted speed limit by 15 or more miles per hour. We will have more to say about how speed was measured in Chapter 6.

RELIABILITY AND VALIDITY

Interrater reliability is well-suited to coding race by observation with multiple observers. In Pennsylvania, Engel et al. required that the two observers had to agree on race classification of drivers. If they did could not agree, the driver's race was recorded as unknown. But this occurred in only 2.7 percent of over 160,000 drivers observed in the Pennsylvania study.

In one sense, reliability in New Jersey was enhanced by having digital photos; they could be reviewed at length. However, taking photos with a stationary camera through the windshield of a car traveling at high speed presented technical challenges. The quality of many images was poor; 24 percent of the 38,747 images were judged to be unusable. Three research assistants independently viewed the remaining images on high-resolution computer monitors. It was required that two of three coders agree on the race of driver. This criterion was met for 89 percent of images that remained after discarding those that were unusable.

We have already touched on the question of validity. If we are interested in whether police decisions to stop drivers are based on a driver's race, then a measure of the appearance of race is more valid than self-identified race. This is not true for measuring Hispanic ethnicity.

a "taxonomy." Typologies are produced by the intersection of two or more variables to create a set of categories or types. We may, for example, wish to classify people according to the range of their experience in criminal court. Assume we have asked a sample of people whether they have ever served as a juror and whether they have ever testified as a witness in criminal court. Table 5.2 shows how the yes/no responses to these two questions can be combined into a typology of experience in court.

Typologies can be more complex—combining scores on three or more measures or combining scores on two measures that take many different values. For an example of a complex typology, consider research by Rolf Loeber and associates

TABLE 5.2   Typology of Court Experience

		Serve on Jury?	
		No	Yes
Testify as Witness?	No	A	B
	Yes	C	D

Typology

    A: No experience with court

    B: Experience as juror only

    C: Experience as witness only

    D: Experience as juror and witness

(1991) on patterns of delinquency over time. The researchers used a longitudinal design in which a sample of boys was selected from Pittsburgh public schools and interviewed many times. Some questions asked about their involvement in delinquency and criminal offending. This approach made it possible to distinguish boys who reported different types of offending at different times.

Loeber and associates first classified delinquent and criminal acts into these ordinal seriousness categories (1991:44):

None:	No self-reported delinquency
Minor:	Theft of items worth less than $5, vandalism, and fare evasion
Moderate:	Theft over $5, gang fighting, and carrying weapons
Serious:	Car theft, breaking and entering, forced sex, and selling drugs

Next, to measure changes in delinquency over time, the researchers compared reports of delinquency from the first screening interview with reports from follow-up interviews. These two measures—delinquency at time one and delinquency at time two—formed the typology, which they referred to as a "dynamic classification of offenders" (1991:44). Table 5.3 summarizes this typology.

The first category in the table, "nondelinquent," includes those boys who reported committing no offenses at both the screening and follow-up interviews. "Starters" reported no offenses at screening and then minor, moderate, or serious delinquency at follow-up, whereas "desistors" were just the opposite. Those who committed the same types of offenses at both times were labeled "stable";

TABLE 5.3   Typology of Change in Juvenile Offending

	Juvenile Offending	
Typology	Screening (Time 1)	Follow-Up (Time 2)
A. Nondelinquent	0	0
B. Starter	0	1, 2, or 3
C. Desistor	1, 2, or 3	0
D. Stable	1	1
D. Stable	2	2
D. Stable	3	3
E. De-escalator	3	2
E. De-escalator	2 or 3	1
F. Escalator	1	2 or 3
F. Escalator	2	3

Juvenile Offending Typology

    0: None

    1: Minor

    2: Moderate

    3: Serious

Source: Adapted from Loeber and associates (1991:43–46).

"de-escalators" reported committing less-serious offenses at follow-up; and "escalators" moved on to more serious offenses.

Notice the efficiency of this typology. Two variables (delinquency at screening and follow-up) with four categories each are reduced to a single variable with six categories. Furthermore, the two measures of delinquency are themselves composite measures, produced by summarizing self-reports of a large number of individual offenses. Finally, notice also how this efficiency is reflected in the clear meaning of the new composite measure. This dynamic typology summarizes information about time, offending, and offense seriousness in a single measure.

An Index of Disorder

"What is disorder, and what isn't?" asks Wesley Skogan (1990:4) in his book on the links between crime, fear, and social problems such as public drinking, drug use, litter, prostitution, panhandling, dilapidated buildings, and groups of boisterous youths. In an influential article titled "Broken Windows," James Wilson and George Kelling (1982) describe disorder as a sign of crime that may contribute independently to fear and crime itself. The argument goes something like this: Disorder is a symbol of urban decay that people associate with crime. Signs of disorder can produce two related problems. First, disorder may contribute to fear of crime, as urban residents believe that physical decay and "undesirables" are symbols of crime. Second, potential offenders may interpret evidence of disorder as a signal that informal social control mechanisms in a neighborhood have broken down and that the area is fair game for mayhem and predation. David Weisburd and associates (2015) discuss these mechanisms in some detail, while describing approaches to evaluating broken-windows policing.

We all have some sort of mental image (conception) of disorder, but to paraphrase Skogan's question: How do we measure it? Let's begin by distinguishing two conceptions of disorder. First, we can focus on the *physical presence* of disorder—whether litter, public drinking, public drug use, and the like are actually evident in an urban neighborhood. We might measure the physical presence of disorder through a series of systematic observations. This is the approach used by Robert Sampson and Stephen Raudenbush (1999) in their study of links between disorder and crime in Chicago. Unfortunately, these authors observed very few examples of disorder and altogether ignored the question of whether such behaviors were perceived as problematic by residents of Chicago neighborhoods.

That brings us to the second conception, one focusing on the *perception* of disorder. Thus, some people might view public drinking as disorderly, whereas others (e.g., New Orleans residents) consider public drinking to be perfectly acceptable. Questionnaires and survey methods are the best suited for measuring perceived disorder.

Having settled on the perceptions of disorder that we will measure through a survey, we must make some more decisions. Consider two versions of a question asking about people loitering on the street. The first is from a series of surveys conducted in three U.S. cities; the second is from a nationwide survey conducted in England and Wales. Each question is paraphrased from the original questionnaire.

1. Are groups of loiterers hanging out on the streets a big problem, some problem, or almost no problem in your neighborhood? (see Skogan and Maxfield, 1981)

2. In your area, how common are loiterers hanging around on the street: very common, fairly common, not very common, or not at all common? (see Maxfield, 1987)

The first question asks about perceptions of loiterers hanging out as a *problem*; the second question asks about perceptions of the *frequency* of people hanging out. Notice also that the first question requires two rather different things of respondents: they must perceive loiterers hanging around, and they must judge that to be a problem. Skogan used the first formulation of the question, reasoning that perception of behavior as a problem is required for it to be perceived as disorder.

Is this a good measure of disorder? The belief that loiterers hanging around is a problem surely has something to do with perceptions of disorder, but there is more to it than that. As it stands, we have a measure of one dimension of disorder, but our measure is quite narrow. In order to represent the concept of disorder more completely, we should measure additional behaviors or characteristics that represent other examples of disorder.

Skogan used questions about nine different examples of disorder and classified them into two groups representing what he calls social and physical disorder (Skogan, 1990:51, 191):

Social Disorder	Physical Disorder
Groups of loiterers	Abandoned buildings
Drug use and sales	Garbage and litter
Vandalism	Junk in vacant lots
Gang activity	
Public drinking	
Street harassment	

Questions corresponding to each of these examples of disorder asked respondents to rate them as big problems (scored 2), some problem (scored 1), or almost no problem (scored 0) in their neighborhood. Together, these nine items measure different

Now I'm going to read you a list of crime-related problems that may be found in some parts of the city. For each one, please tell me how much of a problem it is in your neighborhood. Is it a big problem, some problem, or almost no problem?

	Big problem	Some problem	No problem
(S) Groups of people loitering	②	1	0
(S) People using or selling drugs	2	①	0
(P) Abandoned buildings	2	1	⓪
(S) Vandalism	2	①	0
(P) Garbage and litter on street	②	1	0
(S) Gangs and gang activity	2	1	⓪
(S) People drinking in public	②	1	0
(P) Junk in vacant lots	2	1	⓪
(S) People making rude or insulting remarks	2	①	0

(S) Social = 2 + 1 + 1 + 0 + 2 + 1 = 7
     Index score = $7/6$ = 1.16
(P) Physical = 0 + 2 + 0 = 2
     Index score = $2/3$ = 0.67

FIGURE 5.3 Index of Disorder

types of disorder and appear to have reasonable face validity. However, examining the relationship between each individual item and respondents' fear of crime or experience as a crime victim would be unwieldy at best. So Skogan created two indexes, one for social disorder and one for physical disorder, by adding up the scores for each item and dividing by the number of items in each group. Figure 5.3 shows a hypothetical sample questionnaire for these nine items, together with the scores that would be produced for each index.

This example illustrates how several related variables can be combined to produce an index that has three desirable properties. First, a composite index is a more valid measure of disorder than is a single question. Second, computing and averaging across all items in a category create more variation in the index than we could obtain in any single item. Finally, two indexes are more parsimonious than nine individual variables; data analysis and interpretation can be more efficient.

Measurement Summary

We have covered substantial ground in this chapter, but still have only introduced the important and often complex issue of measurement in criminal justice research. The box "Putting It All Together: Measuring Race" presents an illustration from our running example. More than a step in the research process, measurement involves continuous thinking about what conceptual properties we wish to study, how we will operationalize those properties, and how we will develop measures that are reliable and valid. Often, some type of composite measure better represents underlying concepts and thus enhances validity.

Subsequent chapters pursue issues of measurement further. Part Three of this book describes data collection—how we go about making actual measurements. And Chapter 6 focuses on different approaches to measuring crime.

SUMMARY

- Concepts are mental images we use as summary devices for bringing together observations and experiences that seem to have something in common.

- Our concepts do not exist in the real world, so they can't be measured directly.

- In operationalization, we specify concrete empirical procedures that will result in measurements of variables.

- Operationalization begins in study design and continues throughout the research project, including the analysis of data.

- Categories in a measure must be mutually exclusive and exhaustive.

- Higher levels of measurements specify categories that have ranked order or more complex numerical properties.

- A given variable can sometimes be measured at different levels of measurement. The most appropriate level of measurement used depends on the purpose of the measurement.

- *Precision* refers to the exactness of the measure used in an observation or description of an attribute.

- Reliability and validity are criteria for measurement quality. Valid measures are truly indicators of underlying concepts. A reliable measure is consistent.

- The creation of specific, reliable measures often seems to diminish the richness of meaning our general concepts have. A good solution is to use multiple measures, each of which taps different aspects of the concept.

- Composite measures, formed by combining two or more variables, are often more valid measures of complex criminal justice concepts.

KEY TERMS

Concepts *(p. 111)*
Conception *(p. 110)*
Conceptual definition *(p. 114)*
Conceptualization *(p. 112)*
Construct validity *(p. 128)*
Content validity *(p. 128)*
Criterion-related validity *(p. 127)*
Dimension *(p. 113)*
Face validity *(p. 127)*
Interval measures *(p. 120)*

Nominal measures *(p. 120)*
Operational definition *(p. 114)*
Ordinal measures *(p. 120)*
Ratio measures *(p. 121)*
Reification *(p. 114)*
Reliability *(p. 124)*
Typology *(p. 130)*

REVIEW QUESTIONS AND EXERCISES

1. Review the box titled "What Is Recidivism?". From that discussion, write conceptual and operational definitions for *recidivism*. Summarize how Fabelo proposes to measure the concept. Finally, discuss possible reliability and validity issues associated with Fabelo's proposed measure.

2. On its Web page, "What we investigate" (http://www.fbi.gov/about-us/investigate/terrorism/terrorism-definition), the FBI lists the following definition:

"Domestic terrorism" means activities with the following three characteristics:

(1) involve acts dangerous to human life that violate federal or state law;
(2) Appear intended:
    i. to intimidate or coerce a civilian population;
    ii. to influence the policy of a government by intimidation or coercion; or
    iii. to affect the conduct of a government by mass destruction, assassination or kidnapping; and
(3) Occur primarily within the territorial jurisdiction of the U.S.

This is a conceptual definition. Write an operational definition, then see how it applies to stories about terrorism in a local newspaper or news feed.

3. We all have some sort of mental image of the pace of life. In a fascinating book titled *A Geography of Time*, Robert Levine (1997) operationalized the pace of life in cities around the world with a composite measure of the following:

a. How long it took a single pedestrian to walk 60 feet on an uncrowded sidewalk.
b. What percentage of public clocks displayed the correct time.
c. How long it took to purchase the equivalent of a first-class postage stamp with the equivalent of a $5 bill.

Discuss possible reliability and validity issues with these indicators of pace of life. Be sure to specify a conceptual definition for "pace of life."

CHAPTER 6

Measuring Crime

How do you measure crime? How much crime is there? Researchers and policy makers have developed several different approaches to measure crime—yet there's no definitive answer to the second question. We'll examine a variety of strategies for measuring crime and discuss the strengths and weaknesses of each.

Learning Objectives

1. Recognize how different approaches to measuring crime illustrate general principles of conceptualization, operationalization, and measurement.
2. Understand what crimes are included in different measures.
3. Describe different measures of crime and how they are based on different units of analysis.
4. Understand different purposes for collecting crime data.
5. Explain different measures based on crimes known to police.
6. Describe the main features of victim surveys.
7. Distinguish the main differences between crimes known to police and crimes measured through different types of surveys.
8. Understand why self-report measures are used, and list different types of crimes for which they are appropriate.
9. Summarize the major series of self-reported measures of drug use.
10. Understand how surveillance measures are obtained and used.
11. Explain how different measures of crime satisfy criteria for measurement quality.
12. Recognize that we have different measures of crime because each measure is imperfect.

Measuring Terrorist Incidents

Terrorism is a prominent concern throughout the world; we are all concerned about it at one level or another. And we all know about high-profile terrorist attacks such as 9/11, the attacks in Belgium and Paris in 2015, and the all-too common mass shootings in cities throughout the United States. But what about general measures of terrorism? How common is it? Where does it occur? What kinds of attacks are involved? Or, recalling some of the topics discussed in Chapter 5, what are conceptual and operational definitions of terrorism?

First, researchers and policy makers distinguish terrorism from terrorist incidents. Terrorism is defined by the National Consortium for the Study of Terrorism and Responses to Terrorism (START) as: *"the threatened or actual use of illegal force and violence against a non-state actor to attain a political economic, religious, or other social goal through fear, coercion, or intimidation"* (National Consortium for the Study of Terrorism and Responses to Terrorism [START], 2016:9. emphasis in original).

The next task is to conceptually define examples of terrorism, or how we will measure terrorist incidents. Following the above definition, START states that a terrorist incident must include the first three of following attributes, and two of the next three:

Part 1.   All of:

- The incident must be intentional.
- The incident must entail some level of violence or immediate threat of violence.
- The perpetrators of the incidents must be subnational actors.

Part 2.   And at least two of:

- The act must be aimed at attaining a political, economic, religious, or social goal.
- There must be evidence of an intention to coerce, intimidate, or convey some other message to a larger audience . . . than the immediate victims.
- The action must be outside the context of legitimate warfare activities.

These definitions are used to produce START's Global Terrorism Database (GTD), which is available to researchers and others through the START website.

As you might expect, counting terrorist incidents presents several challenges. Among these are varying definitions and inclusion criteria. For example, the U.S. Department of State publishes an annual report, *Country Reports on Terrorism*. Each year's report uses data from START, but to be consistent with State Department definitions, terrorist incidents are counted only if they meet all three criteria in Part 2.

Here is a sample tabulation from the 2016 report, distinguishing the number of attacks and the number of deaths for the 10 countries that experienced the most terrorist incidents in 2015. We show the total number of attacks and deaths worldwide.

Two things about this table are especially noteworthy. First, these are very large numbers: over 11,700 incidents in 2015. Second, the top 10 countries account for almost three-fourths of all attacks and deaths worldwide. Third, countries in the top 10 are concentrated in three regions: the Middle East, the Indian subcontinent (including Afghanistan), and northern Africa. Finally, in 2015 attacks were much more deadly for some countries (Nigeria and Syria) than for others (Bangladesh and Philippines). Whatever your reaction to this table, we suspect it is something other than "Oh, I knew that." We urge you to read more about measures and counts of terrorist incidents. The 2015 report also includes information on terrorist organizations, targets, types of weapons used, and summary descriptions of incidents in the top 10 countries. Even more narrative detail is available in the annual State Department Report (U.S. Department of State, 2016).

Measuring terrorist incidents is complicated by the fact that standards of definitions developed in the United States may be applied to actions that take place in other countries where definitions and recording rules may be different. Similarly, the definition used by START is slightly different from that specified by the State Department. Try to find at least one other example of that problem in this chapter.

Terrorist Attacks and Deaths

■ Top 10 Countries, 2015

Region	Attacks	Deaths	Deaths per attack
Iraq	2,418	6,932	2.99
Afghanistan	1,708	5,292	3.24
Pakistan	1,009	1,081	1.10
India	791	289	0.38
Nigeria	589	7,531	9.29
Egypt	494	656	1.34
Philippines	485	258	0.54
Bangladesh	459	75	0.16
Libya	428	462	1.24
Syria	382	1,698	7.99
Total top 10	8,763	24,274	
Total worldwide	11,774	32,762	
Top 10%	74%	74%	

Source: Adapted from National Consortium for the Study of Terrorism and Responses to Terrorism (START) 2016, 5.

Introduction

Measures of crime are important for many criminal justice research purposes.

Having discussed the principles of measurement and measurement quality, we now turn to a basic task for criminal justice researchers: measuring crime. Crime is a fundamental variable in criminal justice and criminology. Descriptive and exploratory studies often seek to count how much crime exists in some specific area, a question of obvious concern to criminal justice officials as well as researchers. Explanatory studies, viewing crime as a dependent variable, seek to learn what causes crime; applied studies often focus on what actions might be effective in reducing crime.

Crime can also be an independent variable—for example, in a study of how crime affects fear or other attitudes, or whether people who live in high-crime areas are more likely than are others to favor long prison sentences for drug dealers. Sometimes crime can be both an independent and a dependent variable, as in a study about the relationship between drug use and other offenses.

Whatever our research purpose and whether we're interested in what causes crime or what crime causes, measuring crime clearly is important. It's also difficult; how to measure crime has long been a key research issue in criminology and criminal justice.

We have three objectives in this chapter. First, we'll use the challenge of measuring crime to illustrate the more general measurement issues we considered in Chapter 5. Second, we'll examine a range of available measures of crime and compare the strength and weaknesses of each. Finally, we'll briefly consider some independent measures of crime developed for specific research or policy purposes.

General Issues in Measuring Crime

Researchers must decide on offenses, units of analysis, and purposes before specifying measures of crime.

At the outset, we must acknowledge some broad questions that influence all measures of crime: (1) What offenses should be measured? (2) What units of analysis should be used? and (3) What is the research or policy purpose in measuring crime?

What Offenses?

Let's begin by proposing a conceptual definition of crime—one that will enable us to decide what specific types of crime we'll measure. Recall a definition from Michael Gottfredson and Travis Hirschi (1990:15) mentioned in Chapter 5: "Acts of force or fraud undertaken in pursuit of self-interest." This is an interesting definition, but it is better suited to an extended discussion of theories of crime than to our purposes in this chapter. For example, we would have to clarify what was meant by *self-interest*, a term that has engaged philosophers and social scientists for centuries.

James Q. Wilson and Richard Herrnstein (1985:22) propose a different definition that should get us started: "A crime is any act committed in violation of a law that prohibits it and authorizes punishment for its commission." Although other criminologists (such as Gottfredson and Hirschi) might not agree with this conceptual definition, it has the advantage of being reasonably specific. We could be even more specific by consulting a state or federal code and listing the type of acts for which the law provides punishment.

Our list would be very long. For example, the Indiana Code (IC) includes harvesting ginseng root out of season (IC 14-31-3-16)[1] and selling a switchblade knife (IC 35-47-5-2) as acts punishable by six months' incarceration and a $1,000 fine. Taking Indiana ginseng out of the state without permission (IC 14-31-3-20) and assault resulting in nonserious bodily injury to an adult (IC 35-42-2-1) are equivalent crimes that could bring a year's incarceration and a fine of $5,000. However we decide to measure crime, we certainly want to distinguish acts of violence and the sale of illegal weapons from irregularities concerning rare herbs.

One of the principal difficulties we encounter when we try to measure crime is that many different types of behaviors and actions are included in our conceptualization of crime as an "act committed in violation of a law that prohibits it and authorizes punishment for its commission." Different measures tend to focus on different types of crime, primarily because not all crimes can be measured the same way with any degree of reliability or validity. Therefore, one important step in selecting a measure is deciding what crimes will be included.

What Units of Analysis?

Recall that units of analysis are the specific entities about which researchers collect information. Chapter 4 considered individuals, groups, social artifacts, and other units of analysis. Deciding

---

[1]This citation reflects the standard form of references to a "code"—the body of all laws in effect for a jurisdiction, organized by subject. In this case, "IC" is the abbreviation for Indiana Code; the numbers cite title, article, chapter, and section. So this citation refers to Title 14, article 31, chapter 3, section 16 of the Indiana Code. "USC" refers to the United States Code, that body of federal laws in effect for the United States.

how to measure crime requires that we once again think about these units.

Crimes involve four elements that are often easier to recognize in the abstract than they are to actually measure. The most basic of these elements is the offender. Without an offender, there's no crime, so a crime must, at a minimum, involve an offender. The offender is therefore one possible unit of analysis. We might decide to study burglars, auto thieves, bank robbers, terrorists (or terrorist groups), drug dealers, or people who have committed many different types of offenses.

Crimes also require some sort of victim, the second possible unit of analysis. We could study victims of burglary, auto theft, bank robbery, or assault. Notice that this list of victims includes different types of units: households or businesses for burglary, car owners for auto theft, banks for bank robbery, and individuals for assault. Some of these units are organizations (banks and businesses), some are individual people, some are abstractions (households), and some are ambiguous (individuals or organizations can own automobiles).

UNITS OF ANALYSIS AND MEASURING CRIME

Figuring out the different units of analysis in counting crimes can be difficult and confusing at first. Much of the problem comes from the possibility of what database designers call one-to-many and many-to-many relationships. The same incident can have multiple offenses, offenders, and victims, or just one of each. Fortunately, thinking through some examples usually clarifies the matter. Our two examples are adapted from an FBI publication (2000:18).

Example 1

Two males entered a bar. The bartender was forced at gunpoint to hand over all money from the cash register. The offenders also took money and jewelry from three customers. One of the offenders used his handgun to beat one of the customers, thereby causing serious injury. Both offenders fled on foot.

    1 incident
        1 robbery offense
        2 offenders
        4 victims (bar cash, 3 patrons)
        1 aggravated assault offense
        2 offenders
        1 victim

Even though only one offender actually assaulted the bar patron, the other offender would be charged with assisting in the offense because he prevented others from coming to the aid of the assault victim.

Example 2

Two males entered a bar. The bartender was forced at gunpoint to hand over all money from the cash register. The offenders also took money and jewelry from two customers. One of the offenders, in searching for more people to rob, found a female customer in a back room and raped her there, outside of the view of the other offender. When the rapist returned, both offenders fled on foot.

This example includes two incidents because the rape occurred in a different place and the offenders were not acting in concert. And because they were not acting in concert in the same place, only one offender was associated with the rape incident.

    Incident 1
        1 robbery offense
        2 offenders
        3 victims (bar cash, 2 patrons)
    Incident 2
        1 rape offense
        1 offender
        1 victim

What about so-called victimless crimes like drug use or prostitution? In a legal sense, victimless crimes do not exist because crimes are acts that injure society, organizations, and/or individuals. But studying crimes in which society is the principal victim—prostitution, for example—presents special challenges, and specialized techniques have been developed to measure certain types of victimless crimes. In any event, it's crucial to think about units of analysis in advance. Later, we will examine surveying victims as one approach to counting crime. But surveying individuals, organizations, and society involves fundamentally different tasks.

The final two elements of crimes—offense and incident—are closely intertwined and so will be discussed together. An *offense* is defined as an individual act of burglary, auto theft, bank robbery, and so on. The Federal Bureau of Investigation (FBI) defines *incident* as "one or more offenses committed by the same offender, or group of offenders *acting in concert, at the same time and place*" (Federal Bureau of Investigation, 2000:17; emphasis in original).

Think about the difference between offense and incident for a moment. A single incident can include multiple offenses, but it's not possible to have one offense and multiple incidents. Of course, a single incident could include multiple victims. For example, the opening box shows two different units involved in measuring terrorism: terrorist incidents, and deaths from terrorist attacks. The final column in the sample table shows quite a lot of variation in the numbers of deaths per attack.

To illustrate the different units of analysis—offenders, victims, offenses, and incidents—consider the examples in the box titled "Units of Analysis and Measuring Crime." These examples help distinguish units from each other and illustrate the links among different units.

Notice that we have said nothing about aggregate units of analysis, a topic we examined in Chapter 4. We have considered only individual units, even though measures of crime are often reported for aggregate units of analysis—neighborhoods, cities, counties, states, and so on. As we will see later in this chapter, aggregate counts of crime are among the measures most commonly reported to the general public.

What Purpose?

Different strategies for measuring crime can be distinguished by their general purpose. Measuring crime has at least one of three general purposes: (1) monitoring, (2) agency accountability, and (3) research.

We measure crime for the purpose of monitoring in much the same way that we measure consumer prices, stock market activity, traffic fatalities, birthrates, population, unemployment, and high school graduation rates. This reflects more than a mere compulsion for counting things. We measure a variety of social, economic, demographic, and public health indicators to keep track of social and economic conditions, the size and age distribution of the population, and threats to public health. By the same token, one purpose for measuring crime is to monitor potential threats to public safety and security.

At the national level, two series of crime measures seek to assess "the magnitude, nature, and impact of crime in the Nation [*sic*]" (U.S. Department of Justice, 2003:1). We'll examine the Uniform Crime Reports (UCR) and the National Crime Victimization Survey (NCVS) in detail later in this chapter. Here, we point out that the fundamental purpose for these two measures is monitoring. In the field of public health, this is referred to as a **surveillance system** (Parks et al., 2014). Just as a variety of statistical series administered by the U.S. Public Health Service monitor the incidence of disease and death rates from various causes, the U.S. Department of Justice oversees two nationwide surveillance systems for measuring crime.

The second measurement purpose is agency accountability. Government agencies are obliged to keep records that document their actions and areas of responsibility. Such accountability is a basic principle of the U.S. version of democratic government and is one reason individual police departments measure crime. "You can't manage what you can't measure," states the title page on Idaho's 2015 state crime report, underscoring the significance of accountability (Idaho State Police, 2016).

The final purpose is research; measures of crime are made for research purposes that are distinct from the purpose of surveillance or accountability. We emphasize these different purposes for a reason we'll encounter throughout this and subsequent chapters. Criminal justice research often uses measures of crime that are collected for surveillance or accountability purposes, not for research. It's worth keeping that point in mind when planning a research project that will measure crime with one or more existing data series.

Crimes Known to Police

Police-based crime measures are the most widely used, but they are subject to certain types of error.

The most widely used measures of crime are based on police records and are commonly referred to as **crimes known to police**. This phrase has important implications for understanding what police records do and do not measure. One obvious implication is that crimes not known to police cannot be measured by consulting police records. We can better understand the significance of this by considering the two ways police come to know about crime: observation and reports from other people.

Certain types of crimes are detected almost exclusively by observation, such as traffic offenses and so-called victimless crimes. Police count drug sales because they observe the transaction; they count incidents of prostitution because they witness solicitations. Obviously, police detect traffic offenses through observation. Most other crimes, however, are detected and counted because they are reported to police by other people—victims or witnesses. Victims report burglaries, robberies, assaults, auto thefts, and other offenses to police; witnesses also report crimes.

Recognizing that police measure crime in these two ways—observation and reports by others—we can think readily of crimes that are not well measured by police records. Consider shoplifting,

for example. Many instances of shoplifting are observed neither by police nor by other people who might report them to police. Those instances are not detected and therefore not measured. Shoplifting certainly is included in our conceptual definition—an act committed in violation of a law that prohibits it and that authorizes punishment. However, measuring shoplifting by counting crimes known to police would omit many offenses.

Thinking about crime measured almost exclusively by police observation—victimless crimes and traffic offenses—should make you realize that crimes known to police are not a good measure of these types of offenses either. Most of us have committed traffic offenses and not been caught. Similarly, most instances of drug sales, not to mention drug possession, are not detected.

The other way police measure crime is also imperfect. Many crimes are not reported to police, especially minor thefts and certain types of assaults. People don't report crimes for several reasons, which tend to vary by type of crime. Attempted thefts may not be reported because no property was lost. Many minor assaults or other personal crimes are considered by victims to be private matters that they will settle themselves without involving the police. Other victims may believe that minor losses are not important enough to trouble police or that reporting a crime would make no difference, because police could neither capture the offender nor recover the stolen property (Bureau of Justice Statistics, 2015:7).

Another problem with police measurement of crime undermines the meaning of the phrase "crimes known to police." Research has shown what some people may have personally experienced: Police do not always make official records of crimes they observe or crimes reported to them. Donald Black (1970) and Albert Reiss (1971) described a number of factors that influence police decisions on whether to officially record crimes they know about. For example, assaults between people who know each other well or are related to each other are less likely to be recorded as assaults than are fights between strangers. If a victim urges a police officer not to arrest someone or not to press charges against an offender, the officer is less likely to treat the incident as a crime. Black also found that police more often made

Crimes known to police Crimes reported to police and recorded by police.

official crime reports for incidents that involved victims of higher socioeconomic status. In cases where someone is repeatedly victimized, usually by the same offender, police record later incidents less frequently. Research in India (Belur et al., 2015) and in New Jersey (Mele, 2003) finds nonrecording of repeat incidents for domestic violence.

Similarly, Sean Varano and associates (2009) examined police recording of incidents in different neighborhoods in San Antonio, Texas. After controlling for police workload and crime seriousness, the researchers found that police did not make official records of many types of incidents that had been reported. No differences were found for serious crimes like robbery. However, Varano and associates discovered that offenses such as disturbances and minor property crimes were less likely to become part of official statistics in the more disadvantaged Latino and black neighborhoods of San Antonio. Police non-recording practices have also been studied in Canada. Boivin and Cordeau (2011) examine declines in Montreal recorded crime that correspond with police slowdowns in periods of collective bargaining.

Uniform Crime Reports

Police measures of crime form the basis for the FBI's Uniform Crime Reports (UCR), a data series that has been collected since 1930 and has been widely used by criminal justice researchers. However, certain characteristics and procedures related to the UCR affect how it can be used as a measure of crime. Most of our discussion highlights shortcomings in this regard, but keep in mind that the UCR is still an essential measure for researchers and public officials. Thinking carefully about what the UCR does and does not measure enhances its value as a research tool.

Because UCR data are based on crimes reported to police, they share the measurement problems we have just discussed. However, the FBI crime counts are subject to four additional sources of measurement error.

First, the UCR does not even try to count all crimes reported to police. Eight offense types are recorded if these offenses are reported to police (and recorded by police). These eight types include four violent offenses (murder and non-negligent manslaughter, forcible rape, robbery, and aggravated assault) and four property crime offenses (burglary, larceny-theft, motor vehicle theft, and arson) (Federal Bureau of Investigation, 2012). An additional 20 offenses are counted only if a person has been arrested and charged with a crime. The UCR therefore does not include such offenses as drug sale or use, fraud, prostitution, simple assault, vandalism, receiving stolen property, and all other nontraffic offenses unless someone is arrested. This means that a large number of crimes reported to police are not measured in the UCR.

Second, one of the reasons many offenses are counted only if an arrest is made is that individual states have different definitions of crimes. The operational definition of crime can vary from state to state, and this introduces another source of measurement error into the FBI data. For example, the state of Louisiana includes verbal threats in its counts of assaults, but most other states do not (Justice Research and Statistics Association, 1996:20).

The third source of undercounting is a result of the aggregation of local-level crime reports to the national level. The FBI compiles its UCR figures from data submitted by individual states or local law enforcement agencies. In some states, local police and sheriffs' departments send their crime reports to a state agency, which forwards the data to the FBI. In other states, local law enforcement agencies send crime data directly to the FBI. However, not all local police and sheriffs' departments send complete crime report data to either their state agency or the FBI. Inconsistency also exists in the quality of data submitted. In other words, individual states, cities, and counties vary in the quality and completeness of crime data sent to the FBI and reported in the annual UCR publication, *Crime in the United States*. Just as the decennial census cannot count everyone who lives in the United States, the FBI is not able to reliably count all crimes—either Part I or Part II offenses—that occur in the United States. In some cases, especially since the early 1990s, only a small fraction of law enforcement agencies in a state report under the UCR program. Michael Maltz (1999) describes the scope of this problem and efforts to estimate the amount of missing reports.

Reporting has become more uniform in recent years, but gaps remain for some states. For example, data for forcible rape in Minnesota were only available for the state's two largest cities over the years 2006–2010. Forcible rape was estimated for the rest of Minnesota using national averages broken down by population size (Federal Bureau of Investigation, 2011, Methodology Section, page 13).

UCR data can also suffer from clerical, data processing, and, in some cases, political problems. For example, Henry Brownstein (1996) describes his experience as a senior analyst in the New York Division of Criminal Justice Services, a state agency that compiles local crime reports for submission under the UCR program. The accuracy of data from cities and counties in New York is affected by staff shortages that undermine efforts to verify local reports, maintenance of an aging computer program that compiles UCR reports, and what Brownstein calls the "New York City reconciliation." Here is how he describes that problem (1996:22–23):

> As localities and agencies within localities compete amongst themselves for a greater share of State resources, they all compete to show that they are responsible for a greater share of the problem that the resources will be used to solve. Consequently, everyone wants credit for reported crimes and arrests. In New York City, where there are so many competing jurisdictions and agencies, this translates as a problem of duplicate reporting. So every summer a senior data entry clerk conducts the reconciliation, separating out by hand and by assumption the duplicate reports of the same crimes and arrests submitted by different jurisdictions and agencies.

A more recent example stems from research by John Eterno and Eli Silverman (2010) who interviewed samples of retired New York City police commanders (at the rank of captain or higher). Respondents described how they were pressured by higher-level commanders to continue bringing New York crime rates down. It is claimed that such pressures routinely led police to "downgrade" crime reports to less-serious offenses.

The final source of measurement error in the UCR is produced by the hierarchy rule used by police agencies and the FBI to classify crimes. Under the hierarchy rule, if multiple crimes are committed in a single incident, only the most serious is counted in the UCR. Here's an example from the FBI *Uniform Crime Reporting Handbook* (Federal Bureau of Investigation, 2004:11):

> A burglar broke into a home, stole several items, and placed them in a car belonging to the owner of the home. The homeowner returned and surprised the thief, who in turn knocked the owner unconscious by hitting him over the head with a chair. The burglar drove away in the homeowner's car.
>
> **Applying the Hierarchy Rule to crime reporting:** A Burglary—Forcible Entry (5a), Larceny-theft (6), Robbery—Other Dangerous Weapon (3c), Aggravated Assault—Other Dangerous Weapon (4d), and Motor Vehicle Theft—Auto (7a) occurred in this situation. After classifying the offenses, the reporting agency must score only one offense—Robbery—Other Dangerous Weapon (3c)—the crime appearing first in the list of Part I offenses.

In the examples described in the box "Units of Analysis and Measuring Crime," the UCR would count one offense in each incident: a single robbery in the first example and rape in the second.

The UCR and Criteria for Measurement Quality

Let's now consider how using the UCR to operationalize and measure crime satisfies the criteria for measurement quality we discussed in Chapter 5. Are the UCR data exclusive, exhaustive, valid, and reliable? First, the UCR clearly is neither an exclusive nor an exhaustive measure. Many crimes are not counted (nonexhaustive), and the hierarchy rule means that crime definitions are not strictly exclusive, because only the most serious crime is counted in an incident in which multiple crimes are committed. It does not help us if, for example, we are especially interested in burglary because burglaries are not counted if a rape, robbery, or murder is committed in the same incident.

Because the UCR does not count all crimes, we can rightly question its validity. The UCR does not really measure the concept of crime as we have defined it: any act committed in violation of a law that prohibits it and authorizes punishment for its commission. If we had defined crime more specifically, such as crimes known to police and recorded in police files, the UCR would be a more valid measure.

Finally, is the UCR a reliable measure? Not all law enforcement agencies submit complete reports to the FBI, and the quality of the data submitted varies. Inconsistencies in reporting and pressures to reclassify incidents, such as those reported by Eterno and Silverman (2010), raise questions about the reliability of UCR data.

Recognizing the importance of accurate crime data, the FBI has been pursuing several initiatives to enhance the validity and reliability of crimes known to police. First, under its Quality Assurance Review (QAR) program, staff from the FBI Criminal Justice Information Services Division audit crime data submitted by samples of reporting agencies. Results from this data quality review are shared with staff from state agencies. Under QAR guidelines, state UCR submissions are intended to be reviewed every three years (Federal Bureau of Investigation, 2011). Second, staff from the FBI Crime Statistics Management Unit conduct on-site training to enhance the accuracy and consistency of data submitted by state agencies. A third FBI initiative is actually a from-the-ground-up overhaul of crime reporting, a topic we will examine in the next section. The "UCR Quality Assurance Review" Web page (https://www.fbi.gov/about-us/cjis/ucr/quality-assurance. Accessed 3 July 2016) includes a variety of forms that are designed to enhance the accuracy of Uniform Crime Reports.

Before we move on to other approaches to measuring crime, consider how units of analysis figure into UCR data. The UCR system produces what is referred to as a **summary-based measure** of crime. This means that UCR data include summary, or total, crime counts for reporting agencies; in most cases, these are cities or counties. UCR data, therefore, represent groups as units of analysis. Crime reports are available for cities or counties, and these may be aggregated upward to measure crime for states or regions of the United States. But UCR data available from the FBI cannot represent individual crimes, offenders, or victims as units.

Recall that it is possible to aggregate units of analysis to higher levels, but it is not possible to disaggregate grouped data to the individual level. Because UCR data are aggregates, they cannot be used in descriptive or explanatory studies that focus on individual crimes, offenders, or victims. UCR data are, therefore, restricted to the analysis of such units as cities, counties, states, or regions.

Incident-Based Police Records

The U.S. Department of Justice sponsors two series of police-based crime measures that are based on incidents as units of analysis. The first of these **incident-based measures**, Supplementary Homicide Reports (SHR), was begun in 1961 and is a spin-off from the UCR program, as implied by the word *supplementary*.

Local law enforcement agencies submit detailed information about individual homicide incidents under the SHR program. This includes information about victims and, if known, offenders (age, gender, and race); the relationship between victim and offender; the weapon used; the location of the incident; and the circumstances surrounding the killing.

Notice how the SHR relates to our discussion of units of analysis. Incidents are the basic unit and can include one or more victims and offenders; because the series is restricted to homicides, offense is held constant.

Because the SHR is an incident-based system, investigators can use SHR data to conduct descriptive and explanatory studies of individual events. For example, it's possible to compare the relationship between victim and offender for male victims and female victims, or to compare the types of weapons used in killings by strangers and killings

Summary-based measure Aggregated crime counts such as those submitted to the UCR from law enforcement agencies.

Incident-based measures Police reports based on individual crime incidents.

by non-strangers. Such analyses are not possible if we are studying homicide using UCR summary data. If our unit of analysis is jurisdiction—city or county, for example—we can examine only the aggregate number of homicides in each jurisdiction for a given year; it will not be possible to say anything about individual homicide incidents.

Crime measures based on incidents as units of analysis, therefore, have several advantages over summary measures. It's important to keep in mind, however, that SHR data still represent crimes known to police and recorded by police. Of course, records of homicides will be better represented in police records than will, say, records of shoplifting, but clerical and other errors can still be a factor. Michael Maxfield (1989) discusses some general validity concerns with respect to the SHR. Scott Decker and David Pyrooz (2010) found that SHR on gang-related homicides were less reliable and valid than data from a more specialized series collected by the National Gang Center. Most potential errors in the SHR are due to recording and record-keeping practices, topics we will discuss in Chapter 12.

The National Incident-Based Reporting System

The most ambitious development in police-based measures at the national level is the ongoing effort by the FBI and the Bureau of Justice Statistics (BJS) to convert the UCR to a National Incident-Based Reporting System (NIBRS, pronounced nybers). Planning for replacement of the UCR began in the mid-1980s, but because NIBRS represents major changes, law enforcement agencies continue to shift gradually to the new system.

About 18,000 law enforcement agencies report UCR summary data each year; that's 18,000 annual observations, one for each reporting agency. According to an annual report issued by the Idaho State Police (2016), 107 agencies in Idaho reported UCR data in 2015, so Idaho submitted a maximum of 107 observations for 2015. Under NIBRS, Idaho reported over 80,500 incidents in 2015. So, for Idaho, shifting from the summary UCR system for measuring crime to the incident-based NIBRS system meant shifting

from 107 units (UCR reporting jurisdictions) to more than 80,500 units. In other words, rather than reporting 107 summary crime counts for eight UCR offense types, Idaho reported detailed information on 80,734 individual incidents. And this is Idaho, which ranked 39th among the states in 2013 resident population!

These numbers illustrate the most obvious difference between NIBRS and the UCR system: reporting each crime incident rather than reporting a summary of certain crimes for each law enforcement agency. But the significance of shifting from reporting *aggregate numbers* to reporting *individual incidents* lies in the type of information that is available about each incident. In essence, NIBRS measures many features of each incident, and each of these features is reported individually. Table 6.1 lists most of the "segments" or categories of information recorded for each incident, together with examples of the information recorded within each segment.

TABLE 6.1 Selected Information in National Incident-Based Reporting System Records

Administrative Segment	Offense Segment
Incident date and time	Offense type
Reporting agency ID	Attempted or Completed
Other ID numbers	Offender drug/ alcohol use
	Location type
	Weapon use

Victim Segment	Offender Segment
Victim ID number	Offender ID number
Offense type	Offender age, gender, race
Victim age, gender, race	
Resident of jurisdiction?	
Type of injury	
Relationship to offender	
Victim type:	
Individual person	
Business	
Government	
Society/public	

Source: Adapted from Federal Bureau of Investigation (2000:6–8, 90).

As Table 6.1 shows, NIBRS includes much more detailed information about individual incidents, together with the offenses, offenders, and victims within each incident. Referring back to our earlier discussion of the elements of crime—incidents, offenders, offenses, and victims—notice how the information in Table 6.1 is organized around each incident. Each incident can include one or more offenses, offenders, and victims, as we described in the box, "Units of Analysis and Measuring Crime."

In addition, NIBRS guidelines call for gathering information about a much broader array of offenses. Whereas the UCR reports information about eight offenses, NIBRS is designed to collect detailed information on 49 "Group A" offenses. Table 6.2 demonstrates the significance of this by showing NIBRS crime data for Idaho in 2015. Compare the top part of the table, reporting crime counts for eight UCR offenses, to the bottom part. Additional NIBRS Group A offenses more than double the number of crimes "known to police" in Idaho (32,717 UCR, plus 48,011 additional Group A). Simple assault and drug violations are the most common of these additional offenses, but drug equipment violations accounted for almost 8,800 additional offenses in 2015.

Collecting detailed information on each incident for each offense, victim, and offender, and doing so for a large number of offense types, represents the most significant changes in NIBRS compared with the UCR. Dropping the hierarchy rule is also a major change, but that is a consequence of incident-based reporting. NIBRS incorporates additional important changes. These and data for reporting agencies in 2014 are presented on an FBI NIBRS Web page (Federal Bureau of Investigation, 2015. Accessed 5 July 2016).

1. *Victim type.* Table 6.1 lists most categories for victim type; the most notable of these is "society/public," a category that has the effect of annulling the phrase "victimless crime." Whereas UCR summary data combine all types of victims (individuals, businesses, and others) into one summary measure, NIBRS makes it possible to distinguish different categories of victims.

TABLE 6.2 Crime in Idaho, 2015

UCR Summary Offenses	
Murder, non-negligent manslaughter	30
Rape	537
Robbery	192
Aggravated assault	2,620
Burglary	5,804
Larceny	21,407
Motor vehicle theft	1,888
Arson	239
Subtotal	32,717

Additional NIBRS Group A Offenses	
Simple assault	11,335
Intimidation	1,408
Bribery	3
Counterfeit/forgery	677
Destruction of property	8,582
Drug violations	9,829
Drug equipment violations	8,793
Embezzlement	135
Extortion/blackmail	17
Fraud	4,172
Gambling	0
Kidnapping/abduction	140
Pornography/obscene material	204
Prostitution	34
Forcible sex offenses	1,035
Nonforcible sex offenses	128
Stolen property	499
Weapons violations	1,020
Subtotal	48,011
Group A Total	80,728

Source: Adapted from Idaho State Police, "Crime in Idaho, 2015," https://www.isp.idaho.gov/BCI/CrimeInIdaho/CrimeInIdaho2015/Complete.pdf

2. *Attempted/completed.* UCR summary reports include both attempted and completed offenses, but it's not possible to distinguish them. NIBRS adds a category to indicate whether each offense within each incident was attempted or completed.

3. *Drug-related offenses*. NIBRS includes provisions to assess offender drug use in nondrug offenses and to record whether drugs or drug paraphernalia were seized.

4. *Known offenders*. Much violent crime involves victims and offenders who know each other, and have some sort of prior relationship. Of the almost 1.3 million victims of violence reported in NIBRS in 2014, over 54 percent knew their offenders, but had no family relationship. An additional 25 percent were related to their offenders (Federal Bureau of Investigation, 2015, summary of 2014 crime statistics).

NIBRS and Criteria for Measurement Quality

You now have some idea about the potential wealth of information available from NIBRS and the ways in which this new system represents major changes from the summary-based UCR. How does incident-based reporting fare on our criteria for measurement quality? After considering NIBRS in light of our earlier comments on the summary-based UCR, some improvements are clearly evident. Eliminating the hierarchy rule means that offense classifications are mutually exclusive. Is NIBRS exhaustive? Table 6.2 lists more offenses compared with the UCR, but additional offenses are recorded only for crimes that result in arrest; not all crimes are counted.

In at least one sense, NIBRS data hold the promise of being more reliable. The FBI has produced very thorough documentation on how to record and classify incidents and their component records. Creating auditing standards also enhances reliability. The FBI requires that state records systems be certified before the state can submit incident-based reports. Finally, the Justice Research and Statistics Association (JRSA), an organization that serves state criminal justice statistics agencies, has developed a number of resources that help states develop and implement incident-based data systems.

Victim survey Measure of crime obtained by asking people about their experiences as victims.

Many of these are linked to the JRSA website (http://jrsa.org/ibrrc).

Measuring Crime Through Victim Surveys

Victim surveys are alternative measures of crime, but are still subject to error.

Recognizing the shortcomings associated with using measures of crime known to police, we now consider alternative approaches. Conducting a **victim survey** that asks people whether they have been the victim of a crime is one alternative. Survey research methods will be described in detail in Chapter 9. For now, we assume that you have a general understanding of what a survey involves: presenting a sample of people with carefully worded questions and recording their responses.

Measuring crime through surveys has many strong points. Surveys can obtain information on crimes that were not reported to police. Asking people about victimizations can also measure incidents that police may not have officially recorded as crimes. Asking people about crimes that may have happened to them provides data on victims and offenders (individuals) and on the incidents themselves (social artifacts). Finally, we can compare survey respondents who were victims of different kinds of offenses to respondents who were not victims. Like an incident-based reporting system, therefore, a survey can provide more disaggregated units of analysis. When conducted in a rigorous, systematic fashion, surveys can yield reliable measures.

The National Crime Victimization Survey

Since 1972, the U.S. Census Bureau has conducted national surveys of crime and victimization, currently known as the National Crime Victimization Survey (NCVS). An earlier version of the NCVS was launched following pilot studies in the mid-1960s by President Lyndon Johnson's Commission on Law Enforcement and Administration of Justice, commonly known as the President's Crime Commission. One of the primary reasons for conducting crime surveys was to illuminate what came to be referred to as the **dark figure of unreported crime**. The NCVS is based on a nationally representative sample of households and uses uniform procedures to select and interview respondents, which enhances the reliability of crime measures. Because individual people living in households are interviewed, the NCVS can be used for studies in which individuals or households are the unit of analysis.

The NCVS cannot measure all crimes, however, in part because of the procedures used to select victims. Because the survey is based on a sample of households, it cannot count crimes in which businesses or commercial establishments are the victims. Bank robberies, liquor store holdups, shoplifting, embezzlement, political corruption, and securities fraud are examples of crimes that cannot be systematically counted by interviewing household members. Samples of banks, gas stations, retail stores, business establishments, elected officials, or stockbrokers would be needed to measure those crimes. In much the same fashion, crimes directed at homeless victims cannot be counted by surveys of households like the NCVS.

What about "victimless" crimes? For example, think about how you would respond to a Census Bureau interviewer who asked whether you had been the victim of a drug sale. If you have bought drugs from a dealer, you might think of yourself as a customer rather than as a victim. Or if you lived near a park where drug sales were common, you might think of yourself as a victim even though you did not participate in a drug transaction. The point is that victim surveys are not good measures of victimless crimes because the respondents can't easily be conceived as victims.

Measuring certain forms of delinquency through victim surveys presents similar problems. Status offenses such as truancy and curfew violations do not have identifiable victims who can be included in samples based on households. Homicide and manslaughter are other crimes that are not well measured by victim surveys, for obvious reasons.

Because the NCVS excludes many types of crimes by design, you should recognize potential validity problems. But what about the reliability of crime surveys in general and the NCVS in particular? Because it is a survey, the NCVS is subject to the errors and shortcomings associated with that method of measuring concepts. In the following paragraphs, we will consider some reliability problems that sometimes emerge when surveys are used to count crime.

In the 2014 NCVS, interviewers began the section of the survey on victimization with this introduction: "I'm going to read some examples that will give you an idea about the kinds of crime this study covers. As I go through them, tell me if any of these happened to you in the last six months; that is, since [specific date]." Asking people about crime in this way brings up the possibility of different types of recall error. First, respondents simply may not remember some incidents. This problem is particularly acute for minor crimes such as theft and for people who may have been the victim of more than one crime in the six-month recall period.

The second recall problem, known as telescoping, involves respondents inaccurately recalling when an incident occurred. Forward telescoping means that people may respond to questions by mentioning crimes that occurred more than six months ago, thus bringing past incidents forward into the recall period. In contrast, backward telescoping means that respondents inaccurately recall recent crimes as occurring in the more distant past. Because the NCVS tries to count crimes that occur every six months, forward or backward telescoping can produce unreliable counts. However, the NCVS is designed to reduce the possibility of telescoping, in part by specifying the relatively short recall window of six months.

A different type of recall problem affects people who have been victimized several times during the six-month reference period. The Bureau of Justice Statistics (BJS) describes this as a problem with series victimizations, which are defined as six or more similar but separate crimes that the respondent cannot describe individually to an interviewer (U.S. Census Bureau, 2012). Series victimizations constitute a problem for surveys because it is not clear how they should be counted or combined with individual crimes that the respondent can describe separately. The potential impact of series victimizations is substantial, especially for violent crimes. For example, Michael

Planty and Kevin Strom (2007:191) estimate that if all series incidents involving simple assault were included in NCVS counts, the total number of victimizations could have increased by 81 percent in the year 2000.

Finally, the NCVS potentially underestimates incidents in which the victim and offender know each other—domestic violence or other assaults involving friends or acquaintances, for example. Respondents may not tell interviewers about non-stranger crimes for various reasons. Some domestic violence victims view the assaults as a personal problem, not as a crime, and so may not mention the incidents. Others may feel shame or embarrassment and not wish to talk about their experiences—victims of rape or domestic violence, for example. In addition, respondents who have been victimized by a family member may fear some further assault if they discuss a past incident.

NCVS Redesign

To address these and other concerns about the ability of the NCVS to measure different types of crime, the BJS has periodically revised the survey, most recently in 2006. Changes include how samples are drawn, how questions are phrased, and how interviews are conducted. We describe the most important changes here, primarily to illustrate how revisions to the survey affect measures of crime. Chapter 9 describes different features of surveys in general, and we return to the NCVS to illustrate these survey and sample principles.

Revisions completed in 1993 are the most substantial changes in core questionnaire content. Even though the redesign took effect approximately 20 years ago, we discuss it at some length here because it illustrates how features of survey design and questionnaire construction affect measures of crime. In addition, researchers continue to examine how changes in the NCVS have affected the quality of crime data produced (Cantor and Lynch, 2005; Lauritsen, 2005; Rand and Rennison, 2005).

For the most part, 1993 redesign efforts focused on obtaining better measures of domestic violence and sexual assault, together with methods to help respondents recall a broader range of incidents. Here is a brief summary of major changes undertaken to produce better measures

of victimization (Kinderman et al., 1997; U.S. Census Bureau, 1994):

- Revised screening questions and added cues throughout the interview to help respondents recall and distinguish minor incidents
- More direct questions on rape and other sexual crimes, reflecting the belief that people's willingness to discuss such incidents has increased in recent years
- Greater attention to measuring victimizations by someone the respondent knows, including incidents of domestic violence
- Gradual increase in the use of telephone interviews to replace in-person interviews
- An increase in the threshold for series victimizations from three to six, consistent with other efforts to help respondents distinguish individual victimizations

Before taking a look at how the redesigned NCVS affected victimization rates, let's consider the changes in survey screening questions. These are summarized in Table 6.3. The redesigned NCVS presents more specific questions and cues, in effect encouraging respondents to think about specific types of incidents. Notice in particular the explicit reference to "forced or unwanted sexual acts" in the redesigned survey; the old NCVS made no direct reference to rape or other sexual assaults, implicitly including them in the general categories of "attack you" and "try to attack you." Redesigned NCVS questions also refer more directly to offenses committed by someone known to the respondent:

> People often don't think of incidents committed by someone they know. Did you have something stolen from you OR were you attacked or threatened by
>
> (a) Someone at work or at school
> (b) A neighbor or friend
> (c) A relative or family member
> (d) Any other person you've met or known?

Table 6.4 compares estimates of victimization rates from the first years of the redesigned NCVS with rates from pre-redesign versions. Panel A, reproduced from a study examining violence

TABLE 6.3 Comparison of Old and Redesigned NCVS Screening Questions

General Screening Question

Old NCVS	Redesigned NCVS
Was anything stolen from you while you were away from home—for instance, at work, in a theater or restaurant, or while traveling?	Were you attacked or threatened OR did you have something stolen from you a. At home including the yard or porch b. At or near a friend's or neighbor's home c. At work or school d. In a place such as a shopping mall, laundry room, restaurant, bank, or airport e. While riding in any vehicle f. On the street or in a parking lot g. At such places as a party, theater, gym, picnic area, or while fishing or hunting OR h. Did anyone ATTEMPT to attack or attempt to steal anything belonging to you from any of these places?

Screening Questions for Violent Crimes

Old NCVS	Redesigned NCVS
Did anyone take something from you by using force, such as by a stickup, mugging, or threat? Did anyone TRY to rob you by using force or threatening to harm you? Did anyone beat you up, attack you, or hit you with something such as a rock or bottle? Were you knifed, shot at, or attacked with some other weapon by anyone at all? Did anyone THREATEN to beat you up or threaten you with a knife, gun, or some other weapon, NOT including telephone threats? Did anyone TRY to attack you in some other way?	Has anyone attacked or threatened you in any of these ways a. With any weapon such as a gun or knife b. With anything like a baseball bat, frying pan, scissors, or stick c. By something thrown, such as a rock d. Include any grabbing, punching, or kicking e. Any rape, attempted rape, or other type of sexual assault f. Any face-to-face threats OR g. Any attack or threat or use of force by anyone at all? Please mention it even if you were not certain it was a crime. Incidents involving forced or unwanted sexual acts are often difficult to talk about. Have you ever been forced or coerced to engage in unwanted sexual activity by a. Someone you didn't know before b. A casual acquaintance OR c. Someone you know well?

Source: Adapted from Bachman and Saltzman (1995:8).

against women (Bachman and Saltzman, 1995), shows rates of violent crime victimization by victim–offender relationship for males and females. Notice that the redesigned survey yields higher rates for all categories of relationship, but that the increase tends to be greater for non-stranger offenses. The category "intimate" includes both married persons and those in a quasi-marital or other intimate relationship. Redesigned survey results indicate that just less than 1 percent (9.3 per 1,000) of female respondents reported being the victim of a violent

TABLE 6.4 Comparison of Violent Victimization Rate, Old and Redesigned NCVS

Panel A: Average Annual Rate of Violent Victimizations per 1,000 Persons

Victim–Offender Relationship	Female	Male
Old NCVS (1987–91)		
Intimate	5.4	0.5
Other relative	1.1	0.7
Acquaintance/friend	7.6	13.0
Stranger	5.4	12.2
Redesigned NCVS (1992–93)		
Intimate	9.3	1.4
Other relative	2.8	1.2
Acquaintance/friend	12.9	17.2
Stranger	7.4	19.0

Source: Bachman and Saltzman (1995:8).

Panel B: Rate of Violent Victimizations per 1,000 Persons

Offense	Female	Male
1991 NCVS		
Rape	1.4	0.2
Robbery	3.5	7.8
Aggravated assault	4.4	11.5
Simple assault	13.4	20.9
1994 NCVS		
Rape and sexual assault	3.7	0.2
Robbery	4.1	8.1
Aggravated assault	8.1	15.3
Simple assault	26.6	35.9

Source: Bureau of Justice Statistics (1992:22) (1991 rates); Bureau of Justice Statistics (1996:4) (1994 rates).

offense by an intimate partner or former partner. Therefore, it appears that efforts to uncover more incidents of violence perpetrated by non-strangers have been successful.

Similarly, Panel B in Table 6.4 compares victimization rates for specific violent offenses; estimates of rape and sexual assault victimization rates for females were about 2.5 times higher in 1994 than in 1991. Notice, however, that the redesigned NCVS includes "sexual assault other than rape," so the estimates are not directly comparable. Males are more likely to be victims of both aggravated and simple assault, but as the redesigned NCVS shows, estimates of assault victimization rates increased more for females than for males. This is consistent with redesign efforts to obtain better estimates of violent offenses.

At this point, we want to underscore two general points about the 1993 redesign in particular and the NCVS in general. First, what we learn about crime from the NCVS or any other survey depends on *what* we ask and *how* we ask it. Keep in mind that measures of crime are affected in part by the procedures we use to make those measures. This is another example of an important point from Chapter 5: changing how we operationalize measures can change the values we obtain for those measures. Asking questions about specific kinds of violence discloses more crimes of violence than does asking rather general questions about being attacked by someone. Likewise, when we specifically ask respondents to think of acts committed by someone they know, we will uncover more offenses than if we do not include such cues and prompts. David Cantor and James Lynch (2005) describe other examples of how the redesigned survey affected victimization measures for different subgroups of respondents.

The second point is a consequence of the first: because of the redesigned NCVS, any effort to compare trends and changes in crime over time must account for changes in measurement. BJS analysts are attentive to this and caution readers of their reports to be aware of changes in survey methods: "Data based on the redesign are not comparable to data before 1993. . . . A number of fundamental changes were introduced when the survey was redesigned. These changes were phased into the sample over several years" (Bureau of Justice Statistics, 1996:8).

We emphasize these two points because beginning researchers are often less-critical users of data such as the NCVS than are more experienced researchers; after all, the survey is sponsored by the U.S. Department of Justice and conducted by the Census Bureau. Examining Table 6.4 without being aware of survey changes would suggest that violent victimization rates had increased sharply from 1991 to 1994, a conclusion that would be misleading.

Community Victimization Surveys

Following the initial development of victim survey methods in the late 1960s, the Census Bureau completed a series of city-level surveys. These were discontinued for a variety of reasons, but researchers and officials in the BJS occasionally conducted city-level victim surveys in specific communities. In 1998, the BJS and the Office of Community Oriented Policing Services (COPS) launched pilot surveys in 12 large and medium-sized cities (Smith et al., 1999).

The city-level initiative underscores one of the chief advantages of measuring crime through victim surveys: obtaining counts of incidents not reported to police. In large part, city-level surveys were promoted by BJS and COPS to enable local law enforcement agencies to better understand the scope of crime—reported and unreported—in their communities. Notice also the title of Smith et al.'s report: *Criminal Victimization and Perceptions of Community Safety in 12 Cities, 1998*. We emphasize *perceptions* to illustrate that city-level surveys can be valuable tools for implementing community policing. It is significant that the Department of Justice recognized the potential value of survey measures of crime and perceptions of community safety to develop and evaluate community policing.

The initial BJS/COPS effort was a pilot test of new methods for conducting city-level surveys. These bureaus jointly developed a guidebook and software so that local law enforcement agencies and other groups can conduct their own community surveys (Weisel, 1999). These tools also promise to be useful for researchers who wish to study local patterns of crime and individual responses.

Comparing Victim Surveys and Crimes Known to Police

Before moving on to the next section, let's briefly compare the different ways of measuring crime we have discussed so far.

Researchers have devoted special attention to comparing data from the UCR and the NCVS to determine how the two measures differ along with the strengths and weaknesses of each method are for measuring crime. An early study by Wesley Skogan (1974) recognized that crime surveys and police data take fundamentally different approaches to measuring crime, but that UCR and NCVS counts of robbery and auto theft are moderately related. Michael Rand and Callie Rennison (2002) demonstrate that adjusting NCVS and UCR data for basic design differences produces very similar estimates of violent crime. An even more ambitious effort by David Farrington, Patrick Langan, and Michael Tonry (2004) compares crime measures from police records and victim surveys for eight countries.

Whereas the UCR provides only summary measures of aggregate units, the NCVS yields more disaggregated data on individual victims, offenders, and incidents. This means that the NCVS is better suited to studies of individual factors in the types of incidents covered by the survey.

Because SHR and NIBRS data are incident-based systems, they can also be used to study individual incidents, victims, and offenders. However, the SHR measures one type of crime only. NIBRS holds great promise for the future, but its limited coverage means that it cannot yet serve as a measure of nationwide incidents known to police. For the present, NIBRS data can be used only for those states that currently participate in the program.

By the way, this feature of NIBRS—its availability from only certain local agencies and states—highlights another characteristic of the NCVS worth emphasizing: it is not possible to use survey data to study victimization at the local level. This is because the National Crime Victimization Survey is just that: a *national* survey. It is designed to represent nationwide levels of crime (subject to the limitations we have discussed), but it cannot provide statistically reliable estimates of crime for most cities, counties, or states. A report by Janet Lauritsen and Robin Schaum (2005) examines NCVS data for the nation's three largest cities: New York, Los Angeles, and Chicago. These three cities were also among those where BJS/COPS community victim surveys were conducted, as described by Smith and associates (1999). Researchers have begun to develop ways to produce state-level estimates of victimization. Fay and Diallo (2015) compare NCVS and UCR state-level estimates, as well as estimates for 65 counties with populations over 800,000.

Incident-based measures have great potential for criminal justice research, especially since the coverage of NIBRS continues to increase. In 2014 about one-third of all UCR law enforcement agencies submitted incident-based data, accounting for about 30 percent of all crime reported to the UCR. Like the NCVS, NIBRS yields details about individual incidents. Unlike the NCVS, NIBRS data can be examined for specific geographic areas at the local level and, eventually, for all states. Michael Maxfield (1999) summarizes many of the additional applications of NIBRS data for research and policy. We conclude this section by briefly discussing one area in which NIBRS data measure a type of offense not counted by other annual data series at the national level.

Despite improvements following the NCVS redesign, its sampling plan is still restricted to household residents age 12 and over. We have discussed the significance of a household-based sample. What kinds of offenses might the NCVS miss by not counting victimizations for individuals younger than 12?

Howard Snyder's (2000) analysis of NIBRS sexual assault data from 12 states provides a clue. About 34 percent of some 61,000 victims of sexual assault were under age 12; that means that over 20,000 sexual assault victims would not have been counted by the NCVS (Snyder, 2000:1–2). Furthermore, the expanded information available under NIBRS reveals that over 40 percent of sexual assault victims under age 12 were assaulted by a family member; an additional 50 percent of the offenders were known by the victims. Only about 5 percent of female victims under age 12 were assaulted by strangers.

These figures should make you think of child abuse, or at least child sexual abuse, as an offense type not measured by the NCVS. Of course, child abuse is undercounted by the UCR and NIBRS as well because much child abuse is not reported to police. NIBRS data represent new sources of information about this type of crime and other offenses that affect young victims.

Surveys of Offending

Delinquency, "victimless" crimes, and crimes rarely observed may be measured by self-report surveys.

Just as survey techniques can measure crime by asking people to describe their experiences as victims, **self-report surveys** ask people about crimes they may have committed. Initially we might be skeptical of this technique: How truthful are people when asked about crimes they may have committed? Our concern is justified in one sense. Many people do not wish to disclose illegal behavior to interviewers, even if they are assured of confidentiality. Others might deliberately lie to interviewers and exaggerate the number of offenses they have committed.

Self-report surveys, however, are the best method available for trying to measure certain crimes that are poorly represented by other techniques. Thinking about the other methods we have discussed—crimes known to police and victimization surveys—suggests several examples. Crimes such as prostitution and drug abuse are excluded from victimization surveys and underestimated by police records of people arrested for these offenses. Public order crimes and delinquency are other examples. A third class of offenses that might be better counted by self-report surveys are crimes that are rarely reported to or observed by police. Shoplifting and drunk driving are examples.

Think of it this way; as we saw earlier, all crimes require an offender. Not all crimes have clearly identifiable victims who can be interviewed, however, and not all crimes are readily observed by police, victims, or witnesses. If we can't observe the offense and can't interview a victim, what's the next logical step?

There are no nationwide efforts in the United States to systematically collect self-report measures for a comprehensive variety of crime types. Instead, periodic surveys yield information either on specific types of crime or on crimes committed by a specific target population. We will consider two ongoing self-report surveys here and comment on the validity and reliability of this method for measuring crime.

---

[2]Descriptive information about the National Survey on Drug Use and Health was obtained from the 2015 publication on survey results (Center for Behavioral Health Statistics and Quality 2015), website: https://nsduhweb.rti .org/respweb/homepage.cfm.

National Survey on Drug Use and Health[2]

Like the NCVS, the National Survey on Drug Use and Health (NSDUH) is based on a national sample of households. Both surveys are designed to monitor nationwide patterns. Unlike the victimization survey, however, the central purpose of the NSDUH is to obtain self-reports of drug use.

The survey has been conducted since 1971, with sampling and questioning procedures revised several times since then. The survey is currently sponsored by the Substance Abuse and Mental Health Services Administration in the U.S. Department of Health and Human Services. Persons age 12 and over who live in households are the target population. In the 2014 sample, approximately 67,900 individuals responded to questions regarding their use of illegal drugs, alcohol, and tobacco (Center for Behavioral Health Statistics and Quality, 2015). Because it has been conducted for over four decades, the NSDUH provides information on trends and changes in drug use among respondents.

Think for a moment about what sorts of questions we would ask to learn about people's experiences in using illegal drugs. Among other things, we would probably want to distinguish someone who tried marijuana once from people who used the drug more often. The drug use survey does this by including questions to distinguish *lifetime* use (ever used) of different drugs from *current* use (used within the past month). You may not agree that, for example, use in the past month represents current use, but it is the standard used in regular reports on NSDUH results. That's the operational definition of "current use."

Two potential sources of measurement problems with the NSDUH should come to mind. We have already touched on the first concern: Do people tell the truth when asked about drug use? The NSDUH incorporates certain procedures to encourage candid, truthful responses from individuals. After obtaining basic demographic information about all household residents, interviewers conduct the rest of the interviews in a private area away from other household members. Interviewers do not directly ask about drug use. Instead, these questions, and questions about other illegal behaviors, are administered through computer-assisted self-interviewing. Respondents read questions on a computer screen or listen to questions through earphones and key in their responses. The NSDUH continually revises question format and questionnaire design in an effort to improve the validity of self-report measures.

Although these procedures produce better measures of drug use than do interviews conducted by telephone, the NSDUH still underreports drug use—but it seems to vary by type of drug and age (Gfroerer, Eyerman, and Chromy, 2002). The circumstances of the NSDUH interview appear to affect reporting by adolescents (Gfroerer and Kennet, 2014). In earlier work, Joseph Gfroerer (1993) found higher reported rates of drug use by youths from surveys administered in the classroom compared with surveys administered at home. We will discuss an example of school-based surveys shortly, but let's first briefly consider the second source of concern in using the NSDUH as a measure of drug use.

Recall the earlier point about how the household sample design of the NCVS measures only victimizations that affect households or household residents. Commercial establishments, people in institutional quarters (such as military housing or work-release community corrections centers), and homeless people are not included in household samples. Although the NSDUH makes special efforts to include people living in such facilities as shelters or migrant worker camps, a household survey on drug use excludes many people who do not live in traditional households.

These comments notwithstanding, the NSDUH provides good estimates of drug use. More detail on methods is available on the survey's website: http://www.samhsa.gov/data/population-data-nsduh (accessed 6 July 2016).

Monitoring the Future[3]

Our second example is different in two respects: (1) it targets a specific population, and (2) it asks sampled respondents a broader variety of questions.

---

[3]Descriptive information about Monitoring the Future is drawn primarily from Johnston and associates (2016) and the website: http://monitoringthefuture.org/.

Since 1975, the National Institute on Drug Abuse has sponsored an annual survey of high school seniors, *Monitoring the Future: A Continuing Study of the Lifestyles and Values of Youth,* or Monitoring the Future (MTF) for short. As its long title implies, the MTF survey is intended to monitor the behaviors, attitudes, and values of young people. Researchers and policy makers continue to be interested in drug, alcohol, and tobacco use among youths, and the MTF has been used as something of a sentinel to measure such behaviors.

The MTF actually includes several samples of high school students and others groups, totaling almost 45,000 respondents in 2015 (Johnston et al., 2016). We'll begin with the high school sample, selected from students in 8th, 10th, and 12th grades, and then briefly mention the others.

Each spring, about 400 secondary schools are sampled within particular geographic areas. In larger high schools, samples of up to 350 seniors are selected; in smaller schools, all seniors may participate. The 2015 sample yielded responses from approximately 13,700 high school seniors. Students complete questionnaires containing batteries of questions that include self-reported use of alcohol, tobacco, and illegal drugs. In most cases, students record their answers in classrooms during normal school hours, although in some circumstances, students complete the questionnaires in larger groups. Surveys of students in the 8th and 10th grades are anonymous, whereas those administered to high school seniors are confidential so researchers can contact some respondents in later years.

The core sample of the MTF—surveys of high school seniors—thus provides a cross section for measuring annual drug use and other illegal acts. Each year a subset of about 2,400 MTF respondents from the high school samples is selected to receive a follow-up questionnaire in the mail. The follow-up samples provide MTF data from college students—those high school seniors who went on to college—and from adults.

Now recall our discussion of the time dimension in Chapter 4. Each year, both the MTF and the NSDUH measure drug use for a *cross section* of high school seniors and adults in households, thus providing a snapshot of annual rates of self-reported drug use. Examining annual results from the MTF and the NSDUH over time provides a *time series* or trend study that enables researchers and policy makers to detect changes in drug use among high school seniors, college students, and adults. Finally, the follow-up samples of MTF respondents constitute a series of panel studies whereby changes in drug use among individual respondents can be studied over time.

Because MTF measures for all samples are collected through self-reports, these data share the potential problems we mentioned in connection with the NSDUH. What about sampling procedures for the MTF? In one sense, selecting schools and then students within schools is a sound procedure for sampling high school seniors. But you should be able to think of at least one problem with this approach. Students who are absent on the day the survey is administered are not included and are not eligible for the follow-up sample. We might reasonably expect that students with poor attendance records are absent more often and thus less represented in the sample. And because our interest in the MTF is as a measure of drug use and offending, we might suspect that students with poor attendance records might have higher rates of drug use and offending.

Validity and Reliability of Self-Report Measures

This chapter cannot supply the final word on efforts to validate self-report measures. On the one hand, the final word has not yet been written; on the other, a small number of researchers have examined the issue in some detail. In most cases, the latter studies compare self-reported offending with other measures—usually, records of offending from law enforcement and juvenile justice agencies. You may recognize this as an example of convergent validity, a topic from Chapter 5.

For example, in their study of London delinquents (mentioned in Chapter 5), Donald West and David Farrington (1977:22) compared official criminal records to self-reported delinquent convictions disclosed in interviews with their subjects. Only a small proportion of subjects failed to mention one or more delinquent acts that appeared in criminal records. After further study, West and Farrington concluded that these omissions were due more to memory lapses than to untruthful responses, because most inconsistencies between the sources occurred for high-rate delinquents. A recent follow-up study of these subjects confirmed the validity of self-reports relative to police measures of adult offending (Kazemian and Farrington, 2005).

In another longitudinal study of a sample of Pittsburgh youths, David Farrington and associates (1996) examined convergent validity by again comparing self-reported offending and arrests with official records of arrests and juvenile petitions. Because it was a longitudinal panel study, interviewing the sample at multiple time points, the authors were able to estimate predictive validity by comparing self-reported delinquency at one time period with arrests and juvenile petitions at later times. As you might expect, the relationship is imperfect, but the researchers did find that subjects who self-reported higher levels of more serious offenses at time one were much more likely to have official arrest or delinquency records at time two.

Two additional studies of self-report validity lead us into a summary of this method of measuring crime. Michael Maxfield, Barbara Luntz Weiler, and Cathy Spatz Widom (2000) show that the convergence of self-reported and official records of arrests varies by gender, ethnicity, and type of offense. In a study of the long-term consequences of child abuse, the authors show that female and nonwhite subjects less often report known arrests. All subjects were more likely to self-report offenses that are more common—most notably, drug use.

A special sample that paralleled the NSDUH in 2000 and 2001[4] obtained urine and hair specimens to assess their correspondence with self-reported drug use (Harrison et al., 2007). Researchers found high levels of agreement between self-reported drug use and results from urine tests: 92.5 percent for marijuana use and 98.5 percent for cocaine use in the seven days before the interview.

---

[4]During those years, the survey was called the "National Household Survey of Drug Abuse."

Self-Report Surveys Summarized

Researchers and policy makers are best advised to be *critical users* of measures obtained from self-report surveys. Self-reports can and should be used to measure offending; but researchers, public officials, and others who use such measures should be aware of their strengths and limitations. For example, because MTF and NSDUH sampling and interviewing procedures have remained relatively constant, the surveys provide reasonably consistent information on trends in drug use or offending over time. These two surveys serve better as measures of change than as measures of absolute levels.

Our consideration of these two surveys also highlighted the importance of sampling procedures. Samples based on households may not be readily generalized to other populations, and data obtained from high school seniors in class may differ from data obtained from dropouts or chronic truants.

Also consider that alternative measures of offenses like drug use and delinquency are not readily available for general populations. This leaves three alternatives: (1) carefully using imperfect measures, (2) having no measures of certain types of offenses, or (3) developing new measures. Our strong preference is to pursue both the first and the third alternatives. This echoes recommendations from a recent comparison of self-reported offending and official records by Piquero et al.: "Given the importance of measurement in the field of criminology, researchers should devote . . . [more] attention to issues related to reliability and validity" (2014:24–325). Having read Chapter 5 and worked your way through most of this chapter, you are becoming better equipped to carefully interpret measures of all kinds. Becoming more familiar with self-report methods used in the NSDUH will help you if the need arises to develop new measures.

Drug Surveillance Systems

Surveillance systems have been developed to obtain alternative measures of drug use.

The challenge of developing reliable and valid measures of offenses such as drug use has prompted researchers and policy makers to search for alternative approaches. This has been something of a fitful effort, as various data systems come and go. In this section, we briefly consider examples of focused efforts to monitor drug use and its consequences.

Arrestee Drug Abuse Monitoring[5]

For several years, the National Institute of Justice (NIJ) conducted programs to measure drug use among samples of persons arrested. The most recent version was the Arrestee Drug Abuse Monitoring (ADAM) program, which last collected data in the year 2003. The program was terminated because of lack of funding. In 2007, a scaled-down version was resurrected and relocated to the Office of National Drug Control Policy in the White House. Now ADAM II continues to estimate drug use for a very specific population—persons arrested in five cities: Atlanta, Chicago, Denver, New York, and Sacramento.

Over two 14-day periods each year, participating cities select samples of persons arrested for a variety of offenses. Anonymous interviews and urine specimens are obtained from those who agree to take part in the voluntary study. In 2013, about 1,900 interviews were conducted in the five cities, and almost 1,700 urine specimens were obtained (Office of National Drug Control Policy, 2014).

The main purpose of ADAM II is to provide an ongoing assessment of the prevalence of drug use among persons arrested for criminal offenses. Results for 2013 showed that over 60 percent of adult arrestees tested positive for at least one of 10 drugs. Marijuana was the drug most commonly found in urine samples. ADAM II results vary somewhat by city, with overall positive tests ranging from 63 percent in Atlanta to 83 percent in Chicago.

One of the most interesting aspects of ADAM II and its predecessors is the combination of urinalysis and self-report measures of drug use. Interviews with arrestees include self-report items,

so responses can be compared with urine test results. A variety of additional questions gather information about drug-related policy issues such as perceived dependency and treatment needs, along with respondents' assessment of local drug markets. Charles Katz, Vincent Webb, and Scott Decker (2005) used interview data to examine the links between gang membership and drug use, finding that active gang members used drugs more extensively than did other arrestees.

Any measure of crime is selective; neither all crimes nor all people are included. In what ways is the ADAM II program selective as a measure of drug use? Based on what we have covered so far, three ways should be evident. First, ADAM II operates in only five cities; although these range from New York to Sacramento, we can't assume that participating cities are representatives of other cities. Second, and perhaps most importantly, ADAM II includes only arrested persons. It's obvious that we cannot generalize from people who are arrested to the population at large. It's less obvious that arrest is a selective process. Police exercise discretion in deciding whether to make an arrest, and their priorities can change over time. Third, ADAM II interviews and testing were voluntary, although this did not have much impact on participation. Perhaps surprisingly, a large proportion of 2013 arrestees—approximately 82 percent—agreed to participate.

Even though ADAM II has obvious limits as a measure of drug use among the general population, it is an imaginative attempt to obtain a different type of measure. Data provide information about trends in drug use among arrestees and offer comparisons across cities in different parts of the country. Additional data collected through the interview can be used to analyze drug use by offense, age, gender, and other variables. Asking arrestees about whether they have sought treatment offers insights into needs for such services.

Finally, the fact that ADAM II is restricted to samples of persons arrested is a strength in offering useful information about the co-occurrence of drug use and crime among a group of people at high risk for both. Further, as described in the 2013 report, many arrestees are homeless and will not be included in household-based surveys such as the NSDUH. ADAM II provides an ongoing

---

[5]Descriptive information about Arrestee Drug Abuse Monitoring is drawn primarily from the 2013 report, Office of National Drug Control Policy (2014) and the website: http://www.whitehouse.gov/ondcp/arrestee-drug-abuse-monitoring-program.

system to monitor drug use among high base-rate users of drugs in large cities. Recall our discussion of drug use and crime from Chapter 4, where we described different patterns of drug use among different types of people. Comparing rates of use by people sampled in ADAM II against rates for people sampled in the NSDUH clearly illustrates these different patterns and demonstrates why it is important to have multiple measures.

The Drug Abuse Warning Network

The ADAM II system implicitly assumes that at least some drug users will be involved in other offenses. Our next specialized measure assumes that drug use can produce acute health problems that cause users to seek treatment in hospital emergency rooms. Established in 1972, the Drug Abuse Warning Network (DAWN) collected emergency medical treatment reports for "drug episodes" from samples of hospitals and medical examiners nationwide. In 2009, the DAWN sample included 242 hospitals in 66 metropolitan areas. Participating hospitals submitted information on over 380,000 drug abuse episodes for the year 2009 (Substance Abuse and Mental Health Services Administration, 2011).

Drug episodes are defined as visits to a hospital emergency room that are produced by, or directly related to, the use of illegal drugs or nonmedical use of legal drugs. Included under this definition are direct effects of drug ingestion (overdoses and other physical or psychic reactions), as well as injuries or deaths in which drug intoxication was a contributing factor. Nonfatal episodes are drawn from emergency rooms, whereas drug-related deaths are recorded by medical examiners. Notice that DAWN is based on units of analysis that are only indirectly linked to criminal offenses. The concept of drug episodes is most relevant for studies of public health—and in fact, DAWN was designed as a data system for health surveillance.

Because it was begun in the early 1970s, DAWN is a comparatively long-term time series that monitors the most serious medical consequences of drug use. DAWN is best suited to measuring trends. Like ADAM II, DAWN records include demographic and other information about the individuals whose drug use brings them to hospitals and morgues. But the unusual unit of analysis for DAWN means that one individual can account for multiple drug episodes. This makes it difficult to use DAWN data for research in which individual people are the unit of analysis.

Thomas Mieczkowski (1996:387) points out that DAWN data for a single metropolitan area might serve as indicators of the impact of anti-drug programs. Examining trends in drug episodes involving teenagers, for example, might inform an evaluation of high school education and prevention programs. Or, measures of police cocaine seizures might be compared with changes in cocaine drug emergencies.

Measuring Crime for Specific Purposes

Sometimes, alternative measures of crime are collected for research or policy purposes.

Each of the crime measures discussed so far can be used for a variety of research purposes: exploration, description, explanation, and applied research. However, each has the primary purpose of providing some type of crime count: crimes known to police; victimizations of households and people who live in households; self-reported drug use and other offending; drug use among arrestees and emergency room patients; or qualitative assessments of drug use and availability in specific urban areas. Such measures are useful for criminal justice and public health professionals. Researchers have also made extensive use of data from standard series such as the UCR, SHR, and NCVS.

Often, however, none of these regular series of crime measures meets the needs of researchers, public officials, or others looking for specialized information about crime. At this point, we want to call your attention to examples of crime measures developed for specific research and policy purposes.

Global Terrorism Database

We introduced the Global Terrorism Database (GTD) at the beginning of this chapter as an example of the difficulty of defining and measuring terrorism and terrorist incidents. The GTD also illustrates why independent measures of certain types of crimes must be developed by researchers.

Having read almost through an entire chapter on measuring crime, you should be able to think of several problems in developing measures of terrorism around the world. We cannot conduct victim surveys or self-report offender surveys for obvious reasons. Official police and military sources of terrorist attacks from other countries have the potential to vary in definitions and recording even more than police reports in the United States. Official records are also likely to be classified and unavailable to researchers. The approach adopted by researchers at the National Consortium for the Study of Terrorism and Responses to Terrorism (START) was to develop a type of surveillance system to monitor and tabulate reports of terrorist incidents.

The GTD is based on systematically collected and coded open-source reports of terrorist incidents. Open sources include media reports and other public information on terrorist incidents culled from the Internet. Though you might immediately recognize a version of the reporting problem we have described in this chapter, this is

PUTTING IT ALL TOGETHER

Measuring Traffic Violations

BACKGROUND

The frequency and distribution of certain kinds of offenses underlie many research questions about racial profiling. In the first place, many people trace racial profiling to the use of traffic enforcement to interdict drug and weapons smuggling on the nation's highways. Operation Pipeline, established by the Drug Enforcement Administration in 1986, trained state and local law enforcement officers to recognize features of vehicles that signal possible drug trafficking activity (General Accounting Office, 2000; Verniero and Zoubek, 1999). In many areas it was alleged that race was routinely used as a criterion to make "pretextual" traffic stops. Police were said to use traffic violations as a pretext to stop drivers they suspected of drug trafficking, and this disproportionately targeted nonwhite drivers.

Responses by police and other government agencies varied, ranging from outright denial that race influenced traffic stops, to promises that any racial bias in traffic enforcement would not be tolerated. Whereas some acknowledged interpreting Operation Pipeline as an invitation to target black drivers, many police agencies claimed that drivers were stopped only because of traffic violations, not race.

TRAFFIC VIOLATIONS

This raised the question of how to measure the actual frequency of traffic violations. You will recognize this as a challenging task. Slightly restating two questions presented at the very beginning of this chapter: *How do you measure traffic violations? How many traffic violations are there?* Just as it is virtually impossible to measure all crimes, it is not feasible to measure all traffic violations for two related reasons: Virtually everyone commits some sort of violation at least occasionally; because of this, police have to be selective in deciding which vehicles to stop. Relatively little is known about how police decide which traffic violations to target. Andresen (2005) describes how different troopers in New Jersey tend to concentrate on different kinds of violations.

SPEEDING

Researchers have focused on speeding in an effort to measure the distribution of traffic violation rates. Engel et al. (2004:10) sum up reasons for this in their Pennsylvania study. First, recent national surveys of the general population show that among those who self-report being stopped by police, speeding is the most common reason—55 percent in the NCVS, 65 percent in a U.S. Department of Transportation

less important for the GTD than it may initially seem.

First, unlike many types of crimes, terrorist attacks depend crucially on widespread publicity. It's much more likely that an action meeting the criteria for a terrorist incident will be widely publicized, because that's a principal goal of perpetrators. In other words, non-reporting is less likely to be a problem. An exception will be incidents in countries better able to suppress publicizing such events widely, such as in North Korea.

A second important feature of the GTD is its systematic search, screening, and coding procedures. The GTD Codebook (National Consortium for the Study of Terrorism and Responses to Terrorism (START), 2016) describes these procedures in detail. We mentioned careful definitional criteria at the beginning of this chapter. Since the GTD is based on public reports, screening out duplicate reports is equally important. Units of analysis questions are similar in some ways to those involved in sorting out incidents and offenses. The GTD defines incidents as:

survey (Durose et al., 2005; Royal, 2003). Second, they found that over 75 percent of stops reported by Pennsylvania State Police were for speeding infractions.

Finally, speeding can be measured more easily and reliably than other kinds of driving violations. Just as police can use radar or laser detectors to reliably measure speed, researchers can similarly obtain measures that are accurate and consistent. The Pennsylvania research team used radar equipment issued by state police and measured the speed of cars passing sampled locations. New Jersey researchers placed radar detectors inside unmarked vans together with the digital cameras mentioned in the previous chapter (Lange et al., 2005). North Carolina combined speed metering with the mobile observation of race mentioned in the last chapter (Smith et al., 2003). A van was driven at the posted speed limit, researchers used stop watches to time vehicles passing them, then computed the passing vehicles' speeds.

Of course, police records are also sources of information about speeding and other traffic violations. In all cases researchers examined police records in addition to some other source of data. As we will see in the next chapter, comparing police records to other measures was an important part of efforts to explain race disparity in traffic stops.

The survey data mentioned above can be viewed as something of a self-report survey of offenders. If you think about the rationale for self-report surveys

discussed elsewhere in this chapter, you should be able to see why this method is useful to estimate traffic violation rates. Like drug use and delinquency, traffic violations are not likely to be reported to police. Because speeding and traffic violations are so common, it's not possible for police to detect them all, and the ability of people to evade detection by police may vary. Just as police might not make records of all crimes that come to their attention, their records may not reflect all traffic stops. So we ask people about traffic violating behavior and about their experiences in being stopped by police. Among other things, these measures can be compared to measures from other sources.

Smith et al. (2003) included self-report items in different surveys of North Carolina residents as part of their effort to assess drivers' perceptions of police and experience of being stopped. The researchers also incorporated some clever devices to assess the quality of self-report items. In addition to the general population, they selected some respondents who, according to state police records, had received traffic citations in the previous year. Administering self-report questionnaires to "known offenders" offered a way to estimate the reliability of the survey.

So research on racial profiling used speeding as a measure of traffic violation, and measured that in a variety of ways, just as we have seen in this chapter that a variety of techniques are used to measure different kinds of crime.

Incidents occurring in both the same geographic and temporal point will be regarded as a single incident, but if either the time of occurrence of incidents or their locations are discontinuous, the events will be regarded as separate incidents. (START Codebook, 2016:10).

The codebook lists detailed codes and definitions for information that is recorded. The actual coding process is an example of content analysis, a topic we cover in more detail in Chapter 12.

What results is a specialized research tool for tracking and examining terrorist incidents cross-nationally and over time. In a discussion of different data sources for measuring terrorism, Ivan Sheehan proposes several criteria for evaluating their usefulness. The GTD is an example that, ". . . has the potential to bring rich detailed descriptions that can serve as an alternative to tradition and reliability testing . . . " (Sheehan, 2011:20).

Observing Crime

We have seen that police learn about certain types of crime primarily through observation—for example, drug use and sales, prostitution, public order offenses, and drunk driving. Researchers may face situations in which they need to observe crime independently.

For example, we have pointed out that shoplifting is poorly measured by police records. Victim surveys might reveal some instances of shoplifting, but only if we sampled shops, and then we would learn only about those incidents detected by shop staff. Self-report surveys could tell us something about *shoplifters*, but it would be difficult to use this method to measure *shoplifting incidents*. Terry Baumer and Dennis Rosenbaum (1982) conducted systematic observations of a large department store in Chicago for descriptive and applied purposes. Using ingenious methods, they sought to estimate the frequency of shoplifting and to evaluate the effectiveness of different store security measures. Chapter 11, on field research, describes this study and its findings in detail.

What about assault? Again, police measure assaults that are reported to them, usually by victims or witnesses. The NCVS was redesigned in part to get better counts of assault, but for some research purposes, independent observations may yield better measures.

Ross Homel and associates (Homel and Clark, 1994; Macintyre and Homel, 1996) were interested in the links between drinking and violence in bars and nightclubs. Specifically, they sought to determine which physical features and situations in bars tended to discourage or facilitate violence. For their explanatory studies, they selected samples of public drinking establishments in Sydney, Australia, and dispatched pairs of observers to each site. Observers recorded information about violent incidents they witnessed, together with details about each bar's physical layout, entertainment, and procedures for controlling access and regulating conduct. Researchers were able to make general explanatory statements about how the physical environment and management practices were related to violence.

Police normally learn about drug use or sales only if they witness the acts. Constraints on their ability to make such observations are often cited as obstacles to the enforcement of drug laws. The increased use of closed-circuit television cameras (CCTV) provided an alternative source for Piza and Sytsma (2016) to study drug sales in Newark, NJ. They were especially interested in how dealers took actions to conceal individual sales from observation.

These examples of directed observation have three common characteristics. First, each has a fairly specific research or policy purpose. Baumer and Rosenbaum wanted to obtain estimates of shoplifting frequency and evaluate the effectiveness of certain security measures; Homel and associates wished to learn more about the association between public drinking and violence; Piza and Sytsma studied recordings of individual drug transactions. Second, the three examples focus on relatively small areas—a single department store, a sample of bars and nightclubs, or drug sales in specific locations. Finally, the expected density of incidents made observation an appropriate way to measure crime. Shoplifting happens in shops, and large department stores offer opportunities to observe many incidents; it's well known that public violence is relatively common in bars, and police records can be used to select bars with a history of violence; finally, CCTV cameras in Newark were installed in areas of known drug activity.

Our running example, "Putting It All Together," presents another illustration of measuring crime by observation. Traffic violations are so common that almost everyone is an offender sometime, and some people are frequent offenders.

Measuring Crime Summary

Each measure of crime has strengths and weaknesses.

Table 6.5 summarizes some of what we have considered in this chapter by comparing different measures of crime. Each method has its own strengths and weaknesses. The UCR and SHR provide the best counts for murder and crimes in which the victim is either a business or a commercial establishment. Crimes against persons or households that are not reported to police are best counted by the NCVS. Usually, these are less-serious crimes, many of them UCR Part II incidents that are counted only if a suspect is arrested. Recent changes in NCVS procedures have increased the counts of sexual assault and other violent victimizations. Compared with the UCR, NIBRS potentially provides much greater detail for a broader range of offenses. NIBRS complements the NCVS by including disaggregated incident-based reports for state and local areas and by recording detailed information on crimes against children under age 12.

Self-report surveys are best at measuring crimes that do not have readily identifiable victims and that are less frequently observed by, or reported to, police. The two self-report surveys listed in Table 6.5 sample different populations and use different interview procedures.

Sentinel measures target more narrowly defined populations for the purposes of monitoring and are best seen as measures of change. The

TABLE 6.5 Measuring Crime Summary

	Units	Target Population	Crime Coverage	Best Count for
Known to police				
UCR	Aggregate: reporting agency	All law enforcement agencies, 98% reporting	Limited number reported and recorded crimes	Commercial and business victims
SHR	Incident	All law enforcement agencies; 98% reporting	Homicides only	Homicides
NIBRS	Incident	All law enforcement agencies; limited reporting	Extensive	Details on local incidents; victims under age 12
Surveys				
NCVS	Victimization, individuals and households	Individuals in households	Household and personal crimes	Household and personal crimes not reported to police
NSDUH	Individual respondent, offender	Individuals in households	Drug use	Drug use by adults in households
MTF	Individual respondent, offender	High school seniors; follow-up on sample	Substance use, delinquency, offending	Drug use by high school seniors
Sentinel				
ADAM	Arrested offenders	Quarterly samples arrestees, 35 cities	Drug use	Changes in drug use among arrestees
DAWN	Medical emergency: drug episodes	National sample hospital	Drug-related medical emergencies	Changes in acute drug use problems

two series in Table 6.5 measure drug use in the context of medical and legal crises.

Be aware that Table 6.5 and our discussions throughout this chapter include only a partial listing of crime measures used by researchers and public officials. Each local and state law enforcement agency maintains its own records, which often provide the best measures for research in specific geographic areas. Finally, a specific research purpose may require collecting independent measures of crime.

Don't forget that all crime measures are selective, so it's important to understand the selection process. Despite their various flaws, the measures of crime available to you can serve many research purposes. Researchers are best advised to be critical and careful users of whatever measure of crime best suits their research purpose. This advice is illustrated in this chapter's running example, where researchers tackle the problem of measuring traffic violations.

SUMMARY

- Crime is a fundamental concept in criminal justice research. Different approaches to measuring crime illustrate general principles of conceptualization, operationalization, and measurement.

- Before using any measure of crime, researchers should understand what types of offenses the measure does and does not include.

- Different measures of crime are based on different units of analysis. The UCR is a summary measure that reports totals for individual agencies. Other measures use offenders, victims, incidents, or offenses as the units of analysis.

- Crime data are collected for one or more general purposes: monitoring, agency accountability, and research.

- Crimes known to police have been the most widely used measures. UCR data have been available since the early twentieth century; more detailed information about homicides was added to the UCR in 1961. The FBI has developed an incident-based reporting system that is being adopted gradually by law enforcement agencies.

- Surveys of victims reveal information about crimes that are not reported to police. The NCVS includes very detailed information about personal and household incidents, but does not count crimes against businesses or individual victims under age 12. Although the NCVS is a nationally representative measure, it cannot estimate victimizations for local areas.

- Self-report surveys were developed to measure crimes with unclear victims that are detected by police less frequently. Two such surveys estimate drug use among high school seniors and adults. Self-report surveys do not measure all drug use because of incomplete reporting by respondents and procedures for selecting survey respondents.

- ADAM II and DAWN provide measures of drug use among special populations, but are best suited to monitoring changes in drug use.

- Different measures of crime also are developed for specific research and policy purposes. Many police departments do crime analysis with their own incident-based records.

- We have many different measures of crime because each measure is imperfect. Each measure has its own strengths and weaknesses.

KEY TERMS

Crimes known to police (p. 142)
Dark figure of unreported crime (p. 149)
Incident-based measures (p. 145)
Self-report survey (p. 154)
Summary-based measure (p. 145)
Surveillance system (p. 141)
Victim survey (p. 148)

REVIEW QUESTIONS AND EXERCISES

1. Los Angeles police consider a murder to be gang related if either the victim or the offender is known to be a gang member, whereas Chicago police record a murder as gang related only if the killing is directly related to gang activities (Spergel, 1990). Describe how these different operational definitions illustrate general points about measuring crime discussed in this chapter.

2. Measuring gang-related crime is an example of trying to measure a particular dimension of crime: motive. Other examples are hate crimes, terrorist incidents, and drug-related crimes. Specify conceptual and operational definitions for at least one of these types. Find one mass or social media story and one research report that present an example.

3. How would you measure crime in a specific city if you wanted to evaluate a community policing program that encourages neighborhood residents to report incidents to police?

CHAPTER 7

Experimental and Quasi-Experimental Designs

We'll learn about the experimental approach to social science research, and consider a wide variety of experimental and other designs available to criminal justice researchers.

Learning Objectives

1. Recognize that experiments are well suited for the controlled testing of causal processes and for some evaluation studies.

2. Describe how the classical experiment tests the effect of an experimental stimulus on some dependent variable through the pretesting and posttesting of experimental and control groups.

3. Understand that a group of experimental subjects need not be representative of some larger population, but that experimental and control groups must be similar to each other.

4. Describe how random assignment is the best way to achieve comparability in the experimental and control groups.

5. Describe how the classical experiment with random assignment of subjects guards against most of the threats to internal invalidity.

6. Understand that the controlled conditions under which experiments take place may restrict our ability to generalize results to real-world constructs or to other settings.

7. Recognize how the classical experiment may be modified by changing the number of experimental and control groups, the number and types of experimental stimuli, and the number of pretest or posttest measurements.

8. Know the reasons that quasi-experiments are conducted when it is not possible or desirable to use an experimental design, and be able to describe different categories of quasi-experiments.

9. Understand the differences between case-oriented and variable-oriented research. Time-series designs and case studies are examples of variable-oriented research, in which a large number of variables are examined for one or a few cases.

10. Be able to describe how experiments and quasi-experiments can be customized by using design building blocks to suit particular research purposes.

An Experiment in Spear Phishing

We're willing to bet that any person reading this book has received many offers of riches to be bestowed by bankers and oil ministers from England, Nigeria, Ukraine, and just about everywhere else. Maybe you've wondered how anyone could be so gullible to be taken in by this form of "phishing." Or maybe you, like many people, have responded to or wondered about more sophisticated email phishing attempts. Michael Maxfield was temporarily taken in by the following message: "Your new computer has shipped and will arrive in two days! Click here to review or change payment and delivery information."

Computer scientists at Indiana University conducted an experiment to learn something about what influences people to respond to phishing. Their basic research question was "How easily and effectively can a phisher exploit social networking data found on the Internet to increase the yield of a phishing attack?" (Jagatic et al., 2007).

Tom Jagatic and colleagues searched for publicly available information about 23,000 Indiana students, seeking students who participated in social networking sites such as Facebook. Approximately 1,700 students met the researchers' criteria, which included having several friends or circles of friends on the sites.

They then sent two versions of phishing emails to different groups of students. One group received a *treatment* condition message that mimicked someone in the student's circle of friends; this is sometimes known as "spear phishing." The other group received a *control* message that contained no information, suggesting the sender was part of the receiver's network. For example, assume Maxfield was selected as a treatment subject, and Earl Babbie was among his circle of friends on Facebook. The researchers might have sent Maxfield a message that appeared to be from Babbie, something like: "Hi Mike! I just found this great new website that has copies of hundreds of survey questionnaires. Check it out at: megasurveys.com. Take care, Earl." Or, if Maxfield was a control subject in this experiment, a message might have read: "Dear Professor: Please click on the link below to learn more about our collection of survey questionnaires."

In either case, the message would have redirected Maxfield to some other site—harmless, but clearly not a compilation of survey questionnaires. Which message—treatment or control—do you think would be more likely to prompt recipients to click on the enclosed link?

Jagatic and associates found that a whopping 72 percent of people receiving the treatment message followed the link, compared to 16 percent of those who got the control message. In addition, spear phishing was more effective in cross-gender messages. Females more often clicked on links they believed were from their male friends than to links from female friends; male recipients were similarly duped when they thought messages came from female friends.

This is an excellent example of an experiment. It involved an unambiguous intervention that could be easily controlled: applied to a treatment group, but not to a control group. Researchers could readily determine which subjects were in each group and assign them in a random, unbiased way. As you read this chapter, compare this example to our general discussion of designs and to other examples. What features of the setting for this study facilitated an experimental approach? How is the setting different from the environment in which criminal justice agencies routinely work?

Introduction

Experimentation is an approach to research best suited for explanation and evaluation.

In the most basic sense, research design involves devising a strategy for finding out something. We'll first discuss the experiment as a mode of scientific observation in criminal justice research. In his classic book *The Conduct of Inquiry*, Abraham Kaplan (1964:144) described experimentation as "a process of observation, to be carried out in a situation expressly brought about for that purpose." Essentially, experiments involve (1) taking action and (2) observing the consequences of that action. Social science researchers typically select a group of subjects, do something to them, and observe the effect of what was done.

It is worth noting at the outset that experiments are often used in nonscientific human inquiry as well. We experiment copiously in our attempts to develop a more generalized understanding about the world we live in. We learn many skills through experimentation: riding a bicycle, driving a car, swimming, and so forth. Students discover how much studying is required for academic success through experimentation. Professors learn how much preparation is required for successful lectures through experimentation.

Returning to social science applications, experiments are especially well suited to research projects that involve relatively well-defined concepts and propositions. A further requirement is the ability to control the conditions under which research is conducted. The traditional model of science, discussed in Chapter 2, and the experimental model are closely related.

Experimentation is best suited for hypothesis testing in explanatory or evaluation studies. Suppose we are interested in studying alcohol abuse and discovering ways to reduce it among college students. We might hypothesize that increased student knowledge about the health consequences of binge drinking and long-term alcohol use will have the effect of reducing alcohol abuse. We can test this hypothesis experimentally. To begin, we might ask a group of experimental subjects how much beer, wine, or spirits they drank on the previous day and how frequently, in an average week, they consume alcohol for the specific purpose of getting drunk. Next, we might show these subjects a video depicting the various physiological effects of chronic drinking and binge drinking. Finally—say, one month later—we might again ask the subjects about their use of alcohol in the previous week to determine whether watching the video actually reduced alcohol use.

Because experiments are best suited for hypothesis testing, they can also be appropriate in the study of criminal justice policy. In Chapter 2, we discussed the logical similarity between hypotheses and criminal justice policies, noting that evaluation research is conceptually equivalent to hypothesis testing. The experimental model, therefore, can be a useful design for evaluating criminal justice policy.

You might typically think of experiments as being conducted in laboratories under carefully controlled conditions. Although this is often true in the natural sciences, few social scientific experiments take place in laboratory settings. (The most notable exception to this occurs in the discipline of psychology, in which laboratory experiments are common.) Criminal justice experiments are almost always conducted in field settings outside the laboratory.

The Classical Experiment

Variables, time order, measures, and groups are the central features of the classical experiment.

Like much of the vocabulary of research, the word *experiment* has acquired both a general and a specialized meaning. So far, we have referred to the general meaning, defined by David Farrington, Lloyd Ohlin, and James Q. Wilson (1986:65) as "a systematic attempt to test a causal hypothesis about the effect of variations in one factor (the independent variable) on another (the dependent variable).... The defining feature of an experiment lies in the control of the independent variable by the experimenter." In a narrower sense, the term *experiment* refers to a specific way of structuring research, usually called the **classical experiment**. In this section, we examine the requirements and components of the classical experiment. Later in the chapter, we will consider designs that can be used when

Classical experiment   Research design with three components: pre- and posttests, experimental and control groups, random assignment to groups.

some of the requirements for classical experiments cannot be met.

The most conventional type of experiment, in the natural and the social sciences, involves three major pairs of components: (1) independent and dependent variables, (2) pretesting and posttesting, and (3) experimental and control groups. We will now consider each of those components and the way they are put together in the execution of an experiment.

Independent and Dependent Variables

Essentially, an experiment examines the effect of an **independent variable** on a **dependent variable**. Typically, the independent variable takes the form of an experimental stimulus that is either present or absent—that is, a dichotomous variable, having two attributes. That need not be the case, however, as subsequent sections of this chapter will show. In the example concerning alcohol abuse, the dependent variable is how often subjects used alcohol, and the independent variable is exposure to a video about alcohol's effects. The researcher's hypothesis suggests that levels of alcohol use depend, in part, on understanding its physiological and health effects. The purpose of the experiment is to test the validity of this hypothesis. In the opening vignette, "An Experiment in Spear Phishing," the type of email message a person receives is the independent variable, and whether or not subjects click on a link is the dependent variable.

Keep in mind, however, that a given variable might serve as an independent variable in one experiment and as a dependent variable in another. For example, alcohol abuse is the dependent variable in our example, but it might be the independent variable in an experiment that examines the effects of alcohol abuse on academic performance.

In the terms of our discussion of cause and effect in Chapter 4, the independent variable is the cause and the dependent variable is the effect. Thus, we might say that watching the video *causes* a change in alcohol use or that reduced alcohol use is an *effect* of watching the video. A socially targeted email message causes people to click on an embedded link, and clicking on the link is the effect of the email message.

It is essential that both independent and dependent variables be operationally defined for the purposes of experimentation. Such operational definitions might involve a variety of observation methods. Responses to a questionnaire, for example, might be the basis for defining self-reported alcohol use on the previous day. Alternatively, alcohol use by subjects could be measured with breathalyzer or blood alcohol tests.

Conventionally, in the experimental model, the dependent and independent variables are operationally defined before the experiment begins. However, as we will see in connection with survey research and other methods, it is sometimes appropriate to first make a variety of observations during data collection and then determine the most useful operational definitions of variables during later analyses. Ultimately, however, experimentation requires specific and standardized measurements and observations.

Pretesting and Posttesting

In the simplest experimental design, subjects are measured on a dependent variable (pretested), exposed to a stimulus that represents an independent variable, and then remeasured on the dependent variable (posttested). Differences noted between the first and second measurements on the dependent variable are then attributed to the influence of the independent variable.

In our example of alcohol use, we might begin by pretesting the extent of alcohol use among our experimental subjects. Using a questionnaire, we measure the extent of alcohol use reported by each individual and the average level of alcohol use for the whole group. After showing subjects the video on the effects of alcohol, we administer the same questionnaire again. Responses given in this posttest permit us to measure the subsequent extent of alcohol use by each subject and the average level of alcohol use of the group as a whole. If we discover a lower level of alcohol use on the second administration of the questionnaire, we might conclude that the video indeed reduced the use of alcohol among the subjects.

In the experimental examination of behaviors such as alcohol use, we face a special practical problem relating to validity. As you can imagine, the subjects might respond differently to the questionnaires the second time, even if their level of drinking remained unchanged. During the first administration of the questionnaire, the subjects may have been unaware of its purpose. By the time of the second measurement, however, they may have figured out the purpose of the experiment, become sensitized to the questions about drinking, and changed their answers. Thus, the video might *seem* to have reduced alcohol abuse, although, in fact, it did not.

This is an example of a more general problem that plagues many forms of criminal justice research: The very act of studying something may change it. Techniques for dealing with this problem in the context of experimentation are covered throughout the chapter.

Experimental and Control Groups

The traditional way to offset the effects of the experiment itself is to use a **control group**. Social scientific experiments seldom involve only the observation of an **experimental group** to which a stimulus has been administered. Researchers also observe a control group to which the experimental stimulus has not been administered.

In our example of alcohol abuse, two groups of subjects are examined. To begin, each group is administered a questionnaire designed to measure their alcohol use in general and binge drinking in particular. Then only one of the groups—the experimental group—is shown the video. Later, the researcher administers a posttest of alcohol use to both groups. Figure 7.1 illustrates this basic experimental design.

Using a control group allows the researcher to control for the effects of the experiment itself.

Control group   Subjects in an experiment who do not receive the experimental treatment.

Experimental group   Subjects in an experiment who receive the experimental treatment.

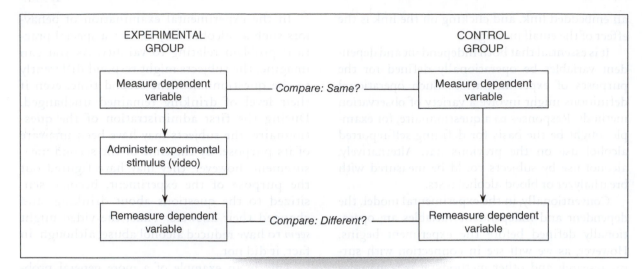

FIGURE 7.1 Basic Experimental Design

If participation in the experiment leads the subjects to report less alcohol use, that should occur in both the experimental and the control groups. On the one hand, if the overall level of drinking exhibited by the control group decreases as much as for the experimental group between the pretest and posttest, then the apparent reduction in alcohol use must be a function of the experiment or of some external factor—not a function of watching the video specifically. In this situation, we can conclude that the video did not cause any change in alcohol use.

On the other hand, if drinking decreases only in the experimental group, then we can say with more confidence that the reduction is a consequence of exposure to the video (because that's the only difference between the two groups). Or, if drinking decreases more in the experimental group than in the control group, then that too is grounds for assuming that watching the video reduced alcohol use.

The need for control groups in social scientific research became clear in a series of employee satisfaction studies conducted by Fritz J. Roethlisberger and William J. Dickson (1939) in the late 1920s and early 1930s. They studied working conditions in the telephone "bank wiring room" of the Western Electric Works in Chicago, attempting to discover what changes in working conditions would improve employee satisfaction and productivity.

To the researchers' great satisfaction, they discovered that improving working conditions consistently increased satisfaction and productivity. When the workroom was brightened by better lighting, for example, productivity went up. Lighting was further improved, and productivity went up again. To substantiate their scientific conclusion, the researchers then dimmed the lights: *Productivity again improved!*

It became evident then that the wiring room workers were responding more to the attention given them by the researchers than to improved working conditions. As a result of this phenomenon, often called the "Hawthorne effect," social researchers have become more sensitive to and cautious about the possible effects of experiments themselves. The use of a proper control group—studied intensively, with the working conditions otherwise unchanged—would have revealed this effect in the wiring room study.

The need for control groups in experimentation has been most obvious in medical research. Time and again, patients who participated in medical experiments appeared to improve, but it was unclear how much of the improvement came from the experimental treatment and how much from the experiment. Now, in testing the effects of new drugs, medical researchers frequently administer a placebo (e.g., sugar pills) to a control group. Thus, the control-group patients believe that they, like members of the experimental group, are receiving an experimental drug—and they often improve! If the new drug is effective, however, those who receive that drug will improve more than those who received the placebo.

In criminal justice experiments, control groups are important as a guard against the effects not only of the experiments themselves, but of events that may occur outside the laboratory during the course of experiments. Suppose the alcohol use experiment was being conducted on your campus, and at that time, a popular athlete was hospitalized for acute alcohol poisoning. This event might shock the experimental subjects and thereby decrease their reported drinking. Because such an effect should happen about equally for members of the control and experimental groups, lower levels of reported alcohol use in the experimental group than in the control group would again demonstrate the impact of the experimental stimulus: watching the video that describes the health effects of alcohol abuse.

Sometimes, an experimental design requires more than one experimental or control group. In the case of the alcohol video, for example, we might also want to examine the impact of participating in group discussions about why college students drink alcohol, with the intent of demonstrating that peer pressure may promote drinking by people who would otherwise abstain. We might design our experiment around three groups. One group would see the video and participate in the group discussions, another would only see the video, and still another would only participate in group discussions; the control group would do neither. With this kind of design, we could determine the impact of each stimulus separately, as well as their combined effect.

Double-Blind Experiments

As we saw with respect to medical experimentation, patients sometimes improve when they think they are receiving a new drug; thus, it is often necessary to administer a placebo to a control group.

Sometimes, experimenters have this same tendency to prejudge results. In medical research, the experimenters may be more likely to "observe" improvements among patients who receive the experimental drug than among those receiving the placebo. That would be most likely, perhaps, for the researcher who developed the drug. A double-blind experiment eliminates this possibility because neither the subjects nor the experimenters know which is the experimental group and which is the control group. In medical experiments, those researchers who are responsible for administering the drug and for noting improvements are not told which subjects receive the drug and which receive the placebo. Thus, both researchers and subjects are "blind" to who is receiving the experimental drug and who is getting the placebo. Another researcher knows which subjects are in which group, but that person is not responsible for administering the experiment.

An experimental study of prison inmate classification offers a good example. Lawrence Bench and Terry Allen (2003) were interested in how security classification might affect the way prison guards viewed inmates and the levels of disciplinary action they took against inmates. You probably have a general understanding of security classification. Persons sentenced to prison are rated on a security risk scale—usually low-, middle-, and high-risk, or something like that. As you might expect, inmates classified as high-risk are treated differently than their low-risk counterparts. But Bench and Allen were interested in whether prison discipline reflected inmate behavior, or the security risk labels applied to inmates. For example, did guards write up high-risk inmates for disciplinary actions because of their behavior or because they were labeled high-risk?

The researchers selected a sample of 200 inmates admitted to prison in Utah and classified at the highest security level. Half of these inmates were randomly assigned to treatment and control groups. Those in the treatment group were placed in medium-security facilities, while control group subjects were assigned to maximum-security sites. In addition, the researchers examined a second control group of prisoners who had been classified as medium security and placed in medium-security facilities.

Analyzing disciplinary actions for one year after prison placement, Bench and Allen found: "Overall, inmates receive about the same number of average weighted disciplinaries regardless of security classification" (2003:377). Interpreting their findings, the researchers argue that classification of inmates into maximum-security is costly and often unnecessary.

The study was double-blinded so that neither prisoners nor guards knew that the treatment group inmates (placed in medium-security) had been classified as maximum-security. Double-blinding allowed researchers to separate the effects of labeling and classification.

Selecting Subjects

Before beginning an experiment, we must make two basic decisions about who will participate. First, we must decide on the target population—the group to which the results of our experiment will apply. If our experiment is designed to determine, for example, whether restitution is more effective than probation in reducing recidivism, our target population is some group of persons convicted of crimes. In our hypothetical experiment about the effects of watching a video on the health consequences of alcohol abuse, the target population might be college students.

Second, we must decide how particular members of the target population will be selected for the experiment. Ideally, the methods used to select subjects must meet the scientific norm of generalizability; it should be possible to generalize from the sample of subjects actually studied to the population those subjects represent.

The cardinal rule of subject selection for experimentation is the comparability of the experimental and control groups. Ideally, the control group represents what the experimental group would have been like had it not been exposed to the experimental stimulus. It is important, therefore, that the experimental and control groups be as similar as possible.

Random Assignment

Having recruited a group of subjects, under the classic experiment we would randomly assign those subjects to either the experimental or the control group. We might accomplish this by numbering all the subjects serially and selecting numbers by means of a random-number table. Or, we might assign the odd-numbered subjects to the experimental group and the even-numbered subjects to the control group.

Random assignment is a central feature of the classical experiment. The most important characteristic of random assignment (sometimes referred to as randomization) is that it produces experimental and control groups that are *statistically equivalent*. Put another way, random assignment reduces sources of systematic bias in assigning subjects to groups. The basic principle is simple: If subjects are assigned to experimental and control groups through a random process such as flipping a coin, the assignment process is said to be unbiased, and the resultant groups are equivalent.

Although the rationale underlying this principle is a bit complex, understanding how random assignment produces equivalent groups is a key point. Farrington, Ohlin, and Wilson (1986:66) compare randomization in criminal justice research to laboratory controls in the natural sciences:

> The control of extraneous variables by randomization is similar to the control of extraneous variables in the physical sciences by holding physical conditions (e.g., temperature, pressure) constant. Randomization insures that the average unit in [the] treatment group is approximately equivalent to the average unit in another [group] before the treatment is applied.

You've surely heard the expression "All other things being equal." Random assignment makes it possible to assume that all other things are equal.

Experiments and Causal Inference

Experiments potentially control for many threats to the validity of causal inference, but researchers must remain aware of these threats.

The central features of the classical experiment are independent and dependent variables, pretesting and posttesting, and experimental and control groups created through random assignment. Think of these features as *building blocks* of a research design to demonstrate a cause-and-effect relationship. This point will become clearer by comparing the criteria for causality, discussed in Chapter 4, to the features of the classical experiment, as shown in Figure 7.2.

The experimental design ensures that the cause precedes the effect in time by taking posttest measurements of the dependent variable after introducing the experimental stimulus. The second criterion for causation—an empirical correlation between the cause-and-effect variables—is determined by comparing the pretest (in which the experimental stimulus is not present) to the posttest for the experimental group (after the experimental stimulus is administered). A change from pretest to posttest measures demonstrates correlation.

The final requirement is to show that the observed correlation between cause and effect is not due to the influence of some third variable. The classical experiment makes it possible to satisfy this criterion for cause in two ways. First, the posttest measures for the experimental group (stimulus present) are compared with those for the control group (stimulus not present). If the observed correlation between the stimulus and the dependent variable is due to some other factor, then the two posttest scores will be similar. Second, random assignment produces experimental and control groups that are equivalent and will not differ on some other variable that could account for the empirical correlation between cause and effect.

Experiments and Threats to Validity

The classical experiment is designed to satisfy the three requirements for demonstrating cause-and-effect relationships. But what about threats to the validity of causal inference discussed in Chapter 4? In this section, we consider each of those threats in more detail and describe how the classical experiment reduces many of them. The book by Donald Campbell and Julian Stanley (1966) is the most frequently cited authority on threats to validity. For a fuller discussion, on which we draw heavily, see the book by William Shadish, Thomas Cook, and Donald Campbell (2002). We present these threats in a slightly different order, beginning with threats to internal validity.

Threats to Internal Validity

The problem of threats to internal validity refers to the possibility that conclusions drawn from experimental results may not accurately reflect what went on in the experiment itself. As we stated in Chapter 4, conclusions about cause and effect may be biased in some systematic way. Shadish, Cook, and Campbell (2002:54–60) pointed to several sources of the problem.

As you read about these different threats to internal validity, keep in mind that each is an example of a simple point: possible ways that researchers might be wrong in inferring causation. Although these threats are well known among researchers and often cited by students as things to memorize, they are simply examples of ways we might be wrong in causal inference.

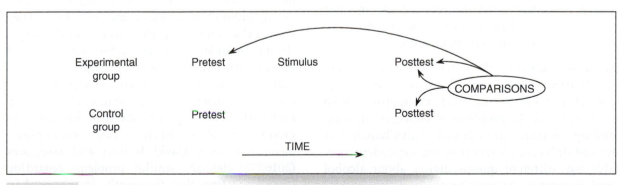

Experimental group — Pretest — Stimulus — Posttest
Control group — Pretest — Posttest
COMPARISONS
TIME

FIGURE 7.2 Another Look at the Classical Experiment

History Historical events may occur during the course of the experiment that confound the experimental results. The hospitalization of a popular athlete for acute alcohol poisoning during an experiment on reducing alcohol use is an example.

Maturation People are continually growing and changing, whether in an experiment or not, and those changes affect the results of the experiment. In a long-term experiment, the fact that the subjects grow older (and wiser?) may have an effect. In shorter experiments, subjects may become tired, sleepy, bored, or hungry, or change in other ways that affect their behavior in the experiment. A long-term study of alcohol abuse might reveal a decline in binge drinking as the subjects mature.

History and maturation are similar in that they represent a correlation between cause and effect that is due to something other than the independent variable. They're different in that history represents something that's outside the experiment altogether, whereas maturation refers to change within the subjects themselves.

Testing Often, the process of testing and retesting influences people's behavior and thereby confounds the experimental results. Suppose we administer a questionnaire to a group as a way of measuring their alcohol use. Then we administer an experimental stimulus and remeasure their alcohol use. By the time we conduct the posttest, the subjects may have become more sensitive to the issue and so may provide different answers. In fact, they may have figured out that we are trying to determine whether they drink too much. Because excessive drinking is frowned on by university authorities, our subjects will be on their best behavior and give answers that they think we want or that will make them look good.

Instrumentation Thus far, we haven't said much about the process of measurement in pretesting and posttesting, and it's appropriate to keep in mind the problems of conceptualization and operationalization discussed in Chapter 5. If we use different measures of the dependent variable (say, different questionnaires about alcohol use), how can we be sure that they are comparable?

Perhaps alcohol use seems to have decreased simply because the pretest measure was more sensitive than the posttest measure. Or, if the experimenters are making the measurements, their procedures may change over the course of the experiment. That would be a problem of reliability.

Instrumentation is always a potential problem in criminal justice research that uses secondary sources of information, such as police records about crime or court records about probation violations. There may be changes in how probation violations are defined or changes in the record-keeping practices of police departments.

The differences between testing and instrumentation threats to internal validity may seem unclear. In general, testing refers to changes in how subjects respond to measurement, whereas instrumentation is concerned with changes in the measurement process itself. If police officers respond differently to pretest and posttest questionnaires about prejudice, for example, that is a testing problem. However, if different questionnaires about prejudice are used in pretest and posttest measurements, instrumentation is a potential threat.

Statistical Regression Sometimes, it's appropriate to conduct experiments on subjects who start out with extreme scores on the dependent variable. A classic example is offered by sentencing policies that target chronic offenders. Charles Murray and L.A. Cox (1979) examined a program to incarcerate high-rate male juvenile offenders. They found that for subjects who had served sentences averaging 11 months, rearrest rates were substantially lower than those for other offenders who were not incarcerated. Michael Maltz and associates (1980) questioned these findings, pointing out that the number of crimes committed by any given offender fluctuates over time. They argued that subjects in the experimental group—chronic offenders—were jailed following a period when their offense rates were abnormally high and that the decline in posttest arrests simply reflected a natural return to less extreme rates of offending. Even without any experimental stimulus, then, the group as a whole was likely to show some improvement over time. David Wilson and associates (2016:175) describe similar problems regarding juvenile curfews that frequently are imposed in response to an increase in crime, or to some highly publicized incident involving groups of youth.

Commonly referred to as "regression to the mean," this threat to validity can emerge whenever researchers are interested in cases that have extreme scores on some variable. Consider hot spots, for example, which are areas where crime appears to be concentrated. Hot spots have become increasingly important in police operations. Michael Townsley and Ken Pease (2002) point out that it is important to consider the number of crimes in a hot spot and the time period over which they are counted. It's common for temporary "spikes" in crime to appear in different areas of large cities, only to disappear in a couple of weeks without any action by police.

Selection Biases Random assignment eliminates the potential for systematic bias in selecting subjects. But subjects may be chosen in other ways that threaten validity. Volunteers are often solicited for experiments conducted on college campuses. Students who volunteer for an experiment may not be typical of students as a whole, however. Volunteers may be more interested in the subject of the experiment and more likely to respond to a stimulus. Or, if experimental subjects are paid a fee, students in greater financial need may participate, although they may not be representative of other students.

A common type of selection bias in applied criminal justice studies results from the natural caution of public officials. Let's say you are a bail commissioner in a large city, and the mayor wants to try a new program to increase the number of arrested persons who are released on bail. The mayor asks you to determine what kinds of defendants should be eligible for release and informs you that staff from the city's criminal justice services agency will be evaluating the program. In establishing eligibility criteria, you will probably try to select defendants who will not be arrested again while on bail and defendants who will most likely show up for scheduled court appearances. In other words, you will try to select participants who are least likely to fail. This common and understandable caution is sometimes referred to as "creaming"—skimming the best risks off the top. Creaming is a threat to validity because the low-risk persons selected for release, although

most likely to succeed, do not represent the jail population as a whole.

Experimental Mortality Experimental subjects often drop out of an experiment before it is completed, and that can affect statistical comparisons and conclusions. This is termed "experimental mortality," sometimes referred to as attrition. In the classical experiment involving an experimental and a control group, each with a pretest and a posttest, suppose that the heavy drinkers in the experimental group are so turned off by the video on the health effects of binge drinking that they tell the experimenter to forget it and leave. Those subjects who stick around for the posttest are less heavy drinkers to start with, and the group results will thus reflect a substantial "decrease" in alcohol use.

In this example, mortality is related to the experimental stimulus itself: Subjects who score highest on the pretest are the most likely to drop out after viewing the video. Mortality may also be a problem in experiments that take place over a long period (people may move away) or in experiments that require a substantial commitment of effort or time by subjects; they may become bored with the study or simply decide it's not worth the effort.

Causal Time Order In criminal justice research, there may be ambiguity about the time order of the experimental stimulus and the dependent variable. Whenever this occurs, the research conclusion that the stimulus caused the dependent variable can be challenged with the explanation that the "dependent" variable actually caused changes in the stimulus. Many early studies of the relationship between different types of punishments and rates of offending exhibited this threat to validity by relying on single interviews with subjects who were asked how they viewed alternative punishments and whether they had committed any crimes.

Diffusion or Imitation of Treatments In the event that experimental- and control-group subjects are in communication with each other, it's possible that experimental subjects will pass on some elements of the experimental stimulus to the control group. David Weisburd, Nancy A. Morris, and Justin Ready (2008:193) describe the potential for spillover effects in their evaluation of targeted community policing in Redlands, California:

> While experimental treatments were restricted to the experimental block groups and juveniles living within them, it is reasonable to expect some degree of diffusion of the treatment effects. One source of that diffusion may have been the Redlands schools. . . . While treatment in the schools was focused only on students in the experimental areas, it is clear that experimental and control students in the same schools would likely interact and pass on information.

Any program that provides a treatment only to some people in a school or other institution and not to others in the same institution is potentially vulnerable to such spillover effects.

Compensatory Treatment In many criminal justice experiments, such as a special job-training program for incarcerated felons, subjects in the control group may be deprived of something of value to them. In such cases, there may be pressures to offer some form of compensation. Recall the discussion in Chapter 4 of how police in the Kansas City Preventive Patrol Experiment patrolled the perimeter of reactive beats—those with no preventive patrol. As we noted, they more often used lights and sirens when responding to calls for service in the reactive beats. Some police officers compensated for the absence of preventive patrol in a way that reduced the differences among proactive, reactive, and control beats.

It's helpful to think of treatment diffusion as the accidental spillover of an experimental stimulus, in contrast to the more intentional compensatory treatment by public officials in the Kansas City case. In applied criminal justice research, such treatment is probably more common, and researchers often take steps to prevent it. For example, in an evaluation of intensive supervision probation (ISP) programs in 11 sites, researchers from the RAND Corporation recognized that probation officers might provide enhanced supervision to clients in the control group, under the assumption that the experimental program (ISP) was better than traditional probation (Petersilia, 1989). This potential for compensation was reduced in two ways. First, researchers explained to program staff why the experimental and control groups should receive different types of services. Second, a type of double-blind procedure was used in which researchers tried to disguise the records of subjects in the control group, so that probation staff could not distinguish subjects who were participating in the experiment from their regular probation caseload.

Compensatory Rivalry In real-life experiments, subjects deprived of the experimental stimulus may try to compensate by working harder. Suppose an experimental career development program for corrections officers is the experimental stimulus; the control group may work harder than before in an attempt to keep pace with the "special" experimental subjects.

Demoralization Feelings of deprivation among the control group may also result in subjects giving up. A career development program for corrections officers may prompt demoralization among control-group subjects who believe their opportunities for advancement will suffer. As a result, it may not be clear whether posttest differences between experimental and control groups in, say, job performance actually reflected program impacts or were due to demoralization among the control group.

Notice that the possibilities of compensatory rivalry and demoralization are based on subjects' reactions to the experiment. Diffusion and compensatory treatment are accidental or intentional extensions of the experimental stimulus to the control group. In studies where agency staff, not researchers, administer an experimental treatment to subjects, there is a greater potential for intentional compensation. In studies where subjects in a control group are aware that other subjects are receiving a desirable treatment, compensatory rivalry or demoralization is possible.

Ruling Out Threats to Internal Validity

These, then, are the threats to internal validity cited by Shadish, Cook, and Campbell. The classical experiment, coupled with proper subject selection and assignment, can potentially handle each of the 12 threats to internal validity.

How do researchers determine whether a particular design rules out threats to internal validity? Shadish, Cook, and Campbell provide excellent advice. Ruling out threats to validity requires a "theory of 'plausibility' so that we know which of the many possible threats are plausible in [a] particular context" (2002:41). In other words, some threats make more sense in some settings than in others. Sorting this out requires theory-based expectations to guide us in figuring out what validity threats might be at work in a particular situation. Let's look again at the classical experiment, presented graphically in Figure 7.2.

Pursuing the example of the educational video as an attempt to reduce alcohol abuse, we should expect two findings if we use the experimental design shown in Figure 7.2. For the experimental group, the frequency of drinking measured in their posttest should be less than in their pretest. In addition, when the two posttests are compared, the experimental group should show less drinking than the control group.

This design guards against the problem of history, because anything occurring outside the experiment that might affect the experimental group should also affect the control group. There should still be a difference between the two posttest results. The same comparison guards against problems of maturation as long as the subjects have been randomly assigned to the two groups. Testing and instrumentation should not be problems, because both the experimental and the control groups are subject to the same tests and experimenter effects. If the subjects have been assigned to the two groups randomly, statistical regression should affect both equally—even if people with extreme scores on drinking (or whatever the dependent variable is) are being studied. Selection bias is ruled out by the random assignment of subjects.

Experimental mortality can be more complicated to handle, because dropout rates between the experimental and control groups may differ. The experimental treatment itself may increase mortality in the group exposed to the video. As a result, the group of experimental subjects that received the posttest will differ from the group that received the pretest. In our example of the alcohol video, it probably would not be possible to handle this problem by administering a placebo, for instance. But in general, the potential for mortality can be reduced by shortening the time between pretest and posttest, by emphasizing to subjects the importance of completing the posttest, or perhaps by offering cash payments for participating in all phases of the experiment.

The remaining problems of internal invalidity can be avoided through the careful administration of a controlled experimental design. The experimental design we've been discussing facilitates the clear specification of independent and dependent variables. Experimental and control subjects can be kept separate to reduce the possibility of diffusion or imitation of treatments. Administrative controls can be applied to avoid compensations given to the control group, and compensatory rivalry can be watched for and considered in evaluating the results of the experiment, as can the problem of demoralization.

We emphasize careful administration here. Random assignment, pretest and posttest measures, and use of control and experimental groups do not automatically rule out threats to validity. This caution is especially true in field studies and evaluation research, in which subjects participate in natural settings and uncontrolled variation in the experimental stimulus may be present. Control over experimental conditions is the hallmark of this approach, but conditions in field settings are usually more difficult to control.

Compare, for example, our hypothetical study of alcohol use among college students with the field experiment on ISP described by Joan Petersilia (1989). In Petersilia's study, more intensive probation was the independent variable, and recidivism was the dependent variable. Subjects were randomly assigned to the experimental group (ISP) or the control group (regular probation).

The alcohol use study could conceivably be completed in about one week, using subjects from a class, dormitory, or house on a single campus. ISP programs were evaluated in 11 sites over four years, using probation clients as subjects. The video on the health effects of alcohol use is a well-defined treatment that is readily standardized and can easily be controlled by researchers. The experimental treatment in the ISP programs was a reduced caseload for probation workers, together with an increased number of regular contacts with each probation client; program staff, not researchers, administered the experimental treatment. There was a great potential for uncontrolled variation in the delivery of ISP treatments; ISP is not a simple dichotomous treatment as is the video/no-video treatment in the alcohol use experiment.

Finally, the alcohol use questionnaire can easily be administered by researchers, providing reliable measures of alcohol use. Probation staff in each of the 11 sites collected data on recidivism for the ISP study. Although recidivism can be readily defined as the number of new arrests after beginning probation, there may have been wide variation in the ability of staff in the 11 sites to reliably detect new arrests.

These remarks are not intended as criticism of the ISP study. In her description of the evaluation, Petersilia (1989) documents the extensive steps taken by RAND Corporation researchers to control possible validity threats. The important point is that field experiments and evaluations can present many obstacles that are not eliminated simply by adopting a randomized experimental design. Careful administration and control throughout the experiment are necessary to reduce potential threats to internal validity.

Generalizability and Threats to Validity

Potential threats to internal validity are only some of the complications faced by experimenters. They also have the problem of generalizing from experimental findings to the real world. Even if the results of an experiment are an accurate gauge of what happened during that experiment, do they really tell us anything about life in the wilds of society? Keeping in mind our examination of cause and effect in Chapter 4, we consider two dimensions of **generalizability**: construct validity and external validity.

Threats to Construct Validity

In the language of experimentation, construct validity is the correspondence between the empirical test of a hypothesis and the underlying causal process that the experiment is intended to represent. Construct validity is thus concerned with generalizing from our observations in an experiment to actual causal processes in the real world. In our hypothetical example, the educational video is how we operationalize the construct of understanding the health effects of alcohol abuse. Our questionnaire represents the dependent construct of actual alcohol use.

Are these reasonable ways to represent the underlying causal process, in which understanding the effects of alcohol use causes people to reduce excessive or abusive drinking? It is a reasonable representation, but certainly it is also incomplete. People develop an understanding of the health effects of alcohol use in many ways. Watching an educational video is one way; having personal experience, talking to friends and parents, taking other courses, and reading books and articles are others. Our video may do a good job of representing the health effects of alcohol use, but it is an incomplete representation of that construct. Alternatively, the video may be poorly produced, too technical, or incomplete. Then the experimental stimulus may not adequately represent the construct we are interested in—educating students about the health effects of alcohol use. There also may be problems with our measure of the dependent variable: questionnaire items on self-reported alcohol use.

Here's another example from *Blink: The Power of Thinking Without Thinking* by popular author Malcolm Gladwell (2005). Part of his book describes how market researchers conduct experiments to test new consumer products. In blind tests of cola drinks, participants were given small samples of different colas without knowing the cola's brand. Market researchers found that people preferred a sweeter type of cola in these experiments. However, in follow-up tests where participants drank 12-ounce servings, more preferred the less sweet formula. A small taste—2 ounces or so—did not represent the construct of cola drinking for most people, who typically drink about 12 ounces. In smaller doses people liked sweeter cola, but that was an artifact of the experiment (2005:165–166).

By this time, you should recognize a similarity between construct validity and some of the measurement issues discussed in Chapter 5. Almost any empirical example or measure of a construct is incomplete. Part of construct validity involves how completely an empirical measure can represent a construct or how well we can generalize from a measure to a construct.

A related issue in construct validity is whether a given level of treatment is sufficient. Perhaps showing a single video to a group of subjects would have little effect on alcohol use, but administering a series of videos over several weeks would have a greater impact. We could test this experimentally by having more than one experimental group and varying the number of videos seen by different groups.

Threats to construct validity are problematic in criminal justice experiments, often because researchers do not clearly specify precisely what constructs are to be represented by particular measures or experimental treatments. Farrington, Ohlin, and Wilson (1986:92) make a related point: "Most treatments in existing experiments are not based on a well-developed theory but on a vague idea about what might influence offending. The treatments given are often heterogeneous, making it difficult to know which element was responsible for any observed effect." These authors also note the importance of thinking about levels of constructs.

The RAND Corporation evaluation of intensive supervision provides a good example. The ISP program explicitly defined enhanced probation as punitive. This leads to the question of how much probation should be enhanced. If a typical probation officer carries an average caseload of 100 clients and sees each an average of twice per month, what workload and contact levels are sufficiently intensive to reduce recidivism? Cutting the workload in half and doubling the number of contacts would be more intensive, but would it be intensive enough to produce a decline in recidivism? Again, an experiment could test this question by including more than one experimental group and giving each a different level of probation supervision.

In summary, three elements in enhancing construct validity are (1) linking constructs and measures to theory, (2) clearly indicating what constructs are represented by specific measures, and (3) thinking carefully about what levels of treatment may be necessary to produce some level of change in the dependent measure.

Threats to External Validity

Will an experimental study, conducted with the kind of control we have emphasized here, produce results that would also be found in more natural settings? Can an intensive probation program shown to be successful in Minneapolis achieve similar results in Miami? External validity represents a slightly different form of generalizability—one in which the question is whether results from experiments in one setting (time and place) will be obtained in other settings, or whether a treatment found to be effective for one population will have similar effects on a different group.

Threats to external validity are greater for experiments conducted under carefully controlled conditions. If the alcohol education experiment reveals that drinking decreased among students in the experimental group, then we can be confident that the video actually reduced alcohol use among our experimental subjects. But will the video have the same effect on high school students or adults if it is broadcast on television? We cannot be certain, because the carefully controlled conditions of the experiment might have had something to do with the video's effectiveness.

In contrast, criminal justice field experiments are conducted in more natural settings. Real probation officers in 11 different local jurisdictions delivered intensive supervision to real probationers in the RAND ISP experiment. Because of the real-world conditions and multiple sites, there were fewer potential threats to external validity. This is not to say that external validity is never a problem in field experiments. The 11 probation agencies that participated in this evaluation may not be typical of probation agencies in other areas; the simple fact that staff were willing to participate suggests that they could be more dedicated or more amenable to trying new approaches. One of the advantages of field experiments in criminal justice is that, because they take place under real-world conditions, results are more likely to be valid in other real-world settings as well.

You may have detected a fundamental conflict between internal and external validity. Conducting experiments under carefully controlled conditions reduces threats to internal validity. But such conditions do not reflect real-world settings, and this restricts our ability to generalize results. Field experiments generally have greater external validity, but their internal validity may suffer because such studies are more difficult to monitor than those conducted in more controlled settings. This is what John Eck (2002:104) refers to as a "diabolical dilemma."

Shadish, Cook, and Campbell (2002:101) offer some useful advice for resolving the potential for conflict between internal and external validity. Explanatory studies that test cause-and-effect theories should place greater emphasis on internal validity; applied studies should be more concerned with external validity. This is not a hard-and-fast rule, because internal validity must be established before external validity becomes an issue. That is, applied researchers must have confidence in the internal validity of their cause-and-effect relationships before they ask whether similar relationships would be found in other settings.

Threats to Statistical Conclusion Validity

The basic principle of *statistical conclusion* validity is simple. Virtually all experimental research in criminal justice is based on samples of subjects that represent a target population. Up to a point, larger samples of subjects are more representative of the target population than are smaller samples. Statistical conclusion validity becomes an issue when findings are based on small samples of cases. Because experiments can be costly and time consuming, they are frequently conducted with relatively small numbers of subjects. In such cases, only large differences between experimental and control groups on posttest measures can be detected with any degree of confidence.

In practice, this means that finding cause-and-effect relationships through experiments depends on two related factors: (1) the number of subjects and (2) the magnitude of posttest differences between the experimental and control groups. Experiments with large numbers of cases may be able to reliably detect small differences, but experiments with smaller numbers can detect only large differences.

Threats to statistical conclusion validity can be magnified by other difficulties in field experiments. If treatment spillover or compensation is a problem, then smaller differences in the experimental stimulus will be delivered to each group. After reviewing a large number of criminal justice experiments, David Weisburd, Cynthia Lum, and Sue-Ming Yang (2003) concluded that more generally, failure to maintain control over experimental conditions reduces statistical conclusion validity—even for studies with large numbers of subjects. Furthermore, these authors found that as sample size increases, so do implementation difficulties, which undermines experimental results in a variety of ways.

Variations in the Classical Experimental Design

The basic experimental design is adapted to meet different research applications.

We now turn to a more systematic consideration of variations on the classical experiment that can be produced by manipulating the building blocks of experiments.

Slightly restating our earlier remarks, four basic building blocks are present in experimental designs: (1) the number of experimental and control groups, (2) the number and variation of experimental stimuli, (3) the number of pretest and posttest measurements, and (4) the procedures used to select subjects and assign them to groups. By illustrating these building blocks and the ways they are used to produce different designs, we adopt the system of notation used by Campbell and Stanley (1966). Figure 7.3 presents this notation and shows how it is used to represent the classical experiment and examples of variations on this design.

In Figure 7.3, the letter *O* represents observations or measurements, and *X* represents an experimental stimulus or treatment. Different time points are displayed as *t* with a subscript to represent time order. Thus, for the classical experiment

```
                              Classical Experiment
Experimental  group            O        X         O
Control group                  O                  O
                               t₁       t₂        t₃
                                       Time
                                              ⟶

                        O = observation or
                              measurement
                        X = experimental stimulus
                         t = time point

                                  Posttest Only
Experimental  group                     X         O
Control group                                     O
                                        t₁        t₂

                                   Factorial
Experimental treatment 1        O       X₁        O
Experimental treatment 2        O       X₂        O
Control                         O                 O
                                t₁      t₂        t₃
```

FIGURE 7.3 Variations in the Experimental Design

shown in Figure 7.3, O at t_1 is the pretest, O at t_3 is the posttest, and the experimental stimulus X is administered to the experimental group at t_2, between the pretest and the posttest. Measures are taken for the control group at times t_1 and t_3, but the experimental stimulus is not administered to the control group.

Now consider the design labeled "Posttest Only." As implied by its name, no pretest measures are made on either the experimental group or the control group. Thinking for a moment about the threats to internal validity, we can imagine situations in which a posttest-only design is appropriate. Testing and retesting might especially influence subjects' behavior if measurements are made by administering a questionnaire, with subjects' responses to the posttest potentially affected by their experience in the pretest. A posttest-only design can reduce the possibility of testing as a threat to validity by eliminating the pretest.

Without a pretest, it is obviously not possible to detect change in measures of the dependent variable, but we can still test the effects of the experimental stimulus by comparing posttest measures

for the experimental group with posttest measures for the control group. For example, if we are concerned about the possibility of sensitizing subjects in a study of an alcohol education video, we might eliminate the pretest and examine the posttest differences between the experimental and control groups. Random assignment is the key to the posttest-only design. If subjects are randomly assigned to experimental and control groups, we expect them to be equivalent. Any posttest differences between the two groups on the dependent variable can then be attributed to the influence of the video.

In general, posttest-only designs are appropriate when researchers suspect that the process of measurement may bias subjects' responses to a questionnaire or other instrument. This is more likely when only a short time elapses between pretest and posttest measurements. The number of observations made on subjects is a design building block that can be varied as needed. We emphasize here that random assignment is essential in a posttest-only design.

Figure 7.3 also shows a factorial design, which has two experimental groups that receive different treatments (or different levels of a single treatment) and one control group. This design is useful for comparing the effects of different interventions or different amounts of a single treatment. In evaluating an ISP program, we might wish to compare how different levels of contact between probation officers and probation clients affect recidivism. In this case, subjects in one experimental group might receive weekly contact (X_1), subjects in the other experimental group might be seen by probation officers twice each week (X_2), and control-group subjects might have normal contact—say, monthly—with probation officers. Because more contact is more expensive, we would be interested in seeing the differing recidivism rates produced by monthly, weekly, and twice-weekly contacts.

Thus, an experimental design may have more than one group receiving different versions or levels of experimental treatment. We can also vary the number of measurements made on dependent variables. No hard-and-fast rules exist for using these building blocks to design a given experiment. A useful rule of thumb, however, is to keep the design as simple as possible to control for potential threats to validity. The specific design for any particular study depends on the research purpose, available resources, and unavoidable constraints in designing and actually carrying out the experiment.

One very common constraint is how subjects or units of analysis are selected and assigned to experimental or control groups. This building block brings us to the subject of quasi-experimental designs.

Quasi-Experimental Designs

When random assignment is not possible, researchers can use different types of quasi-experimental designs.

By now, the value of random assignment in controlling threats to validity should be apparent. However, it is often impossible to randomly select subjects for experimental and control groups and satisfy other requirements. Most often, there may be practical or administrative obstacles. There may also be legal or ethical reasons why random assignment cannot be used in criminal justice experiments.

When random assignment is not possible, the next best choice is often a **quasi-experiment**. The prefix *quasi-*, meaning "to a certain degree," is significant—a quasi-experiment is, to a certain degree, an experiment. In most cases, quasi-experiments do not randomly assign subjects and, therefore, may suffer from the internal validity threats that are so well controlled in true experiments. Without random assignment, the other building blocks of experimental design must be used creatively to reduce validity threats. Following Shadish, Cook, and Campbell (2002), we will group quasi-experimental designs into two categories: (1) nonequivalent-groups designs and (2) time-series designs. Each can be represented with the same O, X, and t notation used to depict experimental designs.

Quasi-experiment Research design that includes most, but not all, elements of an experimental design.

Nonequivalent-Groups Designs

The name for this family of designs is also meaningful. The main strength of random assignment is that it allows us to assume equivalence in experimental and control groups. When it is not possible to create groups through random assignment, we must use some other procedure that is not random. If we construct groups through some nonrandom procedure, however, we cannot assume that the groups are statistically equivalent—hence, the label *nonequivalent-groups design*.

Whenever experimental and control groups are not equivalent, we should select subjects in some way that makes the two groups as comparable as possible. Often, the best way to achieve comparability is through a matching process in which subjects in the experimental group are matched with subjects in a comparison group. The term *comparison group* is commonly used, rather than *control group*, to highlight the nonequivalence of groups in quasi-experimental designs. A comparison group does, however, serve the same function as a control group.

Some examples of research that uses nonequivalent-groups designs illustrate various approaches to matching and the creative use of experimental design building blocks. Examples include studies of child abuse (Widom, 1989), obscene phone calls (Clarke, 1997a), and video cameras for crime prevention (Gill and Spriggs, 2005). Figure 7.4 shows a diagram of each design using the X, O, and t notation. The solid line that separates treatment and comparison groups in the figure signifies that subjects have been placed in groups through some nonrandom procedure.

Child Abuse and Later Arrest Cathy Spatz Widom (1989; also Widom and Maxfield, 2001) studied the long-term effects of child abuse— whether abused children are more likely to be charged with delinquent or adult criminal offenses than are children who were not abused. Child abuse was the experimental stimulus, and the number of subsequent arrests was the dependent variable.

Of course, it is not possible to assign children randomly to groups in which some are abused and others are not. Widom's design called for selecting a sample of children who, according to court records, had been abused. She then matched each

Widom (1989)

Treatment group	X	O
Comparison group		O
	t_1	t_2

X = official record of child abuse
O = counts of juvenile or adult arrest

Clarke (1997a)

Treatment group	O	X	O
Comparison group	O		O
	t_1	t_2	t_3

X = caller identification and call tracing
O = customer complaints of obscene calls

Gill and Spriggs (2005)

Target area 1	O	X_1	O
Comparison area 1	O		O
Target area 2	O	X_2	O
Comparison area 2	O		O
Target area 13	O	X_i	O
Comparison area 13	O		O
	t_1	t_2	t_3

X_i = CCTV installation in area i
O = police crime data, survey data on fear of crime

FIGURE 7.4 Quasi-Experimental Design Examples

abused subject with a comparison subject—of the same gender, race, age, and approximate socioeconomic status (SES)—who had not been abused. The assumption with these matching criteria was that age at the time of abuse, gender, race, and SES differences might confound any observed relationship between abuse and subsequent arrests. Widom found that children who had been abused or neglected were more likely to have juvenile records or adult arrests. But the differences between the treatment and comparison groups were smaller than differences found in most previous research.

You may be wondering how a researcher selects important variables to use in matching experimental and comparison subjects. We cannot provide a definitive answer to that question, any more than we can specify what particular variables

should be used in a given experiment. The answer ultimately depends on the nature and purpose of the experiment. As a general rule, however, the two groups should be comparable in terms of variables that are likely to be related to the dependent variable under study. Widom matched on gender, race, and SES because these variables are correlated with juvenile and adult arrest rates. Age at the time of reported abuse was also an important variable because children abused at a younger age had a longer "at-risk" period for delinquent arrests.

Widom produced experimental and comparison groups by matching individual subjects. It is also possible to construct experimental and comparison groups through aggregate matching, in which the average characteristics of each group are comparable. This is illustrated in our next example.

Deterring Obscene Phone Calls In 1988, the telephone company serving New Jersey introduced caller identification (ID) and instant call tracing in a small number of telephone exchange areas. Now ubiquitous in mobile phones, caller ID was a new technology in 1988. Instant call tracing allows the recipient of an obscene or a threatening call to automatically initiate a procedure to trace the source of the call.

Ronald Clarke (1997a) studied the effects of these new technologies in deterring obscene phone calls. Clarke expected that obscene calls would decrease in areas where the new services were available. To test this, he compared records of formal customer complaints about annoying calls in the New Jersey areas that had caller ID and call tracing to formal complaints in other New Jersey areas where the new services were not available. One year later, the number of formal complaints had dropped sharply in areas serviced by the new technology; no decline was found in other New Jersey Bell areas.

In this study, telephone service areas with new services were the treatment group, and areas without the services were the comparison group. Clarke's matching criterion was a simple one: telephone service by New Jersey Bell, assuming the volume of obscene phone calls was relatively constant within a single phone service area. Of course, matching on telephone service area cannot eliminate the possibility that the volume of obscene phone calls varies from one part of New Jersey to another, but Clarke's choice of a comparison group was straightforward and certainly more plausible than comparing New Jersey to, say, New Mexico.

Clarke's study is a good example of a natural field experiment. The experimental stimulus—caller ID and call tracing—was not specifically introduced by Clarke, but he was able to obtain measures for the dependent variable before and after the experimental stimulus was introduced. This design made it possible for Clarke to infer with reasonable confidence that caller ID and call tracing reduced the number of formal complaints about obscene phone calls.

Another useful lesson from this study is related to the dramatic drop in obscene phone calls. Donald Campbell, whose name has long been associated with experimentation in social science, argues convincingly that researchers can have more confidence in the validity of large changes in dependent variables compared with small changes (Campbell, 1979). Ronald Clarke (2008) refers to this as a "cliff-edge" effect, meaning that some crime prevention measures produce reductions in crime that figuratively fall off the cliff. An example is the virtual end of cell phone cloning after digital cell phones replaced the older technology (Clarke, Kemper, and Wyckoff, 2001).

Cameras and Crime Prevention   U.S. residents have become accustomed to seeing closed-circuit television (CCTV) cameras in stores, at ATMs, and increasingly in other public places. But this technology has been much more widespread in other countries. With an estimated 4 million cameras deployed, CCTV is widely used as a crime prevention and surveillance tool in the United Kingdom (McCahill and Norris, 2003). CCTV enabled the London Metropolitan Police to identify suspects quickly in the Underground bombing attacks that took place in 2005. Cameras are used increasingly to monitor traffic and even record license plates of cars running traffic lights. But does CCTV have any effect in reducing crime?

Martin Gill and Angela Spriggs (2005) conducted an evaluation of 13 CCTV projects installed in a variety of residential and commercial settings in England. These were a mix of small- and large-scale CCTV projects involving multiple cameras. One area on the outskirts of London included over 500 cameras installed to reduce thefts of and from vehicles in parking facilities. Five projects in London and other urban areas placed 10–15 cameras in low-income housing areas, seeking to reduce burglary and robbery. Researchers examined two types of dependent variables before and after cameras were installed: crimes reported to police and fear of crime. Fear was measured through surveys of people living in residential areas and samples of people on local streets for commercial areas and parking facilities.

Measuring police data and fear of crime before and after cameras were installed made it possible for Gill and associates to satisfy two criteria for cause: time order and covariation between the independent variable (CCTV) and dependent variables. Random assignment of areas to treatment (CCTV) or control (no CCTV) groups was not possible. This was because the intervention was planned for only a small number of locations of each type (residential, commercial, and parking) and because CCTV was carefully tailored to each site. Instead, the researchers created two types of comparison areas. First, comparison areas "were selected by similarity on socio-demographic and geographical characteristics and crime problems" (Gill and Spriggs, 2005:123–124). The second type of comparison was "buffer zones," defined as an area in a one-mile radius from the edge of the target area where CCTV cameras were installed; buffer zones were defined only for CCTV areas.

The rationale for comparison areas is clear. If CCTV is effective in reducing crime, we should expect declines in target areas, but not in comparison areas. Alternatively, if posttreatment measures of crime went down in both treatment and comparison areas, we might expect greater declines in the CCTV sites. But what about buffer areas? After defining buffer areas, researchers then subdivided them into concentric rings around a target area (T), as shown in Figure 7.5. The stated purpose was to assess any movement of crime around the target area. If CCTV was effective in reducing crime, any reduction should be greatest in the target area; the size of the reduction should decline moving outward from the target area.[1]

---

[1]Compare this with the Chicago research by Shaw and McKay described in Chapter 2.

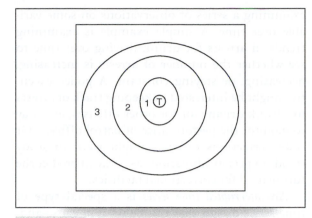

FIGURE 7.5 Buffer Zones in CCTV Quasi-Experiment

Source: Adapted from Gill and Springs (2005:40).

Short-term results found some reduction of some types of crime in some CCTV areas. In other treatment areas, some crimes increased more than in comparison areas. In particular, Gill and Spriggs (2005) found that public order offenses such as drunkenness tended to increase more in CCTV target areas. Overall, significant drops in crime were found in just 2 of 13 target areas. Fear and related attitudes declined in all target and comparison areas, but the authors believed this was largely due to declining crime in all areas.

This example illustrates why nonequivalent comparison groups are important. Because crime declined in most areas and fear declined in all, a simple comparison of pre- and postintervention measures would have been misleading. That strategy would have suggested that CCTV was responsible for reduced crime and fear. Only by adding the comparison and buffer areas to their research were Gill and Spriggs (2005) able to learn that CCTV was probably not the cause of declines, because similar patterns were found in many areas where CCTV systems were not installed.

Together, these three studies illustrate different approaches to research design when it is not possible to randomly assign subjects to treatment and control groups. Lacking random assignment, researchers must use creative procedures for selecting subjects, constructing treatment and comparison groups, measuring dependent variables, and exercising other controls to reduce possible threats to validity.

Cohort Designs

Chapter 4 mentioned cohort studies as examples of longitudinal designs. We can also view cohort studies as nonequivalent-control-group designs. Recall from Chapter 4 that a cohort may be defined as a group of subjects who enter or leave an institution at the same time. For example, a class of police officers who graduate from a training academy at the same time could be considered a cohort. Or we might view all persons who were sentenced to probation in May as a cohort.

Now think of a cohort that is exposed to some experimental stimulus. The May probation cohort might be required to complete 100 hours of community service in addition to meeting other conditions of probation. If we are interested in whether probationers who receive community service sentences are charged with fewer probation violations, we can compare the performance of the May cohort with that of the April cohort or the June cohort or some other cohort not sentenced to community service. Cohorts that do not receive community service sentences serve as comparison groups. The groups are not equivalent because they were not created by random assignment. But if we assume that a comparison cohort does not systematically differ from a treatment cohort on important variables, we can use this design to determine whether community service sentences reduce probation violations.

That last assumption is very important, but it may not be viable. Perhaps a criminal court docket is organized to schedule certain types of cases at the same time, so a May cohort would be systematically different from a June cohort. But if the assumption of comparability can be met, cohorts may be used to construct nonequivalent comparison and experimental groups by taking advantage of the natural flow of cases through some institutional process.

A study by Anthony Braga, Anne Morrison Piehl, and David Hureau (2009) on the effectiveness of a re-entry program for violent offenders released from jail is a good example of a cohort design. The Boston Reentry Initiative (BRI) focused on offenders who were believed to be at high risk of committing violent crimes after release from jail terms. Combining resources from criminal justice, social service, and faith-based organizations, the BRI identified key risk factors (such as gang involvement) and planned return to communities where violent crime was a serious problem. Though the program centered on re-entry, participants were identified when they were first committed to the local jail. This was done so the re-entry services could be started immediately. Beginning in 2002, about 15–20 BRI participants were selected each month.

Jails produce obvious cohorts—people enter and leave through an ongoing process. In the BRI case, those selected for re-entry services in 2002 were the treatment cohort. Offenders who met the same risk factor selection criteria, but began their jail terms one year earlier, were selected as a comparison cohort. Braga and associates used a statistical matching procedure to compare the treatment and comparison cohorts on key measures such as age, prior arrests, prior gang involvement, and history of violent offenses. With the exception of age, no statistically significant differences were found between the two groups. The treatment cohort was slightly younger than the comparison cohort. These similarities enhanced the researchers' confidence in their findings.

Examining data for three years after release, Braga and associates found that BRI participants were 30 percent less likely to be arrested for any offense, and 37 percent less likely to have been arrested for violence. This was particularly encouraging, since those selected for the BRI and those in the comparison cohort were drawn from high-risk groups. You might think this could have signaled a regression artifact. But both treatment and comparison cohorts were from the high-risk group, and rearrest rates declined more sharply for BRI participants. This makes regression and other alternative explanations less plausible.

Time-Series Designs

Time-series designs are common examples of longitudinal studies in criminal justice research. As the name implies, a time-series design involves examining a series of observations on some variable over time. A simple example is examining trends in arrests for drunk driving over time to see whether the number of arrests is increasing, decreasing, or staying constant. A police executive might be interested in keeping track of arrests for drunk driving, or for other offenses, as a way to monitor the performance of patrol officers. Or state corrections officials might want to study trends in prison admissions as a way to predict the future need for correctional facilities.

An *interrupted time series* is a special type of time-series design that can be used in cause-and-effect studies. A series of observations is compared before and after some intervention is introduced. For example, a researcher might want to know whether roadside sobriety checkpoints cause a decrease in fatal automobile accidents. Trends in accidents could be compared before and after the roadside checkpoints are established.

Interrupted time-series designs can be very useful in criminal justice research, especially in applied studies. They do have some limitations, however, just like other ways of structuring research. Shadish, Cook, and Campbell (2002) describe the strengths and limitations of different approaches to time-series designs. We will introduce these approaches with a hypothetical example and then describe some specific criminal justice applications.

Continuing with the example of sobriety checkpoints, Figure 7.6 presents four possible patterns of alcohol-related automobile accidents. The vertical line in each pattern shows the time when the roadside checkpoint program is introduced. Which of these patterns indicates that the new program caused a reduction in car accidents?

If the time-series results looked like pattern 1 in Figure 7.6, we might think initially that the checkpoints caused a reduction in alcohol-related accidents, but there seems to be a general downward trend in accidents that continues after the intervention. It's safer to conclude that the decline would have continued even without the roadside checkpoints.

Pattern 2 shows that an increasing trend in auto accidents has been reversed after the intervention, but apparently this is due to a regular pattern in which accidents have been bouncing up and down. The intervention was introduced at the peak of an upward trend, and the later decline

Time-series design A type of quasi-experimental design where changes in a dependent variable are monitored over some time period.

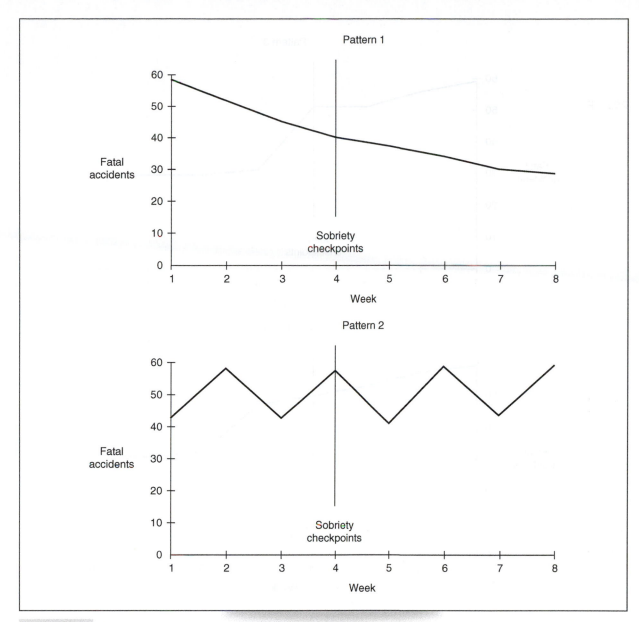

FIGURE 7.6 Four Patterns of Change in Fatal Automobile Accidents (Hypothetical Data) (*Continued*)

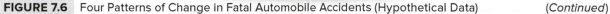

may be an artifact of the underlying pattern rather than of the new program.

Patterns 1 and 2 exhibit some outside trend, rather than an intervention, that may account for a pattern observed over time. We may recognize this as an example of history as a validity threat to the inference that the new checkpoint program caused a change in auto accidents. The general decline in pattern 1 may be due to reduced drunk driving that has nothing to do with sobriety checkpoints. Pattern 2 illustrates what is referred

to as seasonality in a time series—a regular pattern of change over time. Shadish, Cook, and Campbell (2002) describe seasonality as a special case of history. In our example, the data might reflect seasonal variation in alcohol-related accidents that occur around holidays or maybe on football weekends near a college campus.

Patterns 3 and 4 lend more support to the inference that sobriety checkpoints caused a decline in alcohol-related accidents, but the two patterns are different in a subtle way. In pattern 3, accidents

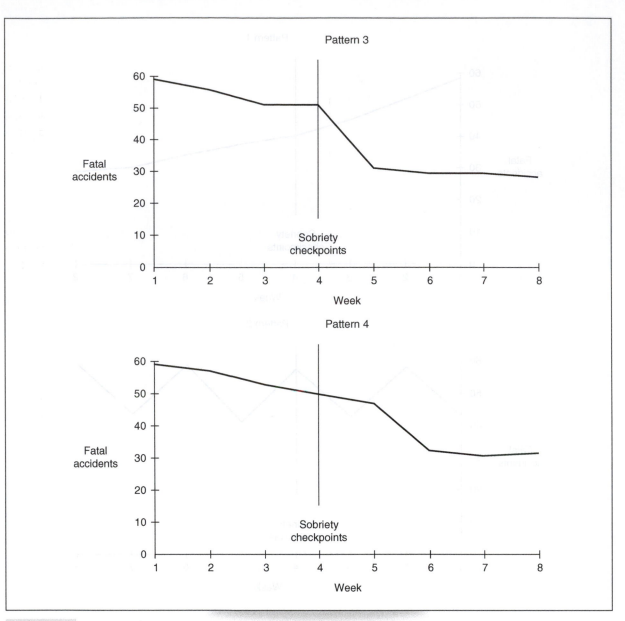

FIGURE 7.6 *(Continued)*

decline more sharply from a general downward trend immediately after the checkpoint program was introduced, whereas pattern 4 displays a sharper decline some time after the new program was established. Which pattern provides stronger support for the inference?

In framing your answer, recall what we have said about construct validity. Think about the underlying causal process these two patterns represent, or consider possible mechanisms that might be at work. Pattern 3 suggests that the program was immediately effective and supports what we might call an incapacitation mechanism; roadside checkpoints enabled police to identify and arrest drunk drivers, thereby getting them off the road and reducing accidents. Pattern 4 suggests a deterrent mechanism; as drivers learned about the checkpoints, they less often drove after drinking, and accidents eventually declined. Either explanation is possible given the evidence presented. This illustrates an important limitation of interrupted time-series designs; they operationalize complex causal constructs in simple ways. Our interpretation depends in large part on how we understand this causal process.

The classic study by Richard McCleary, Barbara Nienstedt, and James Erven (1982) illustrates the need to think carefully about how well time-series results reflect underlying causal patterns. Recall that McCleary and colleagues reported a sharp decline in burglaries immediately after a special burglary investigation unit was established in a large city. This finding was at odds with their understanding of how police investigations could reasonably be expected to reduce burglary. A special unit might eventually be able to reduce the number of burglaries, after investigating incidents over a period of time and making arrests. But it is highly unlikely that changing investigative procedures would have an immediate impact. This discrepancy prompted McCleary and associates to look more closely at the policy change and led to their conclusion that the apparent decline in burglaries was produced by changes in record-keeping practices. No evidence existed of any decline in the actual number of burglaries.

This example illustrates our discussion of instrumentation earlier in this chapter. Changes in the way police counted burglaries produced what appeared to be a reduction in burglary. Instrumentation can be a particular problem in time-series designs for two reasons. First, observations are usually made over a relatively long time period, which increases the likelihood of changes in measurement instruments. Second, time-series designs often use measures that are produced by an organization such as a police department, criminal court, probation office, or corrections department. There may be changes or irregularities in the way data are collected by these agencies that are not readily apparent to researchers and that are, in any case, not subject to their control.

As another example, David Finkelhor and Lisa Jones (2004) systematically examine data showing a nationwide 40 percent decline in child sexual abuse cases from 1990 to 2000. Because child abuse had become a prominent concern in the 1990s, the researchers were especially interested in determining whether any changes in recording practices in

one or more states might account for the decline. They systematically considered such explanations as changing definitions or data collection procedures, more stringent screening of cases by investigators, less reporting of sexual abuse cases, and other possible sources of instrumentation. After comparing different sources of data for a variety of states, Finkelhor and Jones conclude that at least some portion of the decline in reported cases is due to a real decline in the number of child sexual abuse cases. Their careful report is an excellent example of thinking through plausible threats to instrumentation in a time series.

Variations in Time-Series Designs

If we view the basic interrupted time-series design as an adaptation of basic design building blocks, we can consider how modifications can help control for many validity problems. The simplest time-series design studies one group—the treatment group—over time. Rather than making one pretest and one posttest observation, the interrupted time-series design makes a longer series of observations before and after introducing an experimental treatment.

What if we considered the other building blocks of experimental design? Figure 7.7 presents the basic design and some variations using the familiar O, X, and t notation. In the basic design, shown at the top of Figure 7.7, many pretest and posttest observations are made on a single group that receives some treatment. We could strengthen this design by adding a comparison series of observations on some group that does not receive the treatment. If, for example, roadside sobriety checkpoints were introduced all over the state of Ohio but were not used at all in Michigan, then we could compare auto accidents in Ohio (the treatment series) with auto accidents in Michigan (the comparison series). If checkpoints caused a reduction in alcohol-related accidents, we would expect to see a decline in Ohio following the intervention, but there should be no change or a lesser decline in Michigan over the same time period. The second part of Figure 7.7 shows this design—an interrupted time series with a nonequivalent comparison group. The two series are not equivalent because we did not randomly assign drivers

Simple Interrupted Time Series

O   O   O   O   X   O   O   O   O
t_1 t_2 t_3 t_4 t_5 t_6 t_7 t_8

**Interrupted Time Series with
Nonequivalent Comparison Group**

O   O   O   O   X   O   O   O   O

O   O   O   O   O   O   O   O
t_1 t_2 t_3 t_4 t_5 t_6 t_7 t_8

**Interrupted Time Series
with Removed Treatment**

O   O   X   O   O   O   –X   O   O   O
t_1 t_2 t_3 t_4 t_5 t_6 t_7 t_8

**Interrupted Time Series
with Switching Replications**

O   O   O   X   O   O   O   O   O

O   O   O   O   O   X   O   O   O
t_1 t_2 t_3 t_4 t_5 t_6 t_7 t_8

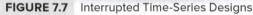

FIGURE 7.7 Interrupted Time-Series Designs

to Ohio or Michigan. Wesley Skogan and associates present a good example of this design in their analysis of police problem solving in Chicago (Skogan et al., 2008). They examined changes in crime for police beats where specific problems were targeted compared with beats where no crime-specific interventions were developed.

A single-series design may be modified by introducing and then removing the intervention, as shown in the third part of Figure 7.7. We might test sobriety checkpoints by setting them up every weekend for a month and then not setting them up for the next few months. If the checkpoints caused a reduction in alcohol-related accidents, we might expect an increase after they were removed. Or the effects of weekend checkpoints might persist even after we removed them.

Because different states or cities sometimes introduce new drunk-driving programs at different times, we might be able to use what Shadish, Cook, and Campbell (2002:192) called a time-series design with switching replications. The bottom of Figure 7.7 illustrates this design. For example, assume that Ohio begins using checkpoints in May 1998 and Michigan introduces

them in July of the same year. A switching replications design could strengthen our conclusion that checkpoints reduce accidents if we saw that a decline in Ohio began in June and a similar pattern was found in Michigan beginning in August. The fact that similar changes occurred in the dependent variable in different states at different times, corresponding to when the program was introduced, would add to our confidence in stating that sobriety checkpoints actually reduced auto accidents.

Nagin and Weisburd present different examples of time-series designs that have what they term "high evidentiary value." (2013:654). This means the designs include building blocks that reduce threats to validity. Because so many justice agencies collect data over time, researchers can often use time-series designs.

Variable-Oriented Research and Scientific Realism

Another way to think about a time-series design is as a study of one or a few cases with many observations. If we design a time-series study of roadside checkpoints in Ohio, we will be examining one case (Ohio) with many observations of auto accidents. Or a design that compares Ohio and Michigan will examine many observations for two cases. Thinking once again about design building blocks, notice how we have slightly restated one of those building blocks. Instead of considering the number of experimental and control groups, our attention centers on the number of subjects or cases in our study. In Figure 7.7, the first and third time-series designs have one case each; the second and fourth designs examine two cases each.

Classical experiments and quasi-experiments with large numbers of subjects are examples of what Charles Ragin (2000) terms **case-oriented research**, in which many cases are examined to understand a small number of variables. Time-series designs and case studies are examples of **variable-oriented research**, in which a large number of variables are studied for a small number of cases or subjects. Suppose we wish to study inmate-on-inmate assaults in correctional facilities. Using a case-oriented approach, we might send a questionnaire to a sample of 500 correctional facilities, asking facility staff to provide information about assaults, facility design, inmate characteristics, and housing conditions. Here, we are gathering information on a few variables from a large number of correctional facilities. Using a variable-oriented approach, we might visit one or a few facilities to conduct in-depth interviews with staff, observe the condition of facilities, and gather information from institutional records. Here, we are collecting information on a wide range of variables from a small number of institutions.

The **case study** design is an example of variable-oriented research. Here, the researcher's attention centers on an in-depth examination of one or a few cases on many dimensions. Robert Yin (2013) points out that the terms *case* and *case study* are used broadly. Cases can be individual people, neighborhoods, correctional facilities, courtrooms, or other aggregations. Our running example of race profiling has many elements of a series of case studies. Researchers gathered information from different sources to measure several types of variables for one state (New Jersey, North Carolina, Pennsylvania, etc.) and a varying number of other cases (state police stations, or counties) in the state.

Robert Yin cautions that the case study design is often misunderstood as representing "qualitative" research or a participant observation study. Instead, Yin advises that the case study is a design strategy and that the labels *qualitative* and *quantitative* are not useful ways to distinguish design strategies. Case studies might appear qualitative because they focus on one or a small number of units. But many case studies employ sophisticated statistical techniques to examine many variables for those units. An example illustrates how misleading it can be to associate case studies with qualitative research.

In what has come to be known as the "Boston Gun Project," Anthony Braga and associates (2001) studied violence by youth gangs in Boston neighborhoods. Theirs was an applied explanatory study. They worked with local officials to better understand gang violence, develop ways to reduce it, and eventually assess the effects of their interventions. Neither a classical experiment nor a nonequivalent-groups design was

possible. Researchers sought to understand and reduce violence by all gangs in the city. Their research centered on gangs, not individuals, although some interventions targeted particular gang members.

Researchers collected a large amount of information about gangs and gang violence from several sources. Earlier reports (Kennedy, Piehl, and Braga, 1996) described something called "network analysis," in which researchers examined relationships between gangs in different neighborhoods and conflicts over turf within neighborhoods. Police records of homicides, assaults, and shootings were studied. Based on extensive data on a small number of gangs, researchers collaborated with public officials, neighborhood organizations, and a coalition of religious leaders—the "faith community." A variety of interventions were devised, but most were crafted from a detailed understanding of the specific nature of gangs and gang violence as they existed in Boston neighborhoods. David Kennedy (1998) summarizes these using the label "pulling levers," signifying that key gang members were vulnerable to intensive monitoring via probation or parole. The package of strategies was markedly successful: Youth homicides were reduced from about 35–40 each year in the 20 years preceding the program to about 15 per year in the first 5 postintervention years (Braga, 2008).

The Boston research is also a good example of the scientific realist approach of Ray Pawson and Nick Tilley (1997). Researchers examined a small number of subjects—gangs and gang members—in a single city and in the context of specific neighborhoods where gangs were active. Extensive data were gathered on the mechanisms of gang violence. Interventions were tailored to those mechanisms in their context.

Braga and associates (2001) emphasize that the success of the Boston efforts was due to the process by which researchers, public officials, and community members collaboratively studied gang violence and then developed appropriate policy actions based on their analyses. Other jurisdictions mistakenly tried to reproduce Boston's interventions, with limited or no success, failing to recognize that the interventions were developed specifically for Boston. In case study language,

The kind of research we have been describing with respect to racial profiling is generally explanatory research. In a sense, we want to learn whether race is associated with differences in police action. Recalling the time-order criterion for demonstrating cause, because an individual's race is determined before any particular experience with traffic enforcement, differences in traffic enforcement by race *may* be explained by race. We emphasize *may*, because time order is only one of the three requirements for demonstrating cause.

Experiments in Racial Profiling?

You may have heard something about field experiments to assess differences between the experiences of black and white people applying for a mortgage, shopping for a new car, renting an apartment, or buying a house. Individuals, or couples in the case of home buying, are matched on age, income, and other criteria relevant to whatever transaction is being tested. Race is systematically varied, acting as an experimental stimulus. The goal is to assess any discriminatory treatment where the only difference between people is race (National Research Council, 2004).

It's not possible to systematically vary race in this kind of experimental fashion and test for different outcomes in criminal justice processing. We can't control or systematically vary the independent variable in the general sense of the word "experiment" as described by Farrington et al. (1986). Imagine, for example, arranging for teams of researchers, half white and half African American, driving identical vehicles at 20 mph above the posted speed limit on an interstate highway. It's interesting to think about doing that kind of research but you will quickly recognize that it can't legally or safely be done. Remember ethics from Chapter 3?

Quasi-Experiments?

Research on race and traffic enforcement is either quasi-experimental or variable-oriented research such as case studies. Because we have been describing research primarily in three states, it might seem that most such efforts are case studies. However, the strongest research—in North Carolina and Pennsylvania—uses a sophisticated series of comparisons to sort out what causes race disparities in traffic stops. These have come to be called benchmarks.

Researchers try to compare a "treatment group," minorities as a proportion of traffic stops, to some benchmark, or comparison group. As Engel et al. (2004:8) put it, the comparison group is intended to reflect: ". . . the 'expected' rate of stops of minorities assuming that no racial discrimination exists." Here are some examples of comparison groups, together with comments on their strengths and weaknesses.

researchers examined many variables for one site and based policy decisions on that analysis. In the words of scientific realism, researchers studied the gang violence mechanism in the Boston context. In other contexts (e.g., Baltimore or Minneapolis), gang violence operated as a different mechanism; the "levers" pulled in Boston did not work elsewhere. Braga and associates emphasize that the problem-solving process is exportable to other settings but that the interventions used in Boston are not (2001:220).

How do case studies address threats to validity? In the most general sense, case studies attempt to isolate causal mechanisms from possible confounding influences by studying very precisely defined subjects. Donald Campbell (2003:ix–x) likened this to laboratory experiments in the natural sciences, in which researchers try to isolate causal variables from outside influences. Case study research takes place in natural field settings, not in laboratories. But the logic of trying to isolate causal mechanisms by focusing on one or a

- Resident population. If nonwhites are 25 percent of drivers stopped, but are only 15 percent of the resident population of a jurisdiction, this suggests a racial disparity. The problem with this comparison is that drivers are mobile by definition. The majority of cars on the southern third of the New Jersey Turnpike have out-of-state license plates. This approach might work on local streets in a large jurisdiction, but even then it ignores the fundamental fact that people are mobile. Researchers in England recognized this in their study of four municipalities (Miller, 2000).

- Driving population. This is better because it compares people stopped by police to people who are actually on the road. In settings like the New Jersey Turnpike, the race of drivers can be observed at tollbooths, as we described in Chapter 5. However, this method produces information about drivers, not traffic violators. Police claim to stop cars because they observe some violation, not because of race.

- Night-time traffic stops. This comparison strategy assumes that police are not able to detect the race of drivers at nighttime. So if the proportion of traffic stops of nonwhite drivers at night is lower than the proportion stopped during the day, some discriminatory targeting might be at work in daylight hours. Even though there is merit in such logic, New Jersey state police tend to make fewer stops at night. There have also been reports of "spotlighting" by state troopers, where they use spotlights, or park their vehicle at right angles to the roadway and shine lights on the face of passing drivers (Verneiro and Zoubek, 1999).

- Radar-timed stops. Similar logic is at work here. If police make stops based on radar readings, it's assumed they will be less likely to stop people based on the appearance of race. In this respect, police are presumed to exercise less discretion in relying solely on radar to decide whom to stop. Again, it's not quite that simple. From their research in New Jersey, Maxfield and Andresen sat in state police cars while troopers used radar. In many cases the racial appearance of drivers was easily visible. Most vehicles were speeding, though some more than others. Together these observations suggest that state police could use race as a factor in deciding which speeding cars to stop and which to ignore.

- Independent observations of speeding. As we saw in the last chapter, researchers in three states collected their own data on speeding. In principle this offers the best comparison against police stop data: comparing the race distribution of police stop data to the race distribution of speeders from data collected independently. If the percentages are similar, it supports police claims that they stop only traffic violators. If they are different, this would be stronger evidence of unexplained disparity.

We say "unexplained disparity" intentionally. Such a disparity would support discrimination as an explanation, but it would not prove that differences were due to discrimination. That's because we cannot be as certain as we would like that all other plausible explanations have been eliminated. Slightly restated, we cannot rule out threats to internal validity of a claim that discrimination causes disparities.

few cases is a direct descendant of the rationale for experimental isolation in laboratories.

Figure 7.8 summarizes advice from Yin (2013:40–42) on how to judge the quality of case study designs in language that should now be familiar. Construct validity is established through multiple sources of evidence, the establishment of chains of causation that connect independent and dependent variables, and what are termed "member checks"—asking key informants to review tentative conclusions about causation.

	Case Study Approach
Construct Validity	Multiple sources of evidence
	Establish chain of causation
	Member checks
Internal Validity	Pattern-matching
	Time-series analysis
External Validity	Replicate through multiple case studies

FIGURE 7.8 Case Studies and Validity

Source: Yin (2013: 42)

Examples of techniques for strengthening internal validity are theory-based pattern matching and time-series analysis. The first criterion follows Shadish, Cook, and Campbell, calling on researchers to make specific theory-based predictions about what pattern of results will support hypothesized causal relationships. Alternative explanations, also termed "rival hypotheses," are less persuasive when specific predictions of results are actually obtained.

For example, Braga and associates (2001) predicted that gun killings among male Boston residents under age 25 would decline following implementation of the package of interventions in the Boston gun strategy. Although other explanations are possible for the observed sharp declines, the specific focus of the researchers' interventions and the concomitant results undermine the credibility of rival hypotheses. Having many measures of variables over time strengthens internal validity if observations support our predicted expectations about cause. We saw earlier how nonequivalent time-series comparisons and switching replications can enhance findings. This is also consistent with pattern matching—we make specific statements about what patterns of results we expect in our observations over time.

Finally, a single case study is vulnerable to external validity threats because it is rooted in the context of a specific site. Conducting multiple case studies in different sites illustrates the principle of replication. By replicating research findings, we accumulate evidence. We may also find that causal relationships are different in different settings, as did researchers who tried to transplant specific interventions from the Boston Gun Project. Although such findings can undermine the generalizability of causality, they also help us understand how causal mechanisms can operate differently in different settings.

Time-series designs and case studies are examples of variable-oriented research. A case study with many observations over time can be an example of a time-series design. Adding one or more other cases offers opportunities to create nonequivalent comparisons. Time-series designs, case studies, and nonequivalent comparisons are quasi-experimental designs; they are conducted in the manner of experiments, using design building blocks in different ways.

Experimental and Quasi-Experimental Designs Summarized

Understanding the building blocks of research design and adapting them accordingly works better than trying to apply the same design to all research questions.

By now, it should be clear that there are no simple formulas or recipes for designing an experimental or quasi-experimental study. Researchers have almost infinite ways of varying the number and composition of groups of subjects, selecting subjects, determining how many observations to make, and deciding what types of experimental stimuli to introduce or study. See the discussion of different approaches in our running example, "Putting It All Together: Evaluating Explanations for Disproportionality in Traffic Stops."

Variations on the classical experimental designs are especially useful for explanatory research and in evaluation studies, but exploratory and descriptive studies usually use other methods. Surveys conducted at one point in time, for example, may be used to explore or describe such phenomena as fear of crime or public attitudes toward punishment. Longitudinal studies of age cohorts are often the best way to examine criminal careers or developmental causes of delinquency.

Even when experimental designs might be the best choice, it is not always possible to construct treatment and control groups, to use random assignment, or even to analyze a series of observations over time. Research on CCTV is an example.

As we stated early in this chapter, experiments are best suited to topics that involve well-defined concepts and propositions. Experiments and quasi-experiments also require that researchers be able to exercise, or at least approximate, some degree of control over an experimental stimulus. Finally, these designs depend on the ability to unambiguously establish the time order of experimental treatments and observations on the dependent variable. Often, it is not possible to achieve the necessary degree of control.

In designing research projects, researchers should be alert to opportunities for using experimental designs. Researchers should also know how quasi-experimental designs can be developed when random assignment is not possible. Experiments and quasi-experiments lend themselves to a logical rigor that is often much more difficult to achieve in other modes of observation. The building blocks of research design can be used in creative ways to address a variety of criminal justice research questions. Careful attention to design issues, and to how design elements can reduce validity threats, is essential to the research process.

SUMMARY

- Experiments are an excellent vehicle for the controlled testing of causal processes. Experiments may also be appropriate for evaluation studies.
- The classical experiment tests the effect of an experimental stimulus on some dependent variable through the pretesting and posttesting of experimental and control groups.
- It is more important that experimental and control groups be similar to each other than that a group of experimental subjects be representative of some larger population.
- Random assignment is the best way to achieve comparability in the experimental and control groups.
- The classical experiment with random assignment of subjects guards against most of the threats to internal invalidity.
- Because experiments often take place under controlled conditions, results may not be generalizable to real-world situations—or findings from an experiment in one setting may not apply to other settings.
- The classical experiment may be modified to suit specific research purposes by changing the number of experimental and control groups, the number and types of experimental stimuli, and the number of pretest or posttest measurements.
- Quasi-experiments may be conducted when it is not possible or desirable to use an experimental design.
- Nonequivalent-groups and time-series designs are two general types of quasi-experiments.
- Time-series designs and case studies are examples of variable-oriented research, in which a large number of variables are examined for one or a few cases.

- Both experiments and quasi-experiments may be customized by using design building blocks to suit particular research purposes.
- Not all research purposes and questions are amenable to experimental or quasi-experimental designs, because researchers may not be able to exercise the required degree of control.

KEY TERMS

Case-oriented research *(p. 190)*
Case study *(p. 191)*
Classical experiment *(p. 168)*
Control group *(p. 169)*
Dependent variable *(p. 168)*
Experimental group *(p. 169)*
Generalizability *(p. 178)*
Independent variable *(p. 168)*
Quasi-experiment *(p. 182)*
Random assignment *(p. 172)*
Time-series design *(p. 186)*
Variable-oriented research *(p. 190)*

REVIEW QUESTIONS AND EXERCISES

1. If you do not remember participating in DARE (Drug Abuse Resistance Education), you have probably heard or read something about it. Describe an experimental design to test the causal hypothesis that DARE reduces drug use. Is your experimental design feasible? Why or why not?

2. Experiments are often conducted in public health research, where a distinction is made between an efficacy experiment and an effectiveness experiment. Efficacy experiments focus on whether some new health program works under ideal conditions; effectiveness experiments test the program under typical conditions that health professionals encounter in their day-to-day work. Discuss how efficacy experiments and effectiveness experiments reflect concerns about internal validity threats on the one hand and generalizability on the other.

3. Crime hot spots are areas where crime reports, calls for police service, or other measures of crime are especially common. Police in departments with a good analytic capability routinely identify hot spots and launch special tactics to reduce crime in these areas. What kinds of validity threats should researchers be especially attentive to in studying the effects of police interventions on hot spots?

Modes of Observation

Having covered the basics of structuring research, from general issues to research design, let's dive into the various observational techniques available for criminal justice research.

Chapter 8 examines how social scientists go about selecting people or things for observation. Our discussion of sampling addresses the fundamental scientific issue of generalizability. As we'll see, it is possible for us to select a few people or things for observation and then apply what we observe to a much larger group of people or things than we actually observed. It is possible, for example, to ask 1,000 people how they feel about using video cameras to enforce traffic laws, and then accurately predict how tens of millions of people feel about it.

Chapter 9 describes survey research and other techniques for collecting data by asking people questions. We'll cover different ways of asking questions and discuss the various uses of surveys and related techniques in criminal justice research.

Chapter 10 describes additional ways to gather information by asking questions. In this chapter, we discuss how to design different types of qualitative interviews, including focus groups.

Chapter 11, on field research, examines what is perhaps the most natural form of data collection: the direct observation of phenomena in natural settings. As we will see, observations can be highly structured and systematic (such as counting pedestrians who walk by some specified point) or less structured and more flexible.

Chapter 12 discusses ways to take advantage of some of the data available all around us. Researchers often examine data collected by criminal justice and other public agencies. Content analysis is a method of collecting data through carefully specifying and counting communications such as news stories, court opinions, or even recorded visual images. Criminal justice researchers may also conduct secondary analysis of data collected by others.

Sampling

CHAPTER 8

Sampling makes it possible to select a few hundred or thousand people for study and discover things that apply to many more people who have not been studied.

Learning Objectives

1. Understand how the logic of probability sampling makes it possible to represent large populations with small subsets of those populations.

2. Recognize that the chief criterion of a sample's quality is the degree to which it represents the population from which it was selected.

3. Summarize the chief principle of probability sampling: Every member of the population has a known, nonzero probability of being selected into the sample.

4. Describe how probability sampling methods make it possible to select samples that will be quite representative.

5. Understand how our ability to estimate population parameters with sample statistics is rooted in the sampling distribution and probability theory.

6. Recognize how simple random sampling is logically the most fundamental technique in probability sampling.

7. Distinguish the variety of probability sampling designs that can be used and combined to suit different populations and research purposes: systematic sampling, stratified sampling, and multistage cluster sampling.

8. Understand the basic features of the National Crime Victimization Survey and the Crime Survey for England and Wales, two national crime surveys based on multistage cluster samples.

Sampling and Election Polls

One of the many interesting features of the 2012 presidential election was the large number of polls that tracked public opinion for several months. Some polls reported just a few days before the election predicted victory by Obama by a razor thin margin, whereas others showed a slight edge for Romney. The small differences in predictions by individual polls illustrate a couple of important principles of sampling. Here's a summary from The Huffington Post web page published on November 3, 2012:

Notice two things about the poll estimates and final election results. First, three poll estimates are very close or tied. Second, two of them show differences of 5 percentage points between the two candidates, but in opposite directions. All polls were completed within two weeks before the election. What accounts for these differences?

	Obama (%)	Romney (%)
Ipsos/Reuters	49	48
ABC/Post	48	49
Rasmussen	48	48
National Journal	50	45
Gallup	46	51
Final election results	51	49

Sources: http://www.huffingtonpost.com/2012/11/03/presidential-polls-2012_n_2068889.html?utm_hp_ref=@pollster; and http://elections.nytimes.com/2012/results/president.

Two things affect the accuracy of poll estimates: sampling and how accurately questions reflect the underlying construct being measured. We examined measurement generally in earlier chapters; Chapter 9 centers on survey research. For now, you should recognize that asking someone how they intend to vote is a pretty simple measurement task that does not vary much across polls: "If the presidential election were being held today and the candidates were Obama and Biden and Romney and Ryan, for whom would you vote?"

Most of the variation in the election poll estimates shown above is due to differences in sampling, the topic of this chapter. The five polls shown above used different sampling techniques. For example, the Rasmussen poll used automated "robo-call" techniques that produced a large number of hang-ups. Further, the Rasmussen and Gallup polls called landline phones only, thus missing the growing proportion of people who use only cell phones (Shepard, 2012;

Silver, 2012). These tend to be younger people and urban residents, both more likely to vote for Obama in the 2012 election.

As we'll see in this chapter, the accuracy of sampling depends on reducing bias in a selection of subjects. Changes in the technology of communication have increased bias in traditional approaches to sampling people by telephone. At the same time, increased use of cell phones and the Internet, the growth of social networks, and mobile computing offer new opportunities to sample and interview people. Later in this chapter, we present some recent data on telephone coverage in households. How many people in your class have landline telephone service?

Introduction

How we collect representative data is fundamental to criminal justice research.

Much of the value of research depends on how data are collected. A critical part of criminal justice research is deciding what will be observed and what won't. If you want to study drug users, for example, which drug users should you study? This chapter discusses the logic and fundamental principles of sampling, and then describes different general approaches for selecting subjects or other units.

Sampling is the process of selecting observations. Sampling is ordinarily used to select observations for one of two related reasons. First, it is often not possible to collect information from all persons or other units we wish to study. We may wish to know what proportion of all persons arrested in U.S. cities have recently used drugs, but collecting all that data would be virtually impossible. Thus, we have to look at a sample of observations.

The second reason for sampling is that it is often not necessary to collect data from all persons or other units. Probability sampling techniques enable us to make relatively few observations and then generalize from those observations to a much wider population. For example, if we are interested in what proportion of high school students have

used marijuana, collecting data from a probability sample of a few thousand students will serve just as well as trying to study every high school student in the country.

Although probability sampling is central to criminal justice research, it cannot be used in many situations of interest. A variety of nonprobability sampling techniques are available in such cases. Nonprobability sampling has its own logic and can provide useful samples for criminal justice inquiry. In this chapter, we examine both the advantages and the shortcomings of such methods, and we discuss where they fit in the larger picture of sampling and collecting data. Keep in mind one important goal of all sampling: to reduce, or at least to understand, potential biases that may be at work in selecting subjects.

The Logic of Probability Sampling

Probability sampling helps researchers generalize from observed to unobserved cases.

In selecting a group of subjects for study, social science researchers often use some type of **sampling**. In general, sampling refers to selecting part of a population. In selecting samples, we want to do two related things. First, we select samples to represent some larger population of people or other things. If we are interested in attitudes about a community correctional facility, for example, we

Sampling Selecting some units of a larger population for study.

might draw a sample of neighborhood residents, ask them some questions, and use their responses to represent the attitudes of all neighborhood residents. Or, in studying cases in a criminal court, we may not be able to examine all cases, so we select a sample to represent that population of all cases processed through some court.

Second, we may want to generalize from a sample to an unobserved population the sample is intended to represent. If we interview a sample of community residents, we may want to generalize our findings to all community residents—those we interviewed and those we did not. We might similarly expect that our sample of criminal court cases can be generalized to the population of all criminal court cases.

A special type of sampling that enables us to make statistical generalizations to a larger population is known as **probability sampling**, a method of selection in which each member of a population has a known chance or probability of being selected. Knowing the probability that any individual member of a population could be selected makes it possible for us to make predictions that our sample accurately represents the larger population.

If all members of a population are identical in all respects—demographic characteristics, attitudes, experiences, behaviors, and so on—there is no need for careful sampling procedures. Any sample will be sufficient. In this extreme case of homogeneity, in fact, a single case will be sufficient as a sample to study characteristics of the whole population. Or, as George Gallup put it: "One spoonful can reflect the taste of the whole pot if the soup is well-stirred" (Best and Radcliff, 2005:716).

In reality, of course, the human beings who make up any real population are heterogeneous, varying in many ways. Figure 8.1 offers a simplified illustration of a heterogeneous population: the 100 members of this small population differ by gender and race. We'll use this hypothetical micropopulation to illustrate various aspects of sampling.

A sample of individuals from a population, if it is to provide useful descriptions of the total population, must contain essentially the same variations that exist in the population. This is not as simple as it might seem. Let's look at some of the possible biases in selection or ways researchers might go astray. Then we will see how probability sampling provides an efficient method for selecting a sample that should adequately reflect variations that exist in the population.

Conscious and Unconscious Sampling Bias

At first glance, it may seem as if sampling is a rather straightforward matter. To select a sample of 100 lawyers, a researcher might simply go to a courthouse and interview the first 100 lawyers who walk through the door. This kind of sampling method is often used by untrained researchers, but it is subject to serious biases. In connection with sampling, bias simply means that those selected are not "typical" or "representative" of the larger populations from which they have been chosen. This kind of bias is virtually inevitable when a researcher picks subjects casually.

Figure 8.2 illustrates what can happen when we simply select people who are convenient for study. Although women make up only 50 percent of our micropopulation, those closest to the researcher (people in the upper-right-hand corner of Figure 8.2) happen to be 70 percent women. Although the population is 12 percent African American, none were selected into this sample of people who happened to be conveniently situated near the researcher.

Moving beyond the risks inherent in simply studying people who are convenient, we need to consider other potential problems as well. Even if the researcher seeks to interview a "balanced" group of lawyers, it's not possible to know the exact proportions of different types of lawyers who make up such a balance.

The researcher might make a conscious effort to interview, say, every tenth lawyer who enters the courthouse, but he still cannot be sure of a

> **Probability sampling** Sampling in which the probability that an element will be included in a sample is known.

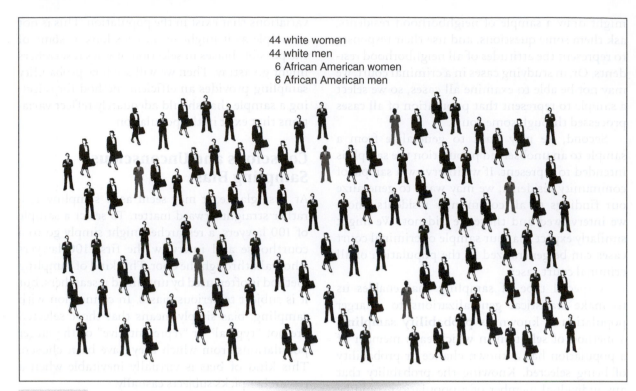

44 white women
44 white men
6 African American women
6 African American men

FIGURE 8.1 A Population of 100 Folks

representative sample—different types of lawyers visit the courthouse with different frequencies, and some never go to the courthouse at all. Thus, the resulting sample will overrepresent lawyers who visit the courthouse more often.

Similarly, polls linked to blogs, text messages, or email cannot be trusted to represent the general population. Blogs tend to be selective; people regularly visit blogs that present views on personal and political issues they endorse (McKenna and Pole, 2008). As a result, the population of people who respond to blog polls can only represent the population of people who regularly visit individual blogs. In the same way, most commercial email services include some type of advertising, and such ads are sometimes cleverly disguised as opinion polls. As a general principle, the more self-selection is involved, the more bias will be introduced into the sample.

The possibilities for inadvertent sampling bias are endless and not always obvious. Fortunately, some techniques can help us avoid bias.

Representativeness and Probability of Selection

Although the term *representativeness* has no precise, scientific definition, it carries a commonsense meaning that makes it useful in the discussion of sampling. As we'll use the term here, a sample is *representative* of the population from which it is selected if the aggregate characteristics of the sample closely approximate those same aggregate characteristics in the population. If the population, for example, contains 50 percent women, a representative sample will also contain "close to" 50 percent women. Later in this chapter, we'll discuss "how close" in detail. Notice that samples need not be representative in all respects; representativeness is limited to those characteristics that are relevant to the substantive interests of the study. This is consistent with the more extensive discussion of what *representative* means in the book by William Shadish, Thomas Cook, and Donald Campbell (2002:354–356).

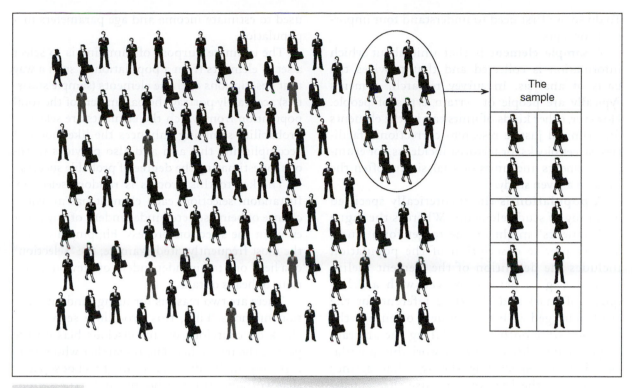

FIGURE 8.2   A Sample of Convenience: Easy, but Not Representative

A basic principle of probability sampling is that a sample will be representative of the population from which it is selected if all members of the population have an equal chance of being selected in the sample. Samples that have this quality are often labeled **equal probability of selection method (EPSEM)** samples. This principle forms the basis of probability sampling.

Even carefully selected EPSEM samples are seldom, if ever, perfectly representative of the populations from which they are drawn. Nevertheless, probability sampling offers two special advantages. First, though never perfectly representative, probability samples are typically more representative than other types of samples because they avoid the biases discussed in the preceding section. In practice, there is a greater likelihood that a probability sample will be representative of the population from which it is drawn than a nonprobability sample will be.

Second, and more importantly, probability sampling permits us to estimate the accuracy or representativeness of the sample. Conceivably, a researcher might select a sample wholly by chance that closely represents the larger population. The odds are against this, however, and we cannot estimate the likelihood that a haphazard sample will achieve representativeness. The probability sample can provide an accurate estimate of success or failure, because probability samples enable us to draw on probability theory.

Probability Theory and Sampling Distribution

Probability theory permits inferences about how sampled data are distributed around the value found in a larger population.

With a basic understanding of the logic of probability sampling in hand, we can examine how probability sampling works in practice. We will then be able to devise specific sampling techniques and assess the results of those techniques.

To do so, we first need to understand four important concepts.

A **sample element** is that unit about which information is collected and that provides the basis of analysis. In survey research, elements typically are people or certain types of people. However, other kinds of units can be the elements for criminal justice research—correctional facilities, street blocks, or terrorist incidents, for example. Elements and units of analysis are often the same in a given study.

A **population** is the theoretically specified grouping of study elements. Whereas the vague "delinquents" might be the target for a study, a more precise description of the population includes the definition of the element "delinquents" (e.g., a person charged with a delinquent offense) and the time referent for the study (charged with a delinquent offense in the previous six months). Translating the abstract "adult drug addicts" into a workable population requires specifying the age that defines "adult" and the level of drug use that constitutes an "addict." Specifying "college student" includes a consideration of full- and part-time students, degree and nondegree candidates, undergraduate and graduate students, and so on.

A **population parameter** is the value for a given variable in a population. The average income of all families in a city and the age distribution of the city's population are parameters. An important portion of criminal justice research involves estimating population parameters on the basis of sample observations.

The summary description of a given variable in the sample is called a **sample statistic**. Sample statistics are used to make estimates of population parameters. Thus, the average income computed from a sample and the age distribution of that sample are statistics, and those statistics are

used to estimate income and age parameters in a population.

The ultimate purpose of sampling is to select a set of elements from a population in such a way that descriptions of those elements (sample statistics) accurately portray the parameters of the total population from which the elements are selected. Probability sampling enhances the likelihood of accomplishing this aim and also provides methods for estimating the degree of probable success.

The key to this process is random selection. In random selection, each element has an equal chance of being selected independent of any other event in the selection process. Flipping a coin is the most frequently cited example; the "selection" of a head or a tail is independent of previous selections of heads or tails.

There are two reasons for using random selection methods. First, this procedure serves as a check on conscious or unconscious bias on the part of the researcher. The researcher who selects cases on an intuitive basis might choose cases that will support his or her research expectations or hypotheses. Random selection erases this danger. Second, and more importantly with random selection we can draw on probability theory—which allows us to estimate population parameters and to estimate how accurate our statistics are likely to be.

The Sampling Distribution of 10 Cases

Suppose there are 10 people in a group, and each has a certain amount of money in his or her pocket. To simplify, let's assume that one person has no money, another has $1, another has $2, and so forth up to the person who has $9. Figure 8.3 illustrates this population of 10 people.[1]

Our task is to determine the average amount of money one person has—specifically, the mean number of dollars. If you simply add up the money shown in Figure 8.3, the total is $45, so the mean is $4.50 (45÷10). Our purpose in the rest of this example is to estimate that mean without actually observing all 10 individuals. We'll do that by

---

Population parameter   The value for a given variable in a population.

Sample statistic   A summary characteristic of a sample, used to estimate a population parameter.

---

[1] We thank Hanan Selvin for this way of introducing probability sampling.

FIGURE 8.3 A Population of 10 People with $0–$9

selecting random samples from the population and using the means of those samples to estimate the mean for the whole population.

To start, suppose we select—at random—a sample of only one person from the 10. Depending on which person we select, we will estimate the group's mean as anywhere from $0 to $9. Figure 8.4 shows a display of those 10 possible samples. The 10 dots shown on the graph represent the 10 "sample" means we will get as estimates of the population. The range of the dots on the graph is the **sampling distribution**, which is defined as the range of sample statistics we will obtain if we select many samples. Figure 8.4 shows how all of our possible samples of 1 are distributed. Obviously, it is not a good idea to select a sample of only 1 because we stand a good chance of missing the true mean of $4.50 by quite a bit.

What if we take samples of 2 each? As you can see from Figure 8.5, increasing the sample size improves our estimations. Once again, each dot represents a possible sample. There are 45 possible samples of two elements: $0/$1, $0/$2, . . . $7/$8, $8/$9. Moreover, some of these samples produce the same means. For example, $0/$6, $1/$5, and $2/$4 all produce means of $3. In Figure 8.5, the

three dots shown above the $3 mean represent those three samples.

Notice that the means we get from the 45 samples are not evenly distributed. Rather, they are somewhat clustered around the true value of $4.50. Only two samples deviate by as much as $4 from the true value ($0/$1 and $8/$9), whereas five of the samples give the true estimate of $4.50, and another eight samples miss the mark by only $0.50 (plus or minus).

Now suppose we select even larger samples. What will that do to our estimates of the mean? Figure 8.6 presents the sampling distributions of samples of 3, 4, 5, and 6. The progression of the sampling distributions is clear. Every increase in sample size improves the distribution of estimates of the mean in two related ways. First, in the distribution for samples of 5, for example, no sample means are at the extreme ends of the distribution. Why? Because it is not possible to select five elements from our population and obtain an average of less than $2 or greater than $7. The second way sampling distributions improve with larger samples is that sample means cluster more and more around the true population mean of $4.50. Figure 8.6 clearly shows this tendency.

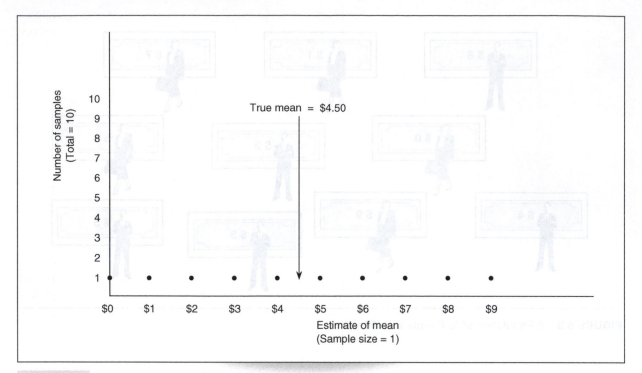

FIGURE 8.4 The Sampling Distribution of Samples of $1

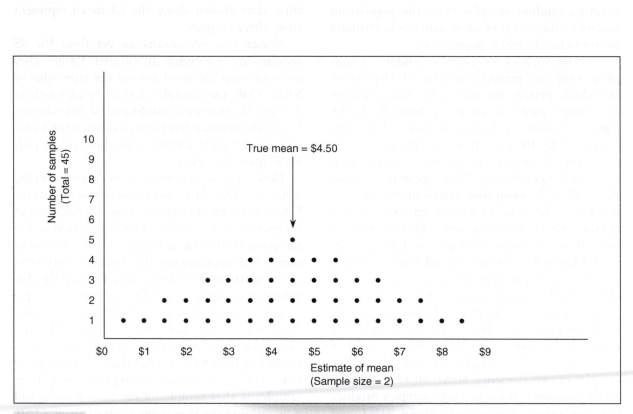

FIGURE 8.5 The Sampling Distribution of Samples of 2

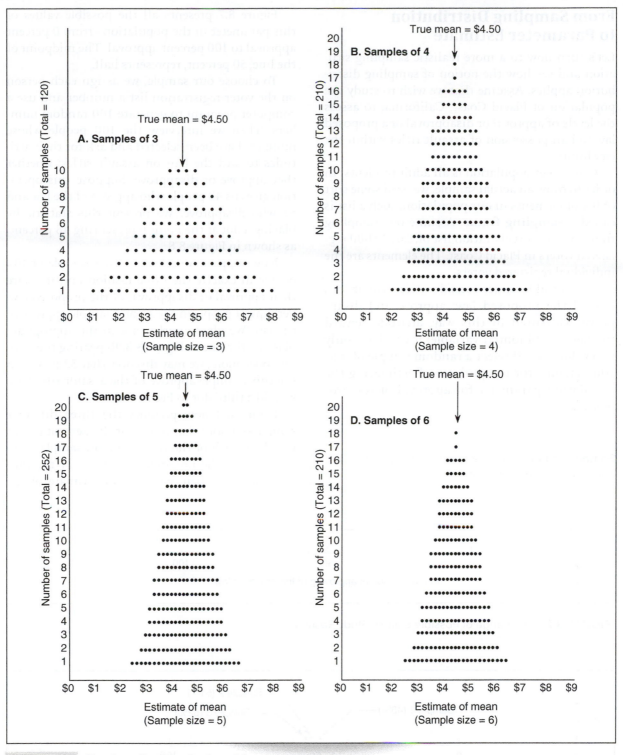

FIGURE 8.6 The Sampling Distribution of Samples of 3, 4, 5, and 6

From Sampling Distribution to Parameter Estimate

Let's turn now to a more realistic sampling situation and see how the notion of sampling distribution applies. Assume that we wish to study the population of Placid Coast, California, to assess the levels of approval or disapproval of a proposed law to ban possession of assault rifles within the city limits.

Our target population is all adult residents. In order to draw an actual sample, we need some sort of list of elements in our population; such a list is called a **sampling frame**. Assume our sampling frame is a voter registration list of, say, 20,000 registered voters in Placid Coast. The elements are the individual registered voters.

The variable under consideration is attitudes toward the proposed law: approve and disapprove. Measured in this way, attitude toward the law is a binomial variable; it can have only two values. We'll select a random sample of, say, 100 persons, for the purpose of estimating the population parameter for approval of the proposed law.

Sampling frame A list or quasi-list of elements in a population that is used to select a sample.

Figure 8.7 presents all the possible values of this parameter in the population—from 0 percent approval to 100 percent approval. The midpoint of the line, 50 percent, represents half.

To choose our sample, we assign each person on the voter registration list a number and use a computer program to generate 100 random numbers. Then we interview the 100 people whose numbers have been selected and ask for their attitudes toward the ban on assault rifles: whether they approve or disapprove. Suppose this operation gives us 48 people who approve of the law and 52 who disapprove. We present this statistic by placing a dot at the point representing 48 percent, as shown in Figure 8.8.

Now suppose we select another sample of 100 people in exactly the same fashion and measure their approval or disapproval of the proposed law. Perhaps 51 people in the second sample approve of the law. We place another dot in the appropriate place on the line in Figure 8.8. Repeating this process once more, we may discover that 52 people in the third sample approve of the assault rifle ban; we add a third dot to Figure 8.8.

Figure 8.8 now presents the three different sample statistics that represent the percentages of people in each of the three random samples who approved of the proposed law. Each of the random samples, then, gives us an estimate of the

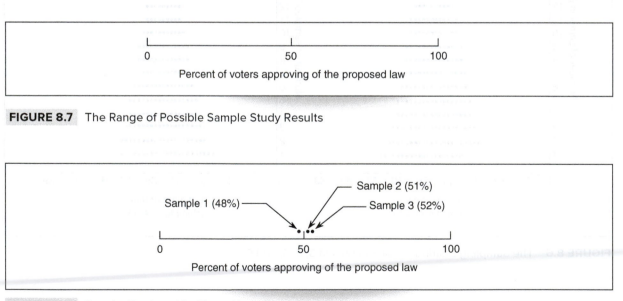

FIGURE 8.7   The Range of Possible Sample Study Results

FIGURE 8.8   Results Produced by Three Hypothetical Samples

percentage of people in the total population of registered voters who approve of the assault rifle law. Unfortunately, we now have three separate estimates.

To rescue ourselves from this dilemma, let's draw more and more samples of 100 registered voters each, question each of the samples concerning their approval or disapproval, and plot the new sample statistics on our summary graph. In drawing many such samples, we discover that some of the new samples provide duplicate estimates, as in our earlier illustration with 10 cases. Figure 8.9 shows the sampling distribution of hundreds of samples. This is often referred to as a normal or bell-shaped curve.

Notice that by increasing the number of samples selected and interviewed, we have also increased the range of estimates provided by the sampling operation. In one sense, we have increased our dilemma in attempting to find the parameter in the population. Fortunately, probability theory provides certain important rules about the sampling distribution shown in Figure 8.9.

Estimating Sampling Error

Probability theory can help resolve our dilemma with some basic statistical concepts. First, if many independent random samples are selected from a population, then the sample statistics provided by those samples will be distributed around the population parameter in a known way. Thus, although Figure 8.9 shows a wide range of estimates, more

of them are in the vicinity of 50 percent than elsewhere in the graph. Probability theory tells us, then, that the true value is in the vicinity of 50 percent.

Second, probability theory gives us a formula for estimating how closely the sample statistics are clustered around the true value:

$$S = \sqrt{\frac{P \times Q}{n}}$$

where S is the **standard error** (defined as a measure of sampling error), n is the number of cases in each sample, and P and Q are the population parameters for the binomial. If 60 percent of registered voters approve of the ban on assault rifles and 40 percent disapprove, then P and Q are 60 percent and 40 percent, or 0.6 and 0.4, respectively.

To see how probability theory makes it possible for us to estimate sampling error, suppose that in reality 50 percent of the people approve of the proposed law and 50 percent disapprove. These are the population parameters we are trying to estimate with our samples. Recall that we have been selecting samples of 100 cases each. When these numbers are plugged into the formula, we get

$$S = \sqrt{\frac{0.5 \times 0.5}{100}} = 0.05$$

The standard error equals 0.05, or 5 percent.

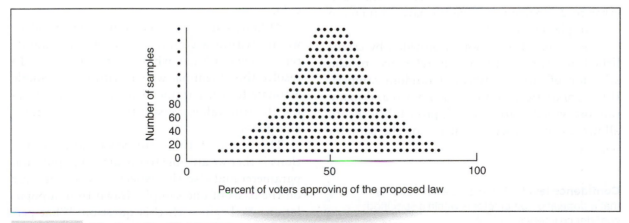

FIGURE 8.9 The Sampling Distribution

The standard error is a valuable piece of information in probability theory, because it indicates how closely the sample estimates will be distributed around the population parameter. The standard error tells us how sample statistics will be dispersed or clustered around a population parameter. Probability theory tells us that approximately 34 percent of the sample estimates will fall within one standard error increment above the population parameter, and another 34 percent will fall within one standard error increment below the parameter. In our example, the standard error increment is 5 percent, so we know that 34 percent of our samples will give estimates of approval between 50 percent (the parameter) and 55 percent (one standard error above); another 34 percent of the samples will give estimates between 50 percent and 45 percent (one standard error below the parameter). Taken together, then, we know that roughly two-thirds (68 percent) of the samples will give estimates between 45 and 55 percent, which is within 5 percent of the parameter.

The standard error is also a function of the sample size—an inverse function. This means that as the sample size increases, the standard error decreases. And as the sample size increases, the several samples will be clustered nearer to the true value. Figure 8.6 illustrates this clustering. Another rule of thumb is evident in the formula for the standard error: because of the square root operation, the standard error is reduced by half if the sample size is quadrupled. In our example, samples of 100 produce a standard error of 5 percent; to reduce the standard error to 2.5 percent, we would have to increase the sample size to 400.

All of this information is provided by established probability theory in reference to the selection of large numbers of random samples. If the population parameter is known and many random samples are selected, probability theory allows us to predict how many of the samples will fall within specified intervals from the parameter.

Of course, this discussion illustrates only the *logic* of probability sampling. It does not describe the way research is actually conducted. Usually, we do not know the parameter; we conduct a sample survey precisely because we want to estimate that value. Moreover, we don't actually select large numbers of samples; we select only one sample. What probability theory does is provide the basis for making inferences about the typical research situation. Knowing what it would be like to select thousands of samples allows us to make assumptions about the one sample we do select and study.

Confidence Levels and Confidence Intervals

Probability theory specifies that 68 percent of that fictitious large number of samples will produce estimates that fall within one standard error of the parameter. As researchers, we can turn the logic around and infer that any single random sample has a 68 percent chance of falling within that range. In this regard, we speak of **confidence levels**; we are 68 percent confident that our sample estimate is within one standard error of the parameter. Or we may say that we are 95 percent confident that the sample statistic is within two standard errors of the parameter, and so forth. Quite reasonably, our confidence level increases as the margin for error is extended. We are virtually positive (99.9 percent) that our statistic is within three standard errors of the true value.

Although at some level we may be confident we are within a certain range of the parameter, we seldom know what the parameter is. To resolve this dilemma, we substitute our sample estimate for the parameter in the formula; lacking the true value, we substitute the best available guess.

The result of these inferences and estimations is that we are able to estimate a population parameter and also the expected degree of error on the basis of one sample drawn from a population. We begin with this question: What percentage of the registered voters in Placid Coast

Confidence level   The estimated probability that a population parameter is within a specified confidence interval.

approve of the proposed ban on assault rifles? We select a random sample of 100 registered voters and interview them. We might then report that our best estimate is that 50 percent of registered voters approve of the assault rifle ban, and that we are 95 percent confident that between 40 and 60 percent (plus or minus two standard errors) approve. The range from 40 to 60 percent is called the **confidence interval**. At the 68 percent confidence level, the confidence interval is 45–55 percent.

The logic of confidence levels and confidence intervals also provides the basis for determining the appropriate sample size for a study. Once we decide on the sampling error we can tolerate, we can calculate the number of cases needed in our sample.

Probability Theory and Sampling Distribution Summed Up

Random selection permits the researcher to use probability theory to estimate the accuracy of findings drawn from a sample. All statements of accuracy in sampling must specify both a confidence level and a confidence interval. The researcher must report that he or she is *x* percent confident that the population parameter is between two specific values.

In this example, we have demonstrated the logic of sampling error using a binomial variable—a variable analyzed in percentages. A different statistical procedure would be required to calculate the standard error for a mean, for example, but the overall logic is the same.

Notice that nowhere in this discussion did we consider the size of the population being studied. This is because the population size is almost always irrelevant. A sample of 2,000 respondents drawn properly to represent residents of Vermont will be no more accurate than a sample of 2,000 drawn properly to represent residents in California—even though the Vermont sample would be a substantially larger proportion of that small state's residents than would the same number chosen to represent the residents of California. The reason for this counterintuitive fact is that the equations for calculating sampling error assume that the populations being sampled are

infinitely large, so all samples would equal zero percent of the whole.

Two cautions are in order before we conclude this discussion of the basic logic of probability sampling. First, the survey uses of probability theory as discussed here technically are not wholly justified. The theory of sampling distributions makes assumptions that almost never apply in survey conditions. The exact proportion of samples contained within specified increments of standard errors, for example, mathematically assumes an infinitely large population, an infinite number of samples, and sampling with replacement—that is, every sampling unit selected is "thrown back into the pot" and could be selected again. Second, our discussion has greatly oversimplified the inferential jump from the distribution of several samples to the probable characteristics of one sample.

We offer these cautions to provide perspective on the uses of probability theory in sampling. Researchers in criminal justice and other social sciences often appear to overestimate the precision of estimates produced by the use of probability theory. Variations in sampling techniques and nonsampling factors may further reduce the accuracy of such estimates. For example, those selected in a sample who fail or refuse to participate further detract from the representativeness of the sample.

Nevertheless, the calculations discussed in this section can be extremely valuable to you in understanding and evaluating your data. Although the calculations do not provide estimates as precise as some researchers might assume, they can be quite valid for practical purposes. They are unquestionably more valid than less-rigorously derived estimates based on less-rigorous sampling methods. Most important, familiarity with the basic logic underlying the calculations can help you react sensibly both to your own data and to those reported by others.

> **Confidence interval**   The range of values that include a population parameter. "Between 34 and 39 percent" is an example.

Probability Sampling

Different types of probability sampling designs can be used alone or in combination for different research purposes.

As researchers and as consumers of research, we need to understand the theoretical foundations of sampling. It is no less important to appreciate the less-than-perfect conditions that exist in the field. Most of what we have considered so far assumes we are using simple random sampling. In reality, researchers have a number of options in choosing their sampling method, each with its own advantages and disadvantages.

Populations and Sampling Frames

Our discussion begins with a more practical consideration of one key feature of all probability sampling designs: the relationship between populations and sampling frames.

A sampling frame is the list or quasi-list of elements from which a probability sample is selected. Put another way, a sampling frame is a list or quasi-list of our target population. We say "quasi-list" because, even though an actual list might not exist, we can draw samples as if there were a list. Properly drawn samples provide information appropriate for describing the population of elements that compose the sampling frame—nothing more. This point is important in view of the common tendency for researchers to select samples from a particular sampling frame and then make assertions about a population that is similar, but not identical, to the study population defined by the sampling frame.

For example, if we want to study the attitudes of corrections administrators toward determinant sentencing policies, we might select a sample by consulting the membership roster of the American Correctional Association. In this case, the membership roster is our sampling frame, and corrections administrators are the population we wish to describe. However, unless all corrections administrators are members of the American Correctional Association and all members are listed in the roster, it would be incorrect to generalize results to *all* corrections administrators.

This example illustrates an important general point with respect to sampling. Samples of people in organizations are often the simplest because organizations typically have membership lists. In such cases, the list of members is often an acceptable sampling frame. If a random sample is selected from a membership list, then the data collected from that sample may be taken as representative of all members—if all members are included in the list. It is, however, imperative that researchers learn how complete or incomplete such lists might be, and limit their generalizations to listed sample elements rather than to an entire population. Membership lists of organizations now typically include email addresses. In such cases, organizations are especially well suited to Web-based sampling and email contacts.

Other lists of individuals may be especially relevant to the research needs of a particular study. Lists of licensed drivers, automobile owners, Medicare recipients, taxpayers, holders of weapons permits, and licensed professionals are just a few examples. Although it may be difficult to gain access to some of these lists, they provide excellent sampling frames for specialized research purposes.

Telephone directories are sometimes still used for "quick and dirty" public opinion polls. Undeniably, they are easy and inexpensive to use, but they have several limitations. A given directory will not include new subscribers or those who have requested unlisted numbers. Sampling is further complicated by the inclusion of nonresidential listings in directories. Moreover, telephone directories are sometimes taken to be a listing of a city's population, which is simply not the case. A growing number of households are served only by wireless phone service and so are not listed in directories. A national study conducted in 2015 reported that 48 percent of adults lived in households with wireless phone service only (Blumberg and Luke, 2016).

Street directories and tax maps may be used as sampling frames for households, but they may also suffer from incompleteness and possible bias. For example, illegal housing units such as subdivided apartments are unlikely to appear on official records. As a result, such units have no chance for selection; sample findings will not be representative of those units, which are often substandard and overcrowded.

In a more general sense, it's worth viewing sampling frames as operational definitions of a study population. Just as operational definitions of variables describe how abstract concepts will be measured, sampling frames serve as a real-world version of an abstract study population. For example, we may want to study how criminologists deal with ethical issues in their research. We don't know how many criminologists exist out there, but we can develop a general idea about the population of criminologists. We could also operationalize the concept by using the membership directory for the American Society of Criminology (ASC)—that list is our operational definition of the population of criminologists.[2] Since most criminologists use email extensively, a sample of email addresses from the ASC directory would suit our purposes nicely.

Simple Random Sampling

Simple random sampling forms the basis of probability theory and the statistical tools we use to estimate population parameters, standard error, and confidence intervals. More accurately, such statistics assume unbiased sampling, and simple random sampling is the foundation of unbiased sampling.

Once a sampling frame has been established, a simple random sample can be produced by assigning a single number to each element in the frame, not skipping any number in the process. A table of random numbers, or a computer program for generating them, is then used to select elements for the sample.

If the sampling frame is a computerized database or some other form of machine-readable data, a simple random sample can be selected automatically by computer. In effect, the computer numbers the elements in the sampling frame, generates its own series of random numbers, and prints out the list of elements selected.

---

[2]You can find the directory on the ASC website: http://asc41.com/director/frame.htm.

Systematic Sampling

Simple random sampling is seldom used in practice, primarily because it is not usually the most efficient method, and it can be tedious if done manually. It typically requires a list of elements. And when such a list is available, researchers usually use **systematic sampling** rather than simple random sampling.

In systematic sampling, the researcher chooses all elements in the list for inclusion in the sample. If a list contains 10,000 elements and we want a sample of 1,000, we select every tenth element for our sample. To ensure against any possible human bias, we should select the first element at random. Thus, to systematically select 1,000 from a list of 10,000 elements, we begin by selecting a random number between 1 and 10. The element having that number, plus every tenth element following it, is included in the sample.

In practice, systematic sampling is virtually identical to simple random sampling. If the list of elements is indeed randomized before sampling, one might argue that a systematic sample drawn from that list is, in fact, a simple random sample.

Systematic sampling has one danger. A periodic arrangement of elements in the list can make systematic sampling unwise; this arrangement is usually called "periodicity." If the list of elements is arranged in a cyclical pattern that coincides with the sampling interval, a biased sample may be drawn. Suppose we select a sample of apartments in an apartment building. If the sample is drawn from a list of apartments arranged in numerical order, there is a danger of the sampling interval coinciding with the number of apartments on a floor or some multiple of it. For example, in Maxfield's apartment building in New York, apartments ending in 01, 02, 03, and 04 have spectacular views and cost more than three times as much as apartments ending in 05, 06, 07, and 08 (Maxfield's number). If the number 02 is selected as a starting point, only the premium apartments will be sampled.

In considering a systematic sample from a list, then, we need to carefully examine the nature of that list. If the elements are arranged in any particular order, we have to figure out whether that order will bias the sample to be selected and take steps to counteract any possible bias.

To summarize, systematic sampling is usually superior to simple random sampling, in terms of convenience if nothing else. Problems in the ordering of elements in the sampling frame usually can be remedied quite easily.

Stratified Sampling

We have discussed two methods of selecting a sample from a list: random and systematic. **Stratification** is not an alternative to these methods, but it represents a possible modification in their use. Simple random sampling and systematic sampling both ensure a degree of representativeness and permit an estimate of the sampling error present. Stratified sampling is a method for obtaining a greater degree of representativeness—decreasing the probable sampling error. To understand why that is the case, we must return briefly to the basic theory of sampling distribution.

Recall that two factors in the sample design reduce sampling error: (1) a large sample produces a smaller sampling error than a small sample does, and (2) a homogeneous population produces samples with smaller sampling errors than a heterogeneous population does. If 99 percent of the population agrees with a certain statement, it is extremely unlikely that any probability sample will greatly misrepresent the extent of agreement. If the population is split 50–50 on the statement, then the sampling error will be much greater. Recall the close vote and close opinion polls in the 2012 presidential election. Larger sampling error was a result, making some polls "too close to call."

Stratified sampling is based on this second factor in sampling theory. Rather than selecting our sample from the total population at large, we select appropriate numbers of elements from homogeneous subsets of that population. To get a stratified sample of university students, for example, we first organize our population by college class and then draw appropriate numbers of freshmen, sophomores, juniors, and seniors. In a nonstratified sample, representation by class is subject to the same sampling error as other variables. In a sample stratified by class, the sampling error on this variable is reduced to zero.

Even more complex stratification methods are possible. In addition to stratifying by class, we might also stratify by gender, grade-point average, and so forth. In this fashion, we could ensure that our sample contains the proper numbers of freshman men with a 4.0 average, freshman women with a 4.0 average, and so forth.

The ultimate function of stratification, then, is to organize the population into homogeneous subsets (with heterogeneity *between* subsets) and to select the appropriate number of elements from each. To the extent that the subsets are homogeneous on the stratification variables, they may be homogeneous on other variables as well. Because age is usually related to college class, a sample stratified by class also will be more representative in terms of age.

The choice of stratification variables typically depends on what variables are available, and which are particularly important for research questions. Gender can often be determined in a list of names. Many local government sources of information on housing units are arranged geographically. Age, race, education, occupation, and other variables are often included on lists of persons who have had contact with criminal justice officials.

In selecting stratification variables, however, we should be concerned primarily with those that are presumably related to the variables we want to represent accurately. Because gender is related to many variables and is often available for stratification, it is frequently used. Age and race are related to many variables of interest in criminal justice research. Income is also related to many variables, but it is often not available for stratification. Geographic location within a city, state, or nation is related to many things. Within a city, stratification by geographic location usually increases representativeness in social class and ethnicity.

Stratified sampling ensures the proper representation of the stratification variables to enhance representation of other related variables. Taken as a whole, then, a stratified sample is likely to be more representative of a number of variables than is a simple random sample.

Disproportionate Stratified Sampling

Another use of stratification is to purposively produce samples that are not representative of a population on some variable, referred to as **disproportionate stratified sampling**. Because the purpose of sampling, as we have been discussing, is to represent a larger population, you may wonder why anyone would want to intentionally produce a sample that was not representative.

To understand the logic of disproportionate stratification, consider again the role of population homogeneity in determining sample size. If members of a population vary widely on some variable of interest, then larger samples must be drawn to adequately represent that population. Similarly, if only a small number of people in a population exhibit some attribute or characteristic of interest, then a large sample must be drawn to produce adequate numbers of elements that exhibit the uncommon condition. Disproportionate stratification is a way of obtaining sufficient numbers of these "rare" cases by selecting a number disproportionate to their representation in the population.

A good example of disproportionate sampling in criminal justice is a national crime survey in which one goal is to obtain some minimum number of crime victims in a sample. Because crime victimization for certain offenses—such as robbery or rape—is relatively rare on a national scale, persons who live in large urban areas, where serious crime is more common, are disproportionately sampled.

The British Crime Survey (BCS) is a nationwide survey of people age 16 and over in England and Wales. Over its first 20 years (since 1982), the BCS selectively oversampled people or areas to yield larger numbers of designated subjects than would result from proportionate random samples of the population of England and Wales. Beginning in 2004, the BCS disproportionately oversampled areas served by smaller police forces to produce a large enough number of cases to statistically represent rural areas (Smith and Hoare, 2009).

Multistage Cluster Sampling

The preceding sections have described reasonably simple procedures for sampling from lists of elements. Unfortunately, however, many interesting research problems require the selection of samples from populations that cannot be listed easily for sampling purposes; that is, sampling frames are not readily available. Examples are the population of a city, state, or nation, and all police officers in the United States. In such cases, the sample design must be much more complex. Such a design typically involves the initial sampling of groups of elements (clusters), followed by the selection of elements within each of the selected clusters. This procedure is called multistage **cluster sampling**.

Cluster sampling may be used when it is either impossible or impractical to compile an exhaustive list of the elements that compose the target population, such as all law enforcement officers in the United States. Often, however, population elements are already grouped into subpopulations, and a list of those subpopulations either exists or can be created.

Population elements, or aggregations of those elements, are referred to as **sampling units**. In the simplest forms of sampling, elements and units are the same thing—usually, people. But for cases in which a listing of elements is not available, we can often use some other unit that includes a grouping of elements.

Because U.S. law enforcement officers are employed by individual cities, counties, or states, it is possible to create lists of those political units. For cluster sampling, then, we could sample the list of cities, counties, and states in some manner as discussed previously (such as a systematic sample stratified by population). Next, we could obtain lists of law enforcement officers from agencies in each of the selected jurisdictions. We could then sample each of the lists to provide samples of police officers for study.

Another typical situation concerns sampling among population areas such as a city. Although there is no single list of a city's population, citizens reside on discrete city blocks or census blocks. It is possible, therefore, to select a sample of blocks initially, create a list of persons who live on each of the selected blocks, and then sample persons from that list. In this case, blocks are treated as the primary sampling unit.

In a more complex design, we might sample blocks, list the households on each selected block, sample the households, list the persons who reside in each household, and, finally, sample persons within each selected household. This multistage sample design will lead to the ultimate selection of a sample of individuals without requiring the initial listing of all individuals in the city's population.

Multistage cluster sampling, then, involves the repetition of two basic steps: listing and sampling. The list of primary sampling units (city blocks) is compiled and perhaps stratified for sampling. Next, a sample of those units is selected. The list of secondary sampling units is then sampled, and the process continues.

A good general guideline for cluster design is to maximize the number of clusters selected while decreasing the number of elements within each cluster. But this scientific guideline must be balanced against practical constraints. The efficiency of cluster sampling is based on the ability to minimize the list of population elements. By initially selecting clusters, we need only list the elements that make up the selected clusters, not all elements in the entire population. Increasing the number of clusters, however, reduces this efficiency in cluster sampling. A small number of clusters may be listed more quickly and more cheaply than a large number. Remember that all the elements in a selected cluster must be listed, even if only a few are to be chosen in the sample.

The final sample design will reflect these two constraints. In effect, we will probably select as many clusters as we can afford. So as not to leave this issue too open-ended, here is a rule of thumb: Population researchers conventionally aim for the selection of five households per census block. If a total of 2,000 households are to be interviewed, researchers select 400 blocks with five household interviews on each. Figure 8.10 presents a graphic overview of this process.

As we turn to more detailed procedures in cluster sampling, keep in mind that this method almost inevitably involves a loss of accuracy. First, a multistage sample design is subject to a sampling error at each stage. Because the sample size is necessarily smaller at each stage than the total sample size, the sampling error at each stage will be greater than it would be for a single-stage random sample of elements. Second, sampling error is estimated on the basis of observed variance among the sample elements. When those elements are drawn from relatively homogeneous clusters, the estimated sampling error will be too optimistic and so must be corrected in light of the cluster sample design.

Multistage Cluster Sampling with Stratification

Thus far, we have looked at cluster sampling as though a simple random sample were selected at each stage of the design. In fact, we can use stratification techniques to refine and improve the sample being selected. The basic options available are essentially the same as those possible in single-stage sampling from a list. In selecting a national sample of law enforcement officers, for example, we might initially stratify our list of agencies by type (state, county, and municipal), geographic region, size, and rural or urban location.

Once the primary sampling units (law enforcement agencies) have been grouped according to the relevant, available stratification variables, either simple random or systematic sampling techniques can be used to select the sample. We might select a specified number of units from each group or stratum, or we might arrange the stratified clusters in a continuous list and systematically sample that list.

To the extent that clusters are combined into homogeneous strata, the sampling error at this stage will be reduced. The primary goal of stratification, as before, is homogeneity.

In principle, stratification can take place at each level of sampling. The elements listed within a selected cluster might be stratified before the next stage of sampling. Typically, however, that is not done because we strive for relative homogeneity within clusters. If clusters are sufficiently similar, it is not necessary to stratify again.

Illustration: Two National Crime Surveys

Two national crime surveys show different ways of designing samples to achieve desired results.

Our discussion of sampling designs suggests that researchers can combine many different techniques

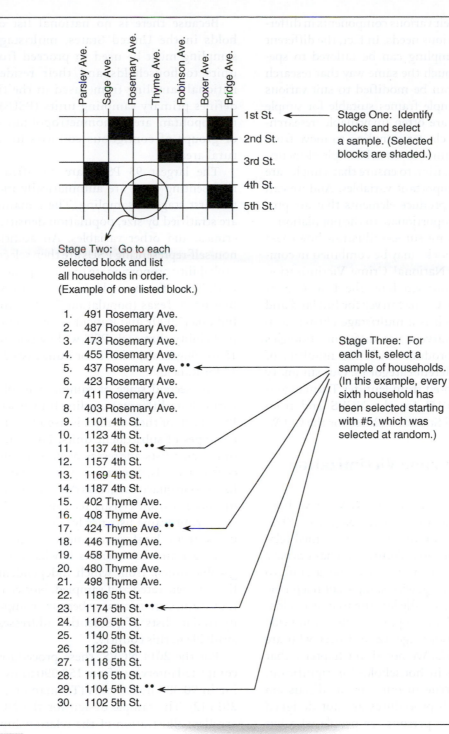

Stage One: Identify blocks and select a sample. (Selected blocks are shaded.)

Stage Two: Go to each selected block and list all households in order. (Example of one listed block.)

1. 491 Rosemary Ave.
2. 487 Rosemary Ave.
3. 473 Rosemary Ave.
4. 455 Rosemary Ave.
5. 437 Rosemary Ave. ••
6. 423 Rosemary Ave.
7. 411 Rosemary Ave.
8. 403 Rosemary Ave.
9. 1101 4th St.
10. 1123 4th St.
11. 1137 4th St. ••
12. 1157 4th St.
13. 1169 4th St.
14. 1187 4th St.
15. 402 Thyme Ave.
16. 408 Thyme Ave.
17. 424 Thyme Ave. ••
18. 446 Thyme Ave.
19. 458 Thyme Ave.
20. 480 Thyme Ave.
21. 498 Thyme Ave.
22. 1186 5th St.
23. 1174 5th St. ••
24. 1160 5th St.
25. 1140 5th St.
26. 1122 5th St.
27. 1118 5th St.
28. 1116 5th St.
29. 1104 5th St. ••
30. 1102 5th St.

Stage Three: For each list, select a sample of households. (In this example, every sixth household has been selected starting with #5, which was selected at random.)

FIGURE 8.10 Multistage Cluster Sampling

of sampling and their various components in different ways to suit various needs. In fact, the different components of sampling can be tailored to specific purposes in much the same way that research design principles can be modified to suit various needs. Because sample frames suitable for simple random sampling are often unavailable, researchers use multistage cluster sampling to move from aggregate sample units to actual sample elements. We can add stratification to ensure that samples are representative of important variables. And we can design samples to produce elements that are proportionate or disproportionate to the population.

Two national crime surveys illustrate how these various building blocks may be combined in complex ways: (1) the National Crime Victimization Survey (NCVS), conducted by the U.S. Census Bureau; and (2) the Crime Survey for England and Wales (CSEW). Each is a multistage cluster sample, but the two surveys use different strategies for sampling to produce sufficient numbers of respondents in different categories. Our summary description is adapted from Jennifer Truman and Lynn Langton (2015) for the NCVS and from Office for National Statistics (2016) for the CSEW.

The National Crime Victimization Survey

Although various parts of the NCVS have been modified since the surveys were begun in 1972, the basic sampling strategies have remained relatively constant. The most significant changes have been fluctuations in sample size and a shift to telephone interviewing, with samples of telephone number listings eventually leading to households.

The NCVS seeks to represent the nationwide population of persons age 12 and over who are living in households. We noted in Chapter 6 that the phrase "living in households" is significant; this is especially true in our current discussion of sampling. NCVS procedures are not designed to sample homeless persons, or people who live in institutional settings such as military group housing or correctional facilities. Also, because the sample targets persons who live in households, it cannot provide estimates of crimes in which a commercial establishment or business is the victim.

Because there is no national list of households in the United States, multistage cluster sampling must be used to proceed from larger units to households and their residents. The national sampling frame used in the first stage defines primary sampling units (PSUs) as large metropolitan areas, nonmetropolitan counties, or groups of contiguous counties (to represent rural areas).

The largest 93 PSUs are specified as "self-representing" and are automatically included in the first stage of sampling. The remaining PSUs are stratified by size, population density, reported crimes, and other variables. An additional 152 non-self-representing PSUs are then selected with a probability proportionate to the population of the PSU. Thus, for example, if one stratum includes Bugtussle, Texas (population 7,000); Punkinseed, Indiana (5,000); and Rancid, Missouri (3,000), the probability that each PSU will be selected is 7 in 15 for Bugtussle, 5 in 15 for Punkinseed, and 3 in 15 for Rancid.

The second stage of sampling involves designating four different sampling frames within each PSU. Each of these frames is used to select different types of subsequent units. First, the housing unit frame lists addresses of housing units from census records. Second, a group quarters frame lists group quarters such as dormitories and rooming houses from census records. Third, a building permit frame lists newly constructed housing units from local government sources. Finally, an area frame lists census blocks (physical geographic units), from which independent address lists are generated and sampled. Notice that these four frames are necessary because comprehensive, up-to-date lists of residential addresses are not available in this country.

For the 2014 NCVS, these procedures yielded completed interviews from 158,090 individuals living in 90,380 households (Truman and Langton, 2015:12). The sample design for the NCVS is an excellent illustration of the relationship between sample size and variation in the target population. Because serious crime is a relatively rare event when averaged across the entire U.S. population, very large samples must be drawn. And because no single list of the target population exists, samples are drawn in several stages.

For further information, consult NCVS documentation maintained by the Bureau of Justice Statistics (http://bjs.ojp.usdoj.gov/index.cfm?ty=dcdetail&iid=245 Accessed 20 July 2016). Also see the "National Crime Victimization Survey Resource Guide," maintained at the National Archive of Criminal Justice Data (http://www.icpsr.umich.edu/NACJD/NCVS Accessed 20 July 2016).

The Crime Survey for England and Wales

We have seen that NCVS sampling procedures begin with demographic units and work down to selection of housing units. CSEW sampling is simplified by the existence of a national list of something close to addresses. The Postcode Address File (PAF) lists postal delivery points nationwide and ". . . is widely accepted as the best general population sampling frame in England and Wales."

Postcode sectors, roughly corresponding to U.S. five-digit zip codes, are easily defined clusters of addresses from the PAF. Samples of addresses are then selected from within these sectors.

Until major budget cuts forced cutbacks in sampling procedures in 2010, the CSEW predecessor (known as the British Crime Survey or BCS) included additional samples to represent particular population groups. BCS researchers used "booster samples" to increase the number of respondents who were ethnic minorities or between the ages of 16 and 24. Victimization experiences of ethnic minorities were of special interest to police and other public officials. Young people were oversampled to complete a special questionnaire of self-report behavior items.

The ethnic minority booster was accomplished by first selecting respondents using formal sampling procedures. Interviewers then sought information about four housing units adjacent to the selected unit in an effort to determine if any residents were nonwhite. If adjacent units housed minority families, one was selected to be interviewed for the ethnic minority booster sample. This is an example of what Steven Thompson (1997) calls "adaptive sampling." Probability samples are first selected, then those respondents are used to identify other individuals who meet some

criterion. Increasing the number of respondents age 16–24 was simpler; interviewers sought additional respondents in that age group within sampled households.

One final sampling dimension in the CSEW reflects the regional organization of police in England and Wales into 42 police areas. The BCS was further stratified to produce about 650 interviews in each police area to support analysis within those areas.

After individual households were selected, one person age 16 or over was randomly chosen to provide information for all household members. Since 2009, children age 10–15 have been sampled from some households. Since 2009, sample sizes have been cut by almost half. The final sample size for the 2014–2015 survey was about 33,350, with a response rate of 70 percent.

Although sampling designs for both the CSEW and the NCVS are more complex than we have represented in this discussion, the important point is how multistage cluster sampling is used in each. The principal difference between the two is that sampling procedures for the CSEW are somewhat simpler than those for the NCVS, largely because a suitable sampling frame exists at the national level.

Probability Sampling in Review

Depending on the field situation, probability sampling can be very simple or extremely complex, time consuming, and expensive. Whatever the situation, however, it is usually the preferred method for selecting study elements. It's worth restating the two main reasons for this.

First, probability sampling avoids conscious or unconscious biases in element selection on the part of the researcher. If all elements in the population have an equal (or unequal and subsequently weighted) chance of selection, there is an excellent chance that the sample thus selected will closely represent the population of all elements.

Second, probability sampling permits estimates of sampling error. Although no probability sample will be perfectly representative in all respects, controlled selection methods permit the researcher to estimate the degree of expected error.

Despite these advantages, it is sometimes impossible to use standard probability sampling methods. Sometimes, it isn't even appropriate to do so. In those cases, researchers turn to nonprobability sampling.

Nonprobability Sampling

In many research applications, nonprobability samples are necessary or advantageous.

You can no doubt envision situations in which it would be either impossible or unfeasible to select the kinds of probability samples we have described. Suppose we want to study auto thieves. There is no list of all auto thieves, nor are we likely to be able to create anything other than a partial and highly selective list. Moreover, probability sampling is sometimes inappropriate even if it is possible. In many such situations, **nonprobability sampling** procedures are called for. Recall that probability samples are defined as those in which the probability that any given sampling element will be selected is known. Conversely, in nonprobability sampling, the likelihood that any given element will be selected is not known.

We'll examine four types of nonprobability samples in this section: (1) purposive or judgmental sampling, (2) quota sampling, (3) the reliance on available subjects, and (4) snowball sampling.

Purposive or Judgmental Sampling

Occasionally, it may be appropriate to select a sample based on our own knowledge of the population, its elements, and the nature of our research aims—in short, based on our judgment and the purpose of the study. Such a sample is called a **purposive sample.**

We may wish to study a small subset of a larger population in which many members of the subset are easily identified, but enumeration of all of them would be nearly impossible. For example, we might want to study members of community crime prevention groups; many members are easily visible, but it is not feasible to define and sample all members of community crime prevention organizations. In studying a sample of the most visible members, however, we may collect data sufficient for our purposes.

Criminal justice research often compares practices in different jurisdictions—cities or states, for example. In such cases, study elements may be selected because they exhibit some particular attribute. For example, Michael Leiber and Jayne Stairs (1999) were interested in how economic inequality combined with race to affect sentencing practices in Iowa juvenile courts. After controlling for economic status, they found that African American defendants received more restrictive sentences than did white defendants. Leiber and Stairs purposively selected three jurisdictions to obtain sample elements with adequate racial diversity in the state of Iowa. The researchers then selected over 5,000 juvenile cases processed in those three courts.

Researchers may also use purposive or judgmental sampling to represent patterns of complex variation. In their study of closed-circuit television (CCTV) systems, Martin Gill and Angela Spriggs (2005) describe how sites were sampled to reflect variation in type of area (residential, commercial, city center, and large parking facilities). Some individual CCTV projects were selected because of certain specific features; they were installed in a high-crime area, or the CCTV setup was notably expensive. One element of this study involved interviews to assess changes in fear of crime following CCTV installation. To do this, the researchers sampled passersby on city-center streets. They first selected purposive samples of areas, then spread their interviews across four day/time periods. This was done to reflect variation in the types of people encountered on different streets at different times. Sampling strategies were thus adapted because of expected heterogeneity that would have been difficult to capture with random selection.

Pretesting a questionnaire is another situation in which purposive sampling is common. If, for example, we plan to study people's attitudes about court-ordered restitution for crime victims, we might want to test the questionnaire on a sample of crime victims. Instead of selecting a probability sample of the general population, we might select some number of known crime victims, perhaps from court records.

Nonprobability sampling Sampling in which the probability that an element will be included in a sample is *not* known.

Quota Sampling

Like probability sampling, **quota sampling** addresses the issue of representativeness, although the two methods approach the issue quite differently. Quota sampling begins with a matrix or table describing the characteristics of the target population we wish to represent. To do this, we need to know, for example, what proportion of the population is male or female, what proportions fall into various age categories, education levels, ethnic groups, and so forth. In establishing a national quota sample, we need to know what proportion of the national population is, say, urban, eastern, male, under 25, white, working class, and all the combinations of these attributes.

Once we have created such a matrix and assigned a relative proportion to each cell in the matrix, we can collect data from people who have all the characteristics of a given cell. We then assign all the persons in a given cell a weight appropriate to their portion of the total population. When all the sample elements are weighted in this way, the overall data should provide a reasonable representation of the total population.

Although quota sampling may resemble probability sampling, it has two inherent problems. First, the quota frame (the proportions that different cells represent) must be accurate, and it is often difficult to get up-to-date information for this purpose. A quota sample of auto thieves or teenage vandals would obviously suffer from this difficulty. Second, biases may exist in the selection of sample elements within a given cell—even though its proportion of the population is accurately estimated. Instructed to interview five persons who meet a given complex set of characteristics, an interviewer may still avoid people who live at the top of seven-story walk-ups, have particularly rundown homes, or own vicious dogs.

Quota and purposive sampling may be combined to produce samples that are intuitively, if not statistically, representative. For example, David Farrington, Trevor Bennett, and Brandon Welsh (2007) designed an experimental evaluation of CCTV impact on perceptions of crime and disorder in Cambridge, England. They wished to represent several characteristics of people who spent time outside in certain areas of the city. A probability sample was rejected because the authors wished to represent characteristics of city-center residents who used city streets, not necessarily people who lived in the city. So researchers selected passersby in target areas of Cambridge to meet quotas of 52 percent male, 40 percent between the ages of 16 and 29, and 92 percent white (2007:190).

Reliance on Available Subjects

Relying on available subjects—that is, stopping people at a street corner or some other location—is sometimes misleadingly called "convenience sampling." University researchers frequently conduct surveys among the students enrolled in large lecture classes. The ease and economy of such a method explain its popularity; however, it seldom produces data of any general value. It may be useful to pretest a questionnaire, but it should not be used for a study purportedly describing students as a whole.

Reliance on available subjects can be an appropriate sampling method in some situations. It is generally best justified if the researcher wants to study the characteristics of people who are passing the sampling point at some specified time. For example, in her study of street lighting as a crime prevention strategy, Kate Painter (1996) interviewed samples of pedestrians as they walked through specified areas of London just before and six weeks after lighting conditions were improved. Painter clearly understood the scope and limits of this sampling technique. Her findings are described as applying to people who actually use area streets after dark, while recognizing that this population may be quite different from the population of area residents. Interviewing a sample of available evening pedestrians is an appropriate sampling technique for generalizing to the population of evening pedestrians, and the population of pedestrians will not be the same as the population of residents. Unlike Farrington and associates, Painter had no specific quotas for subjects in her sample.

In a more general sense, samples like Painter's select elements of a *process*—the process that generates evening pedestrians—rather than elements of a *population*. If we can safely assume that no systematic pattern generates elements of a process, then a sample of available elements as they happen to pass by can be considered to be representative. So if you are interested in studying crimes reported to police, for example, then a sample of, say, every seventh crime report over a two-month period will be representative of the general population of crime reports over that two-month period.

Sometimes nonprobability and probability sampling techniques can be combined. For example, most attempts to sample homeless or street people rely on available subjects found in shelters, parks, or other locations. Salaam Semaan, Jennifer Lauby, and Jon Liebman (2002) suggest that once areas are located where homeless people congregate, individuals found there can be enumerated and then sampled. Here's a semi-hypothetical example.

In recent years, Maxfield has observed that many people who appear to be homeless congregate at the corner of 9th Avenue and 41st Street in Manhattan. An efficient strategy for interviewing samples of homeless people would be a time-space sample where, for example, each hour individuals would be counted and some fraction sampled. Let's say we wished to interview 30 people and spread those interviews over a six-hour period; we would try to interview five people per hour. So each hour we would count the number of people within some specific area (say 20 at 1:00 P.M.) and then divide that number by five to obtain a sampling fraction (four in this case). Recalling our earlier discussion of systematic probability sampling, we would then select a random starting point to identify the first person to interview. Then we would select the fourth person after that, and so on. This approach would yield an unbiased sample that represented the population of street people on one Manhattan corner over a six-hour period. Table 8.1 illustrates how we could complete our 30 interviews, selecting varying fractions of those present at different times.

As it happens, 41st Street and 9th Avenue in Manhattan is the rear entrance to the Port Authority bus terminal. Marcus Felson and associates (1996) described efforts to reduce crime and disorder in the Port Authority terminal, a place they claim is the world's busiest bus station. Among the most important objectives

TABLE 8.1 Systematic Sampling of Available Subjects

Time	People Present	Interviews	Sampling Fraction
10:00 A.M.	15	5	1/3
11:00 A.M.	20	5	1/4
12:00 P.M.	15	5	1/3
1:00 P.M.	30	5	1/6
2:00 P.M.	20	5	1/4
3:00 P.M.	50	5	1/5
Total	135	30	1/4

were to reduce perceptions of crime problems and to improve how travelers felt about the Port Authority terminal. These are research questions appropriate to some sort of survey. Because more than 170,000 passengers pass through the bus station on an average spring day, obtaining a sufficiently large sample of users presents no difficulty.

The problem was how to select a sample. Felson and associates point out that stopping passengers on their way to or from a bus was out of the question. Most passengers are commuters whose journey to and from work is timed to the minute, with none to spare for interviewers' questions. Here's how Felson and associates describe the solution and the sampling strategy it embodied (1996:90–91):

> Response rates would have been low if the Port Authority had tried to interview rushing customers or to hand out questionnaires to be returned later. Their solution was ingenious. The Port Authority drew a sample of outgoing buses . . . and placed representatives aboard. After the bus had departed, he or she would hand out a questionnaire to be completed during the trip . . . [and] collect these questionnaires as each customer arrived at the destination. This procedure produced a very high response rate and high completion rate for each item.

Online samples offer a new and creative way to select high-quality convenience samples. See the box, "Online Sampling via Mechanical Turk" to learn more about this tool for selecting subjects.

Internet-based sampling is a rapidly developing innovation in nonprobability sampling. This type of sampling is closely linked to Web-based surveys, a topic we examine in Chapter 9. The chief advantage of Internet-based samples is the very low cost of obtaining a very large number of sample elements. Here we describe Amazon's Mechanical Turk (MTurk), a service that has emerged as one of the most promising resources for experiments and surveys in social science research (Sheehan and Pittman, 2016).

Amazon maintains MTurk as a type of crowdsourcing platform, introduced by the home page heading, "Mechanical Turk is a marketplace for work." (www .mturk.com/mturk/welcome Accessed 20 July 2016). The MTurk marketplace hosts two types of users: workers and requesters. As you might expect, workers sign on to perform tasks specified by requesters. Perhaps you've signed up as a worker for MTurk or similar Web-based marketplace.

The range of tasks is very broad, as is the number of workers. Here we'll work through a brief example to show how it works. Chapter 9 describes actual research that links a sample recruited through MTurk to online questionnaires administered through another Web-based service.

People sign up as workers and become eligible to perform tasks, labeled Human Intelligence Tasks, or HITs. Workers are paid small amounts of money for completing each HIT. In July 2016, over 1.4 million HITs were listed on the MTurk site. Among these was the following:

> African American Men's Perceptions of Law Enforcement. This task is a research study, which is interested in individuals' perceptions of the fairness of traffic stops. It involves viewing a short picture/audio vignette and answering questions about both the vignette and yourself. Duration: Approx. 15 minutes, Reward 20 cents

A requester, identified by name, designed the survey and submitted it as a task on MTurk. The requester pays 20 cents for each completed and *accepted* response. The accepted part is important since it offers a measure of quality control—questionnaires that are incomplete or exhibit certain inconsistencies can be rejected, and no reward is paid. Workers who accumulate too many rejected HITs are flagged, and may become ineligible for further work. Requesters can specify various characteristics they seek in workers, similar to the process of stratification described in this chapter.

In this case the requester is a researcher studying perceptions of police during traffic stops. In addition to the HIT summarized above, the same researcher sought Latin American men and women to complete similar tasks. This example shows how social science researchers, acting as requesters, can use MTurk to accumulate samples of workers to complete questionnaires and participate in experiments. What results is an enormous pool of potential elements for convenience samples.

MTurk produces convenience samples, but research has found they can be high-quality samples that are more broadly representative than classroom-based student samples and other online methods. For example, Berinsky and associates (2012) compared summary statistics for MTurk samples to other Internet-based convenience samples, as well as high-quality probability samples, finding the MTurk sample to be more representative of the national population than published convenience samples, but less representative than national probability samples. MTurk workers tended to be younger and more ideologically liberal than the general public (2012: 366).

Consider how the spread of Internet access has reduced potential problems with biases that might be associated with online samples. Also, think about how such tools make it possible to produce large samples at very low cost. We'll return to MTurk in Chapter 9, showing how MTurk samples can be coupled with online survey platforms. In the meantime, visit the MTurk website. Even if you have not created a worker account, you can browse the HITs and see examples of surveys and experiments. We found the example described here by searching for "law."

Snowball Sampling

Another type of nonprobability sampling that closely resembles the available-subjects approach is called **snowball sampling**. It is commonly used in field observation studies or qualitative interviewing. Snowball sampling begins by identifying a single subject or small number of subjects and then asking the subject(s) to identify others like him or her who might be willing to participate in a study.

Criminal justice research on active criminals or deviants frequently uses snowball sampling techniques. The researcher often makes an initial contact by consulting criminal justice agency records to identify, say, someone convicted of auto theft and placed on probation. That person is interviewed and asked to suggest other auto thieves whom researchers could contact. Stephen Baron and Timothy Hartnagel (1998) studied violence among homeless youths in Edmonton, Canada, identifying their sample through snowball techniques. Similarly, snowball sampling is often used to study drug users and dealers. Martin Bouchard (2007) began with contacts from colleagues to identify marijuana growers in Quebec, Canada, who then referred him to other active cultivators. Bruce Jacobs and Jody Miller (1998) accumulated a sample of 25 female crack dealers in St. Louis to study specific techniques to avoid arrest.

Contacting an initial subject or informant who will then refer the researcher to other subjects can be especially difficult in studies of active offenders. As in most aspects of criminal justice research, the various approaches to initiating contacts for snowball sampling have advantages and disadvantages. Beginning with subjects who have a previous arrest or conviction is usually the easiest method for researchers, but it suffers from potential bias by depending on offenders who are known to police or other officials (Jacobs, Topalli, and Wright, 2003).

Recent studies by researchers at the University of Missouri–St. Louis offer good examples of snowball samples of offenders that are not dependent on contacts with criminal justice officials. Beginning with a street-savvy ex-offender, these researchers identified samples of burglars (Wright and Decker, 1994), members of youth gangs (Decker and Van Winkle, 1996), armed robbers (Wright and Decker, 1997), and carjackers (Jacobs, 2012). It's especially difficult to identify active offenders as research subjects, but these examples illustrate notably clever uses of snowball sampling techniques.

The study by Richard Wright and Scott Decker (1994) provides a good example. The ex-offender contacted a few active burglars and a few "street-wise noncriminals," who, in turn, referred researchers to additional subjects, and so on. This process is illustrated in Figure 8.11, which shows the chain of referrals that accumulated a snowball sample of 105 individuals.

Starting at the top of Figure 8.11, the ex-offender put researchers in contact with two subjects directly (001 and 003), a small-time criminal, three street-wise noncriminals, a crack addict, a youth worker, and someone serving probation. Continuing downward, the small-time criminal was especially helpful, identifying 12 subjects who participated in the study (005, 006, 008, 009, 010, 021, 022, 023, 025, 026, 030, and 032). Notice how the snowball effect continues, with subject 026 identifying subjects 028 and 029. Notice also that some subjects were themselves "nominated" by more than one source. In the middle of the bottom row in Figure 8.11, for example, subjects 060 and 061 both mentioned subject 064.

Amber Horning describes another good example of snowball sampling in Chapter 10, based on her qualitative interviews with New York City pimps.

Nonprobability Sampling in Review

Snowball samples are essentially variations on purposive samples (we want to sample juvenile gang members) and on samples of available subjects (sample elements identify other sample elements that are available to us). Each of these is a nonprobability sampling technique. And, like other types of nonprobability samples, snowball samples are most appropriate when it is impossible to determine the probability that any given element will be selected in a sample. Furthermore, snowball sampling and related

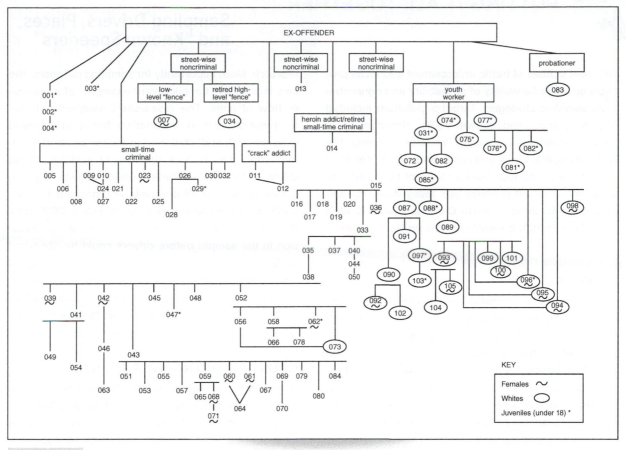

FIGURE 8.11 "Snowball" Referral Chart

Source: Reprinted from Richard T. Wright and Scott H. Decker, *Burglars on the Job: Streetlife and Residential Break-Ins* (Boston: Northeastern University Press, 1994), p. 19. Reprinted by permission of Northeastern University Press.

techniques may be necessary when the target population is difficult to locate or even identify. Approaching pedestrians who happen to pass by, for example, is not an efficient way to select a sample of prostitutes or juvenile gang members. In contrast, approaching pedestrians *is* an appropriate sampling method for studying pedestrians, whereas drawing a probability sample of urban residents to identify people who walk in specific areas of the city would be costly and inefficient.

Like other elements of criminal justice research, sampling plans must be adapted to specific research applications. When it's important to make estimates of the accuracy of our samples,

and when suitable sampling frames are possible, we use probability sampling techniques. When no reasonable sampling frame is available, and we cannot draw a probability sample, we cannot make estimates about sample accuracy. Fortunately, in such situations, we can make use of a variety of approaches for drawing nonprobability samples.

Our running example, "Putting It All Together: Sampling Drivers, Places, and 'Known Speeders,'" illustrates the combination of probability and nonprobability sampling techniques to estimate different types of populations. Take note that only one sample involved a sampling frame. Others represent creative approaches to sampling drivers and road segments.

Different studies of traffic enforcement and racial profiling employed a variety of probability and nonprobability sampling strategies. Target populations included drivers, places, and known traffic offenders. New Jersey researchers sampled vehicles entering the state's turnpike. Engel and colleagues (2005) selected Pennsylvania counties from a range of purposive criteria that reflected roadway use. Many different samples were involved in North Carolina research. We'll consider a stratified sample of "known North Carolina speeders."

DRIVERS

You can probably imagine the population of drivers on a roadway, but how would you define it? Place and time would be important dimensions, for example: "All drivers between milepost 1 and milepost 50 on the New Jersey Turnpike at 4:00 P.M. on Tuesday." Because the New Jersey Turnpike is a toll road with access restricted to a relatively small number of points, that would be a relatively manageable population. Even so, that population would continually change as cars entered and exited the turnpike over the course of an hour or so.

Lange et al. (2005) took advantage of the limited access feature, as well as the fact that vehicles exiting the turnpike had to stop at tollbooths. This slowed vehicles, making it possible for researchers to observe features of cars and drivers that were of interest to their research. More importantly for sampling purposes, the cars leaving the turnpike were examples of a process or flow of units. The researchers sampled vehicles from that process. To accomplish that in an unbiased way, research staff stationed in tollbooths used handheld computers to time the flow of vehicles. About every 2.5 minutes, an alarm sounded on the computer, signaling that the third vehicle approaching the tollbooth after the alarm was to be selected (2005:199). With this procedure, vehicles were selected for inclusion in the sample before drivers could be observed by research staff, thus eliminating any bias that might emerge if researchers chose which vehicles to select. Sampling also included procedures for selecting tollbooth exits to represent different sections of the highway, as well as day of week and time of day.

COUNTIES AND ROAD SEGMENTS

As a relatively uniform highway with few access points, the New Jersey Turnpike produced few sampling challenges. In contrast, Pennsylvania researchers sought locations that represented the considerable variety of roadways and conditions covered by troopers throughout the state. In selecting their sample, Engel and associates (2005) considered several characteristics of Pennsylvania counties that might affect roadway use and attract long-distance travelers. They specified three general constructs to represent, and seven variables to measure those constructs at the county level:

SUMMARY

- The logic of probability sampling forms the foundation for representing large populations with small subsets of those populations.
- The chief criterion of a sample's quality is the degree to which it is representative—the extent to which the characteristics of the sample are the same as those of the population from which it was selected. Samples should be unbiased. But some degree of sampling error always exists.
- The chief principle of probability sampling is that every member of the total population must have some known nonzero probability of being selected into the sample.
- Probability sampling methods provide one excellent way of selecting samples that will be quite representative. They make it possible to estimate the amount of sampling error that should be expected in a given sample.
- Our ability to estimate population parameters with sample statistics is rooted in the sampling distribution and probability theory. If we draw a large number of samples of a given size, sample statistics will cluster around the true population parameter. As sample size increases, the cluster becomes tighter.

- General roadway use
  - County population
  - Total roadway miles within each county
  - Interstate highway miles within each county

- Probable roadway use by minorities
  - County Hispanic population
  - County black population

- Likelihood that county road use did not reflect the residential population
  - Presence of tourist attractions, colleges and universities, or historical sites
  - Presence of seasonal attractions such as amusement parks or ski resorts

These seven variables were combined in a statistical procedure known as factor analysis, to produce summary scores for all Pennsylvania counties. Counties were then sorted into four groups ranging from high to low on the summary scores of roadway use, minority use, and nonlocal driver use. A total of 20 counties were selected from these four groups. An additional seven counties were selected because the racial distribution of drivers stopped was much different than the racial distribution of county residents.

Together, these procedures represented several sampling concepts described in this chapter. Counties were *stratified* by things that affected road use, and likely road use by minorities. Some counties were *purposively* selected based on high proportions of minority traffic stops. Eleven of 20 sampled counties were selected from the high-score group, producing a *disproportionate* number of sample units that had high levels of road use by minorities and nonlocal drivers.

Finally, Engel et al. selected specific road segments within counties where they later conducted observations, resulting in a *multistage* sample design.

KNOWN SPEEDERS

In connection with their research in North Carolina, William Smith and associates (2003) used three general techniques to measure speeding: police records, independent observations, and self-report surveys. Like the Bureau of Justice Statistics survey on contacts with police, one goal of a survey is to sample people who had been stopped, but might not appear in police records. But Smith and associates were also interested in the validity of self-reported speeding and police contacts. How truthful were respondents asked about speeding and traffic stops?

To address this question, the researchers sampled court records of North Carolina residents who had received a speeding ticket between June 1999 and May 2000. Because they wished to include a large number of black drivers ticketed for speeding, the researchers used disproportionate stratified sampling so about half of selected names were for drivers whose race was classified as black on driving records. In this case, the *target population* was persons known to have been cited for speeding. The *sampling frame* was a database containing records of all persons ticket for speeding, together with their address and phone number. Because race was recorded on driver's licenses, it was easier to sort the records then use a random sampling computer procedure to select a sample *stratified* by race.

- Simple random sampling is logically the most fundamental technique in probability sampling, although it is seldom used in practice. A variety of sampling designs can be used and combined to suit different populations and research purposes. Each type of sampling has its own advantages and disadvantages.
- Systematic sampling involves using a sampling frame to select units that appear at some specified interval—for example, every 8th, or 15th, or 1023rd unit. This method is functionally equivalent to simple random sampling.
- Stratification improves the representativeness of a sample by reducing the sampling error.

- Multistage cluster sampling is frequently used when there is no list of all the members of a population.
- The NCVS and the BCS are national crime surveys based on multistage cluster samples. Sampling methods for each survey illustrate different approaches to representing relatively rare events.
- Nonprobability sampling methods are less statistically representative and less reliable than probability sampling methods. However, they are appropriate for many research applications.
- Purposive sampling is used when researchers wish to select specific elements of a population. This may be because the elements are believed to be representative,

or extreme cases, or because they represent the range of variation expected in a population.

- In quota sampling, researchers begin with a detailed description of the characteristics of the total population and then select sample members in a way that includes the different composite profiles that exist in the population.
- Snowball samples accumulate subjects through chains of referrals and are most commonly used in field research.

KEY TERMS

Cluster sampling *(p. 215)*
Confidence intervals *(p. 211)*
Confidence levels *(p. 210)*
Equal probability of selection method (EPSEM) *(p. 203)*
Nonprobability sampling *(p. 220)*
Population *(p. 204)*
Population parameter *(p. 204)*
Probability sampling *(p. 201)*
Purposive sample *(p. 220)*
Quota sampling *(p. 221)*
Sample element *(p. 204)*
Sample statistic *(p. 204)*
Sampling *(p. 200)*
Sampling distribution *(p. 205)*
Sampling frame *(p. 208)*
Sampling units *(p. 215)*
Simple random sampling *(p. 213)*
Snowball sampling *(p. 223)*
Standard error *(p. 209)*
Stratification *(p. 214)*
Systematic sampling *(p. 213)*

REVIEW QUESTIONS AND EXERCISES

1. Review the summary of the Drug Abuse Warning Network (DAWN) program in Chapter 6. Specify the target population, study population, sampling frame, and elements used in the DAWN program. Describe what type of sample DAWN uses, and discuss the advantages and disadvantages of sampling procedures.

2. Stop-and-frisk is a controversial tactic in which police approach persons on the street who appear to act suspiciously, "frisk" them for weapons or contraband, then ask some questions. Research in New York City has shown that young males of color are more often stopped than older people, females, or whites (Jones-Brown, Gill, and Trone 2010). Briefly describe two approaches to sampling subjects for a research study on people's experiences of stop-and-frisk.

3. Discuss possible study populations, elements, sampling units, and sampling frames for drawing a sample to represent the populations listed here. You may wish to limit your discussion to populations in a specific state or other jurisdiction.

   a. Municipal police officers
   b. Felony court judges
   c. Auto thieves
   d. Licensed automobile drivers
   e. State police superintendents
   f. Persons incarcerated in county jails

CHAPTER 9

Survey Research

We'll examine how mail, in-person, and telephone surveys can be used in criminal justice research.

Learning Objectives

1. Understand that survey research involves the administration of questionnaires in a systematic way to a sample of respondents selected from some population.

2. Describe how survey research is especially appropriate for descriptive or exploratory studies of large populations.

3. Describe examples of surveys as the method of choice for obtaining victimization and self-reported offending data.

4. Summarize differences between open-ended or closed-ended questions, and offer examples of the advantages and disadvantages of each.

5. Recognize how bias in questionnaire items encourages respondents to answer in a particular way or to support a particular point of view.

6. Describe different ways to administer questionnaires, and offer examples of how they can be varied.

7. Recognize why it is important for interviewers to be neutral in face-to-face surveys.

8. Provide examples of the advantages and disadvantages of each method of survey administration.

9. Discuss how survey data can be somewhat artificial and potentially superficial.

10. Understand how specialized interviews with a small number of people and focus groups are different from surveys as examples of collecting data by asking questions.

Knowledge and Attitudes about Sex Offenders

by Nerea Marteache, California State University, San Bernardino

In my second year of graduate study at Rutgers University, I worked with Professor Michael Maxfield to do research on what people know about sex offenders and how they believe sex offenders should be punished or treated. It took a lot longer than I thought, but results were finally published in the summer of 2012 (Marteache, 2012). Because it illustrates many features of research discussed in this and earlier chapters of your textbook, Professor Maxfield asked me to write a brief description of the project and how it developed.

Knowledge and attitudes about sex offenders are the kinds of topic that can only be studied by asking questions. State governments in the United States and in other countries, including my native Spain, have reacted to widely publicized stories about sex offenses by increasing penalties for sex offenders and expanding supervision of offenders after they are released from custody. My study had two main goals: (1) to provide detailed data and information about sex offenders to study participants and then assess how their knowledge and attitudes changed, and (2) to assess the stability of attitudes and knowledge after subjects viewed simulated mass media coverage of sex offenses.

My principal questions were as follows:

- Does instruction about sex offenders change knowledge about sex offenders and attitudes toward punishment or treatment?
- Does viewing a sensationalist video about a serious sex offense change knowledge and attitudes less among those who had instruction about sex offenders?

I enlisted the aid of two colleagues in Spain, one at a university in Barcelona and the other at a university in Madrid. They distributed to students questionnaires that I designed at each university. Students completed the questionnaires at three time points over the course of the fall 2009 semester. Students in treatment groups participated in a special class that offered 2 hours of instruction and a debate about sex offenders and treatment. Students in control groups at each university attended a normal class session of the course. With Professor Maxfield's assistance at Rutgers, I designed the instructional materials that were presented by my colleagues in Spain. After participating in a treatment or control class, all subjects completed a second questionnaire.

In the next stage of the project, I developed an intervention to simulate mass media coverage of sex offenders. This was a sensationalist news video about a horrific sex offense case that was widely known in Spain. For the control group, I used a similarly sensationalist video about cocaine use in Spain. Students in Barcelona and Madrid were randomly assigned to view either the sex offense or the drug abuse video. After viewing the videos, students completed a third questionnaire that measured their knowledge and attitudes about sex offenders.

The English version of part of the questionnaire I used is shown below. The questions were part of a battery of items developed by Wesley Church and associates (2008). The reliability of these questions has been established, so I used them rather than make up new questions. Data collection was completed by the end of the fall 2009 semester. I returned to Rutgers after the semester break with 801 completed questionnaires.

This project went pretty much as planned. But it was a lot more work than I initially thought. This was partly due to the complex design, and partly to the logistics of being in New Jersey while two colleagues were collecting the data in Spain.

Survey for University Students About Public Opinion on Sexual Offenders

Our research group is carrying out a project about public opinion on sexual offenders. To do so, we need your help. Please answer the questions below and provide the answer that most accurately expresses your opinion. If you have any doubt about the meaning of a question, just raise your hand and a member of the research group will help you. The information provided will be confidential.

Thank you for participating in this study.

Following are 18 statements about sex offenders and sex offenses. Please select the corresponding number from the rating scale given below for the answer that best describes the way you feel or what you believe.

Most of the statements that follow are difficult to prove or verify in an absolute sense, and many are specifically about your opinion based on what you may have heard, read, or learned; thus, we are less interested in the "right" or "wrong" answers, and more interested in your beliefs and opinions regarding sex offenders.

(Continued)

Even if you have no general knowledge about the issue, please provide an answer to each question.

RATING SCALE:

1 – Strongly disagree   2 – Disagree   3 – Probably disagree   4 – Probably agree   5 – Agree   6 – Strongly agree

Rating

a. With support and therapy, someone who committed a sexual offense can learn to change their behavior. ☐

b. People who commit sex offenses should lose their civil rights (e.g., voting and privacy). ☐

c. People who commit sex offenses want to have sex more often than the average person. ☐

d. Male sex offenders should be punished more severely than female sex offenders. ☐

e. Sexual fondling (inappropriate unwarranted touch) is not as bad as rape. ☐

f. Sex offenders prefer to stay home alone rather than be around lots of people. ☐

g. Most sex offenders do not have close friends. ☐

Source: Church, Wesley T. et al. 2008. "The Community Attitudes Toward Sex Offenders Scale: The Development of a Psychometric Assessment Instrument," *Research on Social Work Practice* 18:251–259.

Introduction

Asking people questions is the most common data collection method in social science.

A little-known survey was attempted among French workers in 1880. A German political sociologist mailed some 25,000 questionnaires to workers to determine the extent of their exploitation by employers. The rather lengthy questionnaire included items such as these:

> Does your employer or his representative resort to trickery in order to defraud you of a part of your earnings? If you are paid piece rates, is the quality of the article made a pretext for fraudulent deductions from your wages?

The survey researcher in this case was not George Gallup but Karl Marx (1880:208). Although

25,000 questionnaires were mailed out, there is no record of any being returned. And you need not know much about survey methods to recognize the loaded questions posed by Marx.

Survey research is perhaps the most frequently used mode of observation in sociology and political science, and surveys are often used in criminal justice research as well. You have no doubt been a respondent in some sort of survey, and you may have conducted a **survey** yourself.

We begin this chapter by discussing criminal justice topics that are most appropriate for survey methods. Next, we cover the basic principles of how to ask people questions for research purposes, including some of the details of questionnaire construction. We describe the three basic ways of administering questionnaires—self-administration, face-to face interviews, and telephone interviews—and summarize the strengths and weaknesses of each method. After discussing more specialized interviewing techniques, such as focus groups, we conclude the chapter with some advice on the benefits and pitfalls of conducting your own surveys.

Survey   A data collection method that applies a standard instrument in a systematic way to take measures from a large number of units.

Topics Appropriate to Survey Research

Surveys have a wide variety of uses in basic and applied criminal justice research.

Surveys may be used for descriptive, explanatory, exploratory, and applied research. They are best suited for studies that have individual people as the units of analysis. They are often used for other units of analysis as well, such as households or organizations. Even in these cases, however, one or more individual people act as **respondent** or informant.

For example, researchers sometimes use victimization incidents as units of analysis in examining data from crime surveys. The fact that some people may be victimized more than once and others not at all means that victimization incidents are not the same units as individuals. However, a survey questionnaire must still be administered to people who provide information about victimization incidents. In a similar fashion, the National Jail Census, conducted every five or so years for the Bureau of Justice Statistics (BJS), collects information about local detention facilities. Jails are the units of analysis, but individuals provide information about each jail. The National Youth Gang Survey has been conducted for many years; although it seeks information about gangs, the survey is sent to law enforcement agencies and the questionnaire is completed by individuals in police departments.

We now consider some broad categories of research applications in which survey methods are especially appropriate.

Counting Crime

Chapter 6 covered this use of surveys in detail. Asking people about victimization is a measure of crime that adjusts for some of the problems found in data collected by police. Of course, survey measures have their own shortcomings. Most of these difficulties, such as recall error and reluctance to discuss victimization with interviewers, are inherent in survey methods. Nevertheless, victim surveys have become important sources of data about the volume of crime in the United States and in other countries.

Self-Reports

Surveys that ask people about crimes they may have committed were also discussed in Chapter 6. Terence Thornberry and Marvin Krohn describe self-report surveys as "an integral part of the way crime and delinquency is studied" (2000:35). For research that seeks to explore or explain why people commit criminal, delinquent, or deviant acts, asking questions is the best method available.

Within the general category of self-report surveys, two different applications are distinguished by their target population and sampling methods. Studies of offenders select samples of respondents known to have committed crimes, often prisoners. Typically, the focus is on the *frequency* of offending—how many crimes of various types are committed by active offenders over a period of time. A study of incarcerated felons by Jan and Marcia Chaiken (1982) is among the best-known self-report surveys of offenders.

The other type of self-report survey focuses on the *prevalence* of offending—how many people commit crimes, in contrast to how many crimes are committed by a target population of offenders. Such surveys typically use samples that represent a broader population, such as U.S. households, adult males, or high school seniors. The National Longitudinal Study of Adolescent Health (Add Health), sponsored by a coalition of over 20 federal agencies and private foundations, began in 1994. The Add Health is a panel study that began with an in-school survey of a national probability sample of students in grades 7–12. The most recent follow-up **interview** with these subjects was conducted in 2007–2008. An additional follow-up wave began in 2016 and is scheduled for completion in 2018. Since the survey's first wave, data from the Add Health study have been used to estimate the prevalence of criminal and delinquent acts, and have appeared in hundreds of publications investigating questions in delinquency and crime. See the Add Health website for lists of publications, details on the study design, and access to survey data (http://www.cpc.unc.edu/projects/addhealth).

General-population surveys and surveys of offenders tend to present different types of difficulties in connection with the validity and reliability of self-reports. Recall error and the reporting of fabricated offenses may be problems in a survey of high-rate offenders, whereas respondents in general-population self-report surveys may be reluctant to disclose illegal behavior. Jennifer Roberts and associates (2005) describe how weekly interviews were required to assess self-reported violence in a sample of psychiatric patients. When we discuss questionnaire construction later in this chapter, we will present examples and suggestions for creating self-report items.

Perceptions and Attitudes

Another application of surveys in criminal justice is to learn how people feel about crime and criminal justice policy. Public views about sentencing policies, gun control, police performance, and drug abuse are often solicited in opinion polls. Begun in 1972, the General Social Survey is an ongoing survey of social indicators in the United States. Questions about fear of crime and other perceptions of crime problems are regularly included. Since the mid-1970s, a growing number of explanatory studies have been conducted on public perceptions of crime and crime problems. A large body of research on fear of crime has grown, in part, from the realization that fear and its behavioral consequences are much more widespread among the population than is actual criminal victimization (Ditton and Farrall, 2007).

The vignette that opens this chapter, "Knowledge and Attitudes About Sex Offenders," illustrates the use of surveys to measure attitudes. Nerea Marteache also describes other features of her research that illustrate principles we address in this chapter.

Targeted Victim Surveys

Victim surveys that target individual cities or neighborhoods are important tools for evaluating policy innovations. Many criminal justice programs seek to prevent or reduce crime in some specific area, but crimes reported to police cannot be used to evaluate many types of programs.

To see why this is so, consider a hypothetical community policing program that encourages neighborhood residents to report all suspected crimes to the police. We saw in Chapter 6 that many minor incidents are not reported because victims believe that police will not want to be bothered. But if a new program stresses that police actually want to be alerted to even the most minor incidents, the proportion of crimes reported may increase—resulting in what appears to be an increase in crime.

The solution is to conduct targeted victim surveys before and after introducing some policy change. Such victim surveys are especially appropriate for evaluating any policy that may increase crime reporting as a side effect.

Consider also that large-scale surveys such as the National Crime Victimization Survey (NCVS) cannot be used to evaluate local crime prevention programs. This is because, as we have seen, the NCVS is designed to represent the national population of persons who live in households.

The community victim surveys designed by the BJS and the Community Oriented Police Services (COPS) office help with each of these needs. Local surveys can be launched specifically to evaluate local crime prevention efforts. Or innovative programs can be timed to correspond to regular cycles of local surveys. In each case, the BJS/COPS (Weisel, 1999) guide presents advice on drawing samples to represent local jurisdictions.

Other Evaluation Uses

Other types of surveys may be appropriate for applied studies. A good illustration of this is a series of neighborhood surveys to evaluate community policing in Chicago. Here's an example of how the researchers link their information needs to surveys (Chicago Community Policing Evaluation Consortium, 2004:2):

> Because it is a participatory program, CAPS depends on the effectiveness of campaigns to bring it to the public's attention and on the success of efforts to get the public involved in beat meetings and other district projects. The surveys enable us to track the public's awareness and involvement in community policing in Chicago.

In general, surveys can be used to evaluate policy that seeks to change attitudes, beliefs, or perceptions. For example, consider a program designed to promote victim and witness cooperation in criminal court by reducing case processing time. At first, we might consider direct measures of case processing time as indicators of program success. If the program goal is to increase cooperation, however, a survey that asks how victims and witnesses perceive case processing time will be more appropriate.

General-Purpose Crime Surveys

As the name implies, these surveys are designed for more than one of the purposes we have mentioned. Since its inception in 1982, the Crime Survey for England and Wales (CSEW), formerly the British Crime Survey, included special batteries of questions about various topics: fear of crime (1984), contacts with the police (1988, 1996, 2000), self-reported drug use (1994), security measures used to protect households and vehicles (1996), and fraud and technology crimes (2002–2003).

The NCVS traditionally has focused on counting crime. In recent years, however, efforts have been devoted to incrementally redesigning the survey to broaden its scope (National Research Council, 2008). Beginning in 1996, the NCVS added a series of questions on police–public contacts other than those in connection with victimization. The most interesting type of such contact is a traffic stop; survey respondents describe their experiences with police in connection with traffic violations. Using the NCVS as a research platform in this way has produced a new source of data with which to assess the scope of race-based disparities in police–public contacts. Lynn Langton and Matthew Durose (2013) draw on this supplement to examine reports of police behavior during stops in 2011. Similarly, supplemental questions on identity theft and school crime victimization have been included in the NCVS in various years.

Guidelines for Asking Questions

How questions are asked is the single most important feature of survey research.

A defining feature of survey methods is that research concepts are operationalized by asking people questions. Several general guidelines can assist in framing and asking questions that serve as excellent operationalizations of variables. It is important also to be aware of pitfalls that can result in useless and even misleading information.

Surveys include a **questionnaire**—an instrument specifically designed to elicit information that will be useful for analysis. Although some of the specific points to follow are more appropriate to structured questionnaires than to the more open-ended questionnaires used in qualitative, in-depth interviewing, the underlying logic is valuable whenever we ask people questions in order to gather data. We'll begin with some of the options available for creating questionnaires.

Open-Ended and Closed-Ended Questions

Researchers have two basic options in asking questions, and each can accommodate certain variations. The first is **open-ended questions**, in which the respondent is asked to provide his or her own answers. For example, the respondent may be asked, "What do you feel is the most important crime problem facing the police in your city today?" and be provided with a space to write in the answer (or be asked to report it orally to an interviewer). The other option is **closed-ended questions**, in which the respondent is asked to select an answer from among a list provided by the researcher.

Closed-ended questions are especially useful because they provide more uniform responses and are more easily processed. They often can be transferred directly into data for analysis. Open-ended responses, by contrast, must be coded before they can be processed for analysis. This coding process often requires that the researcher interpret the meaning of responses, which opens up the possibility of misunderstanding, inconsistencies, and researcher bias. Also, some respondents may give answers that are not directly relevant to the researcher's intent.

The chief shortcoming of closed-ended questions lies in the researcher's structuring of responses. When the relevant answers to a given question are relatively clear, there should be no problem. In some cases, however, the researcher's list of responses may fail to include some important answers. When we ask about "the most important crime problem facing the police in your city today," for example, our checklist might omit certain crime problems that respondents consider important. Chapter 10 on qualitative interviewing offers details on phrasing and using open-ended questions.

In constructing closed-ended questions, we are best guided by two of the requirements for operationalizing variables stated in Chapter 5. First, the response categories provided should be exhaustive; they should include all the possible responses that might be expected. Often, researchers ensure this by adding a category labeled something like "Other (Please specify): _____." Second, the answer categories must be mutually exclusive; the respondent should not feel compelled to select more than one. In some cases, researchers solicit multiple answers, but doing so can create difficulties in subsequent data processing and analysis. To ensure that categories are mutually exclusive, we should carefully consider each combination of categories, asking whether a person could reasonably choose more than one answer. In addition, it is useful to add an instruction that respondents should select the one best answer. However, this is still not a satisfactory substitute for a carefully constructed set of responses.

Questions and Statements

The term *questionnaire* suggests a collection of questions, but a typical questionnaire probably has as many statements as questions. This is because researchers often are interested in determining the extent to which respondents hold a particular attitude or perspective. Researchers try to summarize the attitude in a fairly brief statement; then they present that statement and ask respondents whether they agree or disagree with it. Rensis Likert formalized this procedure through the creation of the Likert scale, a format in which respondents are asked whether they strongly agree, agree, disagree, or strongly disagree, or perhaps strongly approve, approve, and so forth. The sample items from Nerea Marteache's questionnaire illustrate this technique.

Both questions and statements may be used profitably. Using both in a questionnaire adds flexibility in the design of items and can make the questionnaire more interesting as well.

Make Items Clear

It should go without saying that questionnaire items must be clear and unambiguous, but the broad proliferation of unclear and ambiguous questions in surveys makes the point worth stressing here. Researchers often become so deeply involved in the topic that opinions and perspectives that are clear to them will not be at all clear to respondents, many of whom have given little or no thought to the topic. Or, researchers may have only a superficial understanding of the topic and so may fail to specify the intent of a question sufficiently. The question "What do you think about the governor's decision concerning prison furloughs?" may evoke in the respondent a counter-question or two: "Which governor's decision?" "What are prison furloughs?" Questionnaire items should be precise so that the respondent knows exactly what the researcher wants answered.

Frequently, researchers ask respondents for a single answer to a combination question. Such "double-barreled" questions seem to occur most often when the researcher has personally identified with a complex question. For example, the researcher might ask respondents to agree or disagree with the statement "The Department of Corrections should stop releasing inmates for weekend furloughs and concentrate on rehabilitating criminals." Although many people will unequivocally agree with the statement and others will unequivocally disagree, still others will be unable to answer. Some might want to terminate the furlough program and punish—not rehabilitate—prisoners. Others might want to expand rehabilitation efforts while maintaining weekend furloughs; they can neither agree nor disagree without misleading the researcher.

Short Items Are Best

To avoid ambiguity, researchers often create long, complicated items. That should be avoided. In the case of self-administered questionnaires, respondents are often unwilling to study an item in order to understand it. The respondent should be able to read an item quickly, understand its intent, and select or provide an answer without difficulty. In general, it's safe to assume that respondents will read items quickly and give quick answers; therefore, short, clear items that will not be misinterpreted under those conditions are best. Questions read to respondents in person or over the phone should be similarly brief.

Avoid Negative Items

A negation in a questionnaire item paves the way for easy misinterpretation. Asked to agree or disagree with the statement "Drugs such as marijuana should not be legalized," many respondents will overlook the word *not* and answer on that basis. Thus, some will agree with the statement when they are in favor of legalizing marijuana, and others will agree when they oppose it. And we may never know which is which.

Biased Items and Terms

Recall from the earlier discussion of conceptualization and operationalization that there are no ultimately true meanings for any of the concepts we typically study in social science. This general principle also applies to the responses we get from persons in a survey.

The meaning of a given response to a question depends in large part on the wording of the question. That is true of every question and answer. Some questions seem to encourage particular responses more so than other questions. In the context of questionnaires, **bias** refers to any property of a question that encourages respondents to answer in a particular way. Most researchers recognize the likely effect of a question such as "Do you support the president's use of targeted killing by remotely controlled drone aircraft to promote the safety and security of all Americans?" and no reputable researcher would use such an item. The biasing effect of items and terms is far subtler than this example suggests, however.

The mere identification of an attitude or position with a prestigious (or unpopular) person or agency can bias responses. For example, an item that starts with "Do you agree or disagree with the recent Supreme Court decision that . . ." might have this effect. We are not suggesting that such wording will necessarily produce consensus or even a majority in support of the position identified with the prestigious person or agency. Rather, support will likely be greater than what would have been obtained without such identification.

Sometimes, the impact of different forms of question wording is relatively subtle. For example, Kenneth Rasinski (1989) analyzed the results of several General Social Survey studies of attitudes toward government spending. He found that the way programs were identified had an impact on the amount of public support they received. Here are some comparisons:

More Support	Less Support
"Assistance to the poor"	"Welfare"
"Halting the rising crime rate"	"Law enforcement"
"Dealing with drug addiction"	"Drug rehabilitation"
"Protecting Social Security"	"Social Security"

In one poll, for example, 63 percent of respondents said too little money was being spent on "assistance to the poor," whereas in a matched survey, only 23 percent said we were spending too little on "welfare." The main guidance we offer for avoiding bias is that researchers imagine how they would feel giving each of the answers they offer to respondents. If they would feel embarrassed, perverted, inhumane, stupid, irresponsible, or anything like that, then they should give some serious thought to whether others will be willing to give those answers. Researchers must carefully examine the purpose of their inquiry and construct items that will be most useful to it.

We also need to be wary of what researchers call the "social desirability" of questions and answers. Whenever we ask people for information, they answer through a filter of what will make them look good. That is especially true if they are being interviewed in a face-to-face situation. For example, during the 2008 Democratic primary race, many voters who might have been reluctant to vote for an African American (Barack Obama) or a woman (Hillary Clinton) might have been reluctant to admit their racial or gender prejudice to a survey interviewer. Frauke Kreuter, Stanley Presser, and Roger Tourangeau (2008) conducted an experiment on

> **Bias** Measurement that produces a misrepresentation of what is being measured.

the impact of other data-collection techniques on respondents' willingness to provide sensitive information that might not reflect positively on themselves, such as failing a class or being put on probation while in college. Of the three methods tested, respondents were least likely to volunteer such information when interviewed in a conventional telephone interview. They were somewhat more willing when interviewed by an interactive recording, and they were most likely to provide such information when questioned in a Web survey.

Designing Self-Report Items

Social desirability is a particular problem for self-report crime questions in general-population surveys. Adhering to the ethical principles of confidentiality and anonymity, and convincing respondents that we are doing so, is one way of getting more truthful responses to self-report items. Other techniques can help us avoid or reduce problems with self-report items.

One method, used in earlier versions of the BCS, is to introduce a group of self-report items with a disclaimer and to sanitize the presentation of offenses. The self-report section of the 1984 BCS began with this introduction:

> There are lots of things which are actually crimes, but which are done by lots of people, and which many people do not think of as crimes. On this card [printed card handed to respondents] is a list of eight of them. For each one can you tell me how many people you think do it—most people, a lot of people, or no one.

Respondents then read a card, shown in Figure 9.1, that presented descriptions of various offenses. Interviewers first asked respondents how many people they thought ever did X, where X corresponded to the letter for an offense shown in Figure 9.1. Next, respondents were asked whether they had ever done X. Interviewers then moved on down the list of letters for each offense on the card.

This procedure incorporates three techniques to guard against the socially desirable response of not admitting that one has committed a crime. First, the disclaimer seeks to reassure respondents that

A. Taken office supplies from work (such as stationery, envelopes, and pens) when not supposed to.

B. Taken things other than office supplies from work (such as tools, money, or other goods) when not supposed to.

C. Fiddled expenses [*fiddled* is the Queen's English equivalent of *fudged*].

D. Deliberately traveled [on a train] without a ticket or paid too low a fare.

E. Failed to declare something at customs on which duty was payable.

F. Cheated on tax.

G. Used cannabis (hashish, marijuana, ganga, grass).

H. Regularly driven a car when they know they have drunk enough to be well above the legal limit.

FIGURE 9.1 Showcard for Self-Report Items, 1984 British Crime Survey

Source: Adapted from the 1984 British Crime Survey (NOP Market Research Limited, 1985).

"many people" do not really think of various acts as crimes. Second, respondents are asked how many people they think commit each offense before being asked whether they have done so themselves. This takes advantage of a common human justification for engaging in certain kinds of behavior: other people do it. Third, asking whether they "have ever done X" is less confrontational than asking whether they "have ever cheated on an expense account." Again, the foibles of human behavior are at work here, in much the same way that people use euphemisms such as "restroom" and "sleep together" for "toilet" and "have sexual intercourse." It is, of course, not realistic to expect that such ploys will reassure all respondents. Furthermore, disclaimers about serious offenses such as rape or bank robbery would be ludicrous. But such techniques illustrate how thoughtful wording and introductions can be incorporated into sensitive questions.

Self-report surveys of known offenders encounter different problems. Incarcerated persons may be reluctant to admit committing crimes because of the legal consequences. High-rate offenders may have difficulty distinguishing among a number of different crimes or remembering even approximate dates. For many active offenders, promises of immunity from prosecution for offenses revealed in certain forms of sponsored research (as discussed in Chapter 3) can allay the fears of many active offenders. Sorting out dates and details of individual crimes among high-rate offenders requires different strategies.

One technique that is useful in surveys of active offenders is to interview subjects several times at regular intervals. For example, Lisa Maher (1997) interviewed her sample of women addicted to heroin or cocaine repeatedly, sometimes daily, over the course of three years. Each subject was asked about her background, intimate relationships with men, income-generating activities, and drug use habits. Having regular interviews helped respondents recall offending. Research on the use of crime calendars (Roberts et al., 2005) finds that more frequent interviews are necessary for recall by high-rate offenders, and that crime calendars are best suited for tracking more serious offenses.

Obtaining valid and reliable results from self-report items is challenging, but self-report survey techniques are important tools for addressing certain types of criminal justice research questions. As a result, researchers are constantly striving to improve self-report items. See the collection of essays by Joel Kennet and Joseph Gfroerer (2005) for a detailed discussion of issues involved in measuring self-reported drug use through the National Survey on Drug Use and Health. A National Research Council report (2001) discusses self-report survey measures more generally.

Computer technology has made it possible to significantly improve self-reported items. David Matz (2007) describes advances in self-report items from recent surveys that supplement the British Crime Survey. Researchers in Switzerland report more disclosure of delinquent acts by students in school settings using **computer-assisted interviewing (CAI)** compared to paper-and-pencil questionnaires (Lucia, Herrmann, and Killias, 2007). We return to this topic later in the chapter when we describe different modes of survey administration.

Questionnaire Construction

After settling on question content, researchers must consider the format and organization of all items in a questionnaire.

Because questionnaires are the fundamental instruments of survey research, we now turn our attention to some of the established techniques for constructing them. The following sections are best considered as a continuation of our theoretical discussions in Chapter 5 of conceptualization and measurement.

Of course, how a questionnaire is constructed depends on how the questionnaire will be administered to respondents. Later in this chapter, we will consider the three modes of administration: (1) self-administered, (2) in-person interview, and (3) telephone interview.

General Questionnaire Format

The format of a questionnaire is just as important as the nature and wording of the questions. An improperly laid-out questionnaire can cause respondents to miss questions, confuse them about the nature of the data desired, and in the extreme, lead them to throw the questionnaire away.

As a general rule, the questionnaire should be uncluttered. Inexperienced researchers tend to fear that their questionnaire will look too long, so they squeeze several questions onto a single line, abbreviate questions, and try to use as few pages as possible. Such efforts are ill-advised and even counterproductive. Putting more than one question on a line will cause some respondents to miss the second question altogether. Some respondents will misinterpret abbreviated questions. More generally, respondents who have spent considerable time on the first page of what seemed a short questionnaire will be more demoralized than will respondents who quickly completed the first several pages of what initially seemed a long form. Moreover, the latter will have made fewer errors and will not have been forced to reread confusing, abbreviated questions. Nor will they have been forced to write a long answer in a tiny space. The sample questions from Nerea Marteache earlier in this chapter offer a good example of a well-formatted questionnaire.

Computer-assisted interviewing (CAI) Use of computers to record answers keyed in by interviewers or by respondents themselves.

Contingency Questions

Quite often in questionnaires, certain questions are clearly relevant to only some of the respondents and irrelevant to others. A victim survey, for example, presents batteries of questions about victimization incidents that are meaningful only to crime victims.

Frequently, this situation—realizing that the topic is relevant only to some respondents—arises when we wish to ask a series of questions about a certain topic. We may want to ask whether respondents belong to a particular organization, and if so, how often they attend meetings, whether they have held office in the organization, and so forth. Or we might want to ask whether respondents have heard anything about a certain policy proposal, such as opening a youth shelter in the neighborhood, and then investigate the attitudes of those who have heard of it.

The subsequent questions in series such as these are called "contingency questions"; whether they are to be asked and answered is *contingent* on the response to the first question in the series. The proper use of such questions can make it easier for respondents to complete the questionnaire because they do not have to answer questions that are irrelevant to them.

Contingency questions can be presented in several formats. The one shown in Figure 9.2 is probably the clearest and most effective. Note that the questions shown in the figure could have been dealt with in a single question: "How many times, if any, have you smoked marijuana?" The response categories then would be: "Never," "Once," "two

to five times," and so forth. This single question would apply to all respondents, and each would find an appropriate answer category. Such a question, however, might put pressure on some respondents to report having smoked marijuana, because the main question asks how many times they have smoked it. The contingency question format illustrated in Figure 9.2 reduces the subtle pressure on respondents to report having smoked marijuana. This discussion shows how seemingly theoretical issues of validity and reliability are involved in the simple formatting of questions on a piece of paper.

Used properly, even complex sets of questions can be constructed without confusing respondents. Sometimes, a set of contingency questions is long enough to extend over several pages.

Victim surveys typically include many contingency questions. Figure 9.3 presents a few questions from the NCVS questionnaire. All respondents are asked a series of screening questions to reveal possible victimizations. Persons who answer yes to any of the screening questions then complete a crime incident report that presents a large number of items designed to measure details of the victimization incident.

As Figure 9.3 shows, the crime incident report itself also contains contingency questions. You might notice that even this brief adaptation from the NCVS screening and crime incident report questionnaires is rather complex. NCVS questionnaires are administered primarily through computer-assisted telephone interviews, in which the flow of contingency questions is more or less automated. It would be difficult to construct a

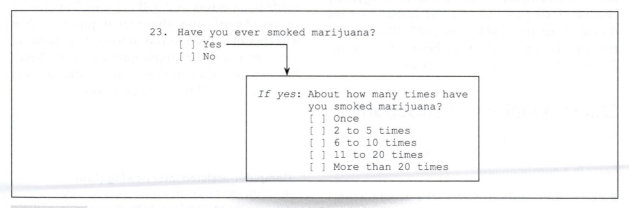

FIGURE 9.2   Contingency Question Format

36a. I'm going to read you some examples that will give you an idea of the kinds of crimes this study covers. As I go through them, tell me if any of these happened to you in the last 6-months, that is, since [date].

Was something belonging to YOU stolen, such as-

(a) Things that you carry, like luggage, a wallet, purse, briefcase, book-
(b) Clothing, jewelry or calculator-
(c) Bicycle or sports equipment-
(d) Things in your home—like a TV, stereo, or tools-
(e) Things outside your home, such as a garden hose or lawn furniture-
(f) Things belonging to children in the household-
(g) Things from a vehicle, such as a package, groceries, camera, or tapes-
OR
(h) Did anyone ATTEMPT to steal anything belonging to you?

Crime Incident Report:

20a. Were you or any other member of this household present when this incident occurred?

___ Yes [ask item 20b]

___ No [skip to 56, page 8]

20b. Which household members were present

___ Respondent only [ask item 21]

___ Respondent and other household member(s) [ask item 21]

___ Only other household member(s) [skip to 59, page 8]

21. Did you personally see an offender?

___ Yes

___ No

. . . .

56. Do you know or have you learned anything about the offender(s)—for instance, whether there was one or more than one offender involved, whether it was someone young or old, or male or female?

___ Yes [ask 57]

___ No [skip to 88, page 11]

FIGURE 9.3   NCVS Screening Questions and Crime Incident Report

Source: Adapted from National Crime Victimization Survey (2004).

self-administered victimization questionnaire with such questions.

Matrix Questions

Often, researchers want to ask several questions that have the same set of answer categories. This happens whenever the Likert response categories are used. Then it is often possible to construct a matrix of items and answers, as illustrated in Figure 9.4.

This format has three advantages. First, it uses space efficiently. Second, respondents probably find it easier to complete a set of questions presented in this fashion. Third, this format may increase the comparability of responses given to different questions for the respondent as well as for the researcher. Because respondents can quickly review their answers against earlier items in the set, they might choose between, say, "strongly agree" and "agree" on a given statement by comparing their strength of agreement with their earlier responses in the set.

Some dangers are inherent in using this format as well. Its advantages may promote structuring an item so that the responses fit into the matrix

17. Beside each of the statements presented below, please indicate whether you Strongly Agree (SA), Agree (A), Disagree (D), Strongly Disagree (SD), or are Undecided (U).

		SA	A	D	SD	U
a.	What this country needs is more law and order	[ ]	[ ]	[ ]	[ ]	[ ]
b.	Police in America should not carry guns	[ ]	[ ]	[ ]	[ ]	[ ]
c.	Repeat drug dealers should receive life sentences	[ ]	[ ]	[ ]	[ ]	[ ]

FIGURE 9.4   Matrix Question Format

format when a different, more idiosyncratic, set of responses might be more appropriate. Also, the matrix question format can generate a response set among some respondents. This means that respondents may develop a pattern, for instance, of agreeing with all the statements without really thinking about what the statements mean. That is especially likely if the set of statements begins with several that indicate a particular orientation (e.g., a conservative political perspective) and then offers only a few subsequent statements that represent the opposite orientation. Respondents might assume that all the statements represent the same orientation and, reading quickly, misread some of them, thereby giving the wrong answers. This problem can be reduced somewhat by alternating statements that represent different orientations and by making all statements short and clear.

A more difficult problem is when responses are generated through respondent boredom or fatigue. This can be avoided by keeping matrix questions and the entire questionnaire as short as possible. Later in this chapter, in the section on comparing different methods of questionnaire administration, we describe a useful technique for avoiding response sets generated by respondent fatigue.

Ordering Questions in a Questionnaire

The order in which questions are asked can also affect the answers given. The content of one question can affect the answers given to later questions,

known as the "halo effect." For example, if several questions ask about the dangers of illegal drug use and then a question asks respondents to volunteer what they believe (open-ended question) to be the most serious crime problems in U.S. cities, drug use will receive more mentions than would otherwise be the case. In this situation, it is preferable to ask the open-ended question first.

If respondents are asked to rate the overall effectiveness of corrections policy, they will answer subsequent questions about specific aspects of correctional institutions in a way that is consistent with their initial assessment. The converse is true as well: If respondents are first asked specific questions about prisons and other correctional facilities, their subsequent overall assessment will be influenced by the earlier question.

The best solution is to be sensitive to the problem. Although we cannot avoid the effect of question order, we should attempt to estimate what that effect will be. Then we will be able to interpret results in a meaningful fashion. If the order of questions seems an especially important issue in a given study, we could construct several versions of the questionnaire that contain the different possible orderings of questions. We could then determine the effects of ordering. At the very least, different versions of the questionnaire should be pretested.

It's common for less experienced researchers to assume that questionnaires must be newly constructed for each application. In contrast, it's almost always possible—and usually preferable—to use an existing questionnaire as a point of departure. See the box "Don't Start from Scratch!" for more on this.

DON'T START FROM SCRATCH!

It's always easier to modify an existing questionnaire for a particular research application than it is to start from scratch. It's also difficult to imagine asking questions that nobody has asked before. Here are examples of websites that present complete questionnaires or batteries of questionnaire items.

- Bureau of Justice Statistics (BJS). In addition to administering the NCVS, the BJS collects information from a variety of justice organizations. Copies of recent questionnaires for all BJS-sponsored surveys are available on the Bureau's website. Look for a ribbon of links near the top of the page. Mouse over "Data Collections" to find a series (e.g., corrections, courts and sentencing, law enforcement, and victims); then click on one of interest. Browse through collections and follow links to find questionnaires for the series. Start at: http://bjs.gov

- California Healthy Kids Survey. This set of questionnaires is useful for assessing behavior routines. Most include items on alcohol, tobacco, and other drug use; fighting; and other behaviors of potential interest for school-based interventions. English and Spanish versions are available for elementary, middle, and high school. In addition, the site includes a page to build custom modules for use in individual schools. http://www.wested.org/administer/download/custom

- Centers for Disease Control (CDC). Various centers within the CDC regularly collect a variety of health-related data through questionnaires and other data collection systems. Copies of instruments are available at https://www.cdc.gov/nchs/data_access/ftp_data.htm

- The Youth Risk Behavior Surveillance System (YRBSS) is an annual CDC survey of middle and high school students that asks questions about behavior that increases the risk of health problems or injuries. It includes questions on drug and alcohol use. Questionnaires are available at http://www.themeasurementgroup.com/evalbttn.htm

- SurveyMonkey Questionnaire Templates. SurveyMonkey is one of the most popular commercial online survey platforms. It offers templates for popular types of surveys. These can be used alone or adapted for specific uses. Most are designed for some type of customer feedback, but some are potentially useful for criminal justice research. https://www.surveymonkey.com/mp/sample-survey-questionnaire-templates/

- The American Association for Public Opinion Research (AAPOR) offers advice and guidelines for best practices in conducting survey research AAPOR also includes tips on question writing and a sample size calculator. http://www.aapor.org/Standards-Ethics/Best-Practices.aspx

Self-Administered Questionnaires

Self-administered questionnaires are generally the least expensive and easiest to complete.

Although the mail survey is the traditional method used in self-administered studies, other methods are now used more often. It may be appropriate to administer the questionnaire to a group of respondents gathered at the same place at the same time, such as police officers at roll call or prison inmates at some specially arranged assembly. The Monitoring the Future survey (see Chapter 6) has students complete self-administered questionnaires in class. You have probably completed questionnaires yourself in college classes.

Some experimentation has been conducted on the home delivery of questionnaires. A research worker delivers the questionnaire to the home of sample respondents and explains the study. Then the questionnaire is left for the respondent to complete, and the researcher picks it up later.

Home delivery and the mail can be used in combination as well. Questionnaires can be mailed to families, and then research workers may visit the homes to pick up the questionnaires and check them for completeness. In the opposite approach, survey packets are hand-delivered by research workers with a request that the respondents mail the completed questionnaires to the research office. In general, when a research worker delivers the questionnaire, picks it up, or both, the completion rate is higher than for straightforward mail surveys.

As the Internet has become an increasingly important part of people's lives, self-administered questionnaires are now more often completed online. Before discussing Web-based questionnaires, let us turn our attention to the fundamentals of mail surveys, which are still used for people without Internet access.

Mail Distribution and Return

The basic method for collecting data through the mail is transmittal of a questionnaire accompanied by a letter of explanation and a self-addressed, stamped envelope for returning the questionnaire. You have probably received a few. As a respondent, you are expected to complete the questionnaire, put it in the envelope, and mail it back. If, by any chance, you have received such a questionnaire and failed to return it, it would be a valuable exercise for you to recall your reasons for not returning it—and keep those in mind any time you plan to send questionnaires to others.

Timing is important to consider in the actual mailing of questionnaires. In most cases, the holiday months of November, December, and January should be avoided. Overall mail volume is greatest during those periods, which can substantially slow down the process of both distribution and return of questionnaires. And because a greater volume of mail is flowing through post offices, people receive more mail of all types. If a questionnaire arrives in the company of glossy gift catalogs, holiday greetings, bills, and assorted junk mail, respondents will be more likely to discard the survey packet.

Warning Mailings and Cover Letters

The U.S. population, especially that proportion residing in urban areas, has always been somewhat mobile. This mobility, together with the fact that sampling frames used to obtain addresses may be dated, has prompted researchers to use warning mailings for the purpose of verifying, or "cleaning," addresses. Certain types of warning mailings can also be effective in increasing a survey's **response rate**, or the number of people participating in a survey divided by the number selected in the sample.

Warning mailings work as follows. After researchers generate a sample, they send a postcard to each selected respondent, with the notation "Address correction requested" printed on the postcard. If the addressee has moved and left a forwarding address, the actual questionnaire is sent to the new address. In cases in which someone has moved and not left a forwarding address, or more than a year has elapsed and the post office no longer has information about a new address, the postcard is returned marked something like "Addressee unknown." Selected persons who still reside at the original listed address are "warned" in suitable language to expect a questionnaire in the mail. In such cases, postcards should briefly describe the purpose of the survey for which the respondent has been selected.

Cover letters accompanying the actual questionnaire offer another opportunity to increase response rates. Two features of cover letters warrant some attention. First, the content of the letter is obviously important. The message should communicate why a survey is being conducted, how and why the respondent was selected, and why it is important for the respondent to complete the questionnaire. In line with our discussion of the protection of ethics in Chapter 3, the cover letter should also truthfully assure respondents that their answers will be confidential.

Second, the cover letter should identify the institutional affiliation or sponsorship of the survey. The two alternatives are (1) some institution that the respondent respects or can identify with or (2) a neutral but impressive-sounding affiliation. For example, if we are conducting a mail survey of police chiefs, printing our cover letter on International Association of Chiefs of Police

(IACP) stationery and having the letter signed by an official in the IACP might increase the response rate. Of course, we cannot adopt such a procedure unless the survey actually is endorsed by the IACP.

Acceptable Response Rates

A question frequently asked about mail surveys concerns the percentage return rate that should be achieved. Note that the body of inferential statistics used in connection with survey analysis assumes that *all* members of the initial sample complete and return their questionnaires. Because this almost never happens, response bias becomes a concern. Researchers must test (and hope for) the possibility that respondents look essentially like a random sample of the initial sample, and thus a somewhat smaller random sample of the total population. For example, if the gender of all people in the sample is known, a researcher can compare the percentages of males and females indicated on returned questionnaires with the percentages for the entire sample.

Nevertheless, overall response rate is one guide to the representativeness of the sample respondents. If the response rate is high, then there is less chance of significant response bias than if the rate is low. But what is a high response rate?

A quick review of the survey literature uncovers a wide range of response rates. Each may be accompanied by a statement like "This is regarded as a relatively high response rate for a survey of this type." Even so, it's possible to state some rules of thumb about return rates. A response rate of at least 50 percent is adequate for analysis and reporting. A response rate of at least 60 percent is good. And a response rate of 70 percent is very good.

Bear in mind, however, that these are only rough guides; they have no statistical basis, and a demonstrated lack of response bias is far more important than a high response rate. Response rates tend to be higher for surveys that target a narrowly defined population; general-population surveys yield lower response rates.

Don Dillman, Jolene Smyth, and Leah Melani Christian (2014) undertook an extensive review of the various techniques survey researchers use to increase return rates on mail surveys, and they evaluated the impact of each. More importantly, Dillman and colleagues stress the necessity of paying attention to all aspects of the study—the "total design method"—rather than one or two special gimmicks.

Computer-Based Self-Administration

As the Internet and Web have permeated work and leisure activities, different types of computer-assisted self-administered surveys have become more common and increasingly sophisticated. In fact, this has contributed to a proliferation of data collection by questionnaire. Think of the last time you visited a government or commercial website and were confronted with a pop-up window asking for feedback on the site.

The most common type is a survey in which respondents are asked to click on a link that eventually takes them to a questionnaire application. The advantages of this method are obvious. Responses are automatically recorded in computer files, saving time and money. Web page design tools make it possible to create attractive questionnaires that include contingency questions, matrixes, and other complex tools for presenting items to respondents.

This potential bias declines each year as more U.S. households gain Internet access. A report issued by the Pew Research Center (Perrin and Duggan, 2016) describes steady growth in Internet use in U.S. households: from 52 percent of adults in 2000 to 84 percent by mid-2015. As you might expect, Internet use is not evenly distributed. In 2015 virtually all younger people (96 percent of those aged 18–29) and those with a college degree (95 percent) had access, compared to 58 percent of those aged 65 and older and 66 percent for people with less than a high school education. Gaps have been closing over the first 15 years of the twenty-first century. Internet use by males and females has been about equal.

Although access is much less of a problem, finding and selecting samples of Internet users remains an important question. Put in terms that should be familiar from the previous chapter, how closely do available sampling frames for online surveys match possible target populations? If, for example, our target population is university students, how can we obtain a list of email addresses or other identifiers that will enable us to survey a representative sample? It's easy to think of other target

AN ONLINE SURVEY WITH MTURK AND QUALTRICS

BY MAWIA KHOGALI and CATHY SPATZ WIDOM
John Jay College of Criminal Justice

Our research questions centered on how people's responses to juvenile behavior varied by two features of the child's appearance: age and race. This was well suited to a survey, in which we presented subjects with descriptions of behavior and a photo of the child, then asked a series of questions about what actions people would take in response to the behavior. By randomly mixing the descriptions of behaviors and the subjects portrayed in images, we conducted a survey-based experiment.

Most of the behavior descriptions were classified as either felony or misdemeanor crimes, while three of the behaviors were ambiguous with respect to illegality. Survey participants were asked to indicate which of several responses they thought they would take if they saw the child engaged in the behavior. These ranged from "do nothing" to "report to police"; other responses included talking to the child directly or trying to find the child's caregivers. This design made it possible for us to see whether people's responses to a range of behaviors differed by the appearance of the child's age (8 or 12 years) and race (Black, Latino, or White.) All images depicted boys.

It's common to conduct such experiments in college classrooms, since students are readily available, but we wanted to examine responses from a more general population. We combined a sample selected through Mechanical Turk (MTurk) with a questionnaire we developed on Qualtrics, an online survey platform for experimental research. Subjects could complete the survey on a computer, or on a tablet device or smartphone.

In MTurk language, our survey was a "Human Intelligence Task" or HIT. MTurk allows the researcher to specify certain requirements from each of the individuals (known on MTurk as "workers") who tried to access the survey. These include the quality of each worker's previous HITs, measured by what percentage of completed HITs was accepted by researchers. Because we wanted workers with experience and demonstrated conscientiousness, we required an acceptance rate of 95 percent. Our HIT posting included a brief description of the purpose of the survey and the link to it on Qualtrics. Workers interested in participating clicked the

populations of interest to criminal justice researchers that might be difficult to reach via email or Web-based questionnaires.

As shown in Chapter 8, services such as Mechanical Turk are increasingly useful for selecting non-probability samples. It's possible to specify certain characteristics that prospective respondents must satisfy, so researchers can exercise a great deal of control over who completes a survey. (Sheehan and Pittman, 2016).

However, rapid growth in Internet use has produced another set of problems for survey researchers. Just as junk mail clutters our physical mailboxes with all sorts of advertising, spam and other kinds of unwanted messages pop up all too often in our email. The proliferation of junk email has led to the development of antispam filters that screen out unwanted correspondence. Unfortunately, such programs also can screen out unfamiliar but well-meaning mail such as email questionnaires. Similar problems with telemarketing and political campaigning have made it increasingly difficult to conduct surveys by telephone.

In yet another example of technology advances accompanied by new threats, the spread of computer viruses and other malware has made people even more cautious about opening email or attachments from unfamiliar sources. This problem, and the electronic version of junk mail, can be addressed with a version of the warning letter described earlier for mail surveys. In the electronic adaptation, researchers distribute email messages from trusted sources to warn recipients to expect to receive a questionnaire or link in a later message.

We should keep one basic principle in mind when considering whether a self-administered

link and were directed to the first page of the Qualtrics survey, which was the informed consent form.

After reading informed consent forms, participants were randomly presented with a photo of a child. After each photo, the next screen presented an accompanying vignette that described 1 of 16 behaviors (e.g. robbing someone at gunpoint and walking down the street alone late at night). The next screen showed a set of response questions about the subject's assessment of how much of a concern the child's behavior was, and what an appropriate response to the behavior would be. This was repeated for all 16 vignettes, followed by demographic items, such as the subject's ethnic and racial background. Overall, it took about two weeks to collect 1,000 responses.

Qualtrics monitors and records responses, including how long it takes subjects to complete the survey. Workers are paid modest amounts for completing each HIT. After we approved each completed HIT, Qualtrics sent a code to MTurk so that workers could receive their payment. We listed a fee of $.25 for each completed and accepted questionnaire. MTurk adds a "collection fee" of $.10 per completed and accepted HIT, so our total cost for data collection was about $350 for 1,000 responses. The Qualtrics software compiled and formatted responses as they were completed. After concluding our HIT, we downloaded responses and began analysis.

Combining the sample selection features of MTurk with the survey design tools of Qualtrics was a very fast and economical way to collect a large number of responses to a complex survey. We ran into some problems in formatting the questionnaire, and found that Qualtrics had more of a learning curve than we expected. Sheehan and Pittman (2016) offer a thorough description of combining MTurk with Qualtrics, together with ways to enhance the quality of samples obtained through MTurk. They also compare Qualtrics to other online survey platforms.

Consider the differences between our survey and what would have been required to obtain 1,000 completed telephone interviews or mail-return questionnaires. Our data are not the result of a probability sample, and we cannot technically estimate parameters and confidence intervals. However, the sample is much more diverse and representative than what would have resulted from using college students. See Buhrmester and associates (2011) and Berinsky and associates (2013) who have compared MTurk samples to other nonprobability samples, and to selected national probability samples.

questionnaire can be distributed electronically: Web-based surveys depend on access to the Web, which, of course, implies having a computer. The use of computers and the Web continues to increase rapidly. Just as telephones eventually spread to larger numbers of households, access to the Internet continues to grow, and Web-based surveys can be readily conducted for many target populations of interest to criminal justice researchers.

For example, in their recommendations for rethinking crime surveys, Maxfield and associates argue that Web-based surveys are well suited for learning more about victims of computer-facilitated fraud. Since only people with Internet access are possible victims, an Internet-based sample is ideal (Maxfield, Hough, and Mayhew, 2007). Mike Sutton (2007) describes other examples of nontraditional crimes for which Internet samples of computer users are appropriate.

Recalling our discussion in Chapter 8, the correspondence between a sampling frame and target population is a crucial feature of sampling. Most justice professionals and criminal justice organizations routinely use the Web and email.

Most important is the rapid growth of online tools for drawing samples, distributing questionnaires, and compiling results. See the box, "An Online Survey with MTurk and Qualtrics" by Mawia Khogali and Cathy Spatz Widom, for an example.

Qualtrics is one example of an online survey service. SurveyMonkey and Google Forms are other examples. Sheehan and Pittman (2016:45–48) describe the strengths and weaknesses of these and other platforms. We suspect most college students have been invited to complete a questionnaire through SurveyMonkey. Staff at John Jay College are enthusiastic users of SurveyMonkey for all sorts of tasks. It's easy to set up a trial account on most services, allowing you to obtain a limited number of responses to a limited number of questions. Each platform includes examples of questionnaire templates that can be adapted for a wide range of uses. The box "Don't Start from Scratch" briefly describes this for SurveyMonkey. Other platforms have even more examples of question banks.

Online sample selection and platforms have become the cheapest and easiest ways to conduct surveys with large numbers of responses. The study described by Khogali and Widom used a complex questionnaire that randomly mixed questions and photographs. However, many research applications still require face-to-face surveys conducted by professional interviewers.

In-Person Interview Surveys

Face-to-face interviews are best for complex questionnaires and other specialized needs.

The in-person **interview survey** is an alternative method of collecting survey data. Rather than asking respondents to read questionnaires and enter their own answers, researchers send interviewers to ask the questions orally and record respondents' answers. Most interview surveys require more than one interviewer, although a researcher might singly undertake a small-scale interview survey.

The Role of the Interviewer

In-person interview surveys typically attain higher response rates than mail surveys do. Respondents seem more reluctant to turn down an interviewer who is standing on their doorstep than to throw away a mail questionnaire. A properly designed and executed interview survey ought to achieve a completion rate of at least 80–85 percent.

The presence of an interviewer generally decreases the number of "don't know" and "no

Interview survey Using a questionnaire in a systematic way to interview a large number of people.

answer" responses. If minimizing such responses is important to the study, the interviewer can be instructed to probe for answers ("If you had to pick one of the answers, which do you think would come closest to your feelings?").

The interviewer can also help respondents with confusing questionnaire items. If the respondent clearly misunderstands the intent of a question, the interviewer can clarify matters and thereby obtain a relevant response. Such clarifications must be strictly controlled, however, through formal specifications.

Finally, the interviewer can observe as well as ask questions. For example, the interviewer can make observations about the quality of the dwelling, the presence of various possessions, the respondent's ability to speak English, and the respondent's general reactions to the study. Interviewers for earlier waves of the British Crime Survey made observations of the physical conditions outside each respondent's home and in the surrounding area (Bolling, Grant, and Donovan, 2009). Items include the physical condition of dwellings, how the sampled unit's condition compares to nearby dwelling units, and what types of locks are evident.

General Rules for Interviewing

The way interviews ought to be conducted will vary somewhat by the survey population and survey content. Nevertheless, some general guidelines apply to most interviewing situations, including sample surveys and more specialized interviewing.

Appearance and Demeanor As a general rule, the interviewer should dress in a fashion similar to that of the people he or she will be interviewing. To the extent that the interviewer's dress and grooming differ from that of the respondents, it should be in the direction of neatness and modesty. Although middle-class standards of dress and grooming are not accepted by all sectors of American society, they remain the norm and are likely to be acceptable to the largest number of respondents.

The importance of considering the target population cannot be overemphasized. "Establishment" attire should be the norm when interviewing most criminal justice officials. However, the middle-class norm in clothing may foster suspicion among street people or incarcerated individuals.

In demeanor, interviewers should be pleasant if nothing else. Because they will be prying into the respondent's personal life and thoughts, they must communicate a genuine interest in getting to know the respondent without appearing to spy. They must be relaxed and friendly without being too casual. Good interviewers also have the ability to quickly determine the kind of person the respondent feels most comfortable with or most enjoys talking to, and they adapt accordingly. Guides for NCVS interviewers offers detail on interacting with respondents, how to dress, and related matters (U.S. Census Bureau, 2012).

Familiarity with the Questionnaire The interviewer must be able to read the questionnaire items to respondents without stumbling over words and phrases. A good model for interviewers is the actor reading lines in a play or film. The interviewer must read the questions as though they are part of a natural conversation, but that "conversation" must precisely follow the language set down in the question.

By the same token, the interviewer must be familiar with the specifications for administering the questionnaire. Inevitably, some questions will not exactly fit a given respondent's situation, and the interviewer must determine how those questions should be interpreted in that situation. The specifications provided to the interviewer should include adequate guidelines in such cases, but the interviewer must know the organization and contents of the specifications well enough to refer to them efficiently.

Probing for Responses Probes are frequently required to elicit responses to open-ended questions. For example, to a question about neighborhood crime problems, the respondent might simply reply, "Pretty bad." The interviewer could obtain an elaboration on this response through a variety of probes. Sometimes, the best probe is silence; if the interviewer sits quietly with pencil poised, the respondent will probably fill the pause with additional comments. Appropriate verbal probes are

"How is that?" and "In what ways?" Perhaps the most generally useful probe is "Anything else?"

In every case, however, it is imperative that the probe be completely neutral. The probe must not in any way affect the nature of the subsequent response. If we anticipate that a given question may require probing for appropriate responses, we should write one or more useful probes next to the item in the questionnaire. This practice has two important advantages. First, it allows for more time to devise the best, most neutral probes. Second, it ensures that all interviewers will use the same probes as needed. Thus, even if the probe is not perfectly neutral, the same stimulus is presented to all respondents. This is the same logical guideline as for question wording. Although a question should not be loaded or biased, it is essential that every respondent be presented with the same question, even if a biased one.

Coordination and Control

Whenever more than one interviewer will administer a survey, it is essential that the efforts be coordinated and controlled carefully. Two ways to ensure this control are by (1) training interviewers and (2) supervising them after they begin work.

Whether the researchers will be administering a survey themselves or paying a professional firm to do it for them, they should be attentive to the importance of training interviewers. The interviewers usually should know what the study is all about. Even though the interviewers may be involved only in the data collection phase of the project, they should understand what will be done with the information they gather and what purpose will be served.

Obviously, training should ensure that interviewers understand the questionnaire. Interviewers should also be clear on procedures to select respondents from among household members. And interviewers should recognize circumstances in which substitute sample elements may be used in place of addresses that no longer exist, families who have moved, or persons who simply refuse to be interviewed.

Training should include practice sessions in which interviewers administer the questionnaire to one another. The final stage of the training should involve some "real" interviews conducted under conditions like those in the actual survey.

While interviews are being conducted, it is a good idea to review questionnaires as they are completed. This may reveal questions or groups of questions that respondents do not understand. Alternatively, reviewing completed questionnaires can signal that an interviewer is encountering difficulties.

Computer-Assisted In-Person Interviews

Just as email and Web-based surveys apply new technology to the gathering of survey data through self-administration, laptop and tablet computers are being used increasingly to conduct in-person interviews. Different forms of computer-assisted interviewing offer major advantages in the collection of survey data. At the same time, CAI has certain disadvantages that must be considered. We'll begin by describing an example of how this technology was adopted in the BCS, one of the earliest uses of CAI in a general-purpose crime survey.

CAI in the British Crime Survey Previous waves of the BCS (a face-to-face interview survey) asked respondents to complete a self-administered questionnaire about drug use, printed as a small booklet that was prominently marked "Confidential." Beginning with the 1994 survey, respondents answered self-report questions on laptop computers. The current Crime Survey for England and Wales (CSEW) includes two related versions of CAI. In computer-assisted personal interviewing (CAPI), interviewers read questions from computer screens and then key in respondents' answers. For self-report items, interviewers hand the computers to subjects, who then key in the responses themselves.

This approach is known as computer-assisted self-interviewing (CASI). In addition, CASI as used in the CSEW is supplemented with audio instructions; selected respondents listen to interview prompts on headphones connected to the computer. After subjects key in their responses to self-report items, the answers are scrambled so the interviewer cannot access them. Notice how this feature of CASI enhances the researcher's ethical obligation to keep responses confidential.

Malcolm Ramsay and associates (2001) report that shifting to CASI produced at least two benefits. First, respondents seem to sense a greater degree of confidentiality when they respond to questions on a computer screen as opposed to questions on a written form. Second, in their first few years of use, laptop computers were something of a novelty that stimulated respondents' interest; this was especially true for younger respondents.

Results from the BCS revealed that CASI techniques produced higher estimates of illegal drug use than those revealed in previous surveys. Table 9.1 compares self-reported drug use from the 1998 BCS (Ramsay and Partridge, 1999) with results from the 1992 BCS (Mott and Mirrlees-Black, 1995), in which respondents answered questions in printed booklets. We present results for only three drugs here, together with tabulations about the use of any drug. For each drug, the survey measured lifetime use ("Ever used?") and use in the past 12 months. Notice that rates of self-reported use were substantially higher in 1998 than in 1992, with the exception of "semeron" use, reported by very few respondents in 1992 and none in 1998. If you've never heard of semeron, you're not alone. It's a fictitious drug, included in the list of real drugs to detect untruthful or exaggerated responses. If someone confessed to using

TABLE 9.1 Self-Reported Drug Use, 1992 and 1998 British Crime Survey

	Percentage of Respondents Ages 16–29 Who Report Use	
	1992	1998
Marijuana or cannabis		
Ever used?	24	42
Used in previous 12 months?	12	23
Amphetamines		
Ever used?	9	20
Used in previous 12 months?	4	8
Semeron		
Ever used?	0.3	0.0
Used in previous 12 months?	0.1	0.0
Any drug		
Ever used?	28	49
Used in previous 12 months?	14	25

Source: 1992 data adapted from Mott and Mirrlees-Black (1995:41–42); 1998 data adapted from Ramsay and Partridge (1999:68–71).

semeron, his or her responses to other self-reported items would be suspect. Notice in Table 9.1 that CASI use in 1998 reduced the number of respondents who admitted using a drug that doesn't exist.

CASI is used in the CSEW to measure sexual assault and domestic violence. Comparing results from earlier procedures, Catriona Mirrlees-Black (1999) found that CASI techniques reveal higher estimates of domestic violence victimization among both females and males.

Advantages and Disadvantages Different types of CAI offer a number of advantages for in-person interviews. The CSEW and other surveys that include self-report items indicate that CAI is more "productive" in that self-reports of drug use and other offending tend to be higher. In 1999, the National Household Survey on Drug Abuse shifted completely to CAI (Wright et al., 2002). Other advantages include the following:

- Responses can be quickly keyed in and automatically reformatted into data files for analysis.
- Complex sequences of contingency questions can be automated. Instead of printing many examples of "If answer is yes, go to question 43a; if no . . .," computer-based questionnaires automatically jump to the next appropriate question contingent on responses to earlier ones.
- CAI offers a way to break up the monotony of a long interview by shifting from verbal interviewer prompts to self-interviewing, with or without an audio supplement.
- Questionnaires for self-interviewing can be programmed in different languages, readily switching to the language appropriate for a particular respondent.
- Audio-supplemented CASI produces a standardized interview, avoiding any bias that might emerge from interviewer effects.
- Audio supplements, in different languages, facilitate self-interviews of respondents who cannot read.

At the same time, CAI has certain disadvantages that preclude its use in many survey applications:

- Although CAI reduces costs in data processing, it requires more up-front investment in programming questionnaires, skip sequences, and the like.

- Proofreading printed questionnaires is straightforward, but it can be difficult to audit a computerized questionnaire. Doing so might require special technical skills.
- Batteries of laptops run down, and computers and software are more vulnerable to malfunctions and glitches than are stacks of printed questionnaires.

In summary, CAI can be costly and requires some specialized skills. As a result, these and related technologies are best suited for use by professional survey researchers or research centers that regularly conduct large-scale in-person interviews. We will return to this issue in the concluding section of this chapter.

Telephone Surveys

Telephone surveys are fast and can be relatively inexpensive.

Despite the growth of online applications, telephone surveys have certain advantages and remain a popular method. Probably the greatest advantages involve money and time. In a face-to-face household interview, a researcher may drive several miles to a respondent's home, find no one there, return to the research office, and drive back the next day—possibly finding no one there again. It's cheaper and quicker to call.

Interviewing by telephone, researchers can dress any way they please, and it will have no effect on the answers respondents give. It may be possible to probe into more sensitive areas, although that is not necessarily the case. People are, to some extent, more suspicious when they can't see the person asking the questions—perhaps a consequence of telemarketing and salespeople conducting bogus surveys prior to making sales pitches.

In computer-assisted telephone interviewing (CATI), interviewers wearing telephone headsets sit at computer workstations. Computer programs dial sampled phone numbers, which can be either generated through random-digit dialing (RDD) or extracted from a database of phone numbers compiled from some source. As soon as phone contact is made, the computer screen displays an introduction ("Hello, my name is . . . calling from the Survey Research Center at Ivory Tower University") and the first question to be asked, often a query about the number of residents who live in the household. As interviewers key in answers to each question, the computer program displays a new screen that presents the next question, until the end of the interview is reached. Perhaps you've occasionally marveled at newspaper stories that report the results of a nationwide opinion poll the day after some major speech or event. The speed of CATI technology makes these instant poll reports possible.

Telephone surveys can give a researcher greater control over data collection if several interviewers are engaged in the project. If all the interviewers are calling from the research office, they can get clarification from the supervisor whenever problems occur, as they inevitably do. Alone in the field, an interviewer may have to wing it between weekly visits with the interviewing supervisor.

A related advantage is rooted in the growing diversity of the United States. Because many areas have growing immigrant populations, interviews may need to be conducted in different languages. Telephone interviews are usually conducted from a central site, so that one or more multilingual interviewers can be quickly summoned if an English-speaking interviewer makes contact with, say, a Spanish-speaking respondent. In-person interview surveys present much more difficult logistical problems in handling multiple languages. And mail surveys require printing and distributing questionnaires in different languages.

Telephone interviewing has its problems, however. As we described in Chapter 8, a growing number of households have only mobile phone service, and regulations restrict the use of random-digit dialing samples using mobile phone numbers. Jan van Dijk (2007) describes how this is especially troublesome in some European countries where mobile-only households are more common.

In addition, phone surveys are much less suitable for individuals not living in households. Homeless people are obvious examples; those who live in institutions are also difficult to reach via telephone.

A related sampling problem involves unlisted numbers. If the survey sample is selected from the pages of a local telephone directory, it totally omits all those people who have requested unlisted numbers. Also, recent movers and transient residents are not well represented in published telephone directories. This potential bias is eliminated through RDD.

RDD samples use computer algorithms to generate lists of random telephone numbers—usually, the last four digits. This procedure gets around the sampling problem of unlisted telephone numbers but may substitute an administrative problem. Randomly generating phone numbers produces numbers that are not in operation or that serve a business establishment. In most cases, businesses are not included in the target population; dialing these numbers and learning that they're out of scope will take time away from producing completed interviews with the target population.

The ease with which people can hang up is, of course, another shortcoming of telephone surveys. Once a researcher is inside someone's home for an interview, that person is unlikely to order the researcher out of the house in mid-interview. It's much easier to terminate a telephone interview abruptly, saying something like "Whoops! Someone's at the door. Gotta go!" or simply hanging up.

Partly as a result of extensive telemarketing in past years, completion rates for telephone surveys have declined. The Pew Research Center (2012) has seen response rates to its telephone surveys decline from 36 percent in 1997 to 9 percent in 2012. Although commercial telemarketing is sharply reduced, people still commonly receive solicitations from charitable organizations, college alumni groups, aggressive political campaigns, and other "soft" telemarketers.

Comparison of the Three Methods

Cost, speed, and question content are issues to consider in selecting a survey method.

We've now examined three ways of collecting survey data: self-administered questionnaires, in-person interviews, and telephone surveys. We have also considered recent changes in each mode of administration. Although we've touched on some of the relative advantages and disadvantages of each, let's take a minute to compare them more directly.

Self-administered questionnaires, especially those administered over the Internet, are generally cheaper to use than interview surveys. Moreover, for self-administered email or online surveys, it costs no more to conduct a national survey than a local one. Obviously, the cost difference between a local and a national in-person interview survey is considerable. Another element of cost savings from online surveys is that they combine data collection and tabulation. The cost of telephone surveys continues to decline, as Internet-based calling services eliminate long-distance toll charges. Mail surveys typically require a small staff. One person can conduct a reasonable mail survey, although it is important not to underestimate the work involved. The cost of postage and printing undermines much of the potential cost savings in mail surveys.

Up to a point, cost and speed are inversely related. In-person interview surveys can be completed very quickly if a large pool of interviewers is available and funding is adequate to pay them. In contrast, if a small number of people are conducting a larger number of face-to-face interviews, costs are generally lower, but the survey takes much longer to complete. Telephone surveys that use CATI technology are usually the fastest, but large online surveys can be conducted very quickly. Khogali and Widom obtained 1,000 completed interviews in about a week.

Self-administered surveys may be more appropriate to use with especially sensitive issues if the surveys offer complete anonymity. Respondents are sometimes reluctant to report controversial or deviant attitudes or behaviors in interviews, but they may be more willing to respond anonymously to a self-administered questionnaire. The successful use of computers for self-report items in the CSEW and the National Household Survey on Drug Abuse indicates that interacting with a machine can promote more candid responses. This is supported by experimental research comparing different modes of questionnaire administration (Kreuter, Presser, and Tourangeaua, 2008).

Interview surveys have advantages, too. For example, in-person or telephone surveys are more appropriate when respondent literacy may be a problem. Interview surveys also result in fewer incomplete questionnaires. Although respondents may skip questions in a self-administered questionnaire, interviewers are trained not to do so. CAI

offers a further check on this in telephone and in-person surveys.

Self-administered questionnaires may be more effective for sensitive issues, but interview surveys are definitely more effective in dealing with complicated ones. Interviewers can explain complex questions to respondents and use visual aids that are not possible in mail or phone surveys.

In-person interviews, especially with computer technology, can also help reduce response sets. Respondents (like students?) eventually become bored listening to a lengthy series of similar types of questions. It's easier to maintain individuals' interest by changing the kind of stimulation to which they are exposed. A mix of questions verbalized by a person, presented on a computer screen, and heard privately through earphones is more interesting for respondents and reduces fatigue.

As mentioned earlier, interviewers who question respondents face to face are also able to make important observations, aside from responses to questions asked. In a household interview, they may summarize characteristics of the neighborhood, the dwelling unit, and so forth. They may also note characteristics of the respondents or the quality of their interaction with the respondents—whether the respondent had difficulty communicating, was hostile, seemed to be lying, and so on. Finally, when the safety of interviewers is an issue, a self-administered or phone survey may be the best option.

Ultimately, researchers must weigh all these advantages and disadvantages of the three methods against research needs and available resources.

Strengths and Weaknesses of Survey Research

Surveys tend to be high on reliability and generalizability, but validity can often be a weak point.

Like other modes of collecting data in criminal justice research, surveys have strengths and weaknesses. It is important to consider these in deciding whether the survey format is appropriate for a specific research purpose.

Surveys are particularly useful in describing the characteristics of a large population. The NCVS and crime surveys in other countries have become important tools for researchers and public officials. A carefully selected probability sample, in combination with a standardized questionnaire, allows researchers to make refined descriptive statements about a neighborhood, a city, a nation, or some other large population.

Standardized questionnaires have an important advantage in regard to measurement. Earlier chapters discussed the ambiguous nature of concepts; they ultimately have no real meaning. One person's view about, say, crime seriousness or punishment severity is quite different from another's. Although we must be able to define concepts in ways that are most relevant to research goals, it's not always easy to apply the same definitions uniformly to all subjects. Nevertheless, the survey researcher is bound to the requirement of having to ask exactly the same questions of all subjects and having to impute the same intent to all respondents giving a particular response.

At the same time, survey research has its weaknesses. First, the requirement for standardization might mean that we are trying to fit round pegs into square holes. Standardized questionnaire items often represent the least common denominator in assessing people's attitudes, orientations, circumstances, and experiences. By designing questions that are at least minimally appropriate to all respondents, we may miss what is most appropriate to many respondents. In this sense, surveys often appear superficial in their coverage of complex topics.

Similarly, survey research cannot readily deal with the specific contexts of social life. Although questionnaires may provide information in this area, the survey researcher seldom develops a feel for the total life situation in which respondents are thinking and acting. This is in contrast to the experiences of the participant observer (Chapter 11). Many researchers are dissatisfied with standard survey questions about important criminal justice concepts such as fear of crime, routine behavior, and crime prevention. NCVS procedures for counting series victimizations remain inadequate even after more than 40 years of experience with the survey.

Using surveys to study crime and criminal justice policy presents special challenges. The target population frequently includes lower-income, transient persons who are difficult to contact through customary sampling methods. For example, homeless persons are excluded from any survey that samples households, but people who live on the street no doubt figure prominently as victims and offenders. Maxfield (1999) describes how new data from the National Incident-Based Reporting System suggest that a number of "nonhousehold-associated" persons are systematically undercounted by sampling procedures used in the NCVS. Research by Census Bureau staff has tried to document how many individuals might be missed in household-based surveys, finding that young males and minorities appear to be most undercounted (Martin, 1999).

Crime surveys such as the NCVS and the BCS have been deficient in getting information about crimes of violence when the victim and offender have some prior relationship. This is particularly true for domestic violence, although Michael Rand and Callie Rennison (2005) report some advantages of large surveys in this regard (2005). Underreporting of domestic violence appears to be due, in part, to the very general nature of large-scale crime surveys. Catriona Mirrlees-Black (1995:8) of the British Home Office summarizes the trade-offs of using survey techniques to learn about domestic violence:

> Measuring domestic violence is difficult territory. The advantage of the BCS is that it is based on a large nationally representative sample, has a relatively high response rate, and collects information on enough incidents to provide reliable details of their nature. One disadvantage is that domestic violence is measured in the context of a crime survey, and some women may not see what happened to them as "crime," or be reluctant to do so. Also, there is little time to approach the topic "gently." A specially designed questionnaire with carefully selected interviewers may well have the edge here.

We have mentioned that national crime surveys cannot be used to estimate the frequency of victimization in local areas like individual cities. For this reason, the Census Bureau conducted a series of victim surveys in cities in the 1970s. City crime surveys suffer problems of their own, however. Because sampling procedures are almost always based on some sample frame of city residents, city-specific surveys are not able to measure crimes that involve nonresident victims. For example, in an RDD survey of Key West, Florida, residents could not possibly count the robbery of a visitor who came down from Cincinnati. This problem still exists in the resurrection of city surveys by the BJS and the COPS office (Smith et al., Steadman, Minton, and Townsend, 1999). City-level surveys are based on samples of residents, and so cannot measure incidents that affect nonresident victims. A report from the National Research Council (2008) on the NCVS describes efforts to conduct state- and local-level victim surveys in a handful of states.

Survey research is generally weaker on validity and stronger on reliability. In comparison with field research, for instance, the artificiality of the survey format puts a strain on validity. As an illustration, most researchers agree that fear of crime is not well measured by the standard question, "How safe do you feel, or would you feel, out alone in your neighborhood at night?" Survey responses to that question are, at best, approximate indicators of what we have in mind when we conceptualize fear of crime.

Reliability is a different matter. By presenting all subjects with a standardized stimulus, survey research goes a long way toward eliminating unreliability in observations made by the researcher.

However, even this statement is subject to qualification. Critics of survey methods argue that questionnaires for standard crime surveys and many specialized studies embody a narrow, legalistic conception of crime that cannot reflect the perceptions and experiences of minorities and women. Survey questions typically are based on male views and do not adequately tap victimization or fear of crime among women (Straus, 1999; Tjaden and Thoennes, 2000). Concern that survey questions might mean different things to different respondents raises important questions about reliability and the generalizability of survey results across subgroups of a population.

Other Ways of Asking Questions

As with all methods of observation, a full awareness of the inherent or probable weaknesses of survey research may partially resolve them. Ultimately, though, we are on the safest ground when we can use several different research methods to study a given topic. For example, in-depth interviews of small numbers of people can yield rich, detailed information about such difficult problems as domestic violence and sexual assault. Similarly, focus groups are semi-structured group interviews used to develop or elaborate understanding of complex topics. The box "Putting It All Together: Asking Questions," presents several examples of surveys and focus groups used to understand different elements of traffic enforcement and racial profiling. Chapter 10, written by Amber Horning, provides a detailed examination of focus groups, qualitative interviews, and other ways of asking questions.

Should You Do It Yourself?

Anyone can do an online or simple telephone survey, but often it's better to use professional survey researchers.

The final issue we address in this chapter is who should conduct surveys. Drawing a sample, constructing a questionnaire, and conducting interviews or distributing self-administered instruments are not especially difficult. Equipped with the basic principles we have discussed so far, you could complete a modest in-person or telephone survey yourself. Self-administered surveys of large numbers of subjects are entirely possible, especially with present-day computer capabilities.

At the same time, the different tasks involved in completing a survey require a lot of work and attention to detail. We have presented many tips for constructing questionnaires, but our guidelines barely scratch the surface. Many books describe survey techniques in more detail, and a growing number focus specifically on Internet-based techniques. In many respects, however, designing and executing a survey of even modest size can be challenging.

Consider the start-up costs involved in face-to-face or telephone interview surveys of any size. Finding, training, and paying interviewers can be time consuming, potentially costly, and may require some degree of expertise. The price of computer equipment continues downward—but a CATI setup or supply of laptops and associated software for interviewers still represents a substantial investment that cannot easily be justified for a single survey.

Research on racial profiling has used surveys and other ways of collecting data by asking questions. One nationally representative survey has been conducted several times. We will say a bit more about the driver survey conducted in New Jersey. Researchers in North Carolina conducted several surveys and focus groups to assess how drivers and the police view each other.

POLICE-PUBLIC CONTACT SURVEY

The Police-Public Contact Survey (PPCS) has its roots in comprehensive anticrime legislation passed in 1994. The law required the Bureau of Justice Statistics (BJS) to collect data on the use of excessive force by police. From the outset it was decided that this would be best accomplished by adding questions to the National Crime Victimization Survey (NCVS). Almost as an afterthought, Jan Chaiken, then director of BJS, decided to include pilot questions asking specifically about traffic stops. As a result, the PPCS became one of the first sources of survey-based information about traffic stops.

Though limited in some respects, using the NCVS as a research platform in this way has several strengths. First, the NCVS has a large sample size, so it produces large numbers of people with some police contact. In the 2002 survey, about 15,700 of 77,000 respondents reported a police contact. Second, not all traffic stops produce a citation, so a survey sample can reveal something about the "dark figure" of unrecorded traffic stops. Third, the race of respondents is recorded, so it's possible to compare experiences of minority drivers to other drivers. Finally, considerable detail about the nature of the traffic stop can be recorded, including police demeanor, and whether or not respondents believed they were treated fairly. All of this is from the perspective of drivers, offering a very different source of information than is obtained from police records of traffic stops.

Results from the 2002 survey are summarized by Durose, Schmitt, and Langan (2005). Note, that these are national estimates. As such they offer useful information about the range of experience throughout the country. But because people are policed by thousands of organizations, any findings about race disparities could not be traced to individual organizations. National findings about police–public contacts have about as much validity as national findings about victimization. They illustrate the broadest patterns of experience, but do not accurately portray patterns of practice for individual agencies.

TOLLBOOTH SURVEY OF DRIVERS

In earlier chapters we mentioned the brief survey of drivers on the New Jersey Turnpike. The mechanics of the survey are especially interesting.

Interviewers were stationed in tollbooths, at a time when all vehicles had to stop and pay cash tolls when exiting the turnpike. Cars were sampled as we described in Chapter 8. Here is how Lange, Johnson, and Voas describe the interview procedure:

> Drivers of selected vehicles would hand the toll collector their Turnpike ticket, and then the surveyor would lean out the booth window and offer the driver $5 to answer a few brief questions. The driver was assured that the survey was voluntary and confidential. A $5 bill was placed inside an envelope that had a contact telephone number on it so drivers could learn more about the survey if they wished. (2005:199)

Drivers were asked where they entered the turnpike, making it possible to associate respondents with specific turnpike segments. They were then asked their age, and racial/ethnic identification from the categories white, black, Hispanic/Latino, Asian, American Indian, or other; follow-up questions further classified those who responded Hispanic/Latino or Asian. Gender was recorded by observation. Interviewers also recorded vehicle license plate numbers and state of registration. This was a hand-held computer-assisted interview.

Questionnaires were programmed into a PDA, and responses tapped in directly. This technique ensured that survey results could be directly uploaded for analysis.

NORTH CAROLINA SURVEYS AND FOCUS GROUPS

Like the PPCS, a statewide telephone survey of North Carolina drivers yielded information on driver behavior, the circumstances surrounding traffic stops, and the character of interactions with police. Unlike the PPCS, it was possible to compare driver experiences across law enforcement organizations. In particular, Smith and associates (2003) report that drivers had generally more favorable attitudes about experience with North Carolina State Highway Patrol compared with police from local agencies. In Chapter 8, we described how a sample of known speeders was included in the survey. This made it possible to test the criterion validity of self-report items. Because the survey sought information about people's experience in traffic stops, its target population was North Carolina drivers. Therefore, a sampling frame was readily available from the state agency that kept driver records. And because telephone numbers were included in these records, a telephone survey was the method of choice.

Multiple focus groups were conducted with North Carolina State Highway Patrol officers and with drivers. Smith and colleagues structured some focus groups so that all participants were African American or all were white. This was to promote open, candid discussion about sensitive topics. Researchers cite focus group literature that advises making respondents feel as comfortable as possible in support of this policy. Six police focus groups of six to nine troopers each were conducted. Six citizen focus groups of 10 people each were convened in large cities throughout North Carolina. Participants in the citizens' groups were selected by a research firm to represent ages between 24 and 60, and included at least four women.

Participants in focus groups of African American citizens felt police generally did a good job, but many also had some personal experience of perceived discrimination. Impolite or demeaning treatment by police was interpreted as signs of bias or discrimination. Drivers had sophisticated views about what sorts of stops were linked to profiling; traffic stops for minor offenses, like rolling through a stop sign, were especially suspect. An excerpt from one of the groups of African American citizens illustrates the kinds of insights that are difficult to get with large-scale surveys:

> I see him (the officer) just looking around my car and what not, and he said, "You know the reason why I pulled you over, don't you?" He said, "Your tag has September '98 on it." I said, "It's only May." He was like, "That's right. My fault." He gave me my driver's license and registration back and said, "You don't have any guns in the car do you?" I said, "No, it's at home with the dope." (2003:359)

Focus groups with troopers also produced candid observations. Most were concerned about increased attention to the racial distribution of people they stopped, feeling that they had to "balance the books" (2003:289). You may recognize how that would increase the role race plays in decisions to stop. These focus group interviews were held in June 2001. The views that two troopers expressed about profiling sound familiar in the post-9/11 world:

> I just want to say that we are all trained and I do not care what law enforcement agency you are in, you are trained to profile and you act on that. It is inherent. This business requires that.
>
> I think stereotyping and violations go together. If you look at a certain group, stereotype a certain group and in that group you deem it to be, have more violations, then naturally you will work more at stopping whatever . . . (2003:287).

Surveys are best at getting a large number of responses to mostly closed-ended questions. Focus groups are valuable sources of richer detail that can explain what people do and how they feel. Surveys are better at tabulating experience with traffic stops. Focus groups are better at explaining how people feel about their experiences.

If interview surveys are beyond a researcher's means, he or she might fall back on a mail or Web-based survey. Few capital costs are involved; most expenses are in consumables such as envelopes, stamps, and stationery. One or two persons can orchestrate a mail survey reasonably well at minimal expense. Perhaps a consultant could be hired to design a Web-based survey at modest cost. But consider two issues.

First, the business of completing a survey involves a great deal of tedious work. In mail surveys, for example, questionnaires and cover letters must be printed, folded, or stuffed into envelopes, stamped, and delivered (finally!) to the post office. It's possible for one individual to do a mail survey, but the researcher must be prepared for lots of work; even then, it will be more work than expected.

The second issue is more difficult to deal with and is often overlooked by researchers. We have examined at some length the advantages and disadvantages of the three methods of questionnaire administration. Some methods are more appropriate than others for different kinds of research questions. If a telephone or an in-person interview survey is best for the particular research needs, conducting a mail or Web-based survey will be a compromise—perhaps an unacceptable one. But excitement at actually beginning the research may lead the researcher to overlook or minimize problems with doing a mail survey on the cheap, in much the same way that researchers often are not in a position to recognize ethical problems with their own work (as we saw in Chapter 3). Doing a mail survey because it's all you can afford does not necessarily make the mail survey worth doing.

The alternative to doing it yourself is to contract with a professional survey research firm or a company that routinely conducts surveys. Most universities have a survey research center or institute, often affiliated with a sociology or political science department. For example, the Eagleton Center for Public Interest Polling at Rutgers University conducts a variety of research and other surveys (http://eagletonpoll.rutgers.edu/index.php). Such institutes are usually available to conduct surveys for government organizations as well as university researchers, and they can often do so very

economically. Private research firms are another possibility. Most have the capability to conduct all types of surveys, as well as focus groups. Finally, online platforms like Qualtrics also design and conduct surveys, sometimes using highly specialized samples.

Using a professional survey firm or institute has several advantages. Chapter 8 described the basic principles of sampling, but actually drawing a probability sample can be complex. Even the BJS/COPS do-it-yourself guidebook for community crime surveys (Weisel, 1999) counsels police departments and others to consult with experts in drawing RDD samples. Professional firms regularly use sampling frames that can represent city, state, and national samples, or whatever combination is appropriate.

We have emphasized the importance of measurement throughout this book. Researchers should develop conceptual and operational definitions and be attentive to all phases of the measurement process. However, constructing an actual questionnaire requires attention to details that may not always be obvious to researchers. After beginning to enter data from her completed questionnaires, Nerea Marteache (see the vignette that opened this chapter) recognized how the format she designed misled some respondents. Survey firms are experienced in preparing standard demographic items, batteries of matrix questions, and complex contingency questions with appropriate skip sequences.

Although it is often best for researchers to discuss specific concepts and even to draft questions, professional firms offer the considerable benefit of experience in pulling it all together. This is not to say that a researcher should simply propose some ideas for questions and then leave the details to the pros. Working together with a survey institute or market research firm to propose questionnaire items, review draft instruments, evaluate pretests, and make final modifications is usually the best approach.

Perhaps the chief benefit of contracting for a survey is that professional firms have a pool of trained interviewers or the equipment to conduct computer-assisted telephone interviews. Survey research centers and other professional organizations have the latest specialized equipment, software, and know-how to take advantage of advances in all forms of CAI. Furthermore, such companies can more readily handle such administrative details as training interviewers, arranging travel for in-person surveys, coordinating mail surveys, and providing general supervision. This frees researchers from much of the tedium of survey research, enabling them to focus on more substantive issues.

Researchers ultimately must decide whether to conduct a survey themselves or to contract with a professional firm. And the decision is best made after carefully considering the pros and cons of each approach. It's becoming increasing easy to conduct large-scale surveys through online samples and questionnaires. But too often, university faculty assume that students can get the job done while overlooking the important issues of how to maintain quality control and whether a survey is a worthwhile investment of students' time. Similarly, criminal justice practitioners may believe that agency staff can conduct phone interviews from the office. Again, compromises in the quality of results, together with the opportunity costs of diverting staff from other tasks, must be considered. The do-it-yourself strategy may seem cheaper in the short run, but it often becomes a false economy when attention turns to data analysis and interpretation.

We'll close this section with an apocryphal story about a consultant's business card; the card reads: "Fast! Low cost! High quality! Pick any two." It's best to make an informed choice that best suits your needs.

SUMMARY

- Survey research involves the administration of questionnaires in a systematic way to a sample of respondents selected from some population.
- Survey research is especially appropriate for descriptive or exploratory studies of large populations, but surveys have many other uses in criminal justice research.
- Surveys are the method of choice for obtaining victimization and self-reported offending data. Continuing efforts to improve self-report surveys include using confidential computer-assisted personal interviews.

- Questions may be open-ended or closed-ended. Each technique for formulating questions has advantages and disadvantages.
- Bias in questionnaire items encourages respondents to answer in a particular way or to support a particular point of view. It should be avoided.
- Questionnaires may be administered in three different ways: self-administered questionnaires, face-to-face interviews, and telephone interviews. Each mode of administration can be varied in several ways.
- Computers make each type of survey easier, and offer other advantages.
- In face-to-face surveys, it is essential that interviewers be neutral. Their presence in the data collection process must not have any effect on the responses given to questionnaire items.
- Each method of survey administration has a variety of advantages and disadvantages.
- Survey research has the weaknesses of being somewhat artificial and potentially superficial.
- Although the particular tasks required to complete a survey are not especially difficult, researchers must carefully consider whether to conduct surveys themselves or contract with a professional organization.

KEY TERMS

Bias *(p. 237)*
Closed-ended questions *(p. 235)*
Computer-assisted interviewing (CAI) *(p. 239)*
Interview *(p. 233)*
Interview survey *(p. 248)*
Open-ended questions *(p. 235)*
Questionnaire *(p. 235)*
Respondent *(p. 233)*
Response rate *(p. 244)*
Survey *(p. 232)*

REVIEW QUESTIONS AND EXERCISES

1. For each of the open-ended questions listed, construct a closed-ended question that could be used in a questionnaire.
   a. What was your family's total income last year?
   b. How do you feel about shock incarceration, or "boot camp" programs?
   c. How do people in your neighborhood feel about the police?
   d. What do you feel is the biggest problem facing this community?
   e. How do you protect your home from burglary?

2. Prepare a brief questionnaire to study perceptions of crime near your college or university. Include

questions asking respondents to describe a nearby area where they either are afraid to go after dark or think crime is a problem. Then use your questionnaire to interview at least 10 students.

3. A recent evaluation of a federal program to support community policing included sending questionnaires to a sample of about 1,200 police chiefs. Each questionnaire included a number of items asking about specific features of community policing and whether they were being used in the department. Almost all the police chiefs had someone else complete the questionnaire. What's the unit of analysis in this survey? What problems might result from having an individual complete such a questionnaire?

4. Open a free SurveyMonkey account. Construct a five-item questionnaire for students in your class, asking them to evaluate this textbook. As much as possible, use survey templates that are available on Survey Monkey. Then use some sampling procedure to select 10 students from your class who will complete the survey. Write a brief report that summarizes your findings.

CHAPTER 10

Qualitative Interviewing

Contributed by Amber Horning, William Paterson University

We'll learn when qualitative interviewing is appropriate, different types of in-depth interviews, how to design questions, and how to interact with participants. Finally, we'll consider different ways to record and analyze data.

Learning Objectives

1. Recognize when to use qualitative interviewing as a data-gathering tool.
2. Understand that there are multiple meanings or constructions about reality.
3. Know the advantages and disadvantages of semi-structured versus unstructured interviews.
4. Understand the use of focus groups or interviewing a group of people simultaneously.
5. Learn how to create interview questions so that data can be gathered effectively.
6. Be able to describe how to approach and interact with participants.
7. Learn how to record or log data.
8. Understand ways to analyze and interpret qualitative data.
9. Recognize how to enhance the quality of information gathered.

Gaining Access to Hard-to-Reach Groups

In 2011–2012, I conducted a study about pimps in Harlem, New York City. Pimps are considered to be a hard-to-reach group, and many people were skeptical that I would find participants. One of the reasons that I thought this study was possible was because one of my colleagues knew someone who had been pimping for over 20 years. Although he agreed to a pilot interview, he was very reluctant to be our contact or to give us sponsorship. He was worried about our intentions and exposing the secrets of the business. It seemed that the study would not be possible or, at the least, that we would have trouble finding participants. We considered going to nonprofit organizations dedicated to helping sex workers to

see if we could find referrals to potential contacts. Sometimes, you can find sponsors by connecting to local organizations.

By a stroke of luck, I needed to have an industrial air conditioner moved, and I asked the same friend if one of her clients (people on probation or parole) would be interested in the job. The person who came over to move my air conditioner turned out to be a former pimp who still had access to many members of this community. We had a nice interaction, and I mentioned the study in casual conversation. He was very interested in the research and agreed to connect me with people who were actively pimping in his neighborhood.

He trusted me because of our mutual connection and the rapport that I established with him. This was a fortuitous moment for the study and illustrates that access can be gained through friends of friends or acquaintances and that even a distant connection can be useful to finding a willing contact. In addition, finding a contact who was formerly involved in a criminal lifestyle can be beneficial because that person may have less fear about the research process.

My contact's presence during the interviews and the fact that the interviews were largely conducting in public spaces (housing project courtyards in New York City) may have allayed some participants' fears. Many of them knew or recognized him from the neighborhood. In addition, they were able to watch interviews taking place and did not witness any adverse consequences. Our presence in the housing project courtyards would have been difficult to navigate without sponsorship. Access can be about connecting with your participants, but sponsorship may also allow you access to spaces that enable participants to feel the trust required for participation.

After working with my contact for several months, he was arrested and sent back to prison. Although I had collected a lot of phone numbers of participants who were interested in the progress of the study, only one person struck me as the right person for continued access. He was one of the first people interviewed and was always hanging around watching interviews and asking questions about the progress of the study. He seemed to be a regular fixture in the community and he knew a lot of people. I texted him to see if he was still interested in connecting us with participants. Through his sponsorship, we were able to interview over 60 more participants. Sometimes your initial sponsor may disappear for various reasons; thus, it is important to connect with other people in the same community. By connecting with other members of the group, you may be able to continue your study should something happen to your original contact.

Introduction

Qualitative interviews are frequently used in criminological research.

Sample surveys are perhaps the best-known method of asking questions in criminal justice research. However, as discussed in Chapter 9, surveys and standardized questionnaires sometimes fall short on validity. A survey would be appropriate to ask people if they have ever been the victim of a robbery, but a survey questionnaire would not be as useful to understand how robbers select victims. To learn what factors robbers consider, you would want to use more specialized interviewing techniques.

To illustrate the difference, suppose you want to study robbery in the shanty settlements of South African townships. You may be interested in the percentage of robberies happening in South African townships between 8:00 p.m. and 8:00 a.m. A victim survey would be a good approach to finding that out. However, you might also want to understand the decision-making process of nighttime robbers who searched for victims in South African townships. You also may be interested in how robbers' actions are influenced by police foot patrols. In that case, it would be best to talk to robbers in person. Generally, when you find yourself wondering about the complexities of any process or the *hows* involving human perspectives, emotions, or decisions, you are usually better off using qualitative interviewing.

Unlike a survey, a **qualitative interview** is an interaction between an interviewer and a respondent where the interviewer has a general plan of inquiry, including the topics to be covered, but not necessarily a specific set of questions that must be asked in a particular order. The qualitative interview can also be thought of as a purposeful conversation (Patton, 2002). You have been conversing your entire life, so you already have a lot of practice and tools at your disposal. Because your purpose is to understand, you are a vigilant conversationalist. You are more aware about how you communicate, how your participant responds, and

Qualitative interview   A verbal interaction between an interviewer and a participant that follows a general plan of inquiry, but not necessarily a specific set of questions.

how your participant feels. At the same time, the qualitative interviewer, like the survey interviewer, should be fully familiar with the questions. This ensures that qualitative interviews consistently cover certain areas, while allowing the interview to proceed smoothly and naturally. As we have seen, survey interviews are based on the use of standardized questions. Qualitative interviews are based on a deliberate plan, but are inherently flexible.

Topics Appropriate for Qualitative Interviewing

Qualitative interviews have many applications and are especially well suited for exploratory research.

Qualitative interviews are crucial to various kinds of studies. They are an important part of field research (to be covered in Chapter 11). Historically, qualitative methods have been used by anthropologists and sociologists for studying other cultures and subcultures. An illustration of this approach is the study by David Brotherton and Luis Barrios (2004) of the Almighty Latin King and Queen Nation in New York City. By attending important meetings, hanging around with key informants, and interviewing gang members, Brotherton and Barrios were able to capture the process of this group's transformation from a street gang to an organized social movement. Another notable study is Lisa Maher's (1997) work on females engaged in sex work within Brooklyn drug markets. She gathered much of her information through informal conversations with these women on the streets. Each of these studies is process oriented—where the purpose is to understand human experiences holistically and in context.

Qualitative interviews can be the sole way of gathering data in criminal justice studies. If you want to understand the perspective of those who are labeled by society as deviant or criminal, your best tactic is to talk to them in person. This is especially true with hard-to-reach populations about which little is known. Through interviews, you can gather firsthand accounts about their impressions of their world that constitute their *lived experience*. For instance, when I began my studies of pimps,

I found very little prior research. I wanted to understand pimps' perspectives about their use of space in urban areas and their views about social interactions with sex workers. Because so little was known about this group, the best way to capture their experiences and feelings was qualitative interviewing through purposeful conversations. Many pimps were engaged in criminal activity and, therefore, only accessible for conversations on the street. Through interviews with 95 pimps in Harlem, New York City, conducted in 2011 and 2012, I learned much about their experiences.

Another example of a topic appropriate for qualitative interviewing is research on how people think about their roles and/or identities. Ferdinand Sutterlüty (2007) wanted to know how young people felt about the process of adopting violent lifestyles, so he interviewed 18 repeat violent offenders in Berlin. He found that some thought of the transition to acting violently as a *turning point*. For some, there was an identity switch from victim to perpetrator. Many had experienced violence within their families and used violence to reclaim power. He also uncovered several different kinds of *violent action schemes*, or ways these young people thought about violence. The most effective way for him to understand meanings of violence and the process of identity change was through in-depth interviews. If you are interested in role or identity construction or reconstruction, it's necessary to interview your participants.

Another reason for choosing qualitative interviewing as part of your design is if your group of interest is part of a "scene." A scene could be a group that is united socially or politically, and you want to understand their perspective in context. To illustrate, Dina Perrone (2009) wanted to get beyond stereotypes of club drug users to understand how the settings of rave clubs influenced drug experience and harm. The best way for her to understand this and get quality interviews was to go where the "dance club kids" hung out. By visiting clubs and attending parties she observed, made connections, and talked to people. Perrone found that unlike popular stereotypes about addicts, the group was largely middle class. Further, many were socially embedded, such as lawyers with families. Club kids who invested in their outside lives had more control over their drug use. In addition, she found the scene to be an escape into a "carnivalesque atmosphere," where lights and music afforded a sharp contrast from typical middle-class routine. This study of dance clubs revealed a social group outside their daily grind within the capitalist machine. This was only apparent because Perrone visited her participants in context.

Understanding an illicit market often requires a longer-term project and interviews with different players involved in the market. After 20 years of field work in New York City, Ric Curtis and Travis Wendel (2007) published an article titled, "You're Always Training the Dog: Strategic Interventions to Reconfigure Drug Markets." This work documented different types of drug markets and the types of systematic violence that were characteristic of each. They found that changes to the market, for better or worse, were often in response to law enforcement interventions. A market is a complex system, and they wanted to understand its variation and changes over time. This required many interviews over the years with police and other people who worked in New York City drug markets.

Sometimes, the only way to obtain the information that you need is through qualitative data collection. Chris Overall, Shalendra Singh, and Bhekekhya Gcina (2008) used crime mapping and other statistical procedures to understand crime hot spots in South Africa. However, they noted that because many poorer South African townships were informal settlements interwoven with formal settlements, these areas could not be understood through standard crime mapping. Overall, Singh and Gcina described how these spaces developed through the interplay between socio-historic events, people, and physical environments. Township spaces were captured through *cognitive maps* that expressed how people understand their environment. Obtaining these maps required qualitative interviews about residents' perceptions of these informal settlements.

I did something very similar in my study of pimps in Harlem. I gave participants a pen and paper and asked them to draw their work space. Pimps' work spaces have traditionally been in open-air markets, similar to lower-level drug dealers (Harocopos and Hough, 2005). Although some sex market facilitation has moved off the street (Venkatesh, 2011), business still occurs in outdoor public space. This method of having pimps draw their work spaces was not only useful for building rapport—there was much discussion about the pictures—but was also a great way to understand how these marginalized men conceived of their everyday work space within the urban landscape. See the box "Maps of an Illicit Economy: Conceptions of Masculinized Outdoor Work Space," for details on cognitive maps by pimps. While you review this box, keep in mind that it's a good illustration of the flexibility available through qualitative interviewing.

Another type of qualitative interview is a focus group: a directed discussion with a small group of people. Focus groups are especially useful in learning about group dynamics. Tarja Pösö, Päivi Honkatukia, and Leo Nyqvist (2008) studied violence in youth residential care facilities in Finnish reform schools. They were interested in how group dynamics affected the ways these young people spoke about violence. The study explored how this knowledge was collectively produced. A focus group with qualitative interviewing was the best approach, because the group format acted as a needed stimulus to generate data. Focus groups can also be used in connection with quantitative studies. For instance, James Nolan and Yoshio Akiyama (1999) studied police routines for making records of hate crimes. In a general sense, they knew what concepts they wanted to measure but were unsure how to operationalize them. They convened five focus groups in different cities—groups that included police administrators, mid-level managers, patrol officers, and civilian employees—to learn about different perspectives on hate crime recording. Analyzing focus group results, Nolan and Akiyama prepared a self-administered questionnaire that was sent to a large number of individuals in four police departments.

Key Features of Qualitative Interviewing

All qualitative interview techniques are rooted in a few basic principles.

Qualitative interviews assume different forms depending on the type of study, but some important principles are consistent regardless of the

Historically, geographers have used maps to understand whether they help people find their way around town, cultural geographers have used maps to understand how social and culture dimensions are shaped by landscapes and vice versa (Jackson, 1989; Sauer, 1925), anthropologists have used maps to understand the perspectives of isolated groups (Madaleno, 2010), and criminologists have used maps to understand crime patterns and decision making (Brantingham and Brantingham, 1984; Canter and Hodge, 2000; Cornish and Clarke, 1986; Lopez and Lukinbeal, 2010) and perceptions of danger (Wallace, 2009). Urban space claimed by lower-class males for work has been documented in Phillippe Bourgois's *In Search of Respect: Selling Crack in El Barrio* on Harlem crack dealers, Mitch Duneier's *Sidewalk* on street vendors in New York City, and Sudhir Vankatesh's *Off the Books: The Underground Economy of the Urban Poor* on how residents in a Chicago housing project make ends meet. Although criminologists have had offenders draw maps to understand offenders' decision making and crime patterns, the types of offenders in these studies often seek out new targets each time. Ethnographers have photographed and described informal economies, but there is very little use of maps drawn by offenders to understand their visual conceptualization and use of their semipermanent, everyday illicit work space.

Pimps, like drug dealers, often work in certain spots or use or claim outdoor space (semi-permanently) to conduct business. If you try to imagine claiming space in the urban environment, you may quickly realize how difficult this could be. If you are female, you may not even be able to conceive of this, as there are few documented examples of women informally claiming outdoor space. Males engaged in the illicit economy may be what James Messerschmidt (1993) calls "doing masculinity;" that is, they are trying to prove their masculine worth through attempts at financial solvency within the capitalist social structure, albeit illicitly. To do this, they sometimes must carve out or at least inhabit public space.

Documentation exists of marginalized males claiming public space, especially in the literature on gangs. For instance, William Foote Whyte's (1993) seminal study on Boston slums distinguished between "corner boys" and "college boys." Often in these accounts, males occupy urban space not only for business purposes, but also to display masculinity and show they have "juice" to establish and maintain street credibility, as discussed in Jack Katz's *Seductions of Crime*. While publicly being involved in "the hustle" for various reasons is well researched, how these predominantly masculine spaces are conceived of and protected has less documentation.

In the maps that the pimps drew, depictions of outdoor work space and conceptions of the self within the larger informal economy showed variation. There were differences in "territory" and the roles taken in order to protect it from competitors, police, and others. These blueprints for the business, including social exchanges with sex workers, were communicated through spatial depictions.

The accompanying figure is a map drawn by a former pimp. Although he was currently living in Harlem, he operated his business in a smaller town in New York State (this is more apparent when you notice the post office and the pharmacy in close proximity). At 8:00 P.M., the *post office, la farmacia* (the pharmacy), and *la bodega* (corner store) closed. Selling sex did not begin until all of these formal businesses closed. The males shown in front of the bodega, depicted by *me* and *pimp*, claimed this public space (one side of a block) from 8:00 P.M. to 6:00 A.M.

This participant was gifted a portion of the business by an uncle; that is, he was given some instruction, a few sex workers, and a place to house them (they all lived together in one large house). Their residence is indicated by the scribbled *ten blocks* as this was the distance from his work space to his house. It is important to note that it was fairly common that related males taught or handed down the business to younger males in the family. Formal and illicit businesses passed down through family generations are well documented as families try to ensure that successive generations are solvent. This test of masculine worth may be more evident with businesses operating in outdoor space where mismanagement or failure becomes displayed quite publicly.

The sex workers stood on a small block near an abandoned building (left-hand side of the drawing). This building and behind the structure are where they took their clients. The participant, along with other pimps, stood in front of the bodega (right-hand side of the drawing). This public work space was split by gender, with females (sex workers) on one part of the block and males (pimps) on the other.

The participant's presence in front of the bodega is a form of "doing masculinity." It is a masculine display showing protection of sex workers, ownership of territory/sex workers, and perhaps performativity for one another. The participant discussed his presence as

being necessary to ensure that everything ran smoothly and to protect the safety of the sex workers. It is interesting to note that he identifies sex workers primarily by their appearance (e.g., *brown hair, hazel eyes*) and age. They are categorized much like a seller would categorize wares. He did not have any major conflicts with other pimps despite standing in close proximity. The act of watching from afar in a group displays many different messages.

Although this was a small street-based business operation, spanning one city block, it was connected to a more elaborate business owned by his uncle. The arrangement was a trial run. Much to his dismay, this participant was unable to succeed in the business. When I asked him specifically why he couldn't continue this work, he said that he didn't like to be rough with the girls, and he hinted that this contributed to him having some trouble controlling them. He claimed that his uncle probably felt that he was a failure. Nonetheless, this illicit business operated in an outdoor public space for 3 years.

design. For the studies discussed earlier, you may have noticed how these project descriptions were highly contextualized. Exploring the complexity of human experience often means examining closely how people live in specific environments.

Richness, Meaning, and Shared Cultural Views

Qualitative interviews involve hearing the richness of human experiences, sifting through layered meaning in context, and recognizing shared cultural meanings.

To illustrate this, Clifford Geertz (1973) makes an important distinction between what he calls thin and thick description. In his seminal work *The Interpretation of Cultures*, Geertz discusses ways to interpret the wink of an eye. In a thin description, the observer would merely state that three different people winked and, therefore, performed the same behavior. Underscoring the importance of interpreting behaviors in context, Geertz (1973:7–8) describes the different meanings of winks.

> The first boy got dust in his eye and his behavior only looked like a wink. Another boy who noticed that it was not a real wink gave a clowning wink to another friend, thereby mocking the boy with dust in his eye. A nearby girl then gave a flirtatious wink to the clowning boy.

This is what Geertz calls "thick" description because it involves not only describing actions, but also understanding meanings of behaviors in context. Qualitative interviews are important tools for producing thick descriptions that help lead to real understanding.

Philippe Bourgois's (2002) work studying crack dealers in East Harlem is another example of research that retains the richness of human experience. Bourgois talks about his relationship with Ray, who was the leader of a local spot where crack was for sale—La Farmacia. Notice the detailed description of behaviors and context in this excerpt

from *In Search of Respect: Selling Crack in El Barrio* (Bourgois, 2002:28).

> Whether Ray was a Gumby Bear, a violent pervert, or an omnipotent street don "with juice," my long-term relationship with the man ultimately uncovered a vulnerability that he kept hidden in his street persona. In his private conversations with me over his aspirations for the future, he often seemed naïve or even learning-disabled. He was completely incapable of fathoming the intricate rules and regulations of legal society despite his brilliant success at directing a retail network for crack distribution. To borrow the French sociologist Pierre Bourdieu's analytical category, Ray lacked the "cultural capital" necessary to succeed in the middle-class or even working-class world.

Often people living in similar communities or subcultures have shared cultural meanings that are transmitted through communication among people (Barth, 2002). For example, the best way to understand why and how people join right-wing extremist groups would be to interact with members of these groups. Members of right-wing extremist groups may come from similar subcultures and have common values even before joining the group. You can learn something about shared meaning and sometimes subcultures through communication with people who, knowingly or unknowingly, belong to certain groups.

The Critical Realist Approach and the Qualitative Interview

It's useful to think of qualitative interviewing as an approach to learning. But it's important to keep in mind that how qualitative interviews are conducted is rooted in our perspective of reality in the social world. In my research on pimps, I obtained multiple perspectives about how they viewed their sex workers. Some viewed workers as friends or girlfriends, others viewed them as business partners, and some viewed them as employees or just products. Even within a single interview, a participant sometimes changed perspectives. However, each of these perspectives contributed to some reality about pimping. This is known as the **critical realist perspective** (Maxwell, 2012). There

Critical realist perspective   A philosophical view that reality exists, but knowledge is constructed through multiple meanings.

are two parts to understanding this position: one involves your stance about the nature of reality and the other about the nature of knowledge (Maxwell, 2012). Although this seems heady, your eventual opinion may influence how you tackle your study.

The nature of reality, or *ontology*, is viewed in two distinct ways: (1) some people believe that a real world exists beyond our perceptions and constructions; and (2) others, known as radical constructivists, think that reality is a construction based on what we perceive reality to be. Critical realists believe that reality does exist, which offers a firmer and less complicated platform to begin research. A belief in reality allows you to have some faith that your findings contribute to something real.

The next part is how you view the nature and scope of knowledge. Critical realists believe that interpretations of the world are constructions derived from many individual perspectives (Maxwell, 2012). There is no way to find a single, "correct" understanding of the world. Critical realists are comfortable with the idea that knowledge is constructed through multiple meanings.

The idea that the nature of knowledge is constructed from many different individual perspectives is not all that surprising if you think about it for a bit. For example, after Hurricane Katrina, two different photos circulated on Internet news sites showing people wading through the water with food or other items. When the people were white, the byline stated, "two residents wade through water after *finding* some bread." But when the photo was of a black man, the caption read, "a young man walks through chest-deep flood water after *looting* groceries" (Sommers et al., 2006:42. Emphasis added). These people were doing exactly the same thing, but the interpretations were quite different. Even if two people look at similar images or hear the same story, they may have very different ways of perceiving what the images or words mean. This example illustrates how peoples' understanding of the world is constructed; knowledge is based on a multiplicity of constructions.

You may be wondering how this influences your overall approach to qualitative interviewing. First, consider how interviewing involves hearing peoples' constructions of lived experiences that give meaning to their life stories. Second, perspectives of lived experience may be shared by members of a group and may be thought of as shared cultural meaning. Third, after listening and being self-aware, you interpret and transmit these meanings to others. This requires the ability to admit that your interpretations are also constructions. There is power to acknowledging your subjectivity; that is, recognizing that your interpretations are influenced by your own social lenses, including biases.

Platform for Creating Questions

Before you create questions, as a part of planning your approach you will want to figure out who you will interview, along with the depth of your interview questions. This is sometimes termed the *substantive frame*. Robert Weiss (1994:41) described the substantive frame as "a sense of the breadth and density of the material we want to collect."

For instance, since the 9/11 terrorist attacks, Muslim communities in many cities have been watched more closely by law enforcement. In 2012, news reports revealed that the New York City Police Department (NYPD) had been monitoring Muslim student organizations for potential ties to terrorist activities. Public outrage emerged about this potential infringement on privacy, and justifications were made about spying in the name of public safety (Baker and Taylor, 2012). Let's say you want to conduct research on Muslim students' perspectives of reported police surveillance, such as their feelings about the violation of their civil rights. You might simply interview the students who belong to Muslim student organizations. However, if you wanted a deeper understanding of the problem, you could interview New York's mayor and members of the NYPD along with those students.

Next, you should familiarize yourself with studies on the same or similar topics. There may be prior research that examined the treatment of Muslim youth in the United States after 9/11. These prior works will be helpful to find the right framework for your interview questions. Once you determine a set of possible questions, you should pilot them on someone from the group of interest. In this example, you may ask members of a Muslim student organization some basic questions about their feelings and experiences about being monitored. An earlier pilot interview might change your approach to how you frame the research and the questions, and put you on a more fruitful road.

Creating a solid platform for interview questions is essential, because it will help you to decide other important steps such as whether your questions are semi-structured or unstructured, whether your interview is one-on-one or in a focus group, and how you should approach your role as interviewer. The execution of these steps will ultimately lead to analysis that is rich in contextualized meaning and shared cultural meanings.

Different Kinds of Qualitative Interviews

As in survey research, qualitative interviews can be conducted in different ways.

Decisions about the form (face-to-face or phone) and type of **interview schedule** influence how in-depth and interactive your interviews should be. Three general types of interview schedules are structured, semi-structured, and unstructured. Most surveys use structured interview schedules. Interviews become more natural, in-depth, and exploratory as you move toward unstructured interviewing. Another important point is that the type of interview schedule you choose often hinges on whether you are testing a specific concept, being guided by existing theory, or doing an exploratory study. If you think of this as a spectrum, unstructured interviewing is the best for an exploratory study where theory may be generated.

Structured and Semi-Structured Interviews

Let's return to the example of Muslim students' perceptions of being monitored by law enforcement. You may already have a preexisting idea that you

Interview schedule   The structure of an interview that may have predetermined questions or topical areas to be discussed with participants.

want to explore. Maybe you theorized that Muslim students' feelings of being monitored by law enforcement could be explained by labeling theory, which holds that being labeled as deviant by society affects the way people view themselves (Becker, 1963). You might ask students how being monitored influenced their self-image in different domains of their lives, such as at home, at work, in school, in the mosque, or in the community more generally. You may decide to use a **structured interview** schedule that consists of predetermined questions and answer sets. The questions, and sometimes the answers, are standardized. The reason for standardizing your interview is to try to give participants the same stimulus so that responses will be comparable. A structured qualitative interview can be thought of as a procedure where slivers of information are retrieved for a very particular purpose. These kinds of answers can also sometimes be quantified. The disadvantages of this approach are a lack of depth, occasionally stilted exchanges with participants, and a limited ability to explore unexpected responses.

Both structured and **semi-structured interview** schedules have standardized questions, but the semi-structured interview allows you to explore themes that emerge in the interview. Semi-structured interviews make it possible to use unscheduled probes, or spontaneous questions that are relevant to the dialogue. During the pilot interview of your study of Muslim students, you may realize that your study could benefit from unscheduled probes and opt for a semi-structured interview schedule. This style of interviewing is usually guided by a specific idea about the group, but allows you to probe beyond participants' answers and your own questions.

Scheduled Question

Interviewer: After finding out about being monitored, did you feel any differently when you were at school?

Participant: I felt that people were looking at me more suspiciously.

Scheduled Probe

Interviewer: Can you give me an example of this happening?

Participant: I was buying lunch, and all of a sudden, I felt that everyone was watching me. It seemed like the cashier was afraid to take my money and didn't want to interact with me. It made me feel like a suspect. There are not many Muslim students at my school, but lately I have gotten to know a few.

Unscheduled Probe

Interviewer: Did you talk with the other Muslim students about being monitored?

Participant: Yes, we were shocked when we discovered that this was going on. We kind of came together in a way. I wasn't that close with them before this.

The semi-structured interview format allows you to ask a spontaneous question and discover an emerging theme. Through the unscheduled probe, you found that the monitoring was not only negatively influencing self-concept in certain social spheres, but also bringing some Muslim students closer together. The semi-structured interview has the benefit of producing more standardized and therefore more comparable answers, while retaining a natural spontaneity where important themes may be discovered.

Unstructured Interviews

For in-depth interviews, the ideal approaches are semi-structured or unstructured. The most open style of interviewing is the **unstructured interview**. This style provides the most breadth, depth, and natural interaction with participants. Perhaps police monitoring only had minimal or no influence on Muslim students' self-image. However, there were other important elements about this experience that you missed because you began with a narrow focus. When there is a lack of existing information about a group's experiences, sometimes in-depth, unstructured interviews yield the best insights. The main drawback is that your interviews are less comparable.

Unstructured interviews take different shapes. Two main approaches to unstructured interviewing are a *conversation* and an *interview guide* (Patton, 2002). A conversation is an informal "chat" where

participants may forget that they are being interviewed and the conversation flows organically. You might be in a local nightclub or hanging out on the street and strike up a conversation with a member of the group of interest. This type of unstructured interview can be used in exploratory studies, but traditionally is used during participant observation or ethnographies. For example, Peter Moskos (2009) joined the Baltimore Police Department to understand police subculture. Moskos obtained much of his data through participant observation and on-the-job conversations with fellow police officers. An interview guide includes a list of topical areas that you want to cover in the conversation. Here, you have a free-flowing conversation that is guided but allows for conversation that is more natural. With this style, you are free to delve deeply into topics that come up during the exchange, but you use the guide as a reference.

Semi-structured interviews are especially useful if two or more people are interviewing, but you still want the option to explore emerging themes. For example, if you and a few other people were interviewing female street sex workers in Los Angeles, it would be best to have the same questions. If you only had a list of topics to be discussed such as *clients*, *business negotiations*, and *safety*, these all could be interpreted in multiple ways. One person may see safety and think that he should ask about safety from clients, whereas another may interpret this to mean safety from pimps or police. Even if this is outlined beforehand, the subtleties of language may dramatically change the meaning of a question. Standardization helps establish continuity across interviews, but open-ended questions with unscheduled probes still leave room to explore new areas.

Moreover, if you are interested in unadulterated views that center on important themes about sex work, you should choose the unstructured interview. A common misperception is that unstructured interviews lack purpose because they resemble a free-flowing conversation. Margot Ely and associates (1991) describe how every interview has a structure. The structure is simply negotiated differently, with the "structured" interview being predetermined. Whether you choose a structured, semi-structured, or unstructured format, preparation for interviews and modifications will need to be made along the way.

Focus Group Interviews

Some researchers opt to interview groups of people at the same time; this method is called a **focus group** interview. This technique originated in market research in the 1950s and is still used by companies to learn from potential customers how to best market their products. Focus groups have come to be widely used by social scientists to gather qualitative data from groups. The group generally consists of 6 to 12 participants and is usually moderated by the researcher (Krueger and Casey, 2000). Focus groups can be used to generate hypotheses. Focus groups can also be combined with other types of data gathering such as participant observation. In these scenarios, focus groups generate research ideas or add support to existing findings from other sources of data. The study by Pösö, Honkatukia, and Nyqvist (2008) on how Finnish youth in reform schools produced knowledge about violence is a good example of how focus groups can generate data about group dynamics.

Group discussions can show how opinions are produced, expressed, and exchanged in everyday life. It is important to keep in mind that the focus group is not a problem-solving session or a decision-making group, but rather an interview (Flick, 2009:196–197). The interview schedule for focus groups can also be structured, semi-structured, or unstructured depending on your purpose. Unstructured focus group interviews are used for research that is more exploratory and are often used to understand a research topic or to generate questions, whereas the more structured interviews use questions to guide the discussion.

Participant Dynamics Two basic types of focus groups are a *natural group* and an *artificial group*. Individuals in a natural group may already be acquainted or have an existing connection; they sometimes also have shared cultural meaning. Let's say that you became interested in the Muslim student who said that monitoring by law enforcement

brought her closer to other Muslim students at school. You may realize that monitoring created a process of unification among Muslim students, and you are interested in how this process works. A natural focus group would be a great way for you to understand how this experience brought this group together. You could ask students if they would be interested in a focus group and then use a type of snowball sample. Although you cannot re-create the initial conversations that they had or see the initial process, you may be able to witness similar dynamics and hear how they collectively reacted to being monitored by their government.

An artificial group includes people selected according to some criteria and brought together for research purposes (Flick, 2009). For instance, maybe you are interested in how men think about avoiding crime. You could create a focus group of men and have them discuss the different ways that they interpret danger and the tactics that they use to stay away from potential crime spots. The only factor that this group has in common is that they are men from urban areas, so it is an artificial group. Artificial groups are best when researchers want to avoid having discussion affected by preexisting relationships.

Designing Qualitative Interview Questions

Qualitative interview questions can assume different forms.

Different approaches to framing interviews depend on how focused and in depth you want your questions to be. One approach is to have a main topic such as *safety* in sex work, with branching questions that you explore at the same level. One line of questioning, such as safety from clients, does not take precedence over other areas, like safety from police. This is called the *tree-and-branch approach*, and it is less exploratory than the *river-and-channel approach* (Rubin and Rubin, 2011). Figure 10.1 provides a graphic illustration of these two approaches.

Focus group A group interview or a guided discussion with a small group of participants.

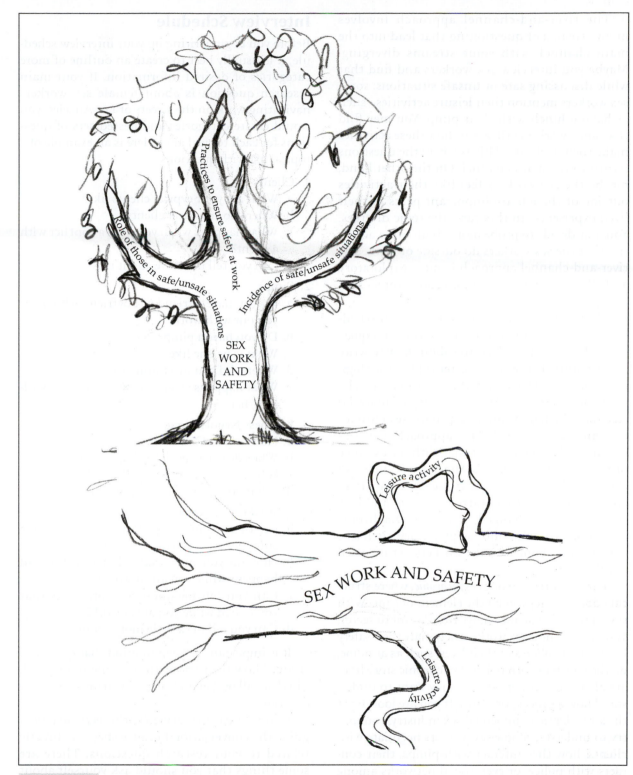

FIGURE 10.1 Tree-and-Branch versus River-and-Channel Approach

The river-and-channel approach involves many streams of questioning that lead into the main channel, with some streams diverging. Maybe you interview sex workers and find that while discussing safe or unsafe situations, some sex workers mention their leisure activities—such as having lunch with their pimp. You may find that some workers talk about how these activities make them feel safe. This is where the questions return to the main channel. On the other hand, maybe the sex workers feel like their activities outside of the job are important parts of their lived experience. In this case, the topic diverges. You may decide to probe more about other activities that the sex workers do outside of work. The river-and-channel approach is more exploratory and allows for a deeper exploration of topics that emerge.

The way that you create your interview schedule mirrors the way you examine research questions. Think of it as deciding about how to write a short story. Is the story better told chronologically, or is it more compelling without the element of time? A *diachronic* delivery of material starts at the beginning and progresses chronologically (Weiss, 1994). This approach may center on developments over time. With the example of the sex workers in Los Angeles, you may ask them to describe how they dealt with safety issues when they first started working and how these may have changed over time. Diachronic story lines are sometimes explanatory, such as a description about why sex workers get involved in selling sex.

The other framework is *synchronic*, where structure does not depend on the element of time. With this approach, you may move from sector to sector. You may ask how sex workers negotiate their safety in different spheres of their lives, such as at home, on the street, or with police. Synchronic story lines are also about function. You may want to understand how a process operates. If you are looking at the street-based commercial sex industry, you may try to understand how sex workers negotiate with clients, how they interact with pimps, their contacts with police, or even social networks among sex workers. Essentially, you are interested in interrelationships between actors within and peripheral to this informal economy.

Interview Schedule

Before you begin writing up your interview schedule, it is usually best to create an outline of more categories of desired information. If your main research question is about female sex workers navigating work on the streets of Los Angeles, you would create categories and nested sets of questions for each topical area. Here is an example of a topical list with questions:

1. Clients
   a. What are your typical clients like?
   b. Where do you meet clients?
   c. What happens when you have a conflict with a client?
   d. Can you tell me more about this?

2. Pimps
   a. Do you have a friend or boyfriend who helps you out with work?
   b. Do you have a pimp?
   c. What is he/she like?
   d. Where did you meet him/her?
   e. What happens when you have a conflict with him/her?

3. Business Negotiations
   a. How do you find clients?
   b. When do you negotiate prices with customers?
   c. Where do you go with customers?
   d. What do you do if something goes wrong?

4. Safety Measures
   a. Are there some things that you do to make sure that you are safe at work?
   b. How do you make sure that nothing bad happens while you are at work?
   c. Can you tell me about any problems that you've had while you are at work?
   d. Can you tell me a little more about this?

It is important to keep in mind that questions "frame" how the participant is going to respond. This list will probably change as you fine-tune your questions.

In qualitative interviews, the *main questions* guide the conversation because they are directly related to your research questions. There are some things that you should ask yourself about your main questions: (1) Do they encompass the overall subject? (2) Is there a good flow in terms of transitions from question to question?

(3) Does the chronology (if synchronic) make sense? (4) Is the language at the appropriate level for your participants? (Rubin and Rubin, 2011) Your main questions generate answers, which are the core of your data, so it's important to think very carefully about them. Table 10.1 offers more guidelines for preparing qualitative interview questions.

How a question is worded can influence how it's answered, so framing questions with care is very important. You can add extra questions that are similar to the main questions in your schedule to check for reliability (Berg, 1998). However, be careful not to overdo this because participants may become annoyed if they think that you are repeating questions; they may think you are not listening or did not like their initial answers.

Different approaches can be used regarding the main questions' placement in the interview. You can put them all together or intersperse them with other questions. One rule of thumb is to avoid placing the main questions in the beginning of the interview. Imagine if you started an interview by asking a sex worker: "How do you make sure that nothing bad happens while you are at work?" It is customary to not begin an interview with emotionally loaded questions. The main questions should come after some level of comfort between you and the participant is established. If necessary, you can use throw-away questions about demographics or less threatening topics to establish rapport at the beginning of an interview (Berg, 1998).

Probes

Probes are important tools for qualitative interviewing, because they prompt participants to elaborate on responses by filling in more detail and therefore depth. Another important purpose of probes is to signal participants that you are actively listening. For example, in the interview

TABLE 10.1 The Nitty-Gritty of Writing Questions

Problems to Avoid		Elements of a Good Question	
Double-barreled questions	These questions simultaneously ask the participant two questions.	**Clear**	Your questions should be very easy to understand.
	Example: How many times have you had sex, and did you use a condom?		*Example: How many times have you had sex? How many of these times did you use a condom?*
Complex questions	Questions that are involved and long should be avoided because the participant may forget part of the question or become annoyed.	**Concise**	Your questions should be short and to the point.
	Example: Once you joined the gang, did you feel that you underwent a transformation where you felt differently from how you felt before you became a gang member?		*Example: After joining the gang, did you feel any differently?*
		Appropriate language level	Language level may vary depending on the participants. Generally, language level should be simple.
Difficult language	Language level should never be overly difficult.		
	Example: Whilst engaging in trysts, did you ever use brute physical force?		*Example: Have you ever hit, punched, or badly hurt someone during casual sex?*
Affective words	Be cautious about using emotional words.	**More neutral words**	When your questions involve sensitive subject matter, use words that are not as emotionally loaded.
	Example: Have you ever beaten someone so badly they were hospitalized?		*Example: Have you ever hurt someone seriously in a fight?*

of sex workers, note the built-in probe at the end of the following question (italicized): "Can you tell me about any problems that you've had with people while you are at work? *Can you tell me a little more about this?*" The built-in probe following this question helps gently prompt participants to reveal sensitive information. However, if the respondent gives a detailed response to the question, then the probe may not be necessary. When you create your interview schedule, it is important to have built-in probes in case you have reluctant or quiet participants.

Think for a moment about how we use probes in regular conversations. If a friend starts telling you some gossip, you might use an *attention probe*, such as leaning in, to signal that you are interested in the information. Or maybe you use a *continuation probe*, such as nod, that acts as another gesture to elaborate. If part of the story is not clear, you might use a *clarification probe*. This type of probe is used when we don't understand something someone says. Probes are standard in regular everyday conversations, and they are essential tools for qualitative interviews.

Follow-up questions are a type of probe that you can use during the initial interview or in a second interview. You may recognize that a theme is emerging after interviews with different participants, and you may want more elaboration. Suppose that one participant in your study of sex workers talks about a client who regularly beats up workers. Maybe the second or third time that you hear this same story, you ask the participant if she has talked with other sex workers about keeping an eye on this client. It may not have occurred to you to ask this during the first interview, or it may have occurred to you near the end of the interview. This may become an important point of inquiry about how sex workers try to protect each other against predatory clients. These follow-ups can occur spontaneously, or even in a second interview. You can add follow-up questions that emerge to your interview schedule. Such flexibility is one of the strengths of qualitative interviewing. If you have recognized an important theme, such as that some sex workers unify and help each other with specific safety issues, you may want to explore that theme further.

Gaining Access to Participants

Arranging access to subjects depends on their role in organizations or subcultures.

Research in criminology can involve participants from various formal organizations, participants who are active offenders, or people involved in a variety of subcultures. In planning qualitative interviews, it's important to think carefully about your role vis-à-vis participants.

Establishing Your Role

One of the first considerations is **insider/outsider status** relative to the group that you want to study. Your level of insiderness depends on how close you are to the group. The more connected you are to the group, the more of an insider you are. Suppose that you want to study the subculture of drug dealers. You could credibly play more of an insider role if you used to sell drugs or have friends who are drug dealers. There are advantages and disadvantages to being an insider. Familiarity with your participants' lives allows you to delve deeply into topics without having to learn the subculture and its associated jargon (Ely et al., 1991). However, as an insider, you may be too close to participants and, therefore, the topics discussed. Biases can result because you already have rooted ideas about the subculture. No consensus exists about whether it is better to be an insider or an outsider, but your role will undoubtedly influence your access to the group and how you conduct your research more generally.

You may already be part of the group of interest, as Dina Perrone (2009) became accepted by the "club kids." With insider status, you can exploit your own experience to gain access because you may know a few people from the group. Or you may at least know enough about some group members to gain access more easily. An example of this is what's referred to as "convict criminology," where people who were formerly incarcerated study aspects of incarceration or prisoner reentry. Other researchers insert themselves into the lives of the group of interest—as exhibited in Jeff Ferrell's (2002) work on graffiti artists, where he engaged in spray painting, drinking, and general socializing with participants. Some researchers are already insiders, whereas others insert themselves into the lives of participants to attain quasi-insider status.

Criminal justice researchers are more commonly outsiders, having no existing connection to the group of interest. In such cases, researchers have to navigate access to participants. Your group of interest influences the way that you gain access. You can use formal channels to gain access if your group is affiliated with an organization or institution. For example, if your subjects are in a treatment program, incarcerated, or part of a police department, then you will probably have to gain access through the institution. But if you are interested in people who are engaged in criminal lifestyles, you may need to find informal access—for example, through sponsorship (gaining the trust of someone on the inside who will vouch for you and introduce you to members of the group). Both formal and informal access usually involve negotiation.

Gaining Access to Formal Organizations

Suppose you decide to conduct research on a community corrections agency in a large city. Let's assume that you do not know a great deal about the agency and that you will identify yourself as an outside researcher to staff and other people you encounter. Your research interests are primarily descriptive; you want to observe the routine operations of the agency in the office and elsewhere. In addition, you want to interview agency staff and persons who are serving community corrections sentences. This section will discuss some of the ways you might prepare before you conduct your interviews and direct observations.

Normally, a formal request and approval are required for research on a criminal justice institution, or on persons who work either in or under the supervision of an institution. One of the first steps in preparing for the field, then, is to arrange access to the community corrections agency.

Obtaining initial approval can be confusing and frustrating. Many criminal justice agencies in large cities have a complex organization, combining a formal hierarchy with a bewildering variety of informal organizational cultures. Criminal courts are highly structured organizations in which a presiding judge may oversee court assignments and case scheduling for judges and many support personnel. At the same time, courts are chaotic organizations in which three constellations of professionals—prosecutors, defense attorneys, and judges—episodically interact to process large numbers of cases.

Continuing with the example of your research on community corrections, the best strategy in gaining access to virtually any formal criminal justice organization is to use a four-step procedure: sponsor, letter, phone call, and meeting. Our discussion of these steps assumes that you will begin your field research by interviewing the agency executive director and gaining that person's approval for subsequent interviews and observations.

Sponsor The first step is to find a sponsor—a person who is personally known to and respected by the executive director. Ideally, a sponsor will be able to advise you on a person to contact, that person's formal position in the organization, and their informal status, including their relationships with other key officials. Such advice can be important in helping you initiate contact with the right person while avoiding people who have bad reputations.

Finding the right sponsor is often the most important step in gaining access. It may require a couple of extra steps, because you might first need to ask a professor whether she or he knows someone. You could then contact that person (with the sponsorship of your professor) and ask for further assistance. For purposes of illustration, we will assume that your professor is knowledgeable, well connected, and happy to act as your sponsor.

Letter Next, write a letter to the executive director. Your letter should have three parts: introduction, brief statement of your research purpose, and action request. See Figure 10.2 for an example. The introduction begins by naming your sponsor, thus immediately establishing your mutual acquaintance.

Next, you describe your research purpose succinctly. This is not the place to give a detailed

Jane Adams
Executive Director
Chaos County Community Corrections
Anxiety Falls, Colorado
1 May 2016

Dear Ms. Adams:

My colleague, Professor Marcus Nelson, suggested I contact you for assistance in my research on community corrections. I will be conducting a study of community corrections programs and wish to include the Chaos County agency in my research.

Briefly, I am interested in learning more about the different types of sentences that judges impose in jurisdictions with community corrections agencies. As you know, Colorado's community corrections statute grants considerable discretion to individual counties in arranging locally administered corrections programs. Because of this, it is generally believed that a wide variety of corrections programs and sentences have been developed throughout the state. My research seeks to learn more about these programs as a first step toward developing recommendations that may guide the development of programs in other states. I also wish to learn more about the routine administration of a community corrections program such as yours.

I would like to meet with you to discuss what programs Chaos County has developed, including current programs and those that were considered but not implemented. In addition, any information about different types of community corrections sentences that Chaos County judges impose would be very useful. Finally, I would appreciate your suggestions on further sources of information about community corrections programs in Chaos County and other areas.

I will call your office at about 10:00 a.m. on Monday, May 8, to arrange a meeting. If that time will not be convenient, or if you have any questions about my research, please contact me at the number below.

Thanks in advance for your help.

Sincerely,

Alfred Nobel
Research Assistant
Institute for Advanced Studies
(201) 555-1212

FIGURE 10.2 Sample Letter for Sponsor

description, as you would in a proposal. If possible, keep the description to one or two paragraphs, as shown in Figure 10.2. If a longer description is necessary to explain what you will be doing, you should *still* include only a brief description in your introductory letter, referring the reader to a separate attachment in which you summarize your research.

The action request describes what immediate role you are asking the contact person to play in your research. You may simply be requesting an interview, or you may want the person to help you gain access to other officials. Notice how the sample in Figure 10.2 mentions both an interview

and "suggestions on further sources of information about community corrections." In any case, you will usually want to arrange to meet or at least talk with the contact person. That leads to the third step.

Phone Call You probably already know that it can be difficult to arrange meetings with public officials (and often professors), or even to reach people by telephone. You can simplify this task by concluding your letter with a proposal for this step: arranging a phone call.

When you make the call, the executive director will have some idea of who you are and what you want. She will also have had the opportunity to contact your sponsor if she wants to verify any information in your introductory letter.

Even if you are not able to talk with the executive director personally, you will probably be able to talk to an assistant and make an appointment for a meeting (the next step). Again, this will be possible because your letter described what you eventually want—a meeting with the executive director—and established your legitimacy by naming a sponsor.

Meeting   The final step is meeting with or interviewing the contact person. Because you have used the letter–phone call–meeting procedure, the contact person may already have taken preliminary steps to help you. For example, because the letter in Figure 10.2 indicates that you wish to interview the executive director about different types of community corrections sentences, she may have assembled some procedures manuals or reports in preparation for your meeting.

This procedure generally works well in gaining initial access to public officials or other people who work in formal organizations. Once initial access is gained, it is up to the researcher to use interviewing skills and other techniques to elicit the desired information. This is not as difficult as it might seem to novice (or apprentice) researchers for a couple of reasons.

First, most people are at least a bit flattered that their work, ideas, and knowledge are of interest to a researcher. And researchers can take advantage of this with the right words of encouragement. Second, criminal justice professionals are often happy to talk about their work with a knowledgeable outsider. Police, probation officers, and corrections workers usually encounter only their colleagues and their clients on the job. Interactions with colleagues become routine and suffused with office politics, and interactions with clients are common sources of stress. Talking with an interested and knowledgeable researcher is often seen as a pleasant diversion.

By the same token, Richard Wright and Scott Decker (1994) report that most members of their sample of active burglars were both happy and flattered to discuss the craft of burglary. Because they were engaged in illegal activities, burglars had to be more circumspect about sharing their experiences,

unlike the way many people talk about events at work. As a result, burglars enjoyed the chance to describe their work to interested researchers who both promised confidentiality and treated them "as having expert knowledge normally unavailable to outsiders" (1994:26).

Gaining Access to Informal Organizations and Subcultures

Research by Wright and Decker (1994) illustrates how gaining access to subcultures—such as active offenders or juvenile gangs—in criminal justice requires tactics that differ in many respects from those used to meet with public officials. Letters, phone calls, and formal meetings are usually not appropriate for initiating field research among active offenders. However, the basic principle of using a sponsor to gain initial access operates in much the same way.

Sponsors in this case may be people whose job involves working with offenders, such as police, juvenile caseworkers, probation officers, attorneys, and counselors at drug clinics. Lawyers who specialize in criminal defense work can be especially useful sources of information about potential subjects. Frances Gant and Peter Grabosky (2001) contacted a private investigator to help locate car thieves and people working in auto-related businesses who were reputed to deal in stolen parts.

Wright and Decker (1994) were fortunate to encounter a former offender who was well connected with active criminals. The ex-offender helped researchers in two related ways. First, he referred them to other people, who in turn found active burglars willing to participate in the study. Second, he was well known and respected among burglars, and his sponsorship of the researchers made it possible for them to study a group of naturally suspicious subjects.

A different approach for gaining access to subcultures is to hang around places where criminals hang out. Wright and Decker rejected that strategy as a time-consuming and uncertain way to find burglars, in part because they were not sure where burglars hung out. In contrast, Bruce Jacobs (1999) initiated contact with street-level drug dealers by hanging around and being noticed in locations known for crack availability. Consider how this tactic might make sense for finding drug dealers, whose illegal work requires customers. In contrast, the offense of burglary is more secretive, and it's more difficult to imagine how one would find an area known for the presence of burglars.

Reviewing field research in several cities, Scott Jacques and Richard Wright (2008) offer general advice on recruiting active offenders. First, more informal social interaction between researchers, criminals, and informants increases the likelihood that offenders will participate. Second, it often helps to pay a small fee in gaining cooperation from offenders who are recruited through a chain of referrals. Third, they recommend that

> . . . criminals who are closest in relational distance to the researcher, especially those who have done previous interviews, are the ones most likely to produce the greatest amount of valid data and are thus the most appropriate persons with whom to discuss the most serious crimes. (Jacques and Wright, 2008:35)

As another example, review the description of gaining access to pimps in the opening vignette for this chapter.

Encouraging Participation

Compensation for access and participation is often required in studies where the researcher is an outsider. At the most basic level, you might compensate participants with payments, goods, or services. Another approach to compensation is to give your contact other stakes in the project. An example is coauthorship of a paper you might write. If your sponsor has more stakes in the project, then you may get richer data. Such arrangements are best established at the outset. Some researchers feel that, on principle, participants should always have a voice in the final product (Denzin, 1997). Member checks, where insiders can review your final product, are the best way to get this input. Participants read your work for incorrect interpretations of meanings and sometimes ask you to eliminate certain information.

Member checks will be discussed in more detail later in this chapter.

Another important question stems from the social roles of participants. Is your group advantaged, such as white-collar offenders, or disadvantaged, such as pimps? Both advantaged and disadvantaged groups tend to be more secretive, albeit for different reasons, and can be hard to reach as a result.

Reluctance to participate usually occurs when participants feel that the study can be a legal, economic, physical, or psychological threat (Adler and Adler, 2001). Participants who engage in illegal behavior, who are currently victims of violence, or who have powerful roles in the community may worry about some combination of these problems. Many qualitative interviews involve sensitive issues; in a sense, any questions about one's personal life are sensitive. It is often possible to allay participants' fears by being informal, carefully explaining confidentiality, and not rushing or pressuring participants into the interview.

Conducting Qualitative Interviews

By their nature, qualitative interviews are conducted in a variety of settings.

As when doing surveys, qualitative interviews can occur face to face, over the phone, or online. Face-to-face interviews are generally the norm. The quality of interaction between phone and face-to-face interviews differs because the former lacks the important social element of physicality. Think about the difference between talking to a friend on the phone versus meeting the friend in person. You may miss a lot of rich information over the phone, such as noticing that your friend is visibly upset when you bring up a certain topic. You might be able to hear this in your friend's voice, but it's usually more evident through a dynamic social exchange that includes nonverbal cues. Phone interviews may be useful for certain types of participants, such as those who live far away or are members of a group that is notably dangerous. Online surveys usually can have only a few open-ended questions. More importantly, self-administered questionnaires lack the interaction and flexibility of a conversation. Overall, interview formats are largely guided by overall research objectives and how you are able to gain access to the group.

Reflexivity

Reflexivity refers generally to your subjectivity in the research process. Recall that reality is constructed through a multiplicity of meanings. In qualitative interviewing, you are the instrument of data collection, which means that you are also involved in constructing meaning. Because you construct meaning based on communication with others, you essentially represent them through your interpretation of their stories. This sounds like a lot of responsibility, and it is. As a result, it's important to understand how to engage in reflexivity before and throughout the research process.

The process of self-reflexivity requires you to be critically conscious of who you are and your feelings. Wanda Pillow (2003) suggests that you should begin by asking yourself a few questions: "Who am I?" and "How do my feelings affect my research?" The first question includes your self-location across gender, race, class, sexuality, and ethnicity. Situating yourself within the larger social structure and being aware of your feelings influence how you relate to participants.

In the example of interviewing female sex workers in Los Angeles, your interviews will likely be influenced by your gender. If you are female, you may be able to identify with your participants about safety issues on a deeper level than if you are male. Even if you have never engaged in sex work, as a female you may have more experience worrying about safety. But over-identification can backfire, because sex workers may have very different conceptions of safety. You should think about how your position intersects with and is different from your participants. Your self-location, whether it involves difference, intersection, or insider status, can influence rapport with participants. If you choose to forego self-reflexivity, your interpretations can suffer from unchecked biases.

However, reflexivity may be overdone and can be viewed as indulgent or narcissistic if overused in the narrative interpretation. Even if reflexivity is not present in your final product, it is still important to be self-aware and keep track of how your feelings influence your research. You may opt for transparency about the process and decide to include how your assumptions shifted in the course of research. In the box "Pimps: Stereotypes, Biases, and Self-Reflexivity," I discuss how parts of this process emerged in my research with pimps.

Rapport

Once you have established access, you must think about your **rapport**, or how you connect with participants. The interaction between the interviewer and the participant is initially influenced by insider/outsider status. Initial rapport may be established through nonthreatening conversation, such as talking about the weather, current events, or anything that allows for informal banter. You can strengthen rapport by finding things that you have in common with participants. Some researchers share personal information about themselves as a way to connect with participants.

Some participants feel more comfortable talking about personal issues with strangers, because they do not have shared social networks and will probably never see each other again. People sometimes feel better about revealing information when there is an element of detachment (Adler and Adler, 2001). Other researchers feel it is important to establish genuine relationships with participants. Sometimes, having multiple conversations with participants yields the richest answers because a deeper level of rapport can be obtained.

Once an interview is underway, you can do a number of things to maintain the rapport necessary for a quality interview. In an article titled "The Great Interview: 25 Strategies for Studying People in Bed," Joseph Hermanowicz (2002) used a sexual metaphor to establish characteristics of a great interview. Some key advice about rapport was as follows:

- *Converse*, as opposed to engage in a mechanistic verbal exchange.

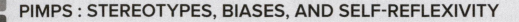

You may begin your research project with preexisting ideas or biases about your group of interest. When I decided to interview pimps, I read as much literature as I could find and also watched a number of films. Although I was not expecting to meet Super Fly, I expected some sort of stereotypical "pimp identity." Media and academic portrayals of pimps shaped some of my preconceptions about pimps until I started interviews. This is where an acute awareness of my subjectivity had to be kept in check, and self-reflexivity throughout the study was crucial to understanding my biases.

Stereotypes about pimps were elevated in the media in 1970s blaxploitation films such as *The Mack*, *Super Fly*, and *Willie Dynamite*, as well as more current movies such as *Hustle and Flow*. These renditions parody the pimp and portray him as flamboyant and comical, yet coldhearted. A few books around this time period—such as Iceburg Slim's semiautobiographical

book *Pimp, The Story of My Life* and Susan Hall's book about the life of Silky titled *Gentleman of Leisure*—also confirmed a lot of these media portrayals. Today, an Internet search for the keyword *pimp* shows that the meaning of the word has broadened. A search will yield quite an array of books and other items centered, for example, on how to coerce women, trick people, and make your car look outlandish.

Very few studies explore pimping from the perspective of a pimp. Many of the articles published focus on the role of the pimp as someone who is coercive, abusive, violent, and even psychopathic (Benoit and Millar, 2001; Greaves et al., 2004; Kennedy et al., 2007; Sanders, 2001; Silbert and Pines, 1981). Most of these inferences were gleaned from interviews with prostitutes or law enforcement and included very few conversations with pimps. The dearth of research and information on actual pimps is surprising and perpetuates our imaginings about pimps.

- *Listen*, or hear the data in the moment.
- *Find all that your date finds important*, or pay attention to meaning.
- *Probe*, or make sure that you get specifics.
- Sometimes *remain quiet* when your date is quiet.
- *Persist* with probes or other inquiries.
- *Play innocent* sometimes because participants may want to help you (don't overdo this because it may seem disingenuous).
- *Don't stay out all night; don't come home too early*, meaning pay attention to the length of the interview.
- *Word questions clearly*.
- *Sequence your moves* so that conversation has a good flow.
- *Be candid*.
- *Show respect*.
- *End on a positive note*.

Great interactions in an interview can be similar to great social exchanges in regular life. Of course, you do not need to take your participants home or become overly intimate with them. Instead, think about the basics of good conversations. Using your existing social abilities to help establish rapport and maintain it throughout the interview can be a great benefit to your research.

Active Interviewing

By this point, you should recognize that qualitative interviewing cannot be objective. A corollary is that dynamic social exchange should not be artificially limited. Active interviewing is a dynamic, two-sided social exchange that serves as a meaning-making context (Holstein and Gubrium, 1995). The social exchange that is the dialogue between you and the participant is what enables the creation of meaning.

A more recent shift in our conception of pimps comes from discourse about sex trafficking. There has been some blurring of sex trafficking and common sex work. Weitzer (2010) discussed this constructed link and referred to the State Department's website that proclaimed that "prostitution is inherently harmful" and that "legal prostitution creates a safe haven for criminals who traffic people into prostitution." With this imposed link between sex work and sex trafficking and the media spotlight on trafficking, the public's perception of pimps and traffickers is also confused. The public gaze is toward the ills of the commercial sex market and sex trafficking, which bolsters and expands our conceptions of the predatory pimp.

When I interviewed pimps, many of them were not sure if they were pimps, some took offense to the term, and a few thought they were pimps because they had sex with a lot of women. In the study by Marcus et al. (2012), which largely involved conversations with boyfriends or friends of sex workers in Atlantic City, we found that these people did not identify as pimps in any shape or form despite their technical qualifications as sex-market facilitators. This is not to say that none of the participants that I interviewed in Harlem embraced being a pimp along with some of the stereotypes, but that many of these portrayals were unfounded. There seemed to be confusion about the term pimp, and among sex-market facilitators, identification as a pimp was definitely not a given. Further, the idea that they could be sex traffickers was outrageous to them (some qualified under the federal Trafficking Victims Protection Act of 2000 because they were older than 18 and had sex workers who were age 17 in New York City or they occasionally traveled to New Jersey or other states with their workers).

At the start of a study, especially involving a group that is hard to reach and has a reputation via the media or academic world, you are bound to begin with some biases. Many of these biases will be dispelled through interaction, and some may be confirmed. I monitored my subjectivity throughout the study by memoing, or keeping a written record. It is important to engage in self-reflexivity throughout the study in order to address your biases and also to document changes in your feeling and thinking.

It's helpful to think of an active interview as collaboration between you and the participant. The boundaries of how you see things become visible through the collaborative interaction. This process is sometimes referred to as *horizons of meaning* because during active interviewing, the interpretive boundaries of you and your participants are discovered (Holstein and Gubrium, 1995). You and the participant may unwittingly push one another's boundaries, and the conflict between boundaries can also generate meaning.

For example, in her study on the narratives of alcoholics, Margaretha Järvinen (2000) analyzed three interviews where the interviewer's and participant's horizons of meaning were in conflict. The aim of the overall project was to talk to alcoholics about their treatment experiences. A few participants, despite their willingness to be in a study of long-term alcohol abusers, were in varying states of denial. For instance, Eric admitted to drinking over 30 beers a day, but the interviewer's interpretation of him as a long-term alcohol abuser clashed with his own self-image. Instead of viewing this as an unsuccessful interview, Järvinen realized that such narratives showed how people with alcohol problems have to negotiate their identities.

The active interview allows for natural conversation that enables spontaneity. You may have an interview guide, but how you use the guide will vary from one interview to the next, and on some occasions, it may be abandoned. For example, I try not to look at my interview schedule while conversing with participants. On my first field outing with pimps in Harlem, I interviewed a higher-level pimp near the end of the day. As the interview was coming to a close, I glanced down at my interview schedule to make sure that I didn't miss any questions. The participant stated, "Why you need to look at that? You have been interviewing pimps all day. You know what questions you want to ask me."

This was an important moment because I realized that some participants are offended when they realize that a conversation has been guided and, in fact, value the naturalness of a typical conversation.

In active interviews, the participant's responses determine which question comes next. They determine whether you are going to shift topic or probe about the same topic. This approach lends itself to a natural conversation where meaning is produced through dialogue, but the interview remains focused. Instead of forcing questions that are unnatural to the dialogue by switching topics, you are flexible.

In my study of New York City pimps, I asked participants early on in the interview to describe a typical workday. In the first example below, the participant brought up money. Instead of ignoring this, I asked some questions about prices, which were actually at the end of the interview guide. In the second example, the participant discussed getting his sex workers ready for work. I used some unscheduled probes to ask more about this. Both examples show that conversation with participants should flow as naturally as possible.

Example 1

Interviewer: *Tell me about a typical day at work.*

Participant: A typical day at work is um we get the clients set up with the girls and um they have to bring home the money to us and at the end of the day, we give them a certain percentage.

Interviewer: What percentage do you give them?

Participant: 10%.

Interviewer: 10%?

Participant: Yeah.

Interviewer: Ok. And what were you charging for stuff?

Participant: 50 dollars for sex.

Interviewer: For anything?

Participant: Yeah.

Example 2

Interviewer: And tell me about a typical day that you would have?

Participant: Well a typical day is getting up in the morning, getting them bitches out to get ready. That was a typical day. If you got a few of them, you gotta get their hair done. They gotta get their nails done. Cause you don't want to put a girl out there that's not attractive. So you gotta take them here to get their hair done.

Interviewer: So that happens early in the morning?

Participant: You try to get there at like 10 o'clock in the morning cause the beauty parlors be jammed if you taking in like 4 to 5 hoes, bitches. You gotta wait for all 4, 5 of them to get done.

Interviewer: So you get them all ready.

Participant: You get 'em all ready. Then you probably go out for breakfast. You know what I mean? Just try to soften the mood cause what you going into at night is very, it's very dangerous. It's exhilarating. It's dangerous. And you can get locked up for it too. So you try to . . . after they get theyselves together, you try to soften the mood cause they know what's coming. I mean you might like soften the mood, so you may take them to breakfast. Then we might just go into the car. Go riding some place. Just to get them out. Get it off their mind. Then you bring 'em back and put them on the track.

Interviewer: So it's like an all day preparation kind of thing.

Participant: All day preparation and not just for them, for yourself too. Cause you gotta get into that frame of mind before you put them out there at night because there's no telling what might happen to them. And whatever happens to them you got to be there.

The Interactive Interview

The active interview can be taken to another level where you are more purposefully interactive. The interactive or dramaturgical interview uses elements and language of theater akin to what Erving Goffman (1959) termed a *social performance*. Consider the idea that everyday social encounters involve some kind of performance, where people are social actors who take on certain roles. The interviewer and participant send and receive messages through nonverbal and verbal communication. Some of these messages are intentional, whereas others are unconscious. With the interactive interview, you must be highly attuned to social cues and your own reflections during the interview.

In an interactive interview, you are simultaneously the *actor*, the *director*, and the *choreographer* (Berg, 1998). As the actor, you must be attuned to your own lines but also respectful of the participant. As the director, you must be conscious of your performance and the participant's performance. Finally, as the choreographer, you must be insightful and constantly evaluating each move. Berg called for a highly self-conscious social performance, but this should not be confused with an entirely staged interaction. Instead of a stilted soap opera production that is overly dramatized, your performance will be similar to improvisational theater—where you are attentive to the moves of participants and yourself to draw out the richest performance.

Conducting Focus Group Interviews

If you are moderating a focus group, you have to embody all the skills of a good interviewer while navigating interactions among participants and generally monitoring the group. Among other things, you are in a balancing act where you must guide the group without being overly directive. In most focus groups, we are interested in spontaneity and the emergence of themes, but this can become difficult because conversations can veer off topic more easily. You must be aware of when you should rein in the group and when you should be silent to allow the flow of conversation among group members.

Planning and Design Considerations A number of design considerations are important in planning focus groups. The first is whether to have a homogenous (natural) or a heterogeneous (artificial) group. A group with existing connections among participants can yield richer information. They already have shared experience and perhaps shared cultural meaning. Second, you have to decide about the physical arrangement of the group. For example, you can put the group in a circle. This not only is more intimate, but also can reduce implied power differentials because no one is in a clear leadership position.

The next consideration is the length of the interview, which usually ranges from 90 minutes to two hours. Here's some rough guidance for a two-hour interview: 15 minutes for introductions and late arrivals, 15 minutes for explaining questions and plans for discussion summary, and 90 minutes of actual questioning and discussion (V. Rajah, personal communication, October 20, 2011). A final consideration is whether to have a natural, less-structured interview or a more formal interview schedule. The natural interview route allows for unscheduled probes, which work well in focus group settings.

Groupthink and Dominant Group Members Two factors to keep track of with respect to group dynamics are *groupthink* and *dominant group members*. Irving Janis (1972) coined the term *groupthink* to describe groups' need for harmony to minimize conflict and reach consensus. If a focus group is exhibiting groupthink, you may not hear opposing opinions, thereby missing alternative viewpoints. To tease out other group members' opinions, you may try probes and questions that are more provocative. A different problem is a dominant group member who takes over the group, perhaps silencing participants who are more reticent. If this is happening, you may direct your questions to people who have not spoken to see if you can change the dynamic. Groupthink and dominant group members occur naturally in any group.

Generating Data on Stigmatized Topics Collecting data from a focus group about sensitive or stigmatized topics such as sexual behaviors, drug use, or criminal activity requires a few special considerations. First, you must realize that your participants are being asked to disclose private information that can result in social censure or disapproval, something that can be upsetting to participants. The focus group format cannot ensure confidentiality, and participants should be aware of this. However, awareness about the lack of privacy may produce biased responses. Kaye Wellings, Patrick Branigan, and Kirsti Mitchell (2000:256) advocate using the focus group format "to reveal conflicts and contradictions between what is personal and private and what is public and open." In the case of sensitive topics, the focus group may be used to show how the collective verbally traverses personal and potentially stigmatizing information about themselves in conversation with others.

Recording Data

Several factors must be considered when recording data from qualitative interviews.

Qualitative interviews may be captured via audio or video recording, photographs, and mapping, supplemented by note taking. After completing interviews, researchers transcribe the dialogue verbatim or summarize it for analysis. Although technology provides you with tools to capture interactions with participants in context, recording or "logging" data is much more involved. A logging record includes transcribed interviews, notes during interviews (you should take some notes even if you are audio recording), field notes, and memoing. As described by John Lofland and Lyn Lofland (1995:67), ". . . the logging record is, in a very real sense, the data." Although creating logging records can be tedious, the kinds of in-depth insights that can be gained from qualitative interviewing depend on the quality of the interview log.

After you return from interviewing, your next task is to write up your field notes. Field notes can include observations and descriptions of interview context, as well as the interview itself. Field notes should be written promptly, because the experience is fresh in your mind and you can record as much detail as possible. Your perceptions and emotions about interviewing experiences may seem so intense that you think that you will not forget anything; but inevitably, your impressions will change as you have more interactions with participants.

If you write about your fieldwork after a few days of work, you will lose nuances of your earlier experiences. Thus, it's important to write up field notes as soon as possible.

Even if other people transcribe interviews verbatim on your behalf, you still have to study each transcript. In any event, it is a good idea to transcribe a few interviews yourself because you may benefit from closely listening to the interview. You may find ways to improve your interview style and have the chance to hear the data closely. As a general rule of thumb, you should spend as much time studying the transcript as you did conducting the interview (Lofland and Lofland, 1995).

Memoing is a technique that involves writing about your research process from beginning to end. Memos allow you to explore decisions that you made as you conducted your research and are a window into your own subjectivity in the interview process. These documents are part of what's called an *audit trail*, or record (Birks, Chapman, and Francis, 2008; Bowen, 2008).

Melanie Birks, Ysanne Chapman, and Karen Francis (2008) describe three types of memos: *operational*, *coding*, and *analytic*. In operational memos, you write about the steps that you took at each stage in your research. Recalling the earlier discussion on reflexivity, memos are a great way to be self-reflexive and keep track of changes in your perception as your research progresses. Coding memos allow you to document the process of coding your data, and analytic memos provide a way for you to explore relationships in the data. These memos become part of your data log and enable you to make sense of your data more easily.

Qualitative projects can produce large data logs, and you may be wondering how you are going to keep track of all of this stuff. Specialized computer applications help organize and make sense of the data you gather. *ATLAS.ti* and *NVivo* are examples of research software that allow you to create memos and link related documents, which contribute to easier coding and analysis. For an example that compares different packages, see Kuş Saillard (2011). It's also possible to create your own system to organize data and notes with a variety of word-processing and other standard applications. Besides keeping meticulous field notes, listening to interviews, and memoing, you should create a system to organize and back up all of your data on separate disks or in the cloud.

Data Analysis and Making Claims

Analyzing nonnumerical data from qualitative interviews allows researchers to make and support claims about what they have found.

Now you have arrived at the point where you are going to analyze your data. The word *analyze* literally means to separate something into parts (Kvale, 1996). You engaged in a meaning-making process with participants, and you must attempt to capture this in your interpretations of the data. Your interviews are conversations that took place between two people, and therefore cannot be reduced to single meanings or a bunch of words. Your mode of description, **analysis**, and interpretation depends on your research objectives—but you should strive to retain richness in the data and uncover meaning in context.

Data Management and Reduction

Analysis usually begins with *data management* and *reduction*. You manage data through visual displays using tables, charts, and other forms of visual display. Data are also managed through various nonvisual techniques. Data reduction involves putting aside information that seems irrelevant (Miles, Huberman, and Saldaña, 2014).

Managing and reducing your data can feel daunting. Luckily, there are a few techniques during and after data collection that can help you focus in order to move deeper into your data.

Making Sense of Data: Thinking Units

Lofland and Lofland (1995) describe how you can use **thinking units** to sort out stories. Thinking units are a simple framework for making sense of all of the stories that emerge from qualitative interviews. You may already have solid categories because you started with a well-structured interpretive framework. However, if your study is less structured or if you who want to check over your data from a different perspective, then you might benefit by using thinking units. Here are examples of common thinking units that Lofland and Lofland suggest as points of departure:

Meanings	Groups
Practices	Organizations
Episodes	Settlements
Encounters	Social Worlds
Roles	Lifestyles

Relationships

Although these units may seem unstructured and vague, they are created this way so that they may apply to different kinds of studies. Your initial thinking units can be adapted to your own study, or these examples can be changed or scrapped altogether for a list more appropriate to your study. You can add a thinking unit entitled *Open* for surprises or confusion that may arise when sifting through the data (Ely et al., 1991). For instance, in your study on sex workers in Los Angeles, you could have thinking units as shown in Table 10.2.

Your thinking units will depend largely on the framework of your study. If you began with a narrow framework, then you will probably create your own thinking units as you go along. But if your study is largely exploratory, then you may use Lofland and Lofland's (1995) suggested thinking units or some modification of them.

Another way to consider thinking units is in their role as **sensitizing concepts**. Sensitizing concepts are general references and guides about what you are looking for (Blumer, 1954). To illustrate, Glenn Bowen (2008) conducted an exploratory study on antipoverty projects in Jamaica that were created to improve social services and community-based organizations. After reviewing the literature, he decided to apply the sensitizing concepts of *citizen participation, social*

TABLE 10.2   Thinking Units

Topic: Sex Workers and Safety

Thinking Units	Topical Areas for Coding Based on Thinking Units
Meanings	How is safety conceptualized by sex workers?
Practices	What practices did they use to ensure safety?
Episodes	Describe periods where they felt things were particularly safe or unsafe (dangerous).
Encounters	What were specific encounters where they felt safe or unsafe (in danger)?
Roles	What were the roles of the players during safe or unsafe situations?
Relationships	What were their relationships to the people involved in safe or unsafe situations?
Groups	What roles did groups or social networks play in these safe or unsafe situations?
Settlements	How did the community negotiate safe or unsafe situations?
Social Worlds	How did their social world or the larger commercial sex market play a role in safety?
Lifestyles	In what ways does this lifestyle increase or decrease safety?
Open	

capital, and *empowerment,* which served as the seeds for theory formulation. It is beneficial to approach your study with some kind of framework for theory generation either through thinking units or sensitizing concepts. It's even better if these predetermined thinking units or sensitizing concepts may already be evident in your interview guide.

Grounded Theory

Recall from Chapter 2 that **grounded theory** stems from an analysis of patterns, themes, and common categories discovered in data. Often developed through qualitative interviewing, grounded theory combines a naturalist approach with a positivist concern for a systematic set of procedures.

According to Anselm Strauss and Juliet Corbin (1994), grounded theory evolves during the actual research, through continuous interplay between analysis and data collection. Grounded theory is a comparative method where you are engaged in constant comparison that is looking for similarities and differences to establish themes. The process is iterative and requires that you collect, code, and analyze your data. This process reveals themes that may ultimately generate theory.

For example, *theoretical sampling,* one of the adaptive sampling techniques discussed in Chapter 8, is part of this theory-generating process. Suppose that in your study on sex workers in Los Angeles, you realize that young sex workers are more apt to use technology such as texting and geographic tracking devices to ensure their safety on the job. As a result, you may decide to interview young sex workers in the hopes of fleshing out the theme of technology as it relates to safety.

Another dimension of generating grounded theory is *theoretical saturation,* the point where you feel that further interviewing will not yield new themes. As a result, you can conclude your qualitative interviewing (Strauss and Corbin, 2007). Unfortunately, little guidance is available to establish when theoretical saturation is achieved (Bowen, 2008). At its most basic form, saturation may be evident when you start to hear repeated or similar stories from the people you interview. You may reach a point where you can almost predict where the conversation is going. Theoretical saturation and theoretical sampling operate in tandem in the research process. For instance, you may begin to hear young sex workers describe the same techniques repeatedly, and you determine that you have reached theoretical saturation. You are not striving for representativeness, but rather adequacy in your development of themes (Bowen, 2008).

Identifying Codes and Themes

Coding information from your interviews assigns units of meaning to data. In a slightly different sense, coding creates categories for the variables that you will analyze. Coding thus involves the organization of raw data into conceptual categories, a process that should be familiar to you from our earlier examination of measurement. Each code is effectively a category into which a piece of data is placed. However, we need to consider a few important dimensions of coding.

First, you engage in a type of *open coding* or brainstorming where you explore all possible meanings before you apply conceptual labels to the data (Corbin and Strauss, 2007:160). For example, research on sex workers might begin with open coding of respondent comments about safety, and later classifying those comments into domains of safety—from johns, police, or predators. Open coding often begins by "chunking" small units of data in an exploratory fashion. You then look at each chunk and try to identify its *properties* and *dimensions*. What you learn from these chunks, or small units, will help direct your next stages in coding.

An alternative to open coding is *microanalysis* (Corbin and Strauss, 2007). For example, in the study on Muslim students who are monitored by law enforcement, your frame of reference was Howard Becker's labeling theory (Becker, 1963); but after looking more deeply at the data, you may see that the effects of labels have many different meanings. You may uncover other important concepts. By going deeper into the data and being open to challenge your original frame of reference, you generate new ideas.

The next step is to use the codes that you developed during the initial open coding or microanalysis to form categories. These codes are more abstract or conceptual. In grounded theory, this is referred to as *axial coding*. After these stages are complete, you engage in *selective coding* to look for patterns in the codes (Corbin and Strauss, 2007). You may begin to ask questions such as whether certain codes can be aggregated under a more general code, or whether you can organize codes sequentially. In addition, you may look for any causal relationships. Once you find yourself in this mode, you are not only becoming more analytical, but you are also starting to develop themes.

Coding often involves both lower-level and higher-level concepts. The higher-level concepts are referred to as **themes** that include a group of lower-level concepts usually produced from open coding (Corbin and Strauss, 2007). Alternatively, you can apply a conceptual name to a group of lower-level concepts that defines a higher-level theme. It's important to begin looking for lower-level concepts

after your first interview. For example, a new theme that you term "solidarity" may emerge from your discussions with Muslim students who have been monitored by police. You may notice that many students began to develop a stronger sense of identity, and this contributes to a theory about the process.

There are many ways to find concepts that become higher-level themes. Finding these concepts requires thinking about the mechanics of coding. Eight techniques for identifying themes are as follows: *similarities and differences, linguistic connectors, repetitions, indigenous typologies, metaphors and analogies, transitions, missing data,* and *theory-related material* (see Ryan and Bernard, 2003, for the full list of techniques).

Identifying *similarities* and *differences* is by far the most popular approach for finding themes, especially for grounded theory. This is generally associated with Barney Glaser and Anselm Strauss's (1967) constant comparison method. The constant comparison method can be used in a couple of different ways. One approach is to engage in a line-by-line analysis where you compare each line of text in an interview to the previous sentence for similarities or differences. Another compares pairs of expressions or longer chunks from the same or different participants. This method allows you to find themes within the data through various forms of comparison.

The next technique is *linguistic connectors*, in which interviews are examined for sentences that suggest causal or conditional relations. Examples of linguistic connectors that signal potential casual relations are words and phrases such as *because, as a result,* and *since* (Ryan and Bernard, 2003). For example, "I started sex work 'cause I needed to pay the rent." A similar type of connector reveals possible time-oriented relations or events where you look for words such as *before, after, then,* and *next*. For example, "After my first guy where nothing bad happened, I started to worry less about safety." Conditional relations connectors involve if - then pairs: "If I go out working with my pimp, then I feel more protected."

It's common to recognize the emergence of a theme in your interviews because you keep hearing something over and over. Even if you hear a concept repeating within a single interview, you can create code and see if it emerges in other interviews.

Repetitions occur when your participant(s) circles around the same kinds of ideas (Ryan and Bernard, 2003). Through coding the interview, you can understand when and how this theme arises in conversation and then see how important the theme is across interviews. The more often you see this concept, the more likely it is a theme.

Another way concepts are identified is by looking for unfamiliar, specialized words, referred to as *indigenous categories* by Michael Patton (2002:454). In your project about sex workers in Los Angeles, you might notice the word *stroll*, a term used to describe an outdoor place or set of street blocks where sex workers find customers. Maybe you recognize through noting the discourse around the word *stroll* that sex workers use this to define physical territory. In terms of safety, you recognize that sex workers describe feeling the safest from clients on the stroll because they are in their comfort zone. For some sex workers, their pimps monitor interactions on the stroll. Perhaps it is only when they go off of the stroll, such as when they get into a car, that their insecurities about safety are heightened.

Metaphors and *analogies* in speech can mark important concepts. In addition, *transitions*, or shifts in content, may signal a change in themes. These two connectors are more useful in unstructured interviews because transitions are less subject to control (Ryan and Bernard, 2003).

Missing data is a different type of connector, where you are alert for what participants do not mention. In your study on sex workers in Los Angeles, maybe most of your sex workers never mention having pimps. This would be unexpected and may prompt you to look for descriptions of relationships with friends or boyfriends. You then realize that although these people are playing the role of a pimp, sex workers think of them as close friends. By recognizing this missing information, you learned about how sex workers construct their interpersonal relationships with sex-market facilitators within this informal economy.

Finally, you should always look for how the data yield *theory-related material*. This may be driven by your understanding of existing theory or may be theory generating. If it is theory generating, James Spradley (1979:199) advises that you can look for:

. . . social conflict, cultural contradictions, informal methods of social control, things people do in managing impersonal social relationships, methods by which people acquire and maintain achieved and ascribed status, and information about how people solve problems.

This list is not exhaustive, but you may have noticed that the examples center on the *hows* of a situation or the processes, which is usually the source of generated theoretical models. You may notice a common theme that sex workers view local residents who are fixtures in the neighborhood around the stroll as a form of protection. Informal social control occurs because others who inhabit the same urban space actively reduce public acts of aggression or violence against sex workers. You may realize that your findings are consistent with Lawrence Cohen and Marcus Felson's (1979) routine activities theory, since local residents act as capable guardians. Social disorganization theory may also be evident, as this process demonstrates how neighborhood networks can reduce crime. As a result, you develop a deeper understanding of how these semipermanent networks monitor and protect those engaged in illicit work within urban space. You may expand upon these theories because you are exploring how capable guardians or networks offer crime prevention for those involved in illegal work. For an example of this process, see the article by Scott Jacques and Danielle Reynald (2012), "The Offenders' Perspective on Prevention."

Tools for Analysis and Interpretation

In qualitative interviewing, we are engaged at different levels of analysis throughout the research process as we discover themes in our data. Eventually we reach a stage where all of this must be transformed into an authoritative written account. Three different levels of presenting qualitative data are as follows: **qualitative description**, or letting the data speak for themselves with minimal commentary; *analysis*, in which we expand beyond a purely descriptive account; and **qualitative interpretation**, or moving beyond what can be explained with a degree of certainty (Wolcott, 1994:10). As you move further away from merely using the raw data as an account, you may notice that you move toward a more interpretive approach.

Some researchers produce a purely descriptive account, whereas others begin with description and move on to analysis and interpretation. Description, analysis, and interpretation are not mutually exclusive. They can all be used in your final authoritative account, but it is important to understand how they differ. We must be aware of which mode or modes we are using and understand the options for each.

In description, participants present their accounts mostly in their own words; some researchers feel this reduces or eliminates bias. However, researchers do choose which descriptions to present and which to exclude, which adds an element of researcher selectivity. When we choose descriptions, it's often best to strive for thick descriptions to avoid losing meaning.

A number of techniques are available to present your description. One example is a *day-in-the-life* approach, where you take your reader through a day of fieldwork. A variation on this is to show a day in the life of some of your participants. Understanding the everyday life of participants is an approachable type of analysis, because one thing that we all have in common is the 24-hour day. Another technique is to identify a *critical* or *key point* to describe activities of participants about pivotal events, such as how they started sex work. You may have heard of something called the *Rashomon Effect*, named after the 1950 Akira Kurosawa film in which a violent event is described from the perspective of four witnesses. This technique centers on telling different sides of a story and is useful if you have interviewed participants from different groups. If you interviewed sex workers, pimps, clients, and police to understand the complexities of the commercial sex market, then this technique can yield insights. Finally, you can follow an *analytic framework*, which adds structure—but in this case, you have to be careful not to force your descriptive material to fit the framework.

In more advanced-level analyses, we not only recognize patterns, but also give them meaning.

Instead of merely presenting a raw account, we strive to systematically display the meanings or shared meanings in the data. One common approach is to identify patterned regularities in the data. We do part of this when identifying themes, but in doing analysis, we assign meaning. Some researchers begin to quantify their findings at this stage, but in most cases, a deeper interpretation of these patterns is warranted in qualitative studies. If your study was guided by theory, you carefully discuss the interplay between these ideas and your actual findings. These are the more basic techniques involved in analysis.

Interpretation is distinguished from analysis because analysis is more systematic and deliberate, whereas interpretation is more speculative and casual (Wolcott, 1994:23). Interpretation is trickier, and it is important to be careful about how far to go in terms of speculation. Nonetheless, interpretations can be a notably refreshing portion of an authoritative account. This is where researchers connect their findings to the larger theoretical body of knowledge and discuss the *coulds*, *maybes*, and *possibilities* that stem from descriptions and analysis.

Several techniques are available for interpretation; Harry Wolcott (1994:40–45) presents an extensive list. The first is to move away from simplistic explanations and perhaps leave the reader with something to think about, or to *extend the analysis*. To illustrate, let's say you find that sex workers seem to feel safer when they have pimps, and you suggest the possibility that pimps are necessary to ensure sex workers' feelings of well-being. This deeper analysis may be somewhat surprising to readers who are accustomed to popular images of pimps as violent scoundrels. Second, you can link your study to relevant theory. For example, Jacques and Reynald (2012) describe how the protective routines of drug dealers are consistent with elements of opportunity theory. Next, you can tell readers what pieces of the puzzle you think are missing or offer alternative possible interpretations. Lastly, you can discuss your own feelings and beliefs or explore alternative formats. It's best to use several of these techniques for a more comprehensive interpretation.

Quality and Rigor in Analyzing Qualitative Interviewing

It is important to consider the reliability and validity of data from qualitative interviews.

There are a number of ways to enhance quality and rigor in interpretations of qualitative interviews. You already have an extensive log of data, including field notes and memos, and these make up your **audit trail**. The audit trail is not only a document of decisions, but important to enhance our confidence in the research (Bowen, 2008). This record is also a sign that your research is of a higher caliber. For situations that involve multiple interviewers, it's important to include some standardized questions to assure a level of consistency across the interviews. In situations where multiple coders are used, we can examine interrater reliability, as discussed in Chapter 5.

An important check used in grounded theory and in qualitative analysis involves looking for *negative cases*. These are cases that contradict emerging themes we have coded and ultimately, our theory. It's common for statistical analysis to eliminate outliers—but in qualitative research, these cases are helpful to check the viability of our emerging theory or to reveal unexpected aspects of the theory.

Another technique for checking our interpretations is the use of *member checks*. In this case, we would ask some of our participants to read draft descriptions to verify the accuracy of our work. This gives participants the chance to analyze the interpretation of their lived reality and provides the opportunity to correct any misinterpretations. Member checks are the best way to establish *truth-value*, or confidence in the truth of the findings in a particular context (Guba, 1981). By incorporating member checks into a design, we can boost the credibility or validity of our findings.

How we interpret consistency in stories, or *stability of results*, is different in qualitative studies because we accept the presence of multiple realities. Instead of interpreting inconsistency in stories as error, qualitative researchers view this as a shift in participant insight. This does not mean we assume all participants are telling the unvarnished truth. Instead, we expect that how participants construct and reconstruct their stories is consistent with multiple interpretations.

Transferability occurs when working hypotheses can be transferred from one context to another (Guba, 1981). Thick description in both contexts is necessary to establish transferability. Qualitative studies are difficult to replicate, and claims about generalizability are tempered because we rarely use representative samples of sufficient size. However, it is common for findings to translate from one setting to another. For instance, you may find that the safety issues discussed by sex workers in Los Angeles, California, are also present among sex workers in Rio de Janeiro, Brazil.

Finally, *neutrality*, rather than objectivity or intersubjective agreement, is commonly a feature of qualitative analysis. Neutrality can be assessed through member checks and transferability.

All of these techniques can be used to ensure that your study is trustworthy, and you can discuss your techniques in detail and depth. The more transparent you are about the research process, including your audit trail, the more your readers will trust and believe in your final product. The techniques that you use to ensure *trustworthiness* of the data and analysis should be known from the moment you decide to start your project. Think about some of the many steps that you take to deliver the best rendition of other peoples' lived experience.

Qualitative Interviewing Summarized

Qualitative interviewing is an interactive data-gathering process that requires thoughtfulness and attentiveness. The researcher is the instrument of data collection, yet in this role, the researcher is also engaged in human interaction. Although this chapter has given you tools to become a skilled qualitative interviewer, practice is the best way to perfect your ability to conduct great interviews.

High-caliber qualitative studies retain richness, recognize meanings and shared meanings, do not lose track of the context, and abide by rigorous standards of data collection and analysis. Many activities bring you to your final authoritative written account, including:

- Formulating questions
- Accessing participants
- Determining your role as an interviewer
- Interacting with participants
- Coding the data for themes
- Retaining the context of data you have collected
- Taking steps to enhance the quality of data

Although your data log will include numerous documents such as interview transcripts, field notes, and memos, you should be clear and precise in your decisions about how to organize and decipher your data. There are many approaches to coding qualitative data, with grounded theory the most popular. As you gain experience, you may think about trying other approaches. You may use some combination of description, analysis, and interpretation in your final write-up. Finally, you may experiment with different techniques to tell the most accurate and compelling rendition of your participants' lived experiences.

SUMMARY

- When you find yourself wondering about the "hows" involving human perspectives, emotions, or lifestyles, you are probably better off using qualitative interviews.
- The critical realist perspective assumes that multiple perspectives about reality exist, rather than a single tangible reality.
- Semi-structured interviews have standardized questions, but include unscheduled probes and spontaneous questions that enable us to explore emerging themes. Resembling natural conversation, unstructured interviews are best for exploratory studies.
- Focus groups involve interviewing groups of people and are best for examining dynamics between group members. The focus group moderator must guide the conversation and be aware of dominant group members and groupthink.
- We must think carefully about how questions are phrased and how they occur in our conversations.
- When conducting qualitative interviewing, it is important to think about whether you are an insider or outsider and how closely you are connected to your group of interest. This will shape how you gain access and how you establish rapport with participants.
- Active interviewing is a two-sided exchange that is dynamic and serves a meaning-making context.

Interactive interviewing also involves a meaning-making context.
- Recording data involves field notes, transcripts, memos, and written records of the research process. Research using qualitative interviews typically produces a large data log.
- Analysis or transforming data happens during and after data collection. Thinking units are important tools for guiding data collection.
- The three types of coding in grounded theory are open, axial, and selective. You start with open coding to find concepts in the data and may move on to selective coding, which involves combining multiple open codes and/or themes.
- Themes are higher-level concepts usually derived from the coding process. The most common way to find these concepts is through constant comparison of similarities and differences in the data to establish themes.
- Qualitative data can be analyzed through description, analysis, and interpretation. Description is closest to raw data, whereas interpretation is more speculative.
- The best way to ensure the quality of your data is to create an audit trail of all coding decisions. Member checks, using negative cases, transferability, and neutrality, are tools for improving data quality.

KEY TERMS

Analysis (p. 287)
Audit trail (p. 292)
Critical realist perspective (p. 268)
Focus groups (p. 272)
Grounded theory (p. 288)
Insider/outsider status (p. 276)
Interview schedule (p. 270)
Memoing (p. 286)
Qualitative description (p. 290)
Qualitative interpretation (p. 290)
Qualitative interview (p. 263)
Rapport (p. 281)
Reflexivity (p. 281)
Semi-structured interview (p. 270)
Sensitizing concepts (p. 287)
Structured interview (p. 270)
Themes (p. 289)
Thinking units (p. 287)
Unstructured interview (p. 271)

REVIEW QUESTIONS AND EXERCISES

1. Watch one of the following movie clips: http://www.youtube.com/watch?v=TQ4y7GPeFBY or http://www.youtube.com/watch?v=ymsHLkB8u3s.

Then write down the main points that you think are conveyed. Compare your interpretation to those of two or three other people in your class.

2. Select a research topic of interest and write an interview schedule; first use an interview guide and then use semi-structured questions. Be sure to include a few scheduled probes in your semi-structured interview schedule.

3. Interview one person using the two interview schedules created in question 2. Write a few paragraphs comparing the two approaches (unstructured and semi-structured). What were the advantages and disadvantages of each approach?

4. Write an operational memo about your self-reflexivity after your interview. Be sure to discuss your insider/outsider status and how this shaped some of your thoughts.

5. Create thinking units or sensitizing concepts about your research project. Then write a coding or analytic memo about your research project.

6. Using one or two interviews, code your data and identify themes. Discuss the process of how you identified themes for your research project. Describe how your themes shifted based on coding one versus two interviews.

CHAPTER 11

Field Observation

The techniques described in this chapter focus on observing life in its natural habitat—going where the action is and watching. We'll consider how to prepare for the field, how to observe, how to make records of what is observed, and how to recognize the relative strengths and weaknesses of field research.

Learning Objectives

1. Be able to describe field research as a data collection method that involves the direct observation of phenomena in their natural settings.

2. Recognize that field observation is usually the preferred data collection method for obtaining information about physical or social settings, behavior, and events.

3. Understand that field research in criminal justice may produce either qualitative or quantitative data.

4. Provide examples of how observations made through field research can be integrated with data collected through interviews and from other sources.

5. Understand why field researchers may or may not identify themselves as researchers to the people they are observing.

6. Recognize what sampling techniques are best suited for field research, and when they can be used.

7. Recognize the alternatives for recording field observations, ranging from video, audio, and other equipment to unstructured field notes.

8. Understand how field notes are taken, and be able to describe different ways to combine structure and flexibility in field notes.

9. Summarize how field research measures up on validity and reliability.

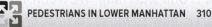
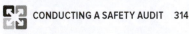

Seaport Operations and Stolen Vehicles

In earlier chapters, we described different elements of research on auto theft and parts-marking conducted by Michael Maxfield, colleague Ronald Clarke, and graduate students at Rutgers University. This research used data from a variety of sources, including fieldwork. Chapter 3 discussed some of the ethical issues faced in field observations of auto body shops. Here we describe fieldwork in an entirely different dimension of auto theft: the export of stolen vehicles through large seaports.

Clarke and Maxfield had learned that over 380,000 vehicles were shipped abroad from Port Newark in 2008. According to vehicle theft records, just under 1 percent of those, about 3,750, had been reported as stolen. For an additional 104,800 vehicles, some irregularity was found with vehicle identification numbers (VINs). So the researchers arranged to visit a large shipping terminal at Port Newark in New Jersey, one of the busiest seaports in the United States. Their general objective was to understand port and shipping operations in an effort to learn more about the export of stolen vehicles. Their role was as complete observers.

They toured the huge facility, a modern port that is exclusively engaged in container handling. A shipping container is basically a semi-truck trailer without its wheels. Thousands of containers move in and out of Port Newark each day, coming by train or truck. Observations began at a portal where all container trucks were weighed and documents were presented. Port and shipping company security staff explained how containers were processed. Incoming containers passed through the portal on their way to an outgoing ship. Outgoing containers had arrived by ship and were leaving the port by truck or train destined to other parts of the United States. In addition to weighing and checking documents, the process for outgoing containers included inspection to screen for contraband and dangerous materials.

Maxfield and Clarke were most interested in containers to be shipped outside of the United States. Cars to be exported were in containers when they arrived at the port; each container was large enough to hold up to three autos. Containers were shuttled around several acres, where they were stacked five containers high. Small trucks fetched the containers for loading on an outbound container ship. At one point, Maxfield and Clarke boarded a 950-foot ship from China to observe loading and unloading operations from the ship's bridge. Three crane towers worked the ship's length, simultaneously moving containers on and off the ship. This was quite a sight. The "round trip"—pick up load on ship pick up place on dock—took only about 90 seconds.

From one morning at the shipping terminal, coupled with qualitative interviews of security and other port staff, the researchers learned several things that appeared to facilitate the export of stolen vehicles through the port:

- An enormous number of containers moved in and out of the port.
- From 800 to 1,000 autos were shipped out each day. Some containers included a car with other types of goods; other containers included only two or three cars.
- Some stolen vehicles mixed with other cargo were not listed as contents of a container.
- Documents for outbound autos were inspected, but rarely compared to VIN numbers identifying individual cars, because
  - containers with cars were mixed with other containers and were difficult to access.
  - adding to their large number, containers were frequently moved around the shipping yard.
  - cars and other goods presented for outbound shipment were available for inspection for 72 hours before being loaded on a ship. But constraints on Immigration and Customs Enforcement staff meant that only a small fraction of containers could be inspected during this period.
  - new technology has been developed to "see" inside containers, much like the widely despised full-body scan technology at airports, but only one such machine was available and rarely used.
  - since the September 11 attacks on the United States, security officials have devoted extensive resources to screening cargo shipped into the country, which undermines the capacity to screen exports.

These are not conclusive findings. Instead, the observations helped Maxfield and Clarke develop tentative explanations for factors that contribute to the export of stolen vehicles. Without these observations, they could not have understood how the enormous scale of operations at the port offers cover for stolen cars commingled among the thousands of other containers handled each day at Port Newark.

You can get a tiny feel for what a modern port is like by typing "port Newark" into Google Earth or a mapping program. Scroll around and zoom in to see a forest of shipping containers. You might also be interested in Marc Levinson's book (2007) on the history of the shipping container. Among other things, Levinson points out how containerized cargo reduces many forms of cargo theft.

Introduction

Field research is often associated with qualitative techniques, although many other applications are possible.

We turn now to what may seem like the most obvious method of making observations: field research. If researchers want to know about something, why not simply go where it's happening and watch it happen?

Field research encompasses two different methods of obtaining data: (1) making direct observation and (2) asking questions. This chapter concentrates on observation, although you should keep in mind the discussion in Chapter 10 on qualitative interviewing, which often accompanies field observation.

Most of the observation methods discussed in this book are designed to produce data appropriate for statistical analysis. Surveys provide data to calculate things like the percentage of crime victims in a population or the mean value of property lost in burglaries. Field research may yield qualitative data—observations not easily reduced to numbers—in addition to quantitative data. For example, a field researcher who is studying burglars may note how many times subjects have been arrested (quantitative) as well as whether individual burglars tend to select certain types of targets (qualitative).

Qualitative field research is often a theory- or hypothesis-generating activity as well. In many types of field studies, researchers do not have precisely defined hypotheses to be tested. Field observation may be used to make sense out of an ongoing process that cannot be predicted in advance. This process involves making initial observations, developing tentative general conclusions that suggest further observations, making those observations, revising the prior conclusions, and so forth.

For example, Ross Homel, Steve Tomsen, and Jennifer Thommeny (1992) conducted field research on violence in bars in Sydney, Australia, and found that certain situations tended to trigger violent incidents. Subsequent studies in Australia and the United Kingdom tested a series of hypotheses about the links between certain situations and violence (Homel and Clark, 1994), and how interior design was related to aggression in dance clubs (Graham and Homel, 2008). Research by James Roberts (2007) expanded these findings by examining management and serving practices in New Jersey bars and clubs. These examples offer another illustration of grounded theory, which is commonly produced from field observations.

Field studies in criminal justice may also produce quantitative data that can be used to test hypotheses or evaluate policy innovations. Typically, qualitative exploratory observations help define the nature of some crime problem and suggest possible policy responses. Following the policy response, further observations are made to assess the policy's impact. For example, we briefly described the situational crime prevention approach in Chapter 2. The first and last of the five steps in a situational crime prevention project illustrate the dual uses of observation for problem definition and hypothesis testing (Clarke, 1997b):

1. Collect data about the nature and dimensions of the specific crime problem.

* * *

5. Monitor results and disseminate experience.

By now, especially if you have experience as a criminal justice professional, you may be thinking that field research is not much different from what police officers and many other people do every day—make observations in the field and ask people questions. Police may also collect data about particular crime problems, take action, and monitor results. So what's new here?

Compared with criminal justice professionals, researchers are more concerned with making generalizations and then using systematic field research techniques to support those generalizations. For example, consider the different goals and approaches used by two people who might observe shoplifters: a retail store security guard and a criminal justice researcher. The security guard wishes to capture a thief and prevent the loss of shop merchandise. Toward those ends, he or she adapts surveillance techniques to the behavior of a particular suspected shoplifter. The researcher's interests are different; perhaps she or he estimates the frequency of shoplifting, describes characteristics of shoplifters, or evaluates some specific measure to prevent shoplifting. In all likelihood, researchers use more standardized methods of observation aimed toward a generalized understanding.

In a sense, we all do field research whenever we observe or participate in social behavior and try to understand it—whether at a corner tavern, in a doctor's waiting room, or on an airplane. When we report our observations to others, we are reporting our field research efforts.

This chapter examines field research methods in some detail, providing a logical overview and suggesting specific skills and techniques that make scientific field research more useful than the casual observation we all engage in. As we cover the various applications and techniques of field research, it's useful to recall the distinction we made, way back in Chapter 1, between ordinary human inquiry and social scientific research. Field methods illustrate how the common observation techniques that we all use in ordinary inquiry can be deployed in systematic ways.

Topics Appropriate to Field Research

When conditions or behavior must be studied in natural settings, field research is usually the best approach.

One of the key strengths of field research is the comprehensive perspective it gives the researcher. This aspect of field research enhances its validity. By going directly to the phenomenon under study and observing it as completely as possible, we can develop a deeper and fuller understanding of it. This mode of observation, then, is especially (though not exclusively) appropriate to research topics that appear to defy simple quantification.

The field researcher may recognize nuances of attitude, behavior, and setting that escape researchers using other methods.

For example, Clifford Shearing and Phillip Stenning (1992:251) describe how Disney World employs subtle but pervasive mechanisms of informal social control that are largely invisible to millions of theme park visitors. It is difficult to imagine any technique other than direct observation that could produce these insights:

> Control strategies are embedded in both environmental features and structural relations. In both cases control structures and activities have other functions that are highlighted so that the control function is overshadowed. For example, virtually every pool, fountain, and flower garden serves both as an aesthetic object and to direct visitors away from, or towards, particular locations. Similarly, every Disney employee, while visibly and primarily engaged in other functions, is also engaged in the maintenance of order.

For another, grittier example of direct observations to understand conditions in field conditions, see the vignette "Seaport Operations and Stolen Vehicles," at the start of this chapter.

Many of the different uses of field observation in criminal justice research are nicely summarized by George McCall in his classic book, *Observing the Law* (1978). Comparing the three principal ways of collecting data—observing, asking questions, and consulting written records—McCall stated that observation is most appropriate for obtaining information about physical or social settings, behaviors, and events.

Observation is not the only way of getting data about settings, behaviors, and events. Information about the number of households on a block (setting) may be found in a city clerk's office; crime surveys routinely ask about victimization (events) and whether crimes were reported to police (behavior). However, in many circumstances, field observation is the preferred method.

Field research is especially appropriate for topics that can best be understood within their natural settings. Surveys may be able to measure behaviors and attitudes in somewhat artificial settings, but not all behavior is best measured this way. For example, field research is a superior method for studying how street-level drug dealers interpret behavioral and situational cues to distinguish potential customers, normal street traffic, and undercover police officers. It would be difficult to study these skills through a survey.

Field research on actual crimes involves obtaining information about events. McCall (1978) pointed out that observational studies of vice—such as prostitution and drug use—are much more common than observational studies of other crimes, largely because these behaviors depend at least in part on being visible and attracting customers. One notable exception is research on shoplifting. A classic study by Terry Baumer and Dennis Rosenbaum (1982) had two goals: (1) to estimate the incidence of shoplifting in a large department store and (2) to assess the effectiveness of different store security measures. Each objective required devising some measure of shoplifting, which Baumer and Rosenbaum obtained through direct observation. Samples of persons were followed by research staff from the time they entered the store until they left. Observers, posing as fellow shoppers, watched for any theft by the person they had been assigned to follow. We'll have more to say about this study later in the chapter.

Many aspects of physical settings are probably best studied through direct observation. The prevalence and patterns of gang graffiti in public places could not be reliably measured through surveys, unless the goal was to measure perceptions of graffiti. The work of Oscar Newman (1972, 1996), Ray Jeffery (1977), and Patricia and Paul Brantingham (Brantingham and Brantingham, 1991) on the relationship between crime and environmental design depends crucially on field observation of settings. If opportunities for crime vary by physical setting, then observation of the physical characteristics of a setting is required.

An evaluation of street lighting as a crime prevention tool in two areas of London illustrates how observation can be used to measure both physical settings and behavior. Kate Painter (1996) was interested in the relationships between street lighting, certain crime rates (measured by victim surveys), fear of crime, and nighttime mobility. Improvements in street lighting were made in selected streets; surveys of pedestrians and households in the affected areas were conducted before and after the lighting improvements. Survey questions included items about victimization, perceptions of crime problems and lighting quality, and reports about routine nighttime behavior in areas affected by the lighting.

Although the pretest and posttest survey items could have been used to assess changes in attitudes and behavior associated with improved lighting, field observations provided better measures of behavior. Painter conducted systematic counts of pedestrians in areas both before and after street lighting was enhanced. Observations like this are better measures of such behavior than are survey items, because people often have difficulty recalling routine actions such as how often they walk through some area after dark.

Painter's research also included provisions to observe physical settings. First, light levels (measured in lux units) were assessed in the experimental areas before and after changes in street lighting equipment. Second, interviewers who conducted household interviews made observations of physical settings in the areas around sampled households.

The Various Roles of the Observer

Field observer roles range from full participation to fully detached observation.

The term *field research* is broader and more inclusive than the common term **ethnography**, which focuses on detailed and accurate description rather than explanation. Field researchers need not always participate in what they are studying, although they usually will study it directly at the scene of the action. Catherine Marshall and Gretchen Rossman (2006:72) point out:

> The researcher may plan to have a role that entails varying degrees of "participantness"— that is, the degree of actual participation in

Ethnography   A report on social life that focuses on detailed and accurate description rather than explanation.

daily life. At one extreme is the full participant, who goes about ordinary life in a role or set of roles constructed in the setting. At the other extreme is the complete observer, who engages not at all in social interaction and may even shun involvement in the world being studied. And, of course, all possible complementary mixes along the continuum are available to the researcher.

The full participant, in this sense, may be a genuine participant in what he or she is studying (e.g., a participant in a demonstration against capital punishment), or at least pretend to be a genuine participant. In any event, if you are acting as a full participant, you let people see you only as a participant, not as a researcher.

That raises an ethical question: Is it ethical to deceive the people we are studying in the hope that they will confide in us as they would not confide in an identified researcher? Do the interests of science—the scientific values of the research—offset any ethical concerns?

Related to this ethical consideration is a scientific one. No researcher deceives his or her subjects solely for the purpose of deception. Rather, it is done in the belief that the data will be more valid and reliable, that the subjects will be more natural and honest if they do not know the researcher is doing a research project. If the people being studied know they are being studied, they might reject the researcher or modify their speech and behavior to appear more respectable than they would otherwise. In either case, the process being observed might radically change.

Alternatively, if we assume the role of complete participant, we may affect what we are studying. To play the role of participant, we must *participate*, yet our participation may affect the social process we are studying. Additional problems may emerge in any participant observation study of active criminals. Legal and physical risks, mentioned in Chapter 3, present obstacles to the complete participant in field research among active offenders or delinquents.

Finally, complete participation in field studies of criminal justice institutions is seldom possible. Although it is common for police officers to become criminal justice researchers, practical constraints on the official duties of police present major obstacles to simultaneously acting as researcher and police officer. Similarly, the responsibilities of judges, prosecutors, probation officers, and corrections workers normally are not compatible with collecting data for research. For a notable exception to this general rule, see the book *Cop in the Hood*, in which Peter Moskos describes how he became a sworn police officer in Baltimore in order to conduct field research for his dissertation (Moskos, 2009).

Because of these considerations—ethical, scientific, practical, and safety—field researchers most often choose a different role. The *participant-as-observer* participates with the group under study, but makes it clear that he or she is also undertaking research. For example, if someone has been convicted of some offense and placed on probation, that might present an opportunity to launch a study of probation officers.

Research by Alice Goffman (2014) offers an example of the complex forms such relations can take. She spent six years living in a distressed neighborhood in Philadelphia, sharing an apartment with young people living near or beyond the edge of the law. In particular, Goffman saw firsthand some of the effects of the government's "war on drugs." Young minorities in poor, urban neighborhoods have been common casualties in this war. Participant observation offered a way to see how the war on drugs was being fought on the ground. Though young, Goffman stood out in the neighborhood and had difficulty reconciling her roles as participant and observer (2014:239–240):

> Beyond being a fly on the wall, I wanted to be a participant observer. I wanted to live and work alongside Mike and his friends and neighbors so that I could understand their everyday worries and small triumphs from the inside. The method of participant observation involves cutting yourself off from your prior life and subjecting yourself as much as possible to the crap that people you want to know about are being subjected to. How do you do this when nobody treats you the same way? When you are a different color, and class, and gender?
>
> At a practical level, the divides between us made participant observation a confusing endeavor. Should I try to take on the attitudes and behaviors and routines of Mike and Chuck and their friends, though I was clearly not a man? Or should I instead try to take on the role of a woman associated with them?

McCall (1978) suggested that field researchers who study active offenders may comfortably occupy positions around the periphery of criminal activity. Acting as a participant in certain types of leisure activities, such as frequenting selected bars or dance clubs, may be appropriate roles. As Amber Horning mentioned in Chapter 10, this approach was used by Dina Perrone (2010) in her research on drug use in New York dance clubs. Furthermore, McCall described how making one's role as a researcher known to criminals and becoming known as a "right square" is more acceptable to subjects than an unsuccessful attempt to masquerade as a colleague. There are dangers in this role also, however. The people being studied may shift their attention to the research project, and the process being observed may no longer be typical. Conversely, a researcher may come to identify too much with the interests and viewpoints of the participants. This is referred to as "going native" and results in a loss of detachment necessary for social science.

The *observer-as-participant* is identified as a researcher and interacts with the participants in the course of their routine activities, but makes no pretense of actually being a participant. Many observational studies of police patrol are examples of this approach. Researchers typically accompany police officers on patrol, observing routine activities and interactions between police and citizens. Spending several hours in the company of a police officer also affords opportunities for unstructured interviewing.

Although the researcher's role in the eyes of police is exclusively observational, people with whom police come into contact may assume that an observer is actually a plainclothes officer. As a consequence, observation of citizens in their encounters with police tends to be less contaminated by the presence of a researcher than is observation of police themselves.

McCall (1978:88) noted that going native is a common tendency among fieldworkers, especially in observational studies of police. For example, observers may become more sympathetic toward officers' behavior and toward the views police express about the people they encounter. Observers may even actively assist officers on patrol. In either case, going native is often the product of the researcher's efforts to be accepted by police and the natural tendency of police to justify their actions to observers.

The *complete observer*, at the other extreme, observes some location or process without becoming a part of it in any way. The subjects of study might not even realize they are being studied because of the researcher's unobtrusiveness. An individual making observations while sitting in a courtroom is an example. Although the complete observer is less likely to affect what is being studied and less likely to go native than the complete participant, he or she may also be less able to develop a full appreciation of what is being studied. A courtroom observer, for example, witnesses only the public acts that take place in the courtroom, not private conferences between judges and attorneys.

McCall (1978:45) pointed out an interesting and often unnoticed trade-off between the role observers adopt and their ability to learn from what they see. If their role is covert (complete participation) or detached (complete observation), they are less able to ask questions to clarify what they observe. As complete participants, they take pains to conceal their observations and must exercise care in querying subjects. Similarly, complete observation means that it is generally not possible to interact with the persons or things being observed. That means it would not be possible to conduct qualitative interviews if one's role is complete observer.

Researchers have to think carefully about the trade-off. If it is most important that subjects not be affected by their role as observer, known as **reactivity**, then complete participation or observation is preferred. If being able to ask questions about what they observe is important, then some role that combines participation and observation is better.

More generally, the appropriate role for observers hinges on what they want to learn and how their inquiry is affected by opportunities and constraints. Different situations require different roles for researchers. Unfortunately, there are no clear guidelines for making this choice; field researchers rely on their understanding of the situation, their judgment, and their experience. In making a decision, researchers must be guided by both methodological and ethical considerations. Because these often conflict, deciding on the appropriate role may be difficult. Often, researchers find that their role limits the scope of their study.

Selecting Cases and Places for Observation

Different types of sampling techniques are adapted to selecting observation targets.

This brings us to the more general question of how to select cases for observation in field research. One common selection technique is snowball sampling. As we mentioned in Chapter 8, with snowball sampling, initial research subjects (or informants) identify other persons who might also become subjects, who in turn suggest more potential subjects, and so on. In this way, a group of subjects is accumulated through a series of referrals.

There are, of course, other ways of selecting subjects for observation. Chapter 8 discussed the more conventional techniques involved in probability sampling and the accompanying logic. Although the general principles of representativeness should be remembered in field research, controlled sampling techniques are often not possible.

As an illustration, consider the potential selection biases involved in a field study of deviants. Let's say we want to study a small number of drug dealers. We have a friend who works in the probation department of a large city who is willing to introduce us to people convicted of drug dealing and sentenced to probation. What selection problems might result from studying subjects identified in this way? How might our subjects not be representative of the general population of drug dealers? If we work our way backward from the chain of events that begins with a crime and ends with a criminal sentence, the answers should become clear.

Reactivity   Research subjects change their behavior as a reaction to being studied.

First, drug dealers sentenced to probation may be first-time offenders or persons convicted of dealing small amounts of "softer" drugs. Repeat offenders and "kingpin" cocaine dealers will not be in this group. Second, it is possible that people initially charged with drug dealing were convicted of simple possession through a plea bargain; because of our focus on people *convicted* of dealing, our selection procedure will miss this group as well. Finally, by selecting dealers who have been arrested and convicted, we may be gaining access only to those less skilled dealers who got caught. More skilled or experienced dealers may be less likely to be arrested in the first place; they may be different in important ways from the dealers we wish to study. Also, if dealers in street drug markets are more likely to be arrested than dealers who work through social networks of friends and acquaintances, a sample based on arrested dealers could be biased in more subtle ways.

To see why this raises an important issue in selecting cases for field research, let's again consider the sample of burglars studied by Richard Wright and Scott Decker (1994). Recall that their snowball sample began with an ex-offender whom they asked to lead them to active burglars (see Chapter 8). An alternative approach would be to select a probability or other sample of convicted burglars, perhaps in prison or on probation. But Wright and Decker rejected this strategy for sampling because of the possibility that they would overlook burglars who had not been caught. After accumulating their sample, the researchers were in a position to test this assumption by examining arrest records for their subjects. Only about one-fourth of the active burglars had ever been convicted of burglary; an additional one-third had been arrested for burglary but not convicted. More than 40 percent had no burglary arrests, and 8 percent had never been arrested for any offense (1994:12).

Putting all this together, Wright and Decker concluded that about three-fourths of their subjects would not have been eligible for inclusion if the researchers had based their sample on persons convicted of burglary. Little overlap existed between the population of active burglars and the population of convicted burglars. This means that studying convicted or even arrested burglars produces a highly selective sample of cases.

It's also possible to use probability sampling methods to select cases or places for observation. For an example, see the box by Shuryo Fujita, "Sampling Streets in Newark, New Jersey."

Purposive Sampling in Field Research

Sampling in field research tends to be more complicated than in other kinds of research. In many types of field studies, researchers attempt to observe everything within their field of study; thus, in a sense, they do not sample at all. In reality, of course, it is impossible to observe everything. To the extent that field researchers observe only a portion of what happens, then, what they do observe is a de facto sample of all possible observations. We can seldom select a controlled sample of such observations. But we can keep in mind the general principles of representativeness and interpret our observations accordingly.

The ability to systematically sample cases for observation depends on the degree of structure and predictability of the phenomenon being observed. This is more of a general guideline than a hard-and-fast rule. For example, the actions of youth gangs, burglars, and auto thieves are less structured and predictable than those of police officers. It is possible to select a probability sample of police officers for observation, because the behavior of police officers in a given city is structured and predictable in many dimensions. Because the population of active criminals is unknown, however, it is not possible to select a probability sample for observation.

This example should call to mind our discussion of sampling frames in Chapter 8. A roster of police officers and their assignments to patrol sectors and shifts could serve as a sampling frame for selecting subjects to observe. No such roster of gang members, burglars, and auto thieves is available. Criminal history records could serve as a sampling frame for selecting persons with previous arrests or convictions, subject to the problems of selectivity we have mentioned.

Now consider the case in which a sampling frame is less important than the regularity of a process. The regular, predictable passage of people on city sidewalks makes it possible to systematically select a sample of cases for observation. There is

SAMPLING STREETS IN NEWARK, NEW JERSEY

BY SHURYO FUJITA, Ph.D.
California State University at San Bernardino

My research on auto theft in Newark, New Jersey, used data from a variety of sources to study what sorts of environmental features of the city were related to the risk of car theft. The most useful data came from observations made on a sample of city streets.

I decided to use Google Street View to assess three measures of neighborhoods: litter, graffiti, and housing condition. Google Street View was also used to count the number of cars parked on sampled streets. After coding car make and approximate model year, I obtained a rough estimate of the number of cars at risk of theft because they were parked on city streets.

Because it was neither practical nor necessary to observe all streets in Newark, I developed a procedure to randomly sample street segments. The first step was to obtain a digital map of the city. Next, I created a grid of 300-by-300-foot cells, or squares, as an overlay to the digital map. That is, the grid of cells was digitally placed on top of the map. The cell size of 300 feet was chosen because the average block length in Newark is about 300 feet. Over one-fourth of Newark's land area includes unpopulated places, such as an international airport, a seaport, warehouse/industrial facilities, and city parks. I excluded these areas, ending up with a total of 4,291 cells.

Next, I selected a random probability sample of 200 cells using a statistical procedure in geographic information system software. The figure below shows the cell grid overlaid on Newark and the 200 randomly selected cells. The white areas are the unpopulated excluded parts of the city. You can see that the selected cells are distributed all over the city. This was important to my research to reduce possible bias from using too many places next to each other. I also wanted to include high-theft and low-theft areas. The random procedure made it possible to avoid both potential sources of bias, in which cells selected had a known, equal probability of being included in the sample.

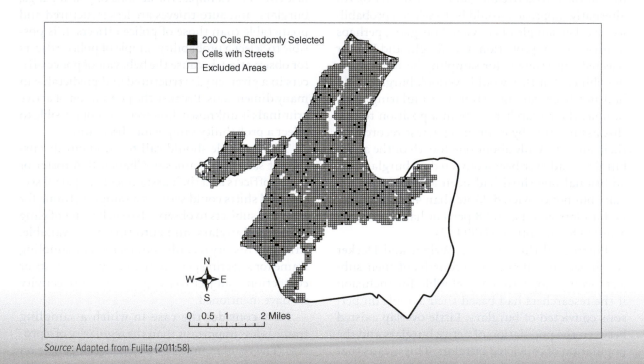

Source: Adapted from Fujita (2011:58).

no sampling frame of pedestrians, but the rhythms of daily life in cities are a process that can be used to reliably sample pedestrians for observation. See the box "Pedestrians in Lower Manhattan," later in this chapter, for an example.

We might also make observations at a number of different locations on different streets. We could pick the sample of locations through standard probability methods; or, more likely, we could use a rough quota system, observing wide streets and narrow ones, busy streets and quiet ones, or samples from different times of day. In a study of pedestrian traffic, we might also observe people in different types of urban neighborhoods—comparing residential and commercial areas, for example.

Michele Kipke and associates (1998) combined purposive and probability sampling techniques for finding street youths. First, places where street youth hung out were identified by observation and by interviewing young people using shelters. Then probability samples of individuals at those locations were selected by counting people who appeared to be ages 12–24 and randomly selecting subjects for interviews. An appendix to the authors' report presents samples of forms to record youth observed at different places and to sample subjects from different-size groups.

Table 11.1 summarizes different sampling dimensions that might be considered in time-space sampling for field research. The behavior of people, together with the characteristics of people and places, can vary by population group, location, time, and weather. We have already touched on the first two in this chapter; now we will briefly discuss how sampling plans might consider time and weather dimensions.

People tend to engage in more out-of-door activities in fair weather than in wet or snowy conditions. In northern cities, people are outside more when the weather is warm. Any study of outdoor activity should, therefore, consider the potential effects of variation in the weather. For example, in Painter's study of pedestrian traffic before and after improvements in street lighting, it was important to consider weather conditions during the times observations were made.

Behavior also varies by time, presented as micro- and macro-dimensions in Table 11.1. City streets in a central business district are busiest during

Table 11.1 Sampling Dimensions in Field Research

Sampling Dimension	Variation in
Population Space	Behavior and characteristics
	Behavior
	Physical characteristics of locations
Time, micro	Behavior by time of day, day of week
	Lighting by time of day
	Business, store, and entertainment activities by time of day, day of week
Time, macro	Behavior by season, holiday
	Entertainment by season, holiday
Weather	Behavior by weather

working hours; more people are in residential areas at other times. And, of course, people do different things on weekends than during the workweek. Seasonal variation, the macro time dimension, may also be important in criminal justice research. Daylight is longer in summer months, which affects the amount of time people spend outdoors. Shopping peaks from Thanksgiving to Christmas, increasing the number of shoppers, who along with their automobiles may become targets for thieves. Marcus Felson and associates (1996) describe variations in the rhythms of activity at New York's Port Authority bus terminal. Time of day, day of week, season, and weather affect the facility's use by bus passengers, transients, and a variety of offenders.

In practice, controlled probability sampling is seldom used in field research. Different types of purposive samples are much more common. Michael Patton (2002:230) describes a broad range of approaches to purposive sampling and offers a useful comparison of probability and purposive samples:

The logic and power of probability sampling derive from statistical probability theory. A random and statistically representative sample permits confident generalization from a sample to a larger population. . . . The logic and power of purposeful sampling lies in selecting *information-rich cases for* study in depth. (emphasis in original)

Nonetheless, if researchers understand the principles and logic of more formal sampling methods, they are likely to produce more effective purposive sampling in field research.

In field research, it is important to bear in mind questions that correspond to two stages of sampling. First, to what extent are the total situations available for observation representative of the more general class of phenomena we wish to describe and explain? (e.g., are the three juvenile gangs being observed representative of all gangs?) Second, are actual observations within those total situations representative of all the possible observations? (e.g., have we observed a representative sample of the members of the three gangs? Have we observed a representative sample of the interactions that took place?) Even when controlled probability sampling methods are impossible or inappropriate, the logical link between representativeness and generalizability still holds. Careful purposive sampling can produce observations that represent the phenomena of interest. However, we cannot make probabilistic statements of representativeness like those examined in Chapter 8.

Recording Observations

Many different methods are available for collecting and recording field observations.

Just as there is great variety in the types of field studies we might conduct, we have many options for making records of field observations. In conducting field interviews, for example, researchers almost certainly write notes of some kind, but they might also record interviews electronically. Video recording may be useful in field interviews to capture visual images of dress and body language. Photographs or videos can be used to make records of visual images, such as a block of apartment buildings before and after some physical design change or to serve as a pretest for an experimental neighborhood cleanup campaign. This technique was used by Robert Sampson and Stephen Raudenbush (1999) in connection with probability samples of city blocks in Chicago. Videotapes were made of

sampled blocks, and the recordings were then viewed to assess physical and social conditions in those areas.

We can think of a continuum of methods for recording observations. At one extreme is traditional field observation and note taking with pen and paper, such as we might use in field interviews. The opposite extreme includes various types of automated and remote measurement, such as videos, devices that count automobile traffic, or computer tabulations of mass transit users. In between is a host of methods that have many potential applications in criminal justice research.

Of course, the methods selected for recording observations are directly related to issues of measurement—especially how key concepts are operationalized. Thinking back to our discussion of measurement in Chapters 5 and 6, you should recognize why this is so. If, for example, we are interested in policies to increase nighttime pedestrian traffic in some city, we might want to know why people do or do not go out at night and how many people stroll around different neighborhoods. Interviews—in connection with field research or a survey—can determine people's reasons for going out or not; video recordings of passersby can provide simple counts. By the same token, a traffic-counting device can produce information about the number of automobiles that pass a particular point on the road, but it cannot measure what the blood alcohol levels of drivers are, whether riders are wearing seat belts, or how fast a vehicle is traveling.

Martin Kurti and associates (2012) were interested in learning about black-market cigarettes in the South Bronx, a low-income area in New York City. They could have conducted interviews with samples of smokers or cigarette dealers. Their novel approach used observations; they collected discarded cigarette packages for a sample of streets in the area, and examined tax stamps. They found that only 19 percent of the 497 collected packets bore stamps from New York, concluding that the illegal cigarette market was extensive.

Cameras and Sound Recorders

Video cameras may be used in public places to record relatively simple phenomena, such as the passage of people or automobiles, or more complex social processes. For several years, London police have monitored traffic conditions at dozens of key intersections using video cameras mounted on building rooftops. In fact, the *2017 Road Atlas for Britain* includes the locations of stationary video cameras on its maps. Since 2003, video cameras have monitored all traffic entering central London as part of an effort to reduce traffic. The license plates of vehicles that do not register paying a toll are recorded, and violation notices are sent to owners. Several studies have used images from speed and red-light cameras in the United States and other countries. Robert Eger and associates (2015) compared the appearance of race in photos from red-light cameras to the racial composition of areas near the cameras, finding that differences between the race of those stopped and people living in surrounding areas varied by county.

In an effort to develop ways to control aggressive panhandling in New York, George Kelling made videotapes of "squeegee people," who wipe the windshields of motorists stopped at intersections and then demand payment for their services. Kelling taped naturally occurring interactions between squeegee people and motorists, and he also staged contacts that involved plainclothes police in unmarked cars. The video recordings made it possible to study the specific tactics used by squeegee people to intimidate motorists and the motorists' reaction to unwanted windshield service (Kelling and Coles, 1996:141–143).

Still photographs may be appropriate to record some types of observations, such as graffiti or litter. Photos have the added benefit of preserving visual images that can later be viewed and coded by more than one person, thus facilitating interrater reliability checks. For example, if we are interested in studying pedestrian traffic on city streets, we might gather data about what types of people we see and how many there are. As the number and complexity of our observations increase, it becomes more difficult to reliably record how many males and females we see, how many adults and juveniles, and so on. Taking photographs of sampled areas will enable us to be more confident in our measurements and will also make it possible for another person to check on our interpretation of the photographs. Some digital cameras are equipped with global positioning devices that automatically record the location of photographs.

In an example of how technology advances offer new opportunities for data collection, Andrew Lemieux (2015) describes different applications of geo-tagged photos. One example combines records from closed-circuit TV (CCTV) cameras with geo-tagged images of graffiti in Amsterdam. He found that graffiti occurred disproportionately in areas with high concentrations of CCTV installations, reasoning the camera placement in areas with many bars and cafes attracted graffiti artists as well as nightlife patrons. An even more creative example is Lemieux's research on wildlife crime in Uganda (2014). Rangers patrolling in protected parks took geo-tagged photos when they encountered signs of poaching. Plotting these images on maps made it possible to identify points of access to parks and the routes poachers appeared to follow.

In addition to their use in interviews, audio recorders are useful for dictating observations. For example, a researcher interested in patterns of activity on urban streets can dictate observations while riding through selected areas in an automobile. It is possible to dictate observations in an unstructured manner, describing each street scene as it unfolds. Smart phones offer apps that make it possible to take time-stamped, geo-tagged photos that can be supplemented with a narrative description of what's shown in the image, or characteristics of the surrounding area.

Field Notes

Even video and audio recordings cannot capture all the relevant aspects of social processes. Most field researchers make some records of observations as written notes, perhaps in a field journal. Field notes should include both empirical observations and interpretations of them. They should record what we "know" we have observed and what we "think" we have observed. It is important, however, that these different kinds of notes be identified for what they are. For example, we might note that person X approached and handed something to person Y, a known drug dealer—that we think this was a drug transaction, and that we think person X was a new customer.

We can anticipate some of the most important observations before we begin the study; others will become apparent as our observations progress. Our note taking will be easier if we prepare standardized recording forms in advance. In a study of nighttime pedestrian traffic, for example, we might anticipate the characteristics of pedestrians who are most likely to be useful for analysis—age, gender, ethnicity, and so forth—and prepare a form on which the actual observations can easily be recorded. Or we might develop a symbolic shorthand in advance to speed up recording. In studying participation at a community crime prevention group meeting, we might want to construct a numbered grid of the different sections of the meeting room; then we could record the locations of participants easily, quickly, and accurately.

None of this advance preparation should limit recording of unanticipated events and aspects of the situation. Quite the contrary, the speedy handling of anticipated observations gives the researcher more freedom to observe the unanticipated.

Every student is familiar with the process of taking notes. Good note taking in field research requires more careful and deliberate attention and involves some specific skills. Three guidelines are particularly important.

First, don't trust your memory any more than you have to; it's unreliable. Even if you pride yourself on having a photographic memory, it's a good idea to take notes, either during the observation or as soon afterward as possible. If you are taking notes during the observation, do it unobtrusively; people are likely to behave differently if they see you writing down everything they say or do.

Second, it's usually a good idea to take notes in stages. In the first stage, you may need to take sketchy notes (words and phrases) to keep abreast of what's happening. Then remove yourself and rewrite your notes in more detail. If you do this soon after the events you've observed, the sketchy notes will help you recall most of the details. The longer you delay, the less likely you are to recall things accurately and fully. In his study of aggression in New Jersey nightclubs, James Roberts (2002, 2007) was reluctant to take any notes while inside clubs, so he went to his car to make sketchy notes about observations and then wrote them up in more detail later.

Third, you will inevitably wonder how much you should record. Is it really worth the effort to write out all the details you can recall right after the observation session? The basic answer is yes. In field research, you can't really be sure what's important and unimportant until you've had a chance to review and analyze a great volume of information, so you should record even things that don't seem important at the time. They may turn out to be significant after all. In addition, the act of recording the details of something "unimportant" may jog your memory on something that is important.

Structured Observations

Field notes may be recorded on highly structured forms in which observers mark items in much the same way a survey interviewer marks a closed-ended questionnaire. For example, Stephen Mastrofski and associates (1998:11) describe how police performance can be recorded on field observation questionnaires:

> Unlike ethnographic research, which relies heavily on the field researcher to make choices about what to observe and how to interpret it, the observer using [structured observation] is guided by . . . instruments designed by presumably experienced and knowledgeable police researchers.

Training for such efforts is extensive and time consuming. But Mastrofski and associates (1998) compared structured observation to closed-ended questions on a questionnaire. If researchers can anticipate in advance that observers will encounter a limited number of situations in the field, those situations can be recorded on structured observation forms. And, like closed-ended survey questions, structured observations have higher reliability.

In their evaluation of hot spots policing in Lowell, Massachusetts, Anthony Braga and Brenda Bond (2008: 587–588) used systematic social observation to assess the presence of social and physical disorder in experimental and control areas. Researchers took photographs from standardized points on each block. Photos were coded, then plotted on maps of study areas to show concentrations of disorder.

Because structured field observation forms often resemble survey questionnaires, their use benefits researchers by enabling them to generate

Date:_____ Day of week:_____ Time:_____

Observer:_____

Street name:_____

Cross streets:_____

1. Street width
   Number of drivable lanes   ____
   Number of parking lanes   ____
   Median present? (yes = 1, no = 2)   ____

2. Volume of traffic flow: (check one)
   a. very light   ____
   b. light   ____
   c. moderate   ____
   d. heavy   ____
   e. very heavy   ____

3. Number of street lights   ____

4. Number of broken street lights   ____

5. Number of abandoned automobiles   ____

6. List all the people on the block and their activities:

Males	Hanging out	Playing	Working	Walking	Other
Young (up to age 12)	____	____	____	____	____
Teens (13–19)	____	____	____	____	____
Adult (20–60)	____	____	____	____	____
Seniors (61+)	____	____	____	____	____
Females					
Young (up to age 12)	____	____	____	____	____
Teens (13–19)	____	____	____	____	____
Adult (20–60)	____	____	____	____	____
Seniors (61+)	____	____	____	____	____

FIGURE 11.1   Example of Environmental Survey

Source: Adapted from Bureau of Justice Assistance (1993:Appendix B).

numeric measures of conditions observed in the field. The Bureau of Justice Assistance (1993:43) has produced a handbook containing guidelines for conducting structured field observations, which are also called **environmental surveys**. The name is significant because observers record information about the conditions of a specified environment:

[Environmental] surveys seek to assess, as systematically and objectively as possible, the overall physical environment of an area. That physical environment comprises the buildings, parks, streets, transportation facilities, and overall landscaping of an area

as well as the functions and conditions of those entities.

Environmental surveys have come to be an important component of problem-oriented policing and situational crime prevention. For example, Figure 11.1 is adapted from an environmental survey form used by the Philadelphia Police

Environmental survey   Applies an observational instrument in a systematic way to record observed features of behavior or the environment.

Pedestrians are more numerous in New York than anywhere else in the United States. If you've visited the city, you would have certainly noticed the crowds of people on sidewalks in many areas. In fact, pedestrian flow and volume are as important in New York as vehicle traffic is in most other cities. For this reason, city officials commissioned the *New York City Pedestrian Level of Service Study* (Bloomberg and Burden, 2006).

In addition to counting pedestrians on different sidewalks in lower Manhattan, the study measured several other dimensions of pedestrian behavior. Here are examples of conceptual and operational definitions.

PEDESTRIAN LEVEL OF SERVICE (LOS)

Conceptual: Volume of pedestrians using a sidewalk segment. *Operational*: Count pedestrians who cross a point over a certain period of time (usually 15 minutes), reducing that figure to pedestrians per minute and then dividing by the effective width of the sidewalk. The resulting figure is called the flow rate. A planner may then look up the flow rate in a table to determine the pedestrian LOS grade, ranging from A (free flow) to F (virtually no movement possible) (Bloomberg and Burden, 2006:5).

TRIP PURPOSE

Conceptual: Reason for pedestrian trip. *Operational*:

- Score = 0 if you are not sure of the pedestrian's trip purpose. This is an extremely important characteristic, so never guess about someone's trip purpose; just indicate "0."

- Score = 1 if the person's primary purpose in the area is tourism. Some characteristics of tourists include casual clothing, visible camera, maps/guidebooks, and looking around.

- Score = 2 if the person's primary purpose in the area is work. This includes people who are going to work, coming from work, taking a lunch/shopping break from work, or actually working. Some signals of work include visible ID card, slightly more formal clothing, or a uniform.

- Score = 3 if the person's primary purpose in the area is nonwork but he or she is not a tourist. This includes people who are shopping or taking a recreational walk. It also includes people whose work entails casual activity: nannies and dog walkers, for example.

WALKING AIDE

Conceptual: Pedestrian using some assistive device. *Operational*:

- Score = 0 if someone is not using a walking aide.
- Score = 1 if someone is using crutches.
- Score = 2 if someone is riding in a wheelchair (that is being pushed by someone else or self-propelled).
- Score = 3 if someone is using a cane or a walker.

Though not directly a criminal justice example, you should recognize how our brief discussion of pedestrian level of service illustrates the many things that have to be considered in measurement. If you read through parts of the full Pedestrian LOS report, you will find more examples of operationalizing pedestrian behavior and the walking environment in New York.

Department in drug enforcement initiatives. Environmental surveys are conducted to plan police strategy in drug enforcement in small areas and to assess changes in conditions following targeted enforcement. Notice that the form can be used to record both information about physical conditions (street width, traffic volume, and streetlights) and counts of people and their activities.

Similar to interview surveys, environmental surveys require that observers be carefully trained in what to observe and how to interpret it. For example, the instructions that accompany the environmental survey excerpted in Figure 11.1 include guidance on coding abandoned automobiles:

> Count as abandoned if it appears nondrivable (i.e., has shattered windows, dismantled body parts, missing tires, missing license plates). Consider it abandoned if it appears that it has not been driven for some time and that it is not going to be for some time to come.

Other instructions provide details on how to count drivable lanes, what sorts of activities constitute "playing" and "working," how to estimate the ages of people observed, and so on.

See the box "Pedestrians in Lower Manhattan" for a good example of some of the challenges involved in conceptualizing and operationalizing structured observations of people walking on city streets.

Linking Field Observations and Other Data

Criminal justice research sometimes combines field research with surveys or data from official records.

Although criminal justice research may use field methods or sample surveys exclusively, a given project will often collect data from several sources. This is consistent with general advice about using appropriate measures and data collection methods. Simply saying "I am going to conduct an observational study of youth gangs" restricts the research focus at the outset to the kinds of information that can be gathered through observation. Such a study may be useful and interesting, but a researcher is better advised to consider what data collection methods are necessary in any particular study.

For example, in their Baltimore study, Ralph Taylor, Sally Shumaker, and Stephen Gottfredson (1985) were interested in the effects of neighborhood physical characteristics on residents' perceptions of crime problems. Collecting data on physical characteristics required field observation, but sample surveys were necessary for gathering data on perceptions. So Taylor and his associates conducted a survey of households in the neighborhoods where observations were made. Finally, they compared census data and crime reports from Baltimore police records with information from observations and household surveys.

These three sources of data provided different types of measures that, in combination, yielded a great deal of information about neighborhoods and neighborhood residents in the study sites. Surveys measured respondents' perceptions and beliefs about crime and other problems. Police records represented crimes reported to police by area residents. Field observations yielded data on physical characteristics and conditions of neighborhoods as rated by outside observers. Census data made it possible to control for the effects of socioeconomic status variables such as income, employment status, and housing tenure.

Finally, Taylor (1999) conducted follow-up field observations and interviews in 1994—13 years after initial data collection. He found that physical conditions had declined since the first series of observations in 1981, but that residents in selected neighborhoods did not perceive that conditions were worse. Thus, Taylor was able to compare changes in conditions observed by researchers in the field to what survey respondents reported to interviewers. The different methods of data collection yielded different results because they measured different dimensions of neighborhoods; field observations measured conditions, whereas surveys measured perceptions.

A long-term research project on community policing in Chicago similarly draws on data from surveys, field observation, and police records (Chicago Community Policing Evaluation Consortium, 2004). As just one example, researchers studied what sorts of activities and discussions emerged at community meetings in 130 of the city's 270 police beats that covered residential areas. Observers attended meetings, making detailed notes and completing structured observation forms. One section of the form (shown in Figure 11.2) instructed observers to make notes of specific types of neighborhood problems that were discussed at the meeting (Bennis, Skogan, and Steiner, 2003). Here is an

5. Location code (circle one)

1. Police station	7. Hospital
2. Park building	8. Public housing facility
3. Library	9. Private facility
4. Church	10. Restaurant
5. Bank	11. Other not-for-profit
6. Other government	

Count the house 30-minutes after the meeting. Exclude police in street clothes... and others that you can identify as non-residents.

8. _____ Total number residents attending

Note Problems Discussed

1. Drugs (include possibles)

___	___	Street sales or use
big	small	Building used for drugs
		Drug-related violence

9. Physical decay

___	___	Abandoned buildings
big	small	Run-down buildings
		Abandoned cars
		Graffiti and vandalism
		Illegal dumping

FIGURE 11.2 Excerpts from Chicago Beat Meeting Observation Form

Source: Adapted from Bennis, Skogan, and Steiner (2003:Appendix 1).

excerpt from the narrative notes that supplemented this section of the form:

> They ... had very serious concerns in regard to a dilapidated building in their block that was being used for drug sales. The drug seller's people were also squatting in the basement of the building. The main concern was that the four adults who were squatting also had three children under the age of four with them. (Chicago Community Policing Evaluation Consortium, 2004:37)

In addition, observers distributed questionnaires to community residents and police officers attending each meeting. Items asked how often people attended beat meetings, what sorts of other civic activities they pursued, and whether they thought various other issues were problems in their neighborhood. As an example, the combination of field observation data and survey questionnaires enabled researchers to assess the degree of general social activism among those who attended beat meetings.

Field research can also be conducted after a survey. For example, a survey designed to measure fear of crime and related concepts might ask respondents to specify any area near their residence that they believe is particularly dangerous. Follow-up field visits to the named areas could then be conducted, during which observers could record information about physical characteristics, land use, numbers of people present, and so forth.

The box titled "Conducting a Safety Audit" describes how structured field observations were combined with a focus group discussion to assess the scope of environmental design changes in Toronto, Canada. A **safety audit**, coupled with surveys or focus groups, is becoming more widely used to assess women's security in public places (Whitzman et al., 2009). Mangai Natarajan (2009) describes her research on sexual harassment of college women in India, known as "eve-teasing." Interviews with college students and police were followed by safety audits of specific areas around students' campuses.

The flexibility of field methods is one reason observation and field interviews can readily be incorporated into many research projects. And field observation often provides a much richer understanding of a phenomenon that is inferred imperfectly through a survey questionnaire.

In their study of home detention, Terry Baumer and Robert Mendelsohn (1990) supplemented interviews with persons sentenced to electronic monitoring by actually wearing the devices themselves for several days. Their participant observation enabled them to experience punitive features of home detention that would have been difficult to appreciate any other way.

Illustrations of Field Research

Examples illustrate different applications of field research to study shoplifting, traffic, and violence in bars.

Before concluding this chapter on field research, let's examine some illustrations of the method in action. These descriptions will provide a clearer sense of how researchers use field observations and interviews in criminal justice research.

Shoplifting

We have briefly mentioned the research on shoplifting by Baumer and Rosenbaum (1982). A fuller discussion of this unusual study illustrates much of the potential of field research, some problems that may be encountered, and the clever approaches to these problems adopted by Baumer and Rosenbaum.

This study was undertaken with two objectives: (1) to estimate the prevalence of shoplifting and (2) to assess the effectiveness of store security in identifying shoplifters. As we noted earlier, it is difficult to obtain reliable counts of offenses such as shoplifting and so-called victimless crimes. Shoplifting is usually counted only when store staff or security personnel witness an offense. Store inventory records could be used to estimate losses by customer theft, but as Baumer and Rosenbaum note, this obscures the difference between shoplifting by customers and employee theft. The approach they adopted was direct observation.

McCall (1978:20) described three difficulties in observational studies of crime. First, most offenses are relatively rare and unpredictable; an observer might spend weeks or months in the field without witnessing a single burglary, for example. Second, unless they are carefully concealed, field observers, by their very presence, are likely to deter criminals anxious to keep their actions from public view. Finally, there is some danger to fieldworkers who attentively observe crimes in progress while taking careful field notes.

Baumer and Rosenbaum reasoned that shoplifting is largely immune from these problems. First, because shoplifting by definition takes place only in certain specific locations, observers can focus their attention there. Baumer and Rosenbaum selected a large department store in downtown Chicago as the site of their research. The second and third problems mentioned by McCall are also largely absent because shoplifters commit their offenses in the presence of other shoppers; the crime is one of stealth, not confrontation. Fieldworkers could readily adopt the participant observation role of shopper with no more fear for their own safety than that experienced by other shoppers.

Field observers could, therefore, be used in much the same way undercover retail security workers are deployed in many stores: pose as a shopper and watch for thefts by other shoppers. When a theft is witnessed, that's shoplifting.

What about selecting subjects for observation? And how can simple counts of observed thefts be used to estimate the prevalence of shoplifting? "Shoplifting prevalence" was defined as the number of shoppers who stole something during their visit to the store divided by the total number of shoppers. This meant that it was necessary to obtain counts of shoppers as well as shoplifters. Because shopping is a predictable activity (if it were not, there would be no shops!), it is possible to use systematic sampling methods to select people to observe.

Baumer and Rosenbaum chose a variety of days and times to conduct observations. During these

CONDUCTING A SAFETY AUDIT

BY GISELA BICHLER
California State University at San Bernardino

A safety audit involves a careful inventory of specific environmental and situational factors that may contribute to feelings of discomfort, fear of victimization, or crime itself. The goal of a safety audit is to devise recommendations that will improve a specific area by reducing fear and crime.

Safety audits combine features of focus groups and structured field observations. To begin, the researcher assembles a small group of individuals (10 or fewer) considered to be vulnerable. Examples include: senior citizens, physically challenged individuals, young women who travel alone, students, youth, and parents with young children. Assembling diverse groups helps to identify a greater variety of environmental and situational factors for the particular area.

After explaining safety audit procedures, an audit leader then takes the group on a tour of the audit site. Since perceptions differ by time of day, at least two audits are conducted for each site—one during daylight and one after dark.

When touring audit sites, individuals do not speak to one another. The audit leader instructs group members to imagine that they are walking through the area alone. Each person is equipped with a structured form for documenting their observations and perceptions. Forms vary, depending on the group and site. In general, however, safety audit participants are instructed to document the following items:

1. Before walking through the area, briefly describe the type of space you are reviewing (e.g., a parking deck, park, shopping district). Record the number of entrances, general volume of users, design of structures, materials used in design, and type of lighting.
2. Complete the following while walking through the area.

General feelings of safety:

- Identify the places in which you feel unsafe and uncomfortable.
- What is it about each place that makes you feel this way?
- Identify the places in which you feel safe.
- What is it about each place that makes you feel this way?

General visibility:

- Can you see very far in front of you?
- Can you see behind you?
- Are there any structures or vegetation that restrict your sightlines?
- How dense are the trees/bushes?

---

times, observers and field supervisors were stationed at each department store entrance. Field supervisors counted everyone who entered the store, and assigned observers to follow selected individuals from the time they entered until they left. Subjects were selected by systematic sampling in which, say, every twentieth person who entered during the observation period was followed by a field observer. Dividing the number of thefts witnessed by the number of shoppers observed yielded an estimate of shoplifting prevalence. For instance, if observers were assigned to follow 500 people, and they witnessed thefts by 20 of them, the prevalence of shoplifting was 4 percent.

Counts of observed thefts also provided one way to assess store security. Comparing the number of thefts witnessed by participant observers to the number detected by store security staff was one obvious way to evaluate store security. Baumer and Rosenbaum devised another method, however, that solved a potential problem with their approach to counting shoplifting. The problem may have already occurred to you.

If you were an observer in this research, how confident would you be in your ability to detect shoplifting? Stated somewhat differently, how reliable would your observations be? Retail thieves are at least somewhat careful to conceal their crime.

- Are there any hiding spots or entrapment zones?
- Is the lighting adequate? Can you see the face of someone 15 meters in front of you?
- Are the paths/hallways open or are they very narrow?
- Are there any sharp corners (90° angles)?

Perceived control over the space:
- Could you see danger approaching with enough time to choose an alternative route?
- Are you visible to others on the street or in other buildings?
- Can you see any evidence of a security system?

Presence of others:
- Does the area seem to be deserted?
- Are there many women around?
- Are you alone in the presence of men?
- What do the other people seem to be doing?
- Are there any undesirables—vagrants (homeless or beggars), drunks, etc.?
- Do you see people who you know?
- Are there any police or security officers present?

General safety:
- Do you have access to a phone or other way of summoning help?
- What is your general perception of criminal behavior?
- Are there any places where you feel you could be attacked or confronted in an uncomfortable way?

Past experience in this space:
- Have you been harassed in this space?
- Have you heard of anyone who had a bad experience in this place (any legends or real experiences)?
- Is it likely that you may be harassed here (e.g., drunk young men coming out of the pub)?
- Have you noticed any social incivilities (minor deviant behavior—i.e., public drinking, vandalism, roughhousing, or skateboarding)?
- Is there much in the way of physical incivilities (broken windows, litter, broken bottles, vandalism)?

Following the site visit, the group finds a secure setting for a focused discussion of the various elements they identified. Harvesting observations about good and bad spaces helps to develop recommendations for physical improvement. Group members may also share perceptions and ideas about personal safety. This process should begin with a brain-storming discussion and finish with identifying the key issues of concern and most reasonable recommendations for addressing those issues.

This method of structured observation has proven to be invaluable. Much of the public space in Toronto including university campuses, public parks, transportation centers, and garages have been improved through such endeavors.

Source: Adapted from materials developed by the Metro Action Committee on Public Violence Against Women and Children (METRAC) (Toronto, Canada: METRAC, 1987). Used by permission.

As a participant observer, you would have to balance your diligence in watching people to whom you were assigned (observation) with care to not appear too interested in what your fellow shoppers were doing (participation).

Baumer and Rosenbaum used an ingenious adaptation of double-blind experimental methods (discussed in Chapter 7) to assess the reliability of field observers. Unknown to field observers, other research staff were employed as confederate shoplifters. Their job was to enter the store and steal something. Field supervisors, knowing when confederates would be entering the store, periodically instructed observers to follow one of these persons.

Confederates committed known thefts and made it possible to determine whether observers were able to detect the incident.

In this way, the researchers could measure the reliability of field observations. If an observer detected 85 percent of the known thefts, that observer's count of shoplifting by real shoppers could be considered 85 percent accurate. Reliability figures were used to adjust estimates of shoplifting prevalence. For example, if the prevalence estimate for all observers was 4 percent and all observers were 85 percent reliable, then the adjusted prevalence rate was 4.7 percent (0.04/0.85).

One of the lessons from this study is that simple observation is often not so simple. This is especially true when researchers are trying to observe people doing something they wish to conceal from observers. Our next example offers similar guidance in planning observations of people who are doing something required by law.

How Many People Wear Seat Belts?

Although nations in Europe and other parts of the world have required drivers to use seat belts for many years, laws mandating seat belt use were rare in the United States until the 1980s. Problems in enforcing such laws, as well as general resistance to regulation, are among the reasons these laws were late in coming. These concerns prompted interest in the degree of compliance with mandated seat belt use.

Indiana University's Transportation Research Center (TRC) conducted pilot studies in Indiana to develop methods of observing seat belt use. One of several research reports issued by TRC (Cornwell et al., 1989) illustrates sampling issues in field observations and offers a good example of why reliability is so important in field research.

The first decision faced by TRC researchers was how to conduct the observations. They opted for stationary observers posted at roadsides rather than mobile observers riding around in cars. The primary reason for this choice was the need to calculate the rates of seat belt use, expressed as the number of people seen to be wearing belts divided by the number of cars observed. Keeping track of the number of vehicles observed is easier when they can be counted as they pass by some stationary point. Trying to count cars in view while the observer is riding in a car is more difficult.

Where to place stationary observers was the next decision. Cornwell and associates describe how detecting seat belt use in moving vehicles is difficult. For this reason, most observers were stationed at controlled intersections—those with a stop sign or traffic light. Because interstate highways do not have intersections, other observers were posted at entrance ramps where cars were traveling more slowly.

Because it is impossible to know the number of autos in operation throughout Indiana at any given time, TRC researchers could not select a probability sample of vehicles to observe. Instead, they used systematic procedures to sample observations on three dimensions that might be associated with seat belt use: time of day, roadway type, and observation site. In addition to considerations about site type, Cornwell and colleagues wished to stratify sites by density of auto ownership. Finding that this was highly correlated with population, they divided Indiana counties into three strata based on population and selected sites within each stratum. Small counties were oversampled to ensure that different geographic areas of the state were represented.

Roadway type included interstate highways, U.S. and state roads, and local streets. Observations were made for each day of the week and at different times of day to represent the various trip purposes. For example, weekday observations at 6:30–7:30 A.M. represented blue-collar home-to-work trips, later morning times were for white-collar commuters, and midday hours represented lunch breaks.

Standing by the roadside and trying to determine whether drivers and front-seat passengers are wearing safety belts was easier than observing shoplifters, but still presented some difficulties. Cornwell and associates describe training procedures and steps taken to maximize the accuracy of observations. All observers completed a training period in which they worked under the supervision of an experienced fieldworker. If you had been a neophyte observer for the seat belt study, here are some of the things you would have been told about your role:

> "First, you realize, of course, that we are complete observers, not participant observers. We don't try to conceal ourselves because we would not be able to see the cars very well if we hid behind signs or something. Sure, drivers can see us standing here with our clipboards, and they may wonder what we're doing. We've posted a sign that says, 'Traffic Safety Research in Progress,' but there's no way they can know that we're checking seat belt use. So try to relax and don't feel self-conscious about standing on the side of the road in your orange vest watching cars.

"Second, remember that you should check only passenger cars and station wagons. Trucks, buses, recreational vehicles, and taxicabs are not covered by the law. Also, this is Indiana, not California, so you won't see too many older cars that don't have shoulder belts. Even if you do, don't try to observe them because they aren't covered by the law either. And remember, we're interested only in front-seat occupants; ignore the back seat.

"Most importantly, record only safety belts that you can see. If you see a belt in use, great; mark a Y for yes on the coding form. If you see a belt that is NOT in use, mark N for no. But if you can't see that someone is wearing a belt and you can't actually see a safety belt that the person is not wearing, mark a U for uncertain. I know you're a good observer; we're all good observers. But sometimes cars go by so fast that you can't see whether a person is wearing a belt. It happens to all of us. Just be sure you mark U when you're uncertain.

"Now, I have been doing this for about six months and I've learned some things that they didn't tell me when I started. We have run into some problems that nobody thought about when they first designed this study. For example, you're lucky to be starting in May, when the weather is good and the sun is up. In wintertime, people are wearing heavy coats, and it's much harder to tell whether they are wearing their safety belt. On cold mornings, the windows on cars can be fogged up, making it hard to see inside. Also, when I started working the 6:30–7:30 A.M. shift in January, it was still dark and we couldn't see anything. We had to revise the time-of-day sampling plan because of that.

"From our site here, we have four lanes of roadway to observe. Concentrate on the traffic lanes closest to us. You will be able to see the cars in those lanes better than you can see those in the far lanes. When traffic is stopped at the light it's not too bad, but when cars are moving you won't be able to observe everybody. Just remember, it's better to observe a smaller number of cars where you can confidently code Y or N than it is to try to see more cars but have to mark U because you can't be sure. There is no reason to expect that drivers in the far lanes will be any different than those in the near lanes. Code cars in all lanes when possible, but when in doubt focus on those closest to you."

The National Highway Traffic Safety Administration (NHTSA) now conducts observation studies of safety belt and motorcycle helmet use in most states. Timothy Pickrell and Ronald Li (2016) present tabulations for 2015, showing an all-time high of 88.7 percent use for passenger car occupants. For further details on how these observations were conducted, see the technical report by Donna Glassbrenner (2005), which also describes how observation procedures have evolved over the years.

Strengths and Weaknesses of Field Research

Validity is usually a strength of field research, but reliability and generalizability are sometimes weaknesses.

As we have seen, field research is especially effective for studying the subtle nuances of behavior and for examining processes over time. For these reasons, the chief strength of this method is the depth of understanding it permits.

Conducting field studies of behavior is often more appropriate than trying to measure behavior through surveys. Counts of seat belt use or theft by shoppers obtained through observation are not subject to the effects of social desirability that we might expect in survey questions about those behaviors.

Flexibility is another advantage of field research. Researchers can modify their research design at any time. In Dina Perrone's words: "I consistently reevaluated my methodology to ensure the highest level of credibility, dependability, and transferability of the data. Coding methods, sampling, observational techniques and [my] interview guide evolved with the research" (2009:37).

Most significantly, qualitative research is a superior method for studying active offenders in field settings. Combining qualitative interviews and observations combines offenders' perspectives and systematic measures collected by researchers. A growing body of research has provided rich detail on the motives of offenders, how they select targets, and what sorts of things they are attentive to as incidents unfold. Researchers have studied drug dealers, robbers, burglars, gang members, carjackers, sex workers, and individuals engaged in a variety of other offenses. Although it's possible to study arrested or convicted offenders in other settings, field research offers many advantages for learning about criminal activity that is untainted by official intervention.

By the same token, field research offers advantages for studying justice officials in natural settings. Scholars have long recognized that the view of police work through a car's windshield offers much richer information about police work than the statistical analysis of arrests or crime reports. Similarly, researchers have interviewed corrections officers for many studies. Ted Conover tried that approach, but was denied access to interview corrections workers in New York state prisons. So he became a corrections officer in New York and wrote up his experiences after working for two years in Sing Sing Correctional Facility. His book, *Newjack: Guarding Sing Sing*, provides insights into life on the job that are unobtainable through any other research method (Conover, 2000).

Field research can be relatively inexpensive. Other research methods may require costly equipment or a large research staff, but field research often can be undertaken by one researcher with a notebook and a pen. This is not to say that field research is never expensive. The shoplifting research, seat belt study, and race profiling research described in our running example, "Putting It All Together: Field Research on Speeding and Traffic Enforcement," required many trained observers. Expensive recording equipment may be needed, or the researcher may wish to travel to South Africa to replicate research by Andrew Lemieux and associates (2014).

Field research has its weaknesses, too. First, qualitative field studies seldom yield precise descriptive statements about a large population.

Observing casual discussions among corrections officers in a cafeteria, for example, does not yield trustworthy estimates about prison conditions. Nevertheless, it could provide important insights into some of the problems facing staff and inmates in a specific institution.

Second, field observation can produce systematic counts of behaviors and reasonable estimates for a large population of behaviors beyond those actually observed. However, because it is difficult to know the total population of given phenomena—shoppers or drivers, for example—precise probability samples normally cannot be drawn. In designing a quantitative field study or assessing the representativeness of some other study, researchers must think carefully about the density and predictability of what will be observed. Then they must decide whether sampling procedures are likely to tap representative instances of cases they will observe.

More generally, the advantages and disadvantages of different types of field studies can be considered in terms of their validity, reliability, and generalizability. As we have seen, validity and reliability are both qualities of measurements. *Validity* concerns whether measurements actually measure what they are supposed to. *Reliability* is a matter of dependability: If researchers make the same measurement again and again, will they get the same result? Note that some examples we described in this chapter included special steps to improve reliability. Finally, *generalizability* refers to whether specific research findings apply to people, places, and things not actually observed. Let's see how field research stacks up in these respects.

Validity

Survey measurements are sometimes criticized as superficial and weak on validity. Observational studies have the potential to yield measures that are more valid. With respect to qualitative field research, "being there" is a powerful technique for gaining insights into the nature of human affairs.

Recall from Chapter 9 our discussion of some limitations of using survey methods to study domestic violence. An alternative is a field study in which the researcher interacts at length with victims of domestic violence. The relative strengths of each approach are nicely illustrated in a pair of articles that examine domestic violence in England. Chapter 9 quoted from Catriona Mirrlees-Black's (1995) article on domestic violence as measured in the British Crime Survey. John Hood-Williams and Tracey Bush (1995) provide a different perspective through their study published in the same issue of the Home Office *Research Bulletin*.

Tracey Bush lived in a London public housing project (termed "housing estate" in England) for about five years. This enabled her to study domestic violence in a natural setting: "The views of men and women on the estate about relationships and domestic violence have been gathered through the researcher's network of friends, neighbours, acquaintances, and contacts" (Hood-Williams and Bush, 1995:11). Through long and patient fieldwork, Bush learned that women sometimes "normalize" low levels of violence, seeing it as an unfortunate but unavoidable consequence of their relationship with a male partner. When violence escalates, victims may blame themselves. Victims may also remain in an abusive relationship in hopes that things will get better:

> She reported that she wanted the companionship and respect that she had received at the beginning of the relationship. It was the earlier, nonviolent man, whom she had met and fallen in love with, that she wanted back. (Hood-Williams and Bush, 1995:13)

Mirrlees-Black (1995) notes that measuring domestic violence is "difficult territory" in part because women may not recognize assault by a partner as a crime. Field research such as that by Hood-Williams and Bush offers an example of this phenomenon and helps us understand why it exists.

Validity is a particular strength of field research. Measurements based on surveys or on simple counts of some phenomenon often give an incomplete picture of the fundamental concept of interest. Survey responses to questions about domestic violence victimization, however carefully phrased, are limited in their ability to count incidents that victims don't recognize as crimes. More importantly, survey methods cannot yield the rich understanding of domestic violence and its context that

Tracey Bush discovered in her five years of field research.

In field research, *validity* often refers to whether the intended meaning of the things observed or people interviewed has been captured accurately. In the case of interviews, Joseph Maxwell (2013) suggests getting feedback on the measures from the people being studied. For example, Wright and Decker (1994) conducted lengthy semistructured interviews with their sample of burglars. The researchers recognized that their limited understanding of the social context of burglary may have produced some errors in interpreting what they learned from subjects. To guard against this, Wright and Decker used member checks (as described in Chapter 10), having some of their subjects review what the researchers thought they had found:

> As the writing proceeded, we read various parts of the manuscript to selected members of our sample. This allowed us to check our interpretations against those of insiders and to enlist their help in reformulating passages they regarded as misleading or inaccurate. . . . The result of using this procedure, we believe, is a book that faithfully conveys the offender's perspective on the process of committing residential burglaries. (1994:33–34)

This approach is possible only if subjects are aware of the researcher's role as a researcher. In that case, having informants review draft field notes or interview transcripts can be an excellent strategy for improving validity.

Reliability

Qualitative field research can have a potential problem with reliability. Suppose you characterize your best friend's political orientation based on everything you know about him or her. There's certainly no question that your assessment of that person's politics is at least somewhat idiosyncratic. The measurement you arrive at will appear to have considerable validity. However, we can't be sure that someone else will characterize your friend's politics in the same way, even with the same amount of observation.

PUTTING IT ALL TOGETHER

Field Research on Speeding and Traffic Enforcement

Field research has been an important element in studies of racial profiling for two reasons. First, field research has provided measures of driver behavior that are not dependent on police records. As we have seen in earlier chapters, it is important to compare police records of stops to some other source of information. Second, field research has provided insights into traffic enforcement, an area of policing not much studied by researchers. Field research has also covered the wide range of applications from highly structured counting to less structured field observation and interviews.

FIELD MEASURES OF SPEED

Studies of racial profiling in three states used highly structured techniques to measure the speed of vehicles. The most sophisticated equipment was used by Lange and associates in New Jersey. Here's how the authors described their setup:

> The digital photographs were captured by TC-2000 camera system, integrated with an AutoPatrol PR-100 radar system, provided by Transcore, Inc. The equipment, other than two large strobe lights, was mounted inside an unmarked van, parked behind pre-existing guide rails along the Turnpike. The camera and radar sensor pointed out of the van's back window toward oncoming traffic. The two strobe lights were mounted on tripods behind the van and directed toward

on-coming traffic. Transcore's employees operated the equipment. (2005:202)

Equipment was programmed to photograph every vehicle exceeding the speed limit by 15 or more miles per hour. Operators also photographed and timed samples of 25–50 other vehicles per hour. Elsewhere we have described the other element of observation—coding the appearance of driver race from photographs.

Pennsylvania researchers also used radar to measure the speed of vehicles in selected locations throughout the state. Their procedures were less automated, relying on teams of two observers in a car parked on the side of sampled roadways. Undergraduate students at Pennsylvania State University served as observers. They were trained by Pennsylvania state police in the use of radar equipment, completing the same classroom training that was required of troopers. Additional training for observers was conducted on samples of roadways by the project director. State police were trained to operate radar equipment, but not to combine it with systematic field observation of driver characteristics. That was an important research task however. Engel et al. (2004) describe training and field procedures in detail. Their simple field observation form is included in an appendix to their report (p. 312).

Smith and associates (2003) tried but rejected stationary observation as a technique for recording speed and observing drivers. They cited the high speed of

Field research measurements—even in-depth measurements—are also often very personal. If, for example, you wished to conduct a field study of bars and clubs near your campus, you might judge levels of disorder on a Friday night to be low or moderate. In contrast, older adults might observe the same levels of noise and commotion and rate levels of disorder as intolerably high. How we interpret the phenomena we observe depends very much on our own experiences and preferences.

The reliability of quantitative field studies can be enhanced by careful attention to the details of observation. We have seen examples of this in studies of shoplifting and seat belt use. Likewise, environmental surveys can promote reliable observations by including detailed instructions on how to classify what is observed. Reviewing the products of field observations can strengthen reliability. In their study of violence in bars and nightclubs, Homel and Clark (1994) sought to increase the reliability of observers'

passing vehicles and glare from windows as problems they encountered. Instead, a research team used mobile observation techniques—observing drivers and timing cars that passed them. Radar was also considered and rejected because it was feared that vehicles having radar detectors, said to be common in North Carolina, would slow down when nearing the research vehicle. Worse, Smith and associates report that truck drivers quickly broadcast word of detected radar, thus eroding the planned unobtrusive measure.

As you can see, the observational component of research in these three states varied quite a lot. Reading the detailed reports from each study offers valuable insights into the kinds of things field researchers must consider.

OBSERVING NEW JERSEY STATE POLICE

Other research in New Jersey used less structured field observation techniques. This was because the research purpose was less structured—learning about the general nature of traffic enforcement on New Jersey highways. Andresen, Kelling, and Maxfield were interested in the mechanics of making traffic stops, and what kinds of things troopers considered in deciding which vehicles to stop. Researchers have long accompanied municipal police on patrol and a number of studies have documented their efforts. But, as Andresen points out, only a handful of studies have examined traffic enforcement, and even fewer considered state police.

To study video recording cameras in state police cars, Maxfield and Andresen (2002) rode with state police and watched the equipment in use. They learned that sound quality of recordings was often poor, for a variety of reasons associated with microphones and wireless transmittal. It was initially hoped that video records might make it possible to classify the race of drivers, but after watching in-car video monitors the researchers confirmed that poor image quality undermined the potential reliability of that approach. The Rutgers University researchers expected that troopers would be on their best behavior. But they did witness actions by troopers to avoid recording sound and/or images on a few occasions. Even though people behave differently when accompanied by researchers, it's not uncommon for police to let their guard down a little.

Andresen accompanied troopers on 57 patrols overall, conducting unstructured interviews during the several hours he spent with individual troopers. He adopted the common practice of using an interview guide, a list of simple questions he planned to ask in the field. He took extensive notes while riding, and repeatedly told troopers they could examine his notes. Andresen observed over 150 traffic stops, writing field notes to document who was involved, reasons for the stop, what actions troopers took, and post-stop comments from troopers. He reports that most troopers seemed to enjoy describing their work. And, as you might imagine, troopers' commentary about traffic enforcement was very interesting.

Semistructured interviews with 57 troopers and field notes from 150 traffic stops produced a large volume of written material. We'll say a bit more about how Andresen summarized that material in Chapter 12.

narrative descriptions by having group discussions about discrepancies in reports by different observers.

Shuryo Fujita took clever steps to enhance the reliability of his measures of street conditions in Newark, New Jersey. The box "Sampling Streets in Newark, New Jersey" earlier in this chapter describes how he selected streets to code. He then used images from Google Street View (GSV) to code variables measuring litter, graffiti, and housing conditions of selected streets. Adapting a technique used for decades to measure street cleanliness in New York City (Mayor's Office of Operations, 2006), Fujita selected sample photographs that showed varying degrees of litter, graffiti, and rundown housing to illustrate the attributes of his scale. These photos served as visual anchors to increase consistency of recording values for each observed measure (Fujita, 2011).

In a similar way, Stephen Mooney and associates (2014) adapted items measuring signs of physical disorder used by Sampson and Raudenbush (1999) in their systematic social observation work in Chicago. Signs of disorder included garbage and litter on the streets, graffiti, abandoned buildings and cars, and a host of similar conditions. Using GSV, Mooney and associates trained "auditors" to virtually code over 1,800 block faces in five cities. Researchers recoded a random sample of 5 percent of block faces to assess interrater reliability. Overall 93 percent of blocks were coded with the same values, but some understandable differences were found in reliability for coding different items. Abandoned buildings were most reliably coded, while the presence of garbage and bottles achieved only "fair agreement." Notice that tools such as GSV make it possible to observe different cities at much lower cost compared to the video recording approach used by Sampson and Raudenbush.

The annual count of homeless people in New York City is another good example of how to enhance the reliability of field observations. Each year, during one overnight period of about 10 hours in January, field researchers are deployed throughout areas of New York where people who appear to be homeless are commonly seen (Silberman School of Social Work, 2013). The count is done at night, under the assumption that people sleeping outdoors in January are likely to be homeless. Observers approach people who meet screening criteria and use a protocol to ask questions about their living arrangements. In an effort to measure observers' abilities in finding and approaching subjects, other research staff are hired as decoys to dress and act like homeless people. Decoys are trained, paid $75 (in 2014) for their work, and deployed to the same areas where observers are assigned. Decoys are known targets, so assessing the number of decoys who are approached and questioned provides an estimate of observer reliability. Check the shadow count website for more information at http://sssw.hunter.cuny.edu/ssw/shadowcount2016/. Consider signing up if you live near New York City and want some (modestly) paid experience in doing field observation!

In a more general sense, reliability will increase as the degree of interpretation required to make actual observations decreases. Participant observation or unstructured interviews may require a considerable degree of interpretation on the part of the observer, and most of us draw on our own experiences and backgrounds in interpreting what we observe. At another extreme, electronic devices and machines can produce very reliable counts of persons who enter a store or of cars that pass some particular point. Somewhere in the middle are fieldworkers who observe shoplifters, motorists, or pedestrians and tabulate some specific behavior.

Generalizability

One of the chief goals of social science is generalization. We study particular situations and events to learn about life in general. Usually, nobody is interested in the specific subjects observed by the researcher. Who cares, after all, about the 18 people who told National Crime Victimization Survey interviewers about their stolen bicycles? We are interested only if their victimization experiences can be generalized to all U.S. households.

Generalizability can be a problem for qualitative field research. It crops up in two forms. First, the personal nature of the observations and measurements made by the researcher can produce results that will not necessarily be replicated by another independent researcher. If the observation depends in part on the individual observers, it is more valuable as a source of particular insight than as a general truth. You may recognize the similarity between this and the more general issue of reliability.

Second, because field researchers get a full and in-depth view of their subject matter, they can reach an unusually comprehensive understanding. By its very comprehensiveness, however, this understanding is less generalizable than results based on rigorous sampling and standardized measurements.

For example, in connection with an investigation of racial profiling, Maxfield has conducted observational research with the New Jersey State Police (Maxfield and Kelling, 2005). This has taken several forms, but one recent experience involved learning about radar speed enforcement on a 50-mile segment of the New Jersey Turnpike. Maxfield accompanied troopers on a thorough tour of this segment, identifying where radar units were routinely stationed (termed "fishing holes" by troopers). In his fieldwork, he also examined physical characteristics of the roadway; patterns of in- and out-of-state travel; and areas where entrance ramps, slight upward grades, and other features affected vehicle speed. Finally, he gained extensive information on priorities and patterns in speed enforcement—learning what affects troopers' decisions to stop certain vehicles.

As a result, Maxfield has detailed knowledge about that 50-mile segment of the New Jersey Turnpike. How generalizable is that knowledge? In one sense, learning about "fishing holes" in very specific terms can help identify such sites on other roads. And learning how slight upward grades can slow traffic in one situation may help us understand traffic on other upward grades. But a detailed, idiosyncratic understanding of 50 miles of highway is just that—idiosyncratic. Knowing all there is to know about a straight, largely level stretch of limited-access toll road with few exits is not generalizable to other roadways—winding roads in mountainous areas, with many exits, for example.

Even quantitative field studies may be weak on generalizability. Baumer and Rosenbaum's (1982) estimates of shoplifting prevalence were based on observations in a single large department store in downtown Chicago. The situation is likely to be different in smaller specialty shops and the department stores in suburban malls that have replaced most urban locations. Similarly, conclusions about seat belt use in Indiana may not apply in New York or Idaho. At the time, Indiana's law called for a $25 fine for not wearing a seat belt and could be invoked only if a driver was stopped for some other reason. Compliance may be different in states that have stiffer penalties and where police are permitted to stop drivers for not wearing seat belts.

At the same time, some field studies are less rooted in the local context of the subject under study. Wright and Decker (1994) studied burglars in St. Louis, and it's certainly reasonable to wonder whether their findings apply to residential burglars in St. Petersburg, Florida. The actions and routines of burglars might be affected by local police strategies, differences in the age or style of dwelling units, or even the type and amount of vegetation screening buildings from the street. However, Wright and Decker draw general conclusions about how burglars search for targets, what features of dwellings signal vulnerability, how opportunistic knowledge can trigger an offense, and what strategies exist for fencing stolen goods. It's likely that their findings about the technology and incentives that affect St. Louis burglars apply generally to residential burglars in other cities.

In reviewing reports of field research projects, it's important to determine where and to what extent the researcher is generalizing beyond her or his specific observations to other settings. Such generalizations may be in order, but it is necessary to judge that. Nothing in this research method guarantees it. As we've seen, field research is a potentially powerful tool for criminal justice research, one that provides a useful balance to surveys.

SUMMARY

- Field research is a data collection method that involves the direct observation of phenomena in their natural settings.
- Field observation is usually the preferred data collection method for obtaining information about physical or social settings, behavior, and events.
- Field research in criminal justice may produce either qualitative or quantitative data. Grounded theory is typically built from qualitative field observations; or, observations that can be quantified may produce measures for hypothesis testing.
- Observations made through field research often can be integrated with data collected from other sources. In this way, field observations can help researchers interpret other data.
- Field researchers may or may not identify themselves as researchers to the people they are observing. Being identified as a researcher may have some effect on what is observed.
- Controlled probability sampling techniques are not usually possible in field research. But in some circumstances, researchers can combine probability and nonprobability sampling.
- Alternatives for recording field observations range from video, audio, and other equipment to unstructured field notes. In between are observations recorded on structured forms; environmental surveys are examples.
- Field notes should be planned in advance to the greatest extent possible. However, note taking should be flexible enough to make records of unexpected observations.
- Compared with surveys, field research measurements generally have more validity but less reliability, and field research results cannot be generalized as safely

as those based on rigorous sampling and standardized questionnaires.

KEY TERMS

Environmental survey *(p. 309)*
Ethnography *(p. 300)*
Reactivity *(p. 302)*
Safety audit *(p. 312)*

REVIEW QUESTIONS AND EXERCISES

1. Review the box titled "Conducting a Safety Audit" by Gisela Bichler. Try conducting a safety audit on your campus or in an area near your campus. If possible, supplement this with satellite photo images of the area where you conduct your audit. See an example for York University: METRAC. 2010. *York University Safety Audit: Leading the Way to Personal and Community Safety.* Toronto, Ontario: Metropolitan Action Committee on Violence against Women and Children. METRAC.

2. This question is linked to Exercise 2 in Chapter 9. After tabulating responses to your questions about nearby areas where respondents feel unsafe or believe crime to be a problem, plan and conduct field observations in those areas. First, visit one or more areas and make detailed field notes about the area's characteristics, thinking especially about how those characteristics might be associated with perceptions of crime problems. Second, use your notes and observations to develop a form for making structured field observations. Third,

visit more areas cited by your respondents and use your form to record area characteristics.

3. We briefly described how Shuryo Fujita sampled street segments and conducted systematic observations using Google Street View. In a paragraph or so, summarize another way to use Google Street View images as a source of field observation data. What are some advantages and disadvantages of this data source? Describe one example of a concept that can be readily measured with Goggle Street View, and one example of a concept that cannot.

4. The Center for Urban Pedagogy (CUP) sponsors a variety of activities to educate New York City students about urban policy, and to involve students in field research projects. One group of students produced a booklet, titled *Field Guide to Federalism: Bushwick, Brooklyn, NY.* In describing their research, students wrote: "We started small and began by looking for signs of federalism in our wallets. Then we took to the streets looking for some evidence of what federal, state, and city government looks like in Bushwick" (Center for Urban Pedagogy, 2011:1). Download the booklet at the CUP website. Briefly describe how the students' research involves techniques of field observation described in this chapter. By the way, CUP projects address a variety of issues in criminal and juvenile justice. For example, see the poster by Danica Navgorodoff, "I got arrested! Now what?" (Navgorodoff, 2010) (http://welcometocup.org/Store?product_id=29).

CHAPTER 12

Agency Records, Content Analysis, and Secondary Data

We'll examine three sources of existing data: agency records, content analysis, and data collected by other researchers. Data from these sources have many applications in criminal justice research.

Learning Objectives

1. Recognize that public organizations produce statistics and data that are often useful for criminal justice researchers.

2. Provide examples of nonpublic agency records that can serve as data for criminal justice research.

3. Understand why the units of analysis represented by agency data may be confusing for researchers.

4. Explain why researchers must be attentive to reliability and validity problems that might stem from agency records.

5. Summarize why "follow the paper trail" and "expect the expected" are useful maxims to follow when using agency records in research.

6. Summarize content analysis as a research method appropriate for studying communications.

7. Describe examples of coding to transform raw data into a standardized, quantitative form.

8. Summarize how secondary analysis refers to the analysis of data collected by another researcher for some other purpose.

9. Be able to access archives of criminal justice data that are maintained by the ICPSR and the NACJD.

10. Understand how the advantages and disadvantages of secondary data are similar to those for agency records.

Terrorist Recruitment

Dr. Niyazi Ekici used agency records and content analysis in his research on recruitment by two terrorist organizations in Turkey (Ekici, 2008). A high-ranking officer in the Turkish National Police, Dr. Ekici had access to official records during his graduate study at Rutgers University. His interests centered on how terrorist organizations initiated contact with potential members, together with what sorts of factors entered into the selection process.

Several organizations that employ terrorist tactics have been active in Turkey. Ekici selected two groups with very different ideologies, expecting that the groups would seek recruits with different qualities. The Revolutionary People's Liberation Party/Front (DHKP/C) is fueled by a Marxist ideology, whereas Turkish Hezbollah is a religious extremist group.

Two sources were used to gather data about active terrorists and those who aspired to join the two groups. Data on active terrorists were obtained from police records of 70 individuals in each of the two organizations who had been arrested and convicted of terrorist offenses. The second source was unique: documents written by individuals who sought to join the organizations, something similar to a letter of application.

These documents, seized in police raids of terrorist cells over a 10-year period, provided information on an individual's family, political and religious beliefs, and reasons for wishing to join the organization. In earlier chapters, we discussed the validity and reliability of self-reports. Ekici writes that these documents are likely to be accurate because "the terrorist organization will not hesitate to kill members who are found to be lying" (2008:92).

Ekici used content analysis to systematically extract information from both police records of active terrorists and seized documents of recruits. He then compared a variety of measures for recruits and active members in Turkish Hezbollah and DHKP/C.

Compared to convicted terrorists, candidate terrorists in both organizations were more likely

- to have criminal records,
- to have family members with criminal records, and
- to have associated with other terrorist organizations.

Ekici interprets this as some measure of selectivity in which loyalty and not being known to police are valued by these two terrorist groups and affect the kinds of people who become members. In contrast, candidates not yet selected are more likely to have criminal records that affect their chances of being accepted.

This is an unusual example of research based on agency records. However, it applies many of the principles of research using agency records and content analysis we discuss in this chapter. A police officer as well as a researcher, Dr. Niyazi Ekici used the tools of social science research to systematically analyze documents maintained by the Turkish National Police and to thus add to knowledge about terrorist recruitment.

Introduction

Agency records, secondary data, and content analysis do not require direct interaction with research subjects.

Except for the complete observer in field research, the modes of observation discussed so far require the researcher to intrude to some degree into whatever he or she is studying. This is most obvious with survey research. As we've seen, even the field researcher can change things in the process of studying them.

Other ways of collecting data do not involve intrusion by observers. In this chapter, we'll consider three different approaches to using information collected by others, often as a routine practice. First, a great deal of criminal justice research uses data collected by state and local agencies such as police, criminal courts, probation offices, juvenile authorities, and corrections departments. National organizations such as the FBI, the Bureau of Justice Statistics (BJS), the Federal Bureau of Prisons, and the National Institute of Corrections compile information about crime problems and criminal justice institutions. In addition, nongovernment organizations such as the National Center for State Courts and the American Prosecutors' Research Institute collect data from members.

Government agencies gather a vast amount of crime and criminal justice data, probably rivaled only by the amount of economic and public health data produced. We refer to such information as "data from agency records." In this chapter, we will describe different types of such data that are available for criminal justice research, together with the promise and potential pitfalls of using information from agency records.

Second, in content analysis, researchers examine a class of social artifacts—written documents or other types of messages. Suppose, for example, you want to contrast the importance of criminal justice policy and health care policy for Americans in 2001 and 2016. One option is to examine public opinion polls from these years. Another method is to analyze articles from newspapers published in each year. The latter is an example of content analysis—the analysis of communications.

Finally, information collected by others is frequently used in criminal justice research, which in this case involves **secondary analysis** of existing data. Investigators who conduct research funded by federal agencies such as the National Institute of Justice are usually obliged to release their data for public use. Thus, if you were interested in developing sentence reform proposals for your state, for example, you might analyze data collected by Nancy Merritt, Terry Fain, and Susan Turner in the study of Oregon's efforts to increase sentence length for certain types of offenders (Merritt, Fain, and Turner, 2006).

Before we begin to explore each of these sources of data in detail, be alert to what researchers call **obtrusive measurement** and **unobtrusive measurement**. When we make obtrusive measures, subjects (usually people) are aware that data are being collected. Administering a questionnaire is an example. In unobtrusive measurement, subjects are not aware that data are being collected.

Secondary analysis   Research in which the data collected and processed by one researcher are analyzed by another.

Observing pedestrian traffic from a park bench could be an example.

When you consult data about persons under correctional supervision or conduct secondary analysis of a prison inmate survey directed by the RAND Corporation, you are not interacting with research subjects. Do not, however, be too quick to describe such measurement as unobtrusive. Inmates interviewed by RAND researchers were certainly aware of their role in providing information for research, even if they had no idea that you would later examine the data. You may gather jail census figures from a Web page, but those data were originally obtained from a survey questionnaire completed by one or more persons directly involved in the measurement process.

In a general sense, then, most data you obtain from agency records or research projects conducted by others are secondary data. Someone else gathered the original data, usually for purposes that will differ from yours. That is certainly the case for research described in the vignette "Terrorist Recruitment" at the opening of this chapter. This vignette briefly describes how Niyazi Ekici used content analysis and agency records collected by the Turkish National Police.

Topics Appropriate for Agency Records and Content Analysis

Agency records support a wide variety of research applications.

Data from agency records or archives originally may have been gathered in any number of ways, from sample surveys to direct observation. As a result, such data may, in principle, be appropriate for just about any criminal justice research topic.

Published statistics and agency records are most commonly used in descriptive or exploratory studies. This is consistent with the fact that many of the criminal justice data published by government agencies are intended to describe something. For instance, BJS publishes annual figures on prison populations. If we are interested in describing differences in prison populations between states or changes in prison populations

from 1995 through 2010, a good place to begin is with the annual data published by BJS. Or, if we wish to learn more about cases of identity theft, we could consult the annual *Consumer Sentinel Network Data Book* that summarizes known cases of identity theft and related frauds (Federal Trade Commission, 2016). Similarly, published figures on crimes reported to police, criminal victimization, felony court caseloads, drug use by high school seniors, and a host of other measures are available over time—for 30 years or longer in many cases.

Agency records may also be used in explanatory studies. Nancy Sinauer and colleagues (1999) examined medical examiner records for over 1,000 female homicide victims in North Carolina to understand the relationship between female homicide and residence in urban versus rural counties. They found that counties on the outskirts of cities had higher female homicide rates than either urban or rural counties.

Agency records are frequently used in applied studies as well. Evaluations of new policies that seek to reduce recidivism might draw on arrest or conviction data for measures of recidivism. A study of drug courts as an alternative way to process defendants with substance abuse problems traced arrest records for experimental and control subjects (Gottfredson et al., 2006). In another study, researchers used data from public sex offender registries in New York to examine the impact of laws restricting where sex offenders could live (Berenson and Appelbaum, 2010). Sometimes, records obtained from private firms can be used in applied studies. Brian Smith (2015) and Ronald Clarke examined records on 7,887 items sold by 204 chain supermarkets in their analysis of shoplifting of selected products with roles in drug use.

In a different type of applied study, James Austin, Wendy Naro, and Tony Fabelo (2007) combined data on prison releases and capacities, reincarcerations, and general-population forecasts to develop a mathematical model that predicts future prison populations. This is an example of forecasting, in which past relationships among arrest rates and prison sentences for different age groups are compared with estimates of future population by age group. Assuming that past associations between age, arrest, and prison sentence will remain constant in future years, demographic models of future population can be used to predict future admissions to prison.

Topics appropriate to research using content analysis center on the important links between communication, perceptions of crime problems, individual behavior, and criminal justice policy. The prevalence of violence in fictional television dramas has long been a concern of researchers and public officials (Anderson and Bushman, 2002). Niyazi Ekici (2008) used content analysis to learn about how terrorists were recruited in Turkey. Mass media also play an important role in affecting policy action by public officials. Many studies have examined the influence of media in setting the agenda for criminal justice policy (see, for example, Chermak and Weiss, 1997).

Research data collected by other investigators, through surveys or field observation, may be used for a broad variety of later studies. National Crime Victimization Survey (NCVS) data have been used by a large number of researchers in countless descriptive and explanatory studies since the 1970s. In a notably ambitious use of secondary data, Robert Sampson and John Laub (1993) recovered life history data on 500 delinquents and 500 nondelinquents originally collected by Sheldon and Eleanor Glueck in the 1940s. Taking advantage of theoretical and empirical advances in criminological research over the ensuing 40 years, Sampson and Laub produced a major contribution to knowledge of criminal career development in childhood.

Existing data may also be considered as a supplemental source of data. For example, a researcher planning to survey correctional facility administrators about their views on the need for drug treatment programs will do well to examine existing data on the number of drug users sentenced to prison terms. Or, if we are evaluating an experimental morale-building program in a probation services department, statistics on absenteeism will be useful in connection with the data our own research will generate.

This is not to say that agency records and secondary data can always provide answers to research questions. If this were true, much of this book would be unnecessary. The key to distinguishing appropriate and inappropriate uses of agency records, content analysis, and secondary data is understanding how these written records are produced. We cannot emphasize this point too strongly. Much of this chapter will underscore the importance of learning where data come from and how they are gathered.

Types of Agency Records

Researchers use a variety of published statistics and nonpublic agency records.

Information collected by or for public agencies usually falls into one of three general categories: (1) published statistics, (2) nonpublic agency records routinely collected for internal use, and (3) new data collected by agency staff for specific research purposes. Each category varies in the extent to which data are readily available to the researcher and in the researcher's degree of control over the data collection process.

Published Statistics

Most government organizations routinely collect and publish compilations of data, which we refer to collectively as **published statistics**. Examples are the Census Bureau, the FBI, the Administrative Office of U.S. Courts, the Federal Bureau of Prisons, and the BJS. Two of these organizations merit special mention. First, the Census Bureau conducts enumerations and sample surveys for several other federal organizations. Notable examples are the NCVS, Census of Children in Custody, Survey of Inmates in Local Jails, Correctional Populations in the United States, and Survey of Justice Expenditure and Employment.

Second, the BJS compiles data from several sources and publishes annual and special reports on most data series. For example, *Criminal Victimization in the United States* reports summary data from the NCVS each year. Table 10.1 presents a sample breakdown of domestic violence victimization rates compiled over the years 2003–2012. The

BJS also issues reports on people under correctional supervision. These are based on sample surveys and enumerations of jail, prison, and juvenile facility populations. Sample tabulations of people serving sentences in state and federal prison in 2012 are shown in Table 10.2. And the series *Federal Criminal Case Processing* reports detailed data on federal court activity.

Until recently, the most comprehensive publication on criminal justice data was the annual *Sourcebook of Criminal Justice Statistics* (http://www.albany.edu/sourcebook), maintained by the Hindelang Criminal Justice Research Center. Since 1972, this report summarized hundreds of criminal justice data series, ranging from public perceptions about crime, to characteristics of criminal justice agencies, to tables on how states execute capital offenders. Data from private sources such as the Gallup Poll are included, with statistics collected by government agencies. The *Sourcebook* also includes notes on data sources and data collection procedures for major series, including the addresses of organizations that either collect or archive original data. As of August 2016, the *Sourcebook* still exists on the University at Albany website, but data do not appear to have been updated since 2014.

Compilations of published data on crime and criminal justice are readily available from many other sources. The BJS website includes summary reports on a number of data series. For information on juvenile justice, see the Statistical Briefing Book compiled by the Office of Juvenile Justice and Delinquency Protection (http://www.ojjdp.gov/ojstatbb/default.asp). And of course, the FBI Uniform Crime Reports series is an important source of published reports on crimes known to police (http://www.fbi.gov/about-us/cjis/ucr/ucr). (Each accessed 18 August 2016.)

However, at this point we want to suggest some possible uses, and limits, of what Herbert Jacob (1984:9) refers to as being "like the apple in the Garden of Eden: tempting but full of danger . . . [for] the unwary researcher."

Referring to Tables 12.1 and 12.2, you may recognize that published data from series such as the NCVS or *Correctional Populations in the United States* are summary data, as discussed in Chapters 4 and 6. This means that data are presented in highly aggregated form and cannot be used to analyze the individuals from or about whom information was originally collected. For example, Table 12.2 shows that in 2012, a total of 13,549 women were serving

TABLE 12.1 Domestic Violence Victimization: Averages 2003–2012

Victim-Offender Relationship	Average Annual Number of Victims	Rate of Violent Victimization per 1,000 Persons		
		Serious Assault	Simple Assault	Total Violent Crime
Known				
Intimate partner	967,710	1.4	2.5	3.9
Spouse	314,430	0.5	0.8	1.3
Ex-spouse	134,690	0.1	0.4	0.05
Boy/girlfriend	518,700	0.8	1.3	2.1
Other family	284,670	0.4	0.7	1.1
Parent	80,900	0.1	0.2	0.3
Child	97,490	0.1	0.3	0.4
Sibling	106,290	0.1	0.3	0.4
Other family	158,950	0.2	0.4	0.6
Acquaintance	2,103,240	2.3	6.1	8.4
Stranger	2,548,860	3.7	6.5	10.2

Source: Adapted from Truman and Morgan (2014), Tables 1 and 2.

TABLE 12.2 Prisoners in Selected States, 2012

	Number			Percent in
			Percent	Private
	Males	Females	Female	Prisons
Alabama	29,782	2,649	8.2%	1.7%
Arizona	36,447	3,633	9.1%	16.1%
California	128,436	6,098	4.5%	0.5%
Florida	94,945	6,985	6.9%	11.5%
New Mexico	6,096	631	9.4%	44.6%
New York	51,963	2,247	4.1%	0%
Texas	152,823	13,549	8.1%	11.2%
Vermont	1,907	127	6.2%	24.8%

Source: Adapted from Carson and Golinelli (2013), Appendix tables 6 and 7.

sentences of one year or more in state correctional institutions in Texas. By comparing that figure with figures from other states, we can make some descriptive statements about prison populations in different states. We can also consult earlier editions of *Correctional Populations* to examine trends in prison populations over time or to compare rates of growth from state to state.

Summary data cannot, however, be used to reveal anything about individual correctional facilities, let alone facility inmates. Individual-level data about inmates and institutions are available from the Census Bureau in electronic form, but published tabulations present only summaries.

This is not to say that published data are useless to criminal justice researchers. Highly aggregated summary data from published statistical series are frequently used in descriptive, explanatory, and applied studies. For example, Eric Baumer and colleagues (1998) examined Uniform Crime Report (UCR), Drug Abuse Warning Network, and Drug Use Forecasting data for 142 U.S. cities from 1984 to 1992. Interested in the relationship between crack cocaine use and robbery, burglary, and homicide rates, the researchers found that high levels of crack cocaine use in the population were found in cities that also had high rates of robbery. In contrast, burglary rates were lower in cities with high levels of crack cocaine use. James Lynch and Lynn

Addington (2007) present a series of studies that examine trends in different measures of crime.

Ted Robert Gurr (1989) used published statistics on violent crime dating back to thirteenth-century England to examine how social and political events affected patterns of homicide through 1984. A long-term decline in homicide rates has been punctuated by spikes during periods of social dislocation, when

> ...significant segments of a population have been separated from the regulating institutions that instill and reinforce the basic Western injunctions against interpersonal violence. They may be migrants, demobilized veterans, a growing population of resentful young people for whom there is no social or economic niche, or badly educated young black men trapped in the decaying ghettos of an affluent society. (1989:48–49)

Published data can, therefore, address questions about highly aggregated patterns or trends: drug use and crime, the covariation in two estimates of crime, or epochal change in fatal violence. Published data also have the distinct advantage of being readily available; a Web search or a trip to the library can quickly place several data series at your disposal. Most publications by the BJS and other Justice Department offices are now available only on the Internet. Selected printed copies have been scanned or otherwise archived.

Many basic crime data can be downloaded from the BJS website in spreadsheet formats or read directly into presentation software. More importantly, complete data series are available in electronic format. Although printed reports of the NCVS limit you to summary tabulations such as those in Table 12.1, the original survey data from over 60,000 respondents are available online. Online analysis tools from the BJS enable researchers to produce custom tabulations from all major data series (http://www.bjs.gov/index.cfm?ty=daa). We will return to these resources later in the chapter.

Of course, before using either original data or tabulations from published sources, researchers must consider the issues of validity and reliability and the more general question of how well these data meet specific research purposes. It would make little sense to use only FBI data on homicides in a descriptive study of domestic violence, because murder records measure only incidents of fatal violence. Data from an annual prison census would not be appropriate for research on changes in sentences to community corrections programs.

Nonpublic Agency Records

Despite the large volume of published statistics in criminal justice, those data represent only the tip of the proverbial iceberg. The FBI publishes the summary UCR, but each of the nation's several thousand law enforcement agencies produces an incredible volume of data not routinely released for public distribution. The BJS publication *Correctional Populations in the United States* presents statistics on prison inmates collected from annual surveys of correctional facilities, but any given facility also maintains detailed case files on individual inmates. The Court Statistics Project, maintained by the National Center for State Courts, contains summary data on cases filed and disposed in state courts; but any courthouse in any large city houses paper or computer files on thousands of individual defendants. Finally, reports on the annual survey of expenditures and employment in criminal justice are sources of summary data on budgets and personnel, but every agency also maintains its own detailed records of expenditures and human resources.

Although we have labeled this data source "nonpublic agency records," many criminal justice organizations will make such data available to criminal justice researchers. However, obtaining agency records is not as simple as scrolling through a list of publications on the BJS website, or clicking a download button on the Census Bureau's Web page.

At the outset, we want to emphasize that the potential promise of agency records is not without cost. Jacob's caution about the hidden perils to unwary researchers who uncritically accept published data applies to nonpublic agency records as well. On the one hand, we could devote an entire book to describing the potential applications of agency records in criminal justice research, together with advice on how to use and interpret such data. On the other hand, we can summarize that unwritten book with one piece of advice: understand how agency records are produced. Restated slightly, researchers can find the road to happiness in using agency records by following the paper trail.

By way of illustrating this humble maxim, we present two types of examples. First, we describe two studies in which nonpublic agency records were used to reveal important findings about the etiology of crime and its spatial distribution. Second, we briefly review two studies in which the authors recognized validity and reliability problems but still were able to draw conclusions about the behavior of criminal justice organizations. At the end of this section, we summarize the promise of agency records for research and note cautions that must be exercised if such records are to be used effectively.

Child Abuse, Delinquency, and Adult Arrests In earlier chapters, we described Cathy Spatz Widom's research on child abuse as an example of a quasi-experimental design. For present purposes, her research illustrates the use of several different types of agency records.

Widom (1989) identified cases of child abuse and neglect by consulting records from juvenile and adult criminal courts in a large Midwestern city. Unlike adult court proceedings, juvenile court proceedings are not open to the public, and juvenile records may not be released. However, after obtaining institutional review board approval, Widom was granted access to these files for research purposes by court authorities. From juvenile court records, she selected 774 cases of neglect, physical abuse, or sexual abuse. Cases of extreme abuse were processed in adult criminal court, where charges were filed against the offender. Criminal court records yielded an additional 134 cases.

As described in Chapter 7, Widom constructed a comparison group of nonabused children through individual matching. Comparison subjects were found from two different sources of agency records. First, abused children who were age 6–11 at the time of the abuse were matched to comparison subjects by consulting public school records. An abused child was matched with a comparison child of the same sex, race, and age (within six months) who attended the same school. Second, children who were younger than six years old at the time of abuse were matched on similar criteria by consulting birth records and selecting a comparison subject born in the same hospital.

These two types of public records and matching criteria—attending the same public school and being born in the same hospital—were used in an attempt to control for socioeconomic status. Although such criteria may be viewed with skepticism today, Widom (1989:360) points out that during this time period (1967–1971), school busing was not used in the area where her study was conducted, and "elementary schools represented very homogeneous neighborhoods." Similarly, in the late 1960s, hospitals tended to serve local communities, unlike contemporary medical-industrial complexes that advertise their services far and wide. Widom assumed that children born in the same hospital were more likely to be from similar socioeconomic backgrounds than children born in different hospitals. Though far from perfect, school and birth records enabled Widom to construct approximate matches on socioeconomic status, illustrating our earlier advice to be creative while being careful. William Shadish, Thomas Cook, and Donald Campbell (2002:129) describe how school- and hospital-based controls can be used more generally in social research.

Widom's research purpose was explanatory—to examine the link between early child abuse and later delinquency or adult criminal behavior. These two dependent variables were measured by consulting additional agency records for information on arrests of abused subjects and comparison subjects for the years 1971 through 1986. Juvenile court files yielded information on delinquency. Adult arrests were measured from criminal history files maintained by local, state, and national law enforcement agencies. In an effort to locate as many subjects as possible, Widom searched for current addresses and Social Security numbers in the files of state motor vehicle bureaus. Finally, "marriage license bureau records were searched to find married names for the females" (Widom, 1989:361).

Findings revealed modest but statistically significant differences between abused and comparison subjects. As a group, abused subjects were more likely to have records of delinquency or adult arrests (Maxfield and Widom, 1996). However, Widom (1992) also found differences in these dependent variables by race and gender.

Now let's consider two potential validity and reliability issues that might be raised by Widom's use of nonpublic agency records. First, data from juvenile and adult criminal courts reveal only cases of abuse that come to the attention of public officials. Unreported and unsubstantiated cases of abuse or neglect are excluded, and this raises a question about the validity of Widom's measure of the independent variable. Second, dependent variable measures are similarly flawed because juvenile and adult arrests do not reflect all delinquent or criminal behavior.

Recognizing these problems, Widom is careful to point out that her measure of abuse probably reflects only the most severe cases, those that were brought to the attention of public officials. She also notes that cases in her study were processed before officials and the general public had become more aware of the problem of child abuse. Widom (1989:365–366) understood the limits of official records and qualified her conclusions accordingly: "These findings, then, are not generalizable to unreported cases of abuse or neglect. Ours are also the cases in which agencies have intervened, and in which there is little doubt of abuse or neglect. Thus, these findings are confounded with the processing factor."

Crime "Hot Spots" Law enforcement officials and criminal justice researchers have long been interested in the spatial concentration of crime. A growing number of police departments employ crime analysts to identify "hot spots"—geographic areas and times of day that signal concentrations of various types of crime (Boba, 2005). Additionally, researchers have recognized that some individual people and places are repeatedly victimized, and that these repeat victims play a major role in producing hot spots (Weisel, 2005).

Research and policy interest in hot spots and repeat victimization can be traced to an influential article by Lawrence Sherman, Patrick Gartin, and Michael Buerger (1989). Their analysis used a long-neglected measure produced in great volume by police departments. Calls for service (CFS) represent the initial reports of crime and other problems to police departments. Most large police departments record basic information about CFS—location, time, and nature of complaint—on audiotapes or computer networks. Telephone operators respond to most CFS by dispatching a patrol car, a process that is automatically recorded on a computer. This produces a source of data on incidents brought to the attention of police.

Truly astonishing numbers of crime victims, witnesses, or people with some sort of noncrime problem telephone police departments each year. Sherman and associates (1989:36) analyzed more than 300,000 such calls to the Minneapolis Police Department in 1986, proposing that "calls to the police provide the most extensive and faithful account of what the public tells the police about crime, with the specific errors and biases that that entails." As we pointed out in Chapter 6, UCR and similar data on recorded crime are subject to validity and reliability problems that reflect decisions by police and complainants. CFS are recorded automatically before most such decisions are made, and so are less subject to screening by police or the public. An additional advantage, and one crucial for Sherman's research on the "criminology of place," is that CFS data provide micro-level information on where incidents occur.

Because Sherman and colleagues (1989:37) were interested in the concentration of calls in certain locations, they required some measure of the number of distinct locations in Minneapolis. After consulting records from the city tax assessor's office, the Administrative Engineering Service, and the Traffic Engineering Office, researchers concluded that it was not possible to obtain a precise count of locations. A denominator of places for computing CFS rates was estimated at 115,000, which included 109,000 street addresses and 6,000 intersections.

In a slight digression, we point out that this approximation illustrates another point made by Jacob (1984:39). Given the many sources of potential error in published statistics and agency records, researchers who use such data should report rounded figures and thereby avoid the illusion of exaggerated accuracy that precise numbers imply. For example, there is no way of knowing whether Minneapolis has 107,037 or 111,252 street addresses because of varying definitions used by different agencies. It is therefore safer to state "about 109,000 street addresses" than to report either a specific estimate or a "precise" average of the two estimates (109,144.5), which falsely inflates the accuracy of data.

Addressing first the general question of concentration, Sherman and colleagues (1989:38) found that about 50 percent of CFS occurred in just 3 percent of Minneapolis locations. A closer look at types of incidents sheds light on the links between type of offense and type of place. For example, hot spots such as discount department stores and large parking lots produced large numbers of shoplifting reports and calls from motorists locked out of their cars. One hotel stood out with a large number of calls for burglary and violent crime, but turned out to be more of a "cool spot" when standardized by the hotel's average daily population of more than 3,000 guests and employees. In contrast, the approximate robbery rate for a single bar that had an estimated daily population of about 300 was 83 per 1,000 persons at risk.

This example is different from Widom's study in many respects. However, the researchers all recognized the potential promise and shortcomings of data from agency records; in each case, they were careful and creative. Despite the advantages of using CFS data, Sherman and associates describe three possible problems: the potential for duplicate records of the same incident; false reports, equivalent to false fire alarms; and misleading hot spots, such as hospitals and police stations, that produce secondary crime reports. After taking these problems into consideration, Sherman and colleagues (1989) concluded that the advantages of CFS data outweigh the disadvantages. Readers can form their own conclusions, aided by the careful description of the paper trail—how CFS data are produced—provided by Sherman and colleagues.

After decades of additional studies of hot spots policing, researchers have concluded that it is among the most effective policing strategies for reducing crime (Braga et al., 2014). In fact, David Weisburd has called for a new "criminology of place," where small places are units of analysis instead of people, which is the case in traditional criminological research. Examining five large cities in the United States and Israel, Weisburd shows that between 1 and 2 percent of small places account for 25 percent of crime incidents. Half of all crime incidents occurred in between 4 and 6 percent of places in the five cities (Weisburd, 2015:144).

Agency Records as Measures of Decision Making Two studies mentioned in earlier chapters illustrate how flaws in agency record-keeping practices can be used to infer something about agency behavior. In earlier chapters, we mentioned the classic study by Richard McCleary, Barbara Nienstedt, and James Erven (1982) as an illustration of measurement problems and the ways in which those problems threaten certain quasi-experimental designs. Recall that McCleary and associates discovered that an apparent reduction in burglary rates was, in fact, due to changes in record-keeping practices. Assigning officers from a special unit to investigate burglaries revealed that earlier investigative procedures sometimes resulted in double counts of a single incident; the special unit also reduced misclassification of larcenies as burglaries.

McCleary and colleagues became suspicious of police records when they detected an immediate decline in burglary rates following the introduction of the special unit, a pattern that was not reasonable given the technology of burglary. Following the paper trail, they were able to discover how changes in procedures affected these measures. In the same article, they describe additional examples—how replacement of a police chief and changes in patrol dispatch procedures produced apparent increases in crime and calls for service. However, after carefully investigating how these records were produced, they were able to link changes in the indicators to changes in agency behavior rather than changes in the frequency of crime.

In a similar type of study, Hugh Whitt (2006) examined mortality data for New York City over 16 years. Although deaths by homicide and accidents varied little from year to year between 1976 and 1992, the number of suicides dropped dramatically from 1984 through 1988, then rose sharply in 1989 to match the numbers in earlier years. Reasoning that such sharp changes in a short period are unlikely to reflect natural variation in suicide, Whitt traced the deviation to a series of personnel and policy changes in the city medical examiner's office. So the sharp, short-term variation was due to changes in how deaths were recorded, not changes in the manner of death.

These two examples point to an important lesson in the use of agency records for criminal justice research: *expect the expected*. If unexpected findings or patterns emerge, review data collection procedures once again before accepting the unexpected. In these two examples, researchers suspected record-keeping problems when data analysis demonstrated sharp discrepancies between results and expectations. Changing the way burglaries are investigated is unlikely to produce a pronounced, immediate decline in burglary. And it is implausible that an experimental program for juvenile offenders will be 99 percent successful. Such clues prompted researchers to inquire further how such suspicious indicators were produced.

New Data Collected by Agency Staff

Thus far, we have concentrated on the research uses of information routinely collected by or for public agencies. Such data are readily available, but researchers have little control over the actual data collection process. Furthermore, agency procedures and definitions may not correspond with the needs of researchers.

It is sometimes possible to use a hybrid source of data in which criminal justice agency staff collect information for specific research purposes. We refer to this as a "hybrid" source because it combines the collection of new data—through observation or interviews—with day-to-day criminal justice agency activities. Virtually all criminal justice organizations routinely document their actions, from investigating crime reports to housing convicted felons. By slightly modifying forms normally used for recording information, researchers may be able to have agency staff collect original data for them.

For example, let's say we are interested in the general question of how many crimes reported to police involve nonresident victims. Reading about violent crime against international tourists in south Florida, we wonder how common such incidents are and decide to investigate the problem systematically. It doesn't take us long to learn that no published data are available on the resident or nonresident status of Dade County crime victims. We next try the Miami and Miami-Dade Police Departments, suspecting that such information might be recorded on crime report forms. No luck here, either. Incident report forms include victim name and address, but we are told that police routinely record the local address for tourists, typically a hotel, motel, or guest house. Staff in the police crime records office inform us that officers sometimes write down something like "tourist, resident

BY MARIE MELE
Monmouth University

An interest in domestic violence led me to learn more about repeat victimization. Research conducted in England has indicated that repeated domestic violence involving the same victim and offender is quite common (Hanmer, Griffiths, and Jerwood, 1999; Farrell, Edmunds, Hibbs, and Laycock, 2000). For example, combining data from four British Crime Surveys, Pease (1998:3) reports that about 1 percent of respondents had four or more personal victimizations and that these victims accounted for 59 percent of all personal victimization incidents disclosed to BCS interviewers. Other studies in England have shown that many other types of offenses are disproportionately concentrated among small groups of victims. Identifying repeat victims and directing prevention and enforcement resources to them has the potential to produce a large decrease in crime rates.

My interest centered on determining the distributions of incidents, victims, and offenders in cases of domestic violence reported to police in a large city in the northeastern United States. Partly this was exploratory research, but I also wished to make policy recommendations to reduce repeat victimization. Working with Michael Maxfield, my initial inquiries found that, although data on assaults and other offenses were available in paper files, it was not possible to efficiently count the number of repeat incidents for victims and offenders. However, seeing the potential value of gathering more systematic information on repeat offenders and victims, senior department staff collaborated with Maxfield and me to produce a database that reorganized existing data on domestic violence incidents. A pilot data system was developed in November 2001. Plans called for the database to be maintained by the department's domestic violence and sexual assault unit (DVSAU); staff would begin entering new incidents in January 2002. In the meantime, I proposed to test the database and its entry procedures by personally entering incidents from August through December 2001. After ironing out a few kinks, the final system was established, and I continued entering new incident reports for a period of time.

of Montreal" in the comments section of the crime report form, but they are neither required nor asked to do this.

Assuming we can gain approval to conduct our study from police and other relevant parties, we may be able to supplement the standard police report form. Adding an entry such as the following will do the trick:

Is complainant a resident of Dade County?
_____ Yes _____ No
If "no," record permanent address here:
_____

A seemingly simple modification of crime report forms may not happen quite so easily. Approval from the department is, of course, one of the first requirements. Individual officers who complete crime report forms must be made aware of the change and told why the new item was added. We might distribute a memorandum that explains the reasons for adopting a new crime report form. It might also be a good idea to have supervisors describe the new form at roll call before each shift of officers heads out on patrol. Finally, we could review samples of the new forms over the first few days they are used to determine the extent to which officers are completing the new item.

Incorporating new data collection procedures into agency routine has two major advantages. First, and most obvious, having agency staff collect data for us is much less costly than fielding a team of research assistants. It is difficult to imagine how original data

This is an admittedly brief description of a process that unfolded over several months. The process began as an attempt to obtain what we thought were existing data. Finding that suitable data were not available, Maxfield had sufficient access to the department to begin discussions of how to supplement existing record-keeping practices to tabulate repeat victimization. Many public agencies will accommodate researchers if such accommodation does not unduly burden the agency. Collecting new data for researchers *does* qualify as unduly burdensome for most public organizations. The key here was collaboration in a way that helped both the researchers and the host organization.

It's obvious that my research benefited from having the department design and ultimately assume responsibility for tabulating repeat victimization. The department benefited in three ways. First, DVSAU staff recognized how a data file that identified repeat *offenders* and victims could produce information that would aid their investigations of incidents. I emphasize *offenders* here because, all other things being equal, police are more interested in offenders than they are in victims. So the database was designed to track people (offenders) of special interest to police and people (victims) of special

interest to my research. Second, recognizing that setting up a new data system is especially difficult in a tradition-bound organization, I was able to ease the transition somewhat by initially entering data myself. One intentional by-product of this was to establish quality-control procedures during a shakedown period. As a criminal justice researcher, I knew that the reliability of data-gathering procedures was important and was able to establish reliable data entry routines for the department.

The DVSAU staff benefited in yet another way that was probably most important of all. This department had incorporated its version of Compstat for about 3 years. Two important components of Compstat are timely data and accountability. Each week, the DVSAU commander was required to present a summary of the unit's activity and was held accountable for the performance of unit staff. Before the database was developed, the DVSAU commander spent several hours compiling data to prepare for each week's Compstat meeting. After the database was operational, preparation time was reduced to minutes. In addition, the DVSAU commander was able to introduce new performance measures— repeat offenders and victims—that came to be valued by the department's chief.

on the resident status of Dade County victims could be collected in any other way. Second, we have more control over the measurement process than we would by relying on agency definitions. Some Dade County officers might note information on victim residence, but most probably they would not. Adding a specific question enhances the reliability of data collection. We might consider using an existing crime report item for "victim address," but the tendency of officers to record local addresses for tourists would undermine measurement validity. A specific "resident/nonresident" item is a more valid indicator.

The box by Marie Mele, titled "Improving Police Records of Domestic Violence," gives an example of this approach to gathering new data from agency records. You should recognize the importance of

collaboration in this example. Less obvious, but equally important, is a lesson we will return to later in this chapter: agency records are not usually intended for research purposes and, as a consequence, are not always well suited to researchers' needs. Sometimes, as was the case for Marie Mele, some subtle tweaking can transform unusable mounds of paper files into computer-based record systems. In any event, researchers are well advised to be careful in not assuming that existing data will meet their needs, and to be creative in seeking ways to improve the quality of agency data.

This approach to data collection has many potential applications. Probation officers or other court staff in many jurisdictions complete some type of presentence investigation on convicted offenders. A researcher might be able to supplement standard interview forms with additional items appropriate for some specific research interest. In their experimental study of intensive probation, Joan Petersilia and Susan Turner (1991) obtained the cooperation of probation staff to complete three data collection forms on each research subject. Intake forms yielded demographic and criminal history information. Review forms completed after 6 and 12 months documented the nature and types of services that probation staff delivered to experimental and control subjects (1991:621). Additional agency records provided data on probationer performance, but the supplementary data were needed to measure the implementation of the intensive probation program.

As we saw in Chapter 6, the Arrestee Dug Abuse Monitoring (ADAM) program sampled persons arrested in each participating city and asked them to voluntarily submit a urine sample for anonymous testing. Results were tabulated to estimate the prevalence of drug use among people arrested for different types of offenses. ADAM was incrementally expanded to become a "research platform." This is illustrated in a study by Scott Decker, Susan Pennell, and Ami Caldwell (1997), which supplemented the interview questionnaire in ADAM sites with questions about firearm availability and use. The researchers found no association between drug use and firearm use, but they did discover that gun use was common among juvenile males and especially widespread among admitted gang members. By piggybacking on ADAM in this way, Decker and associates were able to obtain information from more than 7,000 subjects at very low cost, which illustrates the principal strength of enlisting agency staff in data collection efforts.

At the same time, having agencies collect original research data has some disadvantages. An obvious one is the need to obtain the cooperation of organizations and staff. The difficulty of this varies in direct proportion to the intrusiveness of data collection. Cooperation is less likely if some major additional effort is required of agency personnel, or if data collection activities disrupt routine operations. The potential benefit to participating agencies is a related point. If a research project or an experimental program is likely to economize agency operations or improve staff performance,

as was the case for Marie Mele's research, it will be easier to enlist their assistance.

Researchers have less control over the data collection process when they rely on agency staff. Petersilia (1989:442) points out that agency personnel have competing demands on their time and naturally place a lower priority on data collection than on their primary duties. If you were a probation officer serving a heavy caseload and were asked to complete detailed 6- and 12-month reports on services provided to individual clients, would you devote more attention to keeping up with your clients or filling out data collection forms?

Units of Analysis and Sampling

Researchers must be especially attentive to the units of agency records, particularly in selecting samples for analysis.

After determining that agency records will be suitable for some particular research purpose, several decisions and tasks remain. We will consider two of them briefly because each is covered in more detail elsewhere in the book: units of analysis and sampling.

Units of Analysis

Archives and agency records may be based on units of analysis that are not suitable for particular research questions. If we are interested in studying individual probationers, for example, we need individual-level data about persons sentenced to probation. Summary data on the number of probationers served each week might not meet our research needs. Or if we wish to examine whether probationers convicted of drug offenses are supervised more closely than those convicted of assault, data on individuals sentenced to probation will have to be aggregated into categories based on convicted offense.

A general rule we mentioned in Chapter 4 bears repeating here: it is possible to move from individual to aggregate units of analysis, but not the other way around. Thus, we could aggregate records on individual probationers into groups that reflected convicted offense, but we could not disaggregate weekly reports to produce information about individuals. In any case, researchers using agency records must be attentive to the match or mismatch between the units of analysis required to address specific research questions and the level of aggregation represented in agency records.

Units of analysis can be especially troublesome in studies of criminal justice processes or studies of people moving through some institutional process. This is because criminal justice agencies use different units of count in keeping records of their activities. Figure 12.1, adapted from a report prepared by officials in a New York criminal justice agency (Poklemba, 1988), lists many of the counting units recorded at various stages of processing.

The units listed in Figure 12.1 can be grouped into two different categories: counts of events and counts of cases (Poklemba, 1988:III3). Counts of events—such as an arrest, indictment, or admission—are more straightforward because they are of short duration. Cases, however, may persist over longer times that are bounded by initiating or terminating events. Cases are directly linked to individual persons, although in complex ways. For example, an indictment event begins a court case that does not terminate until a court disposition event. Or a prison admission event begins an inmate case that ends at a prison discharge event. Further complicating matters is the multitude of possible relationships between units of count. For example, a court case can include multiple defendants, each facing multiple counts that can produce multiple dispositions.

The best solution for many research purposes is to define some equivalent to a person—a defendant, for example—as the unit of analysis. This was the approach used by James Eisenstein and Herbert Jacob (1977:175–176) in their study of felony courts:

> Indictments and cases are full of definitional ambiguities that vary from city to city. Some defendants are named in multiple indictments whereas others are not; many defendants are washed out of the process before being indicted but after receiving some punishment. Cases may involve a single defendant or many, and tend to be linked together if there are overlapping defendants or indictments. The concept of "defendants" suffers from none of these ambiguities. Using defendants as our unit of analysis permits us to discern the number of indictments each defendant faced, the number of court cases in which each was involved, and the ultimate [disposition] each [defendant] faced.

Defining individual people as units can resolve the conceptual problems that emerge from complex relationships between different units of count. Practical difficulties may remain in linking individuals to other units of count, however, or in tracing the movement of individuals from one institution to another.

Sampling

It is often necessary to select subsets of agency records for particular research purposes. Just as we would not need to interview every resident of New York City to learn how he or she feels about subway crime, it may not be necessary to examine all court cases to understand patterns of case disposition or sentences.

You will be glad to hear that sampling agency records is relatively simple, once units of analysis are defined. In most cases, a target population and sample frame may be readily defined. If, for example, we want to study the disposition of felony arrests in New York, our target population might be all cases that reached final disposition in the year 2010. We could then get a list or computer file that contains identifying numbers for all 2010

Criminal Activity	Apprehension
Incidents	Arrests
Crimes violated	Offenders
Victims	Charges
Offenders	Counts
Court Activity	Corrections
Defendants	Offenders
Filings	Admissions
Charges and counts	Returns
Cases	Discharges
Appearances	
Dispositions	
Sentences	

FIGURE 12.1   Units of Count in Criminal Justice Data
Source: Adapted from Poklemba (1988:III1–III3).

felony cases and draw a sample using the systematic or other sampling procedures described in Chapter 8. We have to be alert for potential biases in the sample frame, however, such as a recurring pattern in the listing of cases.

Reliability and Validity

Understanding the details of how agency records are produced is the best guard against reliability and validity problems.

The key to evaluating the reliability and validity of agency records, as well as the general suitability of those data for a research project, is to understand as fully as possible how the data were originally collected. Doing so can help researchers identify potential new uses of data. They will also be better equipped to anticipate and detect potential reliability or validity problems in agency records.

Any researcher who considers using agency records will benefit from a careful reading of Jacob's invaluable little guide, *Using Published Data: Errors and Remedies* (1984). In addition to warning readers about general problems with reliability and validity (such as those discussed in Chapter 5), Jacob cautions users of these data to be aware of other potential errors that can be revealed by scrutinizing source notes. Clerical errors, for example, are unavoidable in such large-scale reporting systems as the UCR. These errors may be detected and reported in correction notices appended to later reports.

Users of data series collected over time must be especially attentive to changes in data collection procedures or changes in the operational definitions of key indicators. As you might expect, such changes are more likely to occur in data series that extend over several years. David Cantor and James Lynch (2005) describe how changes in the NCVS, especially the redesign elements introduced in 1992, should be kept in mind for any long-term analysis of NCVS data. In earlier chapters, we described the NCVS redesign that was completed in 1994. If we plan to conduct research on victimization over time, we will have to consider how changes in sample size and design, increased use of telephone interviews, and questionnaire revisions might affect our findings.

Therefore, longitudinal researchers must search diligently for modifications of procedures or definitions over time to avoid attributing substantive meaning to a change in a particular measure. Furthermore, as the time interval under investigation increases, so does the potential for change in measurement. Ted Robert Gurr (1989:24) cites a good example:

> In the first two decades of the 20th century many American police forces treated the fatalities of the auto age as homicides. The sharp increase in "homicide" rates that followed has led to some dubious conclusions. Careful study of the sources and their historical and institutional context is necessary to identify and screen out the potentially misleading effects of these factors on long-term trends.

This example suggests that cross-sectional researchers must be alert for a slightly different type of potential error. Roger Lane (1997) points out that the tendency to classify fatal accidents as homicides was greater in some cities than in others.

The central point here is that researchers who analyze criminal justice data produced by different cities or states or other jurisdictions must be alert to variations in the definitions and measurement of key variables. Even when definitions and measurement seem straightforward, they may run into problems. For example, statisticians at BJS caution potential users of corrections data:

> . . . some jurisdictions have experienced reporting changes for one or more correctional population collections over time. These changes may result because of administrative changes, such as consolidating databases or implementing new information systems, resulting in data review and cleanup; reconciling offender records; reclassifying offenders, including those on probation to parole and offenders on dual community supervision statuses; and including certain subpopulations that were not previously reported. For these reasons, comparisons between jurisdictions and comparisons between years for the same jurisdiction over time may not be valid. (Kaeble et al., 2015:16)

Fortunately, most published reports on regular data series present basic information on definitions and collection procedures. Many BJS publications include copies of the questionnaires used in surveys and enumerations. Researchers should, however, view summary descriptions in printed reports as no more than a starting point in their search for information on how data were collected. Before analyzing published data in earnest, they should contact the issuing organization to obtain details, perhaps in the form of technical reports.

Sources of Reliability and Validity Problems

We conclude this section on agency records by discussing some general characteristics of record keeping by public agencies. Think carefully about each of the features we mention, considering how each might apply to specific types of criminal justice research. It will also be extremely useful for you to think of some additional examples, perhaps discussing them with your instructor or others in your class.

Social Production of Data   Virtually all criminal justice record keeping is a social process. By this we mean that indicators of, say, arrests, juvenile probation violations, court convictions, or rule infractions by prison inmates reflect decisions made by criminal justice officials, in addition to the actual behavior of juvenile or adult offenders. As Terry Baumer, Michael Maxfield, and Robert Mendelsohn state: "Researchers must realize that performance measures are *composites* of offenders' behavior, organizational capacity to detect behavior, and decisions about how to respond to offenders' misbehavior" (1993:139; emphasis added). A small number of classic articles have described the **social production of data** in the form of crime records by police (Black, 1970; Kitsuse and Cicourel, 1963; Seidman and Couzens, 1974). Richard McCleary (1992) describes the social production of data by parole officers. They may fail to record minor infractions to avoid paperwork or, alternatively, may keep careful records of such incidents in an effort to punish troublesome parolees by returning them to prison. More generally, Clive Coleman and Jenny Moynihan (1996) describe the social production of many criminal justice measures.

Discretionary actions by criminal justice officials and others affect the production of virtually all agency records. Police neither learn about all crimes nor arrest all offenders who come to their attention. Similarly, prosecutors, probation officers, and corrections staff are selectively attentive to charges filed or to rule violations by probationers and inmates. At a more general level, the degree of attention state legislatures and criminal justice officials devote to various crime problems varies over time. Levels of tolerance of such behaviors as child abuse, drug use, acquaintance rape, and even alcohol consumption have changed over the years.

Agency Data Are Not Designed for Research   In many cases, criminal justice officials collect data because the law requires them to do so. More generally, agencies tend to collect data for their own use, not for the use of researchers. Court disposition records are maintained in part because of legal mandates, and such records are designed for the use of judges, prosecutors, and other officials. Record-keeping procedures reflect internal needs and directives from higher authorities. As a consequence, researchers sometimes find it difficult to adapt agency records for a specific research purpose.

For example, Maxfield once wished to trace court dispositions for arrests made by individual police officers in Louisville, Kentucky. "No problem," he was assured by a deputy prosecutor, "we keep all disposition records on the computer." Following this electronic version of a paper trail to the county data processing facility, Maxfield discovered that only the previous year's cases were maintained on computer tape, the most common bulk storage medium at the time. Such tapes were said to be expensive (about $17), and nobody had authorized the data processing staff to buy new tapes for each year's files. Instead, voluminous computer printouts from the previous year were microfilmed and saved, whereas the "costly" computer tape was erased for the new year. Maxfield

Social production of data   Data reflect organizational processes and decisions in addition to the concept being measured.

HOW MANY PAROLE VIOLATORS WERE THERE LAST MONTH?

BY JOHN J. POKLEMBA
New York State Division of Criminal Justice Services

Question: How many parole violators were there last month? Answer: It depends. More accurately, it depends on which agency is asked. Each of the three answers below is right in its own way:

New York State Commission of Correction	611
New York Department of Correctional Services	670
New York Division of Parole	356

The State Commission of Correction (SCOC) maintains daily aggregate information on the local under-custody population. Data are gathered from local sheriffs, using a set of common definitions. The SCOC defines a parole violator as follows: an alleged parole violator being held as a result of allegedly having violated a condition of parole—for example, a new arrest. This makes sense for local jails; a special category is devoted to counting alleged parole violators with new arrests. However, New York City does not distinguish between parole violators with and without new arrests, so the SCOC figure includes violators from upstate New York only.

The Department of Correctional Services (DOCS) is less interested in why people are in jail; their concern centers on the backlog of inmates whom they will soon need to accommodate. Furthermore, as far as DOCS is concerned, the only true parole violator is a technical parole violator. This makes sense for DOCS because a parole violator convicted of a new crime will enter DOCS as a new admission, who— from an administrative standpoint—will be treated differently than a parolee returned to prison for a technical violation.

The Division of Parole classifies parole violators into one of four categories: (1) those who have violated

---

abandoned the project after realizing that data collection would involve viewing literally hundreds of thousands of microfilmed case files, instead of running a quick and easy computer search.

Keep in mind that our research needs may not be congruent with agency record-keeping practices. Courts or police departments commonly use idiosyncratic definitions or methods of classifying information that make such records difficult to use. Also, recognize that our conceptual and operational definitions of key concepts, however thoughtful and precise, will seldom be identical to actual measures maintained by criminal justice agencies.

For another example of how definitional differences can be traced to different agency needs, see the box titled "How Many Parole Violators Were There Last Month?"

Tracking People, Not Patterns At the operational level, officials in criminal justice organizations are generally more interested in keeping track of individual cases than in examining patterns. Police patrol officers and investigators deal with individual calls for service, arrests, or case files. Prosecutors and judges are most attentive to court dockets and the clearing of individual cases; corrections officials maintain records on individual inmates. Although each organization produces summary reports on weekly, monthly, or annual activity, officials tend to be much more interested in individual cases. Michael Geerken (1994) makes this point clearly in his discussion of problems researchers are likely to encounter in analyzing police arrest records. Few rap sheet databases are regularly reviewed for accuracy; rather, they simply accumulate arrest records submitted by individual

a condition of parole, (2) those who have absconded, (3) those who have been arrested for a new crime, and (4) those who have been convicted of a new crime. Once again, this makes sense, because the Division of Parole is responsible for monitoring parolee performance and wishes to distinguish different types of parole violations. The Division also classifies a parole violation as either alleged (yet to be confirmed by a parole board) or actual (the violation has been confirmed and entered into the parolee's file). Further differences in the fluid status of parolees and their violations, together with differences between New York City and other areas, add to the confusion.

Taking the varying perspectives and roles of these three organizations into account, answers to the "How many" question can be made more specific:

SCOC: Last month, there were 611 alleged parole violators who were believed to have violated a condition of their parole by being arrested for a new offense and are being held in upstate New York jails.

DOCS: Last month, there were 670 actual parole violators who were judged to have violated a condition of their parole and are counted among the backlog of persons ready for admission to state correctional facilities.

Parole Division: Last month, 356 parolees from the Division's aggregate population were actually removed from the Division's caseload and were en route to DOCS.

One of the major reasons that agency counts do not match is that agency information systems have been developed to meet internal operational needs. A systemwide perspective is lacking. Questions that depend on data from more than one agency are often impossible to answer with confidence. Recognize also that the availability and quality of state data depend on data from local agencies.

As stated above, the best answer to the question is: It depends.

Source: Adapted from Poklemba (1988:11–13).

---

officers. Joel Best (2013) offers additional examples of how small errors in case-by-case record keeping can accumulate to produce compound errors in summary data.

More criminal justice agencies are developing the capability to analyze data in addition to tracing individual cases. Crime analysis by police tracks spatial patterns of recent incidents; prosecutors are attentive to their scorecards; state correctional intake facilities consider prison capacity, security classification, and program availability in deciding where to send new admissions.

As problem-oriented approaches to policing become adopted more widely, many law enforcement agencies have improved their record-keeping and crime analysis practices. New York City's reduction in reported crime has been attributed to police managers' use of timely, accurate crime

data to plan and evaluate specific anticrime tactics (Bratton, 1999; Kelling and Coles, 1996; Maple, 1999). This illustrates an important general principle about the accuracy of agency-produced data: when agency managers routinely use data to make decisions, they will be more attentive to data quality. The box describing Marie Mele's research offers another example: when domestic violence detectives realized how a database would help them prepare for Compstat, they endorsed the effort to improve their record-keeping procedures.

However, record-keeping systems used in most cities today are still designed more to track individual cases for individual departments than to produce data for management or research purposes. Individual agencies maintain what are sometimes called "silo databases," a colorful label that refers to stacks of data that are isolated from each other. Similar problems have been linked to the failure of intelligence agencies to share information about suspicious activities leading up to the 9/11 attacks (Farmer, 2009; National Commission on Terrorist Attacks upon the United States, 2004).

On the other hand, the increasing use of crime and CFS data in planning police actions is a positive development for two reasons. First, the more data are used in decision making and planning, the more attentive officials will be to data quality. They will also be better prepared to detect possible errors or inconsistency. With respect to our consideration of non-public agency records, think about the questions of reliability and validity discussed here and in other chapters. Calls for service are more inclusive than are reported crimes since they include reported incidents that are not classified as crimes. More importantly, calls for service include data on location or place, which drives the definition of hot spots. Police data on place tend to be more reliable than police data on people involved in an incident (Weisburd et al., 2012). So a criminology of place driven by incidents that are highly concentrated uses non-public agency records that are relatively high-quality measures.

Error Increases with Volume   The potential for clerical errors increases as the number of clerical entries increases. This seemingly obvious point is nonetheless important to keep in mind when analyzing criminal justice records. Lawrence Sherman and Ellen Cohn (1989:34) describe the "mirror effect" of duplicate CFS records. Handling a large volume of CFS, phone operators in Minneapolis (or any large city for that matter) are not always able to distinguish duplicate reports of the same incident. An updated report about a CFS may be treated as a new incident. In either case, duplicate data result.

The relationship between volume of data entry and the potential for error can be especially troublesome for studies of relatively rare crimes or incidents. Although murder is rare compared with other crimes, information about individual homicides might be keyed into a computer by the same clerk who inputs data on parking violations. If a murder record is just one case among hundreds of parking tickets and petty thefts awaiting a clerk, there is no guarantee that the rare event will be treated any differently than the everyday ones.

While preparing a briefing for an Indianapolis commission on violence, Maxfield discovered that a single incident in which four people had been murdered in a rural area appeared twice in computerized FBI homicide records. This was traced to the fact that officers from two agencies—sheriff's deputies and state police—investigated the crime, and each agency filed a report with the FBI. But the thousands of murders entered into FBI computer files for that year obscured the fact that duplicate records had been keyed in for one multiple murder in a rural area of Indiana.

In concluding our lengthy discussion of agency records, we do not mean to leave you with the impression that data produced by and for criminal justice organizations are fatally flawed. Thousands of studies making appropriate use of such data are produced each year. However, it is essential that researchers understand potential sources of reliability and validity problems, as well as ways they can be overcome. Public agencies do not normally collect information for research purposes. The data they do collect often reflect discretionary decisions by numerous individuals. And, like any large-scale human activity, making observations on large numbers of people and processes inevitably produces some error.

Content Analysis

Content analysis involves the systematic study of messages.

The Office of Community Oriented Policing Services (COPS) was established by the 1994 Crime Bill, which promoted community policing by providing funds to local law enforcement agencies. In addition to concerns about the effectiveness of these efforts, COPS staff wanted to know something about the public image of community policing as presented in local newspapers. Stephen Mastrofski and Richard Ritti (1999) conducted a content analysis of stories about community policing in newspapers serving 26 cities. The researchers found more than 7,500 stories from 1993 through 1997, with most focusing on a small number of themes: "community, resources, and producing real results for the community. Stories that offer a viewpoint on community policing are nearly always overwhelmingly positive" (1999:10–11).

This is an example of **content analysis**, the systematic study of messages and the meaning those messages convey. For the COPS office, the study by Mastrofski and Ritti was satisfying—many stories about community policing were published in urban newspapers, and most stories presented positive images.

Content analysis methods may be applied to virtually any form of communication. Among the possible artifacts for study are books, magazines, films, songs, speeches, television programs, email, social media posts, letters, laws, and constitutions, as well as any components or collections of these. Content analysis is particularly well suited to answering the classic question of communications research: who says what, to whom, why, how, and with what effect? As a mode of observation, content analysis requires a considered handling of the *what*, and the analysis of data collected in this mode, as in others, addresses the *why* and *with what effect*.

Coding in Content Analysis

Content analysis is essentially a coding operation, and of course, coding represents the measurement process in content analysis. Communications—oral, written, or other—are coded or classified according to some conceptual framework. Thus, for example, newspaper editorials might be coded as liberal or conservative. Radio talk shows might be coded as bombastic or not. Novels might be coded as detective fiction or not. Political speeches might be coded as containing unsupported rhetoric about crime or not. Recall that terms such as these are subject to many interpretations, and the researcher must specify definitions clearly.

Coding in content analysis involves the logic of conceptualization and operationalization we considered in Chapter 4. In content analysis, as in other research methods, researchers must refine their conceptual framework and develop specific methods for observing in relation to that framework.

For all research methods, conceptualization and operationalization typically involve the interaction of theoretical concerns and empirical observations. If, for example, you believe that some newspaper editorials support liberal crime policies and others support conservative ones, ask yourself why you think so. Read some editorials, asking which are liberal and which are conservative. Is the political orientation of a particular editorial most clearly indicated by its manifest content or by its overall tone? Is your decision based on the use of certain terms (such as *moral decay* or *need for rehabilitation*), or on the support or opposition given to a particular issue, such as mandatory prison sentences versus treatment programs for drug users?

As in other decisions relating to measurement, the researcher faces a fundamental choice between depth and specificity of understanding. The survey researcher must decide whether specific closed-ended questions or more general open-ended questions will better suit her or his needs. By the same token, the content analyst has a choice between searching for manifest or for latent content. Coding the **manifest content**—the visible, surface content—of a communication more closely approximates the use of closed-ended items in a survey questionnaire. Alternatively, coding the **latent content** of the communication—its underlying meaning—is an option. In the most general sense, manifest and latent content can be distinguished by the degree of interpretation required in measurement.

Throughout the process of conceptualizing manifest- and latent-content coding procedures, remember that the operational definition of any variable is composed of the attributes included in it. Such attributes, moreover, should be mutually exclusive and exhaustive. A newspaper editorial, for example, should not be described as both liberal and conservative, although we should probably allow for some to be centrist. It may be sufficient

Content analysis The study of recorded communication.

to code television programs as being violent or not violent, but it is also possible that some programs could be antiviolence.

No coding scheme should be used in content analysis unless it has been carefully pretested. We must decide what manifest or latent contents of communications will be regarded as indicators of the different attributes that make up our research variables, write down these operational definitions, and use them in the actual coding of several units of observation. If we plan to use more than one coder in the final project, each of them should independently code the same set of observations so that we can determine the extent of agreement. In any event, we'll want to take special note of any difficult cases—observations that were not easily classified using the operational definition. Finally, we should review the overall results of the pretest to ensure that they are appropriate to our analytic concerns. If, for example, all of the pretest newspaper editorials have been coded as liberal, we should certainly reconsider our definition of that attribute.

Before beginning to code newspapers, crime dramas on television, or detective fiction, we need to make plans to assess the reliability of coding. Fortunately, reliability in content analysis can be readily tested, if not guaranteed, in two related ways. First, interrater reliability can be determined by having two different people code the same message and then computing the proportion of items coded the same. For example, if 20 attributes of newspaper stories about crime are being coded and two coders score 18 attributes identically, their reliability is 90 percent.

The second way to assess coding reliability is the test–retest method, in which one person codes the same message twice. Of course, some time should elapse between the two coding operations. Test–retest procedures can be used when only one person is doing the coding; reliability can be computed in the same way as if the interrater method were being used.

Illustrations of Content Analysis

We now turn to examples of content analysis in action. The first illustration uses content analysis to measure and characterize terrorist incidents.

The second describes content analysis of a different sort of message—video games. The third demonstrates how extracting information from police records is a form of content analysis.

Global Terrorism Database (GTD) We discussed the GTD as an illustration of measurement in Chapter 6. It's also an example of a content analysis project that gathers information about terrorist incidents from public sources, such as media articles and news archives. Although the GTD is a very large-scale project, its basic steps and procedures are straightforward. We summarize how the GTD operates, drawing mostly on the June 2016 edition of its codebook (Start Codebook, 2016).

Each month, broad screening criteria are applied to media articles published on the Internet. The initial filtering process results in about 400,000 possible articles per month. These are further winnowed down by content analysis software, producing about 16,000 monthly articles that are reviewed by researchers (Start Codebook, 2016:7). One important factor in selecting stories for further analysis is the credibility and reliability of sources, something that's learned and regularly updated as articles are screened.

Six teams of coders then review each incident for further screening and coding. In an effort to increase the validity and reliability of coding, specialized teams work on different parts of the GTD codebook, classified by perpetrators, location, weapons and tactics, and other features of incidents. Each team includes a mix of undergraduate and graduate students who are supervised by a team leader. One coding domain is type of attack, which ". . . reflects the broad class of tactics used" (2016:21), coded into one of nine categories. Here is a segment of the codebook instructions, expressing a concept that you should recall from our discussion of Uniform Crime Reports in Chapter 6:

> When multiple attack types may apply, the most appropriate value is determined based on the hierarchy below. For example, if an assassination is carried out through the use of an explosive, the Attack Type is coded as Assassination, not Bombing/Explosion. (2016:21–22)

The codebook then lays out the attack type hierarchy: assassination, hijacking, kidnapping, barricade incident, bombing/explosion, armed assault, unarmed assault, and facility/infrastructure attack.

You can learn a lot about content analysis in general by visiting the site of the GTD parent organization at the University of Maryland, National Consortium for the Study of Terrorism and Responses to Terrorism (www.start.umd.edu). For example, the publications page includes an article titled, "Video Games, Terrorism, and ISIS's Jihad 3.0," that describes how ISIS recruits sympathizers by attracting them to play a video game, "The Clanging of the Swords" (Al-Rawi, 2016).

Violence in Video Games   It seems that whenever some new technology or musical idiom becomes popular, someone becomes interested in linking it to behavior. Examples include television and violence, pornography and sexual assault, and suggestive lyrics in popular music and sexual behavior. It is always difficult to establish causality in such cases, and we will say nothing more about that. But content analysis is the appropriate research tool for classifying content as violent or sexually explicit.

Kimberly Thompson and Kevin Haninger examined the contents of video games rated in categories "E" (suitable for everyone) and "T" (teens, age 13 and up) by the Entertainment Software Rating Board (ESRC). Their first study (Thompson and Haninger, 2001) sampled 55 of over 600 E-rated games available at the time. An undergraduate college student "with considerable video gaming experience" (2001:592) was assigned to play all games for 90 minutes, or until the game reached a natural conclusion. The game player was videotaped, and the tape formed the basis for content analysis. One researcher (also described as an experienced player) and the game player reviewed the video, and coded several dimensions of what was depicted. In this case, the video game was the unit of analysis.

Coders counted the number of violent *incidents* depicted while the game was being played and timed the duration of each violent incident. Violence was defined as "acts in which the aggressor causes or attempts to cause physical injury or death

to another character." This is an example of latent content. The duration of violent acts was manifest content, although researchers had to distinguish short pauses between violent acts. Additional variables coded included the number of deaths; the presence of drugs, alcohol, or tobacco; profanity and sexual behavior; weapon use; and whether any music was included that itself was rated as explicit. Comparing the duration of violent acts and the number of deaths to how long each game was played yielded two standardized measures: violent minutes as a percentage of all minutes and the number of deaths per minute.

Results showed quite a lot of violence. Action games ranged from 3.3 percent violence ("Sonic Adventure") to 91 percent violence ("Nuclear Strike") as a portion of total time. "Paperboy" depicted no deaths, but "Rat Attack" averaged 8.4 deaths per minute. Games classified as "sports" rarely showed violence.

Later research used similar methods to examine violence in a larger number of games rated as suitable for teens (Haninger and Thompson, 2004). These games displayed a wider variety of behaviors in the general domains of violence, obscenity, substance use, and sexual behavior. Again, the authors did not attempt to link such content with behavior. Their content analysis centered on systematically classifying what sorts of things were depicted in video games, thus providing information independent of industry ratings. Of their findings, authors highlight that ESRC ratings did not mention several examples of violence in almost half of the games reviewed.

Classifying Gang-Related Homicides   When is a homicide gang-related? Are there different types of gang-related homicides? These two questions guided research by Richard Rosenfeld, Timothy M. Bray, and Arlen Egley (1999) in attempting to understand how gang membership might facilitate homicide in different ways. To address these questions, the researchers conducted a content analysis of police case files for homicides in St. Louis over a 10-year period.

By now, you should recognize the importance of conceptualization in most criminal justice research. Rosenfeld and associates began by further specifying the ambiguous term *gang-related*. They distinguished *gang-motivated* and *gang-affiliated* homicides. Gang-motivated killings "resulted from gang behavior or relationships, such as an initiation ritual, the 'throwing' of gang signs, or a gang fight" (1999:500). Gang-affiliated homicides involved a gang member as victim or offender, but with no indication of specific gang activity; a gang member killing a nongang person during a robbery is an example. A third category, nongang youth homicide, included all other murders in which no evidence of gang activity was available and the suspected offender was between ages 10 and 24.

Because St. Louis police did not apply the labels *gang-affiliated* or *gang-motivated*, it was necessary for researchers to code each case into one of the three categories using information from case files. This was a form of content analysis—systematically classifying the messages contained in homicide case files. Homicide case files are good examples of police records that are not maintained for research purposes. Recognizing this, Rosenfeld and associates coded the files in a two-stage process, building reliability checks into each stage.

First, one person coded each case as either gang-related or not gang-related. This might seem a step backward, but by simplifying the process, it focused researchers' measurement on the separate dimensions of homicide of interest to them. It was relatively easy to determine whether any evidence of gang activity or membership was present; if not, the case was classified as a nongang youth killing and set aside. Cases that had some evidence of gang involvement were retained for the second coding stage. During this stage, a second researcher randomly selected a 10 percent sample of cases and coded them again, without knowing how the first coder had classified the sampled cases. You will recognize this as an example of interrater reliability.

The second coding stage involved the finer and more difficult classification of cases as either gang-motivated or gang-affiliated. Interrater reliability checks were again conducted, this time on a 25 percent sample of cases. More cases were selected because reliability was lower in this stage—the two coders exhibited less agreement on how to classify gang homicides. Cases in which independent coding produced discrepancies were reviewed and discussed by the two coders until they agreed on how the homicide should be classified.

From these very different examples, we expect that you can think of many additional applications of content analysis in criminal justice research. You might wish to consult Ray Surette's (2006) excellent book *Media, Crime, and Justice: Images, Realities and Policies* to learn more about the scope of topics for which content analysis can be used. The Government Accountability Office (formerly the General Accounting Office) has an excellent guide to content analysis in general (General Accounting Office, 1996).

Secondary Analysis

Data collected by other researchers are often used to address new research questions.

Our final topic encompasses all sources of criminal justice data we have described thus far: content analysis, agency records, field observation, and surveys. We begin with an example of an unusually ambitious use of secondary data by a prolific criminal justice scholar.

For over three decades, Wesley Skogan has examined the influence of crime on the lives of urban residents. In most cases, his research has relied on sample surveys to investigate questions about fear of crime (Skogan and Maxfield, 1981), community crime prevention (Skogan, 1988), and the relationships between urban residents and police (Skogan, 2007), among others. He has long recognized the importance of incivilities—symbols of social disorder—as indicators of neighborhood crime problems and as sources of fear for urban residents.

In 1990, Skogan published a comprehensive study of incivilities, drawing on his own research as well as studies by others (Skogan, 1990). However, instead of conducting new surveys to collect original data, Skogan based his findings on secondary analysis of 40 surveys conducted in six cities from 1977 through 1983. He aggregated responses from about 13,000 individuals and examined questions about the sources of disorder, its impact, and the scope of action by individuals and police.

Secondary analysis of data collected by other researchers has become an increasingly important tool. Like Skogan, numerous criminal justice researchers have reanalyzed data collected by others. Several factors contribute to this trend, including the high cost of collecting original data through surveys or other means. More important, however, is that data for secondary analysis are readily available. We describe two important sources below.

Suppose you are interested in the relationship between delinquency, drug use, and school performance among adolescents. The National Youth Survey (NYS), which includes responses from 1,725 youths interviewed eleven times from 1975 through 2004, might suit your needs nicely. NYS data were originally collected by Delbert Elliott and associates (e.g., Elliott, Huizinga, and Ageton, 1985). However, like Cesar Rebellon and Karen Van Gundy (2005), who used the NYS data to examine links between child maltreatment and delinquency, you may be able to reanalyze the survey data to address your own research questions.

Or perhaps you wish to learn whether there are differences in the sentencing decisions of black and white judges. Cassia Spohn (1990) addressed this question using data originally collected by Milton Heumann and Colin Loftin (1979), who were interested in the effect of a new Michigan law on plea bargaining. Spohn was able to conduct a secondary analysis of the same data to answer a different research question. Let's examine these examples more closely to see how they illustrate the uses and advantages of secondary analysis.

Original NYS data were collected by Elliott and associates (1985:91) for three related research purposes: (1) to estimate the prevalence and incidence of delinquency and drug use among U.S. adolescents, (2) to assess causal relationships between drug use and delinquency, and (3) to test a comprehensive theory of delinquency. The NYS was designed as a panel survey, in which a nationally representative sample of youths age 11–17 in 1976 was interviewed once each year from 1976 through 1989, then in selected years thereafter. As we described in Chapter 4, this is an example of a longitudinal study, and it is especially well suited to disentangling the time ordering of such behaviors as drug use and delinquency.

Rebellon and Van Gundy (2005) were interested in the time order of somewhat different behaviors—physical abuse in childhood and delinquency—that were not directly addressed by the original researchers. A longitudinal design was equally important in this secondary analysis. Given this research interest, they faced two choices: collect original data by conducting a new panel survey, or reanalyze existing data from a panel survey that included questions on victimization and self-reported delinquency. Because the NYS included questions appropriate for their research purpose, Rebellon and Van Gundy were spared the need (and considerable expense) of conducting a new panel study.

The second example mentioned earlier differs in two ways. First, the research questions addressed by Spohn (1990) and by Heumann and Loftin (1979), who collected the original data, are quite different. Heumann and Loftin studied the impact of a new Michigan law that specified mandatory minimum prison sentences for defendants who used firearms in the course of committing a felony offense. Their primary interest was in reductions in plea bargaining by prosecutors in Michigan's largest county following passage of the firearm statute. Spohn, however, used the same data to address the very different question of whether sentences imposed by black judges systematically differed from those imposed by white judges. Her research interest required data from a site with a sufficient number of black criminal court judges, a condition that was met by the Detroit Recorder's Court in Wayne County (Michigan), where Heumann and Loftin had conducted their original research.

You may have already guessed the second difference between our two examples: research by Spohn used data that had been collected from court records, whereas Rebellon and Van Gundy conducted secondary analysis of survey data. Spohn could have gathered original information from court records, in Detroit or some other city, but she was able to address her research question by conducting a new analysis of data that had already been collected from court records.

Sources of Secondary Data

As a college student, you probably would not be able to launch an eight-wave panel study of a national sample of adolescents, or even gather records from some 2,600 felony cases in Wayne County. You do, however, have access to the same data used in those studies, together with data from thousands of other research projects, through the **Interuniversity Consortium for Political and Social Research (ICPSR)** at the University of Michigan.

Since 1962, the ICPSR has served as a central repository of machine-readable data collected by social science researchers. In the early 1960s, "machine-readable" meant punch cards and paper tape. Current holdings include data from thousands of studies conducted by researchers all over the world.

Of particular interest to criminal justice researchers is the **National Archive of Criminal Justice Data (NACJD)**, established by the BJS in cooperation with the ICPSR (http://www.icpsr.umich.edu/icpsrweb/NACJD/ Accessed 20 August 2016). Here you will find the NYS, Heumann and Loftin's sentencing data, and each of the 40 surveys analyzed by Skogan for the book we mentioned earlier. There's much more, including surveys on criminal justice topics by national polling firms, the NCVS from 1972 to the present, periodic censuses of juvenile detention and correctional facilities, a study of thefts from commercial trucks in New York City, and data from Marvin Wolfgang's classic study of a Philadelphia birth cohort. Data from the growing National Incident-Based Reporting System (NIBRS) are available, with an expanding number of participating agencies dating from 1996. Data from a growing number of regular data series are available for online data analysis. Geographic Information Systems (GIS) data and software can also be found. The possibilities are almost endless and grow each year as new data are added to the archives.

Two special features of the NACJD website are important. First, NACJD has developed a number of data resource guides to help researchers understand how data were collected, and how data files are organized. For example, the National Juvenile Corrections Data Resource Guide summarizes important information about data on children being held in residential placement and other facilities (http://www.icpsr.umich.edu/icpsrweb/content/NACJD/guides/ncjd.html Accessed 20 August 2016). Links are included to data series files that have been formatted for analysis. Also included are summary descriptions of samples, data collection procedures, and questionnaires. NACJD offers comprehensive guides to many other data sources, including the Terrorism and Preparedness Data Resource Center.

Second, working with other universities, the NACD has made a variety of data series available for online analysis. Among other things, this means that researchers do not have to download data, format data files, or even have access to any statistical analysis applications. Basic, descriptive analysis can be executed online. Available data include a wide range of series collected by government agencies, as well as selected research studies. See the complete list at http://www.icpsr.umich.edu/icpsrweb/NACJD/studies?sdaAvailable=true (accessed 20 August 2016).

The BJS has also developed data analysis tools for selected series, such as the NCVS, UCR trends since 1960, and tools to examine arrests and prisoner recidivism risk (http://www.bjs.gov/index.cfm?ty=daa Accessed 20 August 2016). These tools are especially useful for obtaining baselines, trends, or current descriptive data. For example, using the arrest analysis tool reveals that in the year 2011, the Ferguson, Missouri Police Department reported arrests for aggravated assault as shown in Table 12.3.

Other sites on the Internet offer a virtually unlimited source of secondary data. For an example, see the box "International Data on the

TABLE 12.3 Number of Arrests for Aggravated Assault, 2011

| | Ferguson, Missouri | | |
Race	Juvenile	Adult	Total
Black	6	18	24
White	0	0	0

Source: http://www.bjs.gov/index.cfm?ty=datool&surl=/arrests/index.cfm# Accessed 25 August 2014.

Correlates of Terrorist Assassinations" by Marissa Mandala, in which she combined data from several sources online. Note Mandala's description highlights some of the advantages and disadvantages of using secondary data, a topic to which we now turn in concluding this chapter.

Advantages and Disadvantages of Secondary Data

The advantages of secondary analysis are obvious and enormous: It is cheaper and faster than collecting original data, and, depending on who did the original study, you may benefit from the work of topflight professionals and esteemed academics.

The National Longitudinal Study of Adolescent Health, known as "Add Health," began in 1994 with a nationally representative sample of people in grades seven–12. Data are available for four waves of follow-up interviews through 2008. Data include survey questions, self-report, and a variety of physiological measures, and many other items (Harris and Udry, 2014). Criminologists have used Add Health to address a variety of questions on offending and substance use. For example, Marie Skubak Tillyer and Emily Wright (2014) examined the co-occurrence of victimization and offending in domestic violence. J.C. Barnes and associates took advantages of some key features of the Add Health sample to explore whether genetic factors might be associated with patterns of offending over time (Barnes, Beaver, and Boutwell, 2011). A new wave of follow-up interviews are planned for 2016–2018 (http://www.cpc.unc.edu/projects/addhealth Accessed 20 August 2016).

Comparative or international research is possible by using data collected by researchers in other countries or by accessing international data sources, as Marissa Mandala did. Marcelo Aebi and Antonia Linde examined long-term trends of police-recorded crime in eight European countries, finding declines for some offenses, but a substantial and steady increase for drug offenses. Aebi and Linde used data compiled in the *European Sourcebook of Crime and Criminal Justice Statistics* (Aebi and Linde, 2012). Graham Farrell and associates combined crime data from the United States, England, and Wales to assess the effects of different requirements for vehicle security on auto theft rates (Farrell, Mailley, and Tilley, 2011). As expected, researchers found the introduction of laws requiring electronic immobilizers in England and Wales produced sharp drops in theft rates compared to that in the United States.

These examples illustrate an important advantage of conducting research with secondary data. Researchers can gain access to information from large-scale studies conducted over an extended period of time, and using complex measures. Additionally, Web-based compilations of secondary data have made it easier to conduct research for populations and sites outside the United States.

Potential disadvantages must be kept in mind, however. The key problem involves the recurrent question of validity. When one researcher collects data for one particular purpose, you have no assurance that those data will be appropriate to your research interests. Typically, you'll find that the original researcher collected data that "come close" to measuring what you are interested in, but you may wish key variables had been operationalized just a little differently. The question, then, is whether secondary data provide valid measures of the variables you want to analyze.

This closely resembles one of the key problems in the use of agency records. Perhaps a particular set of data does not provide a totally satisfactory measure of what interests you, but other sets of data are available. Even if no one set of data provides totally valid measures, you can build up a weight of evidence by analyzing all the possibilities, as illustrated by Marissa Mandala's work. If each of the imperfect measures points to the same research conclusion, you will have developed considerable support for its accuracy. The use of replication lessens the problem.

In general, secondary data are least useful for evaluation studies. This is the case because evaluations are designed to answer specific questions about specific programs. It is always possible to reanalyze data from evaluation studies, but secondary data cannot be used to evaluate an entirely different program. Thus, for example, a number of researchers have reexamined data collected

INTERNATIONAL DATA ON THE CORRELATES OF TERRORIST ASSASSINATIONS

By Marissa Mandala
John Jay College

My dissertation research examines assassination as a terrorist tactic. While terrorism has become recognized as an important policy question relatively recently, assassinations have occurred for millennia. The term "assassination" has been defined as "the murder of (a usually prominent person) by a sudden/secret attack, often for political reasons" (Stolnici and Buda, 2012, p. 907). Under this definition, researchers have begun to classify some assassinations as terrorist attacks.

Several studies have examined country-level characteristics associated with terrorism generally, but few have examined specific types of attacks like assassination. I became interested in whether the country conditions correlated with terrorism are also associated with assassinations. While I already had a comprehensive database of assassinations from the Global Terrorism Database (GTD), which contains information on global terrorist assassinations since 1970, a single database containing all of the possible country-level correlates of terrorism does not exist. As a result, I compiled indicators of various country-level characteristics from different secondary sources and integrated them into one data file to serve as the independent variables in my analyses. My dependent variable was the count of total assassinations in about 200 countries for the years 1995, 2000, 2005, and 2010.

The process of collecting the different correlates of terrorism proved to be challenging in certain respects. I could not conduct a longitudinal analysis, because I was unable to incorporate every independent variable for every year. Some sources were limited in the number of countries they covered, and others were limited in the years they covered. For example, I initially planned to use the Corruption Perceptions Index to include a measure of corruption. However, I discovered that it did not cover a substantial portion of countries, particularly in the years prior to 2003. I searched for another source on corruption and found the Control of Corruption indicator published by the World Governance Indicators (WGI) project. While this source was more comprehensive in its global coverage, it did not contain data for 1995. Similarly, three indicators for Forcibly Displaced Populations published by the Center for Systemic Peace (refugees originating in country, internally displaced persons, and refugees hosted by country) were not available for the 2010 analysis. Another example is the data used to construct the Religious Diversity Index, which summarizes data on the percentage of a country's population

for a series of domestic violence experiments conducted by Lawrence Sherman and others in several cities (see Sherman, 1992a, for a summary). In most cases, these secondary researchers (such as Maxwell, Garner, and Fagan, 2001) wished to verify or reassess findings from the original studies. But it is not possible to use those data to answer questions about domestic violence interventions, other than arrest or to evaluate arrest policies in new cities where the experiments did not take place.

In this book, the discussion of secondary analysis has a special purpose. As we conclude our examination of modes of observation in criminal justice research, you should have developed a full appreciation for the range of possibilities available in finding the answers to questions about crime and criminal justice policy. No single method of getting information unlocks all puzzles, yet there is no limit to the ways you can learn about things. And, more powerfully, you can zero in on an issue from several independent directions, gaining an even greater mastery of it.

This chapter's installment of our running example, "Putting It All Together: Agency Records and Content Analysis," illustrates how researchers have used different sources of data in efforts to understand racial profiling and traffic enforcement.

following different religions. While this source goes as far back as 1945, I could only find its data up through 2010. It also contained data for every five years, rather than every year.

Some sources also altered their methodology, and in some cases added or deleted variables for different years. An example is the Cingranelli-Richards CIRI Human Rights Data Project, from which I decided to use two variables: physical integrity rights and independence of the judiciary. Other variables were changed or deleted after certain years. For example, the indicators representing government respect for human rights changed in 2007, and the variable for women's social rights was retired in 2005.

Because of these changes and discontinuities in indications over time, my analysis focused on four years: 1995, 2000, 2005 and 2010, with different years containing different variables.

Despite these challenges, this approach produced data that made it possible to address my research questions. Each source systematically collects data and operationalizes complex social, political, and economic constructs using consistent definitions. Even with changes in methodology or variables for some sources during certain years, most sources and measures were consistent across several years. Some data sources may be more reliable than others depending on the complexity of the construct being measured. For example,

concepts like economic growth and domestic conflict are easier to measure than more abstract concepts such as a government's control of corruption. While the World Bank's Gross Domestic Product data may not provide a complete economic profile of a country, it is a reliable representation of growth in terms of the total goods and services produced in a given country. Similarly, the variables measuring domestic conflict from the Major Episodes of Political Violence and the Forcibly Displaced Populations datasets can be seen as reliable given how conflict and violence are often well documented, and thus relatively easy to count.

My research ultimately found assassinations to be associated with some of the same variables linked to terrorism generally: religious diversity, major episodes of political violence, physical integrity rights, political stability, and independent judiciaries. As a result, disaggregating specific terrorist tactics, like assassinations, from terrorism in general may assist policy makers and practitioners in their development and implementation of counterterrorism measures.

Sources: Global Terrorism Database (https://www.start.umd.edu/gtd); Corruption Perceptions Index (http://www.transparency.org/research/cpi/overview); World Governance Indicators (http://info.worldbank.org/governance/wgi/index.aspx#home); Center for Systemic Peace (http://www.systemicpeace.org/); Religious Diversity Index (http://www.pewforum.org/2014/04/04/religious-diversity-index-scores-by-country/); and CIRI Human Rights Data Project (http://www.humanrightsdata.com/).

SUMMARY

- Many public organizations produce statistics and data for the public record, and these data are often useful for criminal justice researchers.
- All organizations keep nonpublic records for internal operational purposes, and these records are valuable sources of data for criminal justice research.
- Public organizations can sometimes be enlisted to collect new data—through observation or interviews—for use by researchers.
- The units of analysis represented by agency data may not always be obvious, because agencies typically use different, and often unclear, units of count to record information about people and cases.

- Researchers must be especially attentive to possible reliability and validity problems when they use data from agency records.
- "Follow the paper trail" and "Expect the expected" are two general maxims for researchers to keep in mind when using agency records in their research.
- Content analysis is a research method appropriate for studying human communications. Because communication takes many forms, content analysis can study many other aspects of behavior.
- Coding is the process of transforming raw data—either manifest or latent content—into a standardized, quantitative form.

Data from agency records lie at the heart of research and policy concern about racial profiling. As we have pointed out in earlier chapters, data that show disproportionate numbers of minorities stopped for traffic violations have been repeatedly cited as evidence of discrimination. Some such claims have been based on inappropriate comparisons, such as comparing records of traffic stops on an interstate highway to the population of a state. One interesting side effect of concern about racial profiling has been more careful attention to the characteristics of data on traffic stops.

WHAT WE DON'T KNOW ...

Until 1999, New Jersey State Police records of traffic stops were incomplete, unreliable, and were the foundation of claims that simultaneously documented and denied patterns of racial disparities in traffic stops. State police were supposed to record information on "the racial characteristics of detained motorists" (Verniero and Zoubek, 1999:31), but such information was often missing. Investigations by the New Jersey Attorney General and the U.S. Department of Justice lamented the inconsistent records. In fact, the missing information on race of people stopped was cited by New Jersey State Police, claiming that they had no way of knowing whether black drivers were stopped, searched, and otherwise subject to greater scrutiny than were white drivers. As a result, a formal agreement between the U.S. Department of Justice and the state of New Jersey included broad specifications for improving data collection. Furthermore, data collection in New Jersey was subject to semiannual audits for several years. This is a good example of the principle that the quality of data gathered by public agencies is directly related to the extent those data are used by the agency.

New Jersey was not alone. A 1999 survey by the Bureau of Justice Statistics found that only 9 of 49 state police agencies routinely collected demographic information on the race of drivers for all traffic stops (Strom and Durose, 2000). Growing national interest in racial profiling promoted several states to begin collecting such data, so that by 2004, 22 states recorded demographic information on drivers stopped (Hickman, 2005). The increase in states collecting data was accompanied by attention to data quality. Guides published by the National Institute of Justice (Ramirez, McDevitt, and Farrell, 2000), and the Police Executive Research Forum (Fridell, 2004, 2005) explained how police agencies should collect, audit, and analyze stop data for evidence of racial disparities.

SUPPLEMENTING PENNSYLVANIA DATA

Engel and associates (2004) drew on these resources to design new data collection procedures for the Pennsylvania State Police. This was a laudable effort to enhance the reliability of traffic stop data at the outset of their research. The research team first worked with command staff to gain approval. They then included line officers and union representatives in a collaborative effort to design new data collection forms and procedures. As we mentioned in Chapter 3, the confidentiality of troopers was protected by removing identifying information from traffic stop records. Researchers believed this was an important component of their efforts to enhance the accuracy of data, at the same time supporting their claims that data would not be used to monitor individual troopers.

This kind of attention to detail appeared to pay off. About 327,000 stop records were produced in the first year; missing information was found in only 4 percent. Of the total stops, 75 percent were for speeding, adding support to the authors' decision to use speeding as the primary indicator for traffic violation (2004:24). Residence of driver turned out to be an important item on the data collection form. Almost all drivers (96 percent) were stopped outside the municipality where they lived, and two-thirds were stopped outside their home county (p. 43). An even larger proportion of black drivers were stopped outside their county of residence (82 percent), and half of black drivers lived outside of Pennsylvania. These findings offer strong evidence against using resident population as a benchmark to assess disproportionality in traffic stops.

CITATION ZONES

Examining traffic stop data in North Carolina, Smith et al. (2003) discovered very uneven spatial distributions of stops. They found concentrations of stops on some highway segments, whereas nearby roads had few traffic stops. This led the researchers to conclude that "citation zones" played a major role in where cars were stopped. Another phrase for citation zone is speed trap, but Smith et al. argue that this term oversimplifies a complex process of deciding where to deploy patrol units. Analysis of stop records indicated that citation zones were most often found on interstate highways, and were in fact concentrated in a relatively small number of locations. This proved to be quite important, as data from drivers' surveys (discussed in Chapter 9) revealed that African American drivers were more likely to report traveling on interstate highways, especially in unfamiliar locations. As a result, African American drivers were disproportionately exposed to citation zones; they were more likely to drive in areas where enforcement was concentrated.

Maxfield and Kelling (2005) report similar findings for New Jersey, combining data on traffic stops with data on traffic volume. About 46 percent of traffic stops over the course of one year took place in the southern segment of the turnpike. From earlier chapters, you may recall that the southern segment was an outlier with respect to race of drivers stopped. Consulting traffic volume data from the New Jersey Department of Transportation showed that the southern segment had the lowest volume of traffic, just about one-fourth the average daily volume of the northern segment in the metropolitan New York area. Combining agency records from these different sources suggested that the southern segment was clearly a citation zone.

CONTENT ANALYSIS OF PROBLEMS

In Chapter 10, we mentioned Carsten Andresen's unstructured interviews with troopers. Among the topics he covered was whether certain areas or situations were believed to be particular problems. Here are excerpts from the very detailed coding instructions Andresen used to classify trooper comments (2005:236):

Commercial Attractions: Problems in a specific commercial area in the patrol beat. For example, one trooper complained about an amusement park that attracted scores of people throughout the year and created traffic problems.

Crime Hot Spots: Reference to geographic areas that were the setting for either minor or major crimes. This category does not refer to Commercial Attractions, Low Income Areas, Rest Areas, or Seasonal Areas. Rather this category refers to troopers who said they have to deal with a town full of bars that are filled with drunks, underpasses where people loiter, parks where people do drugs or take prostitutes, and/or sections of back rural roads where drunks travel.

Illegal Immigrants: Reference to illegal aliens or migrant workers. This category is important because some troopers stated that illegal aliens are a difficult group because they do not carry driver's licenses and their cars are illegally registered, which is problematic during a traffic stop, traffic accident, and/or criminal incident.

Seasonal Areas: Problems in seasonal areas during the summer. Specifically, this category captures troopers who complained about increased traffic to the beach, the behavior of people at campsites, or problems with break-ins in summer homes (which are reported at the start of the summer when the summer people first come and find out that someone broke into their house).

- Secondary analysis is the analysis of data collected earlier by another researcher for some purpose other than the topic of the current study.
- Archives of criminal justice and other social data are maintained by the ICPSR and the NACJD for use by other researchers.
- The advantages and disadvantages of using secondary data are similar to those for agency records; data previously collected by a researcher may not match our own needs.

KEY TERMS

Content analysis *(p. 345)*

Interuniversity Consortium for Political and Social Research (ICPSR) *(p. 350)*

Latent content *(p. 345)*

Manifest content *(p. 345)*

National Archive of Criminal Justice Data (NACJD) *(p. 350)*

Obtrusive measurement *(p. 327)*

Published statistics *(p. 329)*

Secondary analysis *(p. 327)*

Social production of data *(p. 341)*

Unobtrusive measurement *(p. 327)*

REVIEW QUESTIONS AND EXERCISES

1. The NACJD includes a variety of data resource guides on its home page (http://www.icpsr.umich.edu/icpsrweb/NACJD/). Each resource guide describes how a data series is collected, along with key features of measures and other information. Choose two data resource guides, and then: (a) summarize in a paragraph or so how data were collected, and what are the units of analysis; and (b) formulate at least one research question that you think can be addressed by data in the series.

2. Visit the FBI UCR website (http://www.ucrdatatool.gov). Use the table-building tool to find violent crime rates and property crime rates for 10 states. Or, examine trends in reported crime for a 20-year period. Briefly write up a summary of results.

3. Many news feed services are available on the Web. Google Alert is one example. Create a news feed on a criminal justice topic of interest, and accumulate stories for a week or so. Be aware of a trade-off between being too narrow (not enough stories) and too broad (being overwhelmed with stories). Write two paragraphs that describe how you would go about conducting a content analysis on concepts of interest in the stories. Focus on manifest content.

PART 4

Application and Analysis

Criminal justice research can be conducted in many ways to answer many types of questions. We have touched on various research purposes throughout the text, but the first chapter in this section examines a specific research purpose more closely. Because crime is an important and seemingly intractable social problem, researchers and public officials alike increasingly are turning to applied research for answers.

Chapter 13 describes evaluation research and problem analysis. As we will see, careful specification of concepts and attention to measures are as important for applied research as they are for other research purposes.

Chapter 14 takes up the question of data analysis. After we have designed a research project, specified measures, and collected data, we will search for patterns and relationships for description, explanation, or evaluation, depending on the research purpose. In Chapter 14, we will take a preliminary look at descriptive and inferential statistics. Our goal is to establish a familiarity with the principles of basic statistical analysis.

CHAPTER 13

Evaluation Research and Problem Analysis

In this chapter, our attention centers on applied criminal justice research. Evaluation studies are conducted to learn whether programs have succeeded or failed, and why. Problem analysis helps officials plan their actions and anticipate the possible effects of new programs.

Learning Objectives

1. Summarize evaluation research and problem analysis as examples of applied research in criminal justice.

2. Describe how different types of evaluation activities correspond to different stages in the policy process.

3. Explain the role of an evaluability assessment.

4. Understand why a careful formulation of the problem, relevant measurements, and criteria of success or failure are essential in evaluation research.

5. Describe the parallels between evaluation research designs and other designs.

6. Explain the advantages, requirements, and limits of randomized field experiments.

7. Summarize the importance of process evaluations conducted independently or in connection with an impact assessment.

8. Describe the role of problem analysis as a planning technique that draws on the same social science research methods used in program evaluation.

9. Explain how the scientific realist approach focuses on mechanisms in context, rather than generalizable causal processes.

10. Present an example of how criminal justice agencies increasingly are using problem analysis tools, crime mapping, and other space-based procedures.

11. Explain how evaluation research entails special logistical, ethical, and political problems.

Evaluating Vehicle Security

Graham Farrell and associates (2011) investigated vehicle theft trends for Australia, Canada, England and Wales, and the United States. This was part of a research project undertaken by Michael Maxfield and Ronald Clarke on the effectiveness of auto parts-marking in the United States.

Vehicle theft had been persistently high in Australia for many years, prompting officials to take a variety of measures to reduce the problem (Carroll, 2004). Farrell and associates took advantage of the staged introduction of security measures in different parts of Australia to conduct an evaluation of the effectiveness of electronic engine immobilizers. These devices prevent a vehicle's engine from being started unless an electronic key code matches the code installed in the vehicle.

The accompanying figure shows trends in motor vehicle theft for Western Australia, one of the country's states and territories, and for the other seven states and territories. Data points are an index set at 100 for the year 1997. Thefts in subsequent years are expressed as change in that base. For example, the value for Western Australia in 1998 was 118, which means vehicle theft had increased 18 percent in 1998 compared to the previous year. By the year 2008, the index for Western Australia had declined to about 40, which means vehicle theft had dropped by about 60 percent from 1997 through 2008.

The figure also shows vertical lines that correspond to government action regarding electronic immobilizers:

■ In 1999, immobilizers were required for *all cars* less than 12 years old registered in Western Australia.
■ In 2001, immobilizers were required for *all new cars* sold throughout Australia.

You can see a clear trend downward in the two series after immobilizer requirements were introduced in different places at different times. The declines correspond roughly with requirements, and the requirements were introduced in different years.

This figure presents an example of an interrupted time series, a type of evaluation often used to assess whether change follows some new law. We describe this and other approaches to evaluation in this chapter. Keep this example in mind as you read our discussion of different types of applied research.

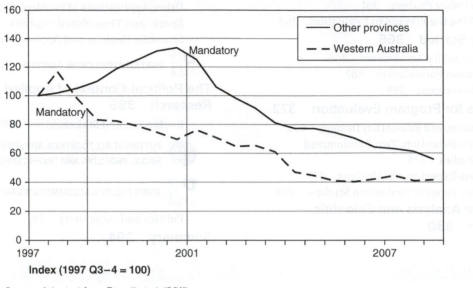

Trends in Australian Vehicle Theft 1997–2007

Index (1997 Q3–4 = 100)

Source: Adapted from Farrell et al. (2011).

Introduction

Evaluation research and problem analysis are increasingly important activities for researchers and public officials alike.

Evaluation research—sometimes called—"program evaluation"—refers to a research purpose rather than a specific research method. Its special purpose is to evaluate the effects of policies such as mandatory arrest for domestic violence, innovations in probation, and new sentencing laws. Another type of evaluation study, **problem analysis**, helps public officials plan and select alternative actions. Virtually all types of designs, measures, and data collection techniques can be used in evaluation research and problem analysis.

Problem analysis An analytic method to help officials plan and select alternative actions.

Evaluation research in criminal justice is probably as old as criminal justice research in general. Whenever people have instituted a new program for a specific purpose, they have paid attention to its actual consequences, even if they have not always done so in a conscious, deliberate, or sophisticated fashion. Over time, the field of evaluation research has become an increasingly important research specialty, which is reflected in the proliferation of associated textbooks, courses, and projects. As a consequence, you are likely to read growing numbers of evaluation reports and, as a researcher, be asked to conduct evaluations.

In part, the growth of evaluation research no doubt reflects rising desire on the part of criminal justice researchers to make a real difference in the world. At the same time, we cannot discount the influence of two additional factors: (1) increased state and federal requirements for program evaluations to accompany the implementation of new programs, and (2) the availability of research funds to meet that requirement.

By the same token, increased interest in program evaluation and problem analysis has followed heightened concern for the accountability of public officials and public policy. Criminal justice agencies are expected to justify the effectiveness and cost of their actions. If traditional approaches to probation supervision, for example, do not deter future lawbreaking, new approaches should be developed and their effectiveness assessed. Or, if using temporary detention facilities fabricated from recycled shipping containers is less costly than constructing new jails, public officials should consider whether the lower-cost alternative would meet their needs for pretrial detention and short-term incarceration.

Justice agencies have come to rely more on **evidence-based policy**, in which the actions of justice agencies are linked to evidence used for planning and evaluation. Traditional practices are being reevaluated against evidence provided by social science research. The Problem-Oriented Guides series summarizes evidence concerning police responses to problems ranging from abandoned buildings (Shane, 2012) to exporting stolen vehicles (Petrossian and Clarke, 2012). The management and accountability practice known as Compstat and its variations design police actions that are based on evidence about the location and circumstances of crime problems. Corrections policies are increasingly evaluated to sort out those that do in fact reduce reoffending (Aos et al., 2011). George Mason University maintains the Center for Evidence-Based Crime Policy (http://cebcp.org [Accessed 21 August 2016]) to help translate applied justice research into state and local initiatives on crime and justice. This trend represents an expansion of applied research that moves beyond collaborations between justice professionals and professional researchers.

Finally, researchers at the John Jay College of Criminal Justice Research and Evaluation Center (REC) have launched an initiative for **evidence generation**. Prompted partly by New York State policies to reform juvenile justice, not-for-profit organizations in New York City have developed innovative programs tailored to the needs of local youths involved in juvenile or criminal justice courts. Researchers at the REC help affiliated organizations evaluate and document their programming, thus generating evidence that can be shared with others. For more information and examples of this collaborative work, see the website johnjayrec.nyc/evgen (Accessed 28 August 2016).

Topics Appropriate for Evaluation Research and Problem Analysis

Problem analysis and evaluation are used to develop justice policy and determine its impact.

Evaluation research is appropriate whenever some policy intervention occurs or is planned. A policy intervention is an action taken for the purpose of producing an intended result. In its simplest sense, evaluation research is a process of determining whether the intended result was produced. Problem analysis focuses more on deciding what intervention should be pursued. Given alternative courses of action, which is likely to be least costly, most effective, or least difficult to implement? Our focus, of course, is on the analysis and evaluation of criminal justice policy and criminal justice agencies. However, it will be useful to first consider a simple general model of the policy-making process in order to understand various topics appropriate to evaluation and problem analysis.

The Policy Process

Figure 13.1 presents our model, adapted from Robert Lineberry's (1977:42–43) classic summary of a policy system. A similar type of "input–output" model is described in a National Institute of Justice publication on evaluation guidelines (McDonald and Smith, 1989). Although we will examine each step in turn, recognize that the policy process is fluid—like the research process in general, as we discussed in Chapter 1—and does not always start at the beginning and conclude at the end.

The policy process begins with some demand that normally appears as support for a new course of action or opposition to existing policy. Such

> **Evidence-based policy**   The use of data and other sources of information to formulate and evaluate justice policy.

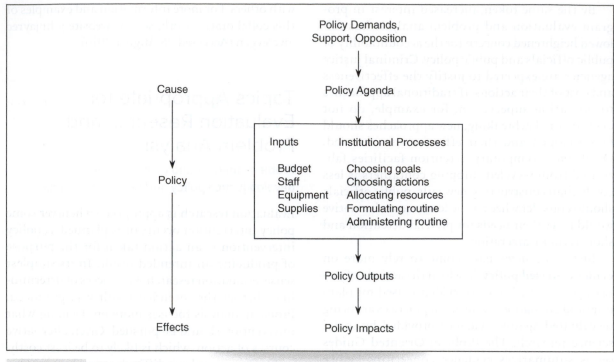

FIGURE 13.1   The Policy Process

Source: Adapted from Lineberry (1977:42–43).

demands can emerge from within a public organization or from outside sources. For example, widely publicized cases of racial discrimination in drug sentencing eventually led to the revision of federal sentencing guidelines for drug offenses (United States Sentencing Commission, 2014). Or, a local prosecutor may independently decide to review all sentence recommendations made by deputies who prosecute drug cases. Before any action can be taken, demands must find a place on the policy agenda. A prosecutor might ignore accusations of discrimination published in an alternative newspaper that is held in low esteem, or she or he may decide not to take actions on suggestions for changes that emerge from within the district attorney's office.

The next step shown in Figure 13.1 actually encompasses several steps. Policy makers consider ultimate goals they wish to accomplish and different means of achieving those goals. Does a prosecutor seek absolute equality in sentences recommended for all white and African American drug defendants, or should there be ranges of permissible variation based on criminal history,

severity of charges, and so on? Resources must be allocated from available inputs, including personnel, equipment, supplies, and even time. Who will review sentence recommendations? How much time will that take, and will additional staff be required? Because the word *policy* implies some standard course of action about how to respond to some recurring problem or issue, routine practices and decision rules must be formulated. Will sentence recommendations for each case be reviewed as they are prepared, or is it sufficient to review all cases on a weekly basis?

Policy outputs refer to what is actually produced, in much the same manner that a manufacturer of office supplies produces paper clips and staples. In our hypothetical example, the prosecutor's policy produces the routine review of sentence recommendations in drug cases. Or, to consider a different example, a selective traffic enforcement program intended to reduce auto accidents on a particular roadway may produce a visible police presence, together with traffic citations for speeding.

In the final stage, we consider the impact of policy outputs. Does the prosecutor's review process actually eliminate disparities in sentences? Are auto accidents reduced in the targeted enforcement area?

The distinction between policy outputs and their impacts is important for understanding applications of evaluation to different stages of the policy process. Unfortunately, this difference is often confusing to both public officials and researchers. *Impacts* are fundamentally related to policy goals; they refer to the basic question of what a policy action is trying to achieve. *Outputs* embody the means to achieve desired policy goals. A prosecutor seeks to achieve equality in sentence recommendations (impact), so a review process is produced as a means to achieve that goal (output). Or a police executive allocates officers, patrol cars, and overtime pay to produce traffic citations (outputs) in the expectation that citations will achieve the goal of reducing auto accidents (impact).

Now consider the left side of Figure 13.1. Our policy model can be expressed as a simple cause-and-effect process, such as we considered in earlier chapters. Some cause has produced the variation in sentences for African American and white defendants, or some cause has produced a concentration of auto accidents. Policies are formulated to produce some effect or impact. In this sense, a policy can be viewed as a hypothesis in which an independent variable is expected to produce change in some dependent variable. Sentence review procedures are expected to produce a reduction in sentence disparities; targeted enforcement is expected to produce a reduction in auto accidents. Goal-directed public policies may therefore be viewed as if-then statements: If some policy action is taken, then we expect some result to be produced.

Linking the Process to Evaluation

By comparing this simple model with a general definition of program evaluation given in one of the most widely used texts on the subject (Rossi, Freeman, and Lipsey, 1999), we get a clearer sense of the topics appropriate to applied research. Peter Rossi, Howard Freeman, and Mark Lipsey (1999:4) define program evaluation as

> . . . the use of social science research procedures to systematically assess the effectiveness of social intervention programs. More specifically,

evaluation researchers (evaluators) use social research methods to study, appraise, and help improve social programs in all their aspects, including the diagnosis of the social problems they address, their conceptualization and design, their implementation and administration, their outcomes, and their efficiency. (emphasis in original)

We have been discussing systematic social science research procedures throughout this book. Now let's substitute criminal justice for social programs, and see how this definition and Figure 13.1 help us to understand program evaluation applications.

Problem Analysis Activities listed under "Institutional Processes" in Figure 13.1 refer to conceptualization and design. For example, faced with a court order to maintain prison populations within established capacity, corrections officials might begin by conceiving and designing different ways to satisfy this demand. Problem analysis is an example of a social science research procedure that can help corrections officials analyze alternative actions, choose among them, and formulate routine practices for implementing policy to comply with a court order.

One approach might be to increase rated capacity through new construction or conversion of existing facilities. Another might be to devise a program to immediately reduce the existing population. Still another might be to cut back on the admission of newly sentenced offenders. The need to protect public safety is a more general goal that would certainly be considered. Each goal implies different types of actions, together with different types and levels of resources, which would be considered within constraints implied by the need to protect public safety. If officials from other organizations—prosecutors, judges, or state legislators—were involved in conceptualization and design, then additional goals, constraints, and policies might be considered.

Increasing capacity by building more prisons would be the most costly approach in financial terms, but it might also be viewed as the most certain way to protect public safety. Early release of current inmates would be cheaper and faster than building new facilities, but this goal implies other decisions, such as how persons would be selected and whether they would be released to parole or to halfway houses. Additionally, each of these alternatives requires some organizational capacity to choose inmates for release, place them in halfway houses, or supervise compliance with parole. Refusing new admissions would be least costly. Political support must be considered for each possible approach. Each alternative—spending money on new construction, accepting responsibility for early release, or tacitly passing the problem on to jails that must house inmates refused admission to state facilities—requires different types of political influence or courage.

Many other topics in criminal justice research are appropriate for problem analysis. Police departments use such techniques to help determine the boundaries of patrol beats. In most large cities, analysts examine the concentration of calls for service in terms of space and time and consider how street layout and obstacles might facilitate or impede patrol car mobility.

A growing number of law enforcement agencies are using computerized crime maps to detect emerging patterns in crime and develop appropriate responses. Producing computer-generated maps that display reported crimes within days after they have occurred is one of the most important policy planning tools for the New York City Police Department (Silverman, 1999). Other departments have taken advantage of funding and technical assistance made available to enhance mapping and other crime analysis capabilities (Santos, 2012). We'll have more to say about mapping later in this chapter.

Court administrators often make changes in the way cases are scheduled for individual judges after estimating what effects such changes will have. Estimates usually are based on analysis of past case volume and predicted future volume. Many states now conduct "prison impact" studies to estimate shifts in prison populations that will result from legislative changes in sentence length.

Program Evaluation Problem analysis takes place in the policy-making stage. In contrast,

program evaluation studies are conducted in later stages and seek answers to two types of questions: (1) Are policies being implemented as planned? and (2) Are policies achieving their intended goals? Evaluation, therefore, seeks to link the intended actions and goals of criminal justice policy to empirical evidence that policies are being carried out as planned, and are having the desired effects. These two types of questions correspond to two related types of program evaluations: process evaluation and impact assessment. Returning to our example of policies to reduce prison population, we will first consider impact assessment and then process evaluation.

Let's assume that corrections department policy analysts select an early-release program to reduce the population of one large institution. Inmates who have less than 120 days remaining on their sentences and who were committed for nonviolent offenses will be considered for early release. Assume further that of those inmates selected for early release, some will be assigned to parole officers and some will serve their remaining sentence in halfway houses—working at jobs during the weekdays but spending evenings and weekends in a community-based facility.

The program has two general goals: (1) to reduce prison population to the court-imposed ceiling and (2) to protect public safety. Whereas the first goal is fairly straightforward, the second is uncomfortably vague. What do we mean by "protecting public safety"? For now, let's say we will conclude that the program is successful in this regard if, after six months, aggregate arrest rates for new offenses by persons in the two early-release conditions are equal to or less than a comparison group of inmates released after completing their sentences.

Our **impact assessment** would examine data on the prison population before and after the new program was implemented, together with arrest records for the two types of early releases and a comparison group. We might obtain something like the hypothetical results shown in Table 13.1 for a subset of 213 evaluation subjects.

Did the program meet its two goals? Your initial reaction might be that it did not, but Table 13.1 presents some interesting findings. The prison population certainly was reduced, but it did not reach the court-imposed cap of 1,350. Those released to halfway houses had lower arrest rates

Impact assessment An evaluation to determine whether a program achieved its intended result.

TABLE 13.1 Hypothetical Results of Early-Prison-Release Impact Assessment

	New Arrests After 6 Months	Number of Inmates Released
Normal release	26%	142
Early release	27%	71
Early release to halfway houses	17%	25
Early parole	33%	46
Total	26%	213

Note: Preprogram population = 1,578; actual population after implementation = 1,402; court-imposed population cap = 1,350.

than all others, but persons placed on early parole had higher arrest rates than those in the normal release condition. Averaging arrest rates for all three groups shows that the total figure is about the same as that for persons released early. Notice also that almost twice as many people were released to early parole as were placed in halfway houses.

The impact assessment results in Table 13.1 would have been easier to interpret if we had conducted a **process evaluation**. A process evaluation focuses on program outputs, as represented in Figure 13.1, seeking answers to the question of whether the program was implemented as intended. If we had conducted a process evaluation of this early-release program, we might have discovered that something was amiss in the selection process. Two pieces of evidence in Table 13.1 suggest that "creaming," one of the selection biases we considered in Chapter 7, might be at work in this program. Recall that creaming is the natural tendency of public officials to choose experimental subjects least likely to fail. In this case, selectivity is indicated by the failure of the early-release program to meet its target number, the relatively small number of persons placed in halfway houses, and the lower rearrest rates for these persons. A process evaluation would have monitored selection procedures and probably revealed evidence of excessive caution on the part of corrections officials in releasing offenders to halfway houses.

Ideally, impact assessments and process evaluations are conducted together. To paraphrase Peter Drucker's (1973) famous comment about efficiency

and effectiveness, the different types of evaluations address similar questions:

- *Process evaluation:* Are we doing things right?
- *Impact evaluation:* Are we doing the right things?

Our example illustrates the important fundamental point that process evaluations make impact assessments more interpretable. In other cases, process evaluations may be conducted when an impact assessment is not possible. To better understand how process evaluations and impact assessments complement each other, let's now look more closely at how evaluations are conducted.

Getting Started

Learning policy goals is a key first step in doing evaluation research.

Several steps are involved in planning any type of research project. This is especially true in applied studies, for which even more planning may be required. In evaluating a prison early-release program, we need to think about design, measurement, sampling, data collection procedures, analysis, and so on. We also have to address such practical problems as obtaining access to people, information, and data needed in an evaluation.

In one sense, however, evaluation research differs slightly in the way research questions are developed and specified. Recall that we equated program evaluation with hypothesis testing; policies are equivalent to if-then statements postulating that some intervention will have some desired impact. Therefore, preliminary versions of research questions already will have been formulated for many types of evaluations. Problem analysis usually considers a limited range of alternative choices, process evaluations focus on whether programs are carried out according to plans, and impact assessments evaluate whether specified goals are attained.

This is not to say that evaluation research is a straightforward business of using social science methods to answer specific questions that

Process evaluation An evaluation to determine whether a program was implemented as intended.

are clearly stated by criminal justice officials. It is often difficult to express policy goals in the form of if-then statements that are empirically testable. Another problem is the presence of conflicting goals. Many issues in criminal justice are complex, involving different organizations and people. And different organizations and people may have different goals that make it difficult to define specific evaluation questions. Perhaps most common and problematic are vague goals. Language describing criminal justice programs may optimistically state goals of "enhancing public safety by reducing recidivism" without clearly specifying (or knowing) what is meant by that objective.

In most cases, researchers have to help criminal justice officials formulate testable goals, something that is not always possible. Other obstacles may interfere with researchers' access to important information. Because of these and similar problems, evaluation researchers must first address the question of whether to evaluate at all.

Evaluability Assessment

An evaluability assessment is described by Rossi, Freeman, and Lipsey (1999:157) as sort of a "pre-evaluation," in which a researcher determines whether conditions necessary for conducting an evaluation are present. One obvious condition is support for the study from organizations delivering program components that will be evaluated. The word *evaluation* may be threatening to public officials, who fear that their own job performance is being rated. Even if officials do not feel personally threatened by an impact assessment or other applied study, evaluation research can disrupt routine agency operations. Ensuring agency cooperation and support is, therefore, an important part of evaluability assessment. Even if no overt opposition exists, officials may be ambivalent about evaluation. This might be the case, for example, if an evaluation is required as a condition of launching some new program.

This and other steps in evaluability assessment may be accomplished by "scouting" a program and interviewing key personnel (Rossi, Freeman, and Lipsey, 1999:135). The focus in scouting and

interviewing should be on obtaining preliminary answers to questions that eventually will have to be answered in more detail as part of an evaluation. What are general program goals and more specific objectives? How are these goals translated into program components? What kinds of records and data are readily available? Who will be the primary consumers of evaluation results? Do other persons or organizations have some direct or indirect stake in the program? Figure 13.2 presents a partial menu of questions that can guide information gathering for the evaluability assessment and later stages.

The answers to these and similar questions should be used to prepare a program description. Although "official" program descriptions may be available, evaluation researchers should always prepare their own description, one that reflects their own understanding of program goals, elements, and operations. Official documents may

1. Goals
   a. What is the program intended to accomplish?
   b. How do staff determine how well they have attained their goals?
   c. What formal goals and objectives have been identified?
   d. Which goals or objectives are most important?
   e. What measures of performance are currently used?
   f. Are adequate measures available, or must they be developed as part of the evaluation?
2. Clients
   a. Who is served by the program?
   b. How do they come to participate?
   c. Do they differ in systematic ways from nonparticipants?
3. Organization and Operation
   a. Where are the services provided?
   b. Are there important differences among sites?
   c. Who provides the services?
   d. What individuals or groups oppose the program or have been critical of it in the past?
4. History
   a. How long has the program been operating?
   b. How did the program come about?
   c. Has the program grown or diminished in size and influence?
   d. Have any significant changes occurred in the program recently?

FIGURE 13.2   Evaluation Questions
Source: Adapted from Stecher and Davis (1987:58–59).

present incomplete descriptions or ones intended for use by program staff, not by evaluators. Even more importantly, official program documents often do not contain usable statements about program goals. As we will see, formulating goal statements that are empirically testable is one of the most important components of evaluation research.

Douglas McDonald and Christine Smith (1989:1) describe slightly different types of questions to be addressed by criminal justice officials and evaluators in deciding whether to evaluate state-level drug control programs:

> How central is the project to the state's strategy?
> How costly is it relative to others?
> Are the project's objectives such that progress toward meeting them is difficult to estimate accurately with existing monitoring procedures?

Such questions are related to setting both program and evaluation priorities. On the one hand, if a project is not central to drug control strategies or if existing information can help determine project effectiveness, then an evaluation probably should not be conducted. On the other hand, costly projects that are key elements in antidrug efforts should be evaluated so that resources can be devoted to new programs if existing approaches are found to be ineffective.

Although Rossi and associates (1999) describe it as a distinct type of research, an evaluability assessment does not need to be a major project in and of itself. Often, a few questions posed to a few people, together with a careful reading of program documents, will yield sufficient information to decide whether to proceed. The questions presented in Figure 13.2 are a good guide for developing a scouting report. If the scouting report indicates that a particular program will not be readily evaluable, it is far better to make that determination before beginning a full-blown study.

Problem Formulation

We mentioned that evaluation research questions may be defined for you. This is true in a general sense, but formulating applied research problems that can be empirically evaluated is an important and often difficult step. Evaluation research is a matter of finding out whether something is or is not there, whether something did or did not happen. To conduct evaluation research, we must be able to operationalize, observe, and recognize the presence or absence of what is under study.

This process normally begins by identifying and specifying program goals. According to Rossi and associates (1999:167), the difficulty of this task revolves around the fact that formal statements of goals are often abstract statements about ideal outcomes. Here are some examples of goal statements paraphrased from actual program descriptions:

- Equip individuals with life skills to succeed (a state-level shock incarceration program; MacKenzie et al., 1993).
- Provide a safe school environment conducive to learning (a school resource officer program; Johnson, 1999).
- Encourage participants to accept the philosophy and principles of drug-free living (an urban drug court; Finn and Newlyn, 1993).
- Provide a mechanism that engages local citizens and community resources in the problem-solving process (a probation–police community corrections program; Wooten and Hoelter, 1998).

Each statement expresses a general program objective that must be clarified before we can formulate research questions to be tested empirically. We can get some idea of what the first example means, but this goal statement raises several questions. The objective is for individuals to succeed, but succeed at what? What is meant by "life—skills"—literacy, job training, time management, self-discipline? We might also ask whether the program focuses on outputs (equipping people with skills) or on impacts (promoting success among people who are equipped with the skills). On the one hand, an evaluation of program outputs might assess individual learning of skills, without considering whether the skills enhance chances for success. On the other hand, an evaluation of program impacts might obtain measures of success such as stable employment or not being arrested within some specified time period.

In all fairness, these goal statements are taken somewhat out of context; source documents expand on program goals in more detail. But they are typical of stated goals, or initial responses we might get to the question, "What are the goals of this program?" Researchers, however, require more specific statements of program objectives.

Wesley Skogan (1985) cautions that official goal statements frequently "oversell" what a program realistically might be expected to accomplish. It's natural for public officials to be positive or optimistic in stating goals, and overselling may be evident in goal statements. Another reason officials and researchers embrace overly optimistic goals is that they fail to develop a micromodel of the program production process (Weiss, 1995)—that is, they do not adequately consider just how some specified intervention will work. Referring back to Figure 13.1, we can see that developing a micromodel can be an important tool for laying out program goals and understanding how institutional processes are structured to achieve those goals. Skogan (1985:38; emphasis in original) describes a micromodel as

> . . . part of what is meant by a "theory-driven" evaluation. Researchers and program personnel should together consider just how each element of a program should affect its targets. If there is not a good reason why "X" *should* cause "Y" the evaluation is probably not going to find that it did! Micromodeling is another good reason for monitoring the actual implementation of programs.

A micromodel can also reveal another problem that sometimes emerges in applied studies: inconsistent goals.

For example, Michael Maxfield and Terry Baumer (1992) evaluated a pretrial home detention program in which persons awaiting trial for certain types of offenses were released from jail and placed on home detention with electronic monitoring. Five different criminal justice organizations played roles in implementation or had stakes in the program. The county sheriff's department (1) faced pressure to reduce its jail population. Under encouragement from the county prosecutor (2) the pretrial release program was established. Criminal court judges (3) had the ultimate authority to release defendants to home detention, following recommendations by bail commissioners in a county criminal justice services agency. (4) Finally, a community corrections department (5) was responsible for actually monitoring persons released to home detention.

Maxfield and Baumer (1992) interviewed persons in each of these organizations and discovered that different agencies had different goals. The sheriff's department was eager to release as many people as possible to free up jail space for convicted offenders and pretrial defendants who faced more serious charges. Community corrections staff, charged with the task of monitoring pretrial clients, were more cautious and sought only persons who presented a lower risk of absconding or committing more offenses while on home detention. The county prosecutor viewed home detention as a way to exercise more control over some individuals who would otherwise be released under less restrictive conditions. Some judges refused to release people on home detention, whereas others followed prosecutors' recommendations. Finally, bail commissioners viewed pretrial home detention as a form of jail resource management, adding to the menu of existing pretrial dispositions (jail, bail, or release on recognizance).

The different organizations involved in the pretrial release program comprised multiple **stakeholders**—persons and organizations with a direct interest in the program. Each stakeholder had different goals for and different views on how the program should actually operate: who should be considered for pretrial home detention, how they should be monitored, and what actions should be taken against those who violated various program rules. After laying out these goals and considering different measures of program performance, Maxfield and Baumer (1992:331) developed a micromodel of home detention indicating that electronic monitoring is suitable for only a small fraction of defendants awaiting trial.

Clearly specifying program goals, then, is a fundamental first step in conducting evaluation studies. If officials are not certain about what a program is expected to achieve, it is not possible to determine whether goals are reached. Or, if multiple stakeholders embrace different goals, evaluators must specify different ways to assess those goals. Maxfield (2001) describes a number of different approaches to specifying clear goals, a crucial first step in the evaluation process.

Measurement

After we identify program goals, our attention turns to measurement, considering first how to measure a program's success in meeting goals. Rossi and associates (1999:83–84) state this in terms that should now be familiar:

> For an evaluation question to be answerable, it must be possible to identify in advance some evidence or "observables" that can realistically be obtained and will be credible as the basis for an answer. This generally means developing questions (1) that involve measurable performance dimensions; (2) that are sufficiently unambiguous so that explicit, noncontroversial definitions can be given for each of their terms; and (3) for which the relevant standards or criteria are specified or obvious.

Obtaining evaluable statements of program goals is conceptually similar to the measurement process, in which program objectives represent conceptual definitions of what a program is trying to accomplish. Chapter 5 began with the following sentence: "This chapter describes the progression from having a vague idea about what we want to study to recognizing and measuring it in the real world." As evaluation researchers, we must similarly recognize the need to state clear conceptual definitions and then describe specific operational definitions.

Specifying Outcomes If a criminal justice program is intended to accomplish something, we must be able to measure that something. If we want to reduce fear of crime, we need to be able to measure fear of crime. If we want to increase consistency in sentences for drug offenses, we need to be able to measure that. But notice that, while outcome measures are derived from goals, they are not the same as goals. Program goals represent desired outcomes, whereas outcome measures are empirical indicators of whether those desired outcomes are achieved. Furthermore, if a program pursues multiple goals, then researchers may have to either devise multiple outcome measures or select a subset of possible measures to correspond with a subset of goals.

Keeping in mind our program-as-hypothesis simile, outcome measures correspond to dependent variables—the Y in a simple XY causal hypothesis. Because we have already considered what's involved in developing measures for dependent variables, we can describe how to formulate outcome measures. Pinning down program goals and objectives results in a conceptual definition. We then specify an operational definition by describing empirical indicators of program outcomes.

In our earlier example, Maxfield and Baumer (1992) translated the disparate interests of organizations involved in pretrial home detention into three more specific objectives: (1) ensure appearance at trial, (2) protect public safety, and (3) relieve jail crowding. These objectives led to corresponding outcome measures: (1) failure-to-appear rates for persons released to pretrial home detention, (2) arrests while on home detention; and (3) estimates of the number of jail beds made available, computed by multiplying the number of persons on pretrial home detention by the number of days each person served on the program. Table 13.2 summarizes the goals, objectives, and measures defined by Maxfield and Baumer.

Let's consider another example. Staff from the Department of the Youth Authority in California conducted an evaluation of a boot camp and intensive parole program known as LEAD—an acronym

TABLE 13.2 Pretrial Home Detention with Electronic Monitoring: Goals, Objectives, and Measures

Actor/Organization	Goals
Sheriff	Release jail inmates
Prosecutor	Increase supervision of pretrial defendants
Judges	Protect public safety
Bail commission	Provide better jail resource management
Community corrections	Monitor defendant compliance
	Return violators to jail

Objectives	Measures
Ensure court appearance	Failure-to-appear courts
Protect public safety	Arrests while on program
Relieve jail crowding	N defendants days served

Source: Adapted from Maxfield and Baumer (1992).

for the qualities of leadership, esteem, ability, and discipline that the program sought to instill in participants. The three major goals of LEAD were to (1) reduce recidivism, (2) ease crowded conditions in juvenile facilities, and (3) provide a cost-effective treatment option (Department of the Youth Authority, 1997:18).

Evaluators assessed the effectiveness of the LEAD program by comparing LEAD participants with other young offenders who were not in LEAD. Data were collected on lengths of stay in each institution, estimated program costs, and rates of recidivism. Measures of recidivism were obtained from official records of arrests and parole violations for 12-, 18-, and 24-month periods after release. Length of incarceration was used to measure the reduction of institutional crowding, as well as cost savings. It was assumed that LEAD participants would have shorter average lengths of incarceration than youths not participating, but that these short-term cost savings would be reduced if LEAD participants were later reincarcerated more rapidly or at higher rates. Recidivism data routinely collected on all subjects were used to examine whether this was the case.

Measuring Program Contexts   Measuring the dependent variables directly involved in an impact assessment is only a beginning. As Ray Pawson and Nick Tilley (1997:69) point out, it is usually necessary to measure the context within which the program is conducted. These variables may appear to be external to the experiment itself, yet they still affect it.

Consider, for example, an evaluation of a job-skills training program coupled with early prison release to a halfway house. The primary outcome measure might be participants' success at gaining employment after completing the program. We will, of course, observe and calculate the subjects' employment rates. We should also be attentive to what has happened to the employment/unemployment rates of the community and state where the program is located. A general slump in the job market should be taken into account in assessing what might otherwise seem to be a low employment rate for subjects. Or, if all the experimental subjects get jobs following the program, that might result more from a general increase in available jobs than from the program itself.

There is no magic formula or set of guidelines for selecting measures of program context, any more than there is for choosing control variables in some other type of research. Just as we read what other researchers have found with respect to some topic we are interested in—say, explanatory research—we should also learn about the production process for some criminal justice program before conducting an evaluation.

Theory also plays an important role. If we study a program to provide job training so that participants can better compete for employment, we need to understand how labor markets operate in general. This is part of a theory-driven evaluation; understanding how a program should work in theory will better enable researchers to specify measures of program contexts that should be considered (Weiss, 1995).

Measuring Program Delivery   In addition to making measurements relevant to the outcomes of a program, it is necessary to measure the program intervention—the experimental stimulus or independent variable. In some cases, this measurement will be handled by assigning subjects to experimental and control groups, if that's the research design. Assigning a person to the experimental group is the same as scoring that person "yes" on the intervention, and assignment to the control group represents a score of "no." In practice, however, it's seldom that simple.

Let's continue with the job-training example. Some inmates will participate in the program through early release; others will not. But imagine for a moment what job-training programs are actually like. Some subjects will participate fully; others might miss sessions or fool around when they are present. So we may need measures of the extent or quality of participation in the program. And if the program is effective, we should find that those who participated fully have higher employment rates than those who participated less.

An evaluation of a drug court operating in Washington, DC, provides an example of uncommonly thorough attention to program delivery (Carver, Boyer, and Hickey, 1996). First, program staff kept attendance records for training activities and classes that participants were required to attend. In addition, evaluators recorded how attentive participants were and how actively they participated in discussions. Assuming that degree of participation in program activities would affect success rates, evaluators expected lower recidivism among drug users who were more attentive and active.

Other factors may further confound the administration of the experimental stimulus. Suppose we are evaluating a new form of counseling designed to cure drug addiction. Several counselors administer it to subjects composing an experimental group. We can compare the recovery rate of the experimental group with that of a control group (a group that received some other type of counseling or none at all). It might be useful to include the names of the counselors who treat specific subjects in the experimental group, as some may be more effective than others. If that turns out to be the case, we must find out why the treatment works better for some counselors than for others. What we learn will further elaborate our understanding of the therapy itself.

Michael Dennis (1990) describes an excellent example of the importance of measuring interventions in this type of study. Intravenous drug users were randomly assigned to receive enhanced treatment (the experimental stimulus) or standard treatment from counselors. Recognizing that some counselors might be more skilled than others, Dennis also randomly assigned counselors to provide either enhanced or standard treatments. There was still some potential for variation in counseling within the enhanced and standard treatment groups, so Dennis tape-recorded sample sessions between patients and counselors. Research staff who were blind to the intended level of counseling then rated each recorded session according to whether they felt it represented enhanced or standard counseling.

Obtaining measures of the experimental intervention is very important for many types of evaluation designs. Variation in the levels of treatment delivered by a program can be a major threat to the validity of even randomized evaluation studies. Put another way, uncontrolled variation in treatment is equivalent to unreliable measurement of the independent variable. Redonna Chandler and associates (2009) describe this as question implementation fidelity, something that's especially important in clinical trials of drug treatment interventions.

Specifying Other Variables   It is usually necessary to measure the population of subjects involved in the program being evaluated. In particular, it is important to define those for whom the program is appropriate. In evaluation studies, such persons are referred to as the program's "target population." If we are evaluating a program that combines more intensive probation supervision with periodic urine testing for drug use, it's probably appropriate for convicted persons who are chronic users of illegal drugs, but how should we define and measure chronic drug use more specifically? The job-skills training program mentioned previously is probably appropriate for inmates who have poor employment histories, but a more specific definition of employment history is needed.

This process of definition and measurement has two aspects. First, the program target population must be specified. This is usually done in a manner similar to the process of defining program goals. Drawing on questions like those in Figure 13.2, evaluators consult program officials to identify the intended targets or beneficiaries of a particular program. Because the hypothetical urine-testing program is combined with probation, its target population will include persons who might receive suspended sentences with probation. However, offenders convicted of crimes that carry nonsuspendible sentences will not be in the target population. Prosecutors and other participants may specify additional limits to the target population—employment or no previous record of probation violations, for example.

Most evaluation studies that use individual people as units of analysis also measure such background variables as age, gender, educational attainment, employment history, and prior criminal record. Such measures are made to determine whether experimental programs work best for males, those over age 25, high school graduates, persons with fewer prior arrests, and so forth.

Second, in providing for the measurement of these different kinds of variables, we need to choose whether to create new measures or use measures already collected in the course of normal program operation. If our study addresses something that's not routinely measured, the choice is easy. More commonly, at least some of the measures we are interested in will be represented in agency records in some form or other. We then have to decide whether agency measures are adequate for our evaluation purposes.

Because we are talking about measurement here, our decision to use our own measures or those produced by agencies should, of course, be based on an assessment of measurement reliability and validity. If we are evaluating the program that combined intensive probation with urinalysis, we will have more confidence in the reliability and validity of basic demographic information recorded by court personnel than in court records of drug use. In this case, we might want to obtain self-report measures of drug use and crime commission from subjects themselves, rather than relying on official records.

By now, it should be abundantly clear that measurement must be taken very seriously in evaluation research. Evaluation researchers must carefully determine all the variables to be measured, and obtain appropriate measures for each. However, such decisions often are not purely scientific. Evaluation researchers frequently must work out their measurement strategy with the people responsible for the program being evaluated.

Designs for Program Evaluation

Designs used in basic research are readily adapted for use in evaluation research.

Chapter 7 presented a good introduction to a variety of experimental and other designs that researchers use in studying criminal justice. Recall that randomly assigning research subjects to experimental or control groups manages many threats to internal validity. Here, our attention turns specifically to the use of different designs in program evaluation.

Randomized Evaluation Designs

To illustrate the advantages of random assignment, consider this dialogue from Lawrence Sherman's book *Policing Domestic Violence: Experiments and Dilemmas* (1992b:67):

When the Minneapolis domestic violence experiment was in its final planning stage,

some police officers asked: "Why does it have to be a randomized experiment? Why can't you just follow up the people we arrest anyway, and compare their future violence risks to the people we don't arrest?"

Since this question reveals the heart of the logic of controlled experiments, I said, "I'm glad you asked. What kind of people do you arrest now?" "Assholes," they replied. "People who commit aggravated POPO."

"What is aggravated POPO?" I asked.

"Pissing off a police officer," they answered. "Contempt of cop. But we also arrest people who look like they're going to be violent, or who have caused more serious injuries."

"What kind of people do you not arrest for misdemeanor domestic assault?" I continued.

"People who act calm and polite, who lost their temper but managed to get control of themselves," came the answer.

"And which kinds of people do you think would have higher risks of repeat violence in the future?" I returned.

"The ones we arrest," they said, the light dawning.

"But does that mean arrest caused them to become more violent?" I pressed.

"Of course not—we arrested them because they were more trouble in the first place," they agreed.

"So just following up the ones you arrest anyway wouldn't tell us anything about the effects of arrest, would it?" was my final question.

"Guess not," they agreed. And they went on to perform the experiment.

Sherman's dialogue portrays the obvious problems of selection bias in routine police procedures for handling domestic violence. In fact, one of the most important benefits of randomization is to avoid the selectivity that is such a fundamental part of criminal justice decision making. Police selectively arrest people, prosecutors selectively file charges, judges and juries selectively convict defendants, and offenders are selectively punished. In a more general sense, randomization is the great equalizer; through probability theory, we can assume that groups created by random assignment will be statistically equivalent.

At the same time, randomized designs are not suitable for evaluating all experimental criminal justice programs. Certain requirements of randomized studies mean that this design cannot be used in many situations. A review of those requirements illustrates many of the limits of randomized designs for applied studies.

Program and Agency Acceptance Random assignment of people to receive some especially desirable or punitive treatment may not be possible for legal, ethical, and practical reasons. We discussed ethics and legal issues in Chapter 3. Sometimes, practical obstacles may also be traced to a misunderstanding of the meaning of random assignment. It is crucial that public officials understand why randomization is desirable and that they fully endorse the procedure.

Richard Berk and associates (2003) describe how researchers obtained cooperation for an evaluation of a new inmate classification system in the California Department of Corrections (CDC) by appealing to the needs of agency managers. Preliminary research suggested that the experimental classification system would increase inmate and staff safety at lower cost than classification procedures then in use. In addition:

> Plans for the study were thoroughly reviewed by stakeholders, including CDC administrators, representatives of prison employee bargaining unions, . . . California State legislative offices, and a wide variety of other interested parties. There was widespread agreement that the study was worth doing. (2003:211)

At the same time, justice agencies have expanding needs for evaluations of smaller-scale programs. John Eck (2002) explains how designs that are less elaborate, less costly, and less disruptive of routine operations are more likely to be accepted by public agencies.

Minimize Exceptions to Random Assignment Exceptions to random assignment are all but inevitable in any real-world delivery of alternative programs or treatments to victims, offenders, or criminal justice agency staff. In a series of experiments on police responses to domestic violence, officers responded to incidents in one of three ways, according to a random assignment procedure (Sherman, 1992b). The experimental treatment was arrest; control treatments included simply separating parties to the dispute or attempting to advise and mediate. Although patrol officers and police administrators accepted the random procedure, exceptions were made as warranted in individual cases, subject to an officer's discretionary judgment.

As the number of exceptions to random assignment increases, however, the statistical equivalence of experimental and control groups is threatened. When police (or others) make exceptions to random assignment, they are introducing bias into the selection of experimental and control groups. Randomized experiments are best suited for programs in which such exceptions can be minimized. The prison classification study by Berk and associates (2003) offers a good example. Random assignment was automatic—inmates having odd identification numbers at intake were assigned to the treatment group; those having even numbers were in the control group. This procedure produced treatment and control groups that were virtually identical in size: 9,662 treatment subjects and 9,656 controls (2003:224–225).

Adequate Case Flow for Sample Size In Chapter 8, we examined the relationship between sample size and accuracy in estimating population characteristics. As sample size increases, up to a point, estimates of population means and standard errors become more precise. By the same token, the number of subjects in groups created through random assignment is related to the researcher's ability to detect significant differences in outcome measures between groups. If each group has only a small number of subjects, statistical tests can detect only very large program effects or differences in outcome measures between the two groups. This is a problem with statistical conclusion validity and sample size, as we discussed in Chapters 7 and 8.

Case flow represents the process through which subjects are accumulated in experimental and control groups. In Sherman's domestic violence evaluations, cases flowed into experimental and control groups as domestic violence incidents were reported to police. Evaluations of other types of programs will generate cases through other processes—for example, offenders sentenced by a court or inmates entering a correctional facility. In a drug court evaluation by Denise Gottfredson and associates (2006), it took 18 months to accumulate 235 cases for the treatment group (drug court). Berk and associates accumulated their 9,662 treatment subjects in six months.

If relatively few cases flow through some process and thereby become eligible for random assignment, it will take a longer time to obtain sufficient numbers of cases. The longer it takes to accumulate cases, the longer it will take to conduct an experiment—and the longer experimental conditions must be maintained. Imagine filling the gas tank of your car with a small cup: It would take a long time, it would test your patience, and you would probably tarnish the paint with spilled gasoline as the ordeal dragged on. In a similar fashion, an inadequate flow of cases into experimental groups risks contaminating the experiment through other problems.

Getting information about case flow in the planning stages of an evaluation is a good way to diagnose possible problems with numbers of subjects. For example, Sherman (1992b:293–295) conducted what he calls a "pipeline" study in Milwaukee to determine whether there were enough suitable domestic violence cases for random assignment to three treatment conditions.

Maintaining Treatment Fidelity *Treatment fidelity* refers to whether an experimental intervention is delivered as intended. Sometimes called "treatment consistency," treatment fidelity is therefore roughly equivalent to measurement reliability. Experimental designs in applied studies often suffer from problems related to treatment inconsistencies. If, for example, serving time in jail is the experimental treatment in a program designed to test different approaches to sentencing drunk drivers, treatment fidelity will be threatened if some defendants are sentenced to a weekend in jail, while others serve 30 days or longer.

Criminal justice programs can vary considerably in the amount of treatment applied to different subjects in experimental groups. For example, Gottfredson and associates (2006) acknowledge that the drug court treatment in Baltimore

County was unevenly implemented. Only about half of those assigned to the experimental group received certified drug treatment. In contrast, the classification system tested by Berk and associates (2003) was a relatively simple treatment that was readily standardized. There was no danger of treatment dilution, as was the case in the drug court experiment.

Midstream changes in experimental programs can also threaten treatment fidelity. Rossi and associates (1999:297) point out that the possibility of midstream changes means that randomized designs are usually not appropriate for evaluating programs in early stages of development, when such changes are more likely. For example, assume we are evaluating an intensive supervision probation program with randomized experimental and control groups. Midway through the experiment, program staff decides to require weekly urinalysis for everyone in the experimental group (those assigned to intensive supervision). If we detect differences in outcome measures between the experimental and control groups—say, arrests within a year after release—we will not know how much of the difference is due to intensive supervision and how much might be due to the midstream change of adding urine tests.

Summing Up the Requirements of Randomized Designs Randomized experiments require that certain conditions be met. Staff responsible for program delivery must accept random assignment and further agree to minimize exceptions to randomization. Case flow must be adequate to produce enough subjects in each group so that statistical tests will be able to detect significant differences in outcome measures. Finally, experimental interventions must be consistently applied to treatment groups and withheld from control groups.

These conditions, and the problems that may result if they are not met, can be summarized as two overriding concerns in field experiments: (1) equivalence between experimental and control groups before an intervention and (2) the ability to detect differences in outcome measures after an intervention is introduced. If there are too many exceptions to random assignment, experimental and control groups may not be equivalent. If there are too few cases, or inconsistencies in administering a treatment, or treatment spillovers to control subjects, outcome measures may be affected in such a way that researchers cannot detect the effects of an intervention.

Although these conditions are related to features of experimental design, more often they are practical issues in experiments in natural settings. David Weisburd, Anthony Petrosino, and Gail Mason (1993) tie many of these issues together by noting something of a paradox. In efforts to gain more precise estimates of treatment effects, researchers commonly increase the size of experimental treatment and control groups. But having larger groups makes experiments more difficult to manage. This, in turn, introduces treatment inconsistencies and other errors that negate the sought-after advantage of a larger sample size.

Let's now look at an example that illustrates both the strengths of random experiments and constraints on their use in criminal justice program evaluations.

Home Detention: Two Randomized Studies

Terry Baumer and Robert Mendelsohn conducted two random experiments to evaluate programs that combine home detention with electronic monitoring (ELMO). In earlier chapters, we examined how different features of these studies illustrated measurement principles; here, our focus is on the mechanics of random assignment and program delivery.

In their first study, Baumer and Mendelsohn evaluated a program that targeted adult offenders convicted of nonviolent misdemeanor and minor felony offenses (Baumer and Mendelsohn, 1990; also summarized in Baumer, Maxfield, and Mendelsohn, 1993). The goal of the program was to provide enhanced supervision of offenders that was more intensive than traditional probation, but less restrictive and less costly than incarceration. Several measures of outcomes and program delivery were examined, as we have described in earlier chapters.

Baumer and Mendelsohn selected a randomized posttest-only design, in which the target population was offenders sentenced to probation. Subjects were randomly assigned to an experimental group in which the treatment was electronically monitored home detention, or to a control group sentenced to home detention without electronic monitoring. Figure 13.3 summarizes case flow into the evaluation experiment. After a guilty plea or trial conviction, probation office staff reviewed offenders' backgrounds and criminal records to inform the recommendation of an appropriate sentence. The next step was a hearing, at which sentences were imposed by a criminal court judge.

Persons sentenced to probation were eligible for inclusion in the experiment. Their case files were forwarded to staff in the community corrections agency responsible for administering the home detention programs. On receiving an eligible case file, community corrections staff telephoned the evaluation researchers, who, having prepared a random list of case numbers, assigned subjects to either the treatment or control group. Subject to two constraints, this process produced 78 treatment subjects and 76 control subjects.

Thinking back on our consideration of ethics in Chapter 3, you should be able to think of one constraint: informed consent. Researchers and program staff explained the evaluation project to subjects and obtained their consent to participate in the experiment. Those who declined to participate in the evaluation study could nevertheless be assigned to home detention as a condition of their probation. The second constraint was made necessary by the technology of electronic monitoring; subjects could not be kept in the treatment group if they did not have a telephone that could be connected to the electronic monitoring equipment.

Notice that random assignment was made after sentencing. Baumer and Mendelsohn began their evaluation by randomizing subjects between stages 2 and 3 in Figure 13.3. This produced problems because judges occasionally overruled presentence investigation recommendations to probation, thus overriding random assignment. After detecting this problem, Baumer and Mendelsohn (1990:27–29) moved randomization "downstream," so that judicial decisions could not contaminate the selection process.

Baumer and Mendelsohn (1990:26) obtained agreement from community corrections staff, prosecutors, and judges to use random assignment by

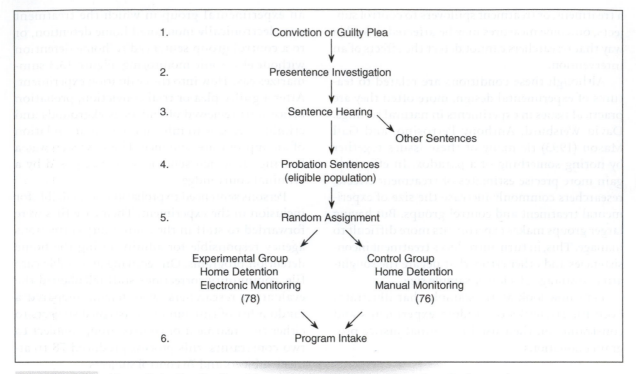

1. Conviction or Guilty Plea
2. Presentence Investigation
3. Sentence Hearing → Other Sentences
4. Probation Sentences (eligible population)
5. Random Assignment

Experimental Group
Home Detention
Electronic Monitoring
(78)

Control Group
Home Detention
Manual Monitoring
(76)

6. Program Intake

FIGURE 13.3 Home Detention for Convicted Adults: Case Flow and Random Assignment

getting all parties to accept an assumption of "no difference":

> That is, in the absence of convincing evidence to the contrary, they were willing to assume that there was no difference between the . . . methods of monitoring. This allowed the prosecutor to negotiate and judges to assign home detention as a condition of probation only, while permitting the community corrections agency to make the monitoring decision.

Convinced of the importance of random assignment, the community corrections agency "delegated" to researchers the responsibility for making the monitoring decision, a "decision" that was randomized.

In this example, the experimental condition (electronic monitoring) was readily distinguished from the control condition (home detention without electronic monitoring). There was no possibility of treatment spillover; control subjects could not unintentionally receive some level of electronic monitoring because they had neither the bracelet nor the home-base unit that embodied the treatment. Electronic monitoring could, therefore, be readily delivered to subjects in the experimental group and withheld from control subjects. This treatment was not necessarily consistent, however.

The second ELMO evaluation conducted by Baumer and Mendelsohn reveals how program delivery problems can undermine the strengths of random assignment (Baumer, Maxfield, and Mendelsohn, 1993). In their study of juvenile burglars, they used similar procedures for randomization, but eligible subjects were placed in one of four groups, as illustrated in the following table:

		Electronic Monitoring?	
		No	Yes
Police Visits?	No	C	E1
	Yes	E2	E3

Juvenile burglars could be randomly assigned to three possible treatments: electronic monitoring only (E1), police visits to their home after school only (E2), or electronic monitoring and police visits (E3). Subjects in the control group (C) were sentenced to home detention only. As in the adult study, outcome measures included arrests after release.

Although there were no problems with random assignment, inconsistencies in the delivery of each of the two experimental treatments produced uninterpretable results (Maxfield and Baumer, 1991:5):

> Observations of day-to-day program operations revealed that, compared with the adult program, the juvenile court and cooperating agencies paid less attention to delivering program elements and using information from . . . the electronic monitoring equipment. Staff were less well-trained in operating the electronic monitoring equipment, and police visits were inconsistent.

The box titled "Home Detention" in Chapter 1 elaborates on differences in the operation of these two programs and a third ELMO program for pretrial defendants. However, the lesson from these studies bears repeating here: *randomization does not control for variation in treatment fidelity and program delivery.*

Randomized experiments can be powerful tools in criminal justice program evaluations. At the same time, it is often impossible to maintain the desired level of control over experimental conditions. This is especially true for complex interventions that may change while an evaluation is under way. Experimental conditions are also difficult to maintain when different organizations work together in delivering some service—a community-based drug treatment provider coupled with intensive probation, for example.

Largely because of such problems, evaluation researchers often use other types of designs that are less "fragile"—less subject to problems if rigorous experimental conditions cannot be maintained.

Quasi-Experimental Designs

Quasi-experiments are distinguished from "true" experiments by the lack of random assignment of subjects to an experimental and a control group. Random assignment of subjects is often impossible in criminal justice evaluations. Rather than forgo evaluation altogether in such instances, it is usually possible to create and execute research designs that will permit evaluation of the program in question.

Quasi-experiments may also be "nested" into experimental designs as backups, should one or more of the requisites for a true experiment break down. For example, William Shadish, Thomas Cook, and Donald Campbell (2002) describe how time-series designs can be nested into a series of random experiments. In the event that case flow is inadequate, or random assignment to enhanced or standard counseling regimes breaks down, the nested time-series design will salvage a quasi-experiment.

In Chapter 7, we considered different classes of quasi-experimental designs—nonequivalent groups, cohorts, and time series—together with examples of each type. Each of these designs has been used extensively in criminal justice evaluation research.

Ex Post Evaluations   Often, a researcher or public official may decide to conduct an evaluation sometime after an experimental program has gone into effect. These so-called ex post evaluations (Rossi, Freeman, and Lipsey, 1999:312) are not usually amenable to random assignment after the fact. For example, if a new job-skills training program is introduced in a state correctional facility, an ex post evaluation might compare rates of employment among released inmates with similar outcome measures for a matched comparison institution. Or an interrupted time-series design might examine records of alcohol-related accidents before and after a new law that allows administrative suspension of driver's licenses to take effect.

Full-Coverage Programs   Interventions such as new national or statewide laws are examples of full-coverage programs in which it is not possible to identify subjects who are not exposed to the intervention, let alone randomly assign persons to receive or not receive the treatment. Quasi-experimental designs may be the strongest possible approach for evaluating such programs. Statewide sentencing guidelines and mandatory minimum sentences are common examples of full-coverage interventions.

Larger Treatment Units   Similarly, some experimental interventions may be designed to affect all persons in some larger unit—a neighborhood crime prevention program, for example. It is not possible to randomly assign some neighborhoods to receive the intervention while withholding it from others. Nor is it possible to control which individuals in a neighborhood are exposed to the intervention.

Different types of quasi-experimental designs can be used in such cases. For example, in a Kansas City program to reduce gun violence, police targeted extra patrols at gun crime "hot spots" (Sherman and Rogan, 1995). Some beats were assigned to receive the extra patrols; comparison beats, selected for their similar frequency of gun crimes, did not get the extra patrols. Several outcome measures were compared for the two types of areas. After 29 weeks, gun seizures in the target area increased by more than 65 percent and gun crimes dropped by 49 percent. There were no significant changes in either gun crimes or gun seizures in the comparison beat. Drive-by shootings dropped from seven to one in the target area and increased from 6 to 12 in the comparison area. Homicides declined in the target area but not in the comparison area. Citizen surveys showed less fear of crime and more positive feelings about the neighborhood in the target area than in the comparison area.

Nonequivalent-Groups Designs As we saw in Chapter 7, quasi-experimental designs lack the built-in controls for selection bias and other threats to internal validity. Nonequivalent-groups designs, by definition, cannot be assumed to include treatment and comparison subjects who are statistically equivalent. For this reason, quasi-experimental program evaluations must be carefully designed and analyzed to rule out possible validity problems.

For evaluation designs that use nonequivalent groups, attention should be devoted to constructing experimental and comparison groups that are as similar as possible on important variables that might account for differences in outcome measures. Rossi and associates (1999) caution that procedures for constructing such groups should be grounded in a theoretical understanding of which individual and group characteristics might confound evaluation results. In a study of recidivism by participants in shock incarceration programs, for example, we certainly want to ensure that equal numbers of men and women are included in groups assigned to shock incarceration and groups that

received some other sentence. Alternatively, we can restrict our analysis of program effects to only men or only women.

David Farrington and associates (1993) conducted a nonequivalent-groups quasi-experiment to evaluate different approaches to preventing shoplifting. The experiment was carried out in nine electronics stores operated in England by the same retail chain. Stores were placed in one of four groups, created by matching the stores on three characteristics: physical size, sales volume, and type of location. Three experimental interventions to prevent shoplifting were tested: (1) physical redesign of store layout to reduce opportunities for shoplifting, (2) electronic tagging of items so that they would trigger sensors at the exit to each shop, and (3) uniformed guards posted at store entrances. In addition, one store in three of the four groups served as a comparison site, where no new measures to prevent shoplifting were introduced.

The outcome measure was based on a system in which labels were placed on certain small items thought to be frequently stolen: audiotapes, videotapes, stereo headphones, and photographic film. Each item was fixed with a sticky label that sales clerks were to remove whenever an item was sold. The total number of labeled items before a store opened for the day was known. Comparing this total with the number of labels accumulated by clerks and the number of items remaining in each store at day's end yielded a count of missing items. Pretest measures were obtained for each store over a three-day period. Two posttest measures were made at most sites, one week and four weeks after introducing prevention measures. Table 13.3 summarizes the grouping of stores with experimental treatments and the results of the evaluation. The figures in this table represent the number of missing tags as a percentage of all items that left the store (sold or stolen).

Notice first the different mixes of stores and experimental treatments. The four groupings of stores reflect within-group similarities and between-group differences in matching criteria. The experimental and control conditions across stores in different groups were mixed to compare prevention effectiveness with store characteristics.

Although we have omitted tests of statistical significance from Table 13.3, some interesting

TABLE 13.3	Situational Crime Prevention of Shoplifting		
	Percentage of Items Stolen		
	Pretest	**Posttest 1**	**Posttest 2**
Group A			
Store 1 (R)	36.5	15.2	27.1
Store 2 (T)	30.8	7.3	4.4
Group B			
Store 3 (T)	17.3	1.4	5.5
Store 4 (G)	10.7	5.8	8.8
Store 5 (C)	15.3	10.4	NA
Group C			
Store 6 (C)	15.4	21.5	15.0
Store 7 (G)	6.9	8.1	18.6
Group D			
Store 8 (R)	24.4	5.0	NA
Store 9 (C)	13.6	29.6	22.0

Note: Experimental treatments: R = store redesign; T = electronic tagging; G = security guard; C = comparison.

Source: Adapted from Farrington and associates (1993:108).

patterns are evident in the results. Electronic tagging (stores 2 and 3) reduced shoplifting in both the one- and four-week posttests. Store redesign was effective only in the first posttest (store 1); a second posttest showed an increase in shoplifting, which suggests that thieves adapted to the new layout (only one posttest was conducted in the other redesign site, store 8). Uniformed guards (stores 4 and 7) had no consistent impact on shoplifting. Shoplifting in the three comparison sites (stores 5, 6, and 9) either increased or declined less than it did in matched experimental sites.

Several features of this evaluation warrant comment. First, randomization was not possible because the experimental treatment was delivered to a small number of large units—electronics stores. Second, Farrington and associates used matching criteria that could reasonably be expected to affect shoplifting rates. A related point is that all sites were franchise stores owned by the same large chain, which minimized differences in inventory mixes, management procedures, and the like. Third, the three experimental conditions were mixed and tested in different groups of matched

stores. This produced a stronger test of the relative effectiveness of different prevention measures.

Finally, consider for a moment the degree of cooperation required between researchers and evaluation clients. On the one hand, Farrington and colleagues required some effort from store staff in collecting and counting tagged items, not to mention implementing different crime prevention measures. On the other hand, you should also see the potential benefits to retail stores from this quasi-experiment to determine what works in preventing shoplifting.

Time-Series Designs Interrupted time-series designs require attention to different issues because researchers cannot normally control how reliably the experimental treatment is actually implemented. Foremost among these issues are instrumentation, history, and construct validity. In many interrupted time-series designs, conclusions about whether an intervention produced change in some outcome measure rely on simple indicators that represent complex causal processes.

In their evaluation of legislation to provide for mandatory minimum sentences in Oregon, Nancy Merritt, Terry Fain, and Susan Turner (2006) examined changes in sentences for different types of offenses. They found that sentences for offenses clearly covered by the law did in fact increase in the first five years after its passage. However, they also found declines in the number of cases filed that were clearly included in the mandatory provisions. Meanwhile, more charges were filed for offenses covered by discretionary provisions. Of course, criminal case prosecution and sentencing are complex processes. The authors could not directly control for different circumstances surrounding cases processed before and after the law took effect. However, their time-series analysis does clearly show changes in case filings, suggesting that prosecutors exercised discretion to evade the mandatory provisions of Oregon's legislation.

Understanding the causal process that produces measures used in time-series analysis is crucial for interpreting results. Such understanding can come in two related ways. First, we should have a sound conceptual grasp of the underlying causal forces at work in the process we are studying. Second, we should understand how the indicators used in any time-series analysis are produced.

Patricia Mayhew, Ronald Clarke, and David Elliott (1989) concluded that laws requiring motorcycle riders to wear helmets produced a reduction in motorcycle theft. This might seem puzzling until we consider the causal constructs involved in stealing motorcycles. Assuming that most motorcycle thefts are crimes of opportunity, Mayhew and associates argue that few impulsive thieves stroll about carrying helmets. Even thieves are sufficiently rational to recognize that a helmetless motorcycle rider will be unacceptably conspicuous—an insight that deters them from stealing motorcycles. Mayhew and colleagues considered displacement as an alternative explanation for the decline in motorcycle theft, but they found no evidence that declines in motorcycle theft were accompanied by increases in either stolen cars or bicycles. By systematically thinking through the causal process of motorcycle theft, Mayhew and associates were able to conclude that helmet laws were unintentionally effective in reducing theft.

Other Types of Evaluation Studies

Earlier in this chapter, we noted how process evaluations are distinct from impact assessments. Whereas the latter seek answers to questions about program effects, process evaluations monitor program implementation, asking whether programs are being delivered as intended.

Process evaluations can be invaluable aids in interpreting results from an impact assessment. We described how Baumer and Mendelsohn were better able to understand outcome measures in their evaluation of ELMO for juvenile burglars because they had monitored program delivery. Similarly, process evaluations were key elements of closed-circuit television (CCTV) evaluations reported by Martin Gill and Angela Spriggs (2005). They were able to describe whether cameras were placed and monitored as intended. In many cases, camera placement was modified, something the authors suggest was related to the relative success of different CCTV installations. Without a process evaluation, information about program implementation cannot be linked to outcome measures.

Process evaluations can also be useful for criminal justice officials whose responsibility centers more on the performance of particular tasks than on the overall success of some program. For example, police patrol officers are collectively responsible for public safety in their beats, but their routine actions focus more on performing specific tasks such as responding to a call for service—or, in community policing, diagnosing the concerns of neighborhood residents. Police supervisors are attentive to traffic tickets written, arrests made, and complaints against individual officers. Probation and parole officers are, of course, interested in the ultimate performance of their clients, but they are also task oriented in their use of records to keep track of client contacts, attendance at substance abuse sessions, or job performance. Process evaluations center on measures of task performance—on the assumption that tasks are linked to program outcomes.

The box "Assessing Gun Violence Reduction Strategies in New York City" incorporates measures for a process evaluation. The Cure Violence project seeks to reduce violence in selected New York City neighborhoods by deploying outreach workers and other resources in the target areas. Whether or not neighborhood residents have seen the workers is a process measure, since worker deployment is an intervention. As you can see from the box, the project uses interesting sampling and interviewing strategies to learn about violence and the project's impact.

Problem Analysis and Scientific Realism

Problem analysis, coupled with scientific realism, helps public officials use research to select and assess alternative courses of action.

Program evaluation differs from problem analysis with respect to the time dimension and where each activity takes place in the policy process. Problem analysis is used to help design alternative courses of action and choose among them.

In reality, there is not much difference between these two types of applied research. Similar types of research methods are used to address problem analysis questions (What would happen? What should we do?) as those brought to bear on

BY SHEYLA A. DELGADO AND JEFFREY A. BUTTS
Research and Evaluation Center
John Jay College of Criminal Justice, CUNY

The Research and Evaluation Center at John Jay College developed a project to evaluate gun violence reduction strategies in New York City neighborhoods. Sponsored by the New York City Council, the project tracked the deployment of gun violence reduction strategies in four areas of the city: South Bronx, Harlem, Jamaica (Queens), and East New York (Brooklyn).

Each pilot program implements Cure Violence, a public health-oriented violence-reduction strategy developed at the University of Illinois-Chicago. In addition to Cure Violence, each site provides support services for at-risk youth, their families, and communities. These include mental health services, school-based conflict mediation, job training and placement, and legal services.

In 2014, the research team began field research in selected areas, conducting interviews with local residents. John Jay researchers (operating under the street brand "NYC-Cure") interviewed young men (ages 18–30) in several city neighborhoods. Interviews were designed to measure each respondent's actual experience of violence as well as his attitudes about violent behavior in varying situations. The project used an innovative sampling method called Respondent-Driven Sampling (RDS). RDS makes it possible to gather data quickly and efficiently from traditionally hard-to-reach populations. The system is based on chains of referrals and field contacts, supported by a visible presence of the research team.

Each data-collection period lasted about 10 continuous days, an important feature to maintain the chain of referrals that sprouted at each interview site. When study participants saw the research team at the same time and location for several days, they were more likely to encourage friends to participate in the study. The combination of RDS and a stable field presence made it possible to interview about 200 young men at each site.

Outreach workers and "violence interruptors" were key interventions in the Cure Violence model. Their role was to circulate through neighborhoods in each research site, using personal contacts to dissuade victims of violence to retaliate or otherwise become involved in serious violence. Outreach workers also helped connect residents with community-based social and educational services that were part of the program.

Because of the central role of community outreach workers in the project, we wanted to learn whether community residents recalled having seen or had talked to them. We assessed this by including items in the survey that showed photos of local outreach workers, and asked respondents whether they had seen or interacted with the people shown in photos. This was a measure of implementation effort—how well known outreach workers had become in the target communities. In all sites, about 80 percent of respondents had seen workers or were otherwise familiar with the anti-violence materials distributed by workers. This varied quite a bit across different parts of New York, ranging from over 90 percent in Brooklyn to about 60 percent in Queens.

Data collection procedures were another key part of our evaluation. Field researchers used tablet devices and a data-collection application to administer the interview protocol. Interview data was collected offline while in the field. Back in the research office tablets were connected to the Internet, data was quickly uploaded, and became readily available for analysis and review. Using tablet-based interview protocols eliminated the need for paper forms and data entry. This helped avoid many of the usual systematic data errors, made coding and cleaning of data much easier for the research team, and generally increased the reliability of data collected in the field. Overall, automating the data collection process was cost-effective and ran much more smoothly than the paper-based interviews and observation forms traditionally used in field research.

A second wave of data collection began in summer 2016. A summary of results from the first part of the evaluation is presented in Delgado and associates (2015). Butts and associates (2015) describe the Cure Violence program itself.

program evaluation questions (What did happen? What have we done?). For example, consider a definition of a similar approach, policy analysis, from a prominent text: "Attempting to bring modern science and technology to bear on society's problems, policy analysis searches for feasible courses of action, generating information and marshaling evidence of the benefits and other consequences that would follow their adoption and implementation" (Quade, 1989:4). Except for the form of the verb—"would follow"—this is not too different from the way we defined program evaluation.

Results from program evaluations are frequently considered in choosing among future courses of action. Problem and policy analysis depend just as much on clearly specifying goals and objectives as does program evaluation. And the achievement of goals and objectives worked out through problem analysis can be tested through program evaluation. Measurement is also a fundamental concern in both types of applied studies.

Problem-Oriented Policing

More than an alternative approach to law enforcement, the core of problem-oriented policing is applying problem analysis methods to public safety problems. Problem-oriented policing depends on identifying problems, planning and taking appropriate action, and then assessing whether those actions achieved intended results.

This approach centers on problems, not individual incidents. For example, traditional policing responds to reports of auto thefts, writing up details about the incident to support an insurance claim, then moving on to the next incident. Let's consider this *incident-oriented policing*. In contrast, **problem-oriented policing** would begin by analyzing a number of auto theft reports. Reports would be examined for similarities, such as where and when they occurred, types of autos stolen, whether stolen cars were eventually recovered, and if so, in what condition. Such analysis would define a more general problem of auto theft. Subsequent steps would consider what kinds of actions might be taken to address the problem.

Problem solving is a fundamental tool in problem-oriented policing. As described by Ronald Clarke and John Eck (2005:Step 7-1), problem solving involves four analytic steps:

(1) carefully define specific problems . . .;
(2) conduct in-depth analysis to understand their causes;
(3) undertake broad searches for solutions to remove these causes and bring about lasting reductions in problems;
(4) evaluate how successful these activities have been.

You can easily see how problem solving merges the application of problem analysis and evaluation (assessment) of the effects of interventions.

Problem-oriented policing is an especially useful example of applied research because a large number of resources are available. We'll briefly describe three categories. Most of the first two categories were prepared with support from the Office of Community Oriented Policing Services (COPS) in the U.S. Department of Justice. The COPS Office has terminated its support of this effort, but the valuable guides remain available at the Center for Problem-Oriented Policing website: http://www.popcenter.org (Accessed 28 August 2016).

How-to-Do-It Guides   Ronald Clarke and John Eck (2005) have prepared a general guide to crime analysis to support problem-oriented policing. Adapted from a document originally prepared for the Jill Dando Institute of Crime Science in London, this publication offers succinct guidance on how to conduct problem analysis and report results. The COPS office also sponsored guides that provide more detail on different problem analysis tools: assessing crime displacement and diffusion (Guerette, 2009); understanding the process of repeat victimization (Weisel, 2005); interviewing offenders (Decker, 2005); and theft of "hot products" (Bowers and Johnson, 2013).

Crime mapping and other methods of space-based analysis are important tools in problem-oriented policing. A book by Spencer Chainey and Jerry Ratcliffe (2005) is an excellent general guide. John Eck and associates (2005) focus on the use of mapping to identify crime hot spots.

Problem and Response Guides   In an earlier chapter, we mentioned that justice agencies frequently adopt programs that appear to have been successful in other jurisdictions. Although this can sometimes be advisable, a key principle of problem-oriented policing is to base local actions on an understanding of *local* problems. Instead of trying an off-the-shelf program, or so-called "best practice," appropriate interventions should be considered only after analyzing data.

This principle is evident in two series of guides that describe what is known about effective responses based on past experience. Problem guides describe how to analyze very specific types of problems (e.g., "Financial Crimes Against the Elderly") and what are known to be effective or ineffective responses. Response guides describe very general kinds of actions that might be undertaken to address different types of problems (e.g., "Video Surveillance of Public Places").

Case Studies and Other Research   One of the hallmarks of applied research is to use research to change practice. The two groups of guides discussed so far were prepared for use by criminal justice professionals, but they were developed following many years of research. Many examples of research that contributed to changes in justice policy have been published in the series *Crime Prevention Studies*. We now turn to an example that illustrates the application of problem analysis, as well as other research principles presented in this and earlier chapters.

Auto Theft in Chula Vista

About seven miles north of the U.S.–Mexico border, Chula Vista is a medium-sized city of just under 200,000 residents, bordered by the Pacific Ocean on the west and sandwiched by San Diego on the north and south. Nanci Plouffe and Rana Sampson (2004) began their analysis of vehicle theft by comparing Chula Vista to other southern California cities. After noting that theft rates tended to be higher for cities closer to the border, they began to disaggregate the problem by searching for areas where vehicle thefts and break-ins were concentrated. Deborah Lamm Weisel (2003) refers to this as "parsing," or breaking down a large-area measure to examine smaller areas.

Plouffe and Sampson first determined that 10 parking lots accounted for 25 percent of thefts and 20 percent of break-ins in the city. Furthermore, 6 of those 10 lots were also among the top 10 calls-for-service locations in Chula Vista. This meant that auto theft hot spots also tended to be hot spots

for other kinds of incidents. Their analysis found other notable patterns:

- Recovery rates for stolen cars and trucks were lower in Chula Vista than in areas to the north.
- Recovery rates in 4 of the 10 hot parking lots were especially low, under 40 percent.
- Smaller pickup trucks and older Toyota Camrys had even lower recovery rates.
- High-risk lots were close to roads that led to the Mexico border.

Together these findings suggested that many cars stolen from the high-risk areas were being driven into Mexico.

Plouffe and Sampson next moved beyond using existing data from police records. This is again consistent with the methods of problem analysis: use existing data to identify problems and their general features, and then collect additional data to better understand the mechanisms of problems. For Plouffe and Sampson that meant conducting environmental surveys of high-risk parking lots, observing operations and interviewing officials at U.S.–Mexico border crossings, and interviewing a small number of individuals arrested for auto theft from target lots. They sought to understand why particular lots were targeted, and whether stolen cars could be easily driven into Mexico.

We described environmental surveys in Chapter 11. In conducting theirs, Plouffe and Sampson discovered that the highest-risk lot was a two-minute drive from vehicle entry points into Mexico. The lot served a midrange general shopping mall with typical open parking. Access was easy, and thieves could expect that vehicles would be unguarded for some time. Information gathered from the border crossing confirmed that few cars entering Mexico were stopped, and vehicle identification documents were rarely requested.

In-person interviews with auto thieves used a 93-item questionnaire, asking about target selection, techniques, and other routines. Thieves preferred older cars because they could be easily stolen—steering column locks wear out and can be broken with simple tools. They watched people entering stores, judged that their vehicle would be unguarded for a time, and then drove the few minutes into Mexico. Cars were rarely stolen from parking garages because thieves would have to produce a ticket in order to exit.

With this and other information, Plouffe and Sampson discussed strategies with Chula Vista police and security staff at parking lots and shopping malls. More diligent screening at the border was rejected, largely because most vehicles had been driven into Mexico before the theft was even discovered. They recommended that high-risk shopping malls install gates at entrance and exit points for parking lots. Drivers would take a ticket upon entering and would have to produce it when leaving. This, it was argued, would substantially increase the effort required to steal vehicles from parking lots near the border.

Other Applications of Problem Analysis

Problem solving is being adopted by other criminal justice agencies, partly because it has proved helpful in law enforcement applications. For example, Veronica Coleman and associates (1999) describe how local and federal prosecutors in several U.S. cities have formed planning teams to identify crime problems and develop appropriate interventions. Teams include U.S. attorneys, researchers, and other criminal justice professionals who pursue a form of problem analysis labeled Strategic Approaches to Community Safety Initiatives (SACSI). SACSI involves five steps, four of which should look familiar (Coleman et al., 1999:18):

1. Form an interagency working group.
2. Gather information and data about a local crime problem.
3. Design a strategic intervention to tackle the problem.
4. Implement the intervention.
5. Assess and modify the strategy as the data reveal effects.

We have only scratched the surface of problem analysis applications in criminal justice. This is an area of applied research that is growing rapidly. Other examples draw on methods of systems analysis, operations research, and economics for such purposes as cost–benefit studies, police patrol allocation, and decisions about hiring probation officers. Cost–benefit analysis, in particular, is used to assess the relative value and expense of alternative policies. Roman and Farrell (2002) describe some examples for crime prevention. Although the mathematical tools that form the base of problem analysis can be sophisticated, the underlying logic is relatively simple.

Space- and Time-Based Analysis

Pin maps are examples of "low-tech" problem analysis that are nonetheless conceptually identical to computer models of hot spots used in many departments to plan police deployment. Computerized mapping systems now permit police to monitor changes in crime patterns on a daily or hourly basis and to develop responses accordingly. Furthermore, simultaneous advances in computing power and declines in the cost of that power make it possible for even small agencies to use mapping tools (Santos, 2012). The ongoing technological advances in mapping have fueled the application of statistical models to geographic clusters of crime problems. Thomas Rich (1999) describes this as analytic mapping, whereby statistical tools supplement the "eyeballing" approach to locating concentrations of crime.

Crime maps usually represent at least four different things: (1) one or more crime types; (2) space or area; (3) some time period; and (4) some dimension of land use, usually streets. The most useful crime maps will show patterns that can help analysts and police decide what sort of action to take. That's part of applied research. An example will illustrate some basic features of crime maps.

Figure 13.4 shows four crime maps prepared by Shuryo Fujita (at the time a graduate student at the Rutgers University School of Criminal Justice) for a midsized city in the northeast United States. All four maps show completed auto theft, but for different areas and time periods. The map in Panel A shows auto thefts for the year 2005 in one of four police precincts in the city. About 1,750 completed thefts are represented, about 33 percent of all thefts in the city. You will probably notice two things about Panel A. First, car theft seems to be everywhere in this area, except for blank spots in

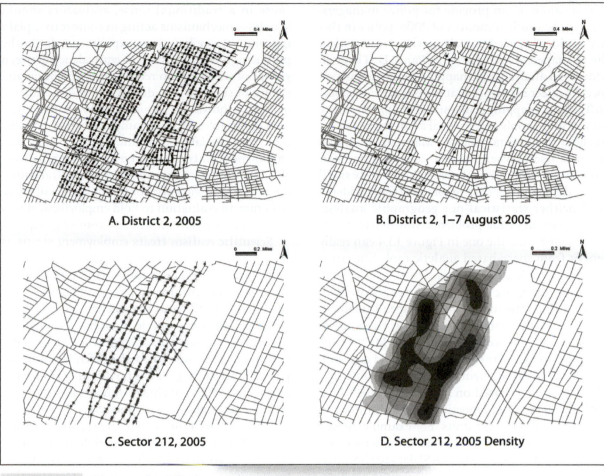

FIGURE 13.4 Mapping Auto Theft

Source: Maps prepared by Shuryo Fujita.

the center and to the right side of the map—a large park and a river, respectively. Second, because car theft seems to be everywhere, the map is not especially useful. Much of the district appears to be a hot spot. Panel B changes the time reference, showing the 30 car thefts that occurred in the first week of August 2005. You might think this is somewhat more useful, showing more theft in the southern part of the district. But whereas Panel A shows too much, Panel B shows smaller numbers that don't seem to cluster very much.

Panel C shifts the geographic focus to one sector within the district, to the left of the park. This sector happens to have the highest volume of car theft, 464 completed thefts in 2005; it's the hottest sector in the hottest precinct in the city. Again, car theft seems to be all over the sector. A closer

look shows more dots on the longer north–south streets than on cross streets. This is clearer in Panel D, which shows a crime density map of the sector. Crime density is a numerical value showing how close some dots are to each other and how distant those clusters are from outlying dots. These values are mapped, showing patterns much more clearly than simple dots. The darker areas of Panel D represent more dense concentrations of car theft. There seem to be two corridors of car theft, running north–south below the diagonal street that bisects the map. These corridors are somewhat connected in the middle, showing a rough H-shape. This shape happens to correspond with some major thoroughfares in the area. You might be able to imagine cruising up, across, and down, looking for cars to steal. That's useful information a crime analyst can provide for police managers. During the summer months of 2006, police in this city deployed special patrols on the streets within the H-shaped area depicted in Panel D. Through additional analysis and mapping, Fujita identified specific street segments that were acute hot spots.

Tools for mapping crime and other problems are similar to the tools of statistical analysis, a topic we consider in the final chapter. Maps and statistics are most useful when we seek to understand patterns in a large number of observations. Very small police departments that report very few incidents need neither statistical nor geographic analysis to understand crime problems. But departments serving cities like the one in Figure 13.4 can really benefit from space-based analytic tools like crime mapping and density analysis.

Crime mapping and other types of problem analysis illustrate another advantage of incident-based data—the potential for use in the kind of problem analysis we have described. Most crime mapping and similar tools are developed and used by individual departments, reflecting the fact that crime analysis is based on locally generated data. With incident-based reporting, crime analysis can be conducted on larger units. For example, Steven Haas and associates (2007) used National Incident-Based Reporting System (NIBRS) data to show that clusters of violent crime in West Virginia are associated with incidents in which illegal guns were seized.

Scientific Realism and Applied Research

Traditional research and evaluation are based on the model of cause and effect we considered in Chapters 4 and 7. An independent variable (cause) produces some change in a dependent variable (effect). Experimental and quasi-experimental designs seek to isolate this causal process from the possible effects of intervening variables. Designs thus try to control for the possible effects of intervening variables.

Problem analysis as we have described it represents a bridge between traditional research approaches and applied research that is the foundation of scientific realism. Ray Pawson and Nick Tilley (1997) propose that, instead of trying to explain

cause in a traditional sense, evaluators should search for mechanisms acting in context to explain outcomes. As we have seen, experiments do this by producing pretest statistical equivalence between groups of subjects who receive an intervention and groups of subjects who do not. Quasi-experiments using nonequivalent groups seek to control intervening variables by, for example, holding possible intervening variables constant. So if we believe that employment status might be an intervening variable in the relationship between arrest and subsequent domestic violence, for example, we will try to structure an evaluation to hold employment status constant between treatment and control groups.

Scientific realism treats employment status as the *context* in which an arrest mechanism operates on the *outcome* of repeat domestic violence. Rather than try to control for employment status, a scientific realist will study the mechanism in context and conclude, for example, that arrest is effective in reducing subsequent violence when an offender is employed but not when the offender is unemployed. This finding will be no different from what Sherman (1992b) concludes in his assessment of a series of randomized experiments.

What is different is that the scientific realist approach is rooted in the principle that similar interventions can naturally be expected to have different outcomes in different contexts. Most notably, this approach is more compatible with the realities of evaluation than is the experimental approach. Pawson and Tilley (1997:81) put it this way: "Ultimately, realist evaluation would be *mechanism* and *context-driven* rather than program-led" (emphasis in original). This means that interventions should be designed not so much as comprehensive programs that apply equally in all situations, but developed for specific contexts—and evaluations of those interventions must consider context as a key factor in whether the intervention achieves the desired outcome.

Situational crime prevention (Clarke, 2017) is an example of the scientific realist approach that bridges problem analysis and evaluation, because it focuses on what mechanisms operate for highly specific types of crime in specific situations. So, rather than develop and evaluate large-scale programs intended to reduce auto theft in general, for example, situational crime prevention seeks specific interventions that will be effective in reducing particular types of auto theft. Ronald Clarke and Patricia Harris (1992) distinguish several types of auto theft by their purposes: joyriding, temporary transportation, resale or stripping, or insurance fraud. Theft of certain models for joyriding may be reduced by modest increases in security, whereas theft of expensive cars for resale or export requires different approaches. And placing attendants at the exits of parking garages can reduce many types of auto theft, but car break-ins may not be affected by that intervention.

As we mentioned in Chapter 7, the realist approach resembles a case study approach. Both are *variable-oriented* strategies for research—they depend on measures of many variables to understand and assess a small number of cases. Detailed data and information are gathered about specific interventions, often in very small areas. Whereas an experimental evaluation uses probability theory to control for intervening variables, the case study approach depends on detailed knowledge to understand the context in which mechanisms operate.

In his discussion of applied research tools for problem solving, John Eck (2002) makes the case even more strongly. Public officials, he argues, are more interested in solving local problems than in identifying robust cause-and-effect relationships. Both problem solving and evaluation are concerned with answering the question "Did the problem decline?" But eliminating alternative explanations for a decline, which is the central concern of internal validity and the rationale for stronger evaluation designs, is important only if officials wish to use the same intervention elsewhere.

In what Eck terms "small-claim, small-area problem solving," analysts develop appropriate interventions for problems in context. This is the essence of the problem-solving process. Like Eck, we emphasize *process*—systematically studying a problem, developing appropriate interventions, and seeing if those interventions have the intended effect. This is quite different from what Eck terms "large-claim interventions"—such as Drug Abuse Resistance Education (DARE) or corrections boot camps—that are developed to apply in a wide variety of settings. Because small-claim, small-scale interventions are tailored to highly specific settings, they cannot easily be transferred intact to different

settings. However, the *process* of diagnosing local problems, selecting appropriate interventions, and then assessing the effects of those interventions can be applied generally. Anthony Braga (2008) offers more examples of this reasoning. Gloria Laycock presents an even stronger case for scientific realism in applied criminal justice research generally (2002) and in making specific plans for crime prevention (Tilley and Laycock, 2002).

Tinus Kruger offers a good example of the strengths of scientific realism for small-claim interventions in the box, "Participatory Crime Analysis." Kruger and colleagues work with community residents in South African urban townships to learn about crime mechanisms in specific context. Each project produces small-claim interventions to reduce threats to public safety. Reading through this example, you should be reminded of our description of safety audits in Chapter 9. Consider also Amber Horning's discussion of qualitative interviewing in Chapter 8. Finally, consider how Kruger and colleagues combine low-tech community-based data collection with more sophisticated analytic techniques.

We might be justifiably skeptical about the generalizability of small-scale evaluations, whether case studies or something else. But the scientific realists respond that generalizability is not really the point, especially in applied research like Kruger's. Instead, they urge combining results from a large number of smaller-scale evaluations as an alternative to trying to generalize from a small number of large-scale evaluations. For example, Graham Farrell and Alistair Buckley (1999) describe how an intervention to reduce repeat victimization among domestic violence victims appeared to have no effect when postintervention counts of domestic violence incidents were examined. Breaking the simple measure of domestic violence incidents down into subsets of repeat victimizations and new victimizations showed that counts of repeat victims were substantially lower, but this was offset by an increase in first-time victimizations. This makes sense if we think through the theory of action implied by this program.

Randomized or quasi-experimental evaluations should be conducted when such designs are appropriate. But it is important to recognize the formidable requirements for deploying these

PARTICIPATORY CRIME ANALYSIS

BY TINUS KRUGER
Council for Scientific and Industrial Research
Pretoria, South Africa

Participatory crime analysis uses community-based mapping and other tools to identify crime hotspots in South African townships. Large numbers of people live in cramped, substandard housing in townships on the outskirts of large cities. Dwellings and streets in townships are not mapped. Townships have limited police protection, and lack water, electricity, and other basic resources of better-off communities. Violence and other types of crime are serious problems that community residents face on a daily basis.

In an effort to reduce crime and increase safety, the Council for Scientific and Industrial Research (CSIR) works with partners to systematically analyze problems and develop crime prevention initiatives tailored to community needs. Our approach is grounded in the belief that people know best the places where they live. The role of CSIR is collaborative, adding analytic skills to local knowledge of problems.

The analysis process maps problems, providing a perspective of local spatial dynamics through the eyes of residents. An important objective is to improve relations between local residents and traditional policing practices.

The process is begun in a one-day workshop that involves the following steps:

1. **Crime prevention concepts**. Workshop participants are introduced to the concept of crime prevention, in particular crime prevention through environmental design (CPTED). Many of the resident community participants have never heard of crime prevention, so this introduction is an import step.

2. **Individual maps**. Community participants draw pictures of areas where they live, indicating the places where they feel unsafe or where they know crime problems are routinely found. The mapping process helps people think about the locations of trouble spots in the community.

3. **Group maps**. Places identified in the drawing are superimposed on aerial photos or detailed maps.

4. **Site visits**. Workshop participants—community residents and CSIR staff—visit selected areas from these maps, and take photos or videos of the areas. During visits to each place, the problems are described by individual(s) who identified the place.

5. **Analysis**. The photos are reviewed and photo maps are created. Information about a particular problem spot is organized according to the crimes that occur there, the victims, the offenders, and the characteristics of the place. The area's spatial relationship to the surrounding environment is also considered. For example, how might a particular feature act as a link (or a barrier) between the houses and their surroundings?

6. **Developing responses**. The problem places are prioritized according to certain criteria, such as the types of crime that occur there, whether these crimes constitute priority crimes, whether other role-players such as the local authority are required to alleviate the problem. The three or four most critical problem areas are then selected and possible responses developed. Some responses might involve the community in cutting grass and cleaning up a dangerous open field. Another type of response engages community residents in lobbying the municipality to provide streetlights, or to demand the closing of an illegal liquor outlet.

The development of a possible intervention is a joint exercise for the whole group. It is important for everybody to realize that the solution is often more complex than just identifying someone, usually the police, to blame for not doing their job. Community residents have a stronger sense of empowerment as a result of the process. Police are better able to address crime problems with the information produced by participatory crime analysis.

Source: Adapted from http://www.saferspaces.org.za/be-inspired/entry/mapping-and-spatial-design-for-community-crime-prevention (Accessed 28 August 2016).

designs. The scientific realist approach to evaluation is flexible and may be appropriate in many situations. A scientific realist evaluation or case study can be especially useful in smaller-scale evaluations in which interest centers more on solving some particular problem in a specific context than on finding generalizable scientific truths. In any case, a variety of approaches can satisfy the definition of program evaluation we discussed early this chapter, by systematically applying social science research procedures to an individual program or agency.

Our general advice in this regard is simple: do the best you can. This requires two things: (1) understanding the strengths and limits of social science research procedures and (2) carefully diagnosing what is needed and what is possible in a particular application. Only by understanding possible methods and program constraints can we judge properly whether any kind of evaluation study is worth undertaking with an experimental, quasi-experimental, or nonexperimental design, or whether an evaluation should not be undertaken at all.

Our running example, "Putting It All Together: Applied Research on Racial Profiling and Traffic Enforcement," illustrates applied research on racial profiling.

The Political Context of Applied Research

Public policy involves making choices, and that involves politics.

Applied researchers bridge the gap between the body of research knowledge about crime and the practical needs of criminal justice professionals—a process that has potential political, ideological, and ethical problems. In the final section of this chapter, we turn our attention to the context of applied research, describing some of the special problems that can emerge in such studies.

Some similarities are evident between this material and our discussion of ethics in Chapter 3. Although ethics and politics are often closely intertwined, the ethics of criminal justice research focuses on the methods used, whereas political issues are more concerned with the substance and use of research findings. Ethical and political aspects of applied research also differ in that there are no formal codes of accepted political conduct comparable to the codes of ethical conduct we examined earlier. Although some ethical norms have political aspects—for example, not harming subjects relates to protection of civil liberties—no one has developed a set of political norms that can be agreed on by all criminal justice researchers.

Evaluation and Stakeholders

Most applied studies involve multiple stakeholders—people who have some direct or indirect interest in the program or evaluation results (Rossi, Freeman, and Lipsey, 1999:204–205). Some stakeholders may be enthusiastic supporters of an experimental program, others may oppose it, and still others may be neutral. Different stakeholder interests in programs can produce conflicting perspectives on evaluations of those programs.

For example, in their study of pretrial home detention, Maxfield and Baumer (1992) found support for the program in the prosecutor's office and sheriff's department. Each was pleased by the prospect of freeing up jail space. However, decision makers in the community corrections agency, responsible for delivering home detention, were less supportive; they expressed concern over the increased workload and feared that too many persons released to pretrial home detention would be bad risks. And some community corrections staff were more worried about the evaluation than the program, feeling that their job performance was under scrutiny. The National Institute of Justice funded the evaluation, hoping that results would document a successful program that could be adopted in other jurisdictions. Community corrections decision makers had a different perspective on the evaluation; they wanted to know what did and did not work.

Emil Posavec and Raymond Carey (2002) describe such problems as dysfunctional attitudes toward program evaluation. Program supporters may have unrealistic expectations that evaluation results will document dramatic success. Conversely, they may worry that negative results will lead to program termination. Agency staff may feel that day-to-day experience in delivering

Virtually all research on racial profiling has been applied in the sense that it addresses important questions of public policy. Research in New Jersey was prompted by lawsuits and the involvement of the U.S. Department of Justice. This was also the case for some municipalities and other states that faced allegations of bias in law enforcement. In contrast, research in North Carolina and Pennsylvania was initiated at the request of state authorities who sought to learn whether racial profiling was a problem, and if so what could be done. You will recognize this as an example of problem analysis and planning.

Little evaluation research has been conducted outside of the problem analysis framework we described in this chapter. Maxfield and Andresen (2002) conducted a process evaluation of the use of video recording equipment in New Jersey State Police patrol vehicles. But this was more of an audit to assess whether or not the equipment was being used properly.

PROBLEM ANALYSIS BY LITIGATION

Most legal action against the New Jersey was captured in a consent decree between the U.S. Department of Justice and state officials (available at http://www.state.nj.us/oag/jointapp.htm). This was essentially a series of specified reforms and other changes in management and operations of the state police. In general, the Division of State Police was compelled to become a more data-driven organization. Here is an example of key provisions in the consent decree:

Management Awareness Program

40. The State shall develop and implement computerized systems for maintaining and retrieving information necessary for the supervision and management of the State Police to promote professionalism and civil rights integrity, to identify and modify potentially problematic behavior, and to promote best practices (hereinafter, the "Management Awareness Program" or "MAP").

41. The MAP shall consist of the following information:
   a. all items of information in connection with all motor vehicle stops that are required to be recorded in a written report, form, or log, or reported to the communications center, pursuant to ¶29 and the protocols listed in ¶29 of this Decree, except that duplicate information need not be entered, and information as to whether the incident was recorded with MVR equipment need not be entered if all patrol cars are equipped with MVR unless a patrol car was equipped with MVR equipment that was not functioning;
   b. information on civilian compliments and other indicia of positive performance; information on misconduct investigations; reports on use of force associated with motor vehicle stops; on-duty and off-duty criminal arrests and criminal charges; civil suits involving alleged misconduct by state troopers while on duty; civil suits in which a trooper is named as a party involving off-duty conduct that alleges

a program imparts a qualitative understanding of its success that cannot be documented by a controlled experiment. Staff and other stakeholders may object that an evaluation consumes scarce resources better spent on actually delivering a program.

We have two bits of advice in dealing with such problems. First, identify program stakeholders, their perspectives on the program, and their likely perspectives on the evaluation. In addition to agency decision makers and staff, stakeholders include program beneficiaries and competitors. For example, store owners in a downtown shopping district might benefit from an experimental program to deploy additional police on foot patrol, whereas people who live in a nearby residential area might

racial bias, physical violence or threats of violence; and

c. implementation of interventions; and training information including the name of the course, date started, date completed and training location for each member receiving training.

As a result of this and other requirements for collecting data, the New Jersey State Police developed what it called a Management Analysis and Professional Performance System (MAPPS) to support periodic reviews of trooper performance at different levels. Essentially the system compiled quarterly data on traffic stops made by each trooper. These were aggregated to the police station level, then further aggregated to a regional level. State police supervisors and managers are required to conduct quarterly reviews based on these performance data. Among other things, MAPPS compares the race of drivers stopped by individual troopers to a norm calculated from stops by all troopers. With MAPPS in place, it's no longer possible for New Jersey officials to claim "We had no way of knowing!" when asked about racial bias in policing.

PURPOSIVE TRAFFIC ENFORCEMENT

Maxfield and Kelling concluded that the higher proportion of black drivers stopped on the southern segment of the New Jersey Turnpike was due to a combination of three things:

- African American drivers are a greater proportion of all drivers on southern segments of the turnpike;
- the proportion of black drivers estimated to be exceeding the speed limit by 15 mph or more is higher on southern segments of the turnpike; and,

- the risk of any vehicle being stopped is substantially greater on southern segments of the turnpike (2005:23).

In the next chapter we will present additional data that led to these statements. For now, and recalling our discussion in Chapter 12, the central point is that traffic enforcement was concentrated on the southern segment of the turnpike, largely because it could be. Traffic volume varies from enormous to very heavy on other segments of the turnpike. Maxfield and Kelling learned that enforcement in those areas tends to be restricted to off-peak times when traffic volume is lighter. It was felt that enforcement during high-volume periods would produce intolerable traffic congestion. This was much less of a problem in the southern segment, so enforcement could be spread more evenly.

Further, from intensive field research, Maxfield discovered that "citation zones" were concentrated in the southern segment. Individual troopers considered a variety of physical features of road segments and the surrounding environment in selecting places to set up radar detection. These conditions were more often present in the more rural southern segments.

Based on their analysis, Maxfield and Kelling recommended that traffic enforcement be considered more purposively. They proposed a series of experiments that would systematically vary the time and place of traffic enforcement. An evaluation of this approach was conducted in Australia (Leggett, 1997), finding that shifting enforcement zones produced a reduction in traffic accidents.

Such purposive action would produce a problem-oriented approach to traffic enforcement that is more rooted in data and analysis.

argue that additional police should be assigned to their neighborhood.

Second, educate stakeholders about why an evaluation should be conducted. This is best done by explaining that applied research is conducted to determine what works and what does not. Various offices in the Department of Justice have issued brief documents that describe how evaluation can

benefit criminal justice agencies by rationalizing their actions (Eck, 2003; Kirchner, Przybylski, and Cardella, 1994; Maxfield, 2001). Such publications, together with examples of completed evaluations, can be valuable tools for winning the support of stakeholders.

For an excellent description of the political and logistical problems involved in a complex

WHEN POLITICS ACCOMMODATES FACTS

BY TONY FABELO

The 1994 federal anticrime bill, and related politics emanating from this initiative, put pressure on the states to adopt certain sentencing policies as a condition for receiving federal funds. Among these policies is the adoption of a "three strikes and you're out" provision establishing a no-parole sentence for repeat violent offenders. Facts have prevented a criminal justice operational gridlock in Texas by delineating to policy makers the operational and fiscal impact of broadly drafted policies in this area. Facts established through policy analysis by the Criminal Justice Policy Council (CJPC) have clearly stated that a broad application of the "three strikes and you're out" policy will have a tremendous fiscal impact.

Therefore, state policy makers have carefully drafted policies in this area. For example, during the last legislative session, the adoption of life with no parole for repeat sex offenders was considered. State policy makers, after considering facts presented by the CJPC, adopted a policy that narrowly defined the group of offenders for whom the law is to apply. They also adopted a 35-year minimum sentence that must be served before parole eligibility, rather than a life sentence with no parole. The careful drafting of this policy limited its fiscal impact while still accomplishing the goal of severely punishing the selected group of sex offenders.

Unlike Texas, politics did not accommodate facts in California, where lawmakers adopted a fiscally unsustainable "three strikes and you're out" policy.

For my part, I need to maintain personal integrity and the integrity of the CJPC in defining the facts for policy makers. I have to be judged not only by "objectivity," which is an elusive concept, but by my judgment in synthesizing complex information for policy makers. To do this, I follow and ask my staff to follow these rules:

1. Consider as many perspectives as possible in synthesizing the meaning of information, including the perspectives of those stakeholders who will be affected.
2. State the limits of the facts and identify areas where drawing conclusions is clearly not possible.
3. Consult with your peers to verify methodological assumptions and meet accepted criteria to pass the scrutiny of the scientific community.
4. Provide potential alternative assumptions behind the facts.
5. Set clear expectations for reviewing reports and releasing information so that facts are not perceived as giving advantage to any particular interest group.
6. Judge the bottom-line meaning of the information for policy action based on a frame of reference broader than that of any particular party or constituency.
7. Finally, if the above are followed, never succumb to political pressure to change your judgment. Integrity cannot be compromised even once. In the modern crowded marketplace of information, your audience will judge you first for your motives and then for your technical expertise.

Source: Adapted from Fabelo (1996:2, 4).

---

evaluation that affects multiple stakeholders, see the appendix to Sherman's (1992b) book on domestic violence experiments. He presents a detailed report on the process of planning one experiment in Milwaukee, from initial negotiations through project completion.

More generally, recognize that applied research is very much a cooperative venture. Accordingly,

researchers and program staff are mutual stakeholders in designing and executing evaluations. Evaluators' interest in a strong design that will meet scientific standards must be balanced against the main concern of program sponsors—obtaining information that is useful for developing public policy. Among other things, the existence of mutual stakeholders' perspectives implies that applied researchers have obligations to program sponsors, their collaborative partners in evaluation studies.

Tinus Kruger's description of participatory crime analysis is an excellent example of how collaboration benefits mutual stakeholders. In their description of the evidence generation initiative, Maxfield and associates (2017) describe extensive collaboration with New York City youth justice organizations from problem conceptualization through evaluation.

The flip side of caution about getting caught in stakeholder conflict is the benefit of applied research in influencing public policy. Evaluation studies can provide support for continuing or expanding successful criminal justice programs, or evidence that ineffective programs should be modified or terminated. And sometimes, problem analysis results can be used to influence actions by public officials. For an example, see the box titled "When Politics Accommodates Facts," in which Tony Fabelo describes how problem analysis dissuaded Texas legislators from costly lawmaking.

Politics and Objectivity

Politics and ideology can color research in ways even more subtle than those described by Fabelo. You may, for example, consider yourself an open-minded and unbiased person who aspires to be an objective criminal justice researcher. However, you might have strong views about different sentencing policies, believing that probation and restitution are preferred over long prison sentences. Because there is no conclusive evidence to favor one approach over the other, your beliefs would be perfectly reasonable.

Now, assume that one of the requirements for the course you are taking is to write a proposal for an evaluation project on corrections policy. In all likelihood, you will prepare a proposal to study a probation program rather than, say, a program on the use of portable jails to provide increased detention capacity. That is natural, and certainly legitimate, but your own policy preferences will affect the topic you choose.

It may sometimes seem difficult to maintain an acceptable level of objectivity about, or distance from, evaluation results in criminal justice research. This task can be complicated further if you have strong views one way or another about a particular program or policy. For example, it is likely that researchers who evaluate an experimental program to prevent offenders from repeating sincerely hope that the program will work. However, substantially less consensus exists about other criminal justice problems and policies. For example, how do you feel about a project to test the effects of restrictive handgun laws or mandatory jail sentences for abortion protesters?

Ronald Clarke (1997b:28) describes political objections to applied studies of situational crime prevention: "Conservative politicians regard it as an irrelevant response to the breakdown in morality that has fueled the postwar rise in crime. Those on the left criticize it for neglecting issues of social justice and for being too accepting of the definitions of crime of those in power." By the same token, electronic monitoring is distrusted for being simultaneously too lenient by allowing offenders to do time at home and too close to a technological nightmare by enabling the government to spy on individuals. Evaluations of situational crime prevention or ELMO programs may be criticized for tacitly supporting either soft-on-crime or heavy-handed police-state ideologies (Lilly, 2006; Nellis, 2006).

It is difficult to claim that criminal justice research, either applied or basic, is value free. Our own beliefs and preferences affect the topics we choose to investigate. Political preferences and ideology may also influence criminal justice research agendas by making funds available for some projects but not others. For example, in 2015 the National Institute of Justice awarded funds for projects to study these topics: "Research on contraband and interdiction modalities used in correctional facilities" and "Los Angeles Police Department DNA capacity enhancement and backlog reduction program." (http://nij.gov/funding/awards/Pages/2015.aspx [Accessed 28 August 2016]). No funds were awarded, however, for such projects as "The Scope of Institutionalized Racism in the War on Drugs" or "Exploratory Research on Torture in Federal Immigrant Detention Camps." It is, of course, possible for researchers—consciously or unconsciously—to become instruments for achieving political or policy objectives in applied research.

In another illustration of how political choices affect applied research, Jeffrey Butts (2015) compares evaluating social policies to pointing a flashlight in a dark room, where one can only see what is illuminated by the flashlight's beam. He writes:

> Research evidence does not emerge from a pristine and impartial search for truth. The evidence we have today is the fruit of previous research investments made by policy makers and funding bodies with goals, beliefs, values, and preferences. Funding provides the flashlight and points it as well. To say that a program or practice is "evidence-based" means that the odds of success are reasonably good. The findings of existing evaluations are like small beams of light in a dark room. They are not sufficient for making all the choices required to formulate and implement social policies. Naive lawmakers who demand irrefutable evidence for every funding decision are simply afraid of the dark.

SUMMARY

- Evaluation research and problem analysis are examples of applied research in criminal justice.
- Different types of evaluation activities correspond to different stages in the policy process—policy planning, process evaluation, and impact evaluation.
- An evaluability assessment may be undertaken as a scouting operation or a preevaluation to determine whether it is possible to evaluate a particular program.
- A careful formulation of the problem, including relevant measurements and criteria of success or failure, is essential in evaluation research.
- Organizations may not have clear statements or ideas about program goals. In such cases, researchers must work with agency staff to formulate mutually acceptable statements of goals before proceeding.
- Evaluation research may use experimental, quasi experimental, or nonexperimental designs. As in studies with other research purposes, designs that offer the greatest control over experimental conditions are usually preferred.
- Randomized designs cannot be used for evaluations that begin after a new program has been implemented or for full-coverage programs in which it is not possible to withhold an experimental treatment from a control group.

- Process evaluations can be undertaken independently or in connection with an impact assessment. Process evaluations are essential for interpreting results from an impact assessment.
- Problem analysis is more of a planning technique. However, problem analysis draws on the same social science research methods used in program evaluation. Many variations on problem analysis are used in applied criminal justice research.
- The scientific realist approach to applied research focuses on mechanisms in context, rather than generalizable causal processes.
- Criminal justice agencies increasingly are using problem analysis tools for tactical and strategic planning. Crime mapping and other space-based procedures are especially useful applied techniques.
- Problem solving, evaluation, and scientific realism have many common elements.
- Evaluation research entails special logistical, ethical, and political problems because it is embedded in the day-to-day events of public policy and real life.

KEY TERMS

Evaluation research (p. 360)
Evidence-based policy (p. 361)
Evidence generation (p. 361)
Impact assessment (p. 364)
Problem analysis (p. 360)
Problem-oriented policing (p. 382)
Problem solving (p. 382)
Process evaluation (p. 365)
Stakeholders (p. 368)

REVIEW QUESTIONS AND EXERCISES

1. In presentations to justice practitioners, Maxfield describes evaluation as answering two questions: "Did you get what you expected?" and "Compared to what?" Discuss how particular sections of this chapter relate to those two questions.

2. When programs do not achieve their expected results, it's due to one of two things: the program was not a good idea to begin with, or it was a good idea but was not implemented properly. Discuss why it is necessary to conduct both a process evaluation and an impact evaluation to learn why a program failed.

3. What are the principal advantages and disadvantages of randomized designs for field experiments? Are such designs used in problem analysis? Explain your answer.

CHAPTER 14

Interpreting Data

We'll examine a few simple statistics frequently used in criminal justice research. We'll also cover the fundamental logic of multivariate analysis. You'll come away from this chapter able to perform a number of simple, though powerful, analyses to describe data and reach research conclusions.

Learning Objectives

1. Understand that descriptive statistics are used to summarize data under study.

2. Describe a frequency distribution in terms of cases, attributes, and variables.

3. Recognize that measures of central tendency summarize data, but they do not convey the detail of the original data.

4. Understand that measures of dispersion give a summary indication of the distribution of cases around an average value.

5. Provide examples of rates as descriptive statistics that standardize some measure for comparative purposes.

6. Describe how bivariate analysis and subgroup comparisons examine relationships between two variables.

7. Compute and interpret percentages in contingency tables.

8. Understand that multivariate analysis examines the relationships among several variables.

9. Explain the logic underlying the proportionate reduction of error (PRE) model.

10. Describe the use of lambda (λ) and gamma (γ), and Pearson's product-moment correlation (r) as PRE-based measures of association for nominal, ordinal, and interval/ration variables, respectively.

11. Summarize how regression equations and regression lines are used in data analysis.

Identity Theft

We have all heard something about identity theft, often from media reports about how it is a growing problem. But how common is it? Or, for that matter, what is identity theft and what forms does it take? The National Crime Victimization Survey (NCVS) added questions on identity theft in 2004. Here we report some basic descriptive statistics on results from the 2010 NCVS (Langton, 2011).

The first table estimates the number of households that experienced different forms of identity theft in 2010. The survey counted victimization for three types of incidents:

1. Unauthorized use or attempted use of existing credit cards

2. Unauthorized use or attempted use of other existing accounts, such as checking or savings

3. Misuse of personal identification to obtain new accounts or loans or to commit other crimes

The last category is what many people think of when they hear the phrase "identity theft." The other two categories are more common, and might just as easily be labeled "credit card fraud" or "checking account fraud." In any event, about 7 percent of households experienced one or more of these three types.

	Estimated Number of Households	Percentage of Households
Total	122,885,200	100%
Identity theft	8,571,900	7.0
Credit card	4,625,100	3.8
Other accounts	2,195,900	1.8
Personal information	775,400	0.6
Multiple types	975,521	0.8

Source: Langton (2011:7).

As is the case for other types of crimes, some variation exists in victimization. The next table shows what percentage of households were victimized by age of household head and income. Like many other types of crime, younger people are at greater risk of identity theft. Victimization risk for those ages 65 or older is one-half or lower than for other age groups. Patterns for income are different from those for other offenses. With the exception of households earning less than $7,500 per year, victimization increases with income. Over 12 percent of households in the highest income category reported identity theft in 2010.

Percentage of Households Victimized	
Age of household head	
18–24	8.5%
25–34	7.6
35–49	7.9
50–64	7.3
65 or older	7.3
Household income	
Less than $7,500	5.3%
$7,500–14,999	4.8
$15,000–24,999	4.6
$25,000–34,999	6.0
$35,000–49,999	6.6
$50,000–74,999	7.9
$75,000 or more	12.3

Source: Langton (2011:3–4).

These simple tables offer examples of univariate statistics (in the first table) and bivariate statistics (in the second table). The univariate table shows the distribution of victimization across households in the United States. The bivariate table shows relationships between identity theft victimization and two other variables—age and income. Think about why these patterns exist: unauthorized use of credit cards is much more common than other types of identity theft; victimization decreases with age, but increases with income.

In this chapter, we describe the basics of how to interpret data and how to compute basic percentage tables. If you wish to try your own hand at this, you can get copies of the tables Langton reports in spreadsheet form at the following Web address: http://bjs.ojp.usdoj.gov/content/pub/sheets/itrh0510.zip.

Introduction

Empirical research usually uses some type of statistical analysis.

Many people are intimidated by empirical research because they feel uncomfortable with mathematics and statistics. Indeed, many research reports are filled with otherwise unspecified computations. The role of statistics in criminal justice research is very important, but it is equally important to view that role in its proper perspective.

Empirical research is, first and foremost, a logical rather than a mathematical operation. Mathematics is not much more than a convenient and efficient language for accomplishing the logical operations inherent in good data analysis. Statistics is the applied branch of mathematics especially appropriate to a variety of research analyses.

We'll be looking at two types of statistics: descriptive and inferential. **Descriptive statistics** are used to summarize and otherwise describe data in manageable forms. **Inferential statistics** help researchers form conclusions from their observations; typically, that involves forming conclusions about a population from studying a sample drawn from it.

Before considering any numbers, we want to assure you that the level of statistics used in this chapter has been proven to be nontoxic and safe for humans. Our introduction to this important phase of criminal justice research is just that—an introduction. Our intent is to familiarize future producers and consumers of empirical criminal justice research with fundamental concepts of

Descriptive statistics Computations that describe either the characteristics of a variable or the relationship among variables.

Inferential statistics Computations for making inferences from findings based on sample observations to some larger population.

quantitative analysis. Many published criminal justice studies use sophisticated statistical techniques that are best learned in specialized courses. But the underlying logic and fundamental techniques of statistics are not at all complicated. It's mostly counting and comparing.

We assume that you are taking a course in research methods for criminology and criminal justice because you are interested in the subjects of crime and criminal justice policy. We suggest that you approach this chapter by thinking about statistics as tools for describing, understanding, and explaining crime and criminal justice policy. Learning how to use these tools will help you better understand this fascinating subject. And learning how to summarize and interpret data about a subject you find inherently interesting is the least painful and most rewarding way to becoming acquainted with statistics.

Univariate Description

The simplest statistics describe some type of average and dispersion for a single variable.

Descriptive statistics represent a method for presenting quantitative descriptions in a manageable form. Sometimes, we want to describe single variables; this procedure is known as univariate analysis. Other times, we want to describe the associations that connect one variable with another. Bivariate analysis refers to descriptions of two variables, and multivariate analysis examines relationships among three or more variables.

Univariate analysis examines the distribution of cases on only one variable at a time. We'll begin with the logic and formats for the analysis of univariate data.

Distributions

The most basic way to present univariate data is to report all individual cases—that is, to list the attribute for each case under study in terms of the variable in question. Suppose we are interested in the ages of criminal court judges; our data might come from a directory of judges prepared by a state bar association. The most direct manner of reporting the ages of judges is simply to list them: 63, 57, 49,

62, 80, 72, 55, and so forth. Such a report will give readers complete details of the data, but it is too cumbersome for most purposes. We could arrange our data in a somewhat more manageable form without losing any of the detail by reporting that five judges are 38 years old, seven are 39, 18 are 40, and so forth. Such a format avoids duplicating data on this variable.

For an even more manageable format—with a certain loss of detail—we might report judges' ages as marginals, which are **frequency distributions** of grouped data: 24 judges under 45 years of age, 51 between 45 and 50 years of age, and so forth. Our readers will have fewer data to examine and interpret, but they will not be able to reproduce fully the original ages of all the judges. Thus, for example, readers will have no way of knowing how many judges are 41 years old.

The preceding example presented marginals in the form of raw numbers. An alternative form is the use of percentages. Thus, for example, we might report that x percent of the judges are younger than 45, y percent are between 45 and 50, and so forth. The following table shows an example:

Ages of Criminal Court Judges (Hypothetical)

Age	Percent
Under 35	9%
36–45	21
46–55	45
56–65	19
65 and older	6
Total	100% = 433
No data	18

In computing percentages, it is necessary to determine the base from which to compute—the number that represents 100 percent. In the most straightforward situation, the base is the total number of cases under study. However, a problem arises whenever some cases have missing data. Let's consider, for example, a survey in which respondents are asked to report their ages. If some respondents fail to answer that question, we have two alternatives. First, we might still base our percentages on the total number of respondents, reporting those who fail to give their ages as a percentage of the total. Second, we might use the number of persons who give an answer as the base from which to compute the percentages; this approach is illustrated in the preceding table. We will still report the number who do not answer, but they will not figure in the percentages.

The choice of a base depends entirely on the purposes of the analysis. If we wish to compare the age distribution of a survey sample with comparable data on the population from which the sample was drawn, we will probably want to omit the "no answers" from the computation. Our best estimate of the age distribution of all respondents is the distribution for those who answered the question. Because "no answer" is not a meaningful age category, its presence among the base categories will only confuse the comparison of sample and population figures.

Measures of Central Tendency

Beyond simply reporting marginals, researchers often present data in the form of summary **averages**, or measures of **central tendency**. Options in this regard include the **mode** (the most frequent attribute, either grouped or ungrouped), the arithmetic **mean** (the sum of values for all observations, divided by the number of observations), and the **median** (the middle attribute in the ranked distribution of observed attributes). Here's how the three averages are calculated from a set of data.

Suppose we are conducting an experiment that involves teenagers as subjects. They range in age from 13 to 19, as indicated in this frequency distribution:

Age	Number
13	3
14	4
15	6
16	8
17	4
18	3
19	3

Now that we know the actual ages of the 31 subjects, how old are these subjects in general, or on average? Let's look at three different ways we might answer that question.

The easiest average to calculate is the mode, the most frequent value. The distribution of our 31 subjects shows there are more 16-year-olds (eight of them) than any other age, so the modal age is 16, as indicated in Figure 14.1.

Figure 14.1 also demonstrates the three steps in calculation of the mean: (1) multiply each age by the number of subjects who are that age, (2) total the results of all those multiplications, and (3) divide that total by the number of subjects. As indicated in Figure 14.1, the mean age in this illustration is 15.87.

The median represents the "middle" value; half are above it and half below. If we had the precise age of each subject (for instance, 17 years and 124 days), we could arrange all 31 subjects in order by age, and the median for the whole group would be the age of the middle subject.

We do not, however, know precise ages; our data constitute "grouped data" in this regard. Three people who are not precisely the same age have been grouped in the category "13 years old," for example.

Figure 14.1 illustrates the logic of calculating a median for grouped data. Because there are 31 subjects altogether, the "middle" subject is number 16 when they are arranged by age; 15 are younger and 17 are older. The bottom portion of Figure 14.1 shows that the middle person is one of the eight 16-year-olds. In the enlarged view of that group, we see that number 16 is the third from the left.

Measures of Dispersion

In the research literature, we find both means and medians presented. Whenever means are presented, we must be aware that they are susceptible to extreme values; a few very large or very small numbers can change the mean dramatically. For this reason, it is usually important to examine measures of **dispersion** about the mean.

Central tendency Clustering of observations to a midpoint in a distribution.

Dispersion The distribution of values around some central value, such as an average.

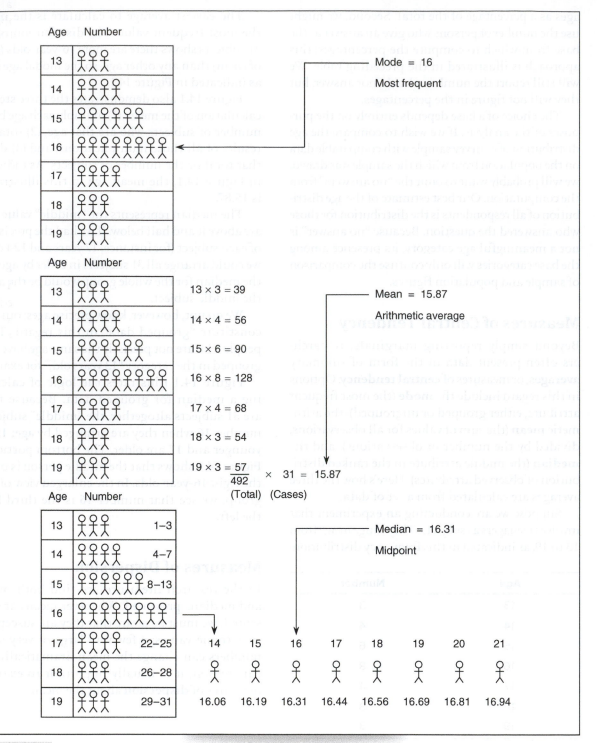

FIGURE 14.1 Three "Averages"

The simplest measure of dispersion is the **range**: the distance separating the highest from the lowest value. Thus, besides reporting that our subjects have a mean age of 15.87, we might also indicate that their ages range from 13 to 19. A somewhat more sophisticated measure of dispersion is the standard deviation, which can be described as the average amount of variation about the mean. If the mean is the average value of all observations in a group, then the **standard deviation** represents the average amount that each individual observation varies from the mean. Table 14.1 presents some hypothetical data on the ages of persons in juvenile and adult courts that will help illustrate the concepts of deviation and average deviation. Let's first consider the top of Table 14.1.

The first column shows the age for each of 10 juvenile court defendants. The mean age for

TABLE 14.1 Standard Deviation for Two Hypothetical Distributions

	Juvenile Court		
	Age	**Deviation from Mean**	**Squared Deviation from Mean**
	12	−2	4
	15	1	1
	14	0	0
	13	−1	1
	15	1	1
	14	0	0
	16	2	4
	16	2	4
	12	−2	4
	13	−1	1
Sum	140	0	20
Average	14	(0)	(2)
Standard deviation			1.41

	Adult Court		
	Age	**Deviation from Mean**	**Squared Deviation from Mean**
	18	−10	100
	37	9	81
	23	−5	25
	22	−6	36
	25	−3	9
	43	15	225
	19	−9	81
	50	22	484
	21	−7	49
	22	−6	36
Sum	280	0	1126
Average	28	(0)	(112.6)
Standard deviation			10.61

these 10 juveniles is 14. The second column shows how much each individual's age deviates from the mean. Thus, the first juvenile is two years younger than the mean, the second is one year older, and the third is the same age as the mean.

You might first think that the average deviation is calculated in the same way as the mean—add up all individual deviations for each case and divide by the number of cases. We did that in Table 14.1, but notice that the total deviation is zero; therefore, the average deviation is zero. In fact, the sum of deviations from the mean will always be zero. This is because some individual deviations will be negative and some will be positive—and the positive and negative values will always cancel each other out.

For this reason (and other reasons too complex to describe here), the standard deviation measure of dispersion is based on the squared deviations from the mean. Squaring any number always produces a positive value, so when we add all the squared deviations together, we will not get zero for the total. Summing these squared deviations in the top of Table 14.1 produces a total of 20, and dividing by the number of observations produces an "average" deviation of 2. This quantity—the sum of squared deviations from the mean divided by the number of cases—is called the "variance." Taking the square root of the variance produces the standard deviation, which is 1.41 for juveniles in Table 14.1.

How should we interpret a standard deviation of 1.41, or any other such value, for that matter? By itself, any particular value for the standard deviation has no intuitive meaning. This measure of dispersion is most useful in a comparative sense. Comparing the relative values for the standard deviation and the mean indicates how much variation there is in a group of cases, relative to the average. Similarly, comparing standard deviations for different groups of cases indicates relative amounts of dispersion within each group.

In our example of juvenile court cases, the standard deviation of 1.41 is rather low relative to the mean of 14. Now compare the data for juvenile court to the bottom half of Table 14.1, which presents ages for a hypothetical group of adult court defendants. The mean is higher, of course, because adults are older than juveniles. More important for illustrating the standard deviation, there is greater variation in the distribution of adult court

defendants, as illustrated by the standard deviation and the columns that show raw deviations and squared deviations from the mean of 28. The standard deviation for adult cases (10.61) is much higher relative to the mean of 28 than are the relative values of the standard deviation and mean for juvenile cases. In this hypothetical example, the substantive reason for this is obvious: there is much greater age variation in adult court than in juvenile court because the *range* for ages of adults is potentially greater (18 to whatever) than the range for ages in juveniles (1 to 17). As a result, the standard deviation for adult defendants indicates greater variation than the same measure for juvenile defendants.

In addition to providing a summary measure of dispersion, the standard deviation plays a role in the calculation of other descriptive statistics, some of which we will touch on later in this chapter. The standard deviation is also a central component of many inferential statistics used to make generalizations from a sample of observations to the population from which the sample was drawn.

Comparing Measures of Dispersion and Central Tendency

Other measures of dispersion can help us interpret measures of central tendency. One useful indicator that expresses both dispersion and grouping of cases is the percentile, which indicates what percentage of cases fall at or below some value. For example, scores on achievement tests such as the SAT are usually reported in both percentiles and raw scores. Thus, a raw score of 630 might fall in the 80th percentile, indicating that 80 percent of persons who take the SAT achieve scores of 630 or less; alternatively, the 80th percentile means that 20 percent of scores were higher than 630. Percentiles may also be grouped into quartiles, which give the cases that fall in the first (lowest), second, third, and fourth (highest) quarters of a distribution.

Table 14.2 presents a distribution of prior arrests for some hypothetical population of, say, probationers to illustrate different measures of central tendency and dispersion. Notice that, although the number of prior arrests ranges from 0 to 55, cases cluster in the lower end of this distribution. Half the cases have four or fewer prior arrests, as indicated by three descriptive statistics in Table 14.2: median, 50th percentile, and 2nd quartile. Only one-fourth of the cases have eight or more prior arrests.

Notice also the different values for our three measures of central tendency. The mode for prior arrests is 2, and the mean or average number is 5.76. Whenever the mean is much higher than the mode, it indicates that the mean is distorted by a small number of persons with many prior arrests. The standard deviation of 6.64 further indicates that our small population has quite a bit of variability. Figure 14.2 presents a graphic representation of the dispersion of cases and the different values for the three measures of central tendency.

Distributions such as those shown in Table 14.2 and Figure 14.2 are known as "skewed distributions." Although most cases cluster near the low end, a few are spread out over very high values for prior arrests. Many variables of interest to criminal justice researchers are skewed in similar ways, especially when examined for some general population. Most people have no prior arrests, but a small number of persons have many. Similarly, most people suffer no victimization from serious crime in any given year, but a small number of persons are repeatedly victimized.

In an appropriately titled article, "Deviating from the Mean," Michael Maltz (1994) cautions that criminologists, failing to recognize high levels of variation, sometimes report means for populations that exhibit a great deal of skewness. When reading reports of criminal justice research, researchers are advised to look closely at measures of both dispersion and central tendency. When the numerical value is high for the standard deviation and low for the mean, the mean is not a good measure of central tendency. Instead, use the median or mode, which are not affected by extreme values.

TABLE 14.2 Hypothetical Data on Distribution of Prior Arrests

Number of Prior Arrests	Number of Cases	Percent of Cases	Percentile Quartile
0	1	0.56	
1	16	8.89	
2	31	17.22	25th/1st
3	23	12.78	
4	20	11.11	50th/2nd
5	16	8.89	
6	19	10.56	
7	18	10.00	75th/3rd
8	11	6.11	
9	14	7.78	
10	5	2.78	
30	3	1.67	
40	2	1.11	
55	1	0.56	
Total	180	100.00%	
Mode	2		
Median	4		
Mean	5.76		
Range	0–55		
Standard deviation	6.64		

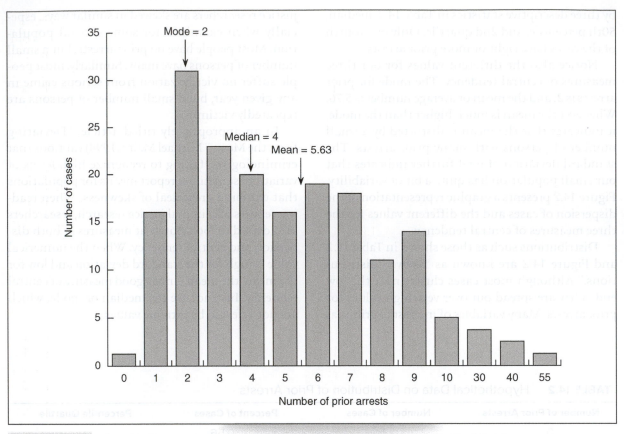

The preceding calculations are not appropriate for all variables. To understand this, we must examine two types of variables: continuous and discrete. Age and number of prior arrests are continuous ratio variables; they increase steadily in tiny fractions instead of jumping from category to category, as does a discrete variable such as gender or marital status. If discrete variables are being analyzed—a nominal or ordinal variable, for example—then some of the techniques discussed previously are not applicable.

Strictly speaking, medians and means should be calculated for only interval and ratio data, respectively. If the variable in question is gender, for instance, raw numbers or percentage marginals are appropriate and useful measures. Calculating the mode is a legitimate, though not very revealing, tool of analysis—but reports of mean, median, or dispersion summaries would be inappropriate.

Computing Rates

Rates are fundamental descriptive statistics in criminal justice research. In most cases, rates are used to standardize some measure for comparative purposes. For example, the following table shows Uniform Crime Report (UCR) figures on total murders for 2014 in four states.

	Total Murders, 2014	2014 Population
California	1,699	38,803,000
Louisiana	477	4,650,000
Missouri	403	6,064,000
New York	617	19,746,000

Source: Federal Bureau of Investigation (2015).

Obviously, California had far more murders than the other three states had, but these figures are difficult to interpret because of large differences in the states' total populations. Computing rates enables us to standardize by population size and make more meaningful comparisons, as the next table shows.

Murder Rates per 100,000 Population, 2014

California	4.4
Louisiana	10.3
Missouri	6.6
New York	3.1

We can see that Louisiana, even with the second fewest murders in 2014 (among the states reported here), had the highest murder rate. Notice also that the murder rate is expressed as the number of murders per 100,000 population. This is a common convention in reporting rates of crime and other rare events. To get the rate of murder *per person*, move the decimal point five places to the left in each of the figures in the second table. If you do that, you can clearly see which version is easier to interpret.

The arithmetic of calculating rates could not be much easier. What is not so simple, and in any event requires careful consideration, is deciding on the two basic components of rates: numerator and denominator. The numerator represents the central concept we are interested in measuring, so selecting the numerator involves all the considerations of measurement we have discussed elsewhere. Murder rates, arrest rates, conviction rates, and incarceration rates are common examples in which the numerator is a relatively straightforward count.

Choosing the right denominator is more a question of measurement than statistics. In most cases, we should compute rates to standardize according to some population eligible for inclusion in the numerator. Sometimes, the choice is fairly obvious, as in our use of each state's total population to compute murder rates. To compute rates of rape or sexual assault, we should probably use the population of adult women in the denominator, although we should also consider how to handle rapes with male victims. Because households are at risk of residential burglary, burglary rates should be computed using some count of households. Similarly, commercial burglaries should be based on some count of commercial establishments, and auto theft on some indicator of registered autos.

More difficult problems can arise in computing rates to express some characteristic of a mobile population. For example, residents of Miami are at risk of criminal victimization in that city, but so are tourists and other visitors to Miami. Because many nonresidents visit or pass through the city in any given year, a measure of Miami's crime rate based only on the city's resident population (such as the U.S. Census) will tend to overestimate the number of crimes standardized by the population at risk; many people at risk will not be counted in the denominator. Or what about estimating the crime rate on a subway system? The population at risk here is users, who, in New York City, amount to millions of persons per day.

Fortunately, data to support better measures of rates are becoming increasingly available. For example, a Census Bureau report estimates the daytime population of individual cities by combining the number of residents who work in the city with the number of nonresidents who work there. For Miami, that produces an estimated daytime population in the year 2000 of 497,536, substantially higher than the resident population of 362,470 (U.S. Census Bureau, 2005). The estimated weekday ridership for New York's subways in 2005 was 4.7 million per day, or 1.449 billion annually (New York City Transit, 2006). Crime totals for 2005 for the entire transit system (including buses and ferries) show 3,383 "major felony crimes," producing a rate per 100,000 of 0.23, or 2.3 major felonies for every million people at risk (City of New York, 2006). If crime data were available for the subway only, the rate would be even lower.

Rates are very useful descriptive statistics that may be easily computed. It is important, however, to be careful in selecting numerators and denominators. Recognize that this caution applies as much to questions of making measurements as it does to questions of computing descriptive statistics. The box titled "Murder on the Job" gives an example of confusion about the meaning of rates.

Detail versus Manageability

In presenting univariate and other data, we are constrained by two often conflicting goals. On the one hand, we should attempt to provide readers with the fullest degree of detail possible regarding

"High Murder Rate for Women on the Job," read the headline for a brief story in the *New York Times*, reporting on a study released by the U.S. Department of Labor. The subhead was equally alarming, and misleading, to casual readers: "40 percent of women killed at work are murdered, but figure for men is only 15 percent." Think about this statement, in light of our discussion of how to percentage a table. You should be able to imagine something like the following:

Cause of Death at Work (Percent)

	Women	Men
Murder	40	15
Other	60	85
Total	100%	100%

This table indicates that, of those women who die while on the job at work, 40 percent are murdered, and is consistent with the opening paragraphs of the story. Notice that so far nothing has been said about how many women and men are murdered, or how many women and men die on the job from all causes. Later on, the story provides more details:

Vehicle accidents caused the most job-related deaths, 18 percent or 1,121 of the 6,083 work-related deaths in 1992. . . . Homicides, including shootings and stabbings, were a close second with 17 percent, or 1,004 deaths, said the study by the department's Bureau of Labor Statistics.

This information enables us to supplement the table by adding row totals: 6,083 people died on the job in 1992; 1,004 of them were murdered and 5,079 died from other causes.

One more piece of information is needed to construct a contingency table: the total number of men and women killed on the job. The story does not tell us that directly, but it provides enough information to approximate the answer: "Although men are 55 percent of the workforce, they comprise 93 percent of all job-related deaths." Men must, therefore, be 93 percent of the 6,083 total workplace deaths, or approximately 5,657; this leaves approximately 426 deaths of women on the job. "Approximate" is an important qualifier here, because computing numbers of cases from percentages creates some inconsistencies due to rounding off percentages reported in the newspaper story. Let's now construct a contingency table to look at the numbers of workplace deaths.

those data. On the other hand, the data should be presented in a manageable form. Because these two goals often run counter to each other, researchers must seek the best compromise. One useful solution is to report a given set of data in more than one form. In the case of age, for example, we might report the marginals on ungrouped ages plus the mean age and standard deviation.

Our introductory discussion of univariate analysis shows how this seemingly simple matter can be rather complex. The lessons of this section will be important as we move now to a consideration of analysis involving more than a single variable.

Describing Two or More Variables

Descriptive statistics applied to two or more variables are tools to understand relationships among those variables.

Univariate analyses describe the units of analysis of a study and, if they are a sample drawn from some larger population, allow us to make descriptive inferences about the larger population. Bivariate and multivariate analyses are aimed primarily at explanation.

The next table shows computed numbers in parentheses. Notice that with the exception of "Total" all numbers have been estimated from the newspaper story's percentages for men and women.

Cause of Death at Work (Number)

	Women (est.)	Men (est.)	Total	Total (est.)
Murder	170	849	1,004	1,019
Other	256	4,808	5,079	5,064
Total	426	5,657	6,083	

The results are interesting. Although a greater percentage of women than men are murdered, a much larger number of men than women are murdered.

Now, recall the story's headline, "High Murder *Rate*." This implies that the *number* of women murdered on the job, divided by the total number of women at risk of murder on the job, is higher than the same computed rate for men. We need more information than the story provides to verify this claim, but there is a clue. Women are about 45 percent of the workforce, so there are about 1.2 men in the workforce for every woman (55 percent ÷ 45 percent). But about five times as many men as women are murdered on the job (849 ÷ 170).

This should tip you off that the headline is misleading. If the ratio of male-to-female murders is 5 to 1, but the ratio of male-to-female workers is 1.2 to 1, how could the murder rate for women be higher? You could compute actual rates of murder on the job by finding a suitable denominator; in this case, the number of men and women in the workforce would be appropriate. Consulting the Census Bureau publication *Statistical Abstract of the United States* would provide this information and enable you to compute rates, as in our final table:

	Women	Men
Civilian workforce (1000s)	53,284	63,593
Murdered at work	170	849
On-the-job murder rate per 100,000 workers	0.319	1.335

So the *New York Times* got it wrong; there is a higher murder rate for men on the job. Women are less often killed on the job by any cause, including murder. But women who die on the job (in much smaller numbers than men) are more likely to die from murder than are men who die on the job. A murder rate expresses the number of people murdered divided by the population at risk.

Rates are often computed with inappropriate denominators. But it is less common to find the term *rate* used so inaccurately.

Sources: Associated Press (1993); and U.S. Bureau of the Census (1992).

Often, it's appropriate to describe subsets of cases, subjects, or respondents. Table 14.3, for example, presents hypothetical data on sentence length for offenders grouped by prior felony record. In some situations, the researcher presents subgroup comparisons purely for descriptive purposes. More often, the purpose of subgroup descriptions is comparative. In this case, comparing sentences for subgroups of convicted offenders implies some causal connection between prior felony record and sentence length. Similarly, if we compare sentence lengths for men and women, it implies that something about gender has a causal effect on sentence length.

TABLE 14.3 Hypothetical Illustration of Subgroup Comparisons: Length of Prison Sentence by Felony Criminal History

Felony Criminal History	Median Sentence Length
No arrests or convictions	6 months
Prior arrests only	11 months
Prior convictions	23 months

Bivariate Analysis

In contrast to univariate analysis, subgroup comparisons constitute a kind of **bivariate analysis** in that two variables are involved. In such situations, we are usually interested in relationships among the variables. Thus, univariate analysis and subgroup comparisons focus on describing the *people* (or other units of analysis) under study, whereas bivariate analysis focuses more on the *variables* themselves.

Notice, then, that Table 14.4 can be regarded as a subgroup comparison; it independently describes gun ownership among male and female respondents in the 2000 General Social Survey. It shows—comparatively and descriptively—that fewer females than males report owning a gun.

The same table viewed as an explanatory bivariate analysis tells a somewhat different story. It suggests that the variable "gender" has an effect on the variable "gun ownership." The behavior is seen as a dependent variable that is partially determined by the independent variable (gender). Explanatory bivariate analyses, then, involve the "variable language" we introduced in Chapter 1. In a subtle shift of focus, we are no longer talking about male and female as different subgroups but about gender as a variable—a variable that has an influence on other variables.

Adding the logic of causal relationships among variables has an important implication for the construction and reading of percentage tables. One of the chief difficulties for novice data analysts is deciding on the appropriate "direction of percentaging" for any given table. In Table 14.4, for example, we divided the group of subjects into two subgroups—male and female—and then described the behavior of each subgroup. That is the correct way to construct this table.

It would have been possible, though inappropriate, to construct the table differently. We could have first divided the subjects into different categories of gun ownership and then described each of those subgroups by the percentage of male and female subjects in each. This method would make no sense in terms of explanation, however; owning a gun does not make someone male or female.

Table 14.4 suggests that gender affects gun ownership. Had we used the other method of construction, the table would have suggested that gun ownership affects whether someone is male or female—which makes no sense.

Another related problem complicates the lives of novice data analysts: How do you read a percentage table? There is a temptation to read Table 14.4 as "Among females, only 25 percent owned a gun, and 75 percent did not; therefore, being female makes you less likely to own a gun." That is not the correct way to read the table, however. The conclusion that gender—as a variable—has an effect on gun ownership must hinge on a comparison between males and females. Specifically, we compare the 25 percent of females with the 42 percent of males and note that women are less likely than men to own a gun. The appropriate comparison of subgroups, then, is essential in reading an explanatory bivariate table.

Percentaging a Table   In constructing and presenting Table 14.4, we have used a convention called "percentage down." This means that we can add the percentages down each column to total 100 percent. We read this form of table across a row. For the row labeled "Yes," what percentage of the males own a gun? What percentage of the females?

The percentage-down convention is just that—a conventional practice. Some researchers prefer to percentage across. They would organize Table 14.4 with "Male" and "Female" on the left side of the table, identifying the two rows, and "Yes" and "No" at the top, identifying the columns. The actual numbers in the table would be moved around accordingly, and each row of percentages would total 100 percent. In that case, we would make our comparisons between males and females by reading down, within table columns, still asking what percentage of males and females owned guns. The logic and the conclusion would be the same in either case; only the form would be different.

In reading a table that someone else has constructed, therefore, it's necessary to find out in

TABLE 14.4   Gun Ownership Among Male and Female Respondents, 2000

	Male	Female
Own a Gun?		
Yes	42%	25%
No	58	75
100% (N) =	(817)	(1,040)

Source: 2000 General Social Survey (available at http://sda.berkeley.edu/archive.htm).

which direction it has been percentaged. Usually, that will be apparent from the labeling of the table or the logic of the variables being analyzed. Sometimes, however, tables are not clearly labeled. In such cases, the reader should add the percentages in each column and each row. If each of the columns totals 100 percent, the table has been percentaged down. If the rows total 100 percent each, the table has been percentaged across. Follow these rules of thumb:

1. If the table is percentaged down, read across.

2. If the table is percentaged across, read down.

By the way, Table 14.4 was constructed from General Social Survey (GSS) data available on the Internet, as you may have guessed from the Internet address shown at the bottom of the table. GSS data from 1972 onward can be accessed directly through the online data analysis capability of the University of California at Berkeley. You can use a simple interactive program at the Berkeley site to construct your own percentage tables for any GSS variables. This will give you invaluable practice in constructing bivariate percentage tables.

Here's another example: suppose we are interested in investigating newspaper editorial policies regarding the legalization of marijuana. We undertake a content analysis of editorials on this subject that have appeared during a given year in a sample of daily newspapers. Each editorial has been classified as favorable, neutral, or unfavorable with regard to the legalization of marijuana. Perhaps we wish to examine the relationship between editorial policies and the types of communities in which the newspapers are published, thinking that rural newspapers might be more conservative than urban newspapers. Thus, each newspaper (and so, each editorial) is classified in terms of the population of the community in which it is published.

Table 14.5 presents some hypothetical data describing the editorial policies of rural and urban newspapers. Note that the unit of analysis in this example is the individual editorial. Table 14.5 tells us that there were 127 editorials about marijuana in our sample of newspapers published in communities with populations under 100,000. (Note: This choice of 100,000 is for simplicity of illustration and does not mean that *rural* refers to a community of less than 100,000 in any absolute sense.) Of these, 11 percent (14 editorials) were favorable

TABLE 14.5 Hypothetical Data Regarding Newspaper Editorials on the Legalization of Marijuana

Editorial Policy Toward Legalizing Marijuana	Community Size	
	Under 100,000	Over 100,000
Favorable	11%	32%
Neutral	29	40
Unfavorable	60	28
100% (N) =	(127)	(438)

toward the legalization of marijuana, 29 percent were neutral, and 60 percent were unfavorable. Of the 438 editorials that appeared in our sample of newspapers published in communities with more than 100,000 residents, 32 percent (140 editorials) were favorable toward legalizing marijuana, 40 percent were neutral, and 28 percent were unfavorable.

When we compare the editorial policies of rural and urban newspapers in our imaginary study, we find—as expected—that rural newspapers are less favorable toward the legalization of marijuana than are urban newspapers. That is determined by noting that a larger percentage of the urban editorials were favorable than rural editorials (32 percent versus 11 percent). We might note, as well, that more rural than urban editorials were unfavorable (60 percent versus 28 percent). Note, too, that this table assumes that the size of a community might affect its newspaper's editorial policies on this issue, rather than that editorial policy might affect the size of communities.

Constructing and Reading Tables Before introducing multivariate analysis, let's review the steps involved in the construction of explanatory bivariate tables:

1. Divide the cases into groups according to attributes of the independent variable.

2. Describe each of these subgroups in terms of attributes of the dependent variable.

3. Read the table by comparing the independent variable subgroups with one another in terms of a given attribute of the dependent variable.

In the example of editorial policies regarding the legalization of marijuana, the size of a community is the independent variable, and a newspaper's editorial policy is the dependent variable. The table is constructed as follows:

1. Divide the editorials into subgroups according to the sizes of the communities in which the newspapers are published.

2. Describe each subgroup of editorials in terms of the percentages favorable, neutral, or unfavorable toward the legalization of marijuana.

3. Compare the two subgroups in terms of the percentages favorable toward the legalization of marijuana.

Bivariate analyses typically have an explanatory purpose. This hypothetical example has hinted at the nature of causation as it is used by social scientists. We hope that the rather simplified approach to causation in these examples will have commonsense acceptability at this point.

Bivariate Table Formats   Tables such as those we've been examining are commonly called **contingency tables**; values of the dependent variable are *contingent* on values of the independent variable. Although contingency tables are commonly used in criminal justice research, their format has never been standardized. As a result, a variety of formats will be found in the research literature. As long as a table is easy to read and interpret, there is probably no reason to strive for standardization; however, these guidelines should be followed in the presentation of most tabular data.

1. Provide a heading or a title that succinctly describes what is contained in the table.

2. Present the original content of the variables clearly—in the table itself if at all possible, or in the text with a paraphrase in the table. This information is especially critical when a variable is derived from responses to an attitudinal question, because the meaning of the responses will depend largely on the wording of the question.

3. Clearly indicate the attributes of each variable. Complex categories need to be abbreviated, but the meaning should be clear in the table, and, of course, the full description should be reported in the text.

4. When percentages are reported in the table, identify the base on which they are computed.

It is redundant to present all the raw numbers for each category, because these could be reconstructed from the percentages and the bases. Moreover, the presentation of both numbers and percentages often makes a table more difficult to read.

5. If any cases are omitted from the table because of missing data (e.g., "no answer"), indicate their numbers in the table.

By following these guidelines and thinking carefully about the kinds of causal and descriptive relationships they want to examine, researchers address many policy and research questions in criminal justice. We want to emphasize, however, the importance of thinking through the logic of contingency tables. Descriptive statistics—contingency tables, measures of central tendency, or rates—are sometimes misrepresented or misinterpreted. See the box titled "Murder on the Job" for an example.

Multivariate Analysis

A great deal of criminal justice research uses multivariate techniques to examine relationships among several variables. Like much statistical analysis, the logic of **multivariate analysis** is straightforward, but the actual use of many multivariate statistical techniques can be complex. A full understanding requires a solid background in statistics and is beyond the scope of this book. In this section, we briefly discuss the construction of multivariate tables—those constructed from three or more variables—and the comparison of multiple subgroups.

Multivariate tables can be constructed by following essentially the same steps outlined previously for bivariate tables. Instead of one independent variable and one dependent variable, however, we will have more than one independent variable. And instead of explaining the dependent variable on the basis of a single independent variable, we'll seek an explanation through the use of more than one independent variable. Let's consider an example from research on victimization.

Multivariate Tables: Lifestyle and Street Crime
If we consult any source of published statistics on victimization (see Chapter 12), we will find several

tables that document a relationship between age and personal crime victimization; younger people are more often victims of assault and robbery, for example. A classic book by Michael Hindelang, Michael Gottfredson, and James Garofalo (1978) suggested a "lifestyle" explanation for this relationship. The lifestyle of many younger people—visiting bars and clubs for evening entertainment, for example—exposes them to street crime and potential predators more than does the less active lifestyle of older people. This is certainly a sensible hypothesis, and Hindelang and associates found general support for the lifestyle explanation in their analysis of data from early versions of the National Crime Victimization Survey. But the U.S. crime survey data did not include direct measures of lifestyle concepts.

Michael Gottfredson (1984) describes questionnaire items in the British Crime Survey (BCS) that provided better measures of individual behaviors. Using these data, Ronald Clarke and associates (1985) examined the link between exposure to risk and victimization, while holding age and gender constant. Specifically, Clarke and colleagues hypothesized that older persons are less often victims of street crime because they spend less time on the streets. The 1982 BCS asked respondents whether they had left their homes in the previous week (i.e., the week before they were interviewed) for any evening leisure or social activities. Those who responded yes were asked which nights they had gone out and what they had done.

Hypothesizing that some types of evening activities are more risky than others, Clarke and associates restricted their analysis to leisure pursuits away from respondents' homes, such as visiting a pub, nightclub, or theater. Their dependent variable—street crime victimization—was also carefully defined to include only crimes against persons (actual and attempted assault, robbery, rape, and theft) that occurred away from victims' homes or workplaces or the homes of friends. Furthermore, because the leisure behavior questions asked about evening activities, only street crime victimizations that took place between 6:00 P.M. and midnight were included.

Clarke and associates therefore proposed a very specific hypothesis that involves three carefully defined concepts and variables: *older persons* are less often *victims* of street crime because they

engage less often in *behavior* that exposes them to risk of street crime. Parts A–C of Table 14.6 present cross-tabulations for the three possible bivariate relationships among these variables: evening street crime victimization by age and by evening leisure pursuits, and evening leisure pursuits by age.

The relationships illustrated in these tables are consistent with the lifestyle hypothesis of personal crime victimization. First, victimization was more common for younger people (ages 16–30) and for those who pursued leisure activities outside their home three or more evenings in the previous week (parts A and B of Table 14.6). Second, as shown in part C, the attributes of young age and frequent exposure to risk were positively related. About 41 percent of the youngest group had gone out three or more nights, compared with 20 percent of those ages 31–60, and only 10 percent of those over age 60.

However, because we are interested in the effects of two independent variables—lifestyle and age—on victimization, we must construct a table that includes all three variables.

Several of the tables we have presented in this chapter are somewhat inefficient. When the dependent variable—street crime victimization—is dichotomous (two attributes), knowing one attribute permits us to easily reconstruct the other. Thus, if we know from Table 14.6A that 1 percent of respondents ages 31–60 were victims of street crime, then we know automatically that 99 percent were not victims. So reporting the percentages for both values of a dichotomy is unnecessary. On the basis of this recognition, Table 14.6D presents the relationship between victimization and two independent variables in a more efficient format. In Table 14.6D, the percentages of respondents who reported a street crime victimization are shown in the cells at the intersections of the two independent variables. The numbers presented in parentheses below each percentage are the numbers of cases on which the percentages are based. Thus, for example, we know that 563 people ages 16–30 did not go out for evening leisure activities in the week before their interview and that 3.9 percent of them were victims of street crime in the previous year. We can calculate from this that 22 of those 563 people were victims and the other 541 people were not victims.

TABLE 14.6A Evening Street Crime Victimization by Age

Street Crime Victim	Age		
	16–30	**31–60**	**61+**
Yes	4.8%	1.0%	0.3%
No	95.2	99.0	99.7
100% (N) =	(2,738)	(4,460)	(1,952)

TABLE 14.6B Evening Street Crime Victimization by Evenings Out During Previous Week

Street Crime Victim	Evenings Out		
	None	**1 or 2**	**3+**
Yes	1.2%	1.6%	3.8%
No	98.9	98.4	96.2
100% (N) =	(3,252)	(3,695)	(2,203)

TABLE 14.6C Evening Out During Previous Week by Age

Evenings Out	Age		
	16–30	**31–60**	**61+**
None	20.6%	35.2%	57.2%
1 or 2	38.6	44.9	32.5
3+	40.9	19.8	10.2
100% (N) =	(2,738)	(4,460)	(1,952)

TABLE 14.6D Evening Street Crime Victimization by Age and Evenings Out

Evenings Out	Age		
	16–30	**31–60**	**61+**
None	3.9%	1.0%	0.2%
	(563)	(1,572)	(1,117)
1 or 2	3.8	0.9	0.2
	(1,056)	(2,004)	(635)
3+	6.2	1.4	1.1
	(1,119)	(884)	(200)
Total (N) =	(2,738)	(4,460)	(1,952)

Note: Percentages and numbers of cases computed from published tabulations.

Source: Adapted from Clarke and associates (1985: Tables 1, 2, and 3).

Let's now interpret the results presented in this table:

- Within each age group, persons who pursue outside evening leisure activities three or more times per week are more often victimized. There is not much difference between those who go out once or twice per week and those who stay home.
- Within each category for evening leisure activities, street crime victimization declines as age increases.
- Exposure to risk through evenings out is less strongly related to street crime victimization than is age.
- Age and exposure to risk have independent effects on street crime victimization. Within a given attribute of one independent variable, different attributes of the second are still related to victimization.
- Similarly, the two independent variables have a cumulative effect on victimization.

Younger people who go out three or more times per week are most often victimized. Returning to the lifestyle hypothesis, what can we conclude from Table 14.6D? First, this measure of exposure to risk is, in fact, related to street crime victimization. People who go out more frequently are more often exposed to risk and more often victims of street crime. As Clarke and associates point out, however, differences in exposure to risk do not account for lower rates of victimization among older persons; within categories of exposure to risk, victimization still declines with age. So lifestyle is related to victimization, but this measure of behavior—exposure to risk of street crime—does not account for all age-related differences in victimization. Furthermore, what we might call lifestyle "intensity" plays a role here. Going out once or twice a week does not have as much impact on victimization as going out more often. The most intensely active night people age 30 or younger are most often victims of street crime.

Multivariate contingency tables are powerful tools for examining relationships between a dependent variable and multiple independent variables measured at the nominal or categorical level. However, contingency tables can become cumbersome and difficult to interpret if independent variables have several categories, or if more than two independent variables are included. In practice, criminal justice researchers often employ more sophisticated techniques for multivariate analysis of discrete or nominal variables. Although the logic of such analysis is not especially difficult, most people learn these techniques in advanced statistics courses.

Multiple-Subgroup Comparisons: Social Disorganization and Boston Neighborhoods
Just as subgroup comparisons can constitute a type of bivariate analysis, comparing values on some dependent variable across multiple subgroups is a type of multivariate analysis. In a sense, Table 14.6D compared victimization for multiple subgroups defined by age and evening leisure activities.

Multiple-subgroup comparisons are most frequently used to compare values for dependent variables measured at the interval or ratio level. For example, we might wish to compare crime rates among urban areas that have been classified according to different attributes. Table 14.7 is adapted from research by Barbara Warner and Glenn Pierce (1993) that examined the relationship between measures of social disorganization and crime problems.

Drawing on earlier studies by Clifford Shaw and Henry McKay (1969) and by William Julius Wilson (1987), Warner and Pierce compared calls for police service from 60 Boston neighborhoods to two measures of social disorganization—poverty and population mobility—with each computed from census data for Boston neighborhoods. Their poverty measure expresses the percentage of neighborhood residents with incomes below the poverty line in 1980; their population mobility measure expresses the percentage of residents who lived in the same dwelling for less than five years. Classifying each neighborhood as high or low on each of these two measures produces the two subgroups shown in Table 14.7. Each cell indicates the mean rate of police calls to report assaults for neighborhoods in each subgroup.

As the table shows, assaults were more common in high-poverty neighborhoods, regardless of residential mobility. No surprises here; this finding is consistent with virtually all research on social disorganization, from Shaw and McKay onward.

TABLE 14.7 Assault Rates per 1,000, Poverty, and Mobility in 60 Boston Neighborhoods

	Mobility		
Poverty	Low	High	Total
Low	12.2	19.5	15.8
	(22)	(21)	(43)
High	43.8	25.0	29.4
	(4)	(13)	(17)
Total	17.1	21.6	19.6
	(26)	(34)	(60)

Note: Row and column total assault rates computed from published tabulations.

Source: Adapted from Warner and Pierce (1993: Table 2).

However, the relationship between mobility and assaults varied, depending on neighborhood poverty levels. In low-poverty areas (the first row of Table 14.7), the mean assault rate was greater for high-mobility neighborhoods, but the opposite was true for high-poverty neighborhoods (the second row). Warner and Pierce refer to Wilson's influential book, *The Truly Disadvantaged: The Inner City, the Underclass, and Public Policy* (1987), to interpret this finding: Assaults were most common in poor, stable neighborhoods—those where poverty was persistent and mobility was limited. As Warner and Pierce (1993:507) state, these are "neighborhoods where people remain because they have no choice. This type of stability appears to have an impact on crime in a very different way. Rather than building cohesiveness, it may build resentment, frustration, and isolation."

Notice also how it is necessary to compare the *combined* categories of poverty and mobility to reveal this finding. If we examined the mean number of assaults for each variable separately, shown in the row and column totals for Table 14.7, we would conclude that assaults are more common in high-poverty and high-mobility neighborhoods. Comparing multiple subgroups defined by the intersection of poverty and mobility is a form of multivariate analysis that enabled Warner and Pierce to sort out the subtle relationships between these two independent variables and neighborhood assault rates. Later in this chapter, we will return to this study to illustrate the use of a more powerful multivariate technique. But multiple subgroup comparisons can provide useful information about the relationship between more than one independent variable and dependent variables measured at the interval or ratio level.

Measures of Association

As we've suggested, descriptive statistics are a method for presenting quantitative descriptions in a manageable form. Sometimes, we want to describe single variables; other times, we want to describe the associations that connect one variable with another.

Bivariate contingency tables are one way to examine the association between two variables. But contingency tables can be quite complex, presenting several different response categories for row and column variables. Nevertheless, a contingency table represents the association between two variables as a data matrix. Table 14.8 presents such a matrix, showing hypothetical data for the joint frequency distribution of education and support for gun control laws. It provides all the information needed to determine the nature and extent of the relationship between education and support for gun control. Notice, for example, that 23 people (1) have no education and (2) scored low on support for gun control; and 77 people (1) have graduate degrees and (2) scored high on support for gun control.

However, this matrix presents more information than we can easily comprehend. Studying the table carefully shows that as education increases from "None" to "Graduate Degree," there is a general tendency for gun control support to increase. A variety of descriptive statistics can summarize this data matrix. Selecting the appropriate measure depends initially on the nature of the two variables.

We'll turn now to some of the options available for summarizing the association between two variables. Each measure of association we'll discuss is based on the same model—**proportionate reduction of error (PRE)**.

To see how this model works, suppose we ask you to guess respondents' attributes on a given variable—for example, whether they answered yes or no to a given questionnaire item. To assist you, let's first assume you know the overall distribution of responses in the total sample—say, 60 percent yes and 40 percent no. You will make the fewest errors in this process if you always guess the modal (most frequent) response: yes.

Second, let's assume you also know the empirical relationship between the first variable and some other variable—say, gender. Now, each time we ask you to guess whether a respondent said yes or no, we'll tell you whether the respondent is a man or a woman. If the two variables are related, you should make fewer errors the second time. It is possible, therefore, to compute the PRE by knowing the relationship between the two variables: the stronger the relationship, the greater the reduction of error.

This basic PRE model is modified slightly to account for different levels of measurement—nominal, ordinal, or interval. The following sections will consider each level of measurement and present one measure of association appropriate to each. However, the three measures discussed are only a partial representation of the many appropriate measures.

Nominal Variables   If the two variables consist of nominal data (e.g., gender, marital status, or race), lambda (λ) is one appropriate measure. Lambda is based on your ability to guess values on one of the variables: the PRE achieved through knowledge of values on the other variable. A simple example will illustrate the logic and method of lambda.

Table 14.9 presents hypothetical data relating gender to a common measure of fear of crime, based on the question "How safe do you feel, or

---

TABLE 14.8   Hypothetical Raw Data on Education and Support for Gun Control Laws

Support for Gun Control	Educational Level				
	None	Grade School	High School	College	Graduate Degree
Low	23	34	156	67	16
Medium	11	21	123	102	23
High	6	12	95	164	77

TABLE 14.9 Hypothetical Data Relating Gender to Fear of Crime

Fear	Men	Women	Total
Safe	900	200	1,100
Unsafe	100	800	900
Total	1,000	1,000	2,000

would you feel, walking alone on your neighborhood streets at night?" Overall, we note that 1,100 people answered "safe" on the fear question, and 900 answered "unsafe." If you try to predict how people will respond to the fear-of-crime question, knowing only the overall distribution on that variable, you will always predict "safe" because that will result in fewer errors than always predicting "unsafe." Nevertheless, this strategy will result in 900 errors out of 2,000 predictions.

But suppose you have access to the data in Table 14.9 and are told each person's gender before making your predictions about fear of crime. Your strategy will change; for every man, you will predict "safe," and for every woman, you will predict "unsafe." In this instance, you will make 300 errors—the 100 men who responded "unsafe" and the 200 women who responded "safe"—600 fewer errors than you would make without knowing the person's gender.

Lambda, then, represents the reduction in errors as a proportion of the errors that would have been made based on the overall distribution. In this hypothetical example, lambda equals 0.67—that is, 600 fewer errors divided by the 900 total errors based on fear of crime alone. In this fashion, lambda measures the statistical association between gender and fear of crime.

If gender and fear were statistically independent, we would find the same distribution of fear of crime for men and women. In this case, knowing gender will not affect the number of errors made in predicting fear, and the resulting lambda will be zero. If, however, all men responded "safe" and all women responded "unsafe," then by knowing gender you can avoid all errors in predicting fear of crime. You will make 900 fewer errors (out of 900), so lambda will equal 1.0—a perfect statistical association.

Lambda is only one of several measures of association appropriate to the analysis of two nominal variables. Any statistics textbook will describe other appropriate measures.

Ordinal Variables If the variables being related are ordinal (e.g., occupational status or education), gamma (γ) is one appropriate measure of association. Like lambda, gamma is based on the ability to guess values on one variable by knowing values on another. Instead of exact values, however, gamma is based on the ordinal arrangement of values. For any given pair of cases, you guess that their ordinal ranking on one variable will correspond (positively or negatively) to their ordinal ranking on the other. For example, if you suspect that political conservatism is negatively related to support for gun control, and if person A is more conservative than person B, then you guess that A is less supportive of gun control than B. Gamma is the proportion of paired comparisons that fits this pattern.

Table 14.10 presents hypothetical data relating political ideology to support for gun control. The general nature of the relationship between these two variables is that, as conservatism increases, support for gun control decreases. There is a negative association between conservatism and support for gun control.

Gamma is computed from two quantities: (1) the number of pairs that have the same ranking on the two variables and (2) the number of pairs that have the opposite ranking on the two variables. The pairs that have the same ranking are computed as follows: the frequency of each cell in the table is multiplied by the sum of all cells appearing below and to the right of it—with all these products being summed. In Table 14.10, the number of pairs with the same ranking is as follows: 200(900 + 300 + 400 + 100) + 500(300 + 100) + 400(400 + 100) + 900(100), or 340,000 + 200,000 + 200,000 + 90,000 = 830,000.

TABLE 14.10 Hypothetical Data Relating Political Ideology and Support for Gun Control

Support for Gun Control	Liberal	Moderate	Conservative
Low	200	400	700
Medium	500	900	400
High	800	300	100

The pairs that have the opposite rankings on the two variables are computed as follows: the frequency of each cell in the table is multiplied by the sum of all cells appearing below and to the left of it—with all these products being summed. In Table 14.10, the number of pairs with opposite rankings is as follows: 700(500 + 800 + 900 + 300) + 400(800 + 300) + 400(500 + 800) + 900(800), or 1,750,000 + 440,000 + 520,000 + 720,000 = 3,430,000. Gamma is computed from the numbers of same-ranked pairs and opposite-ranked pairs as follows:

$$\text{Gamma} = \frac{\text{same} - \text{opposite}}{\text{same} + \text{opposite}}$$

In our example, gamma equals (830,000 − 3,430,000) divided by (830,000 + 3,430,000), or −0.61. The negative sign in this answer indicates the negative association suggested by the initial inspection of the table. Conservatism and support for gun control, in this hypothetical example, are negatively associated. The numerical figure for gamma indicates that 61 percent more of the pairs examined had opposite rankings than the same ranking.

Note that while values of lambda vary from 0 to 1, values of gamma vary from −1 to +1 and represent both the direction and the magnitude of the association. Because nominal variables have no ordinal structure, it makes no sense to speak of the direction of the relationship. A negative lambda indicates that we made more errors in predicting values on one variable (while knowing values on the second) than we made in ignorance of the second, and that's not logically possible.

Interval or Ratio Variables   If interval or ratio variables (such as age, income, or number of arrests) are being analyzed, one appropriate measure of association is Pearson's product-moment correlation (r). The derivation and computation of this measure of association are beyond the scope of this book, so we will make only a few general comments here.

Like both gamma and lambda, r is based on guessing the value of one variable by knowing the other. For a continuous interval or ratio variable, however, it is unlikely that we can predict the precise value of the variable. At the same time, predicting only the ordinal arrangement of values on the two variables does not take advantage of the greater amount of information conveyed by an interval or ratio variable. In a sense, r reflects how closely we can guess the value of one variable through our knowledge of the value of the other.

To understand the logic of r, let's consider how we might hypothetically guess values that particular cases have on a given variable. With nominal variables, we have seen that the best guess is the modal value. But for interval or ratio data, we can minimize our errors by always guessing the mean value of the variable. Although this practice produces few, if any, perfect guesses, it will minimize the extent of our errors.

In the computation of lambda, we noted the number of errors produced by always guessing the modal value. In the case of r, errors are measured in terms of the sum of the squared differences between the actual value and the mean. This sum, called the "total variation," is calculated in much the same way as the standard deviation, discussed earlier in this chapter.

To understand that concept, we must expand the scope of our examination. Let's look at the logic of regression analysis, and we'll return to correlation within that context.

Regression Analysis   The general formula for describing the association between two variables is $Y = f(X)$. This formula is read, "Y is a function of X," which means that values of Y can be explained in terms of variations in the values of X. Stated more strongly, we might say that X causes Y, so the value of X determines the value of Y. **Regression analysis** is a method of determining the specific function relating Y to X. There are several forms of regression analysis, depending on the complexity of the relationships being studied. Let's begin with the simplest.

The regression model can be seen most clearly in the case of a perfect linear association between two variables. Figure 14.3 is a scattergram presenting in graphic form the values of X and Y produced by a hypothetical study. It shows that for the four cases in our study, the values of X and Y are identical in each instance. The case

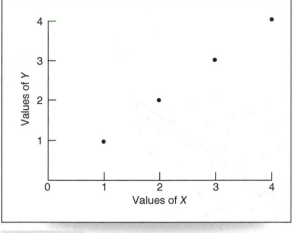

FIGURE 14.3 Simple Scattergram of Values of X and Y

with a value of 1 on X also has a value of 1 on Y, and so forth. The relationship between the two variables in this instance is described by the equation $Y = X$; this is the regression equation. Because all four points lie on a straight line, we can superimpose that line over the points; this is the regression line.

The linear regression model has important descriptive uses. The regression line offers a graphic picture of the association between X and Y, and the regression equation is an efficient form for summarizing that association. The regression model has inferential value as well. To the extent that the regression equation correctly describes the general association between the two variables, it may be used to predict other sets of values. If, for example, we know that a new case has a value of 3.5 on X, then we can predict the value of 3.5 on Y as well.

In practice, of course, studies are seldom limited to four cases, and the associations between variables are seldom as clear as the one presented in Figure 14.3. Figure 14.4 is a somewhat more realistic example that represents a hypothetical relationship between population and crime rate in small-to-medium-size cities. Each dot in the scattergram is a city, and each dot's placement reflects that city's population and its crime rate. As in our previous example, the values of Y (crime rates) generally correspond to those of X (populations), and as values of X increase, so do values of Y. However, the association is not nearly as clear as it was in Figure 14.3.

It is not possible in Figure 14.4 to superimpose a straight line that will pass through all the points in the scattergram. But we can draw an approximate line showing the best possible linear representation of the several points.

If you've ever studied geometry, you know that any straight line on a graph can be represented by an equation of the form $Y = a + bX$, where X and Y are values of the two variables. In this equation, a equals the value of Y when X is zero, and b represents the slope of the line. If we know the values of a and b, we can estimate Y for every value of X.

Regression analysis is a technique for establishing an equation representing the geometric line that comes closest to the distribution of points. This equation is valuable both descriptively and inferentially. First, the regression equation provides a mathematical description of the relationship between the variables. Second, it allows us to infer values of Y when we have values of X. Referring to Figure 14.4, we can estimate crime rates of cities if we know their populations.

To improve our guessing, we construct a regression line, stated in the form of a regression equation that permits the estimation of values on one variable from values on the other. The general format for this equation is $Y' = a + b(X)$, where a and b are computed values, X is a given value on one variable, and Y' is the estimated value on the other. The values of a and b are computed to minimize the differences between the actual values of Y and the corresponding estimates (Y') based on the known value of X. The sum of squared differences between actual and estimated values of Y is called the "unexplained variation," because it represents errors that exist even when estimates are based on known values of X.

The "explained variation" is the difference between the total variation and the unexplained variation. Dividing the explained variation by the total variation produces a measure of the proportionate reduction of error corresponding to the similar quantity in the computation of lambda. In the present case, this quantity is the correlation squared: r^2. Thus, if $r = 0.7$, then $r^2 = 0.49$, which means that about half the variation has been explained.

In practice, we compute r rather than r^2 because the product-moment correlation can take either a positive or a negative sign, depending on the

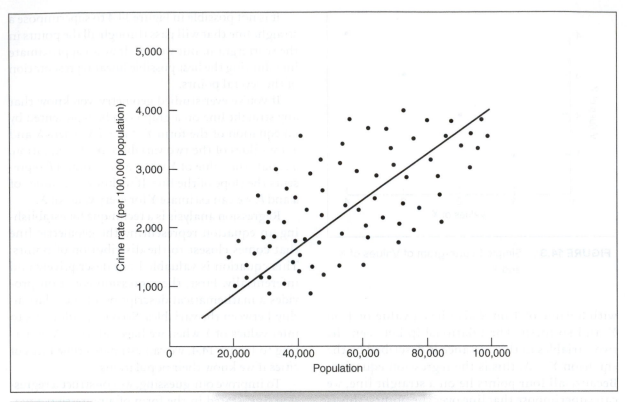

FIGURE 14.4 Scattergram of the Hypothetical Values of Two Variables with Regression Line Added

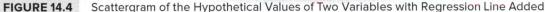

direction of the relationship between the two variables. Computing r^2 and taking a square root will always produce a positive quantity, which means we will lose information about the direction of the relationship between X and Y. Consult any standard statistics textbook for the method of computing r. In practice, this and other measures of association are easily calculated with a variety of computer programs, including popular spreadsheet and database applications.

Inferential Statistics

When we generalize from samples to larger populations, we use inferential statistics to test the significance of an observed relationship.

Many criminal justice research projects examine data collected from a sample drawn from a larger population. A sample of people may be interviewed in a survey; a sample of court records may be coded and analyzed; a sample of newspapers may be examined through content analysis. Researchers seldom, if ever, study samples merely to describe the samples per se; in most instances, their ultimate purpose is to make assertions about the larger population from which the sample has been selected. Frequently, then, we will want to interpret our univariate and multivariate sample findings as the basis for inferences about some population.

This section examines the statistical measures used for making such inferences and their logical bases. We'll begin with univariate data and then move to bivariate.

Univariate Inferences

The opening sections of this chapter dealt with methods of presenting univariate data. Each summary measure was intended to describe the sample studied. Now we will use those measures to make broader assertions about the population. This section will focus on two univariate measures: percentages and means.

If 50 percent of a sample of people say they received traffic tickets during the past year, then 50 percent is also our best estimate of the proportion of people who received traffic tickets in the total population from which the sample was drawn. Our estimate assumes a simple random sample, of course. It is rather unlikely, however, that precisely 50 percent of the population got tickets during the year. If a rigorous sampling design for random selection has been followed, we will be able to estimate the expected range of error when the sample finding is applied to the population.

The section in Chapter 8 on sampling theory covered the procedures for making such estimates, so they will only be reviewed here. The quantity

$$S = \sqrt{\frac{p \times q}{n}}$$

where p is a percentage, q equals $1 - p$, and n is the sample size, is called the "standard error." As noted in Chapter 8, this quantity is very important in the estimation of sampling error. We may be 68 percent confident that the population figure falls within plus or minus 1 standard error of the sample figure, 95 percent confident that it falls within plus or minus 2 standard errors, and 99.9 percent confident that it falls within plus or minus 3 standard errors.

Any statement of sampling error, then, must contain two essential components: the confidence level (e.g., 95 percent) and the confidence interval (e.g., 2.5 percent). If 50 percent of a sample of 1,600 people say they have received traffic tickets during the year, we might say we are 95 percent confident that the population figure is between 47.5 and 52.5 percent.

Recognize in this example that we have moved beyond simply describing the sample into the realm of making estimates (inferences) about the larger population. In doing that, we must be wary of three assumptions.

First, the sample must be drawn from the population about which inferences are being made. A sample taken from a telephone directory, for example, cannot legitimately be the basis for statistical inferences about the population of a city.

Second, the inferential statistics assume simple random sampling, which is virtually never the case in actual sample surveys. The statistics assume sampling with replacement, which is almost never done, but that is probably not a serious problem. Although systematic sampling is used more frequently than random sampling, that, too, probably presents no serious problem if done correctly.

Third, inferential statistics apply to sampling error only; they do not take account of **nonsampling errors**. Thus, although we might correctly state that between 47.5 and 52.5 percent of the population (95 percent confidence) will report getting a traffic ticket during the previous year, we cannot so confidently guess the percentage that had actually received them. Because nonsampling errors are probably larger than sampling errors in a respectable sample design, we need to be especially cautious in generalizing from our sample findings to the population.

Tests of Statistical Significance

There is no scientific answer to the question of whether a given association between two variables is significant, strong, important, interesting, or worth reporting. Perhaps the ultimate test of significance rests with our ability to persuade readers (present and future) of the association's significance. At the same time, a body of inferential statistics—known as parametric tests of significance—can assist in this regard. As the name suggests, *parametric statistics* make certain assumptions about the *parameters* that describe the population from which the sample is selected.

Although **tests of statistical significance** are widely reported in criminal justice literature, the logic underlying them is subtle and often misunderstood. Tests of significance are based on the same sampling logic that has been discussed elsewhere in this book. To understand that logic, let's return to the concept of sampling error with regard to univariate data.

Recall that normally a sample statistic provides the best single estimate of the corresponding population parameter—but the statistic and the parameter are seldom identical. Thus, we report the probability that the parameter falls within a certain range (confidence interval). The degree of uncertainty within that range is due to normal sampling error. The corollary of such a statement is, of course, that it is improbable that the parameter will fall outside the specified range only as a result of sampling error. Thus, if we estimate that a parameter (99.9 percent confidence) lies between 45 and 55 percent, we say by implication that it is extremely improbable that the parameter is actually, say, 70 percent if our only error of estimation is due to normal sampling.

The fundamental logic of tests of statistical significance, then, is this. Faced with any discrepancy between the assumed independence of variables in a population and the observed distribution of sample elements, we may explain that discrepancy in either of two ways: (1) we attribute it to an unrepresentative sample or (2) we reject the assumption of independence. The logic and statistics associated with probability sampling methods offer guidance about the varying probabilities of different degrees of unrepresentativeness (expressed as sampling error). Most simply put, there is a high probability of a small degree of unrepresentativeness and a low probability of a large degree of unrepresentativeness.

The **statistical significance** of a relationship observed in a set of sample data, then, is always expressed in terms of probabilities. Significant at the 0.05 level ($p = .05$) simply means that the probability of a relationship as strong as the one observed being attributable to sampling error alone is no more than 5 in 100. Put somewhat differently, if two variables are independent of each other in the population, and if 100 probability samples were selected from that population, then no more than 5 of those samples should provide a relationship as strong as the one that has been observed.

There is, then, a corollary to confidence intervals in tests of significance, which represent the probability of the measured associations being due only to sampling error. This is called the **level of significance**. Like confidence intervals, levels of significance are derived from a logical model in which several samples are drawn from a given population. In the present case, we assume that no association exists between the variables in the population, and then we ask what proportion of the samples drawn from that population would produce associations at least as great as those measured in the empirical data. Three levels of significance are frequently used in research reports: 0.05,

0.01, and 0.001. These mean, respectively, that the chances of obtaining the measured association as a result of sampling error are no more than 5 in 100, 1 in 100, and 1 in 1,000.

Researchers who use tests of significance normally follow one of two patterns. Some specify in advance the level of significance they will regard as sufficient. If any measured association is statistically significant at that level, they will consider it representative of a genuine association between the two variables. In other words, they are willing to discount the possibility of its resulting from sampling error only.

Other researchers prefer to report the specific level of significance for each association, disregarding the conventions of 0.05, 0.01, and 0.001. Rather than reporting that a given association is significant at, say, the 0.05 level, they might report significance at the 0.023 level, indicating that the chances of its having resulted from sampling error are no more than 23 in 1,000.

Visualizing Statistical Significance

In a Bureau of Justice Statistics publication describing the National Crime Victimization Survey (NCVS) for a nontechnical audience, Michael Maltz and Marianne Zawitz (1998) present an informative graphical display to show statistical significance.

Recall that the NCVS is a national sample designed to estimate nationwide rates of victimization. Maltz and Zawitz use visual displays of estimates and their confidence intervals to demonstrate the relative precision of victimization rates disclosed by the survey.

Figure 14.5, reproduced from Maltz and Zawitz (1998), presents an example of this approach. The figure shows annual rates of change in all violent victimizations from 1973 through 1996. Notice the vertical line in Figure 14.5, representing no change in violent victimization rates for each year. Estimates of annual rates of change are shown in horizontal bars arrayed along the vertical line. The horizontal bars for each year present parameter estimates for annual change, signified by a dot or square, bracketed by the confidence intervals for each parameter estimate at three confidence levels: 68 percent (1 standard error), 90 percent (1.6 standard errors), and 95 percent (2 standard errors).

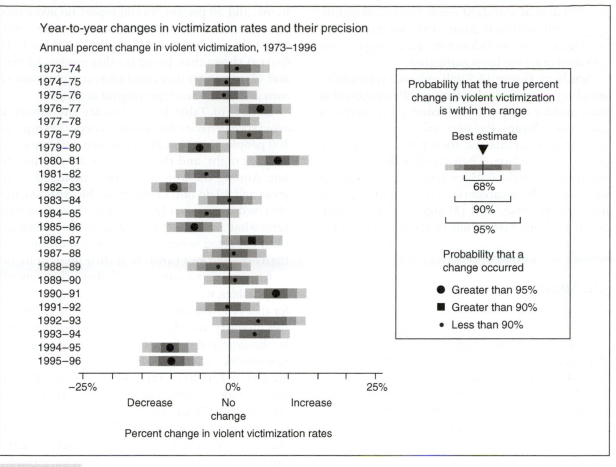

FIGURE 14.5 Point Estimates and Confidence Intervals

Source: Maltz and Zawitz (1998:4).

Consider first the topmost bar, showing estimates for change from 1973 to 1974. The small dot signifying the point estimate (an increase of 1.24 percent) is just to the right of the no-change vertical line. But notice also that the confidence intervals of 1, 1.6, and 2 standard errors cross over the no-change line; the estimate of a 1.24 percent increase is less than 2 standard errors above zero. This means that, using the 0.05 (2 standard errors) criterion, the estimated increase is not statistically significant. To further emphasize this point, notice the key in Figure 14.5, which shows different probabilities that a change occurred each year; the small dot representing the point estimate for 1973–1974 change indicates that the probability that a change actually occurred is less than 90 percent.

Now consider the most recent estimate shown in this figure—change from 1995 to 1996. The point estimate of 29.9 percent is well below the no-change line, and the confidence intervals are well to the left of this line. Bracketing the point estimate by 2 standard errors produces an interval estimate of between 215.7 (point estimate minus 2 standard errors) and 24.05 percent (point estimate plus 2 standard errors). This means we can be 95 percent certain that the violent victimization rate declined from 1995 to 1996 by somewhere between 24.05 and 215.7 percent. Because the point estimate of 29.9 percent is more than 2 standard errors from zero, we can confidently say there was a statistically significant decline in violent victimization.

Displaying point and interval estimates in this way accurately represents the concepts of statistical inference and statistical significance. Sample-based estimates of victimization, or any other variable, are just that—estimates of population values, bounded by estimates of standard error. Statistical significance, in this example, means that our estimates of change are above or below zero, according to some specified criterion for significance.

Studying Figure 14.5 will enhance your understanding of statistical inference. We suggest that you consider the point and interval estimates for each year's change. Pay particular attention to the confidence intervals and their position relative to the no-change line. Then classify the statistical significance (at the 0.05 level) for change each year into one of three categories: (1) no change, (2) significant increase, and (3) significant decrease. You'll find our tabulation in the exercises at the end of this chapter.

Chi Square

Chi square (x^2) is a different type of significance test that is widely used in criminal justice research. It is based on the **null hypothesis**: the assumption that there is no relationship between two variables in a population. Given the observed distribution of values on two variables in a contingency table, we compute the joint distribution that would be expected if there were no relationship between the two variables. The result of this operation is a set of expected frequencies for all the cells in the contingency table. We then compare this expected distribution with the empirical distribution—cases actually found in the data—and determine the probability that the difference between expected and empirical distributions could have resulted from sampling error alone. Stated simply, chi square compares what you get (empirical) with what you expect given a null hypothesis of no relationship. An example will illustrate this procedure.

Let's assume we are interested in the possible relationship between gender and avoidance behavior—that is, in this case whether people avoid areas near their homes because of crime. To test this relationship, we select a sample of 100 people at random. Our sample is made up of 40 men and 60 women; 70 percent of our sample report avoidance behavior, and the remaining 30 percent do not.

If there is no relationship between gender and avoidance behavior, then 70 percent of the men in the sample should report avoiding areas near their home, and 30 percent should report no avoidance behavior. Moreover, women should describe avoidance behavior in the same proportion. Table 14.11 (part I) shows that, based on this model, 28 men and 42 women say they avoid areas at night, with 12 men and 18 women reporting no avoidance.

Part II of Table 14.11 presents the observed avoidance behavior for the hypothetical sample of 100 people. Note that 20 of the men say they avoid areas at night, and the remaining 20 say they do not. Among the women in the sample, 50 avoid areas and 10 do not. Comparing the expected and observed frequencies (parts I and II), we note that somewhat fewer men report avoidance behavior than expected, whereas somewhat more women than expected avoid areas near their home at night.

Chi square is computed as follows: for each cell in the tables, we (1) subtract the expected frequency for that cell from the observed frequency, (2) square this quantity, and (3) divide the squared difference by the expected frequency. This procedure is carried out for each cell in the tables, and the results are added. Part III of Table 14.11 presents the cell-by-cell computations. The final sum is the value of chi square: 12.70 in this example.

This value is the overall discrepancy between the observed distribution in the sample and the distribution we would expect if the two variables were unrelated. Of course, the mere discovery of a discrepancy does not prove that the two variables are related, because normal sampling error might produce discrepancies even when there is no relationship in the total population. The magnitude of the value of chi square, however, permits us to estimate the probability of that having happened.

To determine the statistical significance of the observed relationship, we must use a standard set of chi-square values. That will require the computation of the degrees of freedom. For chi square, the degrees of freedom are computed as follows: the number of rows in the table of observed frequencies, minus 1, is multiplied by the number of columns, minus 1. This may be written as $(r - 1) \times (c - 1)$. In the present example, we have two rows and two columns (discounting the totals), so there is 1 degree of freedom.

Turning to a table of chi-square values (for example, see http://www.statsoft.com/textbook/distribution-tables [Accessed 7 September 2016]), we find that,

TABLE 14.11 Hypothetical Illustration of Chi Square

I. Expected Cell Frequencies

	Men	Women	Total
Avoid areas*	28	42	70
Do not avoid areas	12	18	30
Total	40	60	100

II. Observed Cell Frequencies

	Men	Women	Total
Avoid areas	20	50	70
Do not avoid areas	20	10	30
Total	40	60	100

III. (Observed − Expected)^2 ÷ Expected

	Men	Women	
Avoid areas	2.29	1.52	Chi sq. = 12.70
Do not avoid areas	5.33	3.56	$p < 0.001$

*"Is there any area around here—that is, within a city block—that you avoid at night because of crime?"

for 1 degree of freedom and random sampling from a population in which there is no relationship between two variables, 10 percent of the time we should expect a chi square of at least 2.7. Thus, if we select 100 samples from such a population, we should expect about 10 of those samples to produce chi squares equal to or greater than 2.7. Moreover, we should expect chi-square values of at least 6.6 in only 1 percent of the samples and chi-square values of 10.8 in only 0.1 percent of the samples. The higher the chi-square value, the less probable it is that the value can be attributed to sampling error alone.

In our example, the computed value of chi square is 12.70. If there is no relationship between gender and avoidance behavior, and a large number of samples were selected and studied, we can expect a chi square of this magnitude in fewer than 0.1 percent of those samples. Thus, the probability of obtaining a chi square of this magnitude is less than 0.001 if random sampling has been used and if there is no relationship in the population. We report this finding by saying that the relationship is statistically significant at the 0.001 level. Because it is so improbable that the observed relationship could have resulted from sampling error alone, we are likely to reject the null hypothesis and assume that a relationship does, in fact, exist between the two variables.

Many measures of association can be tested for statistical significance in a similar manner. Standard tables of values permit us to determine whether a given association is statistically significant, and at what level.

Cautions in Interpreting Statistical Significance

Tests of significance provide an objective yardstick against which we can estimate the significance of associations between variables. They assist us in ruling out associations that may not represent genuine relationships in the population under study. However, the researcher who uses or reads reports of significance tests should use caution in their interpretation, for the following reasons.

First, we have been discussing tests of statistical *significance*; there are no objective tests of substantive significance. Thus, we may be legitimately convinced that a given association is not due to sampling error but still assert, without fear of contradiction, that two variables are only slightly related to each other. Recall that sampling error is an inverse function of sample size: the larger the sample, the smaller the expected error. Thus, a correlation of, say, 0.1 might well be significant (at a given level) if discovered in a large sample, whereas the same correlation between the same two variables would not be significant if found in a smaller sample. Of course, that makes perfect sense if one understands the basic logic of tests of significance: In the larger sample, there is less chance that the correlation is simply the product of sampling error.

Consider Table 14.12, for example, in which 20 cases are distributed in the same proportions across row and column categories as in Table 14.11. In each table, 83 percent of women report avoidance behavior (10 out of 12 in Table 14.12, and 50 out of 60 in Table 14.11). But with one-fifth the number of cases in Table 14.12, the computed value of chi square is only one-fifth that obtained in Table 14.11. Consulting the distribution of chi-square values (see table referenced earlier at http://www.statsoft.com/textbook/distribution -tables/), we see that the probability of obtaining a chi square of 2.54 with 1 degree of freedom lies between 0.1 and 0.2. Thus, if there is no relationship between these two variables, we can expect to obtain a chi square of this size in 10–20 percent of samples drawn. Most researchers would not reject the null hypothesis of no relationship in this case.

Recall from Chapter 13 that sample size is especially important for applied studies that use experimental designs. With small sample sizes,

even moderately large differences might result from sampling error. Because randomized experiments are costly and time consuming, they are often conducted with relatively small numbers of subjects in experimental and control groups. With small numbers of subjects, only large differences in outcome variables will be statistically significant.

The distinction between statistical and substantive significance may be illustrated best by those cases in which there is absolute certainty that observed differences cannot be a result of sampling error. That is the case when we observe an entire population. Suppose we are able to learn the age and gender of every murder victim in the United States for 2008. For argument's sake, let's assume that the average age of male murder victims is 25, as compared with, say, 26 for female victims. Because we have the ages of all murder victims, there is no question of sampling error. We know with certainty that the female victims are older than their male counterparts. At the same time, we can say that the difference is of no substantive significance. We conclude, in fact, that they are essentially the same age.

Second, lest you be misled by this hypothetical example, statistical significance should not be calculated on relationships observed in data collected from whole populations. Remember, tests

TABLE 14.12 Hypothetical Illustration of Chi-Square Sensitivity to Sample Size

I. Expected Cell Frequencies

	Men	Women	Total
Avoid areas*	5.6	8.4	14
Do not avoid areas	2.4	3.6	6
Total	8.0	12.0	20

II. Observed Cell Frequencies

	Men	Women	Total
Avoid areas	4	10	14
Do not avoid areas	4	2	6
Total	8	12	20

III. (Observed − Expected)² ÷ Expected

	Men	Women	
Avoid areas	0.46	0.30	Chi sq. = 2.54
Do not avoid areas	1.07	0.71	$10 < p < 20$

*"Is there any area around here—that is, within a city block—that you avoid at night because of crime?"

of statistical significance measure the likelihood of relationships between variables that are only a product of sampling error, which, of course, assumes that data come from a sample. If there's no sampling, there's no sampling error.

Third, tests of significance are based on the same sampling assumptions we used to compute confidence intervals. To the extent that these assumptions are not met by the actual sampling design, the tests of significance are not strictly legitimate.

In practice, tests of statistical significance frequently are used inappropriately. If you were to review any given issue of an academic journal in criminal justice, we'd be willing to bet you would find one or more of these technically improper uses:

- Tests of significance computed for data representing entire populations
- Tests based on samples that do not meet the required assumptions of probability sampling
- Tests applied to measures of association that have been computed in violation of the assumptions made by those measures (e.g., Pearson product-moment correlations computed from ordinal data)
- Interpretation of statistical significance as a measure of association (a "relationship" of $p = 0.001$ is "stronger" than one of $p = 0.05$)

We do not mean to suggest a "purist" approach by these comments. We encourage you to use any statistical technique—any measure of association or any test of significance—on any set of data if it will help you understand your data. In doing so, however, you should recognize what measures of association and statistical significance can and cannot tell you, as well as the assumptions required for various measures. Any individual statistic or measure tells only part of the story, and you should try to learn as much of the story as you can.

Our running example, "Putting It All Together: Stops, Drivers, Speeders, and Citation Zones," shows different approaches to analyzing data on three key concepts: drivers, speeders, and traffic stops. None of the tables are especially complex, but each presents important data for understanding how these three concepts are related. As we stated at the outset of this chapter: "Empirical research

is, first and foremost, a logical rather than a mathematical operation."

Visualizing Discernible Differences

In this spirit, Michael Maltz proposes a compromise in the use of statistical significance tests on populations and on samples that violate the assumptions of probability sampling. Acting on a suggestion by criminologist Alfred Blumstein, Maltz (1994:440) advises researchers to use the phrase "statistically discernible difference" rather than "statistically significant difference" when using significance tests on inappropriate samples or populations. A **statistically discernible difference** is one that would be considered statistically significant if found in a random sample. In another example, James Lange, Mark Johnson, and Robert Voas (2005) use the phrase "statistically reliable difference." Careful use of language in this way alerts readers that, although significance tests are not technically appropriate, they can be used as a gauge to show the magnitude of deviation from the null hypothesis.

Researchers can also use the Maltz and Zawitz (1998) technique for presenting bounded point estimates to assess relationships between two or more variables. For example, Michael Maxfield, Barbara Luntz Weiler, and Cathy Spatz Widom (2000) compared self-reports of arrests to actual records of arrests for Cathy Spatz Widom's (1992) sample of child abuse/neglect victims and matched controls. Their research question centered on the relationship between two measures of offending: official records of arrests and self-reported arrests. Self-report measures, gathered through interviews with almost 1,200 subjects, were compared with arrest records obtained from local, state, and federal law enforcement agencies.

Recall from earlier chapters that Widom's subjects were selected purposively: abuse/neglect victims were identified through court records, and controls were individually matched to victims. Because this sample can in no way be considered random, tests of statistical significance are not technically appropriate.

Figure 14.6 presents point and interval estimates of self-reported arrests for different subgroups of

PUTTING IT ALL TOGETHER

As you probably realize by now, studies of racial profiling and traffic enforcement generated an enormous amount of data. That means some sort of summary analysis is crucial. A good general principle to keep in mind for data analysis is that as the number of data points or observations we make increases, some type of statistical analysis becomes essential. It need not be a sophisticated analysis, though the research reports we have cited include some advanced techniques.

Our final installment of the running example examines two simple tables that illustrate some basic elements of data analysis. We'll offer explanations of what the tables represent and our interpretation of results. It would be extremely value for you to consult the major studies we have mentioned to review other forms of data analysis that are presented in each.

One Population and Two Samples

The table below shows more detailed results from the New Jersey research conducted by Lange and associates:

New Jersey Turnpike, Each Race Category
(2 Standard Errors)

	Stops (Police Data)	Drivers (Tollbooth Survey)	Speeders (Observational Survey)
South			
White	52%	65.9% (3.8)	58.3% (3.0)
Black	29%	15.1% (2.6)	26.0% (2.6)
Central			
White	57%	63.9% (5.0)	60.2% (2.4)
Black	23%	12.5% (2.4)	25.6% (2.1)
North			
White	60%	58.7% (4.2)	68.4% (1.2)
Black	16%	13.1% (2.6)	18.2% (1.0)

Source: Adapted from Lange, Johnson, and Voas (2005:209).

Each of the three segments of the New Jersey Turnpike is presented separately because, as we will see, where you drive makes a difference. Each row represents the percentage of white or black drivers in each of the three segments. Three columns show moving vehicle stops by state police, results from the tollbooth survey of drivers, and results from the observational survey of speeders. So, for example, the first column of the first row indicates that 52 percent of drivers stopped for a moving violation in the southern segment were white; the second row shows black drivers were 29 percent of those stopped in the southern part.

The columns for drivers and speeders also show what percent of drivers are white and black. But the second entry for each category (in parentheses) shows 2 standard errors for each percentage. Recall that these were samples. Samples have standard errors that reflect dispersion around each percentage estimate. We can be 95 percent confident that the percentage for a population lies within 2 standard errors above and below the point estimate. So, for the last column in the first row, we can be 95 percent confident that whites were between 55.3 percent and 61.3 percent of the speeders recorded on the southern segment of the turnpike. Also recall that a statistically significant difference exists between two statistics if their interval estimates do not overlap. Compare the interval estimates for the percentage of drivers who are black and the percentage of speeders who are black:

Make the comparisons within segments, or within columns. Which intervals overlap? Within each segment, the percentage of speeders who are black is

	Drivers	Speeders
South	12.5–17.7%	23.4–28.6%
Central	10.1–14.9%	23.5–27.7%
North	10.5–15.7%	17.2–19.2%

significantly higher than the percentage of drivers who are black. Across the three segments, there are no significant differences in the percentage of drivers who are black. But significantly fewer speeders are black in the northern segment compared to the central or southern segments. If you graph these interval estimates, as Maltz and Zawitz did in Figure 13.5, you should see these patterns clearly.

Estimating Risk of Traffic Stops

The next table simply combines indicators from different sources to compare the relative likelihood of traffic stops in different segments of the turnpike. Row A shows the large difference in traffic volume between segments. The number of traffic stops also varies, but in the opposite direction. After first estimating the number of stops per day (Row C), Maxfield and Kelling standardized estimated daily stops by estimated traffic volume. In this way, row D shows the daily stop rate per 100,000 vehicles, something like a crime rate. The most useful items are in Row E, comparing the risk of being stopped

in the central and southern segments to the risk of being stopped in the north. You can see that drivers in the south are over six times more likely to be stopped compared to those in the north.

Now compare the data we have presented here to the summary findings by Maxfield and Kelling presented in Chapter 12's installment. You should see how these data support those conclusions.

Much more sophisticated analysis is presented in reports for Pennsylvania and North Carolina. The Pennsylvania report includes maps for a large number of counties in the state. One finding common to these reports and research in New Jersey is that patterns of road use and traffic enforcement vary enormously. For that reason, among others, it is very misleading, and bordering on irresponsible, to make summary statements about road use and traffic enforcement for a large geographical area.

We urge you to consult one or more of these reports as one way of continuing to develop your research skills.

New Jersey Turnpike Traffic and Stops

	North	Central	South
A. Average daily volume	262,130	126,020	73,830
B. Moving stops	10,591	11,292	18,794
C. Est. daily stops	29.0	30.9	51.5
D. Moving stops/100,000 vehicles	11.1	24.5	69.7
E. Relative risk of stop	1.0	2.2	6.3

Note:

A. New Jersey Department of Transportation counts for June 2002 at midpoint of segment

B. New Jersey State Police stop data, 1 May 2002–30 April 2003

C. Row B ÷ 365

D. Row C ÷ Row A × 100,000

E. Row D/Row D for North (11.1)

Source: Adapted from Maxfield and Kelling (2005:21).

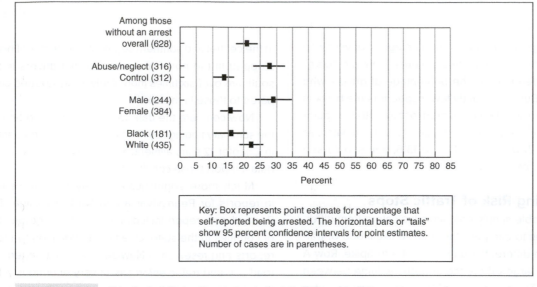

FIGURE 14.6   Displaying Data: Percentage that Self-Reported Arrests

Source: Adapted from Maxfield, Weiler, and Widom (2000:100, Figure 1).

subjects who did not have an official arrest record. The first point estimate shows that, of the 628 subjects with no official arrest record, 21 percent told interviewers that they had been arrested. This estimate is bracketed by 95 percent confidence intervals, showing the point estimate plus or minus 2 standard errors.

Now consider the separate estimates for abuse/neglect victims and their controls. A larger percentage of abuse/neglect victims (28 percent) self-reported arrests compared with control subjects (14 percent). Furthermore, when these point estimates are bounded by 2 standard errors, the "tails" of the two estimates do not overlap. This means that the estimates of self-reported arrests for abuse/neglect victims are more than 2 standard errors higher than those for control subjects. The last pair of subgroupings compares self-reported arrests by black and white subjects, regardless of whether they were abuse/neglect victims or controls. In this case, the tails of bounded estimates for the two groups overlap, indicating that self-reported arrests for black and white subjects are less than 2 standard errors apart. Alex Piquero and associates (2014:19–20) report some updated data, presenting results in a similar way.

Because the analysis shown in Figure 14.6 is not based on a random sample, it violates the assumptions of statistical significance tests. However, it's still possible to assess the relative size of differences in self-reported arrests by comparing bounded point estimates. Following the suggestion of Blumstein and Maltz, we can make the following observation: There is a statistically discernible difference in self-reported arrests between abuse/neglect victims and control subjects, but not between black and white subjects.

SUMMARY

- Descriptive statistics are used to summarize data under study.
- A frequency distribution shows the number of cases that have each of the attributes of a given variable.
- Measures of central tendency reduce data to an easily manageable form, but they do not convey the detail of the original data.
- Measures of dispersion give a summary indication of the distribution of cases around an average value.
- Rates are descriptive statistics that standardize some measure for comparative purposes.
- Bivariate analysis and subgroup comparisons examine some type of relationship between two variables.
- The rules of thumb in making subgroup comparisons in bivariate percentage tables are (1) "percentage down" and "compare across" or (2) "percentage across" and "compare down."
- Multivariate analysis is a method of analyzing the simultaneous relationships among several variables, and may be used to more fully understand the relationship between two variables.

- Many measures of association are based on a proportionate reduction of error (PRE) model, which measures improvement in predictions about one variable, given information about a second variable.
- Lambda (λ) and gamma (γ) are PRE-based measures of association for nominal and ordinal variables, respectively.
- Pearson's product-moment correlation (r) is a measure of association used in the analysis of two interval or ratio variables.
- Regression equations are computed based on a regression line—the geometric line that represents, with the least amount of discrepancy, the actual location of points in a scattergram.
- The equation for a regression line predicts the values of a dependent variable based on values of one or more independent variables.
- Inferential statistics are used to estimate the generalizability of findings arrived at in the analysis of a sample to the larger population from which the sample has been selected.
- Inferences about some characteristic of a population, such as the percentage that favors gun control laws, must contain an indication of a confidence interval (the range within which the value is expected to be—e.g., between 45 and 55 percent favor gun control) and an indication of the confidence level (the likelihood that the value does fall within that range—e.g., 95 percent confidence).
- Tests of statistical significance estimate the likelihood that an association as large as the one observed could result from normal sampling error if no such association exists between the variables in the larger population.
- Statistical significance must not be confused with substantive significance, which means that an observed association is strong, important, or meaningful.
- Tests of statistical significance, strictly speaking, make assumptions about data and methods that are almost never satisfied completely by real social research. Claiming a "statistically discernible relationship" is more appropriate when assumptions are not satisfied.

KEY TERMS

Average *(p. 399)*
Bivariate analysis *(p. 407)*
Central tendency *(p. 399)*
Contingency table *(p. 410)*
Descriptive statistics *(p. 397)*
Dispersion *(p. 399)*
Frequency distributions *(p. 398)*
Inferential statistics *(p. 397)*
Level of significance *(p. 420)*
Mean *(p. 399)*

Median *(p. 399)*
Mode *(p. 399)*
Multivariate analysis *(p. 410)*
Nonsampling error *(p. 419)*
Null hypothesis *(p. 422)*
Proportionate reduction of error (PRE) *(p. 414)*
Range *(p. 401)*
Regression analysis *(p. 416)*
Standard deviation *(p. 401)*
Statistical significance *(p. 420)*
Statistically discernible difference *(p. 425)*
Tests of statistical significance *(p. 419)*
Univariate analysis *(p. 398)*

REVIEW QUESTIONS AND EXERCISES

1. Using the data in the accompanying table, construct and interpret tables showing

   a. the bivariate relationship between age and attitude toward capital punishment.
   b. the bivariate relationship between political orientation and attitude toward capital punishment.
   c. the multivariate relationship linking age, political orientation, and attitude toward capital punishment.

Age	Political Orientation	Attitude Toward Capital Punishment	Frequency
Young	Conservative	Favor	90
Young	Conservative	Oppose	10
Young	Liberal	Favor	60
Young	Liberal	Oppose	40
Old	Conservative	Favor	60
Old	Conservative	Oppose	10
Old	Liberal	Favor	15
Old	Liberal	Oppose	15

2. Distinguish between measures of association and tests of statistical significance.

3. Here are our answers to the question about statistical significance relating to Figure 14.5: 15 years show no significant change in violent victimization; significant increases are shown for three years; violent victimization declines significantly in five years. The increase from 1976 to 1977 and the decrease from 1979 to 1980 are close; notice that the edge of the 95 percent confidence interval borders the no-change line. We recommend that you read the Maltz and Zawitz (1998) publication. It's listed in the bibliography and can be downloaded from the Bureau of Justice Statistics website at http://www.bjs.gov/index.cfm?ty=pbdetail&iid=773 (Accessed 11 September 2016).

Glossary

Aggregate Groups of units—people, prisons, courtrooms, or stolen autos, for example. Although criminal justice professionals are usually most concerned with individual units, social science searches for patterns that are reflected in aggregations of units. For example, a probation officer focuses on probation clients as individuals, whereas a social scientist focuses on groups of probation clients, or aggregates. See Chapter 2.

Anonymity A state in which the identity of a research subject is not known, and it is, therefore, impossible to link data about a subject to an individual's name. Anonymity is one tool for addressing the ethical issue of privacy. Compare to *confidentiality*. See Chapter 3.

Attributes Characteristics of persons or things. See *variables* and Chapter 2.

Audit trail An all-inclusive document of the research process that can include field notes, memos, etc. This record enhances the trustworthiness of research. See Chapter 10.

Average An ambiguous term that generally suggests typical or normal. The mean, median, and mode are specific mathematical averages. See Chapter 14.

Belmont Report A report that proposed three ethical principles to guide the protection of human subjects: respect for persons, beneficence, and justice. Federal regulations for the protection of human subjects are based on this report. See Chapter 3.

Bias That quality of a measurement device that tends to result in a misrepresentation of what is being measured in a particular direction. For example, the questionnaire item "Don't you agree that the president is doing a good job?" would be biased in that it would generally encourage more favorable responses. See Chapter 9.

Bivariate analysis The analysis of two variables simultaneously for the purpose of determining the empirical relationship between them. The construction of a simple percentage table and the computation of a simple correlation coefficient are examples of bivariate analyses. See Chapter 14.

Case-oriented research A research strategy in which many cases are examined to understand a comparatively small number of variables. Examples include experiments (Chapter 7) and surveys (Chapter 9).

Case study A research strategy in which the researcher's attention centers on an in-depth examination of one or a few cases on many dimensions. Case studies can be exploratory, descriptive, or explanatory. Case studies can also be used in evaluation research. See Chapters 7 and 13.

Central tendency Statistical measures that express how observations are clustered in a distribution. See Chapter 14.

Classical experiment A research design well suited to inferring cause, the classical experiment involves three major pairs of components: (1) independent and dependent variables; (2) pretesting and posttesting; and (3) experimental and control groups, with subjects randomly assigned to one group or the other. See Chapter 7.

Closed-ended questions Survey questions in which the respondent is asked to select an answer from a list provided by the researcher. Closed-ended questions are especially popular in surveys because they provide a greater uniformity of responses and are more easily analyzed than *open-ended questions*. See Chapter 9.

Cluster sampling Multistage sampling in which natural groups (clusters) are sampled initially, with the members of each selected group being subsampled afterward. For example, you might select a sample of municipal police departments from a directory, get lists of the police officers at all the selected departments, and then draw samples of officers from each. See Chapter 8.

Cohort study A study in which some specific group is studied over time, although data may be collected from different members in each set of observations. See Chapter 4.

Computer-assisted interviewing (CAI) Survey research by computer, in which questionnaires are presented on computer screens instead of paper. In computer-assisted personal interviewing, an interviewer reads items from the computer screen and keys in responses. In computer-assisted self-interviewing, respondents read (silently) items on the screen of a laptop computer and key in their answers. Another variation is audio-assisted self-interviewing, whereby respondents hear questions through headphones, and then key in their answers. Both types of self-interviewing are especially useful for sensitive questions like self-reports. See Chapter 9.

Concept A word or symbol in language that we use to represent a mental image. "Crime," for example, is a concept that represents our mental images of violence and other acts that are prohibited and punished by government. We use conceptual definitions to specify the meaning of concepts. Compare to *conception*. See Chapter 5.

Conception The mental image we have that represents our thoughts about something we routinely encounter. We use the word *speeding* (a concept) to represent our mental image (conception) of traveling above the posted speed limit. See Chapter 5.

Conceptual definition Defining concepts by using other concepts. The working definition of a concept or term. Concepts are abstract; they are words and symbols used to represent mental images of things and ideas. This means that a conceptual definition uses words and symbols to define concepts. In practice, conceptual definitions represent explicit statements of what a researcher means by a concept. A conceptual definition of "prior record" might be "recorded evidence of one or more convictions for a criminal offense." See also *operational definition* and Chapter 5.

Conceptualization The mental process whereby fuzzy and imprecise notions (concepts) are made more specific and precise. So you want to study fear of crime? What do you mean by fear of crime? Are there different kinds of fear? What are they? See Chapters 1, 5, and 6.

Confidence interval The range of values within which a population parameter is estimated to lie. A survey, for instance, may show that 40 percent of a sample favors a ban on handguns. Although the best estimate of the support that exists among all people is also 40 percent, we do not expect it to be exactly that. We might, therefore, compute a confidence interval (e.g., from 35 to 45 percent) within which the actual percentage of the population probably lies. Note that it is necessary to specify a confidence level in connection with every confidence interval. See Chapters 8 and 14.

Confidence level The estimated probability that a population parameter lies within a given confidence interval. Thus, we might be 95 percent confident that between 35 and 45 percent of all residents of California favor an absolute ban on handguns. See Chapters 8 and 14.

Confidentiality A state in which researchers know the identity of a research subject but promise not to reveal any information that can be attributed to an individual subject. Anonymity is similar, but sometimes researchers need to know subjects' names to link information from different sources. Assuring confidentiality is one way of meeting our ethical obligation to not harm subjects. See Chapter 3.

Construct validity (1) The degree to which a measure relates to other variables as expected within a system of theoretical relationships. See Chapter 5. (2) How well an observed cause-and-effect relationship represents the underlying causal process a researcher is interested in. See Chapters 4 and 7. Also see *validity threats*.

Content analysis The study of recorded communications, such as books, websites, images, mass media messages, and police reports. See Chapter 12.

Content validity The degree to which a measure covers the range of meanings included within the concept. See Chapter 5.

Contingency table A format for presenting the relationship among variables in the form of percentage distributions. See Chapter 14.

Control group In experimentation, a group of subjects to whom no experimental stimulus is administered and who should resemble the experimental group in all other respects. The comparison of the control group and the experimental group at the end of the experiment indicates the effect of the experimental stimulus. See Chapter 7.

Crimes known to police Crime incidents that are *reported* to police, *recorded* by police, and *retained* in police data systems. Crimes known to police are the basis of the FBI Uniform Crime Reports and the most commonly used measures of crime. Compare to the *dark figure of unreported crime* and *victim survey*. See Chapter 6.

Criterion-related validity The degree to which a measure relates to some external criterion. For example, the validity of self-report surveys of drug use can be shown by comparing survey responses to laboratory tests for drug use. See Chapter 5.

Critical realist perspective A philosophical view that reality exists, but knowledge is constructed through multiple meanings. See Chapter 10.

Cross-sectional study A study based on observations that represent a single point in time. Compare to *longitudinal study*. See Chapter 4.

Dark figure of unreported crime Not all crimes are reported to police, and this unknown quantity has been referred to as a "dark figure" because unreported crimes are not counted in measures like the Uniform Crime Reports. Simple assaults and thefts of low-value items are often not reported to police. Victim surveys were developed to measure this "dark figure." See Chapter 6.

Deductive reasoning The logical model in which specific expectations of hypotheses are developed on the basis of general principles. Starting from the general principle that all deans are meanies, you might anticipate that this one won't let you change courses. That anticipation would be the result of deduction. See also *inductive reasoning* and Chapter 2.

Dependent variable The variable assumed to depend on or be caused by another variable (called the independent variable). If you find that sentence length is partly a function of the number of prior arrests, then sentence length is being treated as a dependent variable. See Chapters 2 and 7.

Descriptive statistics Statistical computations that describe either the characteristics of a sample or the relationship among variables in a sample. Descriptive statistics summarize a set of sample observations, whereas inferential statistics move beyond the description of specific observations to make inferences about the larger population from which the sample observations were drawn. See Chapter 14.

Dimension A specifiable aspect or characteristic of a concept. See Chapter 5.

Dispersion The distribution of values around some central value, such as an average. The range is a simple measure of dispersion. Thus, we may report that the mean age of a group is 37.9 and the range is from 12 to 89. See Chapter 14.

Disproportionate stratified sampling Deliberately drawing a sample that overrepresents or underrepresents some characteristic of a population. We may do this to ensure that we obtain a sufficient number of uncommon cases in our sample. For example, believing violent crime to be more common in large cities, we might oversample urban residents to obtain a specific number of crime victims. See Chapter 6.

Ecological fallacy Erroneously drawing conclusions about individuals based solely on the observation of groups. See Chapter 4.

Empirical From experience. Social science is said to be empirical when knowledge is based on what we experience. See Chapter 1.

Environmental survey Structured observations undertaken in the field and recorded on specially designed forms. Note that interview surveys record a respondent's answers to questions, whereas environmental surveys record what an observer sees in the field. For example, a community organization may conduct periodic environmental surveys to monitor neighborhood parks—whether facilities are in good condition, how much litter is present, and what kinds of people use the park. See Chapter 11.

Equal probability of selection method (EPSEM) A sample design in which each member of a population has the same chance of being selected into the sample. See Chapter 8.

Ethical Conforming in behavior to norms and standards embraced by a group or profession. Norms regarding ethical behavior for research on human subjects are often described by professional associations of researchers. See Chapter 3.

Ethnography A report on social life that focuses on detailed and accurate description rather than explanation. See Chapters 10 and 11.

Evaluation research An example of applied research, evaluation involves assessing the effects of some program or policy action, usually in connection with the goals of that action. Determining whether a sex-offender treatment program attained its goal of reducing recidivism by participants would be an example. Compare to *problem analysis*. See Chapter 13.

Evidence-based policy The use of data and other sources of information to formulate and evaluate justice policy. This usually means planning justice actions based on evidence of need, such as deploying police patrols to crime hot spots. It also includes assessing the results of justice policy, such as measuring any change in recidivism among a group of offenders processed through drug court. See Chapter 13.

Evidence generation Collaborative applied research where evaluators and justice professionals build evidence on the effectiveness of community-based interventions. Evidence is then used to manage accountability. See Chapter 13.

Experimental group In experimentation, a group of subjects who are exposed to an experimental stimulus. Subjects in the experimental group are normally compared to subjects in a control group to test the effects of the experimental stimulus. See Chapter 7.

External validity Whether a relationship observed in a specific population, at a specific time, in a specific place would also be observed in other populations, at other times, in other places. External validity is concerned with generalizability from a relationship observed in one setting to the same relationship in other settings. Replication enhances external validity. See Chapters 4 and 7.

Face validity The quality of an indicator that makes it seem a reasonable measure of some variable. That sentence length prescribed by law is some indication of crime seriousness seems to make sense without a lot of explanation; it has face validity. See Chapter 5.

Focus groups Interviews with a group of participants. This format is best for uncovering the perspective of a particular group where group dynamics between group members generate data. See Chapter 10.

Frequency distribution A description of the number of times the various attributes of a variable are observed in a sample. The report that 53 percent of a sample were men and 47 percent were women is a simple example of a frequency distribution. Another example is the report that 15 of the cities studied had populations of less than 10,000, 23 had populations between 10,000 and 25,000, and so forth. See Chapter 14.

Generalizability That quality of a research finding that justifies the inference that it represents something more than the specific observations on which it was based. Sometimes, this involves the generalization of findings from a sample to a population. Other times, it is a matter of concepts: If you are able to discover why people commit burglaries, can you generalize that discovery to other crimes as well? See Chapter 7.

Grounded theory A type of inductive theory that is based on (grounded in) field observation. The researcher makes observations in natural settings and then formulates a tentative theory that explains those observations. See Chapters 2 and 10.

Hypothesis An expectation about the nature of things derived from a theory. It is a statement of something that ought to be observed in the real world if the theory is correct. See *deduction* and Chapters 2 and 7.

Hypothesis testing The determination of whether the expectations that a hypothesis represents are indeed found in the real world. See Chapters 2 and 7.

Idiographic Relating to a mode of causal reasoning that seeks detailed understanding of all factors that contribute to a particular phenomenon. Police detectives trying to solve a particular case use the idiographic mode of explanation. Compare to *nomothetic*. See Chapters 2 and 4.

Impact assessment A type of applied research that seeks to answer the question: Did a public program have the intended effect on the problem it was meant to address? If, for example, a new burglary prevention program has the goal of reducing burglary in a particular neighborhood, an impact assessment would try to determine whether burglary was, in fact, reduced as a result of the new program. Compare to *process evaluation*. See Chapter 13.

Incident-based measure A crime measure that expresses characteristics of individual crime incidents. The FBI Supplementary Homicide Reports are well-known examples, reporting details on each homicide incident. Compare to *summary-based measure*. See Chapter 6.

Independent variable An independent variable is presumed to cause or determine a dependent variable. If we discover that police cynicism is partly a function of years of experience, then experience is the independent variable and cynicism is the dependent variable. Note that any given variable might be treated as independent in one part of an analysis and dependent in another part of the analysis. Cynicism might become an independent variable in the explanation of job satisfaction. See Chapters 2 and 7.

Inductive reasoning The logical model in which general principles are developed from specific observations. Having noted that teenagers and crime victims are less supportive of police than are older people and nonvictims, you might conclude that people with more direct police contact are less supportive of police and explain why. That would be an example of induction. See also *deductive reasoning* and Chapter 2.

Inferential statistics The body of statistical computations relevant to making inferences from findings based on sample observations to some larger population. See also *descriptive statistics* and Chapter 14.

Informed consent Agreement to participate in research after being informed about the research goals, procedures, and potential risks. This information is given before asking subjects to participate. This standard procedure addresses the norm of voluntary participation, a basic tenet of research ethics. See Chapter 3.

Insider/outsider status The researcher's level of closeness to the group of interest, with outsiders having little or no affiliation/relationship to the group. "Insiderness" may be through membership, connection, or similarity to location in the social structure. See Chapter 10.

Internal validity Whether observed associations between two (or more) variables are, in fact, causal associations or are due to the effects of some other variable. The internal validity of causal statements may be threatened by an inability to control experimental conditions. See also *validity threats* and Chapters 4 and 7.

Intersubjective agreement That quality of science (and other inquiries) whereby two different researchers studying the same problem arrive at the same conclusion. Ultimately, this is the practical criterion for what is called objectivity. We agree that something is "objectively true" if independent observers with different subjective orientations conclude that it is "true." See Chapter 2.

Interuniversity Consortium for Political and Social Research (ICPSR) An organization based at the University of Michigan that archives and distributes major social science data collections. Since most universities and many smaller colleges are member institutions, students and faculty have access to vast sources of secondary data. See also the *National Archive of Criminal Justice Data* and Chapter 12.

Interval measure A level of measurement that describes a variable whose attributes are rank-ordered and have equal distances between adjacent attributes. The Fahrenheit temperature scale is an example because the distance between 17 and 18 is the same as that between 89 and 90. See also *nominal measure, ordinal measure,* and *ratio measure* and Chapter 5.

Interview A data collection encounter in which one person (an interviewer) asks questions of another (a respondent). Interviews may be conducted face to face or by telephone. See Chapter 9.

Interview schedule The structure of the interview that may have predetermined questions or topical areas to be discussed with participants. It determines how in depth and interactive an interviewer will be during an interview. See Chapter 10.

Interview survey A survey that uses a questionnaire in a systematic way to interview a large number of people. The National Crime Victimization Survey (NCVS) is an example. Interview surveys can be face to face, over the telephone, or a mix of these two together with computer-assisted interviewing. See also *environmental survey*. See Chapter 9.

Latent content As used in connection with content analysis, this term describes the underlying meaning of communications as distinguished from their *manifest content*. See Chapter 12.

Level of significance In the context of tests of statistical significance, the degree of likelihood that an observed, empirical relationship could be attributable to sampling error. A relationship is significant at the 0.05 level if the likelihood of its being only a function of sampling error is no greater than 5 out of 100. See Chapter 14.

Longitudinal study A study design that involves the collection of data at different points in time, as contrasted to a cross-sectional study. See also *trend study, cohort study,* and *panel study* and Chapter 4.

Manifest content In connection with content analysis, the concrete terms contained in a communication, as distinguished from *latent content*. See Chapter 12.

Mean An average, computed by summing the values of several observations and dividing by the number of observations. If you now have a grade-point average of 4.0 based on 10 courses, and you get an F in this course, then your new grade-point (mean) average will be 3.6. See Chapter 14.

Median Another average, representing the value of the "middle" case in a rank-ordered set of observations. If the ages of five people are 16, 17, 20, 54, and 88, then the median is 20. (The mean is 39.) See Chapter 14.

Memoing The act of writing documents about research decisions made, such as adding a question or creating a code, as well as personal feelings about the process. See Chapter 10.

Methodology The study of methods used to understand something; the science of finding out. See Chapter 1.

Mode Still another average, representing the most frequently observed value or attribute. If a sample contains 1,000 residents from California, 275 from New Jersey, and 33 from Minnesota, then California is the modal category for residence. See Chapter 14.

Multivariate analysis The analysis of the simultaneous relationships among several variables. Examining simultaneously the effects of age, gender, and city of residence on robbery victimization is an example of multivariate analysis. See Chapter 14.

National Archive of Criminal Justice Data (NACJD) A special collection within the Interuniversity Consortium of Political and Social Research that includes data series of special interest to criminal justice researchers and practitioners. The NCVS, Uniform Crime Report (UCR), and data series on correctional populations are included, as are hundreds of other examples of published statistics. The data collection also includes data from most research studies funded by the National Institute of Justice, something that makes the NACJD an excellent source of secondary data. See also the *Interuniversity Consortium of Political and Social Research* and Chapter 12.

Nominal measure A level of measurement that describes a variable whose different attributes are only different, as distinguished from *ordinal, interval,* and *ratio measures.* Gender is an example of a nominal measure. See Chapter 5.

Nomothetic A mode of causal reasoning that tries to explain a number of similar phenomena or situations. Police crime analysts trying to explain patterns of auto thefts, burglaries, or some other offense use nomothetic reasoning. Compare to *idiographic.* See Chapters 2 and 4.

Nonprobability sampling Procedure in which a sample is selected in some fashion other than those suggested by probability theory. Examples are purposive, quota, and snowball sampling. See Chapter 8.

Nonsampling error Imperfections of data quality that are a result of factors other than sampling error. Examples are misunderstandings of questions by respondents, erroneous recordings by interviewers and coders, and data entry errors. See Chapter 14.

Null hypothesis In connection with hypothesis testing and tests of statistical significance, the hypothesis that suggests there is no relationship between the variables under study. You may conclude that the two variables are related after having statistically rejected the null hypothesis. See Chapter 14.

Objectivity Doesn't exist. See also *intersubjective agreement* and Chapter 2.

Obtrusive measurement Research subjects are aware that data are being collected. Administering a questionnaire is an example. See Chapter 12.

Open-ended questions Questions for which the respondent is asked to provide his or her own answers. Compare with *closed-ended questions.* See Chapter 9.

Operational definition A statement specifying what operations should be performed to measure a concept. The operational definition of "prior record" might be "Consult the county (or state or FBI) criminal history records information system. Count the number of times a person has been convicted of committing a crime." See Chapter 5.

Operationalization One step beyond conceptualization. Operationalization is the process of developing operational definitions that describe how actual measurements will be made. See Chapters 1 and 5.

Ordinal measure A level of measurement that describes a variable whose attributes may be rank-ordered along some dimension. An example is socioeconomic status as composed of the attributes high, medium, and low. See also *nominal measure, interval measure,* and *ratio measure* and Chapter 5.

Panel study A type of longitudinal study in which data are collected from the same subjects (the panel) at several points in time. See Chapter 4.

Paradigm A fundamental perspective or model that organizes our view of the world. Thomas Kuhn (1996) coined this term in the philosophy of science. Paradigms affect how we select and define problems for research, together with the methods we use in conducting research. Compare to *theory.* See Chapter 2.

Population All people, things, or other elements we wish to represent. Researchers often study only a subset or sample of a population and then generalize from the people, things, or other elements actually observed to the larger population of all people, things, or elements. See Chapter 8.

Population parameter The summary description of a particular variable in the population. For example, if the mean age of all professors at your college is 43.7, then 43.7 is the population parameter for professors' mean age. Compare to *sample statistic* and *sampling distribution.* See Chapter 8.

Probabilistic Reflecting the causal reasoning that certain factors make outcomes more or less likely to happen. Having been arrested as a juvenile makes it more likely that one will be arrested as an adult. See Chapter 4.

Probability sampling The general term for when samples are selected in accord with probability theory, typically involving some random selection mechanism. Specific types of probability sampling include area probability sampling, equal probability of selection method (EPSEM), simple random sampling, and systematic sampling. See Chapter 8.

Problem analysis Using social science research methods to assess the scope and nature of a problem and then to plan and select actions to address the problem. An example is examining patterns of auto theft to decide what preventive and enforcement strategies should be pursued. Compare to *evaluation research*. See Chapter 13.

Problem-oriented policing An approach to policing that depends on analyzing patterns of incidents and conditions that police are expected to handle and then developing responses based on that analysis. This approach differs from traditional approaches in its focus on patterns rather than individual incidents. See Chapter 13.

Problem solving An example of applied research that combines elements of evaluation and policy analysis. The most widely known approach to problem solving in policing is the SARA model, which stands for scanning, analysis, response, and assessment. See Chapter 13.

Process evaluation A type of applied research that seeks to answer the question: Was a public program implemented as intended? For example, a burglary prevention program might seek to reduce burglaries by having crime prevention officers meet with all residents of some target neighborhood. A process evaluation would determine whether meetings with neighborhood residents were taking place as planned. Compare to *impact assessment*. See Chapter 13.

Proportionate reduction of error (PRE) A logical model for assessing the strength of a relationship by asking how much knowing values on one variable might reduce our errors in guessing values on the other. For example, if we know how much education people have, we can improve our ability to guess how much they earn, thus indicating that there is a relationship between the two variables. See Chapter 14.

Prospective Adjective describing a type of longitudinal study that follows subjects forward in time. "How many people who were sexually abused as children are convicted of a sexual offense as an adult?" is an example of a prospective question. Compare to *retrospective*. See Chapter 4.

Published statistics Summary data collected by public agencies and routinely made available to the public, sometimes referred to as "administrative data." Agencies are often required to keep and publish such measures. See Chapter 12.

Purposive sample A type of nonprobability sample in which you select the units to be observed on the basis of your own judgment about which ones will be best suited to your research purpose. For example, if you were interested in studying community crime prevention groups affiliated with public schools and groups affiliated with religious organizations, you would probably want to select a purposive sample of school- and church-affiliated groups. Most television networks use purposive samples of voting precincts to project winning candidates on election night; precincts that always vote for winners are sampled. See Chapter 8.

Qualitative description Qualitative technique where data are discussed without imposing any system of analysis or interpretation. Letting the data speak for itself. See Chapter 10.

Qualitative interpretation After systematically analyzing data, the discussion of findings that are more speculative or are linked to the larger literature. See Chapter 10.

Qualitative interview Contrasted with survey interviewing, the qualitative interview is based on a set of topics to be discussed in depth rather than based on the use of standardized questions. It's more a verbal interaction between an interviewer and a participant where the interviewer has a general plan of inquiry. See Chapter 10.

Quasi-experiment A research design that includes most, but not all, elements of an experimental design. *Quasi* means "sort of," and a quasi-experiment is sort of an experiment. Two general classes of quasi-experiments are nonequivalent-groups designs and time-series designs. Compare to *classical experiment* and see Chapter 7.

Questionnaire A document that contains questions and other types of items designed to solicit information appropriate to analysis. Questionnaires are used primarily in survey research and also in field research. See Chapter 9.

Quota sampling A type of nonprobability sampling in which units are selected into the sample based on prespecified characteristics so that the total sample will have the same distribution of characteristics as are assumed to exist in the population being studied. See Chapter 8.

Random assignment A technique for randomly assigning experimental subjects to experimental groups and control groups. See Chapter 7.

Range A measure of dispersion, the distance that separates the highest and lowest values of a variable in some set of observations. In your class, for example, the range of ages might be from 17 to 37. See Chapter 14.

Rapport The connection between researcher and participants usually formed through informal conversation. See Chapter 10.

Ratio measure A level of measurement that describes a variable whose attributes have all the qualities of nominal, ordinal, and interval measures and in addition are based on a "true zero" point. Length of prison sentence is an example of a ratio measure. See Chapter 5.

Reactivity The problem that the subjects of social research may react to the fact they are being studied and thus alter their behavior from what it would have been normally. See Chapter 11.

Reflexivity The researcher's awareness of his or her perspectives (i.e., subjectivity), including his or her personal biases. See Chapter 10.

Regression analysis A method of data analysis in which the relationships among variables are represented in the form of an equation called a regression equation. See Chapter 14.

Reification The process of regarding as real things that are not real. This is usually a problem in measurement. See Chapter 5.

Reliability That quality-of-measurement standard whereby the same data should be collected each time in repeated observations of the same phenomenon. We would expect that the question "Did you see a police officer in your neighborhood today?" would have higher reliability than the question "About how many times in the past 6 months have you seen a police officer in your neighborhood?" This is not to be confused with validity. See Chapter 5.

Replication Repeating a research study to test the findings of an earlier study, often under slightly different conditions or for a different group of subjects. Replication results either support earlier findings or cause us to question the accuracy of an earlier study. See Chapter 1.

Respondent A person who provides data for analysis by responding to a survey questionnaire that is self-completed or administered as an interview. See Chapter 9.

Response rate The number of people participating in a survey divided by the number selected in the sample, in the form of a percentage. This is also called the completion rate or, in self-administered surveys, the return rate: the percentage of questionnaires sent out that are returned. See Chapter 9.

Retrospective Adjective describing a type of longitudinal study that looks backward, asking subjects to recall events that happened earlier in their lives or tracing official records of someone's previous actions. "How many current sex offenders were sexually abused as children?" is a retrospective question. Compare to *prospective*. See Chapter 4.

Safety audit A type of environmental survey that focuses on the security and safety of places. Safety audits are often combined with interviews or focus groups to measure *perceptions* of safety among people who regularly use specific places. See Chapter 11.

Sample element That unit about which information is collected and that provides the basis of analysis. Typically, in survey research, elements are people. Other kinds of units can be elements for criminal justice research—correctional facilities, gangs, police beats, or court cases, for example. See Chapter 8.

Sample statistic The summary description of a particular variable in a sample. For example, if the mean age of a sample of 100 professors on your campus is 41.1, then 41.1 is the sample statistic for professors' age. We usually use sample statistics to estimate population parameters. Compare to *sampling distribution*. See Chapter 8.

Sampling distribution The range or array of sample statistics we would obtain if we drew a very large number of samples from a single population. With random sampling, we expect that the sampling distribution for a particular statistic (e.g., mean age) will cluster around the population

parameter for mean age. Furthermore, sampling distributions for larger sample sizes will cluster more tightly around the population parameter. See Chapter 8.

Sampling frame That list or quasi-list of units composing a population from which a sample is selected. If the sample is to be representative of the population, it is essential that the sampling frame include all (or nearly all) members of the population. See Chapter 8.

Sampling units Like sampling elements, these are things that may be selected in the process of sampling; often, sampling units are people. In some types of sampling, however, we often begin by selecting large groupings of the eventual elements we will analyze. *Sampling units* is a generic term for things that are selected in some stage of sampling but are not necessarily the objects of our ultimate interest. See Chapter 8.

Scientific realism An approach to evaluation that studies what's called "local causality." Interest focuses more on how interventions and measures of effect are related in a specific situation. This is different from a more traditional social science interest in finding causal relationships that apply generally to a variety of situations. As explained by Ray Pawson and Nick Tilley (1997), scientific realism is especially useful for evaluating justice programs because it centers on analyzing interventions in local contexts. See Chapters 4, 7, and 13.

Secondary analysis A form of research in which the data collected and processed by one researcher are reanalyzed—often for a different purpose—by another. This is especially appropriate in the case of survey data. Data archives are repositories or libraries for the storage and distribution of data for secondary analysis. See Chapter 12.

Self-report survey A survey that asks people to tell about crimes they have committed. This method is best for measuring drug use and other so-called victimless crimes. Confidentiality is especially important in self-report surveys. See Chapters 6 and 9.

Semi-structured interview An interview that may have standardized questions, but allows for unscheduled probes or spontaneous questions. See Chapter 10.

Sensitizing concepts A term coined by Herbert Blumer (1954), sensitizing concepts are general references and guides about what to look for in data. They are derived from themes or existing theories. See Chapter 10.

Simple random sampling A type of probability sampling in which the units composing a population are assigned numbers, a set of random numbers is then generated, and the units that have those numbers are included in the sample. Although probability theory and the calculations it provides assume this basic sampling method, it is seldom used for practical reasons. An alternative is the systematic sample (with a random start). See Chapter 8.

Snowball sampling A method for drawing a nonprobability sample. Snowball samples are often used in field research. Each person interviewed is asked to suggest additional people for interviewing. See Chapters 8 and 11.

Social production of data Referring mostly to agency records, whose data reflect organization processes and decision rules in addition to the condition measured. Crime reports and probation records are examples. See Chapter 12.

Special populations Groups like juveniles and prisoners who require special protections. Juveniles are considered unable to grant informed consent, just as juveniles are treated differently in most areas of the law. Special rules apply to prisoners because they may feel compelled to participate in research or because they may see participation as especially desirable. See Chapter 3.

Stakeholders Individuals with some interest, or stake, in a specific program. Any particular program may have multiple stakeholders with different interests and goals. See Chapter 13.

Standard deviation A measure of dispersion about the mean. Conceptually, the standard deviation represents an "average" deviation of all values relative to the mean. See Chapter 14.

Standard error A measure of sampling error that gives us a statistical estimate of how much a member of a sample might differ from the population we are studying, solely by chance. Larger samples usually result in smaller standard errors. See Chapters 8 and 14.

Statistical conclusion validity Whether we can find covariation among two variables. This is the first of three requirements for causal inference (see Chapter 4 for the other two). If two variables do not vary together (covariation), there cannot be a causal relationship between them. See Chapters 4 and 7 for more on statistical conclusion validity. Chapter 14 describes the role of sample size in finding statistical significance, which is conceptually related to statistical conclusion validity.

Statistical significance A general term for the probability that relationships observed in a sample could be attributed to sampling error alone. See also *tests of statistical significance* and Chapter 14.

Statistically discernible difference Tests of statistical significance should not normally be used unless our data meet certain assumptions about sampling and variation. Citing a finding as a "statistically discernible difference" allows us to use the tools of statistical inference while alerting readers that the use of these tools is not technically appropriate. See Chapter 14.

Stratification The grouping of the units composing a population into homogeneous groups (or strata) before sampling. This procedure, which may be used in conjunction with simple random, systematic, or cluster sampling, improves the representativeness of a sample, at least in terms of the stratification variables. See Chapter 8.

Structured interview An interview with a set of specific questions and answer choices. See Chapters 9 and 10.

Summary-based measure A crime measure that reports only total crimes for a jurisdiction or other small area. The FBI Uniform Crime Reports is one well-known summary measure. Compare to *incident-based measure*. See Chapter 6.

Surveillance system A routine collection of data to monitor some phenomenon—accidents, injuries, communicable disease incidents, and drug emergencies. U.S. agencies use surveillance measures to obtain estimates of drug use and, more recently, injuries produced by violent crime. See Chapter 6.

Survey A method for collecting data by applying a standard instrument in a systematic way to take measures from a large number of units. See also *interview survey* and *environmental survey*. See Chapter 9.

Systematic sampling A type of probability sampling in which a fraction of units in a list is selected for inclusion in the sample—for example, every 25th student in the college directory of students. We compute the sampling interval by dividing the size of the population by the desired sample size. Within certain constraints, systematic sampling is a functional equivalent of simple random sampling and is usually easier to do. Typically, the first unit is selected at random. See Chapter 8.

Tests of statistical significance A class of statistical computations that indicate the likelihood that the relationship observed between variables in a sample can be attributed to sampling error only. See also *inferential statistics* and Chapter 14.

Themes In grounded theory, they are higher-level concepts (usually derived from selective codes) that include a group of lower-level concepts (usually from open coding). See Chapter 10.

Theory A systematic explanation for the observed facts and laws that relate to a particular aspect of life. For example, routine activities theory (see Cohen and Felson, 1979) explains crime as the result of three key elements coming together: a suitable victim, a motivated offender, and the absence of capable guardians. See Chapter 2.

Thinking units A term coined by John Lofland and Lyn Lofland (1995) to indicate a simple framework or loose coding device used to make sense of narratives. See Chapter 10.

Time-series design A type of quasi-experimental design where changes in a dependent variable are monitored over some time period. See Chapter 7.

Trend study A type of longitudinal study in which a given characteristic of some population is monitored over time. An example is the series of annual Uniform Crime Report totals for some jurisdiction. See Chapter 4.

Typology A classification of observations in terms of their attributes. Sometimes referred to as "taxonomies," typologies are typically created with nominal variables. For example, a typology of thieves might group them according to the types of cars they steal and the types of locations they search to find targets. See Chapter 5.

Units of analysis The "what" or "whom" being studied. Units of analysis may be individual people, groupings of people (a juvenile gang), formal organizations (a probation department), or social artifacts (crime reports). See Chapter 4.

Univariate analysis The analysis of a single variable for purposes of description. Frequency distributions, averages, and measures of dispersion are examples of univariate analysis, as distinguished from bivariate and multivariate analyses. See Chapter 14.

Unobtrusive measurement Research subjects are not aware that data are being collected. Observing pedestrian traffic from a park bench is an example. See Chapter 12.

Unstructured interview An open style of interviewing that is more akin to a conversation, but there may be a list of topical areas for discussion. Compare to *structured interview* and *semi-structured interview* and see Chapters 10 and 11.

Validity (1) Whether statements about cause and effect are true (valid) or false (invalid). See Chapters 4 and 7; also see *validity threats*. (2) A descriptive term used for a measure that accurately reflects what it is intended to measure. For example, police records of auto theft are more valid measures than police records of shoplifting. It is important to realize that the ultimate validity of a measure can never be proved. Yet we may agree as to its relative validity on the basis of face validity, criterion-related validity, content validity, and construct validity. This must not be confused with *reliability*. See Chapter 5.

Validity threats Possible sources of false conclusions about cause or measurement. Four categories of validity threats are linked to fundamental requirements for demonstrating cause: statistical conclusion validity, internal validity, construct validity, and external validity (see separate entries in this Glossary). In general, statistical conclusion validity and internal validity are concerned with bias; construct validity and external validity are concerned with generalization. See Chapters 4 and 7.

Variable-oriented research A research strategy whereby a large number of variables are studied for one or a small number of cases or subjects. Time-series designs and case studies are examples. See Chapter 7.

Variables Logical groupings of attributes. The variable "gender" is made up of the attributes male and female. See Chapter 2.

Victim survey A sample survey that asks people about their experiences as victims of crime. Victim surveys are one way to measure crime, and they are especially valuable for getting information about crimes not reported to police. The National Crime Victimization Survey is an example. See Chapters 6 and 9.

References

Academy of Criminal Justice Sciences. 2000. "Code of Ethics." Greenbelt, MD: Academy of Criminal Justice Sciences, http://www.acjs.org/new_page_13.htm. Accessed 3 May 2016.

Adler, Patricia A, and Peter Adler. 2001. "The Reluctant Respondent." In *The Handbook of Interview Research*, J.F. Gubrium and J. Holstein (Eds.). Thousand Oaks, CA: Sage Publications.

Aebi, Marcelo F., and Antonia Linde. 2012. "Crime Trends in Western Europe According to Official Statistics from 1990 to 2007." In *The International Crime Drop: New Directions in Research*, Jan van Dijk, Andromachi Tslenoi, and Graham Farrell (Eds.). Crime prevention studies, vol. 17. London: Palgrave, 37–75.

American Association of University Professors. 2006. *Protecting Human Beings: Institutional Review Boards and Social Science Research*. AAUP Redbook. Washington, D.C.: American Association of University Professors, http://www.aaup.org/AAUP/comm/rep/A/humansubs.htm. Accessed 18 November 2009.

American Psychological Association. 2010. *Ethical Principles of Psychologists and Code of Conduct*. 2002 Code as amended. Washington, D.C.: American Psychological Association, http://www.apa.org/ethics/index.aspx. Accessed 6 January 2011.

American Society of Criminology. 2016. "Code of Ethics." Columbus, OH: American Society of Criminology, http://asc41.com/code_of_ethics_copies/ASC%20Code%20of%20Ethics.html. Accessed 3 May 2016.

American Sociological Association. 1999. "Code of Ethics." Washington, D.C.: American Sociological Association, http://www.asanet.org/galleries/default-file/Code%20of%20Ethics.pdf.

Anderson, Craig A., and Brad Bushman. 2002. "The Effects of Media Violence on Society." *Science* 295 (29 March):2377–79.

Andresen, W. Carsten. 2005. *State Police: Discretion and Traffic Enforcement*. Unpublished Ph.D., dissertation. Newark, NJ: School of Criminal Justice, Rutgers University.

Aos, Steve, and Elizabeth Drake. 2013. *Prison, Police, and Programs: Evidence-Based Options That Reduce Crime and Save Money*. (Document No. 13-11-1901). Olympia: Washington State Institute for Public Policy, http://www.wsipp.wa.gov.

Associated Press. 1993. "High Murder Rate for Women on the Job." *New York Times*, 3 October.

Austin, James, Wendy Naro, and Tony Fabelo. 2007. *Public Safety, Public Spending: Forecasting America's Prison Population 2007–2011*. Philadelphia: Pew Charitable Trusts.

Babbie, Earl. 2004. *The Practice of Social Research*. 10th ed. Belmont, CA: Wadsworth.

Bachman, Ronet, and Linda E. Saltzman. 1995. *Violence Against Women: Estimates from the Redesigned Survey*. Washington, D.C.: U.S. Department of Justice, Office of Justice Programs, Bureau of Justice Statistics.

Baker, Al, and Kate Taylor. 2012. "Bloomberg Defends Police's Monitoring of Muslim Students on the Web." *New York Times*, 21 February.

Baldus, David C., Catherine M. Grosso, George Woodworth, and Richard Newell. 2011. "Racial Discrimination in the Administration of the Death Penalty: The Experience of the United States Armed Forces (1984–2005)." *Journal of Criminal Law and Criminology* 101(4):1227–335.

Baldus, David C., Charles Pulaski, and George Woodworth. 1983. "Comparative Review of Death Sentences: An Empirical Study of the Georgia Experience." *Journal of Criminal Law and Criminology* 74:661–753.

Barnes, J.C., Kevin M. Beaver, and Brian B. Boutwell. 2011. "Examining the Genetic Underpinnings to Moffitt's Developmental Taxonomy: A Behavioral Genetic Analysis." *Criminology* 49:923–54.

Baron, Stephen W., and Timothy F. Hartnagel. 1998. "Street Youth and Criminal Violence." *Journal of Research in Crime and Delinquency* 35(2):166–92.

Barth, Fredrick. 2002. "Toward a Richer Description and Analysis of Cultural Description." In *Anthropology Beyond Culture*, R.G. Fox and B.J. King (Eds.). Oxford: Berg, 23–36.

Baumer, Eric, Janet L. Lauritsen, Richard Rosenfeld, and Richard Wright. 1998. "The Influence of Crack Cocaine on Robbery, Burglary, and Homicide Rates: A Cross-City Longitudinal Analysis." *Journal of Research in Crime and Delinquency* 35:316–40.

Baumer, Terry L, Michael G. Maxfield, and Robert I. Mendelsohn. 1993. "A Comparative Analysis of Three Electronically Monitored Home Detention Programs." *Justice Quarterly* 10:121–42.

Baumer, Terry L., and Robert I. Mendelsohn. 1990. *The Electronic Monitoring on Non-Violent Convicted Felons: An Experiment in Home Detention*. Final report to the National Institute of Justice. Indianapolis, IN: Indiana University, School of Public and Environmental Affairs.

Baumer, Terry L., and Dennis Rosenbaum. 1982. *Combatting Retail Theft: Programs and Strategies*. Boston: Butterworth.

Beauregard, Eric, D. Kim Rossmo, and Jean Proulx. 2007. "A Descriptive Model of the Hunting Process of Serial Sex Offenders: A Rational Choice Perspective." *Journal of Family Violence* 22:449–63.

Beck, Allen J., et al. 2010. *Sexual Victimization in Prisons and Jails Reported by Inmates, 2008–09*. Washington, D.C.: U.S. Department of Justice, Office of Justice Programs, Bureau of Justice Statistics.

Becker, Howard. 1963. *Outsiders*. New York: Free Press.

Bench, Lawrence L., and Terry D. Allen. 2003. "Investigating the Stigma of Prison Classification: An Experimental Design." *The Prison Journal* 83(4):367–82.

Bennett, Trevor, Katy Holloway, and David Farrington. 2008. "The Statistical Association Between Drug Misuse and Crime: A Meta-Analysis." *Aggression and Violent Behavior* 13:107–18.

Bennett, Trevor, and Katy Holloway. 2005. "Association Between Multiple Drug Use and Crime." *International Journal of Offender Therapy and Comparative Criminology* 49:63–81.

Bennis, Jason, Wesley G. Skogan, and Lynn Steiner. 2003. "The 2002 Beat Meeting Observation Study." Community Policing Working Paper #26. Evanston, IL: Center for Policy Research, Northwestern University, http://www.northwestern.edu/ipr/publications/policing.html. Accessed 27 April 2003.

Benoit, Cecilia, and Alison Millar. 2001. 2nd ed. *Dispelling Myths and Understanding Realities: Working Conditions, Health Status, and Exiting Experiences of Sex Workers—Short Report*. Short rept. Victoria, BC: Prostitutes Empowerment, Education, and Resource Society.

Berg, Bruce L. 1998. "A Dramaturgical Look at Interviewing." In *Qualitative Research Methods for the Social Sciences*, Ed Bruce L. Berg. Needham Heights, MA: Allyn and Bacon, 66–110.

Berinsky, Adam J., Gregory A. Huber, and Gabriel S. Lenz. 2012. "Evaluating Online Labor Markets for Experimental Research: Amazon.com's Mechanical Turk." *Political Analysis* 20:351–66.

Berk, Richard A., Heather Ladd, Heidi Graziano, and Jong-ho Baek. 2003. "A Randomized Experiment Testing Inmate Classification Systems." *Criminology and Public Policy* 2(2, March): 215–42.

Bernstein, Margaret. 2012. "Signs of Human Trafficking Can Stay Hidden in Plain Sight." *Cleveland Plain Dealer*, 12 February.

Best, Joel. 2013. *Stat-Spotting: A Field Guide to Identifying Dubious Data*. Berkeley, CA: University of California Press.

Best, Samuel L., and Benjamin Radcliff. 2005. *Polling America: An Encyclopedia of Public Opinion, Volume II, P-Z*. Westport, CT: Greenwood Press.

Birks, Melanie, Ysanne Chapman, and Karen Francis. 2008. "Memoing in Qualitative Research." *Journal of Research in Nursing* 12(4):68–75.

Black, Donald. 1970. "The Production of Crime Rates." *American Sociological Review* 35:733–48.

Bloomberg, Michael R., and Amanda M. Burden. 2006. *New York City Pedestrian Level of Service Study, Phase 1*. New York: Office of the Mayor and Department of City Planning.

Blumberg, Stephen J., and Julian V. Luke. 2016. *Wireless Substitution: Early Release Estimates from the National Health Interview Survey, July-December 2015*. Atlanta, Georgia: Centers for Disease Control, http://www.cdc.gov/nchs/data/nhis/earlyrelease/wireless201605.pdf.

Blumer, Herbert. 1954. "What Is Wrong with Social Theory?" *Journal of the American Sociological Society* 19(1):3–10.

Blumstein, Alfred, Jacqueline Cohen, Alex R. Piquero, and Christy A. Visher. 2010. "Linking the Crime and Arrest Processes to Measure Variations in Individual Arrest Risk Per Crime (Q)." *Journal of Quantitative Criminology* 26:533–48.

Boba, Rachel. 2005. *Crime Analysis and Crime Mapping*. Thousand Oaks, CA: Sage.

Boivin, Remi, and Gilbert Cordeau. 2011. "Measuring the Impact of Police Discretion on Official Crime Statistics: A Research Note." *Police Quarterly* 14:186–203.

Bolling, Keith, Catherine Grant, and Jeri-Lee Donovan. 2009. *2008–9 British Crime Survey (England and Wales) Technical Report*. Vol. I, 2nd ed. London: Home Office RDS.

Bouchard, Martin. 2007. "A Capture-Recapture Method to Estimate the Size of Criminal Populations and the Risks of Detection in a Marijuana Cultivation Industry." *Journal of Quantitative Criminology* 23:221–41.

Bouchard, Martin, Eric Beauregard, and Margaret Kalacska. 2013. "Journey to Grow: Linking Process to Outcome in Target Site Selection for Cannabis Cultivation." *Journal of Research in Crime and Delinquency* 50:33–52.

Bourgois, Philippe. 2002. *In Search of Respect: Selling Crack in El Barrio (Structural Analysis in the Social Sciences)*. Cambridge: Cambridge University Press.

Bowen, Glenn. 2008. "Supporting a Grounded Theory with an Audit Trail." *International Journal of Social Research Methodology* 12(4):305–16.

Bowers, Kate J., and Shane D. Johnson. 2013. *Understanding Theft of "Hot Products."* Problem solving tools series. Washington, D.C.: U.S. Department of Justice, Office of Community Oriented Policing Services.

Braga, Anthony A. 2008a. *Problem-Oriented Policing and Crime Prevention*, 2nd ed. Monsey, NY: Criminal Justice Press.

Braga, Anthony A. 2008b. "Pulling Levers Focused Deterrence Strategies and the Prevention of Gun Homicide." *Journal of Criminal Justice* 36:332–43.

Braga, Anthony A. 2016. "The Continued Importance of Measuring Potentially Harmful Impacts of Crime Prevention Programs: The Academy of Experimental Criminology 2014 Joan McCord Lecture." *Journal of Experimental Criminology* 12(1):1–20.

Braga, Anthony A., and Brenda J. Bond. 2008. "Policing Crime and Disorder Hot Spots: A Randomized Controlled Trial." *Criminology* 46(3):577–607.

Braga, Anthony A., David M. Kennedy, Elin J. Waring, and Anne Morrison Piehl. 2001. "Problem-Oriented Policing and Youth Violence: An Evaluation of Boston's Operation Ceasefire." *Journal of Research in Crime and Delinquency* 38(3, August):195–225.

Braga, Anthony A., Andrew V. Papachristos, and David M. Hureau. 2014. "The Effects of Hot Spots Policing on Crime: An Updated Systematic Review and Meta-Analysis." *Justice Quarterly* 31:633–63.

Braga, Anthony A., Anne M. Piehl, and David Hureau. 2009. "Controlling Violent Offenders Released to the Community: An Evaluation of the Boston Re-Entry Initiative." *Journal of Research in Crime and Delinquency* 46:411–36.

Brantingham, Paul J., and Patricia L. Brantingham. 1984. *Patterns in Crime*. NY: Macmillan.

Brantingham, Paul J., and Patricia L. Brantingham. 1991. "Introduction." In *Environmental Criminology*. 2nd ed., Paul J. Brantingham and Patricia L. Brantingham (Eds.). Prospect Heights, IL: Waveland.

Brantingham, Paul J., and Patricia L. Brantingham (Eds.). 1991. *Environmental Criminology*. 2nd ed. Prospect Heights, IL: Waveland.

Brantingham, Paul J., and C. Ray Jeffery. 1991. "Afterword: Crime, Space, and Criminological Theory." In *Environmental Criminology*. 2nd ed., Paul J. Brantingham and Patricia L. Brantingham (Eds.). Prospect Heights, IL: Waveland, 227–37.

Bratton, William J. 1999. "Great Expectations: How Higher Expectations for Police Departments Can Lead to a Decrease in Crime." In *Measuring What Matters*. Proceedings from the Policing Research Institute meetings, Robert Langworthy (Ed.). Washington, D.C.: U.S. Department of Justice, Office of Justice Programs, National Institute of Justice, 11–26.

Brotherton, David, and Luis Barrios. 2004. *The Almighty Latin King and Queen Nation*. New York: Columbia University Press.

Brown, Rick, and Ronald V. Clarke. 2004. "Police Intelligence and Theft of Vehicles for Export: Recent U.K. Experience." In *Understanding and Preventing Car Theft*, Michael G. Maxfield and Ronald V. Clarke (Eds.). Crime prevention studies, vol. 17. Monsey, NY: Criminal Justice Press, 173–92.

Brownstein, Henry H. 1996. *The Rise and Fall of a Violent Crime Wave: Crack Cocaine and the Social Construction of a Crime Problem*. Guilderland, NY: Harrow and Heston.

Buhrmester, Michael, Tarcy Kwang, and Samuel D. Gosling. 2011. "Amazon's Mechanical Turk: A New Source of Inexpensive, Yet High-Quality Data?" *Perspectives on Psychological Science* 6:3–5.

Bureau of Justice Assistance. 1993. *A Police Guide to Surveying Citizens and Their Environment*. Washington, D.C.: U.S. Department of Justice, Office of Justice Programs, Bureau of Justice Assistance, NCJ-143711.

Bureau of Justice Statistics. 1996. *Criminal Victimization in the United States, 1993*. Washington, D.C.: U.S. Department of Justice, Office of Justice Programs, Bureau of Justice Statistics.

Burgess, Ernest W. 1925. "The Growth of the City." In *The City: Chicago*, Robert E. Park, Ernest W. Burgess, and Roderic D. McKenzie (Eds.). Chicago, IL: University of Chicago Press.

Butts, Jeffrey. 2015. "Cursing the Darkness," LinkedIn Post.

Butts, Jeffrey A., Catriona Gouvis Roman, Lindsay Bostwick, and Jeremy Porter. 2015. "Cure Violence: A Public Health Model to Reduce Gun Violence." *Annual Review of Public Health* 36:39–53.

Campbell, Donald T. 1979. "Assessing the Impact of Planned Social Change." *Evaluation and Program Planning* 2:67–90.

Campbell, Donald T. 2003. "Introduction." In *Case Study Research: Design and Methods*. 3rd ed., Robert K. Yin. Thousand Oaks, CA: Sage Publications, ix–xi.

Campbell, Donald T., and Julian Stanley. 1966. *Experimental and Quasi-Experimental Designs for Research*. Chicago: Rand McNally.

Canter, David, and Samantha Hodge. 2000. "Criminals' Mental Maps." In *Atlas of Crime: Mapping the Criminal Landscape*, Linda S. Turnbull and Elaine Halsey Hendriz (Eds.). Phoenix, AZ: Oryx Press, 187–91.

Cantor, David, and James P. Lynch. 2005. "Exploring the Effects of Changes in Design on the Analytical Uses of the NCVS Data." *Journal of Quantitative Criminology* 21(3):293–319.

Carson, E. Ann, and Daniela Golinelli. 2013. *Prisoners in 2012*. BJS Bulletin. Washington, D.C.: U.S. Department of Justice, Office of Justice Programs, Bureau of Justice Statistics.

Carver, Jay, Kathryn R. Boyer, and Ronald Hickey. 1996. "Management Information Systems and Drug Courts: The District of Columbia Approach." *Paper presented at the Annual Training Conference of the National Association of Drug Court Professionals*. Washington, D.C.: District of Columbia Pretrial Services Agency.

Center for Behavioral Health Statistics and Quality. 2015. *Behavioral Health Trends in the United States: Results from the 2014 National Survey of Drug Use and Health: Summary of National Findings*. HHS Publication No. SMA 15-4927. Rockville, MD: Center for Behavioral Health Statistics and Quality, Substance Abuse and Mental Health Services Administration, http://www.samhsa.gov/data/sites/default/files/NSDUH -FRR1-2014/NSDUH-FRR1-2014.pdf.

Center for Urban Pedagogy. 2011. *Field Guide to Federalism: Bushwick, Brooklyn, NY*. Comic book. *Brooklyn, NY: Center for Urban Pedagogy, Making Public Policy*, http://welcometocup .org/Store?product_id=29.

Chaiken, Jan M., and Marcia R. Chaiken. 1982. *Varieties of Criminal Behavior*. Santa Monica, CA: Rand.

Chaiken, Jan M., and Marcia R. Chaiken. 1990. "Drugs and Predatory Crime." In *Crime and Justice: A Review of Research: Vol. 13. Drugs and Crime*, Michael Tonry and James Q. Wilson (Eds.). Chicago: University of Chicago Press.

Chainey, Spencer, and Jerry Ratcliffe. 2005. *GIS and Crime Mapping*. New York: Wiley.

Chandler, Redonna K., et al. 2009. "Ensuring Safety, Implementation and Scientific Integrity of Clinical Trials: Lessons from the Criminal Justice-Drug Abuse Treatment Studies Data and Safety Monitoring Board." *Journal of Experimental Criminology* 5:323–44.

Chermak, Steven M., and Alexander Weiss. 1997. "The Effects of the Media on Federal Criminal Justice Policy." *Criminal Justice Policy Review* 8(4): 323–41.

Chicago Community Policing Evaluation Consortium. 2004. *Community Policing in Chicago, Year Ten*. Chicago: Illinois Criminal Justice Information Authority.

Chin, Ko-lin, and James O. Finckenauer. 2012. *Selling Sex Overseas: Chinese Women and the Realities of Prostitution and Global Sex Trafficking*. New York: New York University Press.

Church, Wesley T., et al. 2008. "The Community Attitudes Toward Sex Offenders Scale: The Development of a Psychometric Assessment Instrument." *Research on Social Work Practice* 18:251–59.

City of New York. 2006. "Police Department." Supplementary Tables. In *Preliminary Fiscal 2006 Mayor's Management Report*. City of New York: Office of the Mayor, http://www.nyc.gov/ html/ops/downloads/pdf/_mmr/nypd_wi.pdf.

City University of New York, Human Research Protection Program. 2013. "CUNY HRPP Policy: Prisoners as Research Subjects," http://www.cuny.edu/research/compliance/human-subjects -research-1/hrpp-policies-procedures/Prisoners.pdf.

Clarke, Ronald V. 1997a. "Deterring Obscene Phone Callers: The New Jersey Experience." In *Situational Crime Prevention: Successful Case Studies*. 2nd ed., Ronald V. Clarke (Ed.). New York: Harrow and Heston, 90–97.

Clarke, Ronald V. 1997b. "Introduction." In *Situational Crime Prevention: Successful Case Studies*. 2nd ed., Ronald V. Clarke (Ed.). New York: Harrow and Heston, 2–43.

Clarke, Ronald V. 2008. "Situational Crime Prevention." In *Environmental Criminology and Crime Analysis*, Richard Wortley and Lorraine Mazerolle. (Eds.) Cullompton, Devon, UK: Willan Publishing, 178–220.

Clarke, Ronald V. 2017 (forthcoming). "Situational Crime Prevention." In *Environmental Criminology and Crime Analysis* 2nd ed. Richard Wortley and Michael Townsley (Eds.). PL. London: Routledge.

Clarke, Ronald V., and John Eck. 2005. *Crime Analysis for Problem Solvers in 60 Small Steps*. Washington: U.S. Department of Justice, Office of Community Oriented Policing, http://www .popcenter.org.

Clarke, Ronald V., and Patricia M. Harris. 1992. "Auto Theft and Its Prevention," Michael Tonry (Ed.). Crime and justice: An annual review of research, vol. 16. Chicago, IL: University of Chicago Press, 1–54.

Clarke, Ronald V., Rick Kemper, and Laura Wyckoff. 2001. "Controlling Cell Phone Fraud in the US: Lessons for the UK 'foresight' Initiative." *Security Journal* 14(1, January): 7–22.

Clarke, Ronald V., and Patricia Mayhew. 1980. *Designing Out Crime*. London: Her Majesty's Stationery Office.

Clarke, Ronald V., and Graeme R. Newman. 2006. *Outsmarting the Terrorists*. Westport, CT: Praeger Security International.

Clarke, Ronald V., and Phyllis A. Schultze. 2005. *Researching a Problem*. Tool Guide. Washington, D.C.: U.S. Department of Justice, Office of Community Oriented Policing Services, http://popcenter.org/Tools/tool-researchingProblem.htm.

Clarke, Ronald, Paul Ekblom, Mike Hough, and Pat Mayhew. 1985. "Elderly Victims of Crime and Exposure to Risk." *The Howard Journal* 24(1):1-9.

Cohen, Jaqueline, and Jens Ludwig. 2003. "Policing Crime Guns." In *Evaluating Gun Policy: Effects of Crime and Violence*, Jens Ludwig and Philip J. Cook (Eds.). Washington, D.C.: Brookings Institution Press, 217-39.

Cohen, Lawrence E., and Marcus Felson. 1979. "Social Change and Crime Rate Trends: A Routine Activity Approach." *American Sociological Review* 44:588-608.

Coleman, Clive, and Jenny Moynihan. 1996. *Understanding Crime Data: Haunted by the Dark Figure*. Buckingham: Open University Press.

Coleman, Veronica, et al. 1999. "Using Knowledge and Teamwork to Reduce Crime." *National Institute of Justice Journal* (October): 16-23.

Committee on Science, Engineering, and Public Policy. 2009. *On Being a Scientist: Responsible Conduct in Research*. 3rd ed. Washington, D.C.: National Academy Press.

Conover, Ted. 2000. *Newjack: Guarding Sing Sing*. NY: Random House.

Copes, Heith, Andy Hochstetler, and Michael Cherbonneau. 2012. "Getting the Upper Hand: Scripts for Managing Victim Resistance in Carjackings." *Journal of Research in Crime and Delinquency* 49 (May):249-68.

Corbin, Juliet, and Anselm Strauss. 2007. *Basics of Qualitative Research*. 3rd ed. Thousand Oaks, CA: Sage Publications.

Cornish, D.B., and Ronald V. Clarke (Eds.). 1986. *The Reasoning Criminal: Rational Choice Perspectives on Offending*. New York: Springer-Verlag.

Cornwell, J. Phillip, Michael J. Doherty, Eric L. Mitter, and Scarlet L. Drayer. 1989. *Roadside Observation Survey of Safety Belt Use in Indiana*. Bloomington, Indiana: Indiana University, Transportation Research Center.

Curtis, Ric, and Travis Wendel. 2007. "You're Always Training the Dog: Strategic Interventions to Reconfigure Drug Markets." *Journal of Drug Issues* 37:867-90.

D'Alessio, Stewart J., Lisa Stolzenberg, and W. Clinton Terry. 1999. "'Eyes on the Street': The Impact of Tennessee's Emergency Cellular Telephone Program on Alcohol Related Crashes." *Crime and Delinquency* 45(4):453-66.

Decker, Scott H. 2005. *Using Offender Interviews to Inform Police Problem Solving*. Problem solving tools series. Washington, D.C.: U.S. Department of Justice, Office of Community Oriented Policing Services.

Decker, Scott H., Susan Pennell, and Ami Caldwell. 1997. *Illegal Firearms: Access and Use by Arrestees*. Research in Brief. Washington, D.C.: U.S. Department of Justice, Office of Justice Programs, National Institute of Justice.

Decker, Scott H., and David C. Pyrooz. 2010. "On the Validity and Reliability of Gang Homicide: A Comparison of Disparate Sources." *Homicide Studies* 14:359-76.

Decker, Scott H., and Barrik Van Winkle. 1996. *Life in the Gang: Family, Friends, and Violence*. New York: Cambridge University Press.

del Frate, Anna Alvazzi, and Giulia Mugellini. 2012. "The Crime Drop in 'non-Western' Countries: A Review of Homicide Data." In *The International Crime Drop: New Directions in Research*, Jan van Dijk, Andromachi Tslenoi, and Graham Farrell (Eds.). Crime prevention studies, vol. 17. London: Palgrave, 134-55.

Delgado, Sheyla A., Kwan-Lamar Blount-Hill, Marissa Mandala, and Jeffrey A. Butts. 2015. *Perceptions of Violence: Surveying Young Males in New York City*. NY: Research and Evaluation Center, John Jay College of Criminal Justice, City University of New York.

Dennis, Michael L. 1990. "Assessing the Validity of Randomized Field Experiments: An Example from Drug Abuse Treatment Research." *Evaluation Review* 14:347-73.

Department of the Youth Authority. 1997. *LEAD: A Boot Camp and Intensive Parole Program: The Final Impact Evaluation*. Sacramento, CA: State of California, Department of the Youth Authority.

Dijk, Jan van. 2007. "The International Crime Victims Survey and Complementary Measures of Corruption and Organised Crime." In *Surveying Crime in the 21st Century*, Mike Hough and Mike Maxfield (Eds.). Crime prevention studies, vol. 22. Monsey, NY: Criminal Justice Press, 125-44.

Dillman, Don A., Jolene D. Smyth, and Leah Melani Christian. 2014. *Internet, Mail, and Mixed-Mode Surveys: The Tailored Design Method*. 4th ed. New York: Wiley.

Ditton, Jason, and Stephen Farrall. 2007. "The British Crime Survey and the Fear of Crime." In *Surveying Crime in the 21st Century*, Mike Hough and Mike Maxfield (Eds.). Crime prevention studies, vol. 22. Monsey, NY: Criminal Justice Press, 223-42.

Drucker, Peter F. 1973. *Management: Tasks, Responsibilities, Practices*. New York: Harper & Row, 103-06.

Duneier, Mitchell. 2000. *Sidewalk*. NY: Macmillan.

Durose, Matthew R., Erica L. Schmitt, and Patrick A. Langan. 2005. *Contacts Between Police and the Public: Findings from the 2002 National Survey*. Washington, D.C.: U.S. Department of Justice, Office of Justice Programs, Bureau of Justice Statistics.

Eck, John E. 2002. "Learning from Experience in Problem-Oriented Policing and Situational Prevention: The Positive Functions of Weak Evaluations and the Negative Functions of Strong Ones." In *Evaluation for Crime Prevention*, Nick Tilley (Ed.). Crime prevention studies, vol. 14. Monsey, NY: Criminal Justice Press, 93-117.

Eck, John E. 2003. *Assessing Responses to Problems: An Introductory Guide for Police Problem-Solvers*. Problem-Oriented Guides for Police. Washington, D.C.: U.S. Department of Justice, Office of Community Oriented Policing Services.

Eck, John, et al. 2005. *Mapping Crime: Understanding Hot Spots*. NIJ Special Report. Washington, D.C.: U.S. Department of Justice, Office of Justice Programs, National Institute of Justice.

Eger III, Robert J., C. Kevin Fortner, and Catherine P. Slade. 2015. "The Policy of Enforcement: Red Light Cameras and Racial Profiling." *Police Quarterly* 18(4):397-413.

Eisenberg, Michael. 1999. *Three Year Recidivism Tracking of Offenders Participating in Substance Abuse Treatment Programs*. Austin, TX: Criminal Justice Policy Council.

Eisenstein, James, and Herbert Jacob. 1977. *Felony Justice: An Organizational Analysis of Criminal Courts.* Boston, MA: Little, Brown.

Ekici, Niyazi. 2008. *The Dynamics of Terrorist Recruitment: The Case of the Revolutionary People's Liberation Party/Front (DHKP/C) and the Turkish Hezbollah.* Unpublished Ph.D., dissertation. Newark, NJ: School of Criminal Justice, Rutgers University.

Elliott, Delbert S., David Huizinga, and Suzanne S. Ageton. 1985. *Explaining Delinquency and Drug Use.* Thousand Oaks, CA: Sage.

Ely, Margot, et al. 1991. *Doing Qualitative Research: Circles Within Circles.* Philadelphia: Falmer.

Engel, Robin Shepard, Jennifer M. Calnon, Lin Liu, and Richard Johnson. 2004. *Project on Police-Citizen Contacts: Year 1 Final Report.* Cincinnati, OH: Criminal Justice Research Center, University of Cincinnati.

Engel, Robin Shepard, and Jennifer M. Calnon. 2004. "Comparing Benchmark Methodologies for Police-Citizen Contacts: Traffic Stop Data Collection for the Pennsylvania State Police." *Police Quarterly* 7:97–125, Pdf poldocs.

Engel, Robin Shepard, et al. 2005. *Project on Police-Citizen Contacts: Year 2 Final Report.* Cincinnati, OH: Criminal Justice Research Center, University of Cincinnati.

Eterno, John A., and Ira B. Silverman. 2010. "The NYPD's Compstat: Compare Statistics or Compose Statistics." *International Journal of Police Science and Management* 12(3):426–49.

Fabelo, Tony. 1995. "What Is Recidivism? How Do You Measure It? What Can It Tell Policy Makers?" *Bulletin from the Executive Director, number 19.* Austin, TX: Criminal Justice Policy Council.

Farrell, Graham, and Alistair Buckley. 1999. "Evaluation of a UK Police Domestic Violence Unit Using Repeat Victimisation as a Performance Indicator." *The Howard Journal of Criminal Justice* 38(1, February): 42–53.

Farrell, Graham, Alan Edmunds, Louise Hibbs, and Gloria Laycock. 2000. *RV Snapshot: UK Policing and Repeat Victimisation.* Crime Reduction Research Series, paper 5. London: Home Office, Policing and Reducing Crime Unit, Research, Development and Statistics Directorate.

Farrell, Graham, Andromachi Tseloni, Jen Mailley, and Nick Tilley. 2011. "The Crime Drop and the Security Hypothesis." *Journal of Research in Crime and Delinquency* 48(2):147–75.

Farrington, David P., Patrick A. Langan, and Michael Tonry (Eds.). 2004. *Cross-National Studies in Crime and Justice.* Washington, D.C.: U.S. Department of Justice, Office of Justice Programs, Bureau of Justice Statistics.

Farrington, David P., Trevor H. Bennett, and Brandon C. Welsh. 2007. "The Cambridge Evaluation of the Effects of CCTV on Crime." In *Imagination for Crime Prevention: Essays in Honour of Ken Pease,* Graham Farrell, Kate J. Bowers, Shane D. Johnson, and Michael Townsley (Eds.). Crime prevention studies, vol. 21. Monsey, NY: Criminal Justice Press, 187–201.

Farrington, David P., Patrick A. Langan, Michael Tonry, and Darrick Jolliffe. 2004. "Introduction." In *Cross-National Studies in Crime and Justice,* David P. Farrington, Patrick A. Langan, and Michael Tonry (Eds.). Washington, D.C.: U.S. Department of Justice, Office of Justice Programs, Bureau of Justice Statistics, v–xvi.

Farrington, David P., Lloyd E. Ohlin, and James Q. Wilson. 1986. *Understanding and Controlling Crime: Toward a New Research Strategy.* New York: Springer-Verlag.

Farrington, David P., et al. 1993. "An Experiment in the Prevention of Shoplifting." In *Crime Prevention Studies.* Vol. 1, Ronald V. Clarke (Ed.). Monsey, NY: Criminal Justice Press, 93–119.

Farrington, David P., et al. 1996. "Self-Reported Delinquency and a Combined Delinquency Seriousness Scale Based on Boys, Mothers, and Teachers: Concurrent and Predictive Validity for African-Americans and Caucasians." *Criminology* 34:493–517.

Fay, Robert E., and Mamadou Diallo. 2015. *Developmental Estimates of Subnational Crime Rates Based on the National Crime Victimization Survey.* BJS Research and Development Paper. Washington, D.C.: Bureau of Justice Statistics.

Federal Bureau of Investigation, 2015. *2014 National Incident-Based Reporting System.* Washington, D.C.: U.S. Department of Justice, Federal Bureau of Investigation, Web page: https://www.fbi.gov/about-us/cjis/ucr/nibrs/2014.

Federal Bureau of Investigation. 2000. *National Incident-Based Reporting System.* Volume 1: Data collection guidelines. Washington, D.C.: U.S. Department of Justice, Federal Bureau of Investigation.

Federal Bureau of Investigation. 2002. *Crime in the United States 2001.* Washington, D.C.: U.S. Department of Justice, Federal Bureau of Investigation, http://www.fbi.gov/ucr/01cius.htm.

Federal Bureau of Investigation. 2004. *Uniform Crime Reporting Handbook.* Washington, D.C.: U.S. Department of Justice, Federal Bureau of Investigation.

Federal Bureau of Investigation. 2009. *Crime in the United States 2008.* Washington, D.C.: U.S. Department of Justice, Federal Bureau of Investigation, http://www2.fbi.gov/ucr/cius2008/about/index.html.

Federal Bureau of Investigation. 2011. *Crime in the United States 2010: Methodology.* Washington, D.C.: U.S. Department of Justice, Federal Bureau of Investigation, http://www.fbi.gov.

Federal Bureau of Investigation. 2012. *About Crime in the United States 2012.* Washington, D.C.: U.S. Department of Justice, Federal Bureau of Investigation, http://www.fbi.gov/about-us/ucr/crime-in-the-u.s/2012.

Federal Bureau of Investigation. 2015. *Crime in the United States 2014.* Washington, D.C.: U.S. Department of Justice, Federal Bureau of Investigation, http://www.fbi.gov.

Federal Trade Commission. 2016. *Consumer Sentinel Network Data Book for January - December 2015.* Washington, D.C.: Federal Trade Commission, https://www.ftc.gov/system/files/documents/reports/consumer-sentinel-network-data-book-january-december-2015/160229csn-2015databook.pdf.

Felson, Marcus. 2002. *Crime and Everyday Life.* 3rd ed. Thousand Oaks, CA: Sage.

Felson, Marcus, and Ronald V. Clarke. 1998. *Opportunity Makes the Thief: Practical Theory for Crime Prevention.* Police Research Series, paper 98. London: Home Office, Policing and Reducing Crime Unit, Research, Development and Statistics Directorate.

Felson, Marcus, et al. 1996. "Redesigning Hell: Preventing Crime and Disorder at the Port Authority Bus Terminal." In *Preventing Mass Transit Crime,* Ronald V. Clarke (Ed.). Crime prevention studies, vol. 6. Monsey, NY: Criminal Justice Press, 5–92.

Ferrell, Jeff. 2002. *Tearing Down the Streets: Adventures in Urban Anarchy.* London: Palgrave/Macmillan.

Finkelhor, David, and Lisa M. Jones. 2004. *Explanations for the Decline in Child Sexual Abuse Cases*. Juvenile Justice Bulletin. Washington, D.C.: U.S. Department of Justice, Office of Justice Programs, Office of Juvenile Justice and Delinquency Prevention.

Fisher, Bonnie S., Francis T. Cullen, and Michael G. Turner. 2000. *The Sexual Victimization of College Women*. Washington, D.C.: U.S. Department of Justice, Office of Justice Programs, Burea of Justice Statistics, NCJ-182369.

Flick, Uwe. 2009. *An Introduction to Qualitative Research*. 4th ed. Thousand Oaks, CA: Sage Publications.

Freilich, Joshua D., et al. 2015. "Investigating the Applicability of Macro-Level Criminology Theory to Terrorism: A County-Level Analysis." *Journal of Quantitative Criminology* 31:383–411.

Fridell, Lorie A. 2005. *Understanding Race Data from Vehicle Stops: A Stakeholder's Guide*. Washington, D.C.: Police Executive Research Forum.

Fridell, Lorie. 2004. *By the Numbers: A Guide for Analyzing Race Data from Vehicle Stops*. Washington, D.C.: Police Executive Research Forum.

Fujita, Shuryo. 2011. "Why Are Older Cars Stolen? Examining Motive, Availability, Location, and Security." Unpublished Ph.D., dissertation. Newark, NJ: Rutgers University.

Gant, Frances, and Peter Grabosky. 2001. *The Stolen Vehicle Parts Market*. Trends and Issues, no. 215. Canberra, Australia: Australian Institute of Criminology.

Gau, Jacinta M. 2010. "The Convergent and Discriminant Validity of Procedural Justice and Police Legitimacy: An Empirical Test of Core Theoretical Propositions." *Journal of Criminal Justice* 39:489–98.

Geerken, Michael R. 1994. "Rap Sheets in Criminological Research: Considerations and Caveats." *Journal of Quantitative Criminology* 10(1):3–21.

Geertz, Clifford. 1973. *The Interpretation of Cultures*. NY: Basic Books.

General Accounting Office. 1996. *Content Analysis: A Methodology for Structuring and Analyzing Written Material*. Transfer paper 10.3.1. Washington, D.C.: U.S. General Accounting Office.

Gfroerer, Joseph, and Joel Kennet. 2014. "Collecting Survey Data on Sensitive Topics: Substance Use." Chapter 17. In *Health Survey Methods*, Timothy P. Johnson (Ed.). Hoboken, NJ: John Wiley and Sons.

Gill, Martin, and Angela Spriggs. 2005. *Assessing the Impact of CCTV*. Home Office Research Study, 292. London: Her Majesty's Stationery Office.

Gladwell, Malcolm. 2005. *Blink: The Power of Thinking Without Thinking*. NY: Little, Brown.

Glaser, Barney G., and Anselm Strauss. 1967. *The Discovery of Grounded Theory*. Chicago: University of Chicago Press.

Glassbrenner, Donna. 2005. *Safety Belt Use in 2005: Overall Results*. Research note (DOT HS 809 932). Washington, D.C.: U.S. Department of Transportation, National Highway Traffic Safety Administration, National Center for Statistics and Analysis.

Goffman, Alice. 2014. *On the Run: Fugitive Life in an American City*. Chicago: University of Chicago press.

Goffman, Erving. 1959. *The Presentation of Self in Everyday Life*. NY: Random House.

Gottfredson, Denise C., Stacy S. Najaka, Brook W. Kearly, and Carlos M. Rocha. 2006. "Long-Term Effects of Participation in the Baltimore City Drug Treatment Court: Results from an Experimental Study." *Journal of Experimental Criminology* 2:67–98.

Gottfredson, Michael R. 1984. *Victims of Crime: The Dimensions of Risk*. Home Office Research Study, 81. London: Her Majesty's Stationery Office.

Gottfredson, Michael R., and Travis Hirschi. 1990. *A General Theory of Crime*. Stanford, CA: Stanford University Press.

Grabe, Marie Elizabeth, K.D. Trager, Melissa Lear, and Jennifer Rauch. 2006. "Gender in Crime News: A Case Study Test of the Chivalry Hypothesis." *Mass Communication and Society* 9(2):137–63.

Graham, Kathryn, and Ross Homel. 2008. *Raising the Bar: Preventing Aggression in and Around Bars and Clubs*. Portland, OR: Willan Publishing.

Greaves, Caroline, et al. 2004. "Pimping and Psychopathy." American Psychology and Law Society's Annual Conference. Scottsdale, AZ.

Greenwood, Peter W., and Joan Petersilia. 1975. *The Criminal Investigation Process*. Santa Monica, CA: RAND Corporation.

Guba, Egon G. 1981. "Criteria for Assessing the Trustworthiness of Naturalistic Inquiries." *Educational Communication and Technology* 29(2):75–91.

Guerette, Rob T. 2009. *Analyzing Crime Displacement and Diffusion*. Problem solving tools series. Washington, D.C.: U.S. Department of Justice, Office of Community Oriented Policing Services.

Guerette, Rob T., and Kate J. Bowers. 2009. "Assessing the Extent of Crime Displacement and Diffusion of Benefits." *Criminology* 47(4):1331–68.

Gurr, Ted Robert. 1989. "Historical Trends in Violent Crime: Europe and the United States." In *Violence in America: The History of Crime*, Ted Robert Gurr (Ed.). Thousand Oaks, CA: Sage.

Haney, Craig, Curtis Banks, and Philip Zimbardo. 1973. "Interpersonal Dynamics in a Simulated Prison." *International Journal of Criminology and Penology* 1:69–97.

Haninger, Kevin, and Kimberly M. Thompson. 2004. "Content and Ratings of Teen-Rated Video Games." *Journal of the American Medical Association* 291(7, 18 February):856–65.

Hanmer, Jalna, Sue Griffiths, and David Jerwood. 1999. *Arresting Evidence: Domestic Violence and Repeat Victimisation*. Police Research Series, paper 104. London: Home Office, Policing and Reducing Crime Unit, Research, Development and Statistics Directorate.

Harocopos, Alex, and Mike Hough. 2005. *Drug Dealing in Open-Air Markets*. Problem-Oriented Guides for Police, no. 31. Washington, D.C.: U.S. Department of Justice, Office of Community Oriented Policing Services.

Harris, David A. 1999. "The Stories, the Statistics, and the Law: Why 'Driving While Black' Matters." *Minnesota Law Review* 84:265–326.

Harris, Kathleen Mullan, and J. Richard Udry. 2014. *National Longitudinal Study of Adolescent Health (Add Health)*. Chapel Hill, NC and Ann Arbor, MI: Carolina Population Research Center, University of North Carolina-Chapel Hill, Inter-university Consortium for Political and Social Research, http://doi.org/10.3886/ICPSR21600.v15.

Heeren, Timothy, Robert A. Smith, Suzette Morelock, and Ralph W. Hingson. 1985. "Surrogate Measures of Alcohol

Involvement in Fatal Crashes: Are Conventional Indicators Adequate?" *Journal of Safety Research* 16(3):127–34.

Hempel, Carl G. 1952. "Fundamentals of Concept Formation in Empirical Science." In *International Encyclopedia of Unified Science: Foundations of the Unity of Science*. Vol. 2. Chicago: University of Chicago Press.

Hermanowicz, Joseph C. 2002. "The Great Interview: 25 Strategies for Studying People in Bed." *Qualitative Sociology* 25(4): 479–99.

Hesseling, René B.P. 1994. "Displacement: A Review of the Empirical Literature." In *Crime Prevention Studies*. Vol. 3, Ronald V. Clarke (Ed.). Monsey, NY: Criminal Justice Press, 197–230.

Heumann, Milton, and Colin Loftin. 1979. "Mandatory Sentencing and the Abolition of Plea Bargaining: The Michigan Felony Firearm Statute." *Law and Society Review* 13(2):393–430.

Hickman, Matthew J. 2005. *Traffic Stop Data Collection Policies for State Police, 2004*. Fact Sheet. Washington, D.C.: U.S. Department of Justice, Office of Justice Programs, Bureau of Justice Statistics.

Highfield, Roger, and Paul Carter. 1994. *The Private Lives of Albert Einstein*. NY: Macmillan.

Highway Loss Data Institute. 2011. *Insurance Theft Report: 2008–10 Passenger Cars, Pickups, SUVs, and Vans*. Arlington, VA: Highway Loss Data Institute, http://www.iihs.org/research/hldi/composite_bw.aspx?y=2008-2010&cv=com.

Highway Loss Data Institute. 2016. *Insurance Losses by Make and Model*. Arlington, VA: Highway Loss Data Institute, http://www.iihs.org/iihs/topics/insurance-loss-information. Accessed 3 March 2016.

Hindelang, Michael J., Michael R. Gottfredson, and James Garofalo. 1978. *Victims of Personal Crime: An Empirical Foundation for a Theory of Personal Victimization*. Cambridge, MA: Ballinger.

Holstein, Jaber A., and James F. Gubrium. 1995. *The Active Interview*. Thousand Oaks, CA: Sage Publications.

Homel, Ross, and Jeff Clark. 1994. "The Prediction and Prevention of Violence in Pubs and Clubs." In *Crime Prevention Studies*. Vol. 3, Ronald V. Clarke (Ed.). Monsey, NY: Criminal Justice Press, 1–46.

Homel, Ross, Steve Tomsen, and Jennifer Thommeny. 1992. "Public Drinking and Violence: Not Just an Alcohol Problem." *Journal of Drug Issues* 22(3):679–97.

Hood-Williams, John, and Tracey Bush. 1995. "Domestic Violence on a London Housing Estate." *Research Bulletin* 37:11–18.

Humphreys, Laud. 1975. *The Tearoom Trade*. Enlarged edition with perspectives on ethical issues. Chicago: Aldine.

Hunter, Rosemary S., and Nancy Kilstrom. 1979. "Breaking the Cycle in Abusive Families." *American Journal of Psychiatry* 136(10):1318–22.

Idaho State Police. 2016. *Crime in Idaho 2015*. Meridian, ID: Idaho State Police, Bureau of Criminal Identification, Uniform Crime Reporting Section, https://www.isp.idaho.gov/BCI/CrimeInIdaho/CrimeInIdaho2015.

Inciardi, James A. 1986. *The War on Drugs: Heroin, Cocaine, Crime, and Public Policy*. Palo Alto, CA: Mayfield.

Inciardi, James A. 1993. "Some Considerations on the Methods, Dangers, and Ethics of Crack-House Research." Appendix A, James A. Inciardi, Dorothy Lockwood, and Anne E. Pettieger. In *Women and Crack Cocaine*. New York: Macmillan, 147–57.

Jackson, Peter. 1989. *Maps of Meaning: An Introduction to Cultural Geography*. NY: Routledge.

Jacob, Herbert. 1984. *Using Published Data: Errors and Remedies*. Thousand Oaks, CA: Sage.

Jacobs, Bruce A. 1996. "Crack Dealers' Apprehension Avoidance Techniques: A Case of Restrictive Deterrence." *Justice Quarterly* 13(3):359–81.

Jacobs, Bruce A. 1999. *Dealing Crack: The Social World of Streetcorner Selling*. Boston: Northeastern University Press.

Jacobs, Bruce A. 2012. "Carjacking and Copresence." *Journal of Research in Crime and Delinquency* 49 (May):471–78.

Jacobs, Bruce A., and Jody Miller. 1998. "Crack Dealing, Gender, and Arrest Avoidance." *Social Problems* 45(4):550–69.

Jacobs, Bruce A., Volkan Topalli, and Richard Wright. 2003. "Carjacking, Streetlife and Offender Motivation." *British Journal of Criminology* 43(4):673–88, Pdf autodocs.

Jacobs, Bruce. 2006. "The Case for Dangerous Fieldwork." In *The SAGE Handbook of Fieldwork*. Crime prevention studies, vol. 17. Thousand Oaks, CA: Sage, 157–69.

Jacques, Scott, and Danielle Reynald. 2012. "The Offenders' Perspective on Prevention: Guarding Against Victimization and Law Enforcement." *Journal of Research in Crime and Delinquency* 49(2):269–94.

Jacques, Scott, and Richard Wright. 2008. "Intimacy with Outlaws: The Role of Relational Distance in Recruiting, Paying, and Interviewing Underworld Research Participants." *Journal of Research in Crime and Delinquency* 45 (February):22–38.

Jagatic, Tom N., Nathaniel A. Johnson, Markus Jakobsson, and Filippo Menczer. 2007. "Social Phishing." *Communications of the ACM* 50(10):94–100.

Janis, Irving. 1972. *Victims of Groupthink*. NY: Houghton Mifflin.

Järvinen, Margaretha. 2000. "The Biological Illusion: Constructing Meaning in Qualitative Interviews." *Qualitative Inquiry* 6(3):370–91.

Jeffery, C. Ray. 1977. *Crime Prevention Through Environmental Design*. 2nd ed. Thousand Oaks, CA: Sage.

Johansen, Ditte, Karina Friis, Erik Skovenborg, and Morten Gronbaek. 2006. "Food Buying Habits of People Who Buy Wine or Beer: Cross Sectional Study." *BMJ* 332.7540: 519–322, http://bmj.bmjjournals.com/onlinefirst_date.shtml. BMJ, doi:10.1136/bmj.38694.568981.80.

Johansen, Helle Krogh, and Peter C. Gotzsche. 1999. "Problems in the Design and Reporting of Trials of Antifungal Agents Encountered During Meta-Analysis." *Journal of the American Medical Association* 282(18, 10 November):1752–59.

Johnson, Ida M. 1999. "School Violence: The Effectiveness of a School Resource Officer Program in a Southern City." *Journal of Criminal Justice* 27(2):173–92.

Johnson, Shane D., Aiden Sidebottom, and Adam Thorpe. 2008. *Bicycle Theft*. Problem-Oriented Guides for Police, no. 52. Washington, D.C.: U.S. Department of Justice, Office of Community Oriented Policing Services.

Johnston, Lloyd D., et al. 2016. *Monitoring the Future National Results on Drug Use 1975–2015: Overview, Key Findings on Adolescent Drug Use*. Ann Arbor, MI: Institute for Social Research, The University of Michigan.

Jones-Brown, Delores, Jaspreet Gill, and Jennifer Trone. 2010. *Stop, Question & Frisk Practices in New York City: A Primer*. New York: Center on Race, Crime, and Justice, John Jay College of Criminal Justice.

Justice Research and Statistics Association. 1996. *Domestic and Sexual Violence Data Collection*. Report to Congress under the Violence against Women Act. Washington, D.C.: U.S. Department of Justice, Office of Justice Programs, National Institute of Justice and Bureau of Justice Assistance.

Kaplan, Abraham. 1964. *The Conduct of Inquiry*. San Francisco, CA: Chandler.

Katz, Charles M., Vincent J. Webb, and Scott H. Decker. 2005. "Using the Arrestee Drug Abuse Monitoring (ADAM) Program to Further Understand the Relation Between Drug Use and Gang Membership." *Justice Quarterly* 22:58–88.

Katz, Jack. 1988. *Seductions of Crime: Moral and Sensual Attractions in Doing Evil*. New York: Basic Books.

Kazemian, Lila, and David P. Farrington. 2005. "Comparing the Validity of Prospective, Retrospective, and Official Onset for Different Offending Categories." *Journal of Quantitative Criminology* 21(2):127–47.

Kelling, George L., and Catherine M. Coles. 1996. *Fixing Broken Windows: Restoring Order and Reducing Crime in Our Communities*. New York: Free Press.

Kelling, George L., Tony Pate, Duane Dieckman, and Charles E. Brown. 1974. *The Kansas City Preventive Patrol Experiment: A Technical Report*. Washington, D.C.: Police Foundation.

Kennedy, David M. 1998. "Pulling Levers: Getting Deterrence Right." *National Institute of Justice Journal* 236 (July):2–8.

Kennedy, David M, Anne M. Piehl, and Anthony A. Braga. 1996. "Youth Gun Violence in Boston: Gun Markets, Serious Youth Offenders, and a Use Reduction Strategy." *Law and Contemporary Problems* 59(1, Winter):147–96.

Kennedy, M. Alexis, et al. 2007. "Routes of Recruitment: Pimps' Techniques and Other Circumstances That Lead to Street Prostitution." *Journal of Aggression, Maltreatment, and Trauma* 15(2):1–19.

Kennet, Joel, and Joseph Gfroerer (Eds.). 2005. *Evaluating and Improving Methods Used in the National Survey on Drug Use and Health*. Publication no. SMA 03-3768. DHHS Publication No. SMA 05-4044, Methodology Series M-5. Rockville, MD: Office of Applied Studies, Substance Abuse and Mental Health Services Administration, http://oas.samhsa.gov/nsduh/methods.cfm.

Kessler, David A. 1999. "The Effects of Community Policing on Complaints Against Officers." *Journal of Quantitative Criminology* 15(3):333–72.

Killias, Martin. 1993. "Gun Ownership, Suicide and Homicide: An International Perspective." *Canadian Medical Association Journal* 148(10):1721–25.

Killias, Martin, Marcelo F. Aebi, and Denis Ribeaud. 2000. "Learning Through Controlled Experiments: Community Service and Heroin Prescription in Switzerland." *Crime and Delinquency* 46(2):233–51.

Kindermann, Charles, James Lynch, and David Cantor. 1997. *Effects of the Redesign on Victimization Estimates*. Bureau of Justice Statistics National Crime Victimization Survey rept. Washington, D.C.: U.S. Department of Justice, Office of Justice Programs, Bureau of Justice Statistics.

Kipke, Michele D., Susan O'Connor, Burke Nelson, and John E. Anderson. 1998. "A Probability Sampling for Assessing the Effectiveness of Outreach for Street Youth." In *What We Have Learned from the AIDS Evaluation of Street Outreach Projects: A Summary Document*, Judith B. Greenberg and Mary S. Neumann. Atlanta, GA: U.S. Department of Health and Human Services, Centers for Disease Control and Prevention, 17–28.

Kirchner, Robert A., Roger Przybylski, and Ruth A. Cardella. 1994. Assessing the Effectiveness of Criminal Justice Programs. Assessment and evaluation handbook series, number 1. Washington, D.C.: U.S. Department of Justice, Office of Justice Programs, Bureau of Justice Assistance.

Kitsuse, John I., and Aaron V. Cicourel. 1963. "A Note on the Uses of Official Statistics." *Social Problems* 11:131–38.

Kounadi, Ourania, Kate Bowers, and Michael Leitner. 2014. "Crime Mapping on-Line: Public Perception of Privacy Issues." *European Journal on Criminal Policy and Research* (5, June).

Krueger, Richard A., and Mary Anne Casey. 2000. *Focus Groups: A Practical Guide for Applied Research*. 3rd ed. Thousand Oaks, CA: Sage.

Kreuter, Frauke, Stanley Presser, and Roger Tourangeau. 2008. "Social Desirability Bias in CATI, IVR, and Web Surveys: The Effects of Mode and Question Sensitivity." *Public Opinion Quarterly* 72:847–65.

Kubrin, Charis E., and Ronald Weitzer. 2003. "Retaliatory Homicide: Concentrated Disadvantage and Neighborhood Culture." *Social Problems* 50(2):157–80.

Kuhn, Thomas. 2012. *The Structure of Scientific Revolutions*. Edition no. 4. 50th anniversary edition. Chicago, IL: University of Chicago Press.

Kurti, Marin K., Klaus von Lampe, and Douglas E. Thompkins. 2013. "The Illegal Cigarette Market in a Socioeconomically Deprived Inner-City Area: The Case of the South Bronx." *Tobacco Control* 22:138–40.

Kuş Saillard, Elif. 2011. "Systematic Versus Interpretive Analysis with Two CAQDAS Packages: NVivo and MAXQDA." *Forum: Qualitative Social Research* 12:Art 34, http://nbn-resolving.de/urn:nbn:de:0114-fqs1101345.

Kvale, Steinar. 1996. *Interviews: An Introduction to Qualitative Research Interviewing*. Thousand Oaks, CA: Sage Publications.

Lamberth, John. 1998. "Driving While Black: A Statistician Proves That Prejudice Still Rules the Road." In *Washington Post* 16 August.

Lane, Roger. 1997. *Murder in America: A History*. Columbus, OH: Ohio State University Press.

Lange, James E., Mark B. Johnson, and Robert B. Voas. 2005. "Testing the Racial Profiling Hypothesis for Seemingly Disparate Traffic Stops on the New Jersey Turnpike." *Justice Quarterly* 22(2):193–223.

Langton, Lynn. 2011. *Identity Theft Reported by Households, 2005–2010*. Crime Data Brief. Washington, D.C.: U.S. Department of Justice, Office of Justice Programs, Bureau of Justice Statistics.

Langton, Lynn, and Matthew Durose. 2013. *Police Behavior During Traffic and Street Stops, 2011*. Special Report. Washington, D.C.: U.S. Department of Justice, Office of Justice Programs, Bureau of Justice Statistics.

Larson, Richard C. 1975. "What Happened to Patrol Operations in Kansas City? A Review of the Kansas City Preventive Patrol Experiment." *Journal of Criminal Justice* 3:267–97.

Latané, Bibb, and John M. Darley. 1970. *The Unresponsive Bystander: Why Doesn't He Help?* Englewood Cliffs, NJ: Prentice Hall.

Lauritsen, Janet L., and Robin J. Schaum. 2005. *Crime and Victimization in the Three Largest Metropolitan Areas, 1980–98*. Bureau of Justice Statistics Technical rept. Washington, D.C.: U.S.

Department of Justice, Office of Justice Programs, Bureau of Justice Statistics.

Lauritsen, Janet. 2005. "Social and Scientific Influences on the Measurement of Criminal Victimization." *Journal of Quantitative Criminology* 21:245–66.

Laycock, Gloria. 2002. "Methodological Issues in Working with Policy Advisers and Practitioners." In *Analysis for Crime Prevention*, Nick Tilley (Ed.). Crime prevention studies, vol. 13. Monsey, NY: Criminal Justice Press, 205–37.

Leclerc, Benoit, Richard Wortley, and Stephen Smallbone. 2011. "Getting Into the Script of Adult Child Sex Offenders and Mapping Out Situational Prevention Measures." *Journal of Research in Crime and Delinquency* 48(2):209–37.

Leiber, Michael J., and Jayne M. Stairs. 1999. "Race, Contexts, and the Use of Intake Diversion." *Journal of Research in Crime and Delinquency* 36(1):56–86.

Lemieux, Andrew M. 2015. "Geotagged Photos: A Useful Tool for Criminological Research?" *Crime Science* 4(3).

Lemieux, Andrew M., et al. 2014. "Tracking Poachers in Uganda: Spatial Models of Patrol Intensity and Patrol Efficiency." In *Situational Prevention of Poaching*, Andrew M Lemieux (Ed.). Crime prevention studies, vol. 17. London: Routledge, 102–19.

Lempert, Richard O. 1984. "From the Editor." *Law and Society Review* 18:505–13.

Levine, Robert. 1997. *A Geography of Time: The Temporal Misadventures of a Social Psychologist*. NY: Basic Books.

Levinson, Marc. 2007. *The Box: How the Shipping Container Made the World Smaller and the World Economy Bigger*. Princeton, NJ: Princeton University Press.

Lilly, J. Robert. 2006. "Issues Beyond Empirical EM Reports." *Criminology and Public Policy* 5(1, February):93–102.

Lineberry, Robert L. 1977. *American Public Policy*. New York: Harper and Row.

Loeber, Rolf, Magda Stouthamer-Loeber, Welmoetvan Kammen, and David P. Farrington. 1991. "Initiation, Escalation and Desistance in Juvenile Offending and Their Correlates." *Journal of Criminal Law and Criminology* 82(1):36–82.

Lofland, John, and Lyn H. Lofland (Eds.). 1995. *Analyzing Social Settings: A Guide to Qualitative Observation and Analysis, Part 2*. 3rd ed. Belmont, CA: Wadsworth.

Lopez, Natalie, and Chris Lukinbeal. 2010. "Comparing Police and Residents' Perceptions of Crime in a Phoenix Neighborhood Using Mental Maps in GIS." *Yearbook of the Association of Pacific Coast Geographers* 72:33–55.

Lopez, Patricia. 1992. "'He Said.. She Said..' an Overview of Date Rape from Commission Through Prosecution Through Verdict." *Criminal Justice Journal* 13:275–302.

Lucia, Sonia, Leslie Herrmann, and Martin Killias. 2007. "How Important Are Interview Methods and Questionnaire Designs in Research on Self-Reported Juvenile Delinquency? An Experimental Comparison of Internet Vs Paper-and-Pencil Questionnaires and Different Definitions of the Reference Period." *Journal of Experimental Criminology* 3:39–64.

Lynch, James P., and Lynn A. Addington (Eds.). 2007. *Understanding Crime Statistics: Revisiting the Divergence of the NCVS and the UCR*. NY: Cambridge University Press.

Maass, Dave. 2012. "County Misreports Data About Sexual Violence in Juvenile Jails." *San Diego City Beat*, 25 January.

MacKenzie, Doris Layton, Katherine Browning, Stacy B. Skroban, and Douglas A. Smith. 1999. "The Impact of Probation on the Criminal Activities of Offenders." *Journal of Research in Crime and Delinquency* 36(4):423–53.

MacKenzie, Doris Layton, James W. Shaw, and Voncile B. Gowdy. 1993. *An Evaluation of Shock Incarceration in Louisiana*. Research in Brief. Washington, D.C.: U.S. Department of Justice, Office of Justice Programs, National Institute of Justice.

Madaleno, Isabel Maria. 2010. "How Do Remote Southern Hemisphere Residents Perceive the World? Mental Maps Drawn by East Timorese and Mozambican Islanders." *Scottish Geographical Journal* 126:112–36.

Maher, Lisa. 1997. *Sexed Work: Gender, Race, and Resistance in a Brooklyn Drug Market*. Oxford: Clarendon Press.

Maltz, Michael D. 1994. "Deviating from the Mean: The Declining Significance of Significance." *Journal of Research in Crime and Delinquency* 31(4):434–63.

Maltz, Michael D. 1999. *Bridging Gaps: Estimating Crime Rates from Police Data*. A discussion paper from the BJS Fellows Program. Washington, D.C.: U.S. Department of Justice, Office of Justice Programs, Bureau of Justice Statistics.

Maltz, Michael D., and Marianne W. Zawitz. 1998. *Displaying Violent Crime Trends Using Estimates from the National Crime Victimization Survey*. Bureau of Justice Statistics Technical rept. Washington, D.C.: U.S. Department of Justice, Office of Justice Programs, Bureau of Justice Statistics, http://bjs.ojp.usdoj.gov/content/pub/pdf/dvctue.pdf.

Maltz, Michael, Andrew C. Gordon, David McDowall, and Richard McCleary. 1980. "An Artifact in Pretest-Posttest Designs: How It Can Mistakenly Make Delinquency Programs Look Effective." *Evaluation Review* 4:225–40.

Maple, Jack. 1999. *Crime Fighter: Putting the Bad Guys Out of Business*. In collaboration with Chris Mitchell. NY: Doubleday.

Marcus, Anthony, et al. 2012. "Is Child to Adult as Victim Is to Criminal? Social Policy and Street-Based Sex Work in the USA." *Sexuality Research and Social Policy* 9(2):153–66.

Marshall, Catherine, and Gretchen B. Rossman. 2006. *Designing Qualitative Research, 4th ed*. Thousand Oaks, CA: Sage.

Marteache, Nerea. 2012. "Deliberative Processes and Attitudes Toward Sex Offenders in Spain." *European Journal of Criminology* 9:159–75.

Martin, Elizabeth. 1999. "Who Knows Who Lives Here? Within-Household Disagreements as a Source of Survey Coverage Error." *Public Opinion Quarterly* 63(2):220–36.

Marx, Karl. 1880. "Revue Socialist." Reprinted. In *Karl Marx: Selected Writings in Sociology and Social Philosophy*, T.N. Bottomore and Maximilien Rubel (Eds.). NY: McGraw-Hill.

Mastrofski, Stephen D., and R. Richard Ritti. 1999. "Patterns of Community Policing: A View from Newspapers in the United States." COPS Working Paper #2. Washington: U.S. Department of Justice, Office of Community Oriented Policing Services.

Mastrofski, Stephen D., et al. 1998. *Systematic Observation of Public Police: Applying Field Research Methods to Policy Issues*. Research Report. Washington, D.C.: U.S. Department of Justice, Office of Justice Programs, National Institute of Justice.

Matz, David. 2007. "Development and Key Results from the First Two Waves of the Offending Crime and Justice Survey." In *Surveying Crime in the 21st Century*, Mike Hough and Mike Maxfield (Eds.). Crime prevention studies, vol. 22. Monsey, NY: Criminal Justice Press, 77–98.

Maxfield, Michael G. 1987. *Explaining Fear of Crime: Evidence from the 1984 British Crime Survey*. Research and Planning Unit Paper 43. London: Home Office.

Maxfield, Michael G. 1989. "Circumstances in Supplementary Homicide Reports: Variety and Validity." *Criminology* 26(4):123–55.

Maxfield, Michael G. 1999. "The National Incident-Based Reporting System: Research and Policy Applications." *Journal of Quantitative Criminology* 15(2, June):119–49.

Maxfield, Michael G. 2001. *Guide to Frugal Evaluation for Criminal Justice*. Final report to the National Institute of Justice. Washington, D.C.: U.S. Department of Justice, Office of Justice Programs, National Institute of Justice, ww.ncjrs.org/pdffiles1/nij/187350.pdf.

Maxfield, Michael G., and W. Carsten Andresen. 2004. *Evaluation of New Jersey State Police in-Car Mobile Video Recording System*. Final report to the Office of the Attorney General. Newark, NJ: School of Criminal Justice, Rutgers University.

Maxfield, Michael G., and Terry L. Baumer. 1991. "Electronic Monitoring in Marion County Indiana." *Overcrowded Times* 2:5, 17.

Maxfield, Michael G., and Terry L. Baumer. 1992. "Home Detention with Electronic Monitoring: A Nonexperimental Salvage Evaluation." *Evaluation Review* 16(3):315–32.

Maxfield, Michael G., and George L. Kelling. 2005. *New Jersey State Police and Stop Data: What Do We Know, What Should We Know, and What Should We Do?* W. Carsten Andresen, Wayne Fisher, William Sousa, and Michael Wagers. Newark, NJ: Police Institute at Rutgers-Newark.

Maxfield, Michael G., Barbara Luntz Weiler, and Cathy Spatz Widom. 2000. "Comparing Self-Reports and Official Records of Arrests." *Journal of Quantitative Criminology* 16(1, March):87–110.

Maxfield, Michael G., and Cathy Spatz Widom. 1996. "The Cycle of Violence: Revisited Six Years Later." *Archives of Pediatrics and Adolescent Medicine* 150:390–95.

Maxfield, Mike, Mike Hough, and Pat Mayhew. 2007. "Surveying Crime in the 21st Century: Summary and Recommendations." In *Surveying Crime in the 21st Century*, Mike Hough and Mike Maxfield (Eds.). Crime prevention studies, vol. 22. Monsey, NY: Criminal Justice Press, 303–16.

Maxfield, Mike, et al. 2017 (forthcoming). "Multiple Research Methods for Evidence Generation." In *Advances in Evidence-Based Policing*, Johannes Knutsson and Lisa Tompson (Eds.). Crime Science Series. London: Routledge.

Maxwell, Christopher D., Joel H. Garner, and Jeffrey A. Fagan. 2001. *The Effects of Arrest on Intimate Partner Violence: New Evidence from the Spouse Assault Replication Program*. Research in Brief. Washington, D.C.: U.S. Department of Justice, Office of Justice Programs, National Institute of Justice.

Maxwell, Joseph A. 2012. *A Realist Approach for Qualitative Research*. Thousand Oaks, CA: Sage Publications.

Maxwell, Joseph A. 2013. *Qualitative Research Design: An Interactive Approach*. 3rd ed. Thousand Oaks, CA: Sage Publications.

Maxwell, Sheila Royo. 1999. "Examining the Congruence Between Predictors of Release-on-Recognizance and Failure to Appear." *Journal of Criminal Justice* 27(2):127–41.

Mayhew, Patricia, Ronald V. Clarke, and David Elliott. 1989. "Motorcycle Theft, Helmet Legislation, and Displacement." *Howard Journal* 28(1):1–8.

McCahill, Michael, and Clive Norris. 2003. "Estimating the Extent, Sophistication and Legality of CCTV in London." In *CCTV*, Martin Gill (Ed.). Leicester: Perpetuity Press.

McCall, George J. 1978. *Observing the Law: Field Methods in the Study of Crime and the Criminal Justice System*. New York: Free Press.

McCleary, Richard. 1992. *Dangerous Men: The Sociology of Parole*. 2nd ed. New York: Harrow and Heston.

McCleary, Richard, Barbara C. Nienstedt, and James M. Erven. 1982. "Uniform Crime Reports as Organizational Outcomes: Three Time Series Experiments." *Social Problems* 29(4):361–72.

McDonald, Douglas C., and Christine Smith. 1989. *Evaluating Drug Control and System Improvement Projects*. Washington, D.C.: U.S. Department of Justice, Office of Justice Programs, National Institute of Justice.

McDowall, David, Colin Loftin, and Brain Wiersema. 2000. "The Impact of Youth Curfew Laws on Juvenile Crime Rates." *Crime and Delinquency* 46(1):76–91.

McGarrell, Edmund F., Steven Chermak, Alexander Weiss, and Jeremy Wilson. 2001. "Reducing Firearms Violence Through Directed Police Patrol." *Criminology and Public Policy* 1(1):119–48.

McKenna, Laura, and Antoinette Pole. 2008. "What Do Bloggers Do: An Average Day on an Average Political Blog." *Public Choice* 134(1–2):97–108.

Meriam Library. 2010. "Evaluating Information: Applying the CRAAP Test." Web page. Chico, CA: California State University, http://www.csuchico.edu/lins/handouts/eval_websites.pdf.

Merritt, Nancy, Terry Fain, and Susan Turner. 2006. "Oregon's Get Tough Sentencing Reform: A Lesson in Justice System Adaptation." *Criminology and Public Policy* 5(1, February–March):5–36.

Mertens, Donna M., and Pauline E. Ginsberg (Eds.). 2008. *The Handbook of Social Research Ethics*. Thousand Oaks, CA: Sage.

Mesch, Gustavo S., and Gideon Fishman. 1999. "Entering the System: Ethnic Differences in Closing Criminal Files in Israel." *Journal of Research in Crime and Delinquency* 36(2):175–93.

Messerschmidt, James W. 1993. *Masculinities and Crime*. Baltimore, MD: Rowman and Littlefield.

METRAC. 2010. *York University Safety Audit: Leading the Way to Personal and Community Safety*. Toronto, Ontario: Metropolitan Action Committee on Violence against Women and Children. METRAC.

Mieczkowski, Thomas M. 1996. "The Prevalence of Drug Use in the United States." In *Crime and Justice: An Annual Review of Research*, Michael Tonry (Ed.). Chicago, IL: University of Chicago Press, 349–414.

Miles, Matthew B., A. Michael Huberman, and Johnny Saldaña. 2014. *Qualitative Data Analysis: A Methods Sourcebook*. 3rd ed. Thousand Oaks, CA: Sage Publications.

Milgram, Lester. 1965. "Some Conditions of Obedience to Authority." *Human Relations* 18:57–76.

Mirrlees-Black, Catriona. 1995. "Estimating the Extent of Domestic Violence: Findings from the 1992 BCS." *Research Bulletin* 37:1–9.

Mirrlees-Black, Catriona. 1999. *Domestic Violence: Findings from a New British Crime Survey Self-Completion Questionnaire*. Home Office Research Study. London: Home Office Research, Development, and Statistics Directorate.

Mitford, Jessica. 1973. *Kind and Usual Punishment: The Prison Business.* New York: Random House.

Monahan, John, et al. 1993. "Ethical and Legal Duties in Conducting Research on Violence: Lessons from the MacArthur Risk Assessment Study." *Violence and Victims* 8(4):387–96.

Mooney, Stephen J., et al. 2014. "Validity of an Ecometric Neighborhood Physical Disorder Measure Constructed by Virtual Street Audit." *American Journal of Epidemiology* 180:(626–35).

Moskos, Peter. 2009. *Cop in the Hood.* Princeton: Princeton University Press.

Mott, Joy, and Catriona Mirrlees-Black. 1995. *Self-Reported Drug Misuse in England and Wales: Findings from the 1992 British Crime Survey.* Research and Planning Unit Paper 89. London: Home Office.

Murray, Charles A., and L.A. Cox. 1979. *Beyond Probation: Juvenile Corrections and the Chronic Delinquent.* Thousand Oaks, CA: Sage.

Nagin, Daniel S., and David Weisburd. 2013. "Evidence and Public Policy: The Example of Evaluation Research in Policing." *Criminology and Public Policy* 12:651–79.

National Commission for the Protection of Human Subjects of Biomedical and Behavioral Research. 1979. *The Belmont Report: Ethical Principles and Guidelines for the Protection of Human Subjects of Research.* Washington, D.C.: U.S. Department of Health, Education, and Welfare.

National Consortium for the Study of Terrorism and Responses to Terrorism (START). 2016a. *Annex of Statistical Information, Country Reports on Terrorism, 2015.* College Park, MD: National Consortium for the Study of Terrorism and Responses to Terrorism (START), Website, https://www.start.umd.edu/gtd.

National Consortium for the Study of Terrorism and Responses to Terrorism (START). 2016b. *Global Terrorism Database Codebook: Inclusion Criteria and Variables.* College Park, MD: National Consortium for the Study of Terrorism and Responses to Terrorism (START), Website, https://www.start.umd.edu/gtd.

National Institute of Justice. 2016. *Solicitation: Research and Evaluation in Support of the Recommendations of the President's Task Force on 21st Century Policing.* Washington, D.C.: U.S. Department of Justice, Office of Justice Programs, National Institute of Justice, http://nij.gov/funding/Documents/solicitations/NIJ-2016-9095.pdf.

National Research Council. 1996. *The Evaluation of Forensic DNA Evidence.* Washington, D.C.: National Academy Press.

National Research Council. 2001. *Informing America's Policy on Illegal Drugs: What We Don't Know Keeps Hurting Us.* Committee on Data and Research for Policy on Illegal Drugs. Charles F. Manski, John V. Pepper, and Carol V. Petrie (Eds.). Washington, D.C.: National Academy Press.

National Research Council. 2007. *Parole, Desistance from Crime, and Community Integration.* Committee on Community Supervision and Desistance from Crime. Committee on Law and Justice, Division of Behavioral and Social Sciences. Washington, D.C.: National Academy Press.

National Research Council. 2008. *Surveying Victims: Options for Conducting the National Crime Victimization Survey.* Panel to review the programs of the Bureau of Justice Statistics. Committee on National Statistics and Committee on Law and Justice, Division of Behavioral and Social Sciences. Robert M. Groves and David L. Cork (Eds.). Washington, D.C.: National Academy Press.

National Research Council. 2009. *Strengthening Forensic Science in the United States: A Path Forward.* Washington, D.C.: National Academy Press.

Navgorodoff, Danica. 2010. *I Got Arrested! Now What?* Comic book. Youth Justice Board Center for Court Innovation. Brooklyn, NY: Center for Urban Pedagogy, Making Public Policy, http://welcometocup.org/Store?product_id=14.

Nellis, Mike. 2006. "Surveillance, Rehabilitation, and Electronic Monitoring: Getting the Issues Clear." *Criminology and Public Policy* 5(1, February):103–08.

New York City Transit. 2006. "Police Department." Supplementary Tables. In *Subways.* New York: Metropolitan Transit Authority, http://www.mta.nyc.ny.us/nyct/facts/ffsubway.htm.

Newman, Oscar. 1972. *Defensible Space.* New York: Macmillan.

Newman, Oscar. 1996. *Creating Defensible Space.* Washington, D.C.: U.S. Department of Housing and Urban Development, Office of Policy Development and Research.

Office for National Statistics. 2015. *User Guide to Crime Statistics for England and Wales.* London: Office for National Statistics.

Office of National Drug Control Policy. 2014. *ADAM II 2013 Annual Report Arrestee Drug Abuse Monitoring Program II.* Research rept. Washington, D.C.: Office of National Drug Control Policy, Executive Office of the President, Accessed 20 December 2016 https://www.whitehouse.gov/sites/default/files/ondcp/policy-and-research/adam_ii_2013_annual_report.pdf.

Ostermann, Michael, Laura M. Salerno, and Jordan M. Hyatt. 2015. "How Different Operationalizations of Recidivism Impact Conclusions of Effectiveness of Parole Supervision." *Journal of Research in Crime and Delinquency* 52(6):771–96.

Overall, Chris, Shalendra Singh, and Bhekekhya Gcina. 2008. "Crime Mapping and Analysis: Filling the Gaps." *PositionIT*, May–June, 37–40.

Painter, Kate. 1996. "The Influence of Street Lighting Improvements on Crime, Fear and Pedestrian Street Use After Dark." *Landscape and Urban Planning* 35(2–3):193–201.

Park, Robert E., and Ernest W. Burgess. 1921. *Introduction to the Science of Sociology.* Chicago, IL: University of Chicago Press.

Parks, Sharyn E., Linda L. Johnson, Dawn D McDaniel, and Matthew Gladden. 2014. "Surveillance for Violent Deaths – National Violent Death Reporting System, 16 States, 2010." *Morbidity and Mortality Weekly Report* 63(1):2–33.

Paternoster, Raymond, Jean Marie McGloin, Holly Nguyen, and Kyle J. Thomas. 2013. "The Causal Impact of Exposure to Deviant Peers: An Experimental Investigation." *Journal of Research in Crime and Delinquency* 50(4):476–503.

Paterson, Barbara L., David Gregory, and Sally Thorne. 1999. "A Protocol for Researcher Safety." *Qualitative Health Research* 9(2):259–69.

Patton, Michael Quinn. 2002. *Qualitative Research and Evaluation Methods.* 3rd ed. Thousand Oaks, CA: Sage Publications.

Pawson, Ray, and Nick Tilley. 1997. *Realistic Evaluation.* Thousand Oaks, CA: Sage.

Pease, Ken. 1998. *Repeat Victimisation: Taking Stock. Crime Prevention and Detection Series, paper 90.* London: Police Research Group, Home Office Police Department.

Perrin, Andrew, and Maeve Duggan. 2016. *American's Internet Access: 2000–2015.* Washington, D.C.: Pew Research Center, http://www.pewinternet.org/2015/06/26/americans-internet-access-2000-2015/.

Perrone, Dina. 2009. *The High Life: Club Kids, Harm and Drug Policy*. Qualitative Studies in Crime and Justice. Monsey, NY: Criminal Justice Press.

Perrone, Dina. 2010. "Gender and Sexuality in the Field: A Female Ethnographer's Experience Researching Drug Use in Dance Clubs." *Substance Use and Misuse* 45:717–35.

Petersilia, Joan. 1989. "Implementing Randomized Experiments: Lessons from BJA's Intensive Supervision Project." *Evaluation Review* 13:435–58.

Petersilia, Joan, and Susan Turner. 1991. "An Evaluation of Intensive Supervision in California." *Journal of Criminal Law and Criminology* 82:610–58.

Petrossian, Gohar, and Ronald V. Clarke. 2012. *Export of Stolen Vehicles Across Land Borders*. Problem-Oriented Guides for Police, no. 63. Washington, D.C.: U.S. Department of Justice, Office of Community Oriented Policing Services.

Pew Research Center. 2012. *Assessing the Representativeness of Public Opinion Surveys*. Washington, D.C.: Pew Research Center, http://www.pewinternet.org/2015/06/26/americans-internet-access-2000-2015/.

Pickrell, Timothy M., and Ronald Li. 2016. *Seat Belt Use in 2015: Overall Results*. Research note (DOT HS 812 243). Washington, D.C.: U.S. Department of Transportation, National Highway Traffic Safety Administration, National Center for Statistics and Analysis.

Piquero, Alex R., Carol A. Schubert, and Robert Brame. 2014. "Comparing Official and Self-Report Records of Offending Across Gender and Race/Ethnicity in a Longitudinal Study of Serious Youthful Offenders." *Journal of Research in Crime and Delinquency* 51:526–56.

Piza, Eric L., and Victoria A. Sytsma. 2016. "Exploring the Defensive Actions of Drug Sellers in Open Air Markets: A Systematic Social Observation." *Journal of Research in Crime and Delinquency* 53(a):36–65.

Planty, Michael, and Kevin J. Strom. 2007. "Understanding the Role of Repeat Victims in the Production of Annual US Victimization Rates." *Journal of Quantitative Criminology* 23:179–200.

Plouffe, Nanci, and Rana Sampson. 2004. "Auto Theft and Theft from Autos in Parking Lots in Chula Vista, CA: Crime Analysis for Local and Regional Action." In *Understanding and Preventing Car Theft*, Michael G. Maxfield and Ronald V. Clarke (Eds.). Crime prevention studies, vol. 17. Monsey, NY: Criminal Justice Press, 147–71.

Poklemba, John J. 1988. *Measurement Issues in Prison and Jail Overcrowding*. Albany, NY: New York Division of Criminal Justice Services, Criminal Justice Information Systems Improvement Program.

Pollock, Jocelyn M. 2012. *Ethics in Crime and Justice: Dilemmas and Decisions*. 7th ed. Belmont, CA: Cengage Learning.

Popper, Nathaniel. 2016. "As Marijuana Sales Grow, Start-Ups Step in for Wary Banks." *New York Times*, 17 February, B1.

Posavec, Emil J., and Raymond G. Carey. 2002. *Program Evaluation: Methods and Case Studies*. 6th ed. Englewood Cliffs, NJ: Prentice Hall.

Pösö, Tarja, Päivi Honkatukia, and Leo Nyqvist. 2008. "Focus Groups and the Study of Violence." *Qualitative Research* 8:73–89.

President's Commission on Law Enforcement and Administration of Justice. 1967. *The Challenge of Crime in a Free Society*. Washington, D.C.: U.S. Government Printing Office.

Pudney, Stephen. 2002. *The Road to Ruin? Sequences of Initiation Into Drug Use and Offending by Young People in Britain*. Home Office Research Study, 253. London: Her Majesty's Stationery Office, http://www.crimereduction.gov.uk/drugsalcohol62.htm.

Puzzanchera, Charles. 2014. *Juvenile Arrests 2012*. Juvenile offenders and victims national report. Washington, D.C.: U.S. Department of Justice, Office of Justice Programs, Office of Juvenile Justice and Delinquency Prevention.

Quade, Edward S. 1989. *Policy Analysis for Public Decisions*. 3rd ed. Rev. Grace M. Carter. New York: North-Holland.

Quinn, James W., et al. 2016. "Neighborhood Physical Disorder in New York City." *Journal of Maps* 12(1):53–60.

Ragin, Charles C. 2000. *Fuzzy-Set Social Science*. Chicago: University of Chicago Press.

Ramirez, Deborah, Jack McDevitt, and Amy Farrell. 2000. *A Resource Guide on Racial Profiling Data Collection Systems: Promising Practices and Lessons Learned*. Washington, D.C.: U.S. Department of Justice, Office of Justice Programs, National Institute of Justice and Bureau of Justice Assistance.

Ramsay, Malcolm, and Sarah Partridge. 1999. *Drug Misuse Declared in 1998: Results from the British Crime Survey*. Home Office Research Study, 197. London: Her Majesty's Stationery Office.

Ramsay, Malcolm, et al. 2001. *Drug Misuse Declared in 2000: Results from the British Crime Survey*. Home Office Research Study, 224. London: Her Majesty's Stationery Office.

Rand, Michael R., and Callie M. Rennison. 2005. "Bigger is not Necessarily Better: An Analysis of Violence Against Women Estimates from the National Crime Victimization Survey and the National Violence Against Women Survey." *Journal of Quantitative Criminology* 21(3):267–91.

Rasinski, Kenneth A. 1989. "The Effect of Question Wording on Public Support for Government Spending." *Public Opinion Quarterly* 53:388–94.

Ratcliffe, Jerry H., et al. 2011. "The Philadelphia Foot Patrol Experiment: A Randomized Controlled Trial of Police Patrol Effectiveness in Violent Crime Hotspots." *Criminology* 49(3):795–831.

Ratcliffe, Jerry. 2014. "Towards an Index for Harm-Focused Policing." *Policing* 9:164–82.

Al-Rawi, Ahmed. 2016. "Video Games, Terrorism, and ISISD's Jihad 3.0." *Terrorism and Political Violence* Pre-publication online, http://dx.doi.org/10.1080/09546553.2016.1207633.

Rebellon, Cesar J., and Karen Van Gundy. 2005. "Can Control Theory Explain the Link Between Parental Physical Abuse and Delinquency? A Longitudinal Analysis." *Journal of Research in Crime and Delinquency* 42(3):247–74.

Rennison, Callie Marie. 2002. *Rape and Sexual Assault: Reporting to Police and Medical Attention, 1992–2000*. Bureau of Justice Statistics Selected Findings. Washington, D.C.: U.S. Department of Justice, Office of Justice Programs, Bureau of Justice Statistics.

Reuter, Peter, Robert MacCoun, and Patrick Murphy. 1990. *Money from Crime: A Study of the Economics of Drug Dealing in Washington, D.C.* Santa Monica, CA: Rand.

Reynald, Danielle. 2011. "Factors Associated with the Guardianship of Places: Assessing the Relative Importance of the Spatio-Physical and Sociodemographic Contexts in Generating Opportunities for Capable Guardianship." *Journal of Research in Crime and Delinquency* 48:110–42.

Reynolds, Paul D. 1979. *Ethical Dilemmas and Social Science Research*. San Francisco, CA: Jossey-Bass.

Rich, Thomas F. 1999. "Mapping the Path to Problem Solving." *National Institute of Justice Journal* (October):2–9.

Risler, Edwin A., Tim Sweatman, and Larry Nackerud. 1998. "Evaluating the Georgia Legislative Waiver's Effectiveness in Deterring Juvenile Crime." *Research on Social Work Practice* 8:657–67.

Robb, Paul, Timothy Coupe, and Barak Ariel. 2015. "'Solvability' and Detection of Metal Theft on Railway Property." *European Journal on Criminal Policy and Research* 21:463–84.

Robers, Simone, et al. 2014. *Indicators of School Crime and Safety: 2014*. (NCES 2014-042/NCJ 243299). Washington, D.C.: National Center for Education Statistics, U.S. Department of Education, and Bureau of Justice Statistics, Office of Justice Programs, U.S. Department of Justice.

Roberts, Aki, and Steven Block. 2012. "Explaining Temporary and Permanent Motor Vehicle Theft Rates in the United States: A Crime-Specific Approach." *Journal of Research in Crime and Delinquency* 50(3):445–71.

Roberts, James C. 2002. *Serving Up Trouble in the Barroom Environment*. Unpublished Ph.D. dissertation, Rutgers University School of Criminal Justice. Newark, NJ: School of Criminal Justice, Rutgers University.

Roberts, James C. 2007. "Barroom Aggression in Hoboken, New Jersey: Don't Blame the Bouncers." *Journal of Drug Education* 37(4):429–45.

Roberts, Jennifer, et al. 2005. "A Test of Two Models of Recall for Violent Events." *Journal of Quantitative Criminology* 21(2):175–93.

Roethlisberger, Fritz J., and William J. Dickson. 1939. *Management and the Worker*. Cambridge, MA: Harvard University Press.

Roman, John, and Graham Farrell. 2002. "Cost-Benefit Analysis for Crime Prevention: Opportunity Costs, Routine Savings, and Crime Externalities." In *Evaluation for Crime Prevention*. Vol. 14, Nick Tilley (Ed.). Crime Prevention Studies. Monsey, NY: Criminal Justice Press, 53–92.

Rosenfeld, Richard, Timothy M. Bray, and Arlen Egley. 1999. "Facilitating Violence: A Comparison of Gang-Motivated, Gang-Affiliated, and Nongang Youth Homicides." *Journal of Quantitative Criminology* 15(4):495–516.

Rossi, Peter H., Howard E. Freeman, and Mark W. Lipsey. 1999. *Evaluation: A Systematic Approach*. 6th ed. Thousand Oaks, CA: Sage.

Roth, Andrea. 2010. "Database-Driven Investigations: The Promise—and Peril—of Using Forensics to Solve 'No-Suspect' Cases." *Criminology and Public Policy* 9(2):421–28.

Rubin, Herbert J., and Irene S. Rubin. 2011. 3rd ed. *Qualitative Interviewing: The Art of Hearing*. Thousand Oaks, CA: Sage Publications.

Ryan, Gery W., and H. Russell Bernard. 2003. "Techniques to Identify Themes." *Field Methods* 15(1):85–109.

Sampson, Robert J., and John H. Laub. 1993. *Crime in the Making: Pathways and Turning Points Through Life*. Cambridge, MA: Harvard University Press.

Sampson, Robert J., and Stephen W. Raudenbush. 1999. "Systematic Social Observation of Public Spaces: A New Look at Disorder in Urban Neighborhoods." *American Journal of Sociology* 105(3, November): 603–51.

Sanders, Teela. 2001. "Female Street Sex Workers, Sexual Violence, and Protection Strategies." *Journal of Sexual Aggression* 7:5–8.

Santos, Rachel Boba. 2012. *Crime Analysis with Crime Mapping*. 3rd ed. Thousand Oaks, CA: Sage.

Sauer, Carl. 1925. "The Morphology of Landscape." *University of California Publications in Geography* 2:19–54.

Schuck, Amie M., and Cathy Spatz Widom. 2001. "Childhood Victimization and Alcohol Symptoms in Females: Causal Inferences and Hypothesized Mediators." *Child Abuse and Neglect* 25(8):1069–92.

Seidman, David, and Michael Couzens. 1974. "Getting the Crime Rate Down: Political Pressure and Crime Reporting." *Law and Society Review* 8(3):457–93.

Semaan, Salaam, Jennifer Lauby, and Jon Liebman. 2002. "Street and Network Sampling in Evaluation Studies of HIV Risk-Reduction Interventions." *AIDS Reviews* 4:213–23.

Shadish, William R., Thomas D. Cook, and Donald T. Campbell. 2002. *Experimental and Quasi-Experimental Designs for Generalized Causal Inference*. Boston: Houghton Mifflin.

Shane, Jon. 2012. *Abandoned Buildings and Lots*. Problem-Oriented Guides for Police, no. 64. Washington, D.C.: U.S. Department of Justice, Office of Community Oriented Policing Services.

Shaw, Clifford R., and Henry D. McKay. 1969. *Juvenile Delinquency and Urban Areas*. Rev. ed. Chicago, IL: University of Chicago Press.

Shearing, Clifford D., and Phillip C. Stenning. 1992. "From the Panopticon to Disney World: The Development of Discipline." In *Situational Crime Prevention: Successful Case Studies*, Ronald V. Clarke (Ed.). New York: Harrow and Heston, 249–55.

Sheehan, Ivan Sadcha. 2011. "Assessing and Comparing Data Sources for Terrorism Research." Chapter 17. In *Evidence-Based Counterterrorism Policy*, Cynthia Lum and Leslie W. Kennedy (Eds.). NY: Springer.

Sheehan, Kim Bartel, and Matthew Pittman. 2016. *Amazon's Mechanical Turk for Academics: The HIT Handbook for Social Science Research*. 7th ed. Irvine, CA: Melvin & Leigh.

Sherman, Lawrence W. 1992a. "The Influence of Criminology on Criminal Law: Evaluating Arrests for Misdemeanor Domestic Violence." *Journal of Criminal Law and Criminology* 83:1–45.

Sherman, Lawrence W. 1992b. *Policing Domestic Violence: Experiments and Dilemmas*. New York: Free Press.

Sherman, Lawrence W., and Richard A. Berk. 1984. *The Minneapolis Domestic Violence Experiment*. Washington, D.C.: Police Foundation.

Sherman, Lawrence W., and Cohn Ellen G. 1989. "The Impact of Research on Legal Policy: The Minneapolis Domestic Violence Experiment." *Law and Society Review* 23(1):117–44.

Sherman, Lawrence W., Patrick R. Gartin, and Michael E. Buerger. 1989. "Hot Spots of Predatory Crime: Routine Activity and the Criminology of Place." *Criminology* 27:27–55.

Sherman. Lawrence W., and Heather M. Harris. 2013. "Increased Homicide Victimization of Suspects Arrested for Domestic Assault: A 23-Year Follow-Up of the Milwaukee Domestic Violence Experiment (MilDVE)." *Journal of Experimental Criminology* 9:419–514.

Sherman. Lawrence W., and Heather M. Harris. 2015. "Increased Death Rates of Domestic Violence Victims from Arresting Vs. Warning Suspects in the Milwaukee Domestic Violence Experiment (MilDVE)." *Journal of Experimental Criminology* 11:1–20.

Sherman, Lawrence W., and Dennis P. Rogan. 1995. "Effects of Gun Seizures on Gun Violence: 'Hot Spots' Patrol in Kansas City." *Justice Quarterly* 12(4):673–94.

Sherman, Lawrence W., and David Weisburd. 1995. "General Deterrent Effects of Police Patrol in Crime 'Hot Spots': A Randomized, Controlled Trial." *Justice Quarterly* 12:625–48.

Sherman, Lawrence W., et al. 1992. "The Variable Effects of Arrest on Criminal Careers: The Milwaukee Domestic Violence Experiment." *Journal of Criminal Law and Criminology* 83:137–69.

Shweder, Richard A. 2006. "Protecting Human Subjects and Preserving Academic Freedom." *American Ethnologist* 33(4, November):507–18.

Sieber, Joan E. 2001. *Summary of Human Subjects Protection Issues Related to Large Sample Surveys.* Washington, D.C.: U.S. Department of Justice, Office of Justice Programs, Bureau of Justice Statistics.

Silberman, Charles. 1978. *Criminal Violence, Criminal Justice.* New York: Random House.

Silbert, Mimi H., and Ayala M. Pines. 1981. "Occupational Hazards of Street Prostitutes." *Justice and Behavior* 8:395–99.

Silverman, Eli B. 1999. *NYPD Battles Crime: Innovative Strategies in Policing.* Boston: Northeastern University Press.

Sinauer, Nancy, et al. 1999. "Comparisons Among Female Homicides Occurring in Rural, Intermediate, and Urban Counties in North Carolina." *Homicide Studies* 3(2):107–28.

Singleton, Royce A., Jr., and Bruce C. Straits. 2010. *Approaches to Social Research.* 5th ed. New York: Oxford University Press.

Skogan, Wesley G. 1974. "The Validity of Official Crime Statistics: An Empirical Investigation." *Social Science Quarterly* 55:25–38.

Skogan, Wesley G. 1985. *Evaluating Neighborhood Crime Prevention Programs.* The Hague, Netherlands: Ministry of Justice, Research and Documentation Centre.

Skogan, Wesley G. 1988. "Community Organizations and Crime." In *Crime and Justice: An Annual Review of Research,* Michael Tonry and Norval Morris (Eds.). Chicago, IL: University of Chicago Press, 39–78.

Skogan, Wesley G. 1990. *Disorder and Decline: Crime and the Spiral of Decay in American Neighborhoods.* New York: Free Press.

Skogan, Wesley G. 2007. "Survey Assessments of Police Performance." In *Surveying Crime in the 21st Century,* Mike Hough and Mike Maxfield (Eds.). Crime prevention studies, vol. 22. Monsey, NY: Criminal Justice Press, 165–81.

Skogan, Wesley G., Susan M. Hartnett, Natalie Bump, and Jill Dubois. 2008. *Evaluation of CeaseFire-Chicago.* Assisted by Ryan Hollon and Danielle Morris. Evanston, IL: Center for Policy Research, Northwestern University, http://www.northwestern.edu/ipr/publications/ceasefire.Html.

Skogan, Wesley G., and Michael G. Maxfield. 1981. *Coping with Crime: Individual and Neighborhood Reactions.* Thousand Oaks, CA: Sage.

Smith, Brian T., and Ronald V. Clarke. 2015. "Shoplifting of Everyday Products That Serve Illicit Drug Use." *Journal of Research in Crime and Delinquency* 52(2):245–69.

Smith, Steven K., Greg W. Steadman, Todd D. Minton, and Meg Townsend. 1999. *Criminal Victimization and Perceptions of Community Safety in 12 Cities, 1998.* Washington, D.C.: U.S. Department of Justice, Office of Justice Programs, Bureau of Justice Statistics and Office of Community Oriented Police Services.

Smith, William R., et al. 2003. *The North Carolina Highway Traffic Study.* Final report to the National Institute of Justice. With Harvey McMurray and C. Robert Fenlon. Raleigh, NC: North Carolina State University.

Snyder, Howard N. 2000. *Sexual Assault of Young Children as Reported to Law Enforcement: Victim, Incident, and Offender Characteristics.* NIBRS Statistical Report. Washington, D.C.: U.S. Department of Justice, Office of Justice Programs, Bureau of Justice Statistics.

Sommers, Samuel R., et al. 2006. "Race and Media Coverage of Hurricane Katrina: Analysis, Implications, and Future Research Questions." *Analyses of Social Issues and Public Policy* 6:39–55.

Spergel, Irving A. 1990. "Youth Gangs: Continuity and Change." In *Crime and Justice: An Annual Review of Research,* Norval Morris and Michael Tonry (Eds.). Chicago, IL: University of Chicago Press, 171–275.

Spohn, Cassia. 1990. "The Sentencing Decisions of Black and White Judges: Expected and Unexpected Similarities." *Law and Society Review* 24(5):1197–216.

Spradley, James P. 1979. *The Ethnographic Interview.* NY: Holt, Rinehart, and Winston.

Steenbeek, Wouter, Beate Volker, Henk Flap, and Frank van Oort. 2012. "Local Businesses as Attractors or Preventers of Neighborhood Disorder." *Journal of Research in Crime and Delinquency* 49:213–48.

Stolnici, Constantin B., and Octavian Buda. 2012. "An Unclear Political Assassination: Barbu Catargiu, 1862." *Romanian Journal of Forensic Science* 79(1):907–11.

Straus, Murray A. 1999. "The Controversy Over Domestic Violence by Women: A Methodological, Theoretical, and Sociology of Science Analysis." In *Violence in Intimate Relationships,* Ximena Arriaga and Stuart Oskamp (Eds.). Thousand Oaks, CA: Sage Publications, 17–44.

Strauss, Anselm, and Juliet Corbin. 1994. "Grounded Theory Methodology: An Overview." In *Handbook of Qualitative Research,* Norman K. Denzin and Yvonne S. Lincoln (Eds.). Thousand Oaks, CA: Sage Publications.

Strom, Kevin J., and Matthew R. Durose. 2000. *Traffic Stop Data Collection Policies for State Police, 1999.* Fact Sheet. Washington, D.C.: U.S. Department of Justice, Office of Justice Programs, Bureau of Justice Statistics.

Substance Abuse and Mental Health Services Administration. 2011. *Drug Abuse Warning Network, 2009: National Estimates of Drug-Related Emergency Department Visits.* DAWN Series D-35, Publication No. SMA 11-4659. Rockville, MD: U.S. Department of Health and Human Services, Substance Abuse and Mental Health Services Administration, Office of Applied Studies, http://DAWNinfo.samhsa.gov.

Surette, Ray. 2006. *Media, Crime, and Justice: Images, Realities and Policies.* 3rd ed. Belmont, CA: Wadsworth.

Sutterlüty, Ferdinand. 2007. "The Genesis of Violent Careers." *Ethnography* 8:267–96.

Sutton, Mike. 2007. "Improving National Crime Surveys with a Focus on Fraud, High-Tech Crimes, and Stolen Goods." In *Surveying Crime in the 21st Century,* Mike Hough and Mike Maxfield (Eds.). Crime prevention studies, vol. 22. Monsey, NY: Criminal Justice Press, 243–62.

Taxman, Faye S., and Lori Elis. 1999. "Expediting Court Dispositions: Quick Results, Uncertain Outcomes." *Journal of Research in Crime and Delinquency* 36(1):30–55.

Taylor, Ralph B. 1999. *Crime, Grime, Fear, and Decline: A Longitudinal Look*. Research in Brief. Washington, D.C.: U.S. Department of Justice, Office of Justice Programs, National Institute of Justice.

Taylor, Ralph B., Sally A. Shumaker, and Stephen D. Gottfredson. 1985. "Neighborhood-Level Links Between Physical Features and Local Sentiments." *Journal of Architectural Planning and Research* 2:261–75.

Thompson, Kimberly M., and Kevin Haninger. 2001. "Violence in E-Rated Video Games." *Journal of the American Medical Association* 286(5, 1 August):591–98.

Thompson, Steven K. 1997. *Adaptive Sampling in Behavioral Surveys*. NIDA Monograph no. 167. Bethesda, MD: U.S. Department of Health and Human Services, National Institute of Drug Abuse.

Thornberry, Terence P., and Marvin D. Krohn. 2000. "The Self-Report Method for Measuring Delinquency and Crime." In *Measurement and Analysis of Crime and Justice*. Vol. 4, David Duffee (Ed.). *Criminal Justice 2000 Vol. 4*. Washington, D.C.: U.S. Department of Justice, Office of Justice Programs, National Institute of Justice, 33–83.

Tilley, Nick. 2000. "The Evaluation Jungle." In *Secure Foundations: Key Issues in Crime Prevention, Crime Reduction and Public Safety*, Scott Ballintyne, Ken Pease, and Vic McLaren (Eds.). London: Institute for Public Policy Research, 115–30.

Tilley, Nick, and Gloria Laycock. 2002. *Working Out What to Do: Evidence-Based Crime Reduction*. Crime Reduction Research Series, paper 11. London: Home Office, Policing and Reducing Crime Unit, Research, Development and Statistics Directorate.

Tillyer, Marie Skubak, and Emily M. Wright. 2014. "Intimate Partner Violence and the Victim-Offender Overlap." *Journal of Research in Crime and Delinquency* 51(1):29–55.

Tjaden, Patricia, and Nancy Thoennes. 2000. *Extent, Nature, and Consequences of Intimate Partner Violence*. Findings from the National Violence Against Women Survey. Research Report. Washington, D.C.: U.S. Department of Justice, Office of Justice Programs, National Institute of Justice.

Townsley, Michael, Ross Homel, and Janet Chaseling. 2003. "Infectious Burglaries: A Test of the Near Repeat Hypothesis." *British Journal of Criminology* 43:615–33.

Townsley, Michael, and Ken Pease. 2002. "Hot Spots and Cold Comfort: The Importance of Having a Working Thermometer." In *Analysis for Crime Prevention*, Nick Tilley (Ed.). Crime prevention studies, vol. 13. Monsey, NY: Criminal Justice Press, 59–69.

Truman, Jennifer L., and Lynn. Langton. 2015. *Criminal Victimization, 2014*. Washington, D.C.: U.S. Department of Justice, Office of Justice Programs, Bureau of Justice Statistics, http://www.bjs.ojp.usdoj.gov/content/pub/pdf/cv12.pdf.

Truman, Jennifer L., and Rachel E. Morgan. 2014. *Nonfatal Domestic Violence, 2003–2012*. BJS Special Report. Washington, D.C.: U.S. Department of Justice, Office of Justice Programs, Bureau of Justice Statistics.

United States Bureau of the Census. 1992. *Statistical Abstract of the United States*. Washington, D.C.: U.S. Government Printing Office.

United States Bureau of the Census. 1994. *Technical Background on the Redesigned National Crime Victimization Survey*. Washington, D.C.: U.S. Department of Justice, Office of Justice Programs, Bureau of Justice Statistics.

United States Census Bureau. 2005. *Estimated Daytime Population and Employment-Residence Ratios: 2000*. PHC-T-40. Washington, D.C.: U.S. Bureau of the Census, http://www.census.gov/population/www/socdemo/daytime/daytimepop.html.

United States Census Bureau. 2012. *National Crime Victimization Survey: CAPI Interviewing Manual for Field Representatives. NCVS-550 (12/2012)*. Washington, D.C.: U.S. Bureau of the Census.

United States Department of Justice. 2003. *The Nation's Two Crime Measures*. Washington, D.C.: U.S. Department of Justice, NCJ-122705.

United States Department of State. 2016. *Country Reports on Terrorism 2015*. Washington, D.C.: U.S. Department of State, Bureau of Counterterrorism and Countering Violent Extremism, Website, http://www.state.gov/j/ct/rls/crt/2015/index.htm.

United States Sentencing Commission. 2014. *Amendments to the Sentencing Guidelines*. Washington, D.C.: U.S. Sentencing Commission.

Valdimarsdottir, Margret, and Gunnar Bernburg. 2015. "Community Disadvantage, Parental Network, and Commitment to Social Norms: Multilevel Study of Self-Reported Delinquency in Iceland." *Journal of Research on Crime and Delinquency* 52:213–44.

Van Kirk, Marvin. 1977. *Response Time Analysis*. Washington, D.C.: U.S. Department of Justice, National Institute of Law Enforcement and Administration of Justice.

Varano, Sean P., Joseph A. Schafer, Jeffrey Michael Cancino, and Marc L. Swatt. 2009. "Constructing Crime: Neighborhood Characteristics and Police Recording Behavior." *Journal of Criminl Justice* 37:553–63.

Venkatesh, Sudhir. 2006. *Off the Books: The Underground Economy of the Urban Poor*. Cambridge, MA: Harvard University Press.

Venkatesh, Sudhir. 2011. "How Tech Tools Transformed New York's Sex Trade." *Wired* 19.02 (January).

La Vigne, Nancy G., Sara Debus-Sherrill, Diana Brazzell, and P. Mitchell Downey. 2011. *Preventing Violence and Sexual Assault in Jail: A Situational Crime Prevention Approach*. Washington, D.C.: Urban Institute, Justice Policy Center.

Voas, Robert B., Eduardo Romano, and Raymond Peck. 2009. "Validity of Surrogate Measures of Alcohol Involvement When Applied to Nonfatal Crashes." *Accident Analysis and Prevention* 41:522–30.

Walker, Samuel. 1994. *Sense and Nonsense About Crime and Drugs: A Policy Guide*. 3rd ed. Belmont, CA: Wadsworth.

Wallace, Aurora. 2009. "Mapping City Crime and the New Aesthetic of Danger." *Journal of Visual Culture* 8:5–24.

Walsh, Christine A., et al. 2008. "Measurement of Victimization in Adolescence: Development and Validation of the Childhood Experiences of Violence Questionnaire." *Child Abuse and Neglect* 32(11):1037–57.

Warner, Barbara D., and Glenn L. Pierce. 1993. "Reexamining Social Disorganization Theory Using Calls to Police as a Measure of Crime." *Criminology* 31:493–517.

Weisburd, David. 2015. "The Law of Crime Concentration and the Criminology of Place." *Criminology* 53(2):133–57.

Weisburd, David, Elizabeth R. Groff, and Sue-Min Yang. 2012. *The Criminology of Place: Street Segments and Our Understanding of the Crime Problem*. Oxford: Oxford University Press.

Weisburd, David, Joshua C. Hinkle, Anthony A. Braga, and Alese Wooditch. 2015. "Understanding the Mechanisms

Underlying Broken Windows Policing: The Need for Evaluation Evidence." *Journal of Research in Crime and Delinquency* 52(4):567–88.

Weisburd, David, Cynthia M. Lum, and Sue-Ming Yang. 2003. "When Can We Conclude That Treatments or Programs 'Don't Work'?" *The Annals* 587 (May):31–48.

Weisburd, David, Nancy A. Morris, and Justin Ready. 2008. "Risk-Focused Policing at Places: An Experimental Evaluation." *Justice Quarterly* 25(1, March):163–200.

Weisburd, David, Anthony Petrosino, and Gail Mason. 1993. "Design Sensitivity in Criminal Justice Experiments." In *Crime and Justice: An Annual Review of Research*, Michael Tonry (Ed.). Chicago: University of Chicago Press, 337–79.

Weisel, Deborah Lamm. 2005. *Analyzing Repeat Victimization*. Problem solving tools series. Washington, D.C.: U.S. Department of Justice, Office of Community Oriented Policing Services.

Weisel, Deborah. 1999. *Conducting Community Surveys: A Practical Guide for Law Enforcement Agencies*. Washington, D.C.: U.S. Department of Justice, Office of Justice Programs, Bureau of Justice Statistics and Office of Community Oriented Police Services.

Weiss, Carol H. 1995. "Nothing as Practical as Good Theory: Exploring Theory-Based Evaluation for Comprehensive Community Initiatives for Children and Families." In *New Approaches to Evaluating Community Initiatives: Concepts, Methods, and Contexts*, James P. Connell, Anne C. Kubisch, Lisbeth B. Schorr, and Carol H. Weiss (Eds.). Washington, D.C.: Aspen Institute, 65–92.

Weiss, Robert S. 1994. *Learning from Strangers: The Art and Method of Qualitative Interview Studies*. NY: The Free Press.

Weitzer, Ronald. 2010. "The Movement to Criminalize Sex Work in the United States." *Journal of Law and Society* 37(1):61–84.

Wellings, Kaye, Patrick Branigan, and Kirsti Mitchell. 2000. "Discomfort, Discord, and Discontinuity as Data: Using Focus Groups to Research Sensitive Topics." *Culture, Health, & Sexuality* 2(3):255–67.

West, Donald J., and David P. Farrington. 1977. *The Delinquent Way of Life*. London: Heinemann.

Whitt, Hugh P. 2006. "Where Did the Bodies Go? The Social Construction of Suicide Data, New York City, 1976–1992." *Sociological Inquiry* 76(2):166–87.

Whyte, William Foote. 1993. 4th ed. *Street Corner Society: The Social Structure of an Italian Slum*. Chicago: University of Chicago Press.

Widom, Cathy Spatz. 1989. "Child Abuse, Neglect, and Adult Behavior: Research Design and Findings on Criminality, Violence, and Child Abuse." *American Journal of Orthopsychiatry* 59(3):355–67.

Widom, Cathy Spatz. 1992. *The Cycle of Violence*. Research in Brief. Washington, D.C.: U.S. Department of Justice, Office of Justice Programs, National Institute of Justice.

Widom, Cathy Spatz, Sally J. Czaja, and Mary Ann Dutton. 2008. "Childhood Victimization and Lifetime Revictimization." *Child Abuse and Neglect* 32:785–96.

Widom, Cathy Spatz, and Michael G. Maxfield. 2001. *An Update on the "Cycle of Violence."* Research in Brief. Washington, D.C.: U.S. Department of Justice, Office of Justice Programs, National Institute of Justice.

Widom, Cathy Spatz, Barbara Luntz Weiler, and Linda B. Cotler. 1999. "Childhood Victimization and Drug Abuse: A Comparison of Prospective and Retrospective Findings." *Journal of Consulting and Clinical Psychology* 67(6):867–80.

Wikström, Per-Olof H. 1995. "Preventing City-Center Crimes." In *Building a Safer Society: Strategic Approaches to Crime Prevention*, Michael Tonry and David Farrington (Eds.). Crime and justice: An annual review of research, vol. 19. Chicago, IL: University of Chicago Press, 429–68.

Williams, Kent M. 1991. "Using Battered Woman Syndrome Evidence with a Self-Defense Strategy in Minnesota." *Law and Inequality* 10:107–36.

Wilson, David B., Ajima Olaghere, and Charlotte Gill. 2016. "Juvenile Curfew Effects on Criminal Behavior and Victimization: A Campbell Collaboration Systematic Review." *Journal of Experimental Criminology* 12:167–86.

Wilson, James Q., and Richard J. Herrnstein. 1985. *Crime and Human Nature*. New York: Simon and Schuster.

Wilson, James Q., and George L. Kelling. 1982. "Broken Windows: The Police and Neighborhood Safety." *Atlantic Monthly March* (March):29–38.

Wilson, O.W., and Roy Clinton McLaren. 1963. *Police Administration*. 3rd ed. New York: McGraw-Hill.

Wilson, William Julius. 1987. *The Truly Disadvantaged*. Chicago, IL: University of Chicago Press.

Wilson, William Julius. 1996. *When Work Disappears: The World of the New Urban Poor*. New York: Knopf.

Wolcott, Harry. 1994. *Transforming Qualitative Data: Description, Analysis and Interpretation*. Thousand Oaks, CA: Sage Publications.

Wolfgang, Marvin E., Robert M. Figlio, and Thorsten Sellin. 1972. *Delinquency in a Birth Cohort*. Chicago: University of Chicago Press.

Wolfgang, Marvin E., Robert M. Figlio, Paul E. Tracy, and Simon I. Singer. 1985. *The National Survey of Crime Severity*. Washington, D.C.: U.S. Department of Justice, Office of Justice Programs, Bureau of Justice Statistics, NCJ-96017.

Woodward, Lianne J., and David M. Fergusson. 2000. "Childhood and Adolescent Predictors of Physical Assault: A Prospective Longitudinal Study." *Criminology* 38(1, February):233–61.

Wooten, Harold B., and Herbert J. Hoelter. 1998. "Operation Spotlight: The Community Probation-Community Police Team Process." *Federal Probation* 62(2):30–35.

World Health Organization. 2003. *WHO Ethical and Safety Recommendations for Interviewing Trafficked Women*. Geneva: World Health Organization, http://www.who.int/gender-equity -rights/knowledge/9789242595499/en/.

Wright, Doug, Peggy Barker, Joseph Gfroerer, and Lanny Piper. 2002. "Summary of NHSDA Design Changes in 1999." Chapter 2. In *Redesigning an Ongoing National Household Survey: Methodological Issues*. Publication no. SMA 03-3768, Joseph Gfroerer, Joe Eyerman, and James Chromy (Eds.). Rockville, MD: Office of Applied Studies, Substance Abuse and Mental Health Services Administration, 9–22, http://www .oas.samhsa.gov/redesigningNHSDA.pdf. Accessed 14 December 2006.

Wright, Richard T., and Scott H. Decker. 1994. *Burglars on the Job: Streetlife and Residential Break-Ins.* Boston: Northeastern University Press.

Yin, Robert K. 2013. *Case Study Research: Design and Methods.* 5th ed. Thousand Oaks, CA: Sage Publications.

Yu, Sung-suk Violet. 2011. *Do Bus Stops Increase Crime Opportunities.* El Paso, TX: Lfb Scholarly Publishing.

Zanin, Nicholas, Jon M. Shane, and Ronald V. Clarke. 2004. *Reducing Drug Dealing in Private Apartment Complexes in Newark, New Jersey.* Final report to the Office of Community Oriented Police Services. Washington, D.C.: U.S. Department of Justice, Office of Community Oriented Police Services, Accessed 20 December 2016 http://www.popcenter.org/Library/researcherprojects/DrugsApartment.pdf.

Name Index

Subject Index

Note: Page numbers with f indicate figures; those with t indicate tables.

strengths and weaknesses of, 317–323
structured observations, 308–311
topics appropriate to, 298–300
validity in, 318–319
Focus group interviews, 272, 285–286
conducting, 285–286
data on stigmatized topics, 285–286
dominant group members, 285
groupthink, 285
planning and design considerations, 285
Follow-up questions, 276
Frequency distributions, 398–399
Full-coverage programs, 377

G

Gang-related homicides, 347–348
Generalizability
in field research, 322–323
validity threats and, 178
General-purpose crime surveys, 235
General Social Survey (GSS), 409
Geographic Information Systems (GIS), 350
Global Terrorism Database (GTD), 159–160, 161, 162,
    346–347, 352, 353
Google Street View (GSV), 321–322
Grounded theory, 288
community prosecution and, 47
defined, 44
Groups, as units of analysis, 94
Groupthink, 285

H

Hard-to-reach groups, gaining access to,
    262–263
Historical events during testing, 174
Home detention
with electronic monitoring, 5
randomized studies, 375–377, 376f
Hot spots, agency records, 333–334
How-to-do-it guides, 382
Human trafficking, 54–55
Hypothesis, 39–40, 46
Hypothesis testing, 44

I

Identity theft, data on, 396–397
Ideology, in human inquiry, 11
Idiographic explanations, 36–37
Illicit economy, males engaged in, 266–267
Illogical reasoning, in human inquiry, 11
Imitation of treatments in experiments, 175–176
Impact assessment, 364, 365t, 380
Impacts, 363
Inaccurate observation, in human inquiry, 10

Incident-based measures, 145–148, 146t, 147t
National Incident-Based Reporting System,
    146–148, 146t, 147t, 163t
Supplementary Homicide Reports, 145–146, 163t
Incident-oriented policing, 382
Independent variables, 35, 168–169
Index of disorder, 132–134, 134f
Indigenous categories, 290
Individualistic fallacy, 96
Individuals, as units of analysis, 93–94
Inductive reasoning, 37–38, 50–51
Inductive theory, 44–46
crime concentration, 44–46
in practice, 46
Inferential statistics, 418–428
defined, 397
statistical significance, 419–428
univariate inferences, 418–419
Informal organizations and subcultures, gaining
    access to, 279–280
Informed consent, 69, 70–71
In-person interview surveys, 248–251, 253
appearance and demeanor, 248–249
computer-assisted, 250–251
control, 249–250
coordination, 249–250
defined, 248
familiarity with questionnaire, 249
interviewer's role, 248
probing for responses, 249
rules for, 248–249
Inputs, 362, 362f
Insider/outsider status, 276–277
Institutional review boards (IRBs), 70–71,
    72, 73–75
informed consent, 70–71
requirements and researcher rights, 74–75
special populations, 71, 72, 73–74
Instrumentation in experiments, 174
Interactive interview, 284–285
Internal validity
case studies and, 193f, 194
defined, 88
Internal validity threats, 173–178
causal time order, 175
compensatory rivalry, 176
compensatory treatment, 176
demoralization, 176
diffusion or imitation of treatments, 175–176
experimental mortality, 175
history, 174
instrumentation, 174
maturation, 174
ruling out, 176–178

National Consortium for the Study of Terrorism and
    Responses to Terrorism (START), 137–138, 138t
National crime surveys, examples of designing, 216–220
    Crime Survey for England and Wales, 219
    National Crime Victimization Survey,
        218–219
National Crime Victimization Survey (NCVS), 58, 117,
        141, 148–154, 155
    comparing victim surveys and crimes known to police,
        153–154
    content analysis, 329
    crime incident report, 242f
    as cross-sectional study, 99
    designing samples to achieve desired results, 218–219
    generalization, 322
    identity theft, 396–397
    lifestyle and street crime, 411
    redesign, 150–152, 151t, 152t
    sampling design and, 218–219
    screening questions, 242f, 256
    targeted victim surveys, 234
    visualizing statistical significance, 420
National Criminal Justice Reference Service, 4
National Incident-Based Reporting System (NIBRS),
        146–148, 146t, 147t, 163t
National Institute of Corrections, 327
National Institute of Justice (NIJ), 125, 158, 361
National Institute on Drug Abuse, 156
National Juvenile Corrections Data Resource
        Guide, 350
National Survey on Drug Use and Health (NSDUH), 155,
        163t
National Youth Gang Survey, 98, 99
Natural group, 272
Near-repeats, 45
Necessary cause, 86–87
Negative cases, 292
Neighborhood characteristics, measurement of, 109–110
Neutrality, 292
Newark, New Jersey, sampling streets in, 304
Nominal measures, 120, 122f
Nominal variables, 414–415, 415t
Nomothetic explanations, 36–37
Nonequivalent-groups design, 182–185
    cameras and crime prevention, 184–185
    child abuse and later arrest, 182–183
    deterring obscene phone calls, 183–184
    in quasi-experiments, 378–379, 379t
    time-series designs, 186–190, 187f, 188f
Nonprobability sampling, 220–225
    available subjects, reliance on, 221–222
    defined, 220
    online samples, 222–223
    purposive or judgmental sampling, 220
    quota sampling, 221

in review, 224, 225
    snowball sampling, 224, 225
Nonpublic agency records, 332–335
Nonsampling errors, 419
Null hypothesis, 422, 423, 424, 425

O

Objective, in research proposal, 23
Objectivity
    politics and, 393–394
    in theory, 39
Obscene phone calls, deterring, 183–184
Observations. *See also* Field research
    inaccurate, 10
    modes of, 197
    in research project design, 18
    selective, 10–11
    in traditional model of science, 42–44
Observer-as-participant, 301–302
Observer's roles in field research, 300–302
Obtrusive measurement, 327
Offending promoted by research, 65
Office of National Drug Control Policy, 158
Online samples, 222–223
Open coding, 289
Open-ended questions, 235–236
Operational definition, 114–115
Operationalization, 17–18, 81, 115, 116, 117, 118, 130, 131
Operational memo, 286
Ordering questions, 242
Ordinal measures, 120, 122f
Ordinal variables, 415–416, 415t
Organizations, as units of analysis, 94–95
Organizations, gaining access to formal, 277–279
    letters, 277–278, 278f
    meetings, 279
    phone calls, 278–279
    sponsors, 277, 278f
Outcomes, measurement of, 369–370, 369t
Overgeneralization, 10

P

Panel studies, 100
Paradigms, 40
Parameter estimate, 208–209, 208f
Parameters, 419
Parametric statistics, 419
Parole violators, agency records of, 342, 343
Parsing, 383
Participant-as-observer, 301
Participants in research. *See also* Ethical issues;
        Organizations, gaining access to formal
    anonymity, 62
    confidentiality, 62
    deceiving subjects, 63
    dynamics of, 272

Scattergram, 416–418, 417f, 418f
Schedule, in research proposal, 25
Scholarly research, how to read, 22–23
Science, 1
  causality, 9
  conceptualization in, 41
  observation in, 42–44
  operationalization in, 41–42
  probability, 9
  role of, 7
  theory in, 39–40
  traditional model of, 40–44, 43f
Scientific realism, 91–92, 386–389
Seat belt use, field research on, 316–317
Secondary analysis, 348–351, 352
  advantages and disadvantages of, 351, 352
  defined, 327
  importance of, 349
  introduction, 327–328
  sources of, 350–351, 350t
Selection bias in experiments, 175
Selective coding, 289
Selective observation, 10–11
Self-administered questionnaires, 243–248, 253
  computer-based, 245–248
  mail distribution and return, 244
  response rates, 244–245
  warning mailings and cover letters, 244–245
Self-report, 233–234
Self-report items, 238–239, 238f
Self-report surveys, 154–157
  defined, 154
  Monitoring the Future, 155–156, 163t
  National Survey on Drug Use and Health, 155, 163t
  reliability of, 156–157
  summarized, 157
  validity of, 156–157
Semi-structured interview, 270–271
Sensitizing concepts, 287–288
Sex offenders
  knowledge and attitudes about, 230–232
  theory and, 29–30
Sexual advances in dance club, 60, 61
Sexual assault in prisons and jails, 3–4
Sexual behavior in public restrooms, 75–76
Shoplifting
  field research on, 313, 314, 315–316
  situational crime prevention of, 378–379, 379t
Simple random sampling, 213
Situational crime prevention, 50
Social artifacts, as units of analysis, 95
Social capital, 287–288
Social disorder, 133, 134

Social disorganization and Boston neighborhoods, 413–414, 413t
Social disorganization theory, 40, 41–43, 46–47, 50
Social production of data, 341
Social science, 1
  aggregates *vs.* individuals in, 32
  causation/causality in, 84–87
  exceptions in, 31–32
  foundations of, 30–36
  regularities in, 31
  theory *vs.* philosophy or belief, 30–31
  variables in, 32–36
Social science research
  conducting, 36–39
  deductive reasoning, 37–38
  idiographic explanations, 36–37
  inductive reasoning, 37–38
  nomothetic explanations, 36–37
  qualitative data, 38–39
  quantitative data, 38–39
Social science theory. *See* Theory
Sound recorders, 306–307
Space-based analysis, 384–386
Special populations, 71, 72, 73–74
Split-half method, 126
Stability of results, 292
Staff misbehavior, 65
Stakeholders, 368, 389, 390, 391, 392–393
Standard deviation, 401–402, 401t
Standard error, 209–210, 419
Stanford Prison experiment, 76–78
Statements, questions and, 236
Statistical conclusion validity, 87–88
  experimental threats to, 180
Statistical regression in experiments, 174–175
Statistical significance, 419–428
  chi square, 422–423, 423t
  defined, 420
  interpreting, cautions in, 423–424
  level of significance, 420
  statistically discernible difference, 425, 428, 428f
  tests of, 419–420
  traffic enforcement and racial profiling, 426–427
  visualizing, 420–422, 421f
Statistically discernible difference, 425, 428, 428f
Stereotypes, 282, 283
Stolen vehicles, seaport operations and, 296–297
Strategic Approaches to Community Safety Initiatives (SACSI), 384
Stratification
  defined, 214
  multistage cluster sampling with, 216
Stratified sampling, 214–215
  disproportionate, 215